H   LK

MW01181126

THE CRUISE OF THE BETSEY

OR, A SUMMER RAMBLE AMONG THE
FOSSILIFEROUS DEPOSITS OF THE HEBRIDES

WITH

RAMBLES OF A GEOLOGIST

OR, TEN THOUSAND MILES OVER THE
FOSSILIFEROUS DEPOSITS OF SCOTLAND

Introduction and Notes by
DR MICHAEL A. TAYLOR
NATIONAL MUSEUMS OF SCOTLAND

Foreword by
PROFESSOR T. C. SMOUT
HISTORIOGRAPHER ROYAL IN SCOTLAND

NATIONAL MUSEUMS OF SCOTLAND

Published by NMS Publishing
a division of NMS Enterprises Limited
National Museums of Scotland
Chambers Street, Edinburgh EH1 1JF

Facsimile of Text first published in 1858 © Hugh Miller
Introduction and Notes © Trustees of the National Museums of Scotland
Maps © Jim Lewis

No reproduction permitted without written permission.

ISBN 1-901663-54-X

*No part of this publication may be reproduced, stored in a retrieval system
or transmitted, in any form or by any means, electronic, mechanical, photocopying,
recording or otherwise, without the prior permission of the publisher.*

The right of Michael A. Taylor to be identified
as the author of the Introduction and Notes to this book
has been asserted by him in accordance with the
Copyright, Designs and Patents Act 1988.

British Library Cataloguing in Publication Data
A catalogue record of this book
is available from the British Library.

Cover photographs (credits): Hugh Miller calotype photograph by
David Octavius Hill and Robert Adamson (detail) © Scottish National Photography Collection,
Scottish National Portrait Gallery; sunset, Isle of Eigg © John MacPherson, Stockscotland.com
(cat. no. jm0111320907); fossil fish, *Glyptolepis leptopterus*, Old Red Sandstone, Cromarty:
Hugh Miller Collection (NMS.G1859.33.1315), photograph by Suzie Stevenson,
© Trustees of the National Museums of Scotland

Design by NMS Enterprises Limited – Publishing
Printed and bound in Great Britain by Athenaeum Press, Gateshead, Tyne & Wear

CONTENTS

THE CRUISE OF THE BETSEY

RAMBLES OF A GEOLOGIST

ACKNOWLEDGEMENTS

Dr Michael A. Taylor
NATIONAL MUSEUMS OF SCOTLAND

THIS publication was made possible by the generous financial support of descendants and relatives of Hugh and Lydia Miller, and their spouses, through the National Museums of Scotland Charitable Trust. The Trustees of the National Museums of Scotland therefore wish to acknowledge the kind support of Mrs Rosemary Airey, Mr Richard Beeching, Mrs Bright Gordon, Mr Henry McKenzie Johnston, Mrs Marian McKenzie Johnston, Mr Brian Mackay, Mr Edmond Mansion, and Mr Peter Mansion.

Professors John Hudson, David Oldroyd and Chris Smout critically reviewed the manuscript, and made many valuable suggestions, although I remain responsible for any errors. Ms Camille Dressler and Dr Simon Knell discussed specific problem areas. Specialist advice was given by Mr Hugh Cheape on Gaelic, Mr Graham McKenna on geological maps, Dr Ralph O'Connor on literary quotations, and Dr Roberta Paton on Palaeozoic fishes. I am grateful to many other colleagues for helping me develop an understanding of Miller and his context over the years, and for specific help with this book, including, but not only, Dr Ulrike Al-Khamis, Dr David Alston, Dr Lyall Anderson, Dr Mary Beard, Professor Mike Benton, Dr David Brown, Mr Tom Bryce, Mr John Burnett, Dr Trevor Cowie, Mr John Crompton, Dr Peter Crowther, Dr George Dalgliesh, Mr Peter Davidson, Dr C. H. Emeleus, Professor Sandy Fenton, Dr Krisztina Fenyő, Mr David Forsyth, Dr Henry Gee, Dr David Goldsack, Mrs Frieda Gostwick, Mr Martin Gostwick, Dr Jason Hilton, Mr Nick Holmes, Mr Brian Jackson, Dr Philippe Janvier, Ms Sheila McClure, Mr Henry McKenzie Johnston, Mrs Marian McKenzie Johnston, Dr Gillian King, Dr Andrew Kitchener, Dr Alec Livingstone, Dr Colin MacFadyen, Mr Bob McGowan, Dr Alison Morrison-Low, Dr Bob Nuttall, Ms Edith Philip, Ms Sankurie Pye, Dr Alan Saville, Dr Anne Secord, Professor Jim Secord, Dr Alison Sheridan, Dr Sara Stevenson, Ms Susan Seright, Ms Geoff Swinney, Ms Naomi Tarrant, Dr Nigel Trewin, and Dr Hugh Torrens. Dr Lester Borley and the authors kindly provided advance copies of the geology-related papers from the major conference, marking the bicentenary of Miller's birth, held at Cromarty in October 2002, whose proceedings were published as this book was in proof (Borley, 2003). I would also like to thank Professor David Oldroyd and Professor David Knight for copies of papers in press. I also appreciate the assistance of Mr Andrew Martin, Ms Clare Whittaker, the staff of the Libraries of the National Museums of Scotland, National Library of Scotland, University of Edinburgh New College, and the Scottish Poetry Library, and Lesley Taylor and the staff of NMS Publishing for their careful and patient endeavours.

Finally, I am grateful to Kevin Walton and the Penguin Cruising Club for memorably taking me in the wake of Free Church Yacht *Betsey*, and my partner Helen for accompanying me on the more terrestrial excursions in Miller's tracks.

FOREWORD

Professor T. C. Smout
HISTORIOGRAPHER ROYAL IN SCOTLAND

HUGH Miller epitomised much to the Victorians. He was a self-made working man who made it from being a fatherless youth going to work in a quarry to becoming a figure of national renown. He was a defender of the faith, using his pen as a journalist in the evangelical cause of the Free Church and pitting knowledge as a geologist and palaeontologist against the evolutionary theories of Robert Chambers. He did not have to contend with Charles Darwin, but by 1869, posthumously, *The Testimony of the Rocks* had sold 35,000 copies and *Footprints of the Creator* had run to eleven editions, evidence of the abiding comfort of these anti-evolutionary books to a generation assailed by doubt ten years after the *Origin of Species*. And he was quintessentially a Scot of his day, happy with his country's union with England but confident of its moral and religious superiority, a northerner from Cromarty proud of his roots and fascinated by its folklore, but equally a pillar of the Edinburgh intelligentsia at a time when the capital was a notable centre of British intellectual life. With all these qualities came great literary gifts, a warm humour and a liberal frame of mind.

Great in the nineteenth century, Miller was largely forgotten in the twentieth. The ecclesiastical fights of Victoria's reign were now of small moment to an increasingly secular world. Darwin's paradigm prevailed, and old opponents to evolutionary ideas seemed as dead as the dodo. Miller's discoveries in the *Old Red Sandstone*, no doubt great in their own right, had been made by an amateur a long time ago: modern science was now a matter of professionals, big money, research councils, progress and the future. The mason from Cromarty seemed a footnote in Victorian history, except among a small band of geological enthusiasts and among the local people of the Black Isle, who never forgot the famous man who had once lived among them.

It took another journalist, George Rosie, to begin in 1981 the process of rehabilitating Miller's wider reputation by publishing a volume of selected examples of his prose and emphasising again the scale of his influence on contemporaries, his literary genius and his scientific acumen.* Then a growing academic interest in the history of Victorian ideas, and specifically in geology in formulating a new view of time, helped to restore Miller's place in the pantheon of scientific exploration. In

---

* G. Rosie, *Hugh Miller: Outrage and order: a biography and selected writings* (Mainstream, Edinburgh, 1981).

2000 and 2001, to celebrate the bicentenary of Hugh Miller's birth in 2002, the Cromarty Arts Trust, the National Trust for Scotland, and the National Museums of Scotland came together to hold two conferences and to publish a book of the papers presented there, 're-establishing him as a central figure of nineteenth-century Scotland whose life and writings still have much to tell us today'.** The Cromarty Arts Trust went on to instigate the major bicentenary conference at Cromarty in October 2002 which has done still more to carry on this reassessment.†

This present volume continues this good work, and in the best possible way. No one knows better the importance and the originality of Hugh Miller than Michael Taylor, who, with his colleagues at the National Museums of Scotland, has the task of looking after the fossil collections to which Miller contributed so much with his own original finds. No one better appreciates Miller's ability in making his vast knowledge available and relevant to the public through his skills as a writer, than a curator whose own job is also to make science accessible.

It was an inspired idea to reprint *The Cruise of the Betsey*, and a generous move by descendants and relatives of Hugh and Lydia Miller to support it financially. Of Miller's many writings, none is more engaging than this volume, both learned and discursive: about geology certainly, but also vividly about the social life of the Hebrides and northern Scotland. Set in the immediate aftermath of the Disruption that had rent the Church of Scotland in twain, it is about a rural people in all their poverty and dignity, about the stupendous scenery and nature of the Scottish Highlands and Islands, about science, about storms and about calms. Michael Taylor's careful introduction sets the scene so that the modern reader can find their bearings in a sea of unfamiliar faces and controversies. Once embarked on the *Cruise*, however, the reader will find that Miller's subtle and vivid prose takes over in a truly gripping account of experience and adventure. There are many memorable passages, ranging from the visit to the cave of the massacre on Eigg to the encounter with the little Indian girl at Alness, unfamiliar with the concept of ghosts; from the day the *Betsey* nearly sank with Miller and the Free Church minister on board, to the discovery of the *Asterolepis* near Stromness. Among my favourites is Miller's conversation with the Established Church minister who mistook him for a Lowland shepherd, and was thoroughly taken aback to discover, after several hours' conversation in a gig in the rain, that he was the Editor of *The Witness*, the organ of the archenemy:

> There was a momentary pause. 'Well,' said the minister, 'it's all the same: I'm glad we should have met. Give me, man, a shake of your hand.' And so the conversation went on as before till we parted at Dingwall, – the Establishment clergyman wet to the skin, the Free Church editor in no better condition; but

---

** J. Nightingale, in Borley (2002, p. 5).
† Borley (2003).

both, mayhap, rather less out of conceit with the ride than if it had been ridden alone.

In a cadence of sentences, Miller here expresses so well an incident where common humanity, bad weather and public transport overcame the normal enmities. Indeed, you find in Miller no sour piety trying to keep either old enemies or the modern world at bay, but rather a personality driven always to engagement, whether by enthusiasm and wonder for nature, or by indignation at the injustice of clearance and poverty, or by affection at the qualities of his fellow men and women. It is a delight to have this book available again, as a mirror both to its age and to the qualities of the great man who wrote it.

Notes on Maps

1. Maps are provided to clarify Miller's travels. Larger scale maps, if required, are produced by the Ordnance Survey:

    www.ordsvy.gov.uk
    www.ordnancesurvey.gov.uk

    which also provide free online access at time of writing, as does:

    www.streetmap.co.uk

2. Please note that on the map of Scotland, old county names are in italics; thus *Inverness* denotes the county of Inverness, or (as in this case, but not in some others), Inverness-shire.

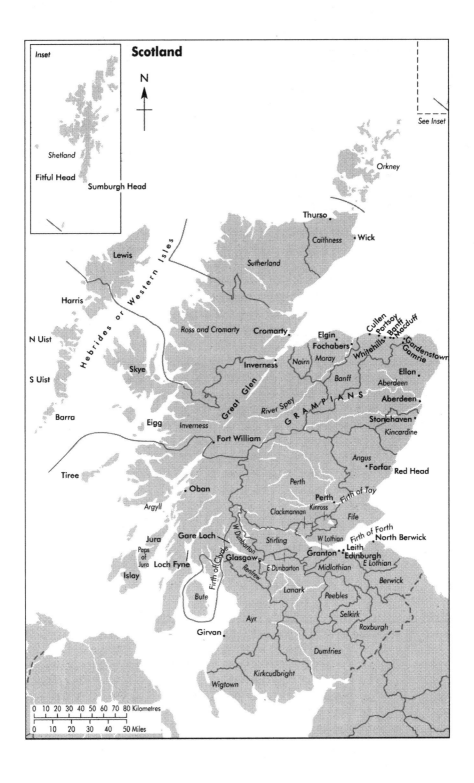

Scotland

N

Inset

Shetland

Fitful Head

Sumburgh Head

See Inset

Orkney

Thurso

Caithness   • Wick

Sutherland

Lewis

Hebrides or Western Isles

Harris

Cromarty

Ross and Cromarty

Cullen   Portsoy
Elgin   Banff Macduff
Fochabers   Whitehills   Gardenstown
              Moray   Gamrie
Nairn
N Uist

Inverness

Skye   Banff   Ellon

Aberdeen

S Uist   Aberdeen

River Spey   G R A M P I A N S

Barra   Stonehaven

Eigg   Kincardine

Inverness

Tiree

Fort William   Angus
                                          • Forfar   Red Head

Perth

Oban   Firth of Tay

Argyll   Perth
                  Clackmannan   Kinross
                                      Fife
Jura
Paps
of   Gare Loch   W Dunbarton   Stirling   W Lothian   Firth of Forth
Jura   Loch Fyne   North Berwick
                        Firth of Clyde   Leith
Islay   Glasgow   Granton • Edinburgh
                              Renfrew   E Lothian
                      E Dunbarton   Midlothian
                  Bute   Berwick

                              Lanark
                                          Peebles
                  Ayr   Selkirk
Girvan   Roxburgh

                              Dumfries

            Kirkcudbright
Wigtown

0 10 20 30 40 50 60 70 80 Kilometres

0   10   20   30   40   50 Miles

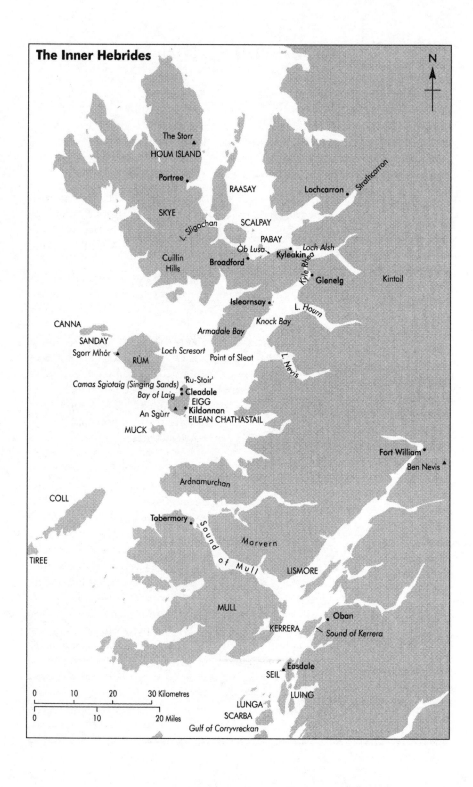

The Inner Hebrides

N

The Storr ▲
HOLM ISLAND

Portree •

RAASAY

Lochcarron • Strathcarron

SKYE

L. Sligachan

SCALPAY

PABAY

Ob Lusa •

Loch Alsh

Broadford •

Kyleakin •

Loch Alsh

Cuillin
Hills

Kyle Rhea

Glenelg •

Kintail

Isleornsay •

L. Hourn

CANNA

Knock Bay

SANDAY

Armadale Bay

Sgorr Mhór ▲

RÙM

Loch Scresort

Point of Sleat

L. Nevis

Camas Sgiotaig (Singing Sands)

'Ru-Stoir'

Bay of Laig

Cleadale

EIGG

An Sgùrr ▲

Kildonnan

EILEAN CHATHASTAIL

MUCK

Fort William •

Ben Nevis ▲

Ardnamurchan

COLL

Tobermory •

Sound of Mull

Morvern

TIREE

LISMORE

MULL

Oban •

KERRERA

Sound of Kerrera

Easdale •

SEIL

LUING

LUNGA

SCARBA

Gulf of Corryvreckan

0   10   20   30 Kilometres

0   10   20 Miles

INTRODUCTION

by Dr Michael A. Taylor

NATIONAL MUSEUMS OF SCOTLAND

CRUISE of the Betsey, with, Rambles of a Geologist (1858) is a classic of Scottish literature and an ideal introduction to its author, Hugh Miller. Here is almost his full range: newspaper editor, religious journalist, social crusader, observer of his life and times, and enthusiast for Scotland's scenery and the exhilaration of discovering fossils. Not surprisingly, *Cruise of the Betsey* is beloved by geologists, often quoted by anthologists, and quarried by historians. Nevertheless it was very much a book of its time, which is perhaps why it has been out of print for many years. This introduction aims to assess it, and to provide the background necessary to make Miller's work newly available to the modern reader.

Hugh Miller was born in 1802 into a rising middle-class family in the small coastal burgh of Cromarty, on the so-called Black Isle, a peninsula north of Inverness. His father, a coasting shipmaster, was drowned in a shipwreck a few years later and the family was plunged into relative poverty. Miller left school early and worked as a stonemason and quarrier, foregoing the chance of a university education in the hope of achieving a literary career during the winter close season. His health was damaged by stone dust, and he took lighter work first as a monumental mason and then as a bank accountant, in his spare time becoming also an author and journalist, and marrying Lydia Fraser. In 1839 he moved to Edinburgh as founding editor of *The Witness*, a newspaper supporting the 'Evangelical' wing of the Church of Scotland, and helped develop the public support essential for the formation of the Free Church of Scotland.

Like all journalists Miller had an insatiable appetite for themes. A keen geologist in his spare time, he sometimes wrote about his geological activities, especially during his usual summer holiday combining a visit to his Cromarty relatives with a tour of interesting geological sites. Writing, probably, in 1849, Miller claimed (p. 476) that to 'acquaint myself with the fossiliferous deposits of Scotland, I have travelled, hammer in hand, during the last nine years, over fully ten thousand miles' – whence the subtitle to *Rambles of a Geologist*. In the first part of this book, *Cruise of the Betsey* proper (whose subtitle was changed later to *A summer holiday in the Hebrides*, as seen, for example, in the 1889 edition), Miller recorded his travels to the Isles of Mull, Eigg, Rùm and Skye, starting in July 1844 (p. 1), then across Scotland to Cromarty and the Moray Firth region. After attending the 1845 General Assembly of the Free Church in Inverness, Miller took a detour on the way home to visit Eigg in June (p. 211), but the weather delayed his departure and he missed the unexpectedly early birth of his daughter Bessie (Sutherland 2002, p. 75). The

A11

second part of the book, *Rambles of a Geologist*, covers his trips of 1846, to Caithness and Orkney via Cromarty (pp. 310, 380–381); and of 1847, from Aberdeen to the Black Isle and Strathpeffer (pp. 231, 380).

Miller originally published articles on these journeys in *The Witness* as serial feature articles (the earlier trips in 1845, the later in 1848–49; Shortland 1996d). He intended to edit them into books, as he had done with others; the articles that ended up in *Rambles* were earmarked for a book on Scottish geology (Lydia Miller in Miller 1859, p xiii). Miller, however, committed suicide in 1856, probably because, ill and overworked, he was suffering hallucinations and believed he was going mad. His widow Lydia started overseeing the posthumous publication of Miller's selected writings, in duty to her husband's memory as well as to provide for the family (McKenzie Johnston and Taylor 2002; Sutherland 2002). However, her own health soon broke down and she went to Malvern, a middle-class health resort, for a 'cure'. Here, Lydia and her daughter Harriet became friends with the Reverend William Symonds, the Anglican rector of Pendock in Herefordshire. Indeed they may have known Symonds already; he was a well-known local geologist and author of popular natural history books (Knight 1999; Oldroyd 2004 in press). As well as providing moral support at Malvern, Symonds helped Lydia by preparing *Cruise of the Betsey ... with Rambles of a Geologist ...* for publication, and it duly appeared in 1858. He also helped Lydia with a revision of *The Old Red Sandstone* (L. Miller in Miller 1899a, p. xi), and with yet another volume, *Sketch-book of Popular Geology* (1859), using the remaining material which Miller had earmarked for his book on Scottish geology (L. Miller in Miller 1859, pp. iii–v, xiii; Sutherland 2002).

When editing Miller's articles for *Cruise of the Betsey*, Symonds presumably had specific target audiences in mind, notably those Scottish readers interested in Miller's writing on the issues of the day (although Symonds deleted some of Miller's polemic), but also the natural history-loving middle classes of the English-speaking world. The book went through numerous 'editions', but in the absence of a formal bibliographical study, it can only be said that the latest known printing was in 1897 (Shortland 1996d) and that the later Edinburgh editions of *Cruise of the Betsey* were still, in 1889, using the same increasingly worn and damaged printing plates as the first edition, although the title page and preface, at least, had at some time been reset. By the end of the nineteenth century the book's geology was obsolete, and during the early years of the twentieth century Miller would soon slip out of fashion. Today, however, with fresh interest in the history of Scotland and of science, one may see *Cruise of the Betsey* as a classic of travel writing comparable to William Cobbett's *Rural Rides*. An evocation of the pleasures of the countryside, it is also a powerful polemic for justice as its author saw it.

In this introduction, I refer to the whole book simply as *Cruise of the Betsey*, without differentiating between *Cruise of the Betsey* proper and *Rambles of a Geologist*, except where specified. Page references given without citing a publication refer to the first edition of *Cruise of the Betsey* as reprinted here in facsimile. Brief explanatory notes are printed integrally with the facsimile; additional explanatory notes, comments, and a glossary are provided after the facsimile.

Miller, folklore and Gaelic culture

Miller had, in 1835, published *Scenes and Legends*, a valuable record of the dying folklore of his native Black Isle (Alston 1996), and in *Cruise of the Betsey* he returned to these 'fossils of the mind' (Mackenzie 1905, p. 60) with the story of the meteor (pp. 322-324), and the use of fossil belemnites as cattle medicine (p. 374). He could glean little folklore on Eigg, perhaps because a past clan massacre had wiped out collective memory (p. 34); no doubt, also, his Free Church contacts were unwilling to dwell on tales that seemed redolent of superstition, prelacy and paganism (pp. 51-52). In any case, Miller did not know Gaelic, which is a Celtic language of the Highlands and western Islands quite different from Scots. In his travels, as he well knew, Miller was exploring a Scotland divided into three, culturally and topographically (pp. 409-410). The so-called Lowlands comprise the Southern Uplands, the Midland Valley and the eastern and northeastern coastlands. This is roughly the original range of the Scots language, then becoming increasingly assimilated into its sister language of English (more correctly, both Scots and English originated during what used to be called the Dark Ages as regional groups of dialects of the same Germanic language group, and modern English in part stems from the dialect spoken by the most powerful and influential parts of society). Indeed, because of the historical quirk of the Reformers' adoption of an English rather than Scots translation of the Bible, written English was already used formally in church, school and law court, though often spoken – as in Miller's own case (Alston 1996) – with a Scots intonation. Cromarty itself was a Lowland enclave, with the Cromarty Firth, a few hundred yards from Miller's birthplace, being a frontier with the Gaelic-speaking Highlands and Islands (p. 92; Withers 1984). As Miller also commented (p. 409), Caithness and the Orkney and Shetland Islands form a third, Scandinavian-Scots, region, speaking a Scots which was deeply influenced by the Norse originally spoken there.

In speech, heart, and mind Miller was certainly 'Saxon', or *Sasannach* as the Gaels called a Lowlander, although he had Gaelic-speaking cousins of whom he thought highly (Miller 1858). His family were long established in the Lowlander town of Cromarty, in contrast to a recent influx of Gaelic speakers from surrounding parishes who provided much of the local industrial workforce (Alston 2002). For him, there was no point in learning Gaelic in a burgh where trade, education and most worship took place in Scots and English. Gaelic language and culture, after all, seemed on the road to extinction, like the Celtic race itself (Fenyő 2000). The only concession was to institute Gaelic worship for those who could not understand English, lest their spiritual needs be ignored. Cromarty therefore had a Gaelic Chapel (Alston 1999, p. 188), and for the same reason Miller's boyhood friend, the Reverend John Swanson, learned the language when he was called to a Highlands parish (Cameron 1877, p. 132).

Although fossils were dearest to Miller's heart, he also took an intelligent interest in antiquities, as on Orkney (pp. 403, 450, and *passim*). He saw human history as being continuous with, rather than separated from, the deep time of geological history (Paradis 1996; Torrens 1998). He thoughtfully analysed a vitri-fied fort near Strathpeffer (pp. 363-372) as he might do with a geological outcrop. Indeed, Miller took particular note of what might be called living (or at least only recently extinct) cultural fossils on Eigg and Rùm: ancient practices which had long died out elsewhere, such as catching fish with brushwood, which he noted as a primitive stage in the evolution of fishing nets (pp. 137-138). This no doubt reflected a then pervasive sense of progress and rapid change, reflected in Walter Scott's development of the historical novels which influenced a whole generation of Scots writers, including Miller himself (Robertson 2002). When Miller noticed another living fossil in the form of 'island shoes' tanned with tormentil (pp. 17-18), he referred to John Stewart, the *Betsey*'s mate, as 'adept in all the multifarious arts of the island', surely alluding to the primitive state of the island economy with its minimal division of labour. Miller found scraps of such a shoe when he explored a cave full of skeletons and debris of a clan massacre some centuries before, as well as yet another cultural fossil, a piece of 'unglazed pottery' (pp. 24-26; now in NMS). This was *crogan* ware, made without a wheel, and produced into the twentieth century in the Outer Hebrides (Cheape 1988). Most evocatively of all (pp. 82-83), Miller visited a shieling, a dwelling used when tending cattle on temporary summer grazing and making butter and cheese for storage (this very hut still stands, although ruinous; Hudson 2000). This is a rare description of the ancient practice of transhumance, the transfer of stock between seasonal pastures, which was already almost extinct in Scotland (Cheape 1995, 1996, 1997).

Unlike many travellers, Miller does not seem to have been unduly biased by romantic preconceptions or by staying with the gentry. We may well regret that Miller did not write more than he did, but, as we shall see, he may have had reason not to dwell overmuch on Gaels' more supposedly 'primitive' traits. In any case, like George Orwell at 'Wigan Pier', he was writing not ethnography, but rather polemics and literature.

Miller, the Disruption, and the Free Church of Scotland

Miller adhered by upbringing and personal conviction to the Church of Scotland, which then dominated Scottish society. However, the Scottish spiritual landscape had just experienced an earthquake in the 'Disruption' of 1843, in which Miller was a key figure, and the aftershocks resonated throughout *Cruise of the Betsey* (main sources for church history are Brown 1893; Drummond and Bulloch 1973, 1975; Brown and Fry 1993; Macleod 1996; Brown 1997; Ansdell 1998; Macleod 2000; and Cheape 2003).

Calvinist and Reformed in doctrine, the Church of Scotland was, and remains, Presbyterian, governed by elders in a way reminiscent of what the Reformers took to be the original Church in Palestine. The emphasis was on the understanding of church doctrine and the Bible, tested by formal catechism. The sermon formed the core of the service, supplemented with prayers and psalms. Good preaching was crucial and seriously appreciated, as when Miller praised Swanson's nautically phrased sermon, admirably directed to its audience of sailors (p. 157). Each parish was run by a kirk session of about a dozen elders, chosen from mature and religious men, and the ordained minister. The session selected the schoolmaster, often a minister in training, who usually became its clerk. The presbytery comprised a minister and an elder from each parish in its area. The presbyteries of a region sent representatives to the region's synod, and also to the Church's annual General Assembly, convened by a Moderator elected annually. Under this structure, the parish ministries were the only fixed positions, and the Church lacked any permanent hierarchy such as the bishops and archbishops of the Roman Catholic Church, headed by the Pope, or of the Church of England, headed by the sovereign.

During the seventeenth century, the Stuart monarchs, starting with James VI (of Scotland) and I (of England), attempted to impose control over the Church of Scotland by supporting such an episcopalian hierarchy. This was abhorred by many Scots as 'Erastianism', the subordination of Church to State, and during the reign of Charles I it led to them signing a public declaration of opposition, the Scottish National Covenant, in 1638. This helped to trigger the successive Wars of the Covenant, which spread into the Civil Wars of Britain and Ireland. During the Union of 1707, the (Presbyterian) Church of Scotland consented to an Anglo-Scottish state on condition that the independence of the Kirk was guaranteed. The ousted 'Jacobite' Stuarts were Catholics, and their supporters in the Highland clans were largely Episcopalian. The final defeat of Charles Stuart ('Bonnie Prince Charlie') and the Jacobites at Culloden in 1746 therefore ensured that the Church of Scotland would stay Presbyterian and pro-Union.

The Cromarty people, including Miller's own grandfather, had watched Culloden's cannon smoke in the distance (Miller 1835, pp. 340-341; 1862, pp. 82-92). Many were independent-minded artisans and traders who had had their own local political and religious struggles, so to speak, which Miller recorded from their (hardly unbiased) viewpoint in *Scenes and Legends* (Miller 1835; Alston 1996, 2002). One critical issue, at Cromarty and elsewhere, was 'patronage'. In Scotland, this was the right of the main local landowner, or 'laird', rather than the congregation, to choose or 'call' the new minister to a vacant parish (a patron could also be a body such as the Crown, *ie* government, or a burgh council). After the Restoration, the Stuarts had reimposed ecclesiastical patronage in 1662. Displaced ministers formed a second Covenanting movement, holding unofficial open air services or 'conventicles' in the face of persecution. Patronage was again abolished in 1690, after James VII and II was overthrown, but it later returned in a modified form, in which the patron proposed a candidate whom the heads of household in the congregation voted to accept or reject. This constrained patrons' freedom to award lucrative livings to favourites and clients, and to ensure acquiescent ministers, thereby exerting control over their domains. Disputes over patronage caused the break-away of the Secession Church in 1733, and the Relief Church in 1761, and recurrent trouble within the Established Church, with court cases, lockouts, boycotts, and public disorder, in Cromarty and elsewhere.

Patronage was still a serious issue when Miller was growing up in the 1820s. The Church of Scotland was polarized into 'Evangelicals' and 'Moderates'. Of course, the late eighteenth and early nineteenth century religious revival was 'evangelical' in the general sense of the word, but 'Evangelical' now became the special label of a party whose members were strongly committed to a fundamentalist view of Christianity, often through a conversion experience in young adulthood, such as Miller himself had (Miller 1858, pp. 373-383). They were aggressively prose-lytising, and opposed patronage, both on principle and because they wanted ministers chosen for competence alone. Their opponents, the 'Moderates', espoused what they saw as tolerance rather than dogmatism, but tended to com-promise with the secular power, and to accept patronage as a right of property.

The Evangelicals sought to follow the Reformers' ideal of a Scotland living by divine law, each parish funding its own schools, poor relief and social support, and its elders supervising the people and enforcing moral discipline. Their leader Thomas Chalmers even experimented with establishing such a 'godly common-wealth' in urban slums. However, the parish system no longer met the changing distribution of population, especially in the expanding cities and new industrial settlements. But the legal problems of reorganizing civil functions such as poor relief and schooling made it hard to reform parish boundaries. To bypass the problem, the Church, under Evangelical influence, established new *quoad sacra* parishes with purely spiritual functions. The Church Extension Campaign now built over two hundred new churches, mostly *quoad sacra*, and mostly without patronage.

In 1834, when the Evangelical wing became dominant, the Church reconfirmed the principle of the congregation's veto on patronage. This started a confrontation known as the 'Ten Years' Conflict'. Local patronage disputes escalated into legal test cases, culminating in a House of Lords judgement delivered by Lord Brougham in 1839, which reasserted patronage by denying the Church's claim to spiritual independence, notably in the selection of ministers. The newspapers of the day, mainly either conservative or whig, were hostile to the Evangelicals, so a group of prominent Evangelicals decided to set up their own newspaper. At this juncture, Miller happened to publish 'A Letter to Lord Brougham', a pamphlet of such striking polemic that he was recruited as editor of what was to become *The Witness*. Its first issue appeared in 1840 and it greatly helped to gather public support for the Evangelical cause.

Matters came to a head in January 1843 when the British Government rejected the Evangelicals' 'Claim of Right' to spiritual independence. The Evangelicals had foreseen the risk of a split in the Church of Scotland, and planned accordingly. At that year's Assembly in Edinburgh, Evangelical ministers, a full third of the clergy, walked out to form the First General Assembly of the Free Church of Scotland, leaving the official Church of Scotland as the 'Establishment'.

In his support for the Evangelicals, Miller was too independent to be a simple message-bearer, but it is probably fair that he, together with Chalmers, should be considered responsible, to a significant degree, for the Disruption. As Macleod

(2002, p. 84) has put it, 'without Miller … [the] people would not have been informed and the ministers would not have had the nerve'. The Disruption's main importance was seen, then and now, as one of spiritual independence, and of Church members upholding the principles in which they believed. Nevertheless, the Disruption had problematic consequences. The Evangelicals lost their hoped-for majority, and the moral force of taking the Church as a whole away from the State, because the middle of the road ministers failed, against expectation, to join them. Instead, the Church was torn down the middle. The Established Church lost many of its most energetic people, and the moral right to speak for the majority of Scots, and, at least in terms of numbers attending, became just one amongst several Presbyterian Churches, as did the Free Church itself.

The Free Churchmen had to sustain the true national Church, as its members saw it, through voluntary contributions alone. One effect of the Disruption was a further profusion of church buildings in the Scottish landscape, as the Free Church energetically started building a parallel network of churches, schools, missions at home and abroad, and a theological college. For instance, Firth and Stennis, Stromness, and Birsay and Harray, three Orkney parishes which Miller visited in the course of his journey, gave rise to five Free Church parishes, needing at least four churches as well as manses, schools and schoolmasters' houses (Ewing 1914). There developed a centralized Free Church bureaucracy to manage funding and the cross-subsidy of poorer parishes through the 'Sustentation Fund'. Under this burden, the Free Church's initial aspirations to be a national Church for the whole of society tended to change over the years towards an essentially 'voluntarist' provision for its members. Miller would have regretted much of this, and the apparent secularisation of Victorian Scotland (Macleod 1996, 2002), reflected for instance by the takeover, by national and local government, of social services and of education (which last, however, Miller would probably have supported). In any case, the entire system remained deeply influenced by the Presbyterian Churches until well into the second half of the twentieth century (Brown 1997).

The Disruption in the Small Isles

Cruise of the Betsey is one of the two great Scots classics describing how the Disruption affected ordinary Scots, the other being William Alexander's *Johnny Gibb of Gushetneuk*. Alexander set his novel in the northeast Lowlands (Alexander 1919; Calder 1993). In contrast, *Cruise of the Betsey* proper dealt with the Disruption in the Highlands and Islands parish of 'Small Isles', and more specifically in Eigg and to a lesser extent Rùm, although this parish comprises all the Small Isles of Inverness-shire, including Canna, Sanday, Muck, and a few smaller islets.

In 1843, at the Disruption, passions were high on both sides. Rather than accept lairds' domination, congregations left their family churches and sought to build Free Churches. A minority found that lairds exerted the rights of feudal superiors under Scots law to forbid such construction, sometimes on all land within walking distance (Ansdell 1998). A congregation on Loch Sunart simply ordered a floating church from Clydeside, mooring their Ark-like creation offshore and noting the success of that day's preacher by the depth of the waterline (Brown 1893, pp. 427-428, 655-657). Unluckier congregations, like that on Eigg (pp. 157-159), worshipped in the open air. Sometimes they were moved on by the laird's men and had to resort to the middle of the public road or the sea shore, where his writ did not run – though this was not a problem on Orkney, with its diverse land ownership (pp. 458-459). It was not just for its geology that Miller and the local Free Church minister examined a cave on Eigg (p. 216): would it do for a temporary church, they wondered?

Only a minority of congregations were seriously hindered by the lairds, however, and the situation soon improved, thanks partly to government intervention and the cooling of tempers. Still, while it lasted, such offensive interference with spiritual conscience damaged the lairds' cause and scored a moral victory for the Free Church. It harked back to the persecution of the Covenanters in the seventeenth century, and even to the wanderings of Christ in Palestine, and the Israelites in the wilderness, a parallel drawn by illustrations in Free Church histories (*eg* Anon. 1877; Brown 1893).

As Robin Jenkins explores in his 1985 novel *The Temptation of George Darroch,* the new Free Church clergy had to abandon what were often comfortable livings. The lawyer Lord Cockburn commented at the time of the Disruption (Drummond and Bulloch 1973, p. 248):

> They have abandoned that public station which was the ambition of their lives, and have descended from certainty to precariousness, and most of them from comfort to destitution, solely for their principles. And the loss of the stipend is the least of it. The dismantling of the manse, the breaking up of all the objects to which the hearts and the habits of the family were attached, the shutting the gate for the last time of the little garden, the termination of all their interest in the humble but respectable kirk – even all these desolations, though they may excite the most immediate pangs, are not the calamities which the head of the house finds it hardest to sustain. It is the loss of station that is the deep and lasting sacrifice, the ceasing to be the most important man in the parish, the closing of the doors of the gentry against him and his family, the altered prospects of his children, the extinction of everything that the State had provided for the decent dignity of the manse and its inmates.

David Octavius Hill chose a minister signing away the richest living in Scotland as the focus for his Disruption painting 'Signing the Deed of Demission' (Stevenson 2002b). Miller, too, emphasised the sacrifice which his boyhood friend John Swanson (1804-1874) made in leaving his position as Minister for Small Isles, with one of the most substantial houses on Eigg and a large and fertile glebe (portion of land allocated to the minister), for the discomfort of a leaky yacht, the eponymous 'Free Church Yacht' *Betsey* (pp. 44-46, 98-99).

Swanson, like Miller, was the son of a Scots coasting captain. He attended Tain Academy. After apprenticeship to a London draper, and trading in Cromarty, he entered King's College, Aberdeen, in 1824 to study for the ministry, doing well in 'natural philosophy' (*ie* physics) and mathematics. In the vacations, he and Miller renewed their friendship, and he encouraged Miller to take personal conviction in his Calvinist faith. They went fossil-hunting together around Cromarty (p.114) and Swanson passed on some of the new ideas he had learnt at Aberdeen, if only informally – 'natural science was not taught' (Miller 1858, pp. 368-370). Apparently Swanson lost interest in geology, or at any rate in maintaining a collection, because he found higher priorities for his time – 'The young minister had greatly more important business to pursue than any which the geologic field furnishes' (p. 115) – but he still retained at least one of Miller's fish from the Old Red Sandstone when Miller visited him in 1844 (p. 114). Whether before this visit or subsequently, Swanson's collection was eventually 'dissipated', though at least some of it was given to Aberdeen University, including some of Miller's earliest finds of Old Red Sandstone fishes (Andrews 1982; Miller 1858, p. 369).*

After a spell as private tutor in the family of a Mr MacIntosh of Nairnshire, Swanson became schoolmaster of Nigg near Cromarty, a typical step towards the ministry, and was licensed (*ie* qualified as a minister) by the Presbytery of Tain. He was 'called' in 1835 to the chapel of Fort William in the parish of Kilmallie, Lochaber, and then on 27 August 1839 to the Small Isles, a living in the gift of Queen Victoria. In 1839 he married Isabella Smith. Swanson was an Evangelical, as shown by his 'coming out' with the Free Church, his social concern (*eg* for a destitute thief, pp. 95-98), and above all by his style of ministry (Cameron 1877, p. 133):

> ... incessant preaching in all the islands, week-day lectures, prayer-meetings, catechising, and schools; and when he wished to get them thoroughly indoctrinated on any important subject he published a brief tract upon it, which he printed with his own hands in his little printing press ....

By Swanson's emotional preaching, one Sunday (Swanson in Cameron 1877, p. 133),

> ... the whole congregation was moved, the house was a place of weeping, as if the promise was literally fulfilled, 'They shall look upon me whom they have pierced, and mourn.' It was an outburst of the whole, so that no mouth was silent, and no eye dry; old and young mourned together, and the blooming and withered cheeks were all wet with tears. The scene was indescribable, and I sat down mayhap to weep too.

---

* Data on Swanson's life from Ewing 1914; Scott 1915-1928; Cameron 1877; the latter gives 1840 for the call to the Small Isles.

Swanson's commitment, as noted above, extended to learning Gaelic. A Gaelic Bible had been published in the eighteenth century, enabling the establishment of schools to teach reading and writing in Gaelic, such as that which Swanson set up informally for adults and children on Eigg.** Swanson's printing press on the 'Free Church Yacht' *Betsey* was important when access to such facilities was difficult physically and politically. Indeed, literacy tended to subvert the lairds' authority. Once Gaels could read the Bible for themselves in the Reformed tradition, they could discuss its teachings and draw their own conclusions – not least about landlords and their allies. This led to the rise, during the later eighteenth and early nineteenth centuries, of *Na Daoine*, 'The Men'. These unofficial lay preachers fused evangelical revivalism with older Celtic traditions of seers and bards, challenging the authority of Moderate ministers and landlords (*eg* Hunter 1995; Ansdell 1998; Cheape 2003). Miller must have known about 'The Men', who feature in his wife Lydia's 1847 novel *Passages in the Life of an English Heiress and Scenes of the Scottish Disruption* (Calder 1993; Sutherland 2002), but, interestingly, they do not appear in *Cruise of the Betsey*. Perhaps he was being discreet; perhaps there had been none in the partly Roman Catholic Small Isles; or perhaps any 'Men' had simply become fully assimilated into the new Free Church.

Evangelicals (in both senses of the word) were deeply hostile to Roman Catholicism, which, by definition, violated key tenets of Protestantism. They were concerned by Catholic proselytisation in the Western Isles, aided by – as they saw it – negligence on the part of ministers such as Swanson's predecessor (p. 94). Swanson's biographer, himself a Free Church minister, described the parish on Swanson's arrival as 'in a half-heathen state, composed of a mixed population of Papists and nominal Protestants, full of all kinds of superstition and ignorance' (Cameron 1877, p. 133). Allegedly the local Catholics obstructed the road to the meeting-house with boulders over which the Protestants fell in the dark – but this probably reflects the sharp deterioration in relationships caused by the new minister's aggressive anti-Catholicism (Dressler 1998).

Swanson published the Gaelic pamphlet *Aideachadh a' Chreidimh Chatholaich agus diultadh Teagasg-Phapa* ('Professing the Catholic faith [presumably in the sense of an universal Christian faith, rather than Roman Catholicism] and denying the teachings of Papacy') (Scott 1915-1928). To edify the reader and raise funds to convert 'idolaters' in India, Swanson also wrote *A leisure hour in the floating manse; or, the story of Niel M– n*. It relates how Niel, an Eigg Roman Catholic, came to the Protestant faith by the chance gift of a Gaelic Bible, despite the efforts of the Roman Catholic priests to 'render the minds of their people rigid in error, like their own [and teach them] to trample reason and Scripture in the dust' (Swanson 1844). Swanson exhorted his readers to donate money for the cause;

** Dressler 1998; this was in parallel to the 'official' parish school, and seems to have been much more successful in teaching literacy, possibly because the official school used English, or because of the failings of the existing schoolmaster, especially if he was the same man who had been there in 1836 (Maclean 1845).

a few pence saved by kitchen economy would pay for a bible that might convert a heathen. But, despite such efforts, Roman Catholicism remained, and today remains, strong in Eigg and Canna, and in certain other parts of the Highlands and Islands.

In *Cruise of the Betsey*, and elsewhere in his writings, Miller forthrightly expressed his deep dislike of Roman Catholicism, for instance attacking it as encouraging blind faith and worship of relics – 'No one not an enthusiastic geologist or a zealous Roman Catholic can really know how vast an amount of interest may attach to a few old bones' (pp. 50, 85). Unfortunate as it may seem from the viewpoint of today's more ecumenical era, Miller's attitude did not, however, arise from the notoriously anti-Irish sectarianism of Lowland Scotland that was partly a reaction to the influx of poor Irish workers which was just then beginning. In fact, around 1830, he disagreed with many of his Cromarty compatriots, refusing to condemn reformist legislation giving increased rights to Roman Catholics and suppressing some of the more blatant advantages of the Anglican Church of Ireland, though this no doubt partly reflected his notorious independence of mind (Miller 1858, pp. 491, 494; David Alston, *pers. comm.* 2000).

When Miller referred to the Celts as a 'race' distinct from the 'Saxon' Lowlanders (*eg* pp. 92, 409), he was simply using language normal for the time; he was not being a prejudiced racist. Indeed, Miller's encounter with a delightful little Parsi girl at Alness gave him the opportunity to emphasise the insignificance of racial differences compared to environment and upbringing, and to denounce the anti-Celtic racism used as justification for the Clearances (pp. 354-356). In *Testimony of the Rocks* (Miller 1857, pp. 256-257), Miller did speak of the inherited degradation of the Irish peasantry, but at once blamed it on the 'iron hand of oppression'. It was then normal to accept the idea of the inheritance of acquired characteristics, at least within the limits of variation set for each species. Such acquired characteristics included the effects of persecution and ill-treatment (pp. 461-464), and we are all too familiar today with the way in which children 'inherit' physical and mental ill-health from families afflicted by social dysfunction, poverty, bad housing, malnutrition, and addiction, even if this 'inheritance' is not coded within the DNA.

To visit Eigg, Miller used the newly available coasting steamboats for long-distance trips. The Small Isles ministers found their little archipelago difficult to tend for want of a local ferry service, and an earlier predecessor of Swanson's bought his own boat (Maclean 1796; not the Maclean who followed him and preceded Swanson; Cameron 1877). Swanson's problems were greatly increased when he and his family left their home at the Disruption. The lairds refused to let him build on a suitable spot (the owner of Eigg claiming to be afraid of perpetuating religious dissension; Brown 1893, p. 421), and Swanson could not get accommodation closer than Isle Ornsay on Skye some 30 kilometres away. Swanson tackled the problem with a floating manse, the 'Free Church Yacht' *Betsey*, in which he even visited the 1843 Free Church Assembly in Glasgow (Brown 1893, pp. 420-421). The Free Church would eventually adopt its own ship, the *Breadalbane*, to ferry ministers and missionaries around the islands (Ansdell 1998).

Nevertheless, F. C. Y. *Betsey* was not the complete answer. Of the Small Isles, only Canna has a decent harbour. Eigg's is exposed from certain quarters, hence the crew's belt and braces approach to mooring (pp. 16-17). Betsey, being a yacht with, apparently, a fore and aft rig, was undoubtedly less dependent on wind direction than some other vessels (pp. 141-142), but still needed fair wind and weather, and could only proceed windward by tacking. On one occasion, Swanson and Miller were stormbound and then becalmed offshore, and it was only because some of the congregation rowed out to tow them in that Swanson could preach (pp. 211-215). In any case, 'docile little Betsey' (p. 15) was in bad condition, and near the end of her useful life (pp. 117, 211), nearly foundering with Miller on board (pp. 224-227): a 'poor vessel of twelve tons burden, some thirty feet in length, by eleven in breadth, utterly unfit to contend with the storms of the Atlantic' with a cabin 'twelve feet by six' (Brown 1893, pp. 420-422). Moreover, Swanson's own health was failing. He declined calls to other parishes but in the end he was forced to accept a second call to Nigg, just over the water from Cromarty, where he remained for the rest of his career (Cameron 1877, p. 135). The Free Church parish of Small Isles was reduced to a preaching station to be visited by a missionary (Ewing 1914, p. 233), and at least in later years it had a resident one (Dressler 1998).

The islands' economy and people

The landscapes in *Cruise of the Betsey* are dramatic scenery, certainly, but they are also inhabited landscapes with a long human history. Miller's tone was doubly detached. First, his landscapes always tended to loom over their contained figures – but then Miller was interested in the scenery. Second, without Gaelic, he could not speak directly to, and therefore for, most of the inhabitants of Eigg – and perhaps he was being discreet lest his informants be persecuted. But he did retain his human sympathy, for he was sending despatches from a disaster area, in some of his earliest public comments on the Highlands. (Main sources for social and economic history: Smout 1969, 1986; Devine 1988, 1994, 1999; Hunter 1995; Gaskell 1996).

Miller's description of the Free Church congregation on Eigg (p. 90), issuing from the door of the building where they are meeting for prayer, 'like carder bees from their nest of dried grass and moss', was evocative of such turf-walled and roofed buildings blending into the landscape. It seems no coincidence that Miller, a careful writer, referred by implication to bees' industrious habits, and he went on to assert that 'The islanders of Eigg are an active, middle-sized race, with well-developed heads, acute intellects, and singularly warm feelings'. This was sympathetic writing, for Miller was effectively presenting the Eigg folk to Lowlander readers as made in their own image. At this time, and even more so after the failure of the potato harvest in 1846 (a year after that in Ireland) started a decade of famine and the ensuing appeals for relief, Scottish large-circulation newspapers usually adopted a tone of contempt for the 'inferior race' of the Highlands and Islands, the supposedly idle, primitive and ungrateful peasants who were blamed for their own destitution (Alston 1999; Devine 1994; Fenyő 2000).

If sometimes such Lowlander contempt was almost in the same breath as glorification of the high romance of the Highland clans, and the bravery of the Highland regiments, then that was just the 'noble' side of the same underlying savage. Another memoir of another 1840s cruise, this time by a well-connected gentleman on a Fisheries Board inspection cruise, commented on the islanders' supposed use of the Massacre Cave (Wilson 1842, p. 237):

> That they are a high-minded and romantic race these islanders, and extremely tenacious of their ancestral glories, is evident from this, that during the potato harvest the pigs are put out of the way of doing mischief by being all cooped up in this same ancestral cave, – and fine mumbling work they will make of it, while grumphing to each other, – *de mortuis nil nisi bones* [*sic*]. Now as the people eat the pigs, and the pigs the people's predecessors, it follows logically that the present natives are a race of cannibals of the very worst description.

I find this tale frankly unbelievable given the cave's inconvenient and marginal location. There was surely a practical joke somewhere along the line, while the victims, as Miller pointed out, were not, of course, 'ancestral' to the islanders. But the point is not so much the story's truth, as the willingness to propagate it.

Under Miller, *The Witness* was almost the only large-circulation newspaper which took a sympathetic attitude to the Gaels, neither romantic nor contemptuous (Fenyő 2000). But Miller, as a boy, had visited the seemingly primitive cottage of his Gaelic aunt and her husband near Lairg in Sutherland, and found, not squalor and idleness, but Christian worship, hard work and intelligent debate. Indeed, it was observation of his cousin, a stonemason who used his spare time in intellectual pursuits, which inspired Miller to take the crucial decision to become a mason (Miller 1858, pp. 94–115).

Cruise of the Betsey fascinatingly depicted Scotland late in the Age of Improvement, in transition from the old agrarian society of communal subsistence farming to the modern cash economy. The Lowlands agricultural revolution was almost complete. The landlords had razed old 'fermtouns' (communal farms) and small-holdings to create heavily capitalized large farms, powered by steam engines and heavy horses, with sheep ranches on higher ground. As we find in *Johnny Gibb of Gushetneuk*, and as Miller found around Cononside (p. 164), the displaced peasants became a mobile rural proletariat in a free labour market of 'farm servants' on fixed contracts, or simply went to the expanding towns. New industries sprang up to meet new demands. Lime, to spread on fields and build farm-steadings, came from kilns like that immolating the fossil fishes of Clune (p. 191), and fields were drained with earthenware drains and pipe-tiles from claypits such as Blackpots (p. 258).

'Improvement' was, however, still in full swing in the other Scottish agrarian society, the Gaelic-speaking Highlands and Islands. The ancient clan structure was founded on a hierarchy of tenants below the chieftain. The lower ranks lived often in communal settlements, growing subsistence crops of oats and potatoes, and raising cattle to pay rent, supplemented with earnings from migrant labour at the Lowland harvest and as soldiers and sailors. The upper classes were increasingly drawn into wider British society, reorganising their estates to maximise cash yields. The resulting transformation varied much from place to place, and *Cruise of the Betsey* captured its later stages in two of the Small Isles.

Many areas, such as Rùm and parts of Eigg, were 'cleared' of their inhabitants and put to intensive sheep farming (Magnusson 1997; Love 2001; Dressler 1998). Economies of scale dictated large flocks of imported Blackface and Cheviot breeds, which needed both the hill grazing and, for wintering the Cheviots, the lower arable land. Far fewer workers were needed, and tended to be incomers as they had to have special experience of the new breeds. Miller was stunned by the resulting 'extermination' of Rùm's human community (pp. 134–135), though it is important to appreciate that he was speaking metaphorically, for there was no hint of the physical violence that compounded some clearances elsewhere. That is not to say, however, that the people were not compelled to leave, taking voyage on ships that were quite probably unsafe, understocked, and disease-ridden, and trying to make a new life in North America without adequate capital (Love 2001). In fact, contrary to Miller's comments, one Rùm-born family did remain, and as Miller noted (p. 134), more had to be brought in when it was realised that the clearances had been too drastic; but later clearances, down to 1852, would again reduce the population to a few dozen, mostly born off-island. Miller's readers would have recognised the sharp edge of his later anecdote (pp. 159–161) of the minister of the Established Church (and by implication a sympathiser with the lairds) on the gig from Lochcarron, and how he mistook Miller 'for a southland shepherd looking out for a farm' and gave him appropriate advice.

What happened to these displaced people, from Rùm and elsewhere? As Miller put it (p. 136), 'a few ... more adventurous spirits' from Rùm had already emigrated to 'America' – which in this context usually meant North America and more specifically what is now Canada (Love 2001) – and elsewhere, as before and since; but it was one thing to emigrate willingly with adequate resources, and quite another to be pushed, or to have to jump at the last moment. Many Gaels, if not those from Rùm, simply crowded into Lowlands towns, especially on the Highlands fringe; Cromarty was one such town. Tenants might also be cleared within a landowner's estate, as on Eigg. They were moved onto a 'croft' or smallholding which was sometimes made deliberately too small for them to survive by farming alone, forcing the tenant to carry out work specified by the landlord. Miller described Sutherland (1871, p. 392, originally published 1843, Shortland 1996d):

> The county has not been depopulated – its population has been merely arranged after a new fashion. The late Duchess found it spread equally over the interior and the sea-coast, and in very comfortable circumstances; – she left it compressed

into a wretched selvage of poverty and suffering, that fringes the county on its eastern and western shores ....

In places this work was fishing, but elsewhere, as on Eigg, it was often kelp-burning (Dressler 1998). 'Kelp' was then the term both for certain types of seaweed and for their alkali ash, which was a crucial feedstock for the chemical industry, notably explosives manufacture, and in glassmaking. Gathering the weed, by wading in the sea, and burning it, all for little pay, was compared unfavourably to work in American slave plantations. When the Napoleonic Wars closed off Continental sources and increased prices and demand, some lairds put even more emphasis on kelping. To maximise their captive cheap labour force, they encouraged subdivision of crofts and squatting by landless 'cottars', and excessive reliance on potatoes (which needed little labour, although now the kelp was burnt rather than used as manure). They also discouraged emigration in the guise of concern for safety.

Yet the Highlands and Islands were remote, their environment variable, and economy marginal. The old mixed economy had allowed some flexibility, as Miller himself noted in 1851 (Miller 1862, pp. 207-217); if one year the oats failed, a family might still pay rent and survive on potatoes and on meal bought with cash from selling some beasts, or from working in the Lowlands harvest, while John Stewart and no doubt other islanders were masters of all the island crafts, in notable contrast to the prevailing philosophy of the division of labour (p. 17). But 'improvement' forced subsistence peasants to become specialists. Successful (if depending always on one's definition of success) in the economically robust Lowlands, this special-isation was disastrous in the Highlands, whose 'improved' economy was vulnerable to external factors. Peace in 1815 threw many soldiers and sailors out of service, and opened the way for imports of kelp substitutes, destroying the market, except for specialist products such as iodine (pp. 155, 431-432). Fisheries were found to be unreliable (p. 99). Yet rents were not reduced to compensate, and indebtedness grew. Before long, the people were destitute and over-dependent on the potato. The final disaster came in 1846 and the following years, when potato blight devastated the crop leading to famine. Total catastrophe on the Irish scale was only averted by charitable agencies, in which the Free Church was prominent, directed by the intelligence network of its ministers. Some lairds bankrupted themselves to help their tenants, but others shocked even Sir Charles Trevelyan, the Civil Service administrator of the relief effort, who exemplified the *laissez-faire* philosophy of the day, requiring applicants for relief to do eight hours' manual work, often stone-breaking for roads, for their daily ration of a pound of meal, lest they become 'idle'.

When sheep farming hit economic trouble, some of the land made available was taken up for game preserves. Miller bitterly condemned the clearance of human communities for game-shooting, and was always opposed to the protection of game as a wasteful luxury which led to injustice and criminalization for ordinary people (Miller 1862). As Miller had feared (pp. 135-136), Rùm was bought by the Marquess of Salisbury in 1845 and converted to a game park. Being more accessible, at least by private yacht, than much of the Highlands before they were opened up by the coming of the railways in the 1840s and 1850s, Rùm was perhaps one of the first estates to satisfy the Victorian craze for Scottish bloodsport, inspired by Walter Scott's audacious reinvention of Scottish culture as quintessentially Highland, and reinforced when Queen Victoria and Prince Albert bought the Balmoral estate on the mainland in 1852 (Tapper 1992).

Initially almost isolated in the Scottish press, Miller went on to publish important attacks on the landlords and appeals for famine relief in *The Witness*. A complication in assessing his impact is that modern studies are apt to credit to *The Witness* articles that were in fact by Miller himself. Many articles were, of course, formally anonymous, and it is not possible to be certain which were his, unless they were later reprinted in book form under his name (Shortland 1996d; Secord 2003). At any rate, Miller reiterated that the Gaels were suffering from bad landlords and their forced dependence on the potato, not their own laziness and degradation (which, in so far as they existed, stemmed from their impossible situation). Miller was thus one of the first newspapermen to condemn the Highlands Clearances publicly and to blame the landed proprietors for oppression and eviction, at a time when the rights of 'Property' were almost unquestioned.

Miller was not, however, the 'radical' which he has sometimes been considered by historians of the Clearances, and he lacked the full-blooded political radicalism of writers such as Thomas Mulock, Robert Somers, and Donald M'Leod (Fenyő 2000). Generally, like many at that time, Miller was hostile to Chartism, socialism and communism (such as it then was) (p. 437; and Miller 1862 *passim*), and to what we would call the politics of class. This is unsurprising: he was a Cromarty burgher at heart, scandalised by the drunken and dissolute urban workmen he had encountered as a mason (Miller 1858). In fact, Miller had no complaints about lairds using power responsibly (Alston 1996). What he did condemn were the abuse of power and wealth, and the neglect of social responsibility, and he even advocated limited land reform (Fenyő 2000). Miller's comments on the Eigg houses (pp. 216–217) were surely influenced by his experiences as a mason lodging in country hovels and in grim bothies, the bare barracks housing unmarried farm-servants and itinerant masons on many Lowlands farms (Miller 1858, 1862). From his experience of sub-middle class life (Alston 2002) he knew that many Scottish landlords failed to use their power benevolently. Instead they ground the poor into the dirt, depriving them of dignity and hope, and sometimes so demoralising them as to drive them into immorality and away from a moral life and any hope of Christian redemption (Miller 1862).

In the longer run, however, *The Witness* never made the Highlands a central issue, and it appears to have reduced coverage from 1850 onwards, although famine and destitution were continuing at a time when argument was raging about the alleged inferiority of the 'Celtic race' (Fenyő 2000). This seems surprising, because of the strength of the Free Church in the Highlands and Islands. There had, however, arisen more radical newspapers such as the *North British Daily Mail*, whose editor from 1849 was Robert Somers, Miller's former assistant. Perhaps Miller came to downplay the Clearances as a personal reaction to Somers (Dr David

Alston, *pers. comm.* 2000), or as a commercial response to position *The Witness* more clearly in its own niche. Maybe his attention simply moved on to other issues. Miller would also have had an eye to commercial reality, in the likely need to avoid alienating the Lowlands middle classes and 'respectable' working classes that would have formed the economic bedrock of the Free Church and *The Witness*'s circulation.

To the Highlands and Islands folk, perhaps the worst part of the whole sorry period was the way in which the chiefs of the clans repudiated what the clansfolk considered their traditional right to their home soil. However, Miller, perhaps unsurprisingly, was not much concerned with this issue in *Cruise of the Betsey*. What offended him was the affront to human dignity, and the extermination of human communities. He was not romantic about the old clan system, which, to him, was linked to the Stuart oppressors and to barbarities such as the massacre in the cave on Eigg. Above all, he did not treat the Highlands and Islands as a romantic fairyland where the rules of real life – as he saw it – were suspended, whether for the clansman harking back to the past, the new laird seeking a private empire, or the tourist drawn by Scott's novels. Instead, he judged them by his own standards, and here, I believe, we come to the root of Miller's view of society.

The 'Godly Commonwealth' in the Small Isles

Miller and his readers lived at a time when society was based far more on the parish than it is today, to the extent that Scotland then has even been called a 'parish state'. The Lowlands, of Miller and many of his readers, had a structured society with an increasingly significant middle class, whose male members had recently gained the parliamentary vote in the Reform Act of 1832, if, as Miller noted approvingly, they had a stake in society in the form of a minimum level of property (p. 167).

In contrast, Miller's account of his time on the Small Isles would, I believe, have given the impression of a society which had collapsed, if indeed it had ever been functional, although his comments are reactions to particular situations rather than a full analysis of social and economic issues. The parish had a dense population of over a thousand (inconceivable to the modern visitor!), but, as in the Highlands and Islands more generally, the former middle classes had mostly escaped by emigration. There was now little between the great mass of the poor and the rich lairds other than the lairds' agents, incoming sheep farmers and the like. Without the vote and without the legally secure, rent-controlled tenancy of the crofting laws of the 1880s, the ordinary peasant was at the landowner's mercy. On an island, or a estate which was so large that it might as well have been an island, the peasant had to accept the laird's policy, or leave home, difficult enough emotionally even if the money was available. Eviction was legally easy, tenures were only annual, and any improvements to the croft might bring higher rents but not necessarily any compensation on removal.

In such a parish, the minister, schoolteacher and doctor might be the only professional men, perhaps the only English speakers, even potentially independent of local magnates. Indeed, sometimes they were one and the same man (Swanson was the 'sole medical man', p. 90). This made patronage even more important. Although the patron of the Small Isles was the Crown rather than the landowner, it seems no coincidence that Donald Maclean, Swanson's predecessor and the brother-in-law of Rùm's tenant, protested little when his father-in-law evicted the population, when, as he put it, 'In 1826, all the inhabitants of the Island of Rum ... found it necessary to leave their native country, and to seek for new abodes in the distant wilds of our colonies in America' (Maclean 1845, p. 152).

As far as one can tell today, the Reverend Maclean was himself a poor minister. Indeed Miller's account (pp. 92-93) was understated, for the Presbytery of Skye had accused Maclean of a range of offences from cursing, swearing, drunkenness, and complete neglect of duty, to violence, wife-beating, adultery, indecent exposure, and sexual assault (Anon. 1835). Maclean had allegedly sworn an 'oath of purgation' regarding a woman. It was probably a formal public denial of adultery, implying a loss of reputation scandalous in itself. On top of this it was sworn before the Catholic priest of all people. The Presbytery's proceedings seem to have been pressed with more energy than expertise, and with witnesses who were perhaps more enthusiastic than they should have been. Maclean resisted for years with legal help, claiming to be 'tired' rather than drunk, denouncing the Presbytery's legal practices, criticising hostile witnesses' statements and bringing his own witnesses, who no doubt had in mind who his relatives were. But, whether or not Maclean had suffered rough justice, he himself summarily resolved the matter by appearing 'senselessly drunk' during his trial at the General Assembly, and was at once deposed (p. 93).

The funding of any Kirk parish contained a potential conflict of interest. The parish session paid the salary of the minister, who was allocated a 'glebe', a stretch of land, to farm or rent out as he wished. The Eigg glebe was particularly good and substantial, and its barn to store the harvest still stands today, converted to a field study centre. The session covered the running costs and maintenance of church and school, and the salary of the schoolteacher. It also supported the poor and infirm, and paid other incidental expenses. To do all this, it was funded partly by teinds (a parish land tax levied on 'heritors', *ie* landowners, in proportion to landholdings), and partly from voluntary donations, particularly for the poor (and partly by poor rates on tenants as well as heritors where these were formally assessed). A landowner wanting to minimise teinds would find it easier to exert pressure if patronage operated and he could choose the minister, especially when (as in much of the Highlands and Islands, though not the Small Isles) the patron was the main, or even the sole, heritor. However, as many lairds themselves recognised, it was an abdication of social responsibility to push teinds below the level at which the parish could function: this would have repudiated the ideal of the Godly Commonwealth to which Miller and the Evangelicals adhered.

The Small Isles parish was evidently in trouble, even before the Disruption. Maclean wrote in 1836, not long before Swanson took over (Maclean 1845, pp. 153-154):

There is no church on any of the islands. In Eigg we assemble in the school-house for public worship; but in the other islands we sometimes meet in the fields .... The only [parish] fund from which [the poor] derive any benefit is one of L. 30 [£30], bequeathed by the late Captain Macaskill .... Any addition to the interest of this sum is made up of fines.

But when Miller visited a poor invalid woman on Eigg (p. 218), he found that:

... not during the ten years in which she had been bed-ridden [including Swanson's Establishment ministry pre-1843] had she received a single farthing from the proprietor, nor, indeed, had any of the poor of the island, and ... the parish had no session-funds. I saw her husband .... They had no means of living, he said, save through the charity of their poor neighbours, who had so little to spare; for the parish or the proprietor had never given them anything.

Miller's Free Church readers would interpret this as showing the lairds' gross neglect of their moral and social duties. Of course, these judgements would have been by Lowlands standards. Yet Miller, no doubt partly as a result of his experiences as a mason, was no more sanguine about the Lowlands, and if anything compared poverty in the Lowlands unfavourably to life in an Eigg shieling (p. 83). Indeed, he pointedly asked, if there really were too many people in Scotland, why it should be the Highlanders who were cleared off abroad, when they could make a living if let alone, rather than the impoverished unemployed of the cities (p. 135).

Miller's emphasis on poverty in *Cruise of the Betsey* was topical: and not just in Gaeldom. The mid-1840s was a time of controversy over how to relieve poverty, and a Royal Commission reported on the matter in 1844 (Miller 1862; Levitt and Smout 1979; Mitchison 2000). Many Scottish Presbyterians regarded statutory relief as a moral evil, shameful and demoralising to the recipient. They advocated voluntary charity organized at the parish level, as being morally superior for both giver and recipient. The minister and elders directed support to the 'deserving', but not those perceived as idle or dissolute, even if failings such as prostitution were a result of poverty. The Old Poor Law of Scotland was partly based on this model (with the option of an assessment or local tax). However, relief was uneven, sometimes giving the poor an unenviable choice between moral starvation and immoral survival. Even if the parish-based system worked in a Lowland agrarian parish (and assuming that the landowners paid up), it was hard to apply in an inner city (as Chalmers's experiments discovered), or an industrial area with periodic mass unemployment, or the economic disaster area of the Highlands and Islands. The alternative, of course, was a modern Poor Law in the English style. Despite rearguard campaigns by Chalmers and his allies, including Miller, who condemned it (Miller 1862, pp. 217-230), such a system was set up in Scotland in 1845. It levied a 'poor rate' on land-owners, who might still delay it in their areas or take it as an incentive for further clearances (Fenyő 2000), and on tenants, which Miller thought discouraged voluntary contributions and taxed the lower classes (p. 353). Even then its implementation was uneven, and the poor found it more difficult to secure their rights in the courts than when they could simply speak to the minister or elder (pp. 218-219).

Miller's sociopolitical critique: a view with hindsight

Miller was certainly expressing strong opinions on the state of the Highlands and Islands in *Cruise of the Betsey*, as he did elsewhere. But crucial questions still remain to be conclusively answered for the Highlands and Islands as a whole, let alone the Small Isles, before we can even begin to assess his judgements beyond tentative conclusions. Plainly, some social and economic change and a dispersal of excess population were essential to avoid a 'Malthusian' disaster, never mind achieve an increase in living standards (not that Lowlands farm servants or industrial workers were much better off). But the people themselves were taking their own steps, by voluntary emigration, migrant labour, and so on. It is also clear that some landlords made the deteriorating situation grossly worse by their actions, for instance by their push towards kelping and their attempt to restrict voluntary emigration. Certainly, the Small Isles lairds could have managed their estates more prudently so as to give their small tenants a better chance at fending for themselves. Nevertheless, in the worsening economic climate, it is not at all clear whether the Small Isles lairds had the resources to make much difference in the long run, without subsidising their estates with income from elsewhere, effectively shifting the burden onto, for instance, Lowlands workers or Indian peasants (cf. Morvern, Gaskell 1996). Indeed, some Highlands and Islands lairds did bankrupt themselves while trying to help their tenants during the famine years; but this is in a sense irrelevant, as the famine was yet to come when Miller was reporting from Eigg during what passed for 'normal' times.

Be all that as it may, the key issue in my view is that *Cruise of the Betsey* does not even try to be a systematic sociopolitical analysis. It is assertions of morality that Miller makes, not arguments from economic theory. Yet economics ruled during that Age of Improvement: many thought that the responsible thing to do was to maximize an estate's financial yield, regardless of any other consideration. Miller did not agree, and this cannot be ascribed to anti-laird prejudice, or to Celtic romanticism. Whether it reflected his high morality and common humanity, or was instead an unrealistic blindness to the 'facts' of free market economics, is perhaps a value judgement for the reader, rather than a question for me to answer on the reader's behalf – at least as a historian. Without doubt, however, it is one of those uncomfortable but vital questions which Miller, 'not a man of easy messages' (Secord 2003, p. 337), asks us even today.†

---

† Note added in press: the proceedings of the major conference marking the bicentenary of Miller's birth in 2002 were published as this edition of *Cruise of the Betsey* went to press (Borley 2003). These include studies on folklore, church, society and politics, all highly relevant to the issues raised by *Cruise of the Betsey*, and to which the interested reader is referred.

At any rate, in the years that followed Miller's trips, the Clearances continued. As *Cruise of the Betsey* showed, the Free Church allied the Highlands and Islands peasantry with the Lowlands industrialists, middle classes and aspiring artisans who read *The Witness*. The strength of the Free Church in Gaeldom had originally stemmed from the evangelical (in the broad sense) revival in the Highlands long before the Disruption. It was not a direct result of class conflict. But being a member of the Free Church came to be seen, then as now, as a defiant rejection – and one within the law – of the lairds' claim to total power, as so well expressed in *Cruise of the Betsey* and, for the Lowlands, in *Johnnie Gibb of Gushetneuk*. In some parishes, only the landlords and major tenants, and their personal servants, were left in the Established Church. Harassment of the Free Church by some landlords simply reinforced the point. The split between the Established and Free Churches therefore tended to reflect the political split between conservative and liberal, landlords versus peasantry. The Free Kirk, or rather its individual members, came to be involved in the debates over the Clearances and, later in the nineteenth century, the crofters' rights movements. Gladstone's Liberal government passed land reforms in the 1880s, giving crofters some security of tenure and fair rents, and making crofting a persisting feature of the Highlands and Islands landscape. This was reinforced by the Congested Districts Boards which bought up more land to convert to crofts in the early twentieth century.

The Free Church itself came under tension as the century went on. The Lowlands middle classes became more liberal in religion but less sympathetic to the Highlanders, while the Highlands peasantry remained conservative in religion. This led to the 'Second Disruption' of 1893 with the secession of the Free Presbyterian Church, notably in the Highlands and Islands (Ansdell 1998; Macleod 2000). In 1900 the union of the Free Church with the United Presbyterian Church to form the United Free Church caused a second secession of Free Church members into a 'Free Church continuing', again with a high proportion of Highlands and Islands members (Ansdell 1998). The United Free Church finally merged in 1929 with the Church of Scotland which had by then long abandoned patronage, but again a proportion stayed out in a United Free Church. To this day, the remaining Free Churches and their descendant bodies, and the Liberal Party and its successor, have remained relatively strong in the crofting areas.

Rùm and Eigg strikingly show the different consequences of landlords' actions two centuries ago. Rùm is still the 'home of wild animals' that Miller foresaw, if now a National Nature Reserve run by Scottish Natural Heritage to study its remarkable geology, and Highlands and Islands ecology (Emeleus 1997; Magnusson 1997; Love 2001). As I write (2002), there is debate about rejecting this solution and putting more emphasis on human settlement – but the original human community which Miller mourned can never be restored. In contrast, Eigg was never totally cleared, although many people were moved from their original settlements, and it shows a hybrid landscape of large farms and small crofts (Dressler 1998). In recent years Eigg saw well-publicized disputes between tenants and successive lairds, with the 1990s newspaper coverage uncannily paralleling Miller's reportage, even to featuring elderly folk in dilapidated cottages. Now the community hold the island in trust, and seek sustainable tourism attracted by the scenery that Miller described. How intrigued Miller would have been, even if he did not always approve of communal holdings!

Miller the travelling geologist

It would have been a relief for the reader of *Cruise of the Betsey*, just as it must have been for Miller, to turn from human miseries to the glories of nature. Many of Miller's geological writings had specific purposes, for instance to argue his views on education, or self-help, or the evolutionary theories of the time. A few are not his most readable works, as the occasional more abstract passages in *Cruise of the Betsey* reveal (*eg* pp. 236-237), and they must sometimes have been arduous to write. But some articles almost write themselves, and much of *Cruise of the Betsey* has this feel to it. It is plain, refreshing geology, for its own sake, and has long been loved by fellow 'votaries of the stony science' (p. 179) (*eg* Hudson 2000, 2003). Indeed, Lydia Miller commented (Miller 1859, pp. xiii-xiv) on *Rambles of a Geologist* and its

> freshness, buoyancy and vigour … the spontaneous utterances of a mind set free from an occupation never very congenial, – that of writing compulsory articles for a newspaper, – to find refreshment amid the familiar haunts in which it delighted, and to seize with a grasp easy, yet powerful, on the recreation of a favourite science ….

Cruise of the Betsey and *Rambles of a Geologist* together offer an insight into the practice of geology by a well-known 'literary geologist' of his time in the countryside that he loved. It shows his exhilaration in exploring new terrain, and his fascination with the evidence, the 'Testimony of the Rocks', that anyone could learn to decipher.

Miller found geology a satisfying and relaxing open air hobby, in the 'mere leisure interstices of a somewhat busy life' (p. 476). He suffered from chronic lung disease, apparently the effects of silicosis contracted while a mason, and perhaps combined with tuberculosis (Miller 1858), which was probably why he had to abandon his customary Scottish expedition in 1845 (p. 381) in favour of a gentler tour of England (Miller 1847), although he did manage a visit to Eigg. In 1846 and 1847 he was still not as robust as he had been (pp. 292, 332). Other folk might have visited a spa such as Strathpeffer (p. 372), or a seaside resort, but Miller did his holidays the hard way, as was *de rigueur* for Victorian naturalists (Allen 1994). The fresh air, exercise, and absence from routine work were themselves curative when cities were polluted from coal smoke and gas lighting.

Miller was travelling at the start of the transport revolution, when the railways were still largely confined to central Scotland. A coasting steamboat, mail coach or gig would take him some of the way, but otherwise he walked. Even as an Edinburgh newspaper editor, Miller was well known for his habitual dress as a Scottish Lowland countryman, in a suit of tweed or similar material, with his rolled maud (a Lowlander's overblanket or wrap, in a plain grey pattern, not a Highland tartan) slung over his shoulder (Geikie in Anon. 1902; Geikie 1906). Miller's outfit was practical. Undoubtedly, also, he was declaring his pride in his origins, and the independence so critical to his editorial freedom, which is surely why Miller travelled incognito, with occasionally ludicrous results, in contrast to gentlemanly geologists such as Roderick Murchison who used their connections to stay in hunting lodges and mansions (Geikie 1875). Some portraits show Miller in a suit of reasonably good quality, such as a farmer might wear in town (Tarrant, *pers. comm.* 2000). But in *Cruise of the Betsey*, Miller's rougher outdoor suit of jacket and trousers, in homespun 'russet', and heavy hobnailed boots were more typical of the Lowlands shepherds and cattle drovers, for whom he was routinely mistaken (pp. 159, 238, 393, 424). Such an outfit might not compare to modern outdoor clothing, or the Reverend Swanson's oilskin, but close-woven wool is surprisingly warm even when wet, and the maud could be unrolled and caped under the umbrella that was needed for the worst Highland weather (p. 250, 375).

Miller's equipment included specimen bag, hammers and chisels, and, to wrap specimens, a supply of 'a fine soft Conservative Edinburgh newspaper, valuable for a quality of preserving old things entire' (p. 1). Miller had a change of smalls or 'linen' (p. 238), but did not always bother with a full change of clothes if travelling light on a side trip (p. 112). The knapsack that held them might have been an ex-Army one judging from the Gardenstown drunk's inquiry (p. 248). The 'microscope' he used (p. 137) was probably his own, a 'botanist's' microscope 'of no great power' with 'three glasses' (Miller 1859, p. 248). It resembled those modern hand lenses with three coaxially pivoted lenses that can be used singly or together, except that the whole was detachably mounted on a stand with a stage for specimens. Such microscopes usually could be taken apart to pack into a flat and conveniently pocket-sized box (cf. Nuttall 1979, p. 27; Morrison-Low and Nuttall 2003). Noticeably missing were a compass and clinometer (to measure the dip of strata), typical of the Victorian professional and modern geologist, but then Miller had neither time nor, probably, inclination for detailed mapping. Miller's brace of pistols were not so much for shooting at porpoises (p. 116), but for self-defence when geologizing alone in crime-ridden countryside (Miller 1847, pp. 245-247).

Miller the fossil collector

To this day Miller's collection, mostly in the National Museums of Scotland, forms a key part of Scotland's geological database. Miller was a collector at a time when the science of geology was thriving all over Britain far beyond the learned societies of the capitals, the universities, and the incipient State survey. It was practised by many people whom we might now, anachronistically for that age with few professional geologists, call amateurs, and, as *Cruise of the Betsey* shows very well, one of the key roles of the provincial geologist was collecting in the field (Knell 2000; Taylor 2000; Knell and Taylor 2003).

Miller was a keen collector in both the field and the cabinet senses of the word, thrilled by discovery and the beauty of his finds, such as the fossil fish 'still as glossy and bright as the japan [enamel] on a *papier-maché* tray' (p. 181). He collected at a time when there were still many small local quarries, like that at Clune (p. 191), rather than today's large centralised operations distributing their product over long distances by mechanised transport. Miller was an important pioneer and locator of fossil sites, his skill at ripping up and breaking open rocks undoubtedly helped by the 'fifteen years' previous practice of the operative mason' (p. 241), which included the location and quarrying of suitable building stone (Miller 1858). However, fossils and good building stone often did not go together (p. 181), and in any case his skills as a fossil collector had to be developed well beyond this (Knell and Taylor 2003). One vital skill is to develop a deep familiarity, layer by layer, with local rocks and more specifically their contained fossils, as Miller did with his home area of Cromarty. This was, of course, best shown in *The Old Red Sandstone* (Miller 1841), but *Cruise of the Betsey* showed him predicting new outcrops of his favourite fossil fishes thereabouts, and seizing temporary opportunities, as when a burst mill–dam scoured clean the bedrock of a ravine, or a storm swept the shingle from a beach (pp. 76, 304, 325-326, 331-332). Miller was also collecting away from his home ground, in the role of travelling collector. Even being at known sites was important: stunning fossil fishes might be destroyed uncollected (pp. 191-192). And in new areas, such as Eigg, he would work systematically through their rocks. Any palaeontologist would be proud of his long day's trek around northern Eigg when, amongst other things, he discovered the first substantial deposit of Scottish Jurassic reptiles. This was not as easy as it sounds, because he was dealing not with skeletons of dinosaurian proportions but small isolated bones and teeth – and finding the actual source stratum took longer (pp. 49 onwards, 77-80, 222-223, Hudson 2003). Indeed, one gets the impression that Miller could never pass by a hole in the ground without investigating, as when he rooted in the foundations of a new Free Church manse (p. 424).

Miller was also well integrated in the network of British geology (Collie 2003; Janvier 2003; Knell and Taylor 2003). For all his diffidence, detestation of being patronized, and independence (he declined an invitation to stay on Orkney to save precious field time, p. 433), he was no misanthrope, and was always happy to talk geology with his friends and Lydia's, including ladies (Bayne 1871; Miller 1858; Sutherland 2002). Miller's enthusiasm for the fossils of Pabay ('Pabba') and Skye (p. 149) presaged his later encouragement of the young Archibald Geikie to investigate this area and make one of his first scientific presentations (Geikie [1856]). This helped to start Geikie's rise to Director-General of the Geological Survey and President of the Royal Society – so, in one sense, Geikie was Miller's greatest 'find' (Oldroyd 1996a). As for the amateur network itself, we find Miller repeatedly connecting into it, through old friends such as Robert Dick, the Thurso baker, and Patrick Duff and his Elgin friends (Willis 2002; Collie 2003), as well as people whom he had never met. He sought local advice on where and what to look for, saving time as at Tobermory (p. 12) and Elgin (p. 200), where he also visited one of the museums then being set up by local societies, as again at Stromness (p. 433): seeing the actual fossils of a district made it easier for him to judge what to look for in the field (Knell and Taylor 2003).

Miller also followed the network of Free Church ministers and elders (*eg* p. 394), which in any case often overlapped with the scientific net, as with the Reverend John Longmuir of Aberdeen (p. 234) and the Orcadians. Nor did Miller disdain Establishment ministers such as the Reverend Charles Clouston (p. 464; Miller 1864, p. 186). Dr Garson of Orkney exemplifies the medical men, another important group of geologically inclined professional men in the countryside. In return, Miller contributed his own expertise and observations, such as the bone of 'Asterolepis' (pp. 414-415). Swanson might have abandoned active geology, but he still showed Miller the Eigg caves, and would surely have pointed out fossils of the kinds which they had hunted together at Eathie in their younger days. Did he, then, also show Miller sites, such as the Jurassic beds of the southern Bay of Laig, which (at least today) are not immediately obvious (J. D. Hudson, *pers. comm.* 2002)? Swanson might have known about them from his own observation, or local report of the activities of geological visitors such as Hay Cunningham. The locals, though not necessarily Swanson, must also have known about the 'musical sands' of Camas Sgiotaig, of which *Cruise of the Betsey* appears to be the first published account.

Miller could also seek information and specimens in return for cash, at least in theory: specialist commercial fossil collectors and dealers seem to have been rare in Scotland compared to England (although Miller employed one at Girvan in south-western Scotland: Miller 1899b, p. 311; McCance 2002; Knell and Taylor 2003). However, there would surely have been casuals seeking supplementary earnings from fossils, from the quarryman putting fossils to one side for beer money, to the labourer digging out the fish bed at Gamrie, who was perhaps the very local guide whom Miller sought at Gardenstown (p. 240).

Miller's geology then and now

Cruise of the Betsey gives a fascinating insight into mid-nineteenth century geology interpreted by a master writer. Miller was both a good journalist and a good palaeontologist, synthesising his own assessment from a critical reading of the older works and of the evidence in the field and the fossil. He was an exceptionally acute observer, and not only for finding fossils. He was much concerned with the details of fossils, even microscopic details, and indeed he corrected the great palaeontologist Louis Agassiz when it came to reconstructing the fish *Coccosteus* (p. 396). In *Cruise of the Betsey* we see Miller as a careful observer of the outcrops of rocks (*eg* pp. 55-58), the structure of bloodstones (pp. 127-132), striated pebbles (pp. 304-306), and the reduction ('bleaching') of iron compounds in bogs (pp. 326-329). Invariably he wondered what bearing his finds had on some, at least, of the great geological

questions of the day, reflecting his characteristic journalistic style, and he often
returned to them in later writings, such as his – apparently – original thoughts on
past climates and tree-rings in fossil wood (Hudson 2003), and the implications for
evolutionary thought of the Orcadian fossils and lochs (*eg* Miller 1857, 1864).

Just because Miller wrote about geology does not, of course, mean that he
originated the entire content of his writings, and it is necessary to distinguish
carefully between Miller the geologist and Miller the journalist. In general, his
main, and most substantial, contribution to palaeontology comprised his discoveries of fossils and their source strata, and his insightful and detailed observations
and reconstructions based on these finds. This was especially so for the fishes from
the Old Red Sandstone of Devonian age which he notably described in *The Old
Red Sandstone* (1841), and which play a smaller part in *Cruise of the Betsey* (Andrews
1982; Oldroyd 1996a; Janvier 2003; Trewin 2003b; Waterston 2002a, 2002b). Miller
also took an interest in fossil plants, for instance (Oldroyd 1996a). Such research
was important, and even more at the 'cutting edge' of science than it might seem
today. Palaeontology and comparative anatomy were examining important, and
unresolved, issues about the diversity of living things and how this might have come
about (*eg* by evolution or divine creation?). For instance, only during the last few
decades had it become clear that there had been a series of mass extinctions during
geological time, with implications not only for science but also for religion. Old Red
Sandstone fishes, many found by Miller, were almost the earliest vertebrates then
known, and he had helped to show that some of them belonged to a new and now
extinct group, the placoderms.

Miller was not a major contributor on the theoretical front, but then not many
geologists ever were – although, interestingly, his prose is noticeably less readable on
theoretical matters than on specific issues such as individual specimens or reconstructions of a past environment. His views on stratigraphy were partly erroneous
and even misleading, yet much (if perhaps not all: see the discussion of Rùm below)
of this simply reflected the immature state of Scottish geology at the time, while his
early death, perhaps misleadingly for later readers, froze his published views into
obsolescence during a period of rapid advancement. For instance, he just missed the
major reorganization of the stratigraphy of the Old Red Sandstone, as is clear from
the editorial changes to posthumous editions of *The Old Red Sandstone* (Oldroyd
1996a). In any case, however, he was a strictly spare-time geologist with limited
opportunities (Knell and Taylor 2003) .

Even as a field collector and observer, Miller was outstandingly good, though
certainly not unique. What really distinguished him from other geologists of the
time was the excellence of his writing (Oldroyd 1996a; Knell and Taylor 2003), and
I will come back to this later. But he published relatively little in what could be called
scientific journals, his few technical contributions tending to be brief and informal,
sometimes even in papers principally written by others (Shortland 1996d, pp. 369-
371). He published many of his observations and insights outside the scientific
mainstream, such as the articles that became *Cruise of the Betsey*. This poses
problems for the historian trying to establish due credit for Miller's geological work.

First, though fine literature, Miller's writing naturally lacked the detailed referencing found in formal academic papers. Such apparatus was irrelevant to popular articles. Direct quotation and internal evidence in *Cruise of the Betsey* show, however, that Miller had read some key works; for instance MacCulloch's book (1819) on the Hebrides, Murchison's papers of 1827 and 1828, and Witham's work (1831) on Eigg's fossil wood. But there is no way to be sure what else Miller had read, and therefore which assertions and observations were original to him, and which he took from previous writers (summarised for the Small Isles by Harker 1908), or deduced independently from looking at the same rocks with the same ideas and theoretical conceptions.

Second, Miller failed, perhaps because of his early death, to publish many of his ideas and observations where they would have made the academic impact they deserved (J. D. Hudson, *pers. comm.* 2001). Given the likely circulation of *The Witness*, an article would be 'lost' to most geologists outside the circle of Scottish Evangelicals, unless and until it was republished in a book.

No doubt this is one reason why Miller's work on Eigg did not receive due credit until, in the 1960s, a much later generation of palaeontologists took up where Miller left off (Hudson 2003). Another reason was the mid-nineteenth century shift of geological interest in the Inner Hebrides to their volcanic rocks, which posed – and still pose – important problems with rewarding solutions (Emeleus 1997; Oldroyd and Hamilton 1997; Hudson 2003). Miller's emphasis on fossils led him to neglect the volcanic rocks overlying his beloved Lias and Oolite on Eigg and Skye. *Cruise of the Betsey*, based admittedly on a very short visit, might lead the reader to think that there was hardly anything to the geology of Rùm except for its glaciation (then a crucial topic, as we will see) and what we might today call the 'geotourist trap' of Bloodstone Hill. Miller even described Rùm's complex geology as 'simple' (p. 120).

The pitchstone veins on Eigg might seem an exception to Miller's emphasis on fossils, but they were another obligatory stop on the 'geotourist trail', as gratifying then as now (Hudson and Allwright 2003). Quite apart from their interest, Miller (pp. 20–21) probably discussed them because they recalled an earlier debate whose embers were only just cold. Abraham Gottlob Werner (1749-1817) taught at the Mining Academy in Freiberg in Saxony, which in the eighteenth century was one of the key centres for studies of the earth. He put forward the 'Neptunist' view that rocks were formed by sequential deposition from a hot primal ocean. This view was promoted in Scotland by Robert Jameson (1774-1854), Professor of Natural History at the University of Edinburgh. By the time of Miller's trips on the *Betsey*, Jameson was an elderly and increasingly isolated figure, out of touch due to personality clashes and his stubborn espousal of Werner's views despite the rising influence of the newer 'Vulcanist' or 'Plutonist' thinking originated by the Scot James Hutton (1726-1797) (Oldroyd 1996b; Waterston 1997; McIntyre and McKirdy 2001; Livingstone 2003). Hutton emphasised the role of the earth's internal heat, for example in the formation of granite and other igneous rocks, and of sedimentation in deriving new rocks in turn from these. A critical supporting observation was that veins of rocks such as granite and basalt (then often called 'trap') could only be explained as having solidified from melted rock injected into cracks in previously existing rock. The pitchstone veins would have been just such strong evidence: they could not have been laid down from solution, and what was more, they were obviously related to volcanic rocks, producing pumice when heated, as Miller noted (pp. 21, 41-43).

Of course, Miller was entitled to take an interest in whatever he liked: he was on holiday and, as he willingly admitted (p. 271), he was 'not much of a mineralogist'. But his emphasis on fossils – the remains of living things – also reflected the geology of the 1830s and '40s, after the decisive victory of the principle of using fossils to correlate strata and rank them in relative temporal order, first put forward by the English geologist William Smith. The alternative method, of using rock type (*eg* sandstone) and composition (*ie* minerals constituting the rock), was flawed, because similar rocks could have been formed at different times – as will be seen. The imperative at the time was to correlate as many rock strata as possible to expand the understanding of the geology of Britain and the world. This was important theoretically and economically, especially in the search for coal (Torrens 2002, 2003). Miller had evidently read Murchison's work (1827, 1828) on rocks similar to Eigg's on Skye, and Murchison's mistake in dating the East Coast Jurassic as 'Liassic' was almost certainly the source of Miller's error in dating similar rocks at Laig (p. 53). Such errors, reflecting an initial coarseness of technique, were inevitable in the early stages of comparing strata in geographically distant locations. Indeed, Miller himself transposed the relative position of certain Old Red Sandstone beds (Oldroyd 1996a). Miller's perceptive comments on the 'estuarine' nature of the Eigg fossil deposits and on relevant modern comparisons (pp. 54-55, 69-71, 178-179, *etc*) were apparently original for that locality (J. D. Hudson, *pers. comm.* 2001; Hudson 2003) – but they also focused on a critical issue complicating the use of fossils for dating rocks (discussed, for instance, by Murchison 1827; Lyell 1830-1833; and Forbes 1851b). This was (and still is) that deposits of the same age might nevertheless have different fossils if laid down in different environmental conditions (for instance, brackish water rather than open sea).

However, seeking fossils meant emphasizing rocks with fossils, and conversely ignoring rocks without fossils. Miller downplayed previous researchers who had failed to make full use of fossils, such as Hay Cunningham (1839) (*eg* p. 111) and John MacCulloch (1773-1835), although the latter in particular is nowadays given rather more credit (Waterston 1959; Cumming 1977, 1981, 1985; Oldroyd 1990; Oldroyd and Hamilton 1997; Livingstone 2003). Indeed, Miller's contemporary, Roderick Murchison, tended to ignore the large unfossiliferous regions in the Highlands and Islands, in favour of focusing on the correlation, through fossils, of isolated sedimentary basins (Cumming 1985). Yet Miller, by any standards, made a bad lapse when he explicitly described Rùm as a microcosm of Scottish geology, with the Old Red Sandstone a coastal fringe 'framing' the rocks of the interior mountains. He was, for Rùm and the whole of northern Scotland, equating the Torridonian Sandstone of the west of Scotland (which occurs on Rùm) with the much younger Old Red Sandstone of eastern Scotland (which does not occur on

Rùm) (*eg* pp. 120–122; and Oldroyd 1996a). But the sandstone of Rùm has no fossils, as he himself said, and it would surely have been more prudent to leave the question open. Generally, in fact, Miller's work on stratigraphy and structure was his weakest area, though he mapped and sectioned the simple structure around Cromarty most successfully (Oldroyd 1996a).

On the whole, Miller and his contemporaries emerge as drawing the best conclusions they could from the available information and theoretical evidence. Miller was of course writing about his 1840s readings of the then known evidence (sporadically updated to the 1850s by Symonds's footnotes). For instance, he interpreted the Old Red Sandstone as a marine deposit, when it is now considered to have been laid down in and around a large freshwater lake. Nevertheless, it is bad history always to blame Miller for these 'errors' – if they should be called that at all, given a century and a half of hindsight. They comprised his own often excellent observations, plus interpretations founded on the consensus opinions of geologists of the time, which, like ours today, stemmed from a complex interplay of observation and collection, reportage, theoretical preconceptions, and scientific authority, not to mention the vagaries of fieldwork and personal interests. There are two main reasons why, as Miller wryly noted (p. 476), 'what is discovery to-day will be but rudimentary fact to the tyro-geologists of the future':

1. Less evidence than today, including prior research. There were far fewer geologists and fewer facts had been cumulatively discovered. Fewer fossils were known from fewer sites. The state Geological Survey only started mapping Scotland in 1854 (Geikie 1895), following on from MacCulloch's Government-subsidised work several decades earlier (Cumming 1985).
2. Fewer developed concepts. Geology was still a relatively young science in the 1840s. It has since grown enormously, with new evidence and old reinterpreted with new concepts.

An instance of such a 'rudimentary fact' is the fossil wood of An Sgùrr – Miller's 'Scuir' – on Eigg, whose geology, it should be remembered, was then only imperfectly known to geologists (Oldroyd and Hamilton 1997; Hudson 2003). To the modern reader, Miller does not seem at his best here: as far as one can tell from his oblique comments, in what was after all a travel book, he apparently regarded the wood as laid down on a 'sea bottom' covered in old lava flows, and sealed by another lava flow, all these rocks (or at any rate the earlier ones) being 'Oolitic' – our Jurassic – in age (pp. 35, 37, 222). But that was consensual: Forbes (1851b) and Geikie (1861) also described the nearby basalts of Skye as 'Oolitic'. Indeed, underwater lava flows intercalated with sediments featured in Charles Lyell's *Principles of Geology* (Lyell 1830–1833, *eg* vol. I, pp. 128, 390–393), which geologists used for its facts even if they disagreed with its theoretical conclusions (and which may well have inspired Miller's comments on human artifacts as fossils, whether Roman remains in today's rocks, p. 35, or the field drains of Improvement as fossils for the future: p. 258, cf. Lyell 1830–1833, II, ch. 17).

To talk anachronistically for a moment about geology after Miller, the lavas 'intercalated' with the Jurassic sediments are in fact now considered to be 'sills' 'intruded' while still molten during Tertiary times, forcing their way between the pre-existing strata. This theoretical possibility had been well known ever since Hutton's time, and Forbes (1851b) would soon try, and fail, to find evidence for it on Skye. We do not know whether Miller had done this on Eigg, or simply accepted the consensus view. But no doubt his acceptance of an 'Oolitic' date for the wood was reinforced by his mistaken identification of it as the same as that which he had collected from the 'Oolite' of the north coast of the Moray Firth. The picture started to change in 1851 with the discovery of unequivocally Tertiary plants in the lavas of the Isle of Mull (Argyll 1851; Forbes 1851a). Eventually, much later in the century, in a *tour de force* which became a textbook example, Geikie radically reinterpreted the Sgùrr as a pitchstone lava flow filling a river valley eroded into basalt lavas, all of Tertiary age. Of course Miller, like others, had looked at the same rocks (or at any rate had the opportunity), and failed to draw this conclusion. But, quite apart from being a full-time geologist, Geikie had the advantages of a more developed knowledge of local geology, and the essential concept of valleys eroded by river action over immense periods of time – something not fully part of geological thinking in Miller's time. In any case, even Geikie's view is being significantly modified and refined in detail (Oldroyd 1996; Emeleus 1997; Oldroyd and Hamilton 1997; Hudson 2003; Hudson and Allwright 2003; D. R. Oldroyd, *pers. comm.* 2003).

One key theoretical concept not available to Miller was Darwinian evolution by means of natural selection, for Charles Darwin did not publish *The Origin of Species* until 1859. However, pre-Darwinian evolutionary theories did exist, and they were highly topical when Miller was writing. *Vestiges of the Natural History of Creation* was published in late 1844, with a cheap popular edition in 1847. Written anonymously by Miller's Edinburgh contemporary and fellow Scots journalist, Robert Chambers, it advanced a concept of progressive evolution from simple to complex organisms (Chambers 1994; Secord 1994, 2000). Miller did not say much about it in *Cruise of the Betsey*, but he was clearly brooding on it, judging from his periodic sideswipes, and above all his reaction on finding the 'Asterolepis' on Orkney in 1846 (p. 426), when, unable to extract it from the rock, he ensured that the local geologists would take care of the matter. His emphasis on the fish's large size, complexity, and apparently early date seem irrelevant to his geological ramble, but he evidently realized that these attributes made 'Asterolepis' a counter-example refuting Chambers's naïvely progressionist model of evolution. It is almost certain (p. 426) that he was deliberately seeking just such a fossil in what then appeared to be the lowest, and oldest, beds of the Old Red Sandstone (but which are in fact Middle Old Red Sandstone: Oldroyd 1996a). At any rate, Miller soon deployed 'Asterolepis' to make – so he felt – the breakthrough in his assault on Chambers, in *Footprints of the Creator* (subtitled *The Asterolepis of Stromness*: Miller 1864, published 1849). Miller's musings on the aquatic life in the lochs at Stenness in the Orkney Islands (pp. 448-450) likewise presaged a passage in *Footprints* in which he used the discontinuous distribution of species on a gradual salinity gradient to attack the concept of transmutation of species (Oldroyd 1996a; Henry 1996). However, after Miller's death, Darwin published an analysis of the evidence for evolution and a new mechanism for it in the form of natural selection, changing the debate in favour of evolution, as some Free Churchmen recognised (Macleod 2000).

Miller was something of a 'catastrophist', like many geologists of his day, notably Murchison (Geikie 1875; Davies [1969]; Oldroyd 1996b). Rocks often bear evidence of great physical forces, being faulted, crushed and distorted, and so on. Catastrophists supposed that such changes had happened in short but intense 'convulsions' (*eg* pp. 6, 240). This made good sense: if the earth had cooled down from a molten ball, then earthquakes, for instance, must have been more powerful in the past. Only the discovery of radioactivity around the end of the nineteenth century made it clear that the earth itself generated heat and therefore did not cool down nearly as fast as had been thought (Bowler 1989; Oldroyd 1996b). Today, most geological changes are considered the cumulative effect, over an extremely long period, of many small changes such as minor earth movements. This is more like, but does not go as far as, the extreme anti-catastrophist or 'uniformitarian' doctrine of Charles Lyell who stressed the enormous transformations produced by even the slowest processes visible today if they operate over immensely long geological time (Lyell 1830-1833). However, Lyell also made the logically distinct assertion that the evidence of the past should where possible be explained by known present-day processes, and Miller happily did this whenever it seemed sensible (*eg* p. 9; Oldroyd 1996a).

Miller was also deeply interested in what we would now call the Ice Ages, with their glaciers and raised beaches. *Cruise of the Betsey* was written at a time of great debate (Davies [1969]; Oldroyd 1996b) on what caused the intense erosion visible over most of Scotland, 'that comparatively modern geologic agent' (p. 233) whose action was distinctively directional, from parallel scratches on rocks to the linear landscape features of gouged valleys, and 'tails' of soft rock in the lee of crags of hard rock. It left a 'drift' or 'boulder clay' of ground-up local rock, containing pebbles and boulders, some of which had 'travelled' for long distances. There were also widespread deposits of silt, sand, and gravel. Miller (1859, p. 65) summed up the consensus interpretation adopted by most geologists such as Darwin and Lyell:

> A foundering land under a severe sky, beaten by tempests and lashed by tides, with glaciers half choking up its cheerless valleys, and with countless icebergs brushing its coasts and grating over its shallows ....

The land, it seemed, had been deeply inundated by the sea in Arctic climatic conditions, the erosive effect of water currents enhanced by rock- and grit-laden icebergs which dropped rocks down-current as they melted. Such phenomena had been observed on a small scale, for instance in Nova Scotia (Lyell in Miller 1859, pp. 38-39). Much of Scotland indeed shows evidence for changing sea levels in the form of raised beaches, former beaches and their associated cliffs and sea-caves, high and dry above present sea level, and this was a natural explanation for problematical higher-level deposits such as those of Linksfield near Elgin, and the flints of Banffshire and Aberdeenshire (pp. 176-177, 234-235; cf. modern accounts in Bridgland *et al.* 1997; Merritt, Connell and Bridgland 2000). (Miller did *not* equate this inundation to Noah's Flood, which he considered a local Middle Eastern event: Miller 1857, pp. 267-350). There were also lower relative sea levels to take into account, as evidenced by the sunken peat bed at Oban (p. 5), and reconstructed in his tale of the Clach Mhallaichte (p. 349).

The Swiss geologist and palaeontologist Louis Agassiz put forward an alternative view in 1837, repeating it in a specifically Scottish context at the 1840 meeting of the British Association in Glasgow. But, even before that, Miller himself had publicized Agassiz's ideas in *The Witness* (Finnegan 2003). Agassiz's belief was that much of Europe was formerly covered by a huge icecap, distorting and flowing under its own weight to gouge the underlying rocks. This would, eventually, be seen as the best explanation for phenomena such as the sand and gravel deposits caused by the floods from melting ice, the placement of cold-water shells on Welsh hills by moving land-ice, and the relative changes of sea level as Scotland was depressed by the weight of the ice, versus the fall in sea level as water was sequestrated into the global icecaps.

Miller's long discussion of the boulder clay (pp. 299-322) in *Cruise of the Betsey* showed geologists of the time struggling with the intractably complex superficial deposits. When Miller observed beds of clay, sand and gravel, he wrongly ascribed some, at least, to the effects of marine erosion (pp. 320-321), whereas we now consider that they were laid down by floodwaters arising from melting snow and ice, carrying glacial debris downstream. Geologists of his time found themselves in dead ends such as the problem of the relative rates of sea level rise and fall, given that sea-borne icebergs could not very well scratch the bedrocks of high hills and low ground at the same time (p. 318) – but this problem vanished with a glacial icecap which could have scratched at many heights at once. Miller's comments on Rùm (pp. 123-124) and Strathcarron (p. 159) reflected, as did the quotation given earlier, the hybrid position he, like many other British geologists, adopted, of an iceberg-laden inundation complemented by local glaciers on high ground. It would take a long time for Agassiz's glacial option to be completely accepted. Andrew Ramsay, a key Scottish supporter, adopted it only in 1861, after seeing modern glaciers abroad, and in the face of criticism from older geologists (Geikie 1895).

The moral value of natural science

Miller recommended a science such as geology as part of one's self-improvement programme. One reason for its appeal to the Victorians was that it was a constructive recreation, not frivolous amusement. The physical and mental labour of finding, collecting and studying fossils provided exercise for body and mind, often in fresh air – a real benefit in those days of limited facilities and expensive books. Miller was a man of his time, imbued with Calvinist Presbyterianism, with its abhorrence of idleness and emphasis on hard work. Miller was not in top physical form in the 1840s, as noted above, but his original 'thirty miles per day' (p. 381) would not have been unusual, given the Victorians' physical and mental stamina (Allen 1994).

To study nature was, in any case, a serious business. To Miller, science and revealed religion were but two aspects of the same truth, as he argued extensively elsewhere, especially in *Testimony of the Rocks* (Miller 1857). The hand of God could be discerned in the functional design (pp. 173-175, and especially 284-286), and the beauty of fossils. Such interpretations of fossils as works of a divine Creator contributed to a 'natural theology' complementing the 'revealed theology' of the Bible in those days before the publication of Darwinian natural selection (Buckland 1836; Brooke 1996; Henry 1996). But otherwise Miller did not, in fact, discuss the relationship of science and religion very much in *Cruise of the Betsey*, compared to some of his other writings. Occasional comments do however show how topical an issue it was, for instance when he asserted (p. 236) that the competent theologian needed to understand 'natural history and geology', lest these sciences might be perverted by enemies. Professor John Fleming (1785-1857) had just started teaching natural science to trainee ministers at the new Free Church College, Edinburgh (Andrews 1982, pp. 57-58; Livingstone 2003). Such teaching was not just to combat evolutionists, for Miller and his allies were opposed to religious obscurantists who denied the truth of scientific evidence, even when it seemed to contradict literal readings of the Bible. With his unimpeachable Free Church credentials, Miller's 'genial ardour and irresistible eloquence swept away the last remnants of the barrier of orthodox prejudice against geology in this country', Geikie later asserted (in Anon. 1902, p. 61).

Nevertheless religion was a higher priority than geology (p. 115). For instance, in *Cruise of the Betsey* Miller never described himself collecting on a Sunday. To adopt the criterion of the Shorter Catechism, natural science was a work of neither necessity nor mercy, whether one wanted to do it oneself or ask others to work on their Sabbath, as a German tourist, mentioned by Miller, found (pp. 482-483). This seems hard on those who had to work six long days a week, and wanted to engage in some scientific recreation, but the mores of the day did not permit otherwise.

More generally, Miller's life, notably as described in his autobiography *My Schools and Schoolmasters* (Robb 1996; Vincent 1996), inspired young Scots to make the best of themselves through hard work and self-education: 'life itself is a school, and Nature always a fresh study – and ... the man who keeps his eyes and his mind open will always find fitting, though, it may be, hard schoolmasters, to speed him on in his lifelong education' (Miller 1858, p. 562). Such self-development was not unusual in Scotland – the Moderate minister on the mail-gig regarded Miller as a shepherd even after Miller had discussed the local glacial moraines (p. 159). Robert Chambers had encouraged the young Miller with 'pleasing sympathy ... with struggling merit' (p. 189; Miller 1858, p. 525; Secord 2000). Miller in his turn was notably careful in *Cruise of the Betsey* to commend those who tried their best, whatever their station in life, such as Mr Joss the mailcoach guard (p. 276), and Robert Dick the baker (pp. 180-189). But, in contrast to Miller, Dick's activities contributed to his alienation from his fellow townsfolk of Thurso (Smiles 1878; Alston 1996; Oldroyd 1996a). Was Miller's extensive quotation of Dick's work, perhaps, a deliberate expression of support?

Miller the writer on geology and landscape: an appreciation

Miller was a good geologist, but an even better writer, and in that combination lay, perhaps, his greatest contribution to science. From 1840 he was a busy journalist and editor. Geology, and the writing of articles and books on it, were secondary to the main business of the newspaper. What astounds us today is the quality of his writing and that he did it on top of editing a newspaper (Shortland 1996c, 1996d). Given the common understanding of Miller among modern geologists, people are often surprised to learn that his geological writings formed only a fraction of his output (Oldroyd 1996a, Shortland 1996b). A proportion of these writings comprised books which I suspect he felt it his duty – both moral and commercial – to write, notably those on the 'geology versus religion' controversies of the time, *Footprints of the Creator* and *Testimony of the Rocks*. Neither was recycled from previous articles from the paper (though the latter was partly based on previous lectures). What little remaining time he had for geology he spent in what he enjoyed most, which was being out in the field looking at rocks and collecting fossils. This is the Miller of *Cruise of the Betsey*.

Miller did use his editorial position to create the geological articles and popular books that gave him his lasting fame within geology; and if many people only came across geology because they were seeking his literary, political and religious writings, then that was to the good. However much it might have reduced his formal contributions to science, Miller was regarded as a great popularizer of geology. His books were said to inspire a generation of geologists across the English-speaking world, being 'found in the remotest log-hut of the Far West, and on both sides of the Atlantic ideas of the nature and shape of geology were largely drawn from them' (Geikie in Leask 1896, p. 149). Indeed, he appears to have influenced no less a man than John Muir, the expatriate Scot and pioneering American conservationist of the nineteenth century (Taylor 2002a).

Miller caught a powerful wave, as the new middle classes of Victorian Britain espoused natural history. Other palaeontological writers included Gideon Mantell of Sussex and *Iguanodon* fame, while marine biology had Philip Gosse, immortalised in his son Edmund's *Father and Son*, and Charles Kingsley, whose *Water Babies* charmingly parodied the movement while imparting important moral and social messages. Indeed, like Gosse and Kingsley, Miller was, I believe, one of the 'evangelical naturalists' – evangelical in the broad sense, not that of the pre-Disruption Kirk – who, Allen (1994) observes, came to dominate natural history.

Miller was an outstanding writer heuristically, a competent journalist speaking to the intelligent but not necessarily knowledgeable reader. He used charmingly everyday analogies, such as the geological map modelled by the slovenly painter (pp.

277-278). Or his extraordinary visual imagination painted a vivid picture of some past or present landscape: the glacier problem, to Miller, literally 'summoned up doubtful, ever-shifting visions' (p. 124). His style (*eg* pp. 296-297) had much in common with landscape painting and more generally with Victorian narrative art (Mackenzie 1905; Merrill 1989; Stevenson 2002a, 2002b; O'Connor 2003). Although Miller's work usually eschewed pictorial illustrations other than fossil specimens, his writing, so to speak, created illustrated books out of printed text, and appropriate modern comparisons could well include the Hebridean photographs of Paul Strand and John Sibbick's exquisitely detailed paintings of carefully reconstructed Mesozoic animals. Miller's verbal skills, if not now redundant, are at least less important today with the development of photography and the cheaper printing of illustrations – but, revealingly, Miller was fascinated by that new technique of photography and made penetrating comments on it (p. 300; Stevenson 2002a, 2002b).

Reading Miller is often to be taken on a personal tour, whether in space, through the dramatic scenery of the Small Isles and along Orkney beaches, or in time to wander the shores of primeval seas, just as Kingsley and Gosse took their readers amidst today's rockpools (Merrill 1989). Moreover, Miller had been influenced, like almost all Scottish writers and artists, by Walter Scott's interpretation of human history (Robertson 2002). No wonder, therefore, that Miller sometimes seemed to write like a historical novelist of the natural world, penetrating deep time as with his little novella of a single boulder (pp. 341-349). Yet Miller's imagination was always rooted in the actuality of evidence, and he always returned to real fossils, and real landscapes, all still recognizable today whether in museum collections or in the actual terrain (Knell and Taylor 2003).

Readers were willing to read more intensively than is usual today, to put more into reading a book and learning from it (cf. Secord 2000), and if Miller's books resemble sermons in their density and tone, then that is not surprising in a world where preaching was seriously appreciated. Miller may have used rather too many technical terms for the modern reader, but the Victorians were hardy beings. Nor was humour absent, even if Miller's wit is not always evident at first reading. Miller's style differed from the colloquial, almost conversational, John-Bullish manner of William Cobbett, his equally peripatetic and indignant English contemporary. It owed much to the Augustan style of Addison and other writers of the eighteenth century. Miller's prose was beautifully crafted, and could be read aloud to the family around the fire. Indeed that, in a way, is how much of his writing was composed. A family friend recalled him working at home in the evening: 'He never sat, but walked up and down, repeating his sentences until they were moulded to his liking; occasionally coming up to his wife and saying, "Do you think this is the best way to put it?" and when satisfied went to his desk and wrote' (H. Taylor in Sutherland 2002, p. 173).

To some extent, *Cruise of the Betsey* retains the feel of its origins in *The Witness*, with numerous allusions that were topical in the 1840s. We can also discern traces of its serial origins in the tantalising climax of several chapters. The convoluted and, perhaps appropriately, rambling storyline was inevitable in a volume that, in a sense, contained one whole book and fragments of another. No doubt its author might have revised it had he lived. The numerous minor errors in Miller's quotations – many very likely drawn from his elephantine memory, and at least one perhaps cribbed from another book – may be charitably ascribed to emendations, consciously or otherwise made to ease them into the cadences of Miller's sentences. But these are matters of detail. What the quotations also show is Miller's wide reading in many fields, both in contemporary books – some no doubt review copies sent to *The Witness* – and in the classics, which to him included the Presbyterian divines as well as the Augustan essayists and eighteenth-century pastoral poets whom he so loved. Indeed, the brevity of some of his allusions reveals a mutual community of reading which we have now lost.

How far did Miller write for effect rather than accuracy? Mackenzie (1905, p.122), perhaps unreasonably, complained that Miller claimed that 'the gigantic Scuir of Eigg rests on the remains of a prostrate forest' (p. 32). But Miller was indeed guilty of some exaggeration when he transmogrified one or two pieces of wood into a lattice foundation (note to p. 32). Yet, as his collection in the National Museums of Scotland shows, Miller did find a substantial amount of fossil wood on a short visit, and no doubt he expected that there was more to be found. In another sense, Miller was undoubtedly writing for effect rather than precision, at least where the latter was not needed. Maddening as this often is to the modern reader, he often failed to give precise dates, justify his views on the origin of the fossil wood of Eigg, or go into more detail about some fascinating social custom; but he was not writing a geologist's or anthropologist's field diary, with its observations recorded day by day in strict chronological sequence. Quite the opposite: he blended foresight and hindsight with actual travel in a literary, but effective, manner. For instance, his account of a single visit to the valley behind Rosemarkie (pp. 295-299) incorporated observations made by night and by day, and almost certainly on more than one occasion. Nevertheless, as with the specimens mentioned earlier, his writing remained rooted in actual scenery, so much so that his travels can be retraced today, and one may even have a feeling of *déjà vu* as when, for instance, first seeing the 'fertile meniscus' of Cleadale on Eigg after reading about it (pp. 50, 68). Even – especially! – at its richest, around Cromarty, Miller's mental landscape still maps onto the real landscape. To him, 'every little locality, and every more striking feature in the landscape, ha[d] its associated tradition' (p. 294). And now Miller has himself become part of that tradition, accreted onto it like the latest stratum of the geological succession.

Cruise of the Betsey shows how Hugh Miller the geologist was firmly located in two related mainstreams: the field geologists; and the evangelical natural history writers. The book confirms his importance in the first field and his crucial importance in the other. Although *Cruise of the Betsey* was a travel book, philosophical and religious questions were never far below the surface, as when Miller found 'Asterolepis' on the Stromness shore in the Orkney Islands. Miller was writing, as he always did, for the ordinary reader who wanted to know not only about exciting new scientific discoveries, but also what they might mean for our view of life, the universe and everything: the great question of 'why are we here?'

Nevertheless, to say that Miller wrote 'popular science', self-help tracts, and so on, risks invoking today's spurious division between science and literature. The Victorians, least of all Miller, did not see the world like that (O'Connor 2003; Secord 2003). Miller was a 'man of letters' at a time when seminal works of science, such as Lyell's *Principles of Geology* and Miller's own *The Old Red Sandstone*, were still literature, ornamented with classical or poetical quotations as much as by sketches of volcanoes and fossils (Lyell 1830-1833; Secord 1997; Secord 2000).

Conclusion

Perhaps most of all his books, *Cruise of the Betsey* reveals, to the modern reader, the range of Hugh Miller – the Free Church activist, folklorist, social commentator, researcher, field geologist, popular science writer, visionary of the past, self-help propagandist, and so on. Yet the fact that these aspects melded so well in *Cruise of the Betsey* shows the futility of trying to analyse him thus. It is like trying to cut quicksilver, given Miller's eclectic mind, and his integrated outlook on the world (Knell and Taylor 2003).

This is not a superficial statement. Consider *Cruise of the Betsey*'s three main strands: Kirk, society, and science. Obviously, Miller's Calvinist worldview informed his religious faith. But less obviously, and as Henry (1996) insightfully argued in an outstanding paper, it also formed Miller's attitude to society, notably his rejection of *laissez-faire* socio-economic philosophy, for instance the notion that the poor were poor because of their own moral failings (and so poverty was their own fault, and should not be relieved). Again not so obviously, Miller's Calvinism also informed his attitude to science and the interpretation of divine Creation, such as his attacks on pre-Darwinian theories of evolution – but also his defence of science. Despite its rambling style, *Cruise of the Betsey* can therefore be seen to have a remarkable internal consistency, strikingly linking Miller's observation of the Free Church's struggle for religious liberty, his indignation at the miserable cottage on Eigg, and the glee with which he pounces on the fossil fish 'Asterolepis' on an Orcadian shore.

As he had intended from his youngest days, Hugh Miller wrote great literature about the world as he saw it, and *Cruise of the Betsey* was part of that literary oeuvre. It is, I submit, a treasure of Scottish culture.

FOLLOWING
IN THE FOOTSTEPS
OF HUGH MILLER TODAY

MANY of the places that Miller visited in *Cruise of the Betsey* are rich in scenery, wildlife, geology and history, quite apart from their Millerian associations. They make rewarding visits, mostly well off the beaten tourist track. For instance, despite intense social and economic change, the dramatic scenery of **Eigg**, **Rùm**, and **Skye** is much as it was when Miller visited them. **Cromarty** superbly retains the atmosphere of a Scottish coastal burgh of Miller's time. Guides are available from the Cottage and the Cromarty Courthouse Museum, which is recommended for local history. Miller's unmissable birthplace cottage is held by the National Trust for Scotland which is also opening a new exhibition on Hugh Miller in 2004 in Miller House next door. There are many other places in the area with Millerian associations, such as **Eathie** where he sought Jurassic fossils. **Rosemarkie** still has its jackdaws on Kaes' Craig and other 'scaurs', and a visit is recommended to the Fairy Glen and to Groam House Museum for Pictish stones and local history. **Strathpeffer** retains its spa atmosphere, and there is an excellent walk up to Knockfarril's vitrified ramparts. At **Elgin** the Museum is still run by the same society (albeit under a different name) as when Miller visited it. At **Portsoy** the former 'marble' quarries can still be seen some 300m east of the old harbour. **Gardenstown** on Gamrie Bay has good exposures of the Old Red Sandstone as do **Caithness** and the **Orkney Islands**, where the Old Red's dramatic scenery is well developed and where Stromness Museum still stands.

 Miller's fossil collection is mostly held by the National Museums of Scotland. It is not on display as a whole, but a selection of specimens from it, or found by others at the same sites, can normally be seen in the Royal Museum and the Museum of Scotland, Edinburgh. Hugh Miller's Cottage in Cromarty also displays some of his finds.

 Recommended reading includes Miller's *My Schools and Schoolmasters, Scenes and Legends of the North of Scotland*, and *Testimony of the Rocks*. These are currently in print (Miller 1993, 1994, 2001); the first two are good on the Black Isle in his time, as is his local journalism (Miller 1997). Recent brief accounts of Miller's life include Rudwick (1974), Waterston (1978); Gostwick (1993); and Taylor (2002b, 2004 in press). Shortland (1996a) and Borley (2002, 2003) are valuable collections of studies, the latter two being particularly accessible to the non-specialist.

 On the history and archaeology of some areas which Miller visited in *Cruise of the Betsey*, I have found the following useful: Omand (1989); Magnusson (1997); Dressler (1998); Alston (1999); Love (2001); Rixson (2001); Thomson (2001); and the appropriate regional guides by the Royal Commission on Ancient and Historical Monuments for Scotland, Historic Scotland, and the Royal Incorporation of Architects in Scotland.

On modern geology, basic introductions are McKirdy and Crofts (1999) and other booklets in the Scottish Natural Heritage series *A Landscape Fashioned by Geology*. More specialist are Trewin (2003a) and the geological maps and associated memoirs of the British Geological Survey, such as Fletcher *et al.* (1996) and Emeleus (1997). Some of the geological sites mentioned in *Cruise of the Betsey* are covered in modern field guides such as Mykura (1976); Emeleus and Forster (1979); Bell and Harris (1986); Trewin *et al.* (1987); Trewin and Hurst (1993); Morton and Hudson (1995); Merritt, Connell and Bridgland (2000); and Hudson and Allwright (2003). There is also useful information on some sites in the relevant Survey memoirs, and in the Joint Nature Conservation Committee's Geological Conservation Review Series such as Emeleus and Gyopari (1992); Gordon and Sutherland (1993); Dineley and Metcalf (1999); and Cox and Sumbler (2002).

Some useful websites

Hugh Miller . . . . **www.hughmiller.org**
National Trust for Scotland (which
  holds Hugh Miller's Cottage) . . . . . . **www.nts.org.uk**
National Museums of Scotland . . . . . . **www.nms.ac.uk**
Scottish Museums Council . . . . **www.scottishmuseums.org.uk**
Scottish Natural Heritage
  (including Rùm) . . . . **www.snh.org.uk**
Scottish geology . . . . **www.scottishgeology.com**
Scottish history and culture
  and some geology . . . . **www.scran.ac.uk**
24 Hour Museum **http://www.24hourmuseum.org**

VisitScotland . . . . **http://www.visitscotland.com**
Highlands Tourist Board . . . . **http://www.host.co.uk/**

Aberdeenshire
  (including Banff and Buchan) . . . . . . **www.aberdeenshire.gov.uk**
                                           www.buchanweb.org
Caithness . . . . **www.caithness.org**
Cromarty . . . . **www.cromarty-courthouse.org.uk**
Eigg . . . . **www.isleofeigg.org**
Invergordon . . . . **http://www.invergordon.org/home.htm**
Moray . . . . **http://www.moray.org/**
Mull . . . . **www.isleofmull.com**
Nairn . . . . **http://www.cali.co.uk/HIGHEXP/Nairn/**

Orkney . . . . www.orkney.org
Ross-shire Online . . . . http://www.ross-shire.com/
Skye . . . . http://www.skye.co.uk/
Strathpeffer & Dingwall . . . . http://www.undiscoveredscotland.co.uk

A note on fossil and mineral collecting

The reader must not always expect to collect fossils where Miller did, quite apart from the effects of 150 years of collecting, erosion and quarry infill. When Miller ridiculed (p. 36) 'the idea of a fossil preserve ... [and] a great fossil act for the British empire, framed on the principles of the game-laws', he was thinking of how these unjust laws made a public resource into a private benefit. We are today far more aware of how limited the nation's fossil resources are and of the need to conserve them for public benefit. Readers must not emulate his attitude to seeking landowners' permission, which was legally unsound even then.

Publication of this reprint is no indication of safe or legal access to any site Miller mentions, or of permission to collect. It is impractical in a book such as this to give details of surviving individual sites, or their ownership, conservation and access requirements, but the field guides listed elsewhere may be useful. You must obtain permission from the relevant landowner and occupier (and, where separately held, the holder of the mineral rights); this is especially the case for sites protected under conservation law, such as Sites of Special Scientific Interest and National Nature Reserves. *Many sites mentioned in this book are protected in this way, including the Cromarty foreshore site, Eathie, the whole of Rùm, and several on Eigg.* However, collecting *is* encouraged at some sites, such as Achanarras Quarry in Caithness, a classic Old Red Sandstone fish locality owned by Scottish Natural Heritage. Responsible collecting at this site is possible through the permit system operated by the SNH office in Golspie (tel: 01408 633602).

If you must collect at those sites where collecting permission has been granted, then please collect only from loose rock, and leave sites undamaged for other people to see. Please always follow the Country Code and Code of Geological Fieldwork, and avoid disturbing or damaging crops and livestock. Take appropriate safety precautions, go equipped for what can be wild and exposed terrain far from help, and watch for hazards such as tides and wet grassy slopes.

Please take some time to visit the following websites for further information concerning the conservation of Scotland's natural heritage:

www.snh.org.uk
www.scottishgeology.com

REFERENCES
AND FURTHER READING

AGASSIZ, J. L. R. 1844-1845. *Monographie des Poissons fossiles du Vieux Grès Rouge ou Système Dévonien (Old Red Sandstone) des Îles Britanniques et de la Russie.* Neuchatel.

AIKMAN, J. 1827. *The History of Scotland translated from the Latin of George Buchanan; with notes and a continuation to the Union in the reign of Queen Anne.* 4 vols. Blackie, Fullarton & Co., Glasgow.

ALEXANDER, W. 1919 (first published 1871). *Johnny Gibb of Gushetneuk* [with introduction and appreciation by A. MACKIE]. David Douglas, Edinburgh [reprinted 1995 by Tuckwell Press, East Linton].

ALLAN, R. 1834. *A manual of mineralogy comprehending the more recent discoveries in the mineral kingdom.* Black, Edinburgh.

ALLEN, D. E. 1994. *The naturalist in Britain. A social history.* 2nd edition. Princeton University Press, Princeton, New Jersey.

ALLEN, D. E. 2000. 'Walking the swards: medical education and the rise and spread of the botanical field class', in *Archives of Natural History* 27, 335-367.

ALSTON, D. 1996. 'The fallen meteor: Hugh Miller and local tradition', pp. 206-229 in SHORTLAND (1996a).

ALSTON, D. 1999. *Ross and Cromarty. A historical guide.* Birlinn, Edinburgh.

ALSTON, D. 2002. 'Hugh Miller: the Cromarty years. The social background', pp. 10-16 in BORLEY (2002).

ANDERSON, G. and ANDERSON, P. 1863. (first published 1834). *Guide to the Highlands and Western Islands of Scotland, including Orkney and Zetland.* 4th edition. 3 vols. Black, Edinburgh.

ANDREWS, S. M. 1982. *The discovery of fossil fishes in Scotland up to 1845 with checklists of Agassiz's figured specimens.* Royal Scottish Museum, Edinburgh.

ANON. 1835. *In the General Assembly. Case for the Rev. Donald Maclean, Minister of the Parish of Small Isles, Appellant, in the prosecution against him, at the instance of the Presbytery of Skye respondents.* Oliver and Boyd, Edinburgh. [Copy in the Library of New College, University of Edinburgh.]

ANON. [GREIG, J.] (ed.) 1877. *Disruption worthies of the Highlands. Another memorial of 1843.* John Greig and Son, Edinburgh [the preface is signed J. G.].

ANON. 1902. *The centenary of Hugh Miller being an account of the celebration held at Cromarty on 22nd August, 1902.* Maclehose, Glasgow.

ANSDELL, D. 1998. *The people of the Great Faith. The Highland Church, 1690-1900.* Acair, Stornoway.

APPLEBY, J. H. 1999. 'Woronzow Greig (1805-1865), F.R.S., and his scientific interests', in *Notes and Records of the Royal Society of London* 53, 95-106.

ARGYLL, DUKE OF. 1851. 'On Tertiary leaf-beds in the Isle of Mull', in *Quarterly Journal of the Geological Society of London* 7, 88-103.

ARMIT, I. 1997. *Celtic Scotland*. Batsford, London (Historic Scotland series).

BAILLIE, R. 1841. *The Letters and Journals of Robert Baillie, A. M. Principal of the University of Glasgow. M.DC.XXXVII.-M.DC.LXII.* 3 vols. Privately published, Bannatyne Club, Edinburgh.

BAYNE, P. 1871. *The life and letters of Hugh Miller*. 2 vols. Strahan & Co., London.

BELL, B. R. and HARRIS, J. W. 1986. *An excursion guide to the geology of the Isle of Skye*. Geological Society of Glasgow, Glasgow.

BENTON, M. J. 1982. 'Progressionism in the 1850s: Lyell, Owen, Mantell and the Elgin fossil reptile *Leptopleuron (Telerpeton)*', in *Archives of Natural History* 11, 123-136.

BENTON, M. J. 1995a. 'The Elgin reptiles', pp. 51-82 in KEILLAR and SMITH (1995).

BENTON, M. J. 1995b. 'Gordon and Huxley: the exploitation of the Elgin reptiles, 1850-1890', pp. 83-104 in KEILLAR and SMITH (1995).

BORLEY, L. (ed.) 2002. *Hugh Miller in context: geologist and naturalist: writer and folklorist. A collection of papers presented at two conferences* 'The Cromarty Years' (2000) *and* 'The Edinburgh Years' (2001). Cromarty Arts Trust, Cromarty.

BORLEY, L. (ed.) 2003. *Celebrating the life and times of Hugh Miller. Scotland in the early 19th century, ethnography and folklore, geology and natural history, church and society*. Cromarty Arts Trust, Cromarty, and Elphinstone Institute of the University of Aberdeen, Aberdeen.

BOWLER, P. J. 1989. *Evolution. The history of an idea*. Revised edition. University of California Press, Berkeley.

BRIDGLAND, D. R., SAVILLE, A. and SINCLAIR, J. M. 1997. 'New evidence for the origin of the Buchan Ridge Gravel, Aberdeenshire', in *Scottish Journal of Geology* 33, 43-50.

BREWSTER, D. 1845. '*Des Sciences Occultes, ou Essai sur la Magie, les Prodiges, et les Miracles.* Par Eusebe Salverte. Paris, 1829. 2 vols. 8vo' [essay review], *North British Review* 3, 1-39 [published anonymously; for authorship see Houghton and Houghton (1966-1979, I, p. 668)].

BROOKE, J. H. 1996. 'Like minds: the God of Hugh Miller', pp. 171-186 in SHORTLAND (1996a).

BROWN, C. G. 1997. *Religion and Society in Scotland since 1707*. Edinburgh University Press, Edinburgh.

BROWN, S. J. and FRY, M. (eds.) 1993. *Scotland in the age of the Disruption*. Edinburgh University Press, Edinburgh.

BROWN, T. 1893. *Annals of the Disruption; with extracts from the narratives of ministers who left the Scottish Establishment in 1843*. New edition. Macniven & Wallace, Edinburgh.

BUCKLAND, W. 1836. *Geology and Mineralogy considered with reference to Natural Theology*. Pickering, London.

BURNET, [G.] 1838. *Bishop Burnet's History of his own Time; from the restoration of Charles II to the Treaty of Peace at Utrecht, in the Reign of Queen Anne*. New edition. Smith, London.

CALDER, A. 1993. 'The Disruption in fiction', pp. 113-132 in BROWN and FRY (1993).

CAMERON, A. 1877. 'Rev. John Swanson', pp. 126-136 in ANON. (1877).

CHAMBERS, R. 1994 [originally published 1844]. *Vestiges of the Natural History of Creation and other writings* [with introduction by J. A. SECORD]. Chicago University Press, Chicago.

CHEAPE, H. 1988. 'Food and liquid containers in the Hebrides: a window on the Iron Age', pp. 6-27 in A. FENTON and J. MYRDAL (eds.) *Food and drink and travelling accessories. Essays in honour of Gösta Berg*. John Donald, National Museums of Scotland and Skansen and Nordiska Museet, Edinburgh.

CHEAPE, H. 1995. '"A few summer shielings or cots". Material culture and buildings of the '45', in *Clan Donald Magazine* 13, 64-70.

CHEAPE, H. 1996. 'Royal refuges of the Forty-five', in *Scottish Local History* 36, 13-19.

CHEAPE, H. 1997. 'Shielings in the Highlands and Islands of Scotland: prehistory to the present', in *Folk life* 35, 7-24.

CHEAPE, H. 2003. '"A hotbed of bigotry" and "a sea of difficulties": the Free Church in Hugh Miller's Scotland', pp. 306-320 in BORLEY (2003).

CHECKLAND, S. G. 1975. *Scottish banking. A history*. Collins, London.

CLEEVELY, R. 1983. *World Palaeontological Collections*. British Museum (Natural History) and Mansell, London.

COLLIE, M. 2003. 'Hugh Miller's dealings with contemporary scientists', pp. 227-236 in BORLEY (2003).

CORLETT, E. 1975. *The iron ship. The history and significance of Brunel's Great Britain*. Moonraker Press.

COX, B. M. and SUMBLER, M. G. (eds.) 2002. *British Middle Jurassic stratigraphy. Geological Conservation Review Series* 26. Joint Nature Conservation Committee, Peterborough.

CUMMING, D. A. 1977. '*A Description of the Western Islands of Scotland*: John MacCulloch's successful failure', in *Archives of Natural History* 8, 270-285.

CUMMING, D. A. 1981. 'Geological maps in preparation: John MacCulloch on western islands', in *Archives of Natural History* 10, 255-271.

CUMMING, D. A. 1985. 'John MacCulloch, blackguard, thief, and high priest, reassessed', pp. 77-85 in A. WHEELER and J. BROWNE (eds.) *From Linnaeus to Darwin: commentaries on the history of biology and geology .... Society for the Bibliography of Natural History Special Volume* 3.

DAVIES, G. L. [1969]. *The Earth in decay. A history of British geomorphology 1578-1878*. Macdonald Technical and Scientific, London.

DEVINE, T. M. 1988. *The Great Highland Famine. Hunger, emigration and the Scottish Highlands in the nineteenth century*. John Donald, Edinburgh.

DEVINE, T. M. 1994. *Clanship to crofter's war. The social transformation of the Scottish Highlands*. Manchester University Press, Manchester.

DEVINE, T. M. 1999. *The Scottish Nation 1700-2000*. Allen Lane, The Penguin Press, London.

DINELEY, D. L. and METCALF, S. J. 1999. *Fossil fishes of Great Britain. Geological Conservation Review Series* 16. Joint Nature Conservation Committee, Peterborough.

DRESSLER, C. 1998. *Eigg. The story of an island.* Polygon, Edinburgh.

DRUMMOND, A. L. and BULLOCH, J. 1973. *The Scottish Church 1688-1843. The age of the Moderates.* Saint Andrew Press, Edinburgh.

DRUMMOND, A. L. and BULLOCH, J. 1975. *The Church in Victorian Scotland 1843-1874.* Saint Andrew Press, Edinburgh.

DUFF, P. 1842. *Sketch of the Geology of Moray.* Forsyth and Young, Elgin.

EGERTON, P. de M. G. 1848. 'Palichthyologic notes supplemental to the works of Prof. Agassiz', in *Quarterly Journal of the Geological Society of London* 4, 302-314.

EMELEUS, C. H. 1997. *Geology of Rum and the adjacent islands. Memoirs of the British Geological Survey,* Sheet 60 (Scotland). Stationery Office, London.

EMELEUS, C. H. and FORSTER, R. M. 1979. *Field guide to the Tertiary igneous rocks of Rhum.* Nature Conservancy Council, Newbury.

EMELEUS, C. H. and GYOPARI, M. C. 1992. *British Tertiary Volcanic Province. Geological Conservation Review Series* 4. Chapman and Hall, London.

EWING, W. 1914. *Annals of the Free Church of Scotland 1843-1900.* 2 vols. Clark, Edinburgh.

FENYŐ, K. 2000. *Contempt, sympathy and romance. Lowland perceptions of the Highlands and the Clearances during the Famine Years, 1845-1855.* Tuckwell Press, East Linton.

FINNEGAN, D. 2003. 'Edinburgh and the reception of early glacial theory', in *Edinburgh Geologist* 40, 3-11.

FLEMING, J. 1828. *A History of British Animals, exhibiting the descriptive characters and systematical arrangement of the genera and species of quadrupeds, birds, reptiles, fishes, mollusca, and radiata of the United Kingdom; including the indigenous, extirpated, and extinct kinds, together with periodical and occasional visitants.* Bell and Bradfute, Edinburgh.

FLETCHER, T. P., AUTON, C. A., HIGHTON, A. J., MERRITT, J. W., ROBERTSON, S. and ROLLIN, K. E. 1996. *Geology of the Fortrose and eastern Inverness district. Memoirs of the British Geological Survey,* Sheet 84W (Scotland). HMSO, London.

FORBES, E. 1851a. 'A note on the vegetable remains from Ardtun Head', in *Quarterly Journal of the Geological Society of London* 7, 103 only.

FORBES, E. 1851b. 'On the Estuary Beds and the Oxford Clay at Loch Staffin, in Skye', in *Quarterly Journal of the Geological Society of London* 7, 104-113.

GASKELL, P. 1996. *Morvern transformed. A Highland parish in the nineteenth century.* Cambridge University Press.

GEIKIE, A. [1856]. 'Exhibition of a collection of Liassic fossils from Pabba and Skye', in *Proceedings of the Royal Physical Society of Edinburgh,* 1, 6-7.

GEIKIE, A. 1861. 'On the chronology of the trap rocks of Scotland', in *Transactions of the Royal Society of Edinburgh* 22, 633-653.

GEIKIE, A. 1875. *Life of Sir Roderick I. Murchison Bart.; K.C.B., F.R.S.; sometime Director-General of the Geological Survey of the United Kingdom. Based on his journals and letters with notices of his scientific contemporaries and a sketch of the rise and growth of Palaeozoic geology in Britain.* 2 vols. John Murray, London.

GEIKIE, A. 1895. *Memoir of Sir Andrew Crombie Ramsay.* Macmillan, London.

GEIKIE, A. 1906. *Scottish reminiscences.* Cheap edition. Maclehose, Glasgow.

GOLDSACK, D. E., LEACH, M. F, and KILKENNY, C. 1997. 'Natural and artificial "singing" sands', in *Nature* 386, 29 only.

GOLDSMID, E. (ed.) 1885. *The Norwegian account of King Haco's expedition against Scotland AD MCCLXIIII and literally translated ... by the Rev. James Johnstone, A. M.* Privately published, Edinburgh.

GORDON, J. E. and SUTHERLAND, D. G. (eds.) 1993. *Quaternary of Scotland. Geological Conservation Review Series* 6. Joint Nature Conservation Committee, Peterborough, and Chapman and Hall, London.

GOSTWICK, M. 1993. *The legend of Hugh Miller.* Cromarty Courthouse, Cromarty.

HARKER, A. 1908. *Memoirs of the Geological Survey. Scotland. The geology of the Small Isles of Inverness-shire (Rum, Canna, Eigg, Muck, etc.)* Sheet 60 (Scotland). HMSO, Glasgow.

HAY CUNNINGHAM, R. J. 1839. 'On the geognosy of the Isle of Eigg', in *Memoirs of the Wernerian Society* 8, 144-163.

HEDDLE, M. FORSTER (ed. by J. G. GOODCHILD) 1901. *The Mineralogy of Scotland.* 2 vols. David Douglas, Edinburgh.

HENDERSON, L. and COWAN, E. J. 2001. *Scottish fairy belief: a history.* Tuckwell, East Linton.

HENRY, J. 1996. 'Palaeontology and theodicy: religion, politics and the *Asterolepis* of Stromness', pp. 151-170 in SHORTLAND (1996a).

HEWISON, W. S. 1998. *Who was who in Orkney.* Bellavista Publications, Kirkwall.

HIBBERT, S. 1831. 'Memoirs on the tings of Orkney and Shetland', in *Archaeologia Scotica* 3, 103-120.

HOGG, J. 1995 [first published 1819 onwards] (ed. by MACK, D. S.). *The Shepherd's Calendar.* Edinburgh University Press, Edinburgh.

HOLMES, N. M. McQ. 1988. *Trinity College Church, Hospital and Apse.* City of Edinburgh Museums and Art Galleries, Edinburgh.

HOUGHTON, W. E. and HOUGHTON, E. R. (eds.) 1966-1979. *The Wellesley Index to Victorian Periodicals 1824-1900.* 3 vols. University of Toronto Press and Routledge Kegan Paul, Toronto and London.

HUDSON, J. D. 2000. 'That man is little to be envied ....', in *Scottish Journal of Geology* 36, 1-3.

HUDSON, J. D. 2003. 'Hugh Miller's geological discoveries and observations on the Isle of Eigg, as recorded in *The Cruise of the Betsey* and in the light of modern knowledge', pp. 197-213 in BORLEY (2003).

HUDSON, J. D. and ALLWRIGHT, A. 2003. *The geology of Eigg.* Revised edition. Isle of Eigg Heritage Trust, Eigg.

HUTTON, J. 1795. *Theory of the Earth with proofs and illustrations.* 2 vols. Cadell, Edinburgh.

HUNTER, J. 1995. *The making of the crofting community.* Paperback edition. John Donald, Edinburgh.

JAMESON, R. 1800. *Outline of the mineralogy of the Scottish Isles; with mineralogical observations made in different parts of the mainland of Scotland, and dissertations upon peat and kelp.* 2 vols. Stewart, Edinburgh.

JAMESON, R. 1813. *Mineralogical travels through the Hebrides, Orkney and Shetland Islands, and mainland of Scotland, and dissertations upon peat and kelp.* 2 vols. Constable, Edinburgh.

JANVIER, P. 1996. *Early vertebrates.* Clarendon Press, Oxford.

JANVIER, P. 2003. 'Armoured fish from deep time: from Hugh Miller's insights to current questions of early vertebrate evolution', pp. 177-196 in BORLEY (2003).

JOHNSON, S. 1775. *Journey to the Western Islands of Scotland.* Strahan and Cadell, London.

JOBLING, J. A. 1991. *A dictionary of scientific bird names.* Oxford University Press, Oxford.

KEAY, J. and KEAY, J. 2000. *Collins Encyclopaedia of Scotland.* 2nd edition. HarperCollins, London.

KEILLAR, I. and SMITH, J. S. 1995. *George Gordon: man of science.* Centre for Scottish Studies, University of Aberdeen, Aberdeen.

KNELL, S. J. 2000. *The culture of English geology, 1815-1851.* Ashgate, Aldershot.

KNELL, S. J. and TAYLOR, M. A. 2003. 'Hugh Miller, the fossil discoverer and collector', pp. 156-167 in BORLEY (2003).

KNIGHT, D. M. 1999. 'Old Bones and New Ideas: the Rector of Pendock, Revd. W. S. Symonds, seen in his *Notes for Young Naturalists*, 1861', pp. 145-151 in N. COOPER (ed.) *John Ray and his successors. The clergyman as naturalist.* John Ray Trust, Braintree.

LAWSON, J. P. 1842. *The descriptive atlas of Scotland with a scientific view of its geology accompanied by a coloured map by William A. Rhind.* Edinburgh Printing and Publishing Co., Edinburgh.

LEASK, W. K. 1896. *Hugh Miller.* Oliphant Anderson and Ferrier, Edinburgh.

LEVITT, I. and SMOUT, T. C. 1979. *The state of the Scottish working class in 1843: a statistical and spatial enquiry based on the data from the Poor Law Commission Report of 1844.* Scottish Academic Press, Edinburgh.

LINDSAY, J. F., CRISWELL, D. R., CRISWELL, T. L., and CRISWELL, B. S. 1976. 'Sound-producing dune and beach sands', in *Geological Society of America Bulletin* 87, 463-473.

LIVINGSTONE, A. 2003. *Minerals of Scotland.* NMS Enterprises Limited, National Museums of Scotland, Edinburgh.

LONG, J. A. 1995. *The rise of fishes. 500 million years of evolution.* Johns Hopkins University Press, Baltimore.

LONGMUIR, J. 1848. 'The Lias clay – a visit to Blackpots', *Hogg's Weekly Instructor*, New Series 1, 349-351 [published anonymously; for authorship see *Cruise of the Betsey*, p. 259fn].

LOVE, J. A. 2001. *Rum. A landscape without figures.* Birlinn, Edinburgh.

LYELL, C. 1830-1833. *Principles of Geology, being an attempt to explain the former causes of the Earth's surface, by reference to causes now in operation.* 3 vols. Murray, London [1990-1991 facsimile reprint with introduction and notes by M. J. S. RUDWICK, University of Chicago Press, Chicago].

LYELL, C. 1841. *Elements of Geology.* 2nd edition. 2 vols. Murray, London.

McCANCE, M. 2002. 'Hugh Miller, 1802-1856, geologist and writer: his links with 19th century Girvan', in *Ayrshire Notes* 23, 20-23.

M'CRIE, T. P. (ed.) 1848. *The Bass Rock. Its Civil and Ecclesiastical History ....* W. P. Kennedy, Edinburgh.

MacCULLOCH, J. 1819. *A description of the Western Islands of Scotland, including the Isle of Man: comprising an account of their geological structure; with remarks on their agriculture, scenery, and antiquities.* 3 vols. Constable, Edinburgh, and Hurst, Robinson and Co., London.

MacCULLOCH, J. 1824. *Highlands and Western Isles of Scotland containing descriptions of their scenery and antiquities ....* 4 vols. Longman, London.

McINTYRE, D. B. and McKIRDY, A. 2001. *James Hutton. The founder of modern geology.* NMS Enterprises Limited, National Museums of Scotland, Edinburgh.

MACKENZIE, W. M. 1905. *Hugh Miller. A critical study.* Hodder and Stoughton, London.

McKENZIE JOHNSTON, M. A. and TAYLOR, M. A. 2002. 'Lydia Miller and the posthumous reputation', pp. 103-111 in BORLEY (2002).

McKIRDY, A. and CROFTS, R. 1999. *Scotland: the creation of its natural landscape. A landscape fashioned by geology.* Scottish Natural Heritage. Perth.

MacLEAN, D. 1796. 'Parish of Small Isles ....', vol. 17, pp. 272-294 in *The Statistical Account of Scotland.* Creech, Edinburgh, and http://edina.ac.uk/StatAcc

MacLEAN, D. 1845. 'Parish of Small Isles ....', vol. 14, pp. 145-154 in *The New Statistical Account of Scotland.* Blackwood, Edinburgh, and http://edina.ac.uk/StatAcc

MACLEOD, D. 1996. 'Hugh Miller, the Disruption, and the Free Church of Scotland', pp. 187-205 in SHORTLAND (1996a).

MACLEOD, D. 2002. 'Miller and the Disruption', pp. 80-84 in BORLEY (2002).

MACLEOD, J. L. 2000. *The Second Disruption. The Free Church in Victorian Scotland and the origins of the Free Presbyterian Church.* Tuckwell Press, East Linton.

MACPHERSON. H. G. 1989. *Agates.* NMS Enterprises Limited, National Museums of Scotland, Edinburgh.

MAGNUSSON, M. 1997. *Rum: Nature's island.* Luath Press, Edinburgh.

MALCOLM, J. [1905]. *Poems, Tales and Sketches* [with essay by G. GILFILLAN]. Peace, Kirkwall.

MANTELL, G. A. 1844. *The Medals of Creation; or, First Lessons in Geology, and in the study of Organic Remains.* 2 vols. Bohn, London.

MARTILL, D. M. 1988. 'Preservation of fishes in the Cretaceous Santana Formation of Brazil', in *Palaeontology* 31, 1-18.

MELVILLE [or MELVILL], J. 1829. *The diary of Mr James Melvill 1556-1601.* Privately published, Bannatyne Club, Edinburgh.

MERRILL, L. L. 1989. *The romance of Victorian natural history.* Oxford University Press, Oxford.

MERRITT, J. W., CONNELL, E. R. and BRIDGLAND, D. R. (eds.) 2000. *The Quaternary of the Banffshire coast and Buchan. Field Guide.* Quaternary Research Association, London.

MERRITT, J. W., CONNELL, E. R., HALL, A. M. and PEACOCK, J. D. 2000. 'An introduction to the Cainozoic geology of coastal Morayshire, Banffshire and Buchan', pp. 1-20 in MERRITT, CONNELL and BRIDGLAND (2000).

MILLER, H. 1835. *Scenes and Legends of the North of Scotland; or, The Traditional History of Cromarty.* Black, Edinburgh.

MILLER, H. 1841. *The Old Red Sandstone, or, New Walks in an old field.* John Johnstone, Edinburgh.

MILLER, H. 1847. *First Impressions of England and its People.* John Johnstone, London.

MILLER, H. 1857. *The Testimony of the Rocks, or, Geology in its bearings on the two theologies, natural and revealed.* Constable, Edinburgh.

MILLER, H. 1858 [first published 1854]. *My Schools and Schoolmasters, or, The story of my education.* Constable, Edinburgh.

MILLER, H. 1859. *Sketch-book of Popular Geology.* 1st edition. Constable, Edinburgh.

MILLER, H. 1862. *Essays, historical and biographical, political and social, literary and scientific.* A. & C. Black, Edinburgh; Hamilton, Adams & Co., London.

MILLER, H. 1864 [first published 1849]. *Footprints of the Creator or, the Asterolepis of Stromness.* Black, Edinburgh.

MILLER, H. 1871. *Leading articles on various subjects.* 3rd edition. Nimmo, Edinburgh.

MILLER, H. 1891a [first published 1864]. *Edinburgh and its neighbourhood, geological and historical.* Nimmo, Hay and Mitchell, Edinburgh.

MILLER, H. 1891b. 'A voice from the Greyfriars', pp. 191-205 in MILLER (1891a).

MILLER, H. 1891c. 'Trinity College Church versus Burns' Monument', pp. 206-218 in MILLER (1891a).

MILLER, H. 1899a. *The Old Red Sandstone.* 7th edn. Nimmo, Hay and Mitchell, Edinburgh.

MILLER, H. 1899b. 'On the ancient Grauwacke rocks of Scotland', pp. 296-324 in MILLER (1899a).

MILLER, H. 1993 [first published 1854]. *My schools and schoolmasters* [reprint with introduction and notes by J. ROBERTSON]. B&W Publishing, Edinburgh.

MILLER, H. 1994 [first published 1835]. *Scenes and legends of the north of Scotland* [reprint of revised 1850 edition with introduction and notes by J. ROBERTSON]. B&W Publishing, Edinburgh.

MILLER, H. 1997. *A noble smuggler and other stories.* [reprint of earlier journalism from Miller's Cromarty days, ed. and with introduction by M. GOSTWICK]. *Inverness Courier*, Inverness.

MILLER, H. 2001 [first published 1857]. *The Testimony of the Rocks, or, Geology in its bearings on the two theologies, natural and revealed* [reprint with introductions by P. FOSTER and M. A. TAYLOR]. St Matthew Publishing, Cambridge.

MITCHISON, R. 2000. *The Old Poor Law in Scotland. The experience of poverty, 1574-1845.* Edinburgh University Press, Edinburgh.

MOIR, D. G. 1973-1983. *The early maps of Scotland to 1850.* 2 vols. Royal Scottish Geographical Society, Edinburgh.

MORRISON-LOW, A. D. and CHRISTIE, J. R. R. 1984. *'Martyr of Science': Sir David Brewster 1781-1868. Proceedings of a bicentenary symposium held at the Royal Scottish Museum ....* Royal Scottish Museum, Edinburgh.

MORRISON-LOW, A. D. and NUTTALL, R. H. 2003. 'Hugh Miller in an age of microscopy', pp. 214-226 in BORLEY (2003).

MORTON, N. and HUDSON, J. D. 1995. 'Field guide to the Jurassic of the Isles of Raasay and Skye, Inner Hebrides, NW Scotland', pp. 209-280 in P. D. TAYLOR (ed.) *Field geology of the British Jurassic.* Geological Society Publishing House, Bath.

MURCHISON, R. I. 1827. 'On the coal-field of Brora in Sutherlandshire, and some other stratified deposits in the North of Scotland', in *Transactions of the Geological Society of London* (2)2(2), 293-325.

MURCHISON, R. I. 1828. 'Supplementary remarks on the strata of the Oolitic Series, and the rocks associated with them, in the counties of Sutherland and Ross, and in the Hebrides', in *Transactions of the Geological Society of London* (2)2(3), 353-368.

MYKURA, W. 1976. *British Regional Geology. Orkney and Shetland.* HMSO, Edinburgh.

NORI, F., SHOLTZ, P. and BRETZ, M. 1997. 'Booming sand', in *Scientific American* 277(3) for October, 64-69.

NEILL, P. 1806. *A tour through some of the islands of Orkney and Shetland, with a view chiefly to objects of natural history ....* Constable, Edinburgh.

NUTTALL, R. H. 1979. *Microscopes from the Frank Collection 1800-1860.* A. Frank, Jersey, Channel Islands.

O'CONNOR, R. 2003. 'Hugh Miller and geological spectacle', pp. 237-258 in BORLEY (2003).

OLDROYD, D. R. 1990. *The Highlands Controversy.* University of Chicago Press, Chicago.

OLDROYD, D. R. 1996a. 'The geologist from Cromarty', pp. 76-121 in SHORTLAND (1996a).

OLDROYD, D. R. 1996b. *Thinking about the Earth. A history of ideas in geology.* Athlone, London.

OLDROYD, D. R. 2004 in press. 'Symonds, William Samuel (1818-1887)', in *Oxford Dictionary of National Biography.* Oxford University Press, Oxford.

OLDROYD, D. R. and HAMILTON, B. 1997. 'Geikie and Judd, and controversies about the igneous rocks of the Scottish Hebrides: theory, practice and power in the geological community', in *Annals of Science* 54, 221-268.

OMAND, D. (ed.) 1989. *The New Caithness Book.* North of Scotland Newspapers, Wick.

PALEY, W. 1809. *Natural Theology; or, evidences of the existence and attributes of the Deity collected from the appearances of Nature.* 12th edition. J. Faulder, London.

PARADIS, J. G. 1996. 'The natural historian as antiquary of the world: Hugh Miller and the rise of literary natural history', pp. 122-150 in SHORTLAND (1996a).

PARIS, J. A. 1818. 'On a recent formation of sandstone, occurring in various parts of the northern coasts of Cornwall', in *Transactions of the Royal Geological Society of Cornwall* 1, 1-19.

PRESTWICH, J. 1840. 'On the structure of the neighbourhood of Gamrie, Banffshire, particularly on the deposit containing ichthyolites', in *Transactions of the Geological Society of London* (2) 5, 139-148.

RALSTON, I. 1986. 'The Yorkshire Television vitrified wall experiment at East Tullos, City of Aberdeen District', in *Proceedings of the Society of Antiquaries of Scotland* 116, 17-40.

RIXSON, D. 2001. *The Small Isles, Canna, Rum, Eigg and Muck.* Birlinn, Edinburgh.

ROBB, D. 1996. 'Stand, and unfold yourself': *My schools and schoolmasters*, pp. 246-264 in SHORTLAND (1996a).

ROBERTSON, J. 2002. 'Scenes and legends of the north: feeding a youthful imagination', pp. 17-25 in BORLEY (2002).

ROBINS, N. S. and McMILLAN, A. A. 1989. 'The Strathpeffer Spa Waters: an appraisal at the end of the 19th century by Ben N. Peach and John Horne', in *The Edinburgh Geologist* 22, 1-14.

ROSIE, G. 1981. *Hugh Miller: Outrage and order: a biography and selected writings.* Mainstream, Edinburgh.

RUDWICK, M. J. S. 1974. 'Miller, Hugh', vol. 9, pp. 388-390 in C. C. GILLISPIE (ed.) *Dictionary of Scientific Biography.* Charles Scribner's Sons, New York.

SARJEANT, W. A. S. 1980-1996. *Geologists and the history of geology. An international bibliography from the origins to 1978.* 10 vols. Macmillan, London (first five volumes), and Krieger, Malabar, Florida (second five volumes).

SCOTT, H. 1915-1928. *Fasti Ecclesiae Scoticanae: the succession of ministers in the Church of Scotland from the Reformation.* New edition. 7 vols. Oliver & Boyd, Edinburgh.

SECORD, J. A. 1986. *Controversy in Victorian Geology. The Cambrian-Silurian Dispute.* Princeton University Press, Princeton, New Jersey.

SECORD, J. A. 1994. 'Introduction', pp. ix-xlviii in CHAMBERS (1994).

SECORD, J. A. 1997. 'Introduction', pp. ix-xlii in C. LYELL, *Principles of Geology.* Abridged edition. Penguin Books, London.

SECORD, J. A. 2000. *Victorian sensation. The extraordinary publication, reception, and secret authorship of Vestiges of the Natural History of Creation.* University of Chicago Press, Chicago.

SECORD, J. A. 2003. 'From Miller to the Millennium', pp. 328-337 in BORLEY (2003).

SHERIDAN, A., DAVIS, M., CLARK, I., and REDVERS-JONES, H. 2002. 'Investigating jet and jet-like artifacts from prehistoric Scotland: the National Museums of Scotland project', in *Antiquity* 76, 812-825.

SHORTLAND, M. (ed.) 1996a. *Hugh Miller and the controversies of Victorian science.* Oxford University Press, Oxford.

SHORTLAND, M. 1996b. 'Bonneted mechanic and narrative hero: the self-modelling of Hugh Miller', pp. 14-75 in SHORTLAND (1996a).

SHORTLAND, M. 1996c. 'Hugh Miller's contribution to the *Witness*: 1840-56', pp. 287-300 in SHORTLAND (1996a).

SHORTLAND, M. 1996d. 'Appendix: a bibliography of Hugh Miller', pp. 301-384 in SHORTLAND (1996a).

SMILES, S. 1878. *Robert Dick baker, of Thurso, geologist and botanist* [also including Charles Peach]. John Murray, London.

SMITH, G. 1879. *The life of John Wilson, D. D., F. R. S. for fifty years philanthropist and scholar in the East.* 2nd edition. John Murray, London.

SMITH, J. 1907. *Annals of the Church of Scotland in Orkney from 1560. History of the U. P. Church in Orkney until 1906. And also the Episcopal Church from 1694.* W. R. Mackintosh, Kirkwall.

SMOUT, T. C. 1969. *A history of the Scottish people 1560-1830.* Collins, London.

SMOUT, T. C. 1986. *A century of the Scottish people 1830-1950.* Collins, London.

SOWERBY, J. and SOWERBY, J. de C. 1812-1829. *The Mineral Conchology of Great Britain; or coloured figures and descriptions of those remains of testaceous animals or shells, which have been preserved at various times and depths in the Earth.* Sowerby, London.

STEVENSON, S. 1981. *David Octavius Hill and Robert Adamson. Catalogue of their calotypes taken between 1841 and 1847 in the collection of the Scottish National Portrait Gallery.* National Galleries of Scotland, Edinburgh.

STEVENSON, S. 2002a. 'Hugh Miller in focus: the art of Hill and Adamson', pp. 72-79 in BORLEY (2002).

STEVENSON, S. 2002b. *The personal art of David Octavius Hill.* Yale University Press, New Haven.

STORRS, G. W. 1994. 'Fossil vertebrate faunas of the British Rhaetian (latest Triassic)', in *Zoological Journal of the Linnean Society of London* 112, 217-259.

SUTHERLAND, E. 2002. *Lydia, wife of Hugh Miller of Cromarty.* Tuckwell. East Linton.

SWANSON, J. 1844. *A leisure hour in the floating manse; or, the story of Niel M–n.* John Johnstone, Edinburgh. [Copy in the Library of New College, University of Edinburgh.]

TAPPER, S. 1992. *Game heritage. An ecological review from shooting and gamekeeping records.* Game Conservancy, Fordingbridge.

TAYLOR, M. A. 2000. 'Mary Anning, Thomas Hawkins and Hugh Miller, and the realities of being a provincial fossil collector', in *Edinburgh Geologist* 34, 28-37.

TAYLOR, M. A. 2002a. 'Fellow Scots: John Muir and Hugh Miller', in *John Muir Trust Journal and News* 32, 12-17, 68-69; **www.jmt.org/news/2002/32/muirmiller.html**

TAYLOR, M. A. 2002b. 'Hugh Miller and his fossils – a bicentenary appreciation', in *Edinburgh Geologist* 38, 10-19; **www.edinburghgeolsoc.org**

TAYLOR, M. A. 2004 in press. 'Hugh Miller (1802-1856)', in *Oxford Dictionary of National Biography.* Oxford University Press, Oxford.

TAYLOR, M. A. and CHEAPE, H. 1999. 'Fossil folk', in *Geology Today* 15, 23 only.

TAYLOR, M. A. and CRUICKSHANK, A. R. I. 1993. 'A plesiosaur from the Linksfield Erratic (Rhaetian, Upper Triassic) near Elgin, Morayshire', in *Scottish Journal of Geology* 29, 191-196.

TAYLOR, M. A. and GOSTWICK, M. 2003. 'Hugh Miller's collection – a memorial to a great geological Scot', in *Edinburgh Geologist* 40, 24-29; **www.edinburghgeolsoc.org**

THOMSON, W. P. L. 2001. *The new history of Orkney.* Mercat, Edinburgh.

TORRENS, H. S. 1997. 'Politics and paleontology: Richard Owen and the invention of dinosaurs', pp. 175-190 in J. O. FARLOW and M. K. BRETT-SURMAN (eds.), *The complete dinosaur.* Indiana University Press, Bloomington.

TORRENS, H. S. 1998. 'Geology and the natural sciences: some contributions to archaeology in Britain 1780-1850', pp. 35-59 in V. BRAND (ed.) *The study of the past in the Victorian Age. Oxbow Monograph* 73. Oxbow Books, Oxford.

TORRENS, H. S. 2002. *The practice of British geology, 1750-1850.* Ashgate, Aldershot.

TORRENS, H. S. 2003. 'William Smith (1769-1839) and the search for English raw materials: some parallels with Hugh Miller and with Scotland', pp. 137-155 in BORLEY (2003).

TREWIN, N. H. 1973. 'Hugh Miller's graptolites', in *Scottish Journal of Geology* 9, 163-164.

TREWIN, N. H. 1986. 'Palaeoecology and sedimentology of the Achanarras fish bed of the Middle Old Red Sandstone, Scotland', in *Transactions of the Royal Society of Edinburgh – Earth Sciences* 77, 21-46.

TREWIN, N. H. (ed.) 2003a. *The geology of Scotland.* 4th edition. Geological Society Publishing House, Bath.

TREWIN, N. H. 2003b. 'Hugh Miller's fish; the "winged *Pterichthys*"', pp. 168-176 in BORLEY (2003).

TREWIN, N. H. and DAVIDSON, R. G. 1999. 'Lake-level changes, sedimentation and faunas in a Middle Devonian basin-margin fish bed', in *Journal of the Geological Society, London*, 156, 535-548.

TREWIN, N. H. and HURST, A. 1993. *Excursion guide to the geology of East Sutherland and Caithness.* Geological Society of Aberdeen and Scottish Academic Press, Edinburgh.

TREWIN, N. H., KNELLER, B. C. and GILLEN, C. 1987. *Geology of the Aberdeen area.* Geological Society of Aberdeen and Scottish Academic Press, Edinburgh.

VINCENT, D. 1996. 'Miller's improvement: a classic tale of self-advancement?', pp. 230-245 in SHORTLAND (1996a).

WALKER, J. (ed. by H. W. SCOTT) 1966. *Lectures on geology including hydrography, mineralogy and meteorology with an introduction to biology.* University of Chicago Press, Chicago and London.

WATERSTON, C. D. 1959. 'Robert James Hay Cunningham (1815-1842)', in *Transactions of the Edinburgh Geological Society* 17, 260-272.

WATERSTON, C. D. 1978. 'Hugh Miller', pp. 160-169 in J. CALDER (ed.) *The Enterprising Scot.* Royal Museum of Scotland and Her Majesty's Stationery Office, Edinburgh.

WATERSTON, C. D. 1997. *Collections in context. The Museum of the Royal Society of Edinburgh and the inception of a National Museum for Scotland.* NMS Enterprises, National Museums of Scotland, Edinburgh.

WATERSTON, C. D. 2002a. 'Hugh Miller as a geologist and naturalist', pp. 26-31 in BORLEY (2002).

WATERSTON, C. D. 2002b. 'An awakening interest in geology,' pp. 85-91 in BORLEY (2002).

WATTERS, M., CORMACK, W. and CORMACK, S. 1996. *Notes on George Petrie 1818-1875 antiquary and Sheriff Clerk.* Privately published (copy in NMS Library).

WILLIS, D. 2002. 'Enlightenment in the north: the role of the amateur natural historian in the early 19th century', pp. 32-36 in BORLEY (2002).

WILSON, J. 1842. *A voyage round the coasts of Scotland and the Isles.* 2 vols. Black, Edinburgh.

WITHAM, H. T. M. 1831. *Observations on fossil vegetables, accompanied by representations of their internal structure, as seen through the microscope.* Edinburgh.

WITHERS, C. W. J. 1984. *Gaelic in Scotland 1698-1981. The geographical history of a language.* John Donald, Edinburgh.

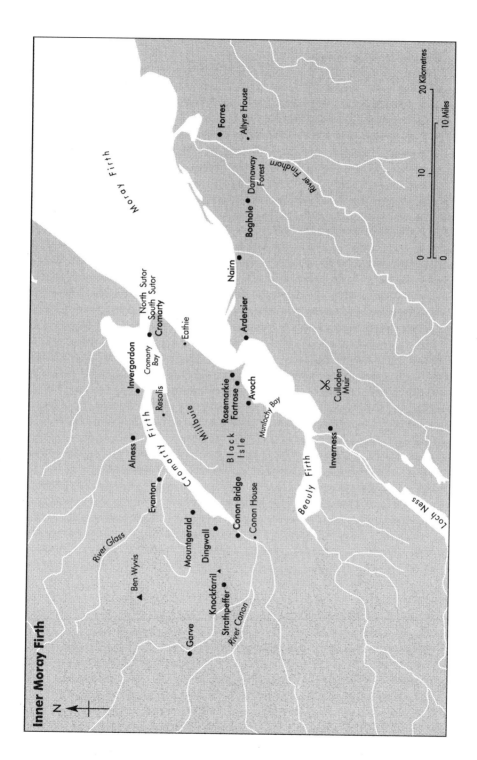

Inner Moray Firth

N

Moray Firth

Forres
Altyre House

Boghole
Darnaway Forest
River Findhorn

North Sutor
South Sutor
Cromarty
Eathie

Nairn

Ardersier

Invergordon
Cromarty Bay

Resolis

Millbuie

Rosemarkie
Fortrose
Avoch

Munlochy Bay

Culloden Muir

Alness

Cromarty Firth

Black Isle

Inverness

Evanton

Conon Bridge
Conon House

Beauly Firth

Mountgerald
Dingwall

River Glass

Ben Wyvis

Knockfarril

Loch Ness

Garve
Strathpeffer
River Conon

0   10   20 Kilometres
0   10 Miles

A63

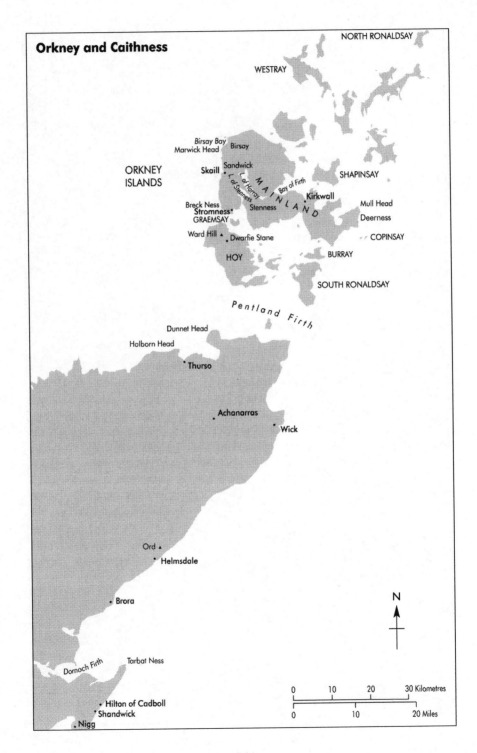

Orkney and Caithness

NORTH RONALDSAY

WESTRAY

ORKNEY ISLANDS

Birsay Bay
Marwick Head
Birsay
Skaill
Sandwick
L. of Harray
L. of Stenness
MAINLAND
Bay of Firth
SHAPINSAY

Kirkwall

Breck Ness
Stromness
GRAEMSAY
Stenness
Mull Head
Deerness

Ward Hill
Dwarfie Stane
COPINSAY

HOY
BURRAY

SOUTH RONALDSAY

Pentland Firth

Dunnet Head

Holborn Head
Thurso

Achanarras

Wick

Ord
Helmsdale

Brora

N

Dornoch Firth
Tarbat Ness

Hilton of Cadboll
Shandwick
Nigg

| 0 | 10 | 20 | 30 Kilometres |

| 0 | 10 | 20 Miles |

THE

CRUISE OF THE BETSEY;

OR,

A SUMMER RAMBLE AMONG THE FOSSILIFEROUS
DEPOSITS OF THE HEBRIDES.

WITH

RAMBLES OF A GEOLOGIST;

OR,

TEN THOUSAND MILES OVER THE FOSSILIFEROUS
DEPOSITS OF SCOTLAND.

BY HUGH MILLER,

AUTHOR OF "THE OLD RED SANDSTONE," "MY SCHOOLS AND SCHOOL-
MASTERS," "THE TESTIMONY OF THE ROCKS," ETC.

EDINBURGH: THOMAS CONSTABLE AND CO.
HAMILTON, ADAMS, AND CO., LONDON.
MDCCCLVIII.

PREFACE.

NATURALISTS of every class know too well how HUGH MILLER died,—the victim of an overworked brain ; and how that bright and vigorous spirit was abruptly quenched for ever.

During the month of May (1857) Mrs Miller came to Malvern, after recovering from the first shock of bereavement, in search of health and repose, and evidently hoping to do justice, on her recovery, to the literary remains of her husband. Unhappily the excitement and anxiety naturally attaching to a revision of her husband's works proved over much for one suffering under such recent trial, and from an affection of the brain and spine which ensued ; and, in consequence, Mrs Miller has been forbidden, for the present, to engage in any work of mental labour.

Under these circumstances, and at Mrs Miller's request, I have undertaken the editing of " The Cruise of the Betsey, or a Summer Ramble among the Fossiliferous Deposits of the Hebrides," as well as " The Rambles of a Geologist," hitherto unpublished, save as a series of articles in the "Witness" newspaper. The style and arguments of HUGH MILLER are so peculiarly his own, that I have not presumed to alter the text, and have merely corrected some statements incidental to the condition of geological knowledge at the time this work was penned. The "Cruise of the Betsey" was written for that well-known paper the "Witness" during the period when a disputation productive of much bitter feeling waged between the Free and Established Churches of Scotland ; but as the Disruption and its history possesses little interest to a large class of the readers of this work, who will rejoice to follow their favourite author among the isles and rocks of the " bonnie land," I have expunged *some* passages, which I am assured the author would have omitted had he lived to reprint this interesting narrative of his geological rambles. Hugh Miller battled nobly for his faith while living. The sword is in the scabbard : let it rest !

W. S. SYMONDS.

Pendock Rectory, October 1, 1857.

THE CRUISE OF THE BETSEY.

CHAPTER I.

THE pleasant month of July had again come round, and for full five weeks I was free. Chisels and hammers, and the bag for specimens, were taken from their corner in the dark closet, and packed up with half a stone weight of a fine *soft* Conservative Edinburgh newspaper, valuable for a quality of preserving old things entire. And at noon on St Swithin's day (Monday the 15th), I was speeding down the Clyde in the Toward Castle steamer, for Tobermory in Mull. In the previous season I had intended passing direct from the Oolitic deposits of the eastern coast of Scotland, to the Oolitic deposits of the Hebrides. But the weeks glided all too quickly away among the ichthyolites of Caithness and Cromarty, and the shells and lignites of Sutherland and Ross. My friend, too, the Rev. Mr Swanson of Small Isles, on whose assistance I had reckoned, was in the middle of his troubles at the time, with no longer a home in his parish, and not yet provided with one elsewhere ; and I concluded he would have but little heart, at such a season, for breaking into rocks, or for passing from the too pressing monstrosities of an existing state of things, to the old lapidified monstrosities of the past. And so my design on the Hebrides had to be postponed for a twelvemonth.   But my friend, now afloat in his Free Church yacht, had got a home on the sea beside his island charge, which, if not very secure when nights were dark and winds loud, and the little vessel tilted high to the long roll of the Atlantic, lay at least beyond the reach of man's intolerance, and not beyond the protecting care of the Almighty.   He had written me that he would run down his vessel from Small Isles to meet me at Tobermory, and in consequence of the arrangement I was now on my way to Mull.

St Swithin's day, so important in the calendar of our humbler meteorologists, had in this part of the country its alternate fits of sunshine and shower.   We passed gaily along the green banks of the Clyde, with their rich flat fields glittering in moisture, and their lines of stately trees, that, as the light flashed out, threw their shadows over the grass. The river expanded into the estuary, the estuary into the open sea ; we left behind us beacon, and obelisk, and rock-perched castle ;—

> " Merrily down we drop
> Below the church, below the tower,
> Below the lighthouse top ;"

and, as the evening fell, we were ploughing the outer reaches of the Frith, with the ridgy table-land of Ayrshire stretching away green on the one side, and the serrated peaks of Arran rising dark and high on the other.   At sunrise next morning our boat lay, unloading a portion of her cargo, in one of the ports of Islay, and we could see the Irish coast resting on the horizon to the south and west, like a long undulating bank of thin blue cloud ; with the island of Rachrin—famous for the asylum it had afforded the Bruce when there was no home for him in Scotland—presenting in front its mass of darker azure.   On and away !   We swept past Islay, with its low fertile hills of mica-schist and slate ; and Jura, with its flat dreary moors, and its far-seen gigantic paps, on one

---

humbler meteorologists: in folk tradition rain on St Swithin's day presaged a long period of bad weather; 'merrily ... ': from Samuel Taylor Coleridge's 'Rime of the Ancient Mariner' of which, in the last age, Professor Walker of Edinburgh set water a-boil with six degrees of heat less than he found necessary for the purpose on the plain below.   The Professor describes the view from the summit, which includes in its wide circle at once the Isle of Skye and the Isle of Man, as singularly noble and imposing : two such prospects more, he says, would bring under the eye the whole island of Great Britain, from the Pentland Frith to the English Channel. We sped past Jura.   Then came the Gulf of Coryvrekin, with the bare mountain island of Scarba overlooking the fierce, far-famed whirlpool that we could see from the deck breaking in long lines of foam, and sending out its waves in wide rings on every side, when not a speck of white was visible elsewhere in the expanse of sea around us.   And then came an opener space, studded with smaller islands,—mere hill-tops rising out of the sea, with here and there insulated groupes of pointed rocks, the skeletons of perished hills, amid which the tides chafed and fretted, as if labouring to complete on the broken remains their work of denudation and ruin.

The disposition of land and water on this coast suggests the idea that the Western Highlands, from the line in the interior whence the rivers descend to the Atlantic, with the islands beyond to the outer Hebrides, are all parts of one great mountainous plain, inclined slantways into the sea. First, the long withdrawing valleys of the main land, with their brown mossy streams, change their character as they dip beneath the sea-level, and become salt-water lochs.   The lines of hills that rise over them jut out as promontories, till cut off by some transverse valley, lowered still more deeply into the brine, and that exists as a kyle, minch, or sound, swept twice every tide by powerful currents.   The sea deepens as the plain slopes downward ; mountain-chains stand up out of the water as larger islands, single mountains as smaller

last age: previous century; **set water a-boil**: in 1764 John Walker (1731-1803), later Professor of Natural History at the University of Edinburgh (Waterston 1997; Livingstone 2003), made the first quantitative demonstration of how the lower air pressure on top of the mountain reduced the boiling point of water (Walker 1966)

ones, lower eminences as mere groupes of pointed rocks ; till
at length, as we pass outwards, all trace of the submerged
land disappears, and the wide ocean stretches out and away
its unfathomable depths.   The model of some alpine country
raised in plaster on a flat board, and tilted slantways at a low
angle into a basin of water, would exhibit on a minute scale
an appearance exactly similar to that presented by the western
coast of Scotland and the Hebrides.   The water would rise
along the hollows, longitudinal and transverse, forming sounds
and lochs, and surround, island-like, the more deeply submerged eminences.   But an examination of the geology of
the coast, with its promontories and islands, communicates a
different idea.   These islands and promontories prove to be
of very various ages and origin.   The *outer* Hebrides may
have existed as the inner skeleton of some ancient country
contemporary with the main land, and that bore on its upper
soils the productions of perished creations, at a time when
by much the larger portion of the *inner* Hebrides,—Skye, and
Mull, and the Small Isles,—existed as part of the bottom of
a wide sound, inhabited by the Cephalopoda and Enaliosaurians of the Lias and the Oolite.   Judging from its components, the Long Island, like the Lammermoors and the
Grampians, may have been smiling to the sun when the Alps
and the Himalaya Mountains lay buried in the abyss ; whereas the greater part of Skye and Mull must have been, like
these vast mountain-chains of the Continent, an oozy sea-
floor, over which the ligneous productions of the neighbouring lands, washed down by the streams, grew heavy and sank,
and on which the belemnite dropped its spindle and the ammonite its shell.   The idea imparted of *old* Scotland to the
geologist here,—of Scotland, proudly, aristocratically, super-
eminently old,—for it can call Mont Blanc a mere upstart,
and Dhawalageri, with its twenty-eight thousand feet of elevation, a heady fellow of yesterday,—is not that of a land

---

Long Island: Outer Hebrides (Lewis, Harris, The Uists, *etc*); **Lammermoors**: hills in
East Lothian and Berwickshire; **ligneous productions**: here, driftwood; **Dhawalageri**:
the Himalayan mountain, now Dhawalagiri

settling down by the head like a foundering vessel, but of a
land whose hills and islands, like its great aristocratic families,
have arisen from the level in very various ages, and under
the operation of circumstances essentially diverse.

We left behind us the islands of Lunga, Luing, and Seil,
and entered the narrow Sound of Kerrera, with its border of
Old Red conglomerate resting on the clay-slate of the district. We had passed Esdaile near enough to see the workmen employed in the quarries of the island so extensively
known in commerce for their roofing slate, and several small
vessels beside them, engaged in loading ; and now we had
got a step higher in the geological scale, and could mark from
the deck the peculiar character of the conglomerate, which, in
cliffs washed by the sea, when the binding matrix is softer
than the pebbles which it incloses, roughens, instead of being
polished, by the action of the waves, and which, along the eastern side of the Sound here, seems as if formed of cannon-shot
of all sizes embedded in cement. The Sound terminates in
the beautiful bay of Oban, so quiet and sheltered, with its two
island breakwaters in front,—its semicircular sweep of hill
behind,—its long white-walled village, bent like a bow, to
conform to the inflection of the shore,—its mural precipices
behind, tapestried with ivy,—its rich patches of green pasture,—its bosky dingles of shrub and tree,—and, perched on
the seaward promontory, its old, time-eaten keep. "In one
part of the harbour of Oban," says Dr James Anderson, in
his "Practical Treatise on Peat Moss," (1794), "where the
depth of the sea is about twenty fathoms, the bottom is found
to consist of quick peat, which affords no safe anchorage." I
made inquiry at the captain of the steamer regarding this
submerged deposit, but he had never heard of it. There are,
however, many such on the coasts of both Britain and Ireland. We staid at Oban for several hours, waiting the arrival of the Fort-William steamer ; and, taking out hammer and

---

Old Red: *ie* part of the Old Red Sandstone, of Devonian age chisel from my bag, I stepped ashore to question my ancient acquaintance the Old Red conglomerate, and was fortunate enough to meet on the pier-head, as I landed, one of the best of companions for assisting in such work, Mr Colin Elder of Isle Ornsay,—the gentleman who had so kindly furnished my friend Mr Swanson with an asylum for his family, when there was no longer a home for them in Small Isles. " You are much in luck," he said, after our first greeting : " one of the villagers, in improving his garden, has just made a cut for some fifteen or twenty yards along the face of the precipice behind the village, and laid open the line of junction between the conglomerate and the clay-slate.   Let us go and see it."

I found several things worthy of notice in the chance section to which I was thus introduced.   The conglomerate lies unconformably along the edges of the slate strata, which present under it an appearance exactly similar to that which they exhibit under the rolled stones and shingle of the neighbouring shore, where we find them laid bare beside the harbour for several hundred yards.   And, mixed with the pebbles of various character and origin of which the conglomerate is mainly composed, we see detached masses of the slate, that still exhibit on their edges the identical lines of fracture characteristic of the rock, which they received, when torn from the mass below, myriads of ages before.   In the incalculably remote period in which the conglomerate base of the Old Red Sandstone was formed, the clay-slate of this district had been exactly the same sort of rock that it is now. Some long anterior convulsion had upturned its strata ; and the sweep of water, mingled with broken fragments of stone, had worn smooth the exposed edges, just as a similar agency wears the edges exposed at the present time.   Quarries might have been opened in this rock, as now, for a roofing slate, had there been quarriers to open them, or houses to roof over : it was in every respect as ancient a looking stone then as in

---

unconformably: alluding – especially on p. 7 – to the eighteenth century Scots geologist James Hutton's key insight, classically at Siccar Point in Berwickshire, that such unconformities between differently oriented strata indicate huge gaps of time between their deposition, which is necessary for the lower rock layers to have been tilted from their originally horizontal position (McIntyre and McKirdy 2001) the present late age of the world. There are no sermons that seem stranger or more impressive to one who has acquired just a little of the language in which they are preached, than those which, according to the poet, are to be found in stones : a bit of fractured slate, embedded among a mass of rounded pebbles, proves voluble with idea of a kind almost too large for the mind of man to grasp. The eternity that hath passed is an ocean without a further shore, and a finite conception may in vain attempt to span it over. But from the beach, strewed with wrecks, on which we stand to contemplate it, we see far out towards the cloudy horizon many a dim islet and many a pinnacled rock, the sepulchres of successive eras, —the monuments of consecutive creations : the entire prospect is studded over with these landmarks of a hoar antiquity, which, measuring out space from space, constitute the vast whole a province of time ; nor can the eye reach to the open shoreless infinitude beyond, in which only God existed : and—as in a sea-scene in nature, in which headland stretches dim and blue beyond headland, and islet beyond islet, the distance seems not lessened, but increased, by the crowded objects—we borrow a larger, not a smaller idea of the distant eternity, from the vastness of the measured periods that occur between.

Over the lower bed of conglomerate, which here, as on the east coast, is of great thickness, we find a bed of gray stratified clay, containing a few calcareo-argillaceous nodules. The conglomerate cliffs to the north of the village present appearances highly interesting to the geologist. Rising in a long wall within the pleasure-grounds of Dunolly Castle, we find them wooded atop and at the base ; while immediately at their feet there stretches out a grassy lawn, traversed by the road from the village to the castle, which sinks with a gradual slope into the existing sea-beach, but which ages ago must have been a sea-beach itself. We see the bases of the

---

poet ... in stones: Shakespeare, *As You Like It*, Act 2, Scene 1. Duke Senior, in exile in the Forest of Arden, reflects, '... our life exempt from public haunt/Finds tongues in trees, books in the running brooks,/Sermons in stones and good in every thing' precipices hollowed and worn, with all their rents and crevices widened into caves ; and mark, at a picturesque angle of the rock, what must have been once an insulated sea-stack, some thirty or forty feet in height, standing up from amid the rank grass, as at one time it stood up from amid the waves. Tufts of fern and sprays of ivy bristle from its sides, once roughened by the serrated kelp-weed and the tangle. The Highlanders call it M'Dougall's Dog-stone, and say that the old chieftains of Lorne made use of it as a post to which to fasten their dogs,—animals wild and gigantic as themselves, —when the hunters were gathering to rendezvous, and the impatient beagles struggled to break away and begin the chace on their own behalf.   It owes its existence as a stack —for the precipice in which it was once included has receded from around it for yards—to an immense boulder in its base, —by far the largest stone I ever saw in an Old Red conglomerate.   The mass is of a rudely rhomboidal form, and measures nearly twelve feet in the line of its largest diagonal.   A second huge pebble in the same detached spire measures four feet by about three.   Both have their edges much rounded, as if, ere their deposition in the conglomerate, they had been long exposed to the wear of the sea ; and both are composed of an earthy amygdaloidal trap.   I have stated elsewhere ["Old Red Sandstone," Chapter XII.], that I had scarce ever seen a stone in the Old Red conglomerate which I could not raise from the ground ; and ere I said so I had examined no inconsiderable extent of this deposit, chiefly, however, along the eastern coast of Scotland, where its larger pebbles rarely exceed two hundredweight.   How account for the occurrence of pebbles of so gigantic a size here?   We can but guess at a solution, and that very vaguely.   The islands of Mull and Kerrera form, in the present state of things, inner and outer breakwaters between what is now the coast of Oban and the waves of the Atlantic ; but Mull, in the times of even the Oolite, must have existed as a mere sea-bottom ; and Kerrera, composed mainly of trap, which has brought with it to the surface patches of the conglomerate, must, when the conglomerate was in forming, have been a mere sea-bottom also. Is it not possible, that when the breakwaters *were not*, the Atlantic *was ;* and that its tempests, which in the present time can transport vast rocks for hundreds of yards along the exposed coasts of Shetland and Orkney, may have been the agent here in the transport of these huge pebbles of the Old Red conglomerate ? " Rocks that two or three men could not lift," say the Messrs Anderson of Inverness, in describing the storms of Orkney, " are washed about even on the tops of cliffs which are between sixty and a hundred feet above the surface of the sea when smooth ; and detached masses of rock, of an enormous size, are well known to have been carried a considerable distance between low and high-water mark." " A little way from the Brough," says Dr Patrick Neill, in his " Tour through Orkney and Shetland, " we saw the prodigious effects of a late winter storm : many great stones, one of them of several tons weight, had been tossed up a precipice twenty or thirty feet high, and laid fairly on the green sward." There is something farther worthy of notice in the stone of which the two boulders of the Dog-stack are composed. No species of rock occurs more abundantly in the embedded pebbles of this ancient conglomerate than rocks of the trap family. We find in it trap-porphyries, greenstones, clinkstones, basalts, and amygdaloids, largely mingled with fragments of the granitic, clay-slate, and quartz rocks. The Plutonic agencies must have been active in the locality for periods amazingly protracted ; and many of the masses protruded at a very early time seem identical in their composition with rocks of the trap family, which in other parts of the country we find referred to much later eras. There occur in this deposit

---

Atlantic: see 'Geology then and now'; Andersons: see Additional Notes; Brough: *ie* Brough of Birsay, an Orkney islet at the north end of the Bay of Birsay. The quote is from Neill (1806, p. 25); amygdaloids: here, amygdaloidal basalts; Plutonic agencies: here, volcanic activity and the effect of heat deep down in the earth rolled pebbles of a basalt which in the neighbourhood of Edinburgh would be deemed considerably more modern than the times of the Mountain Limestone, and in the Isle of Skye, considerably more modern than the times of the Oolite.

The sun-light was showering its last slant rays on island and loch, and then retreating upwards along the higher hills, chased by the shadows, as our boat quitted the bay of Oban, and stretched northwards, along the end of green Lismore, for the Sound of Mull. We had just enough of day left as we reached mid sea, to show us the gray fronts of the three ancient castles,—which at this point may be at once seen from the deck,—Dunolly, Duart, and Dunstaffnage ; and enough left us as we entered the Sound, to show, and barely show, the Lady Rock, famous in tradition, and made classic by the pen of Campbell, raising its black back amid the tides, like a belated porpoise. And then twilight deepened into night, and we went snorting through the Strait with a stream of green light curling off from either bow in the calm, towards the high dim land, that seemed standing up on both sides like tall hedges over a green lane. We entered the Bay of Tobermory about midnight, and cast anchor amid a group of little vessels. An exceedingly small boat shot out from the side of a yacht of rather diminutive proportions, but tantly rigged for her size, and bearing an outrigger astern. The water this evening was full of phosphoric matter, and it gleamed and sparkled around the little boat like a northern aurora around a dark cloudlet. There was just light enough to show that the oars were plied by a sailor-like man in a Guernsey frock, and that another sailor-like man,—the skipper, mayhap,—attired in a cap and pea-jacket, stood in the stern. The man in the Guernsey frock was John Stewart, sole mate and half the crew of the Free Church yacht Betsey ; and the skipper-like man in the pea-jacket was my friend the minister of the Protestants of Small Isles. In five minutes more

---

Lady Rock … Campbell: the tradition of the drowning of a chieftain's wife on the rock inspired the poem 'Glenara' by Thomas Campbell (1777-1874), popular poet and author of 'The Last Man', 'Gertrude of Wyoming' and 'Lord Ullin's Daughter'; **tantly** and **outrigger**: see Additional Notes; **phosphoric matter**: phosphorescent matter – here, in fact, bioluminescent (light-emitting) plankton

I was sitting with Mr Elder beside the little iron stove in the cabin of the Betsey ; and the minister, divested of his cap and jacket, but still looking the veritable skipper to admiration, was busied in making us a rather late tea.

The cabin,—my home for the greater part of the three following weeks, and that of my friend for the greater part of the previous twelvemonth,—I found to be an apartment about twice the size of a common bed, and just lofty enough under the beams to permit a man of five feet eleven to stand erect in his nightcap. A large table, lashed to the floor, furnished with tiers of drawers of all sorts and sizes, and bearing a writing desk bound to it a-top, occupied the middle space, leaving just room enough for a person to pass between its edges and the narrow coffin-like beds in the sides, and space enough at its fore-end for two seats in front of the stove. A jealously-barred skylight opened above ; and there depended from it this evening a close lanthorn-looking lamp, sufficiently valuable, no doubt, in foul weather, but dreary and dim on the occasions when all one really wished from it was light. The peculiar furniture of the place gave evidence to the mixed nature of my friend's employment. A well-thumbed chart of the Western Islands lay across an equally well-thumbed volume of Henry's "Commentary." There was a Polyglot and a spy-glass in one corner, and a copy of Calvin's "Institutes," with the latest edition of "The Coaster's Sailing Directions," in another ; while in an adjoining state-room, nearly large enough to accommodate an arm-chair, if the chair could have but contrived to get into it, I caught a glimpse of my friend's printing-press and his case of types, canopied overhead by the blue ancient of the vessel, bearing in stately six-inch letters of white bunting, the legend, " FREE CHURCH YACHT. " A door opened which communicated with the forecastle ; and John Stewart, stooping very much to accommodate himself to the low-roofed passage, thrust in a plate of fresh herrings,

---

Henry's 'Commentary': Matthew Henry's *Commentary on the Whole Bible* (1706-1721); Polyglot: Bible with parallel texts in different languages (*eg* Greek, Latin and Hebrew); spy-glass: telescope; 'Institutes': John Calvin's *Institutes of the Christian Religion*, a major Reformation work. All these were means of navigation, maritime or spiritual; ancient: here, ensign or flag

splendidly toasted, to give substantiality and relish to our
tea. The little rude forecastle, a considerably smaller apartment than the cabin, was all a-glow with the bright fire in
the coppers, itself invisible : we could see the chain-cable
dangling from the hatchway to the floor, and John Stewart's
companion, a powerful-looking, handsome young man, with
broad bare breast, and in his shirt sleeves, squatted full in
front of the blaze, like the household goblin described by
Milton, or the "Christmas Present" of Dickens. Mr Elder
left us for the steamer, in which he prosecuted his voyage
next morning to Skye ; and we tumbled in, each to his narrow
bed,—comfortable enough sort of resting-places, though not
over soft ; and slept so soundly, that we failed to mark Mr
Elder's return for a few seconds, a little after daybreak. I
found at my bedside, when I awoke, a fragment of rock which
he had brought from the shore, charged with Liasic fossils ;
and a note he had written, to say that the deposit to which
it belonged occurred in the trap immediately above the vil-
lage-mill ; and further, to call my attention to a house near
the middle of the village, built of a mouldering red sandstone which had been found *in situ* in digging the foundations. I had but little time for the work of exploration in
Mull, and the information thus kindly rendered enabled me
to economize it.

The village of Tobermory resembles that of Oban. A
quiet bay has its secure island-breakwater in front ; a line of
tall, well-built houses, not in the least rural in their aspect,
but that seem rather as if they had been transported from
the centre of some stately city entire and at once, sweeps
round its inner inflection like a bent bow ; and an amphitheatre of mingled rock and wood rises behind. With all its
beauty, however, there hangs about the village an air of melancholy. Like some of the other western-coast villages, it
seems not to have grown piecemeal, as a village ought, but

---

household goblin: the 'brownie' who does the chores at night and then has a rest in
John Milton's 'L'Allegro': 'Then lies him down the lubber fiend,/And, stretch'd out all
the chimney's length/Basks at the fire his hairy strength'; **'Christmas Present'**: from *A
Christmas Carol*; **Liasic**: Liassic

to have been made wholesale, as Frankenstein made his man ;
and to be ever asking, and never more incessantly than when
it is at its quietest, why it should have been made at all ?
The remains of the Florida, a gallant Spanish ship, lie off its
shores, a wreck of the Invincible Armada, " deep whelmed,"
according to Thomson,

" What time,
Snatched sudden by the vengeful blast,
The scattered vessels drove, and on blind shelve,
And pointed rock that marks th' indented shore,
Relentless dashed, where loud the northern main
Howls through the fractured Caledonian isles."

Macculloch relates, that there was an attempt made, rather
more than a century ago, to weigh up the Florida, which
ended in the weighing up of merely a few of her guns, some
of them of iron greatly corroded ; and that, on scraping them,
they became so hot under the hand that they could not be
touched, but that they lost this curious property after a few
hours' exposure to the air.   There have since been repeated
instances elsewhere, he adds, of the same phenomenon, and
chemistry has lent its solution of the principles on which it
occurs ; but in the year 1740, ere the riddle was read, it
must have been deemed a thoroughly magical one by the
simple islanders of Mull.   It would seem as if the guns,
heated in the contest with Drake, Hawkins, and Frobisher,
had again kindled, under some supernatural influence, with
the intense glow of the lost battle.

The morning was showery ; but it cleared up a little after
ten, and we landed to explore.   We found the mill a little
to the south of the village, where a small stream descends, all
foam and uproar, from the higher grounds along a rocky
channel half-hidden by brushwood ; and the Liasic bed occurs
in an exposed front directly over it, coped by a thick bed of
amygdaloidal trap. The organisms are numerous ; and, when
we dig into the bank beyond the reach of the weathering in-

Frankenstein: hero of Mary Shelley's novel (1818) who made an artificial man from adult
body parts; 'What time ...': from 'Britannia' by James **Thomson** (1700-1748);
Macculloch: MacCulloch (1819, I, 536-537fn. or 1824, IV, 243); **contest**: with English
forces led by **Drake, Hawkins and Frobisher** in the English Channel, 1588 – the *Florida*
was later wrecked on the Armada's return round-about Scotland; **organisms**: here, fossils

fluences, we find them delicately preserved, though after a
fashion that renders difficult their safe removal.   Originally
the bed must have existed as a brown argillaceous mud, somewhat resembling that which forms in the course of years
under a scalp of muscles ; and it has hardened into a mere
silt-like clay, in which the fossils occur, not as petrifactions,
but as shells in a state of decay, except in some rare cases in
which a calcareous nodule has formed within or around them.
Viewed in the group, they seem of an intermediate character
between the shells of the Lias and Oolite.   One of the first
fossils I disinterred was the Gryphæa obliquata,—a shell characteristic of the Liasic formation ; and the fossil immediately
after, the Pholadomya æqualis,—a shell of the Oolitic one.
There occurs in great numbers a species of small Pecten,—
some of the specimens scarce larger than a herring scale ; a
minute Ostrea, a sulcated Terebratula, an Isocardia, a Pullastra, and groupes of broken serpulæ in vast abundance.   The
deposit has also its three species of Ammonite, existing as mere
impressions in the clay ; and at least two species of Belemnite,
—one of the two somewhat resembling the Belemnites ab-
breviatus, but smaller and rather more elongated ; while the
other, of a spindle form, diminishing at both ends, reminds
one of the Belemnites minimus of the Gault.   The Red Sandstone in the centre of the village occurs detached, like this
Liasic bed, amid the prevailing trap, and may be seen *in situ*
beside the southern gable of the tall, deserted-looking house
at the hill-foot, that has been built of it.   It is a soft, coarse-
grained, mouldering stone, ill fitted for the purposes of the
architect ; and more nearly resembles the New Red Sandstone
of England and Dumfriesshire than any other rock I have
yet seen in the north of Scotland.   I failed to detect in it
aught organic.

    We weighed anchor about two o'clock, and beat gallantly
out the Sound, in the face of an intermittent baffling wind

Gryphaea ... Gault: Miller compared his finds with fossils of known age elsewhere, in
the still standard technique for finding the age of the deposit; **aught organic**: *ie* any
fossils

and a heavy swell from the sea.   I would fain have approached nearer the precipices of Ardnamurchan, to trace along their inaccessible fronts the strange reticulations of trap figured by Macculloch ; but prudence and the skipper forbade our trusting even the docile little Betsey on one of the most formidable lee shores in Scotland, in winds so light and variable, and with the swell so high.   We could hear the deep roar of the surf for miles, and see its undulating strip of white flickering under stack and cliff.   The scenery here seems rich in legendary association.   At one tack we bore into Bloody Bay, on the Mull coast,—the scene of a naval battle between two island chiefs ; at another, we approached, on the mainland, a cave inaccessible save from the sea, long the haunt of a ruthless Highland pirate.   Ere we rounded the headland of Ardnamurchan, the slant light of evening was gleaming athwart the green acclivities of Mull, barring them with long horizontal lines of shadow, where the trap terraces rise step beyond step, in the characteristic stair-like arrangement to which the rock owes its name ; and the sun set as we were bearing down in one long tack on the Small Isles.   We passed the Isle of Muck, with its one low hill ; saw the pyramidal mountains of Rum looming tall in the offing ; and then, running along the Isle of Eigg, with its colossal Scuir rising between us and the sky, as if it were a piece of Babylonian wall, or of the great wall of China, only vastly larger, set down on the ridge of a mountain, we entered the channel which separates the island from one of its dependencies, Eilean Chaisteil, and cast anchor in the tideway about fifty yards from the rocks.   We were now at home,— the only home which the proprietor of the island permits to the islanders' minister ; and, after getting warm and comfortable over the stove and a cup of tea, we did what all sensible men do in their own homes when the night wears late,—got into bed.

---

reticulations of trap: branching and superimposed veins of intrusive basalt now exposed by erosion in the face of the cliff (MacCulloch 1819, II, p. 469; III, p. 55, pl. XXXIII, fig. 1)

CHAPTER II.

WE had rich tea this morning. The minister was among his
people ; and our first evidence of the fact came in the agreeable form of three bottles of fine fresh cream from the shore.
Then followed an ample baking of nice oaten cakes. The
material out of which the cakes were manufactured had been
sent from the minister's store aboard,—for oatmeal in Eigg is
rather a scarce commodity in the middle of July ; but they
had borrowed a crispness and flavour from the island, that
the meal, left to its own resources, could scarcely have communicated ; and the golden-coloured cylinder of fresh butter
which accompanied them was all the island's own. There
was an ample supply of eggs too, as one not quite a conjuror
might have expected from a country bearing such a name,—
eggs with the milk in them ; and, with cream, butter, oaten
cakes, eggs, and tea, all of the best, and with sharp-set sea-
air appetites to boot, we fared sumptuously. There is properly no harbour in the island. We lay in a narrow channel, through which, twice every twenty-four hours, the tides
sweep powerfully in one direction, and then as powerfully in
the direction opposite ; and our anchors had a trick of getting
foul, and canting stock downwards in the loose sand, which,
with pointed rocks all around us, over which the currents ran
races, seemed a very shrewd sort of trick indeed. But a

anchor ... stock: see Additional Notes

kedge and halser, stretched thwartwise to a neighbouring crag, and jambed fast in a crevice, served in moderate weather to keep us tolerably right. In the severer seasons, however, the kedge is found inadequate, and the minister has to hoist sail and make out for the open sea, as if served with a sudden summons of ejectment.

Among the various things brought aboard this morning, there was a pair of island shoes for the minister's cabin use, that struck my fancy not a little. They were all around of a deep madder-red colour, soles, welts, and uppers ; and, though somewhat resembling in form the little yawl of the Betsey, were sewed not unskilfully with thongs ; and their peculiar style of tie seemed of a kind suited to furnish with new idea a fashionable shoemaker of the metropolis. They were altogether the production of Eigg, from the skin out of which they had been cut, with the lime that had prepared it for the tan, and the root by which the tan had been furnish-ed, down to the last on which they had been moulded, and the artizan that had cast them off, a pair of finished shoes. There are few trees, and, of course, no bark to spare, in the island ; but the islanders find a substitute in the astringent lobiferous root of the *Tormentilla erecta*, which they dig out for the purpose among the heath, at no inconsiderable expense of time and trouble. I was informed by John Stewart, an adept in all the multifarious arts of the island, from the tan-ning of leather and the tilling of land, to the building of a house or the working of a ship, that the infusion of root had to be thrice changed for every skin, and that it took a man nearly a day to gather roots enough for a single infusion. I was further informed that it was not unusual for the owner of a skin to give it to some neighbour to tan, and that, the process finished, it was divided equally between them, the time and trouble bestowed on it by the one being deemed equivalent to the property held in it by the other. I wished to call a pair of these primitive-looking shoes my own, and no sooner was the wish expressed than straightway one islander furnished me with leather, and another set to work upon the shoes. When I came to speak of remuneration, however, the islanders shook their heads. " No, no, not from the *Witness :* there are not many that take our part, and the *Witness* does." I hold the shoes, therefore, as my first retainer, determined, on all occasions of just quarrel, to make common cause with the poor islanders.

The view from the anchoring ground presents some very striking features. Between us and the sea lies Eilean Chaisteil, a rocky trap islet, about half a mile in length by a few hundred yards in breadth ; poor in pastures, but peculiarly rich in sea-weed, of which John Stewart used, he informed me, to make finer kelp, ere the trade was put down by act of Parliament, than could be made elsewhere in Eigg. This islet bore, in the remote past, its rude fort or dun, long since sunk into a few grassy mounds ; and hence its name. On the landward side rises the island of Eigg proper, resembling in outline two wedges placed point to point on a board. The centre is occupied by a deep angular gap, from which the ground slopes upward on both sides, till, attaining its extreme height at the opposite ends of the island, it drops suddenly on the sea. In the northern rising ground the wedge-like outline is complete ; in the southern one it is somewhat modified by the gigantic Scuir, which rises direct on the apex of the height, *i. e.,* the thick part of the wedge ; and which, seen bows-on from this point of view, resembles some vast donjon-keep, taller from base to summit, by about a hundred feet, than the dome of St Paul's. The upper slopes of the island are brown and moory, and present little on which the eye may rest, save a few trap terraces with rudely columnar fronts ; its middle space is mottled with patches of green, and studded with dingy cottages, each of which this morning, just a little

---

Act of Parliament: it reduced duties on foreign imports, enabling them to compete more strongly with home-produced kelp – see Introduction; **Eilean Chaisteil**: an alternative rendering of *Eilean Chathastail*, 'Castle Island'; **columnar**: see Glossary before the breakfast hour, had its own blue cloudlet of smoke diffused around it ; while along the beach, patches of level sand, alternated with tracts of green bank, or both, give place to stately ranges of basaltic columns, or dingy groupes of detached rocks.   Immediately in front of the central hollow, as if skilfully introduced to relieve the tamest part of the prospect, a noble wall of semicircular columns rises some eighty or a hundred feet over the shore ; and on a green slope, directly above, we see the picturesque ruins of the Chapel of St Donan, one of the disciples of Columba, and the Culdee saint and apostle of the island.

One of the things that first struck me, as I got on deck this morning, was the extreme whiteness of the sand.   I could see it gleaming bright through the transparent green of the sea, three fathoms below our keel, and, in a little flat bay directly opposite, it presented almost the appearance of pulverized chalk.   A stronger contrast to the dingy trap-rocks around which it lies could scarce be produced, had contrast for effect's sake been the object.   On landing on the exposed shelf to which we had fastened our halser, I found the origin of the sand interestingly exhibited.   The hollows of the rock, a rough trachyte, with a surface like that of a steel rasp, were filled with handfuls of broken shells thrown up by the surf from the sea-banks beyond ; fragments of echini, bits of the valves of razor-fish, the island cyprina, mactridæ, buccinidæ, and fractured periwinkles, lay heaped together in vast abundance.   In hollow after hollow, as I passed shorewards, I found the fragments more and more comminuted, just as, in passing along the successive vats of a paper-mill, one finds the linen rags more and more disintegrated by the cylinders ; and immediately beyond the inner edge of the shelf, which is of considerable extent, lies the flat bay, the ultimate recipient of the whole, filled to the depth of several feet, and to the extent of several hundred yards, with a pure shell-sand,

Columba: also written as Colum Cille, the Irish missionary and saint who brought Christianity to the Hebrides the greater part of which had been thus washed ashore in handfuls, and ground down by the blended agency of the trachyte and the surf. Once formed, however, in this way it began to receive accessions from the exuviæ of animals that love such localities,—the deep arenaceous bed and soft sand-beach ; and these now form no inconsiderable proportion of the entire mass. I found the deposit thickly inhabited by spatangi, razor-fish, gapers, and large well-conditioned cockles, which seemed to have no idea whatever that they were living amid the debris of a charnel-house. Such has been the origin here of a bed of shell-sand, consisting of many thousand tons, and of which at least eighty per cent. was once associated with animal life. And such, I doubt not, is the history of many a calcareous rock in the later secondary formations. There are strata not a few of the Cretaceous and Oolitic groupes, that would be found—could we but trace their beginnings with a certainty and clearness equal to that with which we can unravel the story of this deposit—to be, like it, elaborations from dead matter, made through the agency of animal secretion.

We set out on our first exploratory ramble in Eigg an hour before noon. The day was bracing and breezy, and a clear sun looked cheerily down on island, and strait, and blue open sea. We rowed southwards in our little boat through the channel of Eilean Chaisteil, along the trap-rocks of the island, and landed under the two pitchstone veins of Eigg, so generally known among mineralogists, and of which specimens may be found in so many cabinets. They occur in an earthy, greenish-black amygdaloid, which forms a range of sea-cliffs varying in height from thirty to fifty feet, and that, from their sad hue and dull fracture, seem to absorb the light ; while the veins themselves, bright and glistening, glitter in the sun, as if they were streams of water traversing the face of the rock. The first impression they imparted, in viewing

---

later secondary formations: rocks formed during the later Mesozoic Era, roughly our Jurassic and Cretaceous; pitchstone: volcanic rock somewhat glassy in texture, resembling solidified pitch. Forced under pressure into cracks in pre-existing rock, the Eigg vein pitchstone cooled more quickly, and so became glassier, at the 'chilled margins' next to the cool surrounding rock; amygdaloid: here, amygdaloidal or vesicular basalt them from the boat, was, that the inclosing mass was a pitch cauldron, rather of the roughest and largest, and much begrimed by soot, that had cracked to the heat, and that the fluid pitch was forcing its way outward through the rents. The veins expand and contract, here diminishing to a strip a few inches across, there widening into a comparatively broad belt some two or three feet over; and, as well described by M'Culloch, we find the inclosed pitch-stone changing in colour, and assuming a lighter or darker hue, as it nears the edge or recedes from it. In the centre it is of a dull olive green, passing gradually into blue, which in turn deepens into black; and it is exactly at the point of contact with the earthy amygdaloid that the black is most intense, and the fracture of the stone glassiest and brightest. I was lucky enough to detach a specimen, which, though scarce four inches across, exhibits the three colours characteristic of the vein,—its bar of olive green on the one side, of intense black on the other, and of blue, like that of imperfectly fused bottle-glass, in the centre. This curious rock,—so nearly akin in composition and appearance to obsidian,—a mineral which, in its dense form, closely resembles the coarse dark-coloured glass of which common bottles are made, and which, in its lighter form, exists as pumice,—constitutes one of the links that connect the trap with the unequivocally volcanic rocks. The one mineral may be seen beside smoking crater, as in the Lipari Isles, passing into pumice; while the other may be converted into a substance almost identical with pumice by the chemist. "It is stated by the Honourable George Knox of Dublin," says Mr Robert Allan, in his valuable mineralogical work, "that the pitchstone of Newry, on being exposed to a high temperature, loses its bitumen and water, and is converted into a light substance in every respect resembling pumice." But of pumice in connection with the pitchstones of Eigg, more anon.

Leaving our boat to return to the Betsey at John Stewart's

M'Culloch: MacCulloch (1819, II, p. 518); Allan: the mineralogist and Edinburgh stockbroker Robert Allan (1806–1863) (Livingstone 2003). The quote may be Allan (1834, p. 189); pumice: pitchstone is essentially obsidian containing water. When pitchstone melts, the water vaporises and bubbles unless it is under pressure. This bubbling creates pumice when the melt cools and solidifies

leisure, and taking with us his companion to assist us in car
rying such specimens as we might procure, we passed westwards for a few hundred yards under the crags, and came
abreast of a dark angular opening at the base of the precipice, scarce two feet in height, and in front of which there
lies a little sluggish, ankle-deep pool, half-mud, half-water,
and matted over with grass and rushes.   Along the mural
face of the rock of earthy amygdaloid there runs a nearly vertical line, which in one of the stratified rocks one might perhaps term the line of a fault, but which in a trap-rock may
merely indicate where two semi-molten masses had pressed
against each other without uniting,—just as currents of cooling lead poured by the plumber from the opposite ends of a
groove, sometimes meet and press together, so as to make a
close, polished joint, without running into one piece.   The
little angular opening forms the lower termination of the line,
which, hollowing inwards, recedes near the bottom into a shallow cave, roughened with tufts of fern and bunches of long
silky grass, here and there enlivened by the delicate flowers
of the lesser rock-geranium.   A shower of drops patters from
above among the weeds and rushes of the little pool.   My
friend the minister stopped short.   "There," he said, pointing to the hollow, "you will find such a bone-cave as you
never saw before. Within that opening there lie the remains
of an entire race, palpably destroyed, as geologists in so many
other cases are content merely to imagine, by one great catastrophe.   That is the famous cave of Frances (Uamh Fhraing),
in which the whole people of Eigg were smoked to death by
the M'Leods."
    We struck a light, and, worming ourselves through the
narrow entrance, gained the interior,—a true rock gallery,
vastly more roomy and lofty than one could have anticipated
from the mean vestibule placed in front of it.   Its extreme
length we found to be two hundred and sixty feet ; its ex-

---

bone-cave: caves containing bones, often of Ice Age mammals (sometimes former hyena
dens), were a major field of research during the early nineteenth century (Torrens 1998;
Knell 2000); catastrophe: see Additional Note for p. 39

treme breadth twenty-seven feet ; its height, where the roof
rises highest, from eighteen to twenty feet. The cave seems
to have owed its origin to two distinct causes. The trap-rocks
on each side of the vertical fault-like crevice which separates
them are greatly decomposed, as if by the moisture percolating from above ; and directly in the line of the crevice must
the surf have charged, wave after wave, for ages ere the last
upheaval of the land. When the dog-stone at Dunolly existed
as a sea-stack, skirted with algæ, the breakers on this shore
must have dashed every tide through the narrow opening of
the cavern, and scooped out by handfuls the decomposing trap
within. The process of decomposition, and consequent enlargement, is still going on inside, but there is no longer an
agent to sweep away the disintegrated fragments. Where
the roof rises highest, the floor is blocked up with accumulations of bulky decaying masses, that have dropped from above ;
and it is covered over its entire area by a stratum of earthy
rubbish, which has fallen from the sides and ceiling in such
abundance, that it covers up the straw beds of the perished
islanders, which still exist beneath as a brown mouldering
felt, to the depth of from five to eight inches. Never yet was
tragedy enacted on a gloomier theatre. An uncertain twilight glimmers gray at the entrance, from the narrow vestibule ; but all within, for full two hundred feet, is black as
with Egyptian darkness. As we passed onward with our one
feeble light, along the dark mouldering walls and roof which
absorbed every straggling ray that reached them, and over
the dingy floor, roppy and damp, the place called to recollection that hall in Roman story, hung and carpeted with black,
into which Domitian once thrust his senate in a frolic, to
read their own names on the coffin-lids placed against the wall.
The darkness seemed to press upon us from every side, as if
it were a dense jetty fluid, out of which our light had scooped
a pailful or two, and that was rushing in to supply the vacuum ;

---

that hall in Roman story: presumably, ultimately from the classical historian Dio
Cassius, book 67, chapter 9

and the only objects we saw distinctly visible were each other's heads and faces, and the lighter parts of our dress.

The floor, for about a hundred feet inwards from the narrow vestibule, resembles that of a charnel-house. At almost every step we come upon heaps of human bones grouped together, as the Psalmist so graphically describes, " as when one cutteth and cleaveth wood upon the earth." They are of a brownish, earthy hue, here and there tinged with green ; the skulls, with the exception of a few broken fragments, have disappeared ; for travellers in the Hebrides have of late years been numerous and curious ; and many a museum,—that at Abbotsford among the rest,—exhibits, in a grinning skull, its memorial of the Massacre at Eigg. We find, too, further marks of visitors in the single bones separated from the heaps and scattered over the area ; but enough still remains to show, in the general disposition of the remains, that the hapless islanders died under the walls in families, each little group separated by a few feet from the others. Here and there the remains of a detached skeleton may be seen, as if some robust islander, restless in his agony, had stalked out into the middle space ere he fell ; but the social arrangement is the general one. And beneath every heap we find, at the depth, as has been said, of a few inches, the remains of the straw-bed upon which the family had lain, largely mixed with the smaller bones of the human frame, ribs and vertebræ, and hand and feet bones ; occasionally, too, with fragments of unglazed pottery, and various other implements of a rude housewifery. The minister found for me, under one family heap, the pieces of a half-burned, unglazed earthen jar, with a narrow mouth, that, like the sepulchral urns of our ancient tumuli, had been moulded by the hand without the assistance of the potter's wheel ; and to one of the fragments there stuck a minute pellet of gray hair. From under another heap he disinterred the handle-stave of a child's wooden porringer *(bicker)*, per-

---

Psalmist: many of Miller's readers would know the full verse, Bible, Psalm 141:7 'Our bones are scattered at the grave's mouth, as when one cutteth and cleaveth wood upon the earth'; **charnel-house**: the cave was cleared later in the nineteenth century and the bones buried; **Abbotsford**: Sir Walter Scott's house in the Borders; **earthen jar**: *crogan* – see Introduction forated by a hole still bearing the mark of the cord that had hung it to the wall; and beside the stave lay a few of the larger, less destructible bones of the child, with what for a time puzzled us both not a little,—one of the grinders of a horse. Certain it was, no horse could have got there to have dropped a tooth,—a foal of a week old could not have pressed itself through the opening; and how the single grinder, evidently no recent introduction into the cave, could have got mixed up in the straw with the human bones, seemed an enigma somewhat of the class to which the reel in the bottle belongs. I found in Edinburgh an unexpected commentator on the mystery, in the person of my little boy,—an experimental philosopher in his second year. I had spread out on the floor the curiosities of Eigg,—among the rest, the relics of the cave, including the pieces of earthen jar, and the fragment of the porringer; but the horse's tooth seemed to be the only real curiosity among them in the eyes of little Bill. He laid instant hold of it; and, appropriating it as a toy, continued playing with it till he fell asleep. I have now little doubt that it was first brought into the cave by the poor child amid whose mouldering remains Mr Swanson found it. The little pellet of gray hair spoke of feeble old age involved in this wholesale massacre with the vigorous manhood of the island; and here was a story of unsuspecting infancy amusing itself on the eve of destruction with its toys. Alas for man! "Should not I spare Nineveh, that great city," said God to the angry prophet, "wherein are more than six thousand score persons that cannot discern between their right hand and their left?" God's image must have been sadly defaced in the murderers of the poor inoffensive children of Eigg, ere they could have heard their feeble wailings, raised, no doubt, when the stifling atmosphere within began first to thicken, and yet ruthlessly persist in their work of indiscriminate destruction.

Various curious things have from time to time been picked

---

experimental philosopher: *ie* investigative scientist; **Nineveh**: Bible, Jonah 4:11

up from under the bones. An islander found among them, shortly before our visit, a sewing needle of copper, little more than an inch in length ; fragments of Eigg shoes, of the kind still made in the island, are of comparatively common occurrence ; and Mr James Wilson relates, in the singularly graphic and powerful description of *Uamh Fraingh* which occurs in his "Voyage round the Coasts of Scotland" (1841), that a sailor, when he was there, disinterred, by turning up a flat stone, a "buck-tooth" and a piece of money,—the latter a rusty copper coin, apparently of the times of Mary of Scotland. I also found a few teeth : they were sticking fast in a fragment of jaw ; and, taking it for granted, as I suppose I may, that the dentology of the murderous M'Leods outside the cave must have very much resembled that of the murdered M'Donalds within, very harmless-looking teeth they were for being those of an animal so maliciously mischievous as man. I have found in the Old Red Sandstone the strong-based tusks of the semi-reptile Holoptychius ; I have chiselled out of the limestone of the Coal Measures the sharp, dagger-like incisors of the Megalichthys ; I have picked up in the Lias and Oolite the cruel spikes of the crocodile and the Ichthyosaurus ; I have seen the trenchant, saw-edged teeth of gigantic Cestracions and Squalidæ that had been disinterred from the Chalk and the London Clay ; and I have felt, as I examined them, that there could be no possibility of mistake regarding the nature of the creatures to which they had belonged ;—they were teeth made for hacking, tearing, mangling,—for amputating limbs at a bite, and laying open bulky bodies with a crunch : but I could find no such evidence in the human jaw, with its three inoffensive-looking grinders, that the animal it had belonged to,—far more ruthless and cruel than reptile-fish, crocodiles, or sharks,—was of such a nature that it could destroy creatures of even its own kind by hundreds at a time, when not in the least incited by

---

coin: now in NMS. Sir Thomas Dick Lauder (1784–1848), of the Grange (now in south Edinburgh) and Relugas in Morayshire, landowner, geologist, and author of *The Moray Floods in 1829*, befriended the young Miller on the latter's first visit to Edinburgh as a mason. He was the Secretary of the Fisheries Board on the cruise described by Wilson (1842) who mentions what is apparently this coin; **semi-reptile**: see Additional Notes hunger, and with no ultimate intention of eating them. Man must surely have become an immensely worse animal than his teeth show him to have been designed for : his teeth give no evidence regarding his real character. Who, for instance, could gather from the dentology of the M'Leods the passage in their history to which the cave of Francis bears evidence?

We quitted the cave, with its stagnant damp atmosphere and its mouldy unwholesome smells, to breathe the fresh sea-air on the beach without. Its story, as recorded by Sir Walter in his "Tales of a Grandfather," and by Mr Wilson in his "Voyage," must be familiar to the reader ; and I learned from my friend, versant in all the various island traditions regarding it, that the less I inquired into its history on the spot, the more was I likely to feel satisfied that I knew something about it. There seem to have been no chroniclers in this part of the Hebrides in the rude age of the unglazed pipkin and the copper needle ; and many years seem to have elapsed ere the story of their hapless possessors was committed to writing : and so we find it existing in various and somewhat conflicting editions. "Some hundred years ago," says Mr Wilson, "a few of the M'Leods landed in Eigg from Skye, where, having greatly misconducted themselves, the Eiggites strapped them to their own boats, which they sent adrift into the ocean. They were, however, rescued by some clansmen ; and soon after, a strong body of the M'Leods set sail from Skye, to revenge themselves on Eigg. The natives of the latter island feeling they were not of sufficient force to offer resistance, went and hid themselves (men, women, and children) in this secret cave, which is narrow, but of great subterranean length, with an exceedingly small entrance. It opens from the broken face of a steep bank along the shore ; and, as the whole coast is cavernous, their particular retreat would have been sought for in vain by strangers. So the Skye-men finding the island uninhabit-

---

Wilson: quoted from Wilson (1842, I, pp. 232-234) with errors, mainly 'boat' for 'boats'

ed, presumed the natives had fled, and satisfied their revenge-
ful feelings by ransacking and pillaging the empty houses.
Probably the *moveables* were of no great value.   They then
took their departure and left the island, when the sight of a
solitary human being among the cliffs awakened their suspi-
cion, and induced them to return.   Unfortunately a slight
sprinkling of snow had fallen, and the footsteps of an individual were traced to the mouth of the cave.   Not having been
there ourselves at the period alluded to, we cannot speak with
certainty as to the nature of the parley which ensued, or the
terms offered by either party ; but we know that those were
not the days of protocols.   The ultimatum was unsatisfac-
tory to the Skye-men, who immediately proceeded to 'adjust
the preliminaries' in their own way, which adjustment consisted in carrying a vast collection of heather, ferns, and
other combustibles, and making a huge fire just in the very
entrance of the *Uamh Fhraing,* which they kept up for a
length of time ; and thus, by 'one fell smoke,' they smothered
the entire population of the island."

Such is Mr Wilson's version of the story, which, in all its
leading circumstances, agrees with that of Sir Walter.   According, however, to at least one of the Eigg versions, it was
the M'Leod himself who had landed on the island, driven
there by a storm.   The islanders, at feud with the M'Leods
at the time, inhospitably rose upon him, as he bivouacked on
the shores of the Bay of Laig ; and in a fray, in which his
party had the worse, his back was broken, and he was forced
off half-dead to sea.   Several months after, on his partial recovery, he returned, crook-backed and infirm, to wreak his
vengeance on the inhabitants, all of whom, warned of his coming by the array of his galleys in the offing, hid themselves
in the cave, in which, however, they were ultimately betrayed
—as narrated by Sir Walter and Mr Wilson—by the track
of some footpaths in a sprinkling of snow ; and the impla-

---

the M'Leod himself: *ie* The Macleod, chief of the Clan Macleod cable chieftain, giving orders, on the discovery, to unroof the houses in the neighbourhood, raised high a pile of rafters against the opening, and set it on fire. And there he stood in front of the blaze, hump-backed and grim, till the wild hollow cry from the rock within had sunk into silence, and there lived not a single islander of Eigg, man, woman, or child. The fact that their remains should have been left to moulder in the cave is proof enough of itself that none survived to bury the dead. I am inclined to believe, from the appearance of the place, that smoke could scarcely have been the real agent of destruction : then, as now, it would have taken a great deal of pure smoke to smother a Highlander. It may be perhaps deemed more probable, that the huge fire of rafter and roof-tree piled close against the opening, and rising high over it, would draw out the oxygen within as its proper food, till at length all would be exhausted ; and life would go out for want of it, like the flame of a candle under an upturned jar. Sir Walter refers the date of the event to some time " about the close of the sixteenth century ;" and the coin of Queen Mary, mentioned by Mr Wilson, points at a period at least not much earlier : but the exact time of its occurrence is so uncertain, that a Roman Catholic priest of the Hebrides, in lately showing his people what a very bad thing Protestantism is, instanced, as a specimen of its average morality, the affair of the cave. The *Protestant* M'Leods of Skye, he said, full of hatred in their hearts, had murdered wholesale their wretched brethren the *Protestant* M'Donalds of Eigg, and sent them off to perdition before their time.

Quitting the beach, we ascended the breezy hill-side on our way to the Scuir,—an object so often and so well described, that it might be perhaps prudent, instead of attempting one description more, to present the reader with some of the already existing ones. "The Scuir of Eigg," says Professor Jamieson, in his " Mineralogy of the Western Islands,"

---

smother: peat smoke from the open central hearth pervaded any black house; **Sir Walter**: Scott the novelist; **Jamieson**: Robert Jameson – see Introduction; '**Mineralogy** ...': perhaps conflating Jameson (1800) and (1813) – actually the same book. Miller's quote matches vol. 2, pp. 231-232, with variations, especially the beneficial insertion of 'when viewed from below', seen also in Wilson (1842, I, pp. 231-232) and Maclean (1845, written 1836) "is perfectly mural, and extends for upwards of a mile and a-half, and rises to a height of several hundred feet. It is entirely columnar, and the columns rise in successive ranges until they reach the summit, where, from their great height, they appear, when viewed from below, diminutive. Staffa is an object of the greatest beauty and regularity ; the pillars are as distinct as if they had been reared by the hand of art ; but it has not the extent or sublimity of the Scuir of Eigg. The one may be compared with the greatest exertions of human power ; the other is characteristic of the wildest and most inimitable works of nature." "The height of this extraordinary object is considerable," says M'Culloch, dashing off his sketch with a still bolder hand ; "yet its powerful effect arises rather from its peculiar form, and the commanding elevation which it occupies, than from its positive altitude. Viewed in one direction, it presents a long irregular wall, crowning the summit of the highest hill, while in the other it resembles a huge tower. Thus it forms no natural combination of outline with the surrounding land, and hence acquires that independence in the general landscape which increases its apparent magnitude, and produces that imposing effect which it displays. From the peculiar position of the Scuir, it must also inevitably be viewed from a low station. Hence it everywhere towers high above the spectator ; while, like other objects on the mountain outline, its apparent dimensions are magnified, and its dark mass defined on the sky so as to produce all the additional effects arising from strong oppositions of light and shadow. The height of this rock is sufficient in this stormy country frequently to arrest the passage of the clouds, so as to be further productive of the most brilliant effects in landscape. Often they may be seen hovering on its summit, and adding ideal dimensions to the lofty face, or, when it is viewed on the extremity, conveying the impression of a tower the height of which is such

McCulloch: MacCulloch (1819, I, pp. 508-509)

as to lie in the regions of the clouds. Occasionally they sweep along the base, leaving its huge and black mass involved in additional gloom, and resembling the castle of some Arabian enchanter, built on the clouds, and suspended in air." It might be perhaps deemed somewhat invidious to deal with pictures such as these in the style the connoisseur in the "Vicar of Wakefield" dealt with the old painting, when, seizing a brush, he daubed it over with brown varnish, and then asked the spectators whether he had not greatly improved the tone of the colouring. And yet it is just possible, that in the case of at least M'Culloch's picture, the brown varnish might do no manner of harm. But a homelier sketch, traced out on almost the same leading lines, with just a little less of the aerial in it, may have nearly the same subduing effect; I have, besides, a few curious touches to lay in, which seem hitherto to have escaped observation and the pencil; and in these several circumstances must lie my apology for adding one sketch more to the sketches existing already.

The Scuir of Eigg, then, is a veritable Giant's Causeway, like that on the coast of Antrim, taken and magnified rather more than twenty times in height, and some five or six times in breadth, and then placed on the ridge of a hill nearly nine hundred feet high. Viewed sideways, it assumes, as described by M'Culloch, the form of a perpendicular but ruinous rampart, much gapped above, that runs for about a mile and a quarter along the top of a lofty sloping talus. Viewed endways, it resembles a tall massy tower,—such a tower as my friend Mr D. O. Hill would delight to draw, and give delight by drawing,—a tower three hundred feet in breadth by four hundred and seventy feet in height, perched on the apex of a pyramid, like a statue on a pedestal. This strange causeway is columnar from end to end; but the columns, from their great altitude and deficient breadth, seem mere rodded shafts in the Gothic style : they rather resemble bun-

---

'Vicar of Wakefield': the novel by Oliver Goldsmith; **Giant's Causeway**: the outcrop of columnar basalt on the coast of Antrim; **Hill**: David Octavius Hill (1802-1870), landscape painter and pioneer photographer – see Additional Note for p. 208

dles of rods than well-proportioned pillars.   Few of them
exceed eighteen inches in diameter, and many of them fall
short of half a foot ; but, though lost in the general mass of
the Scuir as independent columns, when we view it at an
angle sufficiently large to take in its entire bulk, they yet impart to it that graceful linear effect which we see brought
out in tasteful pencil-sketches and good line-engravings.   We
approached it this day from the shore in the direction in
which the eminence it stands upon assumes the pyramidal
form, and itself the tower-like outline.   The acclivity is barren and stony,—a true desert foreground, like those of Thebes
and Palmyra ; and the huge square shadow of the tower
stretched dark and cold athwart it.   The sun shone out
clearly.   One half the immense bulk before us, with its delicate vertical lining, lay from top to bottom in deep shade,
massive and gray ; one half presented its many-sided columns
to the light, here and there gleaming with tints of extreme
brightness, where the pitch-stones presented their glassy
planes to the sun ; its general outline, whether pencilled by
the lighter or darker tints, stood out sharp and clear ; and a
stratum of white fleecy clouds floated slowly amid the delicious blue behind it.   But the minuter details I must reserve for my next chapter.   One fact, however, anticipated
just a little out of its order, may heighten the interest of the
reader.   There are massive buildings,—bridges of noble span,
and harbours that abut far into the waves,—founded on
wooden piles ; and this hugest of hill-forts we find founded
on wooden piles also.   It is built on what a Scotch architect
would perhaps term a pile-*brander* of the *Pinites Eiggensis*,
an ancient tree of the Oolite.   The gigantic Scuir of Eigg
rests on the remains of a prostrate forest.

---

brander: Miller exaggerated somewhat – see Introduction

CHAPTER III.

As we climbed the hill-side, and the Shinar-like tower before us rose higher over the horizon at each step we took, till it seemed pointing at the middle sky, we could mark peculiarities in its structure which escape notice in the distance. We found it composed of various beds, each of which would make a Giant's Causeway entire, piled over each other like storeys in a building, and divided into columns, vertical, or nearly so, in every instance except in one bed near the base, in which the pillars incline to a side, as if losing footing under the superincumbent weight. Innumerable polygonal fragments,—single stones of the building,—lie scattered over the slope, composed, like almost all the rest of the Scuir, of a peculiar and very beautiful stone, unlike any other in Scotland,—a dark pitchstone-porphyry, which, inclosing crystals of glassy feldspar, resembles in the hand-specimen a mass of black sealing-wax, with numerous pieces of white bugle stuck into it. Some of the detached polygons are of considerable size ; few of them larger and bulkier, however, than a piece of column of this characteristic porphyry, about ten feet in length by two feet in diameter, which lies a full mile away from any of the others, in the line of the old burying-ground, and distant from it only a few hundred yards. It seems to have .been carried there by man : we find its bearing from

---

Shinar: Babylon, and by extension the Tower of Babylon, Bible, Genesis 9:3

the Scuir lying nearly at right angles with the direction of
the drift-boulders of the western coast, which are, besides, of
rare occurrence in the Hebrides : nor has it a single neighbour ; and it seems not improbable, as a tradition of the
island testifies, that it was removed thus far for the purpose
of marking some place of sepulture, and that the catastrophe
of the cave arrested its progress after by far the longer and
rougher portion of the way had been passed.   The dry arm-
bones of the charnel-house in the rock may have been tugging
around it when the galleys of the M'Leod hove in sight.   The
traditional history of Eigg, said my friend the minister, compared with that of some of the neighbouring islands, presents a decapitated aspect : the M'Leods cut it off by the
neck.   Most of the present inhabitants can tell which of
their ancestors, grandfather or great-grandfather, or great-
great-grandfather, first settled in the place, and where they
came from ; and, with the exception of a few vague legends
about St Donan and his grave, which were preserved apparently among the people of the other Small Isles, the island
has no early traditional history.

We had now reached the Scuir.   There occur, intercalated
with the columnar beds, a few bands of a buff-coloured non-
columnar trap, described by M'Culloch as of a texture intermediate between a greenstone and a basalt, and which, while
the pitchstone around it seems nearly indestructible, has
weathered so freely as to form horizontal grooves along the
face of the rock from two to five yards in depth.   One of
these runs for several hundred feet along the base of the
Scuir, just at the top of the talus, and greatly resembles a
piazza lacking the outer pillars.   It is from ten to twelve
feet in height, by from fifteen to twenty in depth ; the columns
of the pitchstone-bed immediately above it seem perilously
hanging in mid air ; and along their sides there trickles, in
even the driest summer weather,—for the Scuir is a con-

---

drift-boulders: a pillar moved naturally would have followed the broadly *westward* movement of boulders by, it is now known, glaciers; trap **'along the base'**: see Additional
Notes; **McCulloch**: MacCulloch (1819, I, p. 520)

denser on an immense scale,—minute runnels of water, that
patter ceaselessly in front of the long deep hollow, like rain
from the eaves of a cottage during a thunder-shower.   Inside, however, all is dry, and the floor is covered to the depth
of several inches with the dung of sheep and cattle, that find,
in this singular mountain-piazza, a place of shelter. We had
brought a pickaxe with us ; and the dry and dusty floor, composed mainly of a gritty conglomerate, formed the scene of
our labours.   It is richly fossiliferous, though the organisms
have no specific variety ; and never certainly have I found
the remains of former creations in a scene in which they
more powerfully addressed themselves to the imagination. A
stratum of peat-moss, mixed with fresh-water shells, and resting on a layer of vegetable mould, from which the stumps
and roots of trees still protruded, was once found in Italy
buried beneath an ancient tesselated pavement ; and the
whole gave curious evidence of a kind fitted to picture to the
imagination a back-ground vista of antiquity, all the more
remotely ancient in aspect from the venerable age of the object in front.   Dry ground covered by wood, a lake, a morass,
and then dry ground again, had all taken precedence, on the
site of the tesselated pavement, in this instance, of an old
Roman villa.   But what was antiquity in connection with a
Roman villa, to antiquity in connection with the Scuir of
Eigg ?   Under the old foundations of this huge wall we find
the remains of a pine-forest, that, long ere a single bed of
the porphyry had burst from beneath, had sprung up and decayed on hill and beside stream in some nameless land,—had
then been swept to the sea,—had been entombed deep at the
bottom in a grit of the Oolite,—had been heaved up to the
surface, and high over it, by volcanic agencies working from
beneath,—and had finally been built upon, as moles are built
upon piles, by the architect that had laid down the masonry
of the gigantic Scuir in one fiery layer after another.   The

mountain-wall of Eigg, with its dizzy elevation of four hundred and seventy feet, is a wall founded on piles of pine laid
crossways ; and, strange as the fact may seem, one has but
to dig into the floor of this deep-hewn piazza, to be convinced
that at least it *is* a fact.

Just at this interesting stage, however, our explorations
bade fair to be interrupted.   Our man who carried the pick-
axe had lingered behind us for a few hundred yards, in earnest conversation with an islander ; and he now came up,
breathless and in hot haste, to say that the islander, a Roman
Catholic tacksman in the neighbourhood, had peremptorily
warned him that the Scuir of Eigg was the property of Dr
M'Pherson of Aberdeen, not ours, and that the Doctor would
be very angry at any man who meddled with it.   " That
message," said my friend, laughing, but looking just a little
sad through the laugh, " would scarce have been sent us when
I was minister of the Establishment here ; but it seems al-
lowable in the case of a poor Dissenter, and is no bad specimen of the thousand little ways in which the Roman Catholic population of the island try to annoy me, now that
they see my back to the wall."   I was tickled with the idea
of a fossil preserve, which coupled itself in my mind, through
a trick of the associative faculty, with the idea of a great
fossil act for the British empire, framed on the principles of
the game-laws ; and, just wondering what sort of disreputable vagabonds geological poachers would become under its
deteriorating influence, I laid hold of the pickaxe, and broke
into the stonefast floor.   And thence I succeeded in abstract-
ing,—feloniously, I dare say, though the crime has not yet
got into the statute-book,—some six or eight pieces of the
Pinites Eiggensis, amounting in all to about half a cubic foot
of that very ancient wood—value unknown.   I trust, should
the case come to a serious bearing, the members of the London Geological Society will generously subscribe half-a-crown

---

piazza: in the (erroneous) sense of a sheltered walkway with pillars, which last are lacking
here; **pine forest**: possibly an exaggeration – see Introduction; **tacksman**: chief tenant

a-piece to assist me in feeing counsel.   There are more interests than mine at stake in the affair.   If I be cast and committed,—I, who have poached over only a few miserable districts in Scotland,—pray, what will become of some of them, —the Lyells, Bucklands, Murchisons, and Sedgwicks,—who have poached over whole continents ?

We were successful in procuring several good specimens of the Eigg pine, at a depth, in the conglomerate, of from eight to eighteen inches.   Some of the upper pieces we found in contact with the decomposing trap out of which the hollow piazza above had been scooped ; but the greater number, as my set of specimens abundantly testify, lay imbedded in the original Oolitic grit in which they had been locked up, in, I doubt not, their present fossil state, ere their upheaval, through Plutonic agency, from their deep-sea bottom.   The annual rings of the wood, which are quite as small as in a slow-growing Baltic pine, are distinctly visible in all the better pieces I this day transferred to my bag.   In one fragment I reckon sixteen rings in half an inch, and fifteen in the same space in another.   The trees to which they belonged seem to have grown on some exposed hill-side, where, in the course of half a century, little more than from two to three inches were added to their diameter.   The *Pinites Eiggensis*, or Eigg pine, was first introduced to the notice of the scientific world by the late Mr Witham, in whose interesting work on "The Internal Structure of Fossil Vegetables" the reader may find it figured and described.   The specimen in which he studied its peculiarities "was found," he says, "at the base of the magnificent mural escarpment named the Scuir of Eigg, not, however, *in situ*, but among fragments of rocks of the Oolitic series."   The authors of the "Fossil Flora," where it is also figured, describe it as differing very considerably in structure from any of the coniferæ of the Coal Measures.   "Its medullary rays," say Messrs Lindley and Hutton, "appear to

---

cast and committed: convicted and sent to prison: **Lyells, Bucklands, Murchisons and Sedgwicks**: eminent British geologists – see Additional Notes; **Witham**: Henry T. M. Witham (1779-1844), pioneering researcher on fossil plants; **authors of the 'Fossil Flora'**: John Lindley (1799-1865) and William Hutton (1797-1860), also pioneering researchers on fossil plants

be more numerous, and frequently are not continued through
one zone of wood to another, but more generally terminate
at the concentric circles.   It abounds also in turpentine vessels, or lacunæ, of various sizes, the sides of which are distinctly defined." Viewed through the microscope, in transparent slips, longitudinal and transverse, it presents, within
the space of a few lines, objects fitted to fill the mind with
wonder.   We find the minutest cells, glands, fibres, of the
original wood preserved uninjured.   *There* still are those
medullary rays entire that communicated between the pith
and the outside,—*there* still the ring of thickened cells that
indicated the yearly check which the growth received when
winter came on,—*there* the polygonal reticulations of the cross
section, without a single broken mesh,—*there*, too, the elongated cells in the longitudinal one, each filled with minute
glands that take the form of double circles,—*there* also, of
larger size and less regular form, the lacunæ in which the
turpentine lay : every nicely organized speck, invisible to
the naked eye, we find in as perfect a state of keeping in the
incalculably ancient pile-work on which the gigantic Scuir is
founded, as in the living pines that flourish green on our hill-
sides.   A net-work, compared with which that of the finest
lace ever worn by the fair reader would seem a net-work of
cable, has preserved entire, for untold ages, the most delicate
peculiarities of its pattern.   There is not a mesh broken, nor
a circular dot away !

   The experiments of Mr Witham on the Eigg fossil furnish
an interesting example of the light which a single, apparently
simple, discovery may throw on whole departments of fact.
He sliced his specimen longitudinally and across, fastened the
slices on glass, ground them down till they became semi-transparent, and then, examining them under reflected light by the
microscope, marked and recorded the specific peculiarities of
their structure.   And we now know, in consequence, that the

------

turpentine: here, resin; **transparent slips**: *ie* cut into thin enough slices to be transparent when viewed under the microscope, in order to make their internal structure visible
(Morrison-Low and Nuttall 2003)

ancient Eigg pine, to which the detached fragment picked up at the base of the Scuir belonged,—a pine alike different from those of the earlier carboniferous period and those which exist contemporary with ourselves,—was, some *three creations* ago, an exceedingly common tree in the country now called Scotland,—as much so, perhaps, as the Scotch fir is at the present day.   The fossil-trees found in such abundance in the neighbourhood of Helmsdale that they are burnt for lime,— the fossil-wood of Eathie in Cromartyshire, and that of Shandwick in Ross,—all belong to the *Pinites Eiggensis*.   It seems to have been a straight and stately tree, in most in- stances, as in the Eigg specimens, of slow growth.   One of the trunks I saw near Navidale measured two feet in diame- ter, but a full century had passed ere it attained to a bulk so considerable ; and a splendid specimen in my collection from the same locality, which measures twenty-one inches, exhibits even *more* than a hundred annual rings.   In one of my spe- cimens, and one only, the rings are of great breadth.   They differ from those of all the others in the proportion in which I have seen the annual rings of a young vigorous fir that had sprung up in some rich moist hollow, differ from the annual rings of trees of the same species that had grown in the shal- low hard soil of exposed hill-sides.   And this one specimen furnishes curious evidence that the often-marked but little understood law, which gives us our better and worse seasons in alternate groupes, various in number and uncertain in their time of recurrence, obtained as early as the age of the Oolite. The rings follow each other in groupes of lesser and larger breadth.   One group of four rings measures an inch and a quarter across, while an adjoining group of five rings measures only five-eighth parts ; and in a breadth of six inches there occur five of these alternate groupes.   For some four or five years together, when this pine was a living tree, the springs were late and cold, and the summers cloudy and chill, as in

---

three creations: see Additional Notes; all belong: Eathie, Shandwick, Navidale and Helmsdale fossil woods are Jurassic, different from the Eigg 'pine' which is of Palaeocene, early Tertiary, age; one specimen: Miller later found other fossil woods with clumped variations of annual rings, but it is not clear that any actually came from Eigg (Miller 1859, pp. 137-143; Hudson 2003) that group of seasons which intervened between 1835 and 1841 ; and then for four or five years more springs were early and summers genial, as in the after group of 1842, 1843, and 1844.   An arrangement in nature,—first observed, as we learn from Bacon, by the people of the low countries, and which has since formed the basis of meteoric tables, and of predictions, and elaborate cycles of the weather,— bound together the twelvemonths of the Oolitic period in alternate bundles of better and worse : vegetation throve vigorously during the summers of one group, and languished in those of another in a state of partial development.

Sending away our man shipwards, laden with a bag of fossil-wood, we ascended by a steep broken ravine to the top of the Scuir.   The columns, as we pass on towards the west, diminish in size, and assume in many of the beds considerable variety of direction and form.   In one bed they belly over with a curve, like the ribs of some wrecked vessel from which the planking has been torn away ; in another they project in a straight line, like muskets planted slantways on the ground to receive a charge of cavalry ; in others the inclination is inwards, like that of ranges of stakes placed in front of a sea-dyke, to break the violence of the waves ; while in yet others they present, as in the eastern portion of the Scuir, the common vertical direction.   The ribbed appearance of every crag and cliff imparts to the scene a peculiar character : every larger mass of light and shadow is corded with minute stripes ; and the feeling experienced among the more shattered peaks, and in the more broken recesses, seems nearer akin to that which it is the tendency of some magnificent ruin to excite, than that which awakens amid the sublime of nature.   We feel as if the pillared rocks around us were like the Cyclopean walls of Southern Italy,—the erections of some old gigantic race passed from the earth for ever.   The feeling must have been experienced on former occasions amid the innumerable

----

Bacon: Francis Bacon, Elizabethan statesman and writer: 'Lord Bacon remarks in ... the Essay on the Vicissitude of Things, – that it was a circumstance first observed in the Low Countries (the provinces of the Netherlands), that there were certain meteorological cycles of seasons ...' (Miller 1859, pp. 138-139)

pillars of the Scuir ; for we find M'Culloch, in his description, ingeniously analyzing it.   "The resemblance to architecture here is much increased," he says, " by the columnar
structure, which is sufficiently distinguishable even from a
distance, and produces a strong effect of artificial regularity
when seen near at hand.   To this vague association in the
mind of the efforts of art with the magnitude of nature, is
owing much of that sublimity of character which the Scuir
presents.   The sense of power is a fertile source of the sublime ; and as the appearance of power exerted, no less than
that of simplicity, is necessary to confer this character on architecture, so the mind, insensibly transferring the operations
of nature to the efforts of art where they approximate in character, becomes impressed with a feeling rarely excited by her
more ordinary forms, where these are even more stupendous."

The top of the Scuir, more especially towards its eastern
termination, resembles that of some vast mole not yet levelled over by the workmen ; the pavement has not yet been
laid down ; and there are deep gaps in the masonry, that run
transversely from side to side, still to fill up.   Along one of
these ditch-like gaps, which serves to insulate the eastern and
highest portion of the Scuir from all its other portions, we
find fragments of a rude wall of uncemented stones, the remains of an ancient hill-fort ; which, with its natural rampart
of rock on three of its four sides, more than a hundred yards
in sheer descent, and with its deep ditch and rude wall on
the fourth, must have formed one of the most inaccessible in
the kingdom.   The masses of pitchstone atop, though so intensely black within, are weathered on the surface into almost
a pure white ; and we found lying detached among them, fragments of common amygdaloid and basalt, and minute slaty
pieces of chalcedony that had formed apparently in fissures
of the trap.   We would have scrutinized more narrowly at
the time had we expected to find anything more rare ; but I

did not know, until full four months after, that aught more
rare was to be found.   Had we examined somewhat more
carefully, we might possibly have done what Mr Woronzow
Greig did on the Scuir about eighteen years previous,—picked
up on it a piece of *bona fide* Scotch pumice.   This gentleman, well known through his exertions in statistical science,
and for his love of science in general, and whose tastes and
acquirements are not unworthy the son of Mrs Somerville,
has kindly informed me by letter regarding his curious discovery.   "I visited the island of Eigg," he says, "in 1825
or 1826, for the purpose of shooting, and remained in it several days ; and as there was a great scarcity of game, I
amused myself in my wanderings by looking about for natural curiosities. I knew little about Geology at the time, but,
collecting whatever struck my eye as uncommon, I picked up
from the sides of the Scuir, among various other things, a bit
of fossil-wood, and, nearly at the summit of the eminence, a
piece of pumice of a deep brownish-black colour, and very
porous, the pores being large and round, and the substance
which divided them of a uniform thickness.   This last specimen I gave to Mr Lyell, who said that it could not originally
have belonged to Eigg, though it might possibly have been
washed there by the sea,—a suggestion, however, with which
its place on the top of the Scuir seems ill to accord.   I may
add, that I have since procured a larger specimen from the
same place."   This seems a curious fact, when we take into
account the identity, in their mineral components, of the
pumice and obsidian of the recent volcanoes ; and that pitchstone, the obsidian of the trap-rocks, is resolvable into a
pumice by the art of the chemist. If pumice was to be found
anywhere in Scotland, we might *a priori* expect to find it in
connection with by far the largest mass of pitchstone in the
kingdom.   It is just possible, however, that Mr Greig's two
specimens may not date farther back, in at least their exist-

---

Mr Woronzow Greig: Woronzow Greig F. R. S. (1805-1865), barrister, statistician and
amateur scientist. In 1825-1826 an undergraduate at the University of Cambridge
(Appleby 1999); Mrs Somerville: Mrs Mary Somerville (1780-1862), the mathematician
and scientist; Lyell: see Additional Note for p. 37; by the art of the chemist: here,
heating in the laboratory

ing state, than the days of the hill-fort. Powerful fires would
have been required to render the exposed summit of the Scuir
at all comfortable ; there is a deep peat-moss in its immediate
neighbourhood, that would have furnished the necessary fuel ;
the wind must have often been sufficiently high on the summit to fan the embers into an intense white heat ; and if it
was heat but half as intense as that which was employed in
fusing into one mass the thick vitrified ramparts of Craig
Phadrig and Knock Ferril, on the east coast, it could scarce
have failed to anticipate the experiment of the Hon. Mr Knox
of Dublin, by converting some of the numerous pitchstone
fragments that lie scattered about, "into a light substance in
every respect resembling pumice."

It was now evening, and rarely have I witnessed a finer.
The sun had declined half-way adown the western sky, and
for many yards the shadow of the gigantic Scuir lay dark beneath us along the descending slope. All the rest of the
island, spread out at our feet as in a map, was basking in
yellow sunshine ; and with its one dark shadow thrown from
its one mountain-elevated wall of rock, it seemed some immense fantastical dial, with its gnomon rising tall in the
midst. Far below, perched on the apex of the shadow, and
half lost in the line of the penumbra, we could see two indistinct specks of black, with a dim halo around each,—specks
that elongated as we arose, and contracted as we sat, and
went gliding along the line as we walked. The shadows of
two gnats disporting on the edge of an ordinary gnomon would
have seemed vastly more important, in proportion, on the
figured plane of the dial, than these, our ghostly representatives, did here. The sea, spangled in the wake of the sun
with quick glancing light, stretched out its blue plain around
us ; and we could see included in the wide prospect, on the
one hand, at once the hill-chains of Morven and Kintail, with
the many intervening lochs and bold jutting headlands that

---

vitrified ramparts: see p. 363 and Additional Notes; Mr Knox: see p. 21; dial: here,
sundial

give variety to the mainland ; and, on the other, the various-
ly-complexioned Hebrides, from the Isle of Skye to Uist and
Barra, and from Uist and Barra to Tiree and Mull.   The
contiguous Small Isles, Muck and Rum, lay moored immediately beside us, like vessels of the same convoy that in some
secure roadstead drop anchor within hail of each other.   I
could willingly have lingered on the top of the Scuir until
after sunset ; but the minister, who ever and anon, during
the day, had been conning over some notes jotted on a paper
of wonderfully scant dimensions, reminded me that this was
the evening of his week-day discourse, and that we were more
than a particularly rough mile from the place of meeting, and
within half an hour of the time.   I took one last look of
the scene ere we commenced our descent.   There,—in the
middle of the ample parish glebe, that looked richer and
greener in the light of the declining sun than at any former
period during the day,—rose the snug parish manse ; and
yonder,—in an open island channel, with a strip of dark
rocks fringing the land within, and another dark strip fringing the barren Eilean Chaisteil outside,—lay the Betsey, looking wonderfully diminutive, but evidently a little thing of
high spirit, tant-masted, with a smart rake aft, and a spruce
outrigger astern, and flaunting her triangular flag of blue in
the sun.   I pointed first to the manse, and then to the yacht.
The minister shook his head.

"'Tis a time of strange changes," he said : "I thought to
have lived and died in that house, and found a quiet grave in
the burying-ground yonder beside the ruin ; but my path was
a clear though a rugged one ; and from almost the moment
that it opened up to me, I saw what I had to expect.   It
has been said that I might have lain by here in this out-of-
the-way corner, and suffered the Church question to run its
course, without quitting my hold of the Establishment.   And
so I perhaps might.   It is easy securing one's own safety, in

---

rake aft: the *Betsey*'s mainmast is tilted slightly to the rear even the worst of times, if one look no higher ; and I, as I had no opportunity of mixing in the contest, or of declaring my views respecting it, might be regarded as an unpledged man.   But the principles of the Evangelical party were my principles ; and it would have been consistent with neither honour nor religion to have hung back in the day of battle, and suffered the men with whom in heart I was at one to pay the whole forfeit of our common quarrel.   So I attended the Convocation, and pledged myself to stand or fall with my brethren.   On my return I called my people together, and told them how the case stood, and that in May next I bade fair to be a dependent for a home on the proprietor of Eigg. And so they petitioned the proprietor that he might give me leave to build a house among them,—exactly the same sort of favour granted to the Roman Catholics of the island.   But month after month passed, and they got no reply to their petition ; and I was left in suspense, not knowing whether I was to have a home among them or no.   I did feel the case a somewhat hard one.   The father of Dr M'Pherson of Eigg had been, like myself, a humble Scotch minister ; and the Doctor, however indifferent to his people's wishes in such a matter, might have just thought that a man in his father's station in life, with a wife and family dependent on him, was placed by his silence in cruel circumstances of uncertainty. Ere the Disruption took place, however, I came to know pretty conclusively what I had to expect.   The Doctor's factor came to Eigg, and, as I was informed, told the islanders that it was not likely the Doctor would permit a *third* place of worship on the island : the Roman Catholics had one, and the Establishment had a kind of one, and there was to be no more.   The factor, an active messenger-at-arms, useful in raising rents in these parts, has always been understood to speak the mind of his master ; but the congregation took heart in the emergency, and sent off a second petition to Dr M'Pher-

son, a week or so previous to the Disruption. Ere *it* received
an answer, the Disruption took place ; and, laying the whole
circumstances before my brethren in Edinburgh, who, like
myself, interpreted the silence of the Doctor into a refusal,
I suggested to them the scheme of the Betsey, as the only
scheme through which I could keep up unbroken my connection with my people. So the trial is now over ; and here we
are, and yonder is the Betsey."

We descended the Scuir together for the place of meeting,
and entered, by the way, the cottage of a worthy islander,
much attached to his minister. "We are both very hungry,"
said my friend : "we have been out among the rocks since
breakfast time, and are wonderfully disposed to eat. Do not
put yourself about, but give us anything you have at hand."
There was a bowl of rich milk brought us, and a splendid
platter of mashed potatoes, and we dined like princes. I observed for the first time in the interior of this cottage, what
I had frequent occasion to remark afterwards, that much of
the wood used in buildings in the smaller and outer islands
of the Hebrides must have drifted across the Atlantic, borne
eastwards and northwards by the great gulf-stream. Many
of the beams and boards, sorely drilled by the *Teredo navalis,*
are of American timber, that from time to time has been cast
upon the shore,—a portion of it apparently from timber-laden
vessels unfortunate in their voyage, but a portion of it also,
with root and branch still attached, bearing mark of having
been swept to the sea by Transatlantic rivers. Nuts and
seeds of tropical plants are occasionally picked up on the
beach. My friend gave me a bean or nut of the *Dolichos
urens,* or cow-itch shrub of the West Indies, which an islander
had found on the shore some time in the previous year, and
given to one of the manse children as a toy ; and I attach
some little interest to it, as a curiosity of the same class with
the large canes and the fragment of carved wood found float-

ing near the shores of Madeira by the brother-in-law of Columbus, and which, among other similar pieces of circumstantial evidence, led the great navigator to infer the existence of a western continent. Curiosities of this kind seem still more common in the northern than in the western islands of Scotland. " Large exotic nuts or seeds," says Dr Patrick Neill, in his interesting " Tour," quoted in a former chapter, " which in Orkney are known by the name of Molucca beans, are occasionally found among the rejectamenta of the sea, especially after westerly winds. There are two kinds commonly found : the larger (of which the fishermen very generally make snuff-boxes) seem to be seeds from the great pod of the *Mimosa scandens* of the West Indies ; the smaller seeds, from the pod of the *Dolichos urens*, also a native of the same region. It is probable that the currents of the ocean, and particularly that great current which issues from the Gulf of Florida, and is hence denominated the Gulf Stream, aid very much in transporting across the mighty Atlantic these American products. They are generally quite fresh and entire, and afford an additional proof how impervious to moisture, and how imperishable, nuts and seeds generally are."

The evening was fast falling ere the minister closed his discourse; and we had but just light enough left, on reaching the Betsey, to show us that there lay a dead sheep on the deck. It had been sent aboard to be killed by the minister's factotum, John Stewart ; but John was at the evening preaching at the time, and the poor sheep, in its attempts to set itself free, had got itself involved among the cords, and strangled itself. " Alas, alas !" exclaimed the minister, " thus ends our hope of fresh mutton for the present, and my hapless speculation as a sheep-farmer for ever more." I learned from him afterwards, over our tea, that shortly previous to the Convocation he had got his glebe,—one of the largest in Scotland, —well stocked with sheep and cattle, which he had to sell,

Neill: (1806, pp. 60-61), slightly edited

immediately on the Disruption, in miserably bad condition, at a loss of nearly fifty per cent. He had a few sheep, however, that would not sell at all, and that remained on the glebe in consequence, until his successor entered into possession. And he, honest man, straightway impounded them, and got them incarcerated in a dark, dirty hole, somewhat in the way Giant Despair incarcerated the pilgrims,—a thing he had quite a legal right to do, seeing that the mile-long glebe, with its many acres of luxuriant pasture, was now as much his property as it had been Mr Swanson's a few months before, and seeing Mr Swanson's few sheep had no right to crop his grass. But a worthy neighbour interfered,—Mr M'Donald of Keil, the principal tenant in the island. Mr M'Donald,—a practical commentator on the law of kindness, —was sorely scandalized by what he deemed the new minister's gratuitous unkindness to a brother in calamity ; and, relieving the sheep, he brought them to his own farm, where he found them board and lodging on my friend's behalf, till they could be used up at leisure. And it was one of the last of this unfortunate lot that now contrived to escape from us by anticipating John Stewart. "A black beginning makes a black ending," said Gouffing Jock, an ancient border shepherd, when his only sheep, a black ewe, the sole survivor of a flock smothered in a snow-storm, was worried to death by his dogs. Then, taking down his broad sword, he added, "Come awa, my auld friend ; thou and I maun e'en stock Bowerhope-Law ance mair !" Less warlike than Gouffing Jock, we were content to repeat over the dead, on this occasion, simply the first portion of his speech; and then, betaking ourselves to our cabin, we forgot all our sorrows over our tea.

Giant Despair: a character in John Bunyan's *Pilgrim's Progress*; Keil: Kildonnan Farm; Gouffing Jock: see Additional Notes

CHAPTER IV.

THERE had been rain during the night ; and when I first got on deck, a little after seven, a low stratum of mist, that completely enveloped the Scuir, and truncated both the eminence on which it stands and the opposite height, stretched like a ruler across the flat valley which indents so deeply the middle of the island. But the fogs melted away as the morning rose, and ere our breakfast was satisfactorily discussed, the last thin wreath had disappeared from around the columned front of the rock-tower of Eigg, and a powerful sun looked down on moist slopes and dank hollows, from which there arose in the calm a hazy vapour, that, while it softened the lower features of the landscape, left the bold outline relieved against a clear sky. Accompanied by our attendant of the previous day, bearing bag and hammer, we set out a little before eleven for the north-western side of the island, by a road which winds along the central hollow. My friend showed me as we went, that on the edge of an eminence, on which the traveller journeying westwards catches the last glimpse of the chapel of St Donan, there had once been a rude cross erected, and another rude cross on an eminence on which he catches the last glimpse of the first ; and that there had thus been a chain of stations formed from sea to sea, like the sights of a land-surveyor, from one of which a

---

chapel of St Donan: Kildonnan

second could be seen, and a third from the second, till, last
of all, the emphatically holy point of the island,—the burial-
place of the old Culdee,—came full in view.   The unsteady
devotion, that journeyed, fancy-bound, along the heights, to
gloat over a dead man's bones, had its clue to carry it on in
a straight line.   Its trail was on the ground ; it glided snake-
like from cross to cross, in quest of dust ; and, without its
finger-posts to guide it, would have wandered devious.   It is
surely a better devotion that, instead of thus creeping over
the earth to a mouldy sepulchre, can at once launch into the
sky, secure of finding Him who arose from one.   In less than
an hour we were descending on the Bay of Laig, a semicircular indentation of the coast about a mile in length, and,
where it opens to the main sea, nearly two miles in breadth ;
with the noble island of Rum rising high in front, like some
vast breakwater ; and a meniscus of comparatively level land,
walled in behind by a semicircular rampart of continuous
precipice, sweeping round its shores.   There are few finer
scenes in the Hebrides than that furnished by this island bay
and its picturesque accompaniments,—none that break more
unexpectedly on the traveller who descends upon it from the
east ; and rarely has it been seen to greater advantage than
on the delicate day, so soft, and yet so sunshiny and clear, on
which I paid it my first visit.

    The island of Rum, with its abrupt sea-wall of rock, and its
steep-pointed hills, that attain, immediately over the sea, an
elevation of more than two thousand feet, loomed bold and high
in the offing, some five miles away, but apparently much nearer.
The four tall summits of the island rose clear against the
sky, like a group of pyramids ; its lower slopes and precipices,
variegated and relieved by graceful alternations of light and
shadow, and resting on their blue basement of sea, stood out
with equal distinctness ; but the entire middle space from end
to end was hidden in a long horizontal stratum of gray cloud,

edged atop with a lacing of silver. Such was the aspect of
the noble breakwater in front. Fully two-thirds of the semicircular rampart of rock which shuts in the crescent-shaped
plain directly opposite lay in deep shadow ; but the sun shone
softly on the plain itself, brightening up many a dingy cottage, and many a green patch of corn ; and the bay below
stretched out, sparkling in the light. There is no part of the
island so thickly inhabited as this flat meniscus. It is composed almost entirely of Oolitic rocks, and bears atop, especially where an ancient oyster-bed of great depth forms the subsoil, a kindly and fertile mould. The cottages lie in groupes ;
and, save where a few bogs, which it would be no very difficult matter to drain, interpose their rough shag of dark
green, and break the continuity, the plain around them waves
with corn. Lying fair, green, and populous within the sweep
of its inaccessible rampart of rock, at least twice as lofty as
the ramparts of Babylon of old, it reminds one of the suburbs of some ancient city lying embosomed, with all its dwellings and fields, within some roomy crescent of the city wall.
We passed, ere we entered on the level, a steep-sided narrow
dell, through which a small stream finds its way from the
higher grounds, and which terminates at the upper end in an
abrupt precipice, and a lofty but very slim cascade. " One
of the few superstitions that still linger on the island," said
my friend the minister, " is associated with that wild hollow.
It is believed that shortly before a death takes place among
the inhabitants, a tall withered female may be seen in the
twilight, just yonder where the rocks open, washing a shroud
in the stream. John, there, will perhaps tell you how she
was spoken to on one occasion, by an over-bold, over-inqui-
sitive islander, curious to know whose shroud she was preparing ; and how she more than satisfied his curiosity, by telling him it was his own. It is a not uninteresting fact," added the minister, " that my poor people, since they have become

---

crescent-shaped plain: *ie* Cleadale on Eigg, not Rùm

more earnest about their religion, think very little about
ghosts and spectres : their faith in the realities of the unseen
world seems to have banished from their minds much of their
old belief in its phantoms."

In the rude fences that separate from each other the little
farms in this plain, we find frequent fragments of the oyster-
bed, hardened into a tolerably compact limestone.   It is seen
to most advantage, however, in some of the deeper cuttings
in the fields, where the surrounding matrix exists merely as
an incoherent shale ; and the shells may be picked out as entire as when they lay, ages before, in the mud, which we still
see retaining around them its original colour.   They are small,
thin, triangular, much resembling in form some specimens of
the *Ostrea deltoidea*, but greatly less in size.   The nearest
resembling shell in Sowerby is the *Ostrea acuminata*,—an
oyster of the clay that underlies the great Oolite of Bath.
Few of the shells exceed an inch and half in length, and the
majority fall short of an inch.   What they lack in bulk, however, they make up in number.   They are massed as thickly
together, to the depth of several feet, as shells on the heap
at the door of a Newhaven fisherman, and extend over many
acres.   Where they lie open we can still detect the triangular
disc of the hinge, with the single impression of the adductor
muscle ; and the foliaceous character of the shell remains in
most instances as distinct as if it had undergone no mineral
change.   I have seen nowhere in Scotland, among the secondary formations, so unequivocal an oyster-bed ; nor do such
beds seem to be at all common in formations older than the
Tertiary in England, though the oyster itself is sufficiently
so.   We find Mantell stating, in his recent work ("Medals of
Creation"), after first describing an immense oyster-bed of the
London Basin, that underlies the city (for what is now London was once an oyster-bed), that in the chalk below, though
it contains several species of Ostrea, the shells are diffused

---

Sowerby: presumably the then standard reference work on fossil shells, *Mineral conchology*
(Sowerby 1812-1829, *etc*), by James Sowerby (1757-1822) and his family; **Mantell**:
Gideon Mantell (1790-1852), doctor, geologist and popular writer on geology – referring
to Mantell (1844, I, pp. 385-386)

promiscuously throughout the general mass.   Leaving, however, these oysters of the Oolite, which never net inclosed nor
drag disturbed, though they must have formed the food of
many an extinct order of fish,—mayhap reptile,—we pass
on in a south-western direction, descending in the geological
scale as we go, until we reach the southern side of the Bay
of Laig.   And there, far below tidemark, we find a dark-
coloured argillaceous shale of the Lias, greatly obscured by
boulders of trap,—the only deposit of the Liasic formation in
the island.

A line of trap-hills that rises along the shore seems as if
it had strewed half its materials over the beach.   The rugged blocks lie thick as stones in a causeway, down to the line
of low ebb,—memorials of a time when the surf dashed
against the shattered bases of the trap-hills, now elevated
considerably beyond its reach ; and we can catch but partial
glimpses of the shale below.   Wherever access to it can be
had, we find it richly fossiliferous ; but its organisms, with
the exception of its Belemnites, are very imperfectly preserved.   I dug up from under the trap-blocks some of the
common Liasic Ammonites of the north-eastern coast of Scotland, a few of the septa of a large Nautilus, broken pieces of
wood, and half-effaced casts of what seems a branched coral ;
but only minute portions of the shells have been converted
into stone ; here and there a few chambers in the whorls of
an Ammonite or Nautilus, though the outline of the entire
organism lies impressed in the shale ; and the ligneous and
polyparious fossils we find in a still greater state of decay.
The Belemnite alone, as is common with this robust fossil,—
so often the sole survivor of its many contemporaries,—has
preserved its structure entire.   I disinterred from the shale
good specimens of the Belemnite *sulcatus* and Belemnite
elongatus, and found, detached on the surface of the bed, a
fragment of a singularly large Belemnite, a full inch and a

Lias: this site is now known to be Upper Jurassic (Oxfordian), not true Lias (Lower
Jurassic) – Miller compared it through its fossils with the 'Liassic' rocks of the east coast,
presumably following the erroneous dating by Murchison (1827)

quarter in diameter, the species of which I could not determine.

Returning by the track we came, we reach the bottom of
the bay, which we find much obscured with sand and shingle;
and pass northwards along its side, under a range of low sandstone precipices, with interposing grassy slopes, in which the
fertile Oolitic meniscus descends to the beach.   The sandstone, white and soft, and occurring in thick beds, much resembles that of the Oolite of Sutherland.   We detect in it
few traces of fossils ; now and then a carbonaceous marking,
and now and then what seems a thin vein of coal, but which
proves to be merely the bark of some woody stem, converted
into a glossy bituminous lignite, like that of Brora.   But in
beds of a blue clay, intercalated with the sandstone, we find
fossils in abundance, of a character less obscure.   We spent
a full half-hour in picking out shells from the bottom of a
long dock-like hollow among the rocks, in which a bed of clay
has yielded to the waves, while the strata on either side stand
up over it like low wharfs on the opposite sides of a river.
The shells, though exceedingly fragile,—for they partake of
the nature of the clayey matrix in which they are embedded,
—rise as entire as when they had died among the mud, years,
mayhap ages, ere the sandstone had been deposited over them ;
and we were enabled at once to detect their extreme dissimilarity, as a group, to the shells of the Liasic deposit we
had so lately quitted.   We did not find in this bed a single
Ammonite, Belemnite, or Nautilus ; but chalky Bivalves, resembling our existing Tellina, in vast abundance, mixed with
what seem to be a small Buccinum and a minute Trochus,
with numerous rather equivocal fragments of a shell resembling an Oiliva.   So thickly do they lie clustered together in
this deposit, that in some patches where the sad-coloured argillaceous ground is washed bare by the sea, it seems marbled
with them into a light gray tint.   The group more nearly

resembles in type a recent one than any I have yet seen in
a secondary deposit, except perhaps in the Weald of Moray,
where we find in one of the layers a Planorbis scarce distinguishable from those of our ponds and ditches, mingled with
a Paludina that seems as nearly modelled after the existing
form.   From the absence of the more characteristic shells of
the Oolite, I am inclined to deem the deposit one of estuary
origin.   Its clays were probably thrown down, like the silts
of so many of our rivers, in some shallow bay, where the
waters of a descending stream mingled with those of the sea,
and where, though shells nearly akin to our existing periwinkles and whelks congregated thickly, the Belemnite, scared
by the brackish water, never plied its semi-cartilaginous fins,
or the Nautilus or Ammonite hoisted its membranaceous sail.

We pass on towards the north.   A thick bed of an extremely soft white sandstone presents here, for nearly half a
mile together, its front to the waves, and exhibits, under the
incessant wear of the surf, many singularly grotesque combinations of form.   The low precipices, undermined at the base,
beetle over like the sides of stranded vessels.   One of the projecting promontories we find hollowed through and through
by a tall rugged archway ; while the outer pier of the arch,
—if pier we may term it,—worn to a skeleton, and jutting
outwards with a knee-like angle, presents the appearance of
a thin ungainly leg and splay foot, advanced, as if in awk-
ward courtesy, to the breakers.   But in a winter or two,
judging from its present degree of attenuation, and the yielding nature of its material, which resembles a damaged mass
of arrowroot consolidated by lying in the leaky hold of a
vessel, its persevering courtesies will be over, and pier and
archway must lie in shapeless fragments on the beach.
Wherever the surf has broken into the upper surface of this
sandstone bed, and worn it down to nearly the level of the
shore, what seem a number of double ramparts, fronting each

Weald: see Additional Notes; membranaceous sail: from earlier notions that nautiluses
and ammonites floated on the surface, using a membrane to drift with the wind, much as
a Portuguese Man o' War does

other, and separated by deep square ditches exactly parallel
in the sides, traverse the irregular level in every direction.
The ditches vary in width from one to twelve feet ; and the
ramparts, rising from three to six feet over them, are perpendicular as the walls of houses, where they front each
other, and descend on the opposite sides in irregular slopes.
The iron block, with square groove and projecting ears, that
receives the bar of a railway, and connects it with the stone
below, represents not inadequately a section of one of these
ditches with its ramparts.   They form here the sole remains
of dykes of an earthy trap, which, though at one time in a
state of such high fusion that they converted the portions of
soft sandstone in immediate contact with them into the con-
sistence of quartz rock, have long since mouldered away,
leaving but the hollow rectilinear rents which they had occupied, surmounted by the indurated walls which they had
baked.   Some of the most curious appearances, however, connected with the sandstone, though they occur chiefly in an
upper bed, are exhibited by what seem fields of petrified
mushrooms, of a gigantic size, that spread out in some places
for hundreds of yards under the high-water level.   These
apparent mushrooms stand on thick squat stems, from a foot
to eighteen inches in height : the heads are round, like those
of toad-stools, and vary from one foot to nearly two yards in
diameter.   In some specimens we find two heads joined together in a form resembling a squat figure of *eight*, of what
printers term the Egyptian type, or, to borrow the illustration of M'Culloch, " like the ancient military projectile
known by the name of double-headed shot ;" in other specimens three heads have coalesced in a trefoil shape, or rather
in a shape like that of an ace of clubs divested of the stem.
By much the greater number, however, are spherical.   They
are composed of concretionary masses, consolidated, like the
walls of the dykes, though under some different process, into

---

railway: *ie* track. The **block**, a cast iron 'chair', held the rail – Miller's **bar** – to the
sleeper, then often of **stone**, more recently wood. Nowadays rails are clasped directly to
concrete sleepers; **dykes**: unusually, the dykes here stand out not though the hardness of
the basalt, but because the sandstone next to the basalt was baked and hardened by the
molten rock and is more resistant to erosion, hence the 'double ramparts'

a hard siliceous stone, that has resisted those disintegrating influences of the weather and the surf under which the yielding matrix in which they were embedded has worn from around them.   Here and there we find them lying detached on the beach, like huge shot, compared with which the greenstone balls of Mons Meg are but marbles for children to play with ; in other cases they project from the mural front of rampart-like precipices, as if they had been showered into them by the ordnance of some besieging battery, and had stuck fast in the mason-work.   Abbotsford has been described as a romance in stone and lime : we have here, on the shores of Laig, what seems a wild but agreeable tale, of the extravagant cast of " Christabel," or the " Rhyme of the Ancient Mariner," fretted into sandstone.   But by far the most curious part of the story remains to be told.

The hollows and fissures of the lower sandstone bed we find filled with a fine quartzose sand, which, from its pure white colour, and the clearness with which the minute particles reflect the light, reminds one of accumulations of potato-flour drying in the sun.   It is formed almost entirely of disintegrated particles of the soft sandstone ; and as we at first find it occurring in mere handfuls, that seem as if they had been detached from the mass during the last few tides, we begin to marvel to what quarter the missing materials of the many hundred cubic yards of rock, ground down along the shore in this bed during the last century or two, have been conveyed away.   As we pass on northwards, however, we see the white sand occurring in much larger quantities, —here heaped up in little bent-covered hillocks above the reach of the tide,—there stretching out in level, ripple-marked wastes into the waves,—yonder rising in flat narrow spits among the shallows.   At length we reach a small, irregularly-formed bay, a few hundred feet across, floored with it from side to side ; and see it, on the one hand, descending deep

---

Mons Meg: a huge bombard (the largest calibre of cannon), presented to James II by the Duke of Burgundy in 1457. Still at Edinburgh Castle today; 'Christabel': the poem by Coleridge

into the sea, that exhibits over its whiteness a lighter tint
of green, and, on the other, encroaching on the land, in the
form of drifted banks, covered with the plants common to
our tracts of sandy downs.   The sandstone bed that has been
worn down to form it contains no fossils, save here and there
a carbonaceous stem ; but in an underlying harder stratum
we occasionally find a few shells ; and, with a specimen in my
hand charged with a group of bivalves resembling the existing conchifera of our sandy beaches, I was turning aside this
sand of the Oolite, so curiously reduced to its original state,
and marking how nearly the recent shells that lay embedded
in it resembled the extinct ones that had lain in it so long
before, when I became aware of a peculiar sound that it yielded to the tread, as my companions paced over it.   I struck
it obliquely with my foot, where the surface lay dry and incoherent in the sun, and the sound elicited was a shrill sonorous note, somewhat resembling that produced by a waxed
thread, when tightened between the teeth and the hand, and
tipped by the nail of the forefinger.   I walked over it, striking
it obliquely at each step, and with every blow the shrill note
was repeated.   My companions joined me ; and we performed
a concert, in which, if we could boast of but little variety in
the tones produced, we might at least challenge all Europe
for an instrument of the kind which produced them.   It
seemed less wonderful that there should be music in the granite of Memnon, than in the loose Oolitic sand of the Bay
of Laig.   As we marched over the drier tracts, an incessant
woo, woo, woo, rose from the surface, that might be heard in
the calm some twenty or thirty yards away ; and we found
that where a damp semi-coherent stratum lay at the depth of
three or four inches beneath, and all was dry and incoherent
above, the tones were loudest and sharpest, and most easily
evoked by the foot.   Our discovery,—for I trust I may regard it as such,—adds a third locality to two previously

---

carbonaceous stem: *ie* of a fossil plant; conchifera: here, shellfish; Memnon: a colossal
statue at Luxor in Egypt that 'sang' at dawn due to thermal expansion in the sun; Bay of
Laig: actually, the 'Singing Sands' (as they are known today) are in the adjacent small bay
of Camas Sgiotaig (Hudson 2003; Hudson and Allwright 2003)

known ones, in which what may be termed the musical sand,
—no unmeet counterpart to the "singing water" of the tale,
—has now been found.   And as the island of Eigg is considerably more accessible than *Jabel Nakous* in Arabia Petræa,
or *Reg-Rawan* in the neighbourhood of Cabul, there must be
facilities presented through the discovery which did not exist
hitherto, for examining the phenomenon in acoustics which
it exhibits,—a phenomenon, it may be added, which some of
our greatest masters of the science have confessed their inabi-
lity to explain.

Jabel Nakous, or the "Mountain of the Bell," is situated
about three miles from the shores of the Gulf of Suez, in that
land of wonders which witnessed for forty years the journeyings of the Israelites, and in which the granite peaks of Sinai
and Horeb overlook an arid wilderness of rock and sand.   It
had been known for many ages by the wild Arab of the desert, that there rose at times from this hill a strange, inexplicable music.   As he leads his camel past in the heat of the
day, a sound like the first low tones of an Æolian harp stirs
the hot breezeless air.   It swells louder and louder in progressive undulations, till at length the dry baked earth seems
to vibrate under foot, and the startled animal snorts and rears,
and struggles to break away.   According to the Arabian
account of the phenomenon, says Sir David Brewster, in his
"Letters on Natural Magic," there is a convent miraculously
preserved in the bowels of the hill ; and the sounds are said
to be those of the "*Nakous*, a long metallic ruler, suspended
horizontally, which the priest strikes with a hammer, for the
purpose of assembling the monks to prayer."   There exists
a tradition that on one occasion a wandering Greek saw the
mountain open, and that, entering by the gap, he descended
into the subterranean convent, where he found beautiful gardens and fountains of delicious water, and brought with him
to the upper world, on his return, fragments of consecrated

Brewster: (1781-1868), Principal of the University of St Andrews, scientist,
writer, and Free Churchman (Morrison-Low and Christie 1984; Livingstone 2003).
Amongst other things, he sought natural explanations for apparently magical or
supernatural events, such as optical effects for ghosts

bread.   The first European traveller who visited *Jabel Nakous*,
says Sir David, was M. Seetzen, a German.   He journeyed
for several hours over arid sands, and under ranges of precipices inscribed by mysterious characters, that tell, haply, of
the wanderings of Israel under Moses.   And reaching, about
noon, the base of the musical fountain, he found it composed
of a white friable sandstone, and presenting on two of its
sides sandy declivities.   He watched beside it for an hour
and a quarter, and then heard, for the first time, a low undulating sound, somewhat resembling that of a humming top,
which rose and fell, and ceased and began, and then ceased
again ; and in an hour and three quarters after, when in the
act of climbing along the declivity, he heard the sound yet
louder and more prolonged.   It seemed as if issuing from
under his knees, beneath which the sand, disturbed by his
efforts, was sliding downwards along the surface of the rock.
Concluding that the sliding sand was the cause of the sounds,
not an effect of the vibrations which they occasioned, he
climbed to the top of one of the declivities, and, sliding downwards, exerted himself with hands and feet to set the sand in
motion.   The effect produced far exceeded his expectations :
the incoherent sand rolled under and around in a vast sheet ;
and so loud was the noise produced, that " the earth seemed
to tremble beneath him to such a degree, that he states he
should certainly have been afraid if he had been ignorant of
the cause."   At the time Sir David Brewster wrote (1832),
the only other European who had visited *Jabel Nakous* was
Mr Gray, of University College, Oxford.   This gentleman
describes the noises he heard, but which he was unable to
trace to their producing cause, as " beginning with a low continuous murmuring sound, which seemed to rise beneath his
feet," but " which gradually changed into pulsations as it became louder, so as to resemble the striking of a clock, and
became so strong at the end of five minutes *as to detach the*

sand." The Mountain of the Bell has been since carefully explored by Lieutenant J. Welsted of the Indian navy ; and the reader may see it exhibited in a fine lithograph, in his travels, as a vast irregularly-conical mass of broken stone, somewhat resembling one of our Highland cairns, though, of course, on a scale immensely more huge, with a steep angular slope of sand resting in a hollow in one of its sides, and rising to nearly its apex. " It forms," says Lieutenant Welsted, " one of a ridge of low calcareous hills, at a distance of three and a half miles from the beach, to which a sandy plain, extending with a gentle rise to their base, connects them. Its height, about four hundred feet, as well as the material of which it is composed,—a light-coloured friable sandstone, —is about the same as the rest of the chain ; but an inclined plane of almost impalpable sand rises at an angle of forty degrees with the horizon, and is bounded by a semicircle of rocks, presenting broken, abrupt, and pinnacled forms, and extending to the base of this remarkable hill. Although their shape and arrangement in some respects may be said to resemble a whispering gallery, yet I determined by experiment that their irregular surface renders them but ill adapted for the production of an echo. Seated at a rock at the base of the sloping eminence, I directed one of the Bedouins to ascend ; and it was not until he had reached some distance that I perceived the sand in motion, rolling down the hill to the depth of a foot. It did not, however, descend in one continued stream ; but, as the Arab scrambled up, it spread out laterally and upwards, until a considerable portion of the surface was in motion. At their commencement the sounds might be compared to the faint strains of an Æolian harp when its strings first catch the breeze : as the sand became more violently agitated by the increased velocity of the descent, the noise more nearly resembled that produced by drawing the moistened fingers over glass. As it reached the base, the reverberations attained the loudness of distant thunder, causing the rock on which we were seated to vibrate ; and our camels,—animals not easily frightened,—became so alarmed, that it was with difficulty their drivers could restrain them."

" The hill of *Reg-Rawan*, or the ' Moving Sand,' " says the late Sir Alexander Burnes, by whom the place was visited in the autumn of 1837, and who has recorded his visit in a brief paper, illustrated by a rude lithographic view, in the " Journal of the Asiatic Society" for 1838, " is about forty miles north of Cabul, towards Hindu-kush, and near the base of the mountains." It rises to the height of about four hundred feet, in an angle formed by the junction of two ridges of hills ; and a sheet of sand, "pure as that of the sea-shore," and which slopes in an angle of forty degrees, reclines against it from base to summit. As represented in the lithograph, there projects over the steep sandy slope on each side, as in " the Mountain of the Bell," still steeper barriers of rock ; and we are told by Sir Alexander, that though "the mountains here are generally composed of granite or mica, at *Reg-Rawan* there is sandstone and lime." The situation of the sand is curious, he adds : it is seen from a great distance ; and as there is none other in the neighbourhood, " it might almost be imagined, from its appearance, that the hill had been cut in two, and that the sand had gushed forth as from a sand-bag." " When set in motion by a body of people who slide down it, a sound is emitted. On the first trial we distinctly heard two loud hollow sounds, such as would be given by a large drum ;"—" there is an echo in the place ; and the inhabitants have a belief that the sounds are only heard on Friday, when the saint of *Reg-Rawan*, who is interred hard by, permits." The phenomenon, like the resembling one in Arabia, seems to have attracted attention among the inhabitants of the country at an early period ; and the notice

---

Sir Alexander Burnes: (1805-1841), Oriental traveller and political agent at Kabul, who died in the insurrection there of an eastern annalist, the Emperor Baber, who flourished late in the fifteenth century, and, like Cæsar, conquered and recorded his conquests, still survives. He describes it as the *Khwaja Reg-Rawan*, "a small hill, in which there is a line of sandy ground reaching from the top to the bottom," from which there "issues in the summer season the sound of drums and nagarets." In connection with the fact that the musical sand of Eigg is composed of a disintegrated sandstone of the Oolite, it is not quite unworthy of notice that sandstone and lime enter into the composition of the hill of *Reg-Rawan*,—that the district in which the hill is situated is not a sandy one,—and that its slope of sonorous sand seems as if it had issued from its side. These various circumstances, taken together, lead to the inference that the sand may have originated in the decomposition of the rock beneath. It is further noticeable, that the *Jabel Nakous* is composed of a white friable sandstone, resembling that of the white friable bed of the Bay of Laig, and that it belongs to nearly the same geological era. I owe to the kindness of Dr Wilson of Bombay, two specimens which he picked up in Arabia Petræa, of spines of Cidarites of the mace-formed type so common in the Chalk and Oolite, but so rare in the older formations. Dr Wilson informs me that they are of frequent occurrence in the desert of Arabia Petræa, where they are termed by the Arabs petrified olives ; that nummulites are also abundant in the district ; and that the various secondary rocks he examined in his route through it seem to belong to the Cretaceous group. It appears not improbable, therefore, that all the sonorous sand in the world yet discovered is formed, like that of Eigg, of disintegrated sandstone ; and at least two-thirds of it of the disintegrated sandstone of secondary formations, newer than the Lias. But how it should be at all sonorous, whatever its age or origin, seems yet to be discovered. There are few substances that appear worse suited than sand to com-

---

Dr Wilson: John Wilson (1804–1875), 'learned Free Church missionary to the Parsees of India' (Miller 1857, p. 42; Smith 1879); he promoted the teaching of science and took an interest in geology and palaeontology, although this was evidently subordinate to his main religious and antiquarian work; **how it should be at all sonorous**: see Additional Notes municate to the atmosphere those vibratory undulations that are the producing causes of sound : the grains, even when sonorous individually, seem, from their inevitable contact with each other, to exist under the influence of that simple law in acoustics which arrests the tones of the ringing glass or struck bell, immediately as they are but touched by some foreign body, such as the hand or finger. The one grain, ever in contact with several other grains, is a glass or bell on which the hand always rest. And the difficulty has been felt and acknowledged. Sir John Herschel, in referring to the phenomenon of the *Jabel Nakous*, in his " Treatise on Sound," in the " Encyclopædia Metropolitana," describes it as to him "utterly inexplicable ;" and Sir David Brewster, whom I had the pleasure of meeting in December last, assured me it was not less a puzzle to him than to Sir John. An eastern traveller, who attributes its production to " a reduplication of impulse setting air in vibration in a focus of echo," means, I suppose, saying nearly the same thing as the two philosophers, and merely conveys his meaning in a less simple style.

I have not yet procured what I expect to procure soon,—sand enough from the musical bay at Laig to enable me to make its sonorous qualities the subject of experiment at home. It seems doubtful whether a small quantity set in motion on an artificial slope will serve to evolve the phenomena which have rendered the Mountain of the Bell so famous. Lieutenant Welsted informs us, that when his Bedouin first set the sand in motion, there was scarce any perceptible sound heard ;—it was rolling downwards for many yards around him to the depth of a foot, ere the music arose ; and it is questionable whether the effect could be elicited with some fifty or sixty pounds weight of the sand of Eigg, on a slope of but at most a few feet, which it took many hundredweight of the sand of *Jabel Nakous*, and a slope of many yards, to produce. But in the stillness of a close room, it is just pos-

---

Sir John Herschel: (1792-1871), mathematician, astronomer and physicist sible that it may.   I have, however, little doubt, that from small quantities the sounds evoked by the foot on the shore may be reproduced : enough will lie within the reach of experiment to demonstrate the strange difference which exists between this sonorous sand of the Oolite, and the common unsonorous sand of our sea-beaches ; and it is certainly worth while examining into the nature and producing causes of a phenomenon so curious in itself, and which has been characterized by one of the most distinguished of living philosophers as " the most celebrated of all the acoustic wonders which the natural world presents to us."   In the forthcoming number of the " North British Review,"—which appears on Monday first,*—the reader will find the sonorous sand of Eigg referred to, in an article the authorship of which will scarce be mistaken.   " We have here," says the writer, after first describing the sounds of *Jabel Nakous*, and then referring to those of Eigg, " the phenomenon in its simple state, disembarrassed from reflecting rocks, from a hard bed beneath, and from cracks and cavities that might be supposed to admit the sand ; and indicating as its cause, either the accumulated vibrations of the air when struck by the driven sand, or the accumulated sounds occasioned by the mutual impact of the particles of sand against each other.   If a musket-ball passing through the air emits a whistling note, each individual particle of sand must do the same, however faint be the note which it yields ; and the accumulation of these infinitesimal vibrations must constitute an audible sound, varying with the number and velocity of the moving particles.   In like manner, if two plates of silex or quartz, which are but large crystals of sand, give out a musical sound when mutually struck, the impact or collision of two minute crystals or particles of sand must do the same, in however inferior a degree ; and the union of all these sounds, though singly

* March 31, 1845.

authorship: Brewster; see note for p. 59. The quote is from Brewster (1845, pp. 25-26) imperceptible, may constitute the musical notes of the Bell Mountain, or the lesser sounds of the trodden sea-beach at Eigg."

Here is a vigorous effort made to unlock the difficulty. I should, however, have mentioned to the philosophic writer, —what I inadvertently failed to do,—that the sounds elicited from the sand of Eigg seem as directly evoked by the slant blow dealt it by the foot, as the sounds similarly evoked from a highly waxed floor, or a board strewed over with ground rosin. The sharp shrill note follows the stroke, altogether independently of the grains driven into the air. My omission may serve to show how much safer it is for those minds of the observant order, that serve as hands and eyes to the reflective ones, to prefer incurring the risk of being even tediously minute in their descriptions, to the danger of being inadequately brief in them. But, alas ! for purposes of exact science, rarely are verbal descriptions other than inadequate. Let us just look, for example, at the various accounts given us of *Jabel Nakous*. There are strange sounds heard proceeding from a hill in Arabia, and various travellers set themselves to describe them. The tones are those of the convent *Nakous*, says the wild Arab ;—there must be a convent buried under the hill. More like the sounds of a humming top, remarks a phlegmatic German traveller. Not quite like them, says an English one in an Oxford gown ; they resemble rather the striking of a clock. Nay, listen just a little longer and more carefully, says a second Englishman, with epaulettes on his shoulder : " the sounds at their commencement may be compared to the faint strains of an Æolian harp when its strings first catch the breeze," but anon, as the agitation of the sand increases, they " more nearly resemble those produced by drawing the moistened fingers over glass." Not at all, exclaims the warlike Zahor Ed-Din Muhammad Baber, twirling his whiskers : "I know a similar hill in the country towards Hindu-kush : it is the sound of drums and nagarets that issues from the sand." All we really know of this often-described music of the desert, after reading all the descriptions, is, that its tones bear certain analogies to certain other tones,—analogies that seem stronger in one direction to one ear, and stronger in another direction to an ear differently constituted, but which do not exactly resemble any other sounds in nature. The strange music of *Jabel Nakous*, as a combination of tones, is essentially unique.

CHAPTER V.

WE leave behind us the musical sand, and reach the point of the promontory which forms the northern extremity of the Bay of Laig. Wherever the beach has been swept bare, we see it floored with trap-dykes worn down to the level, but in most places accumulations of huge blocks of various composition cover it up, concealing the nature of the rock beneath. The long semicircular wall of precipice which, sweeping inwards at the bottom of the bay, leaves to the inhabitants between its base and the beach their fertile meniscus of land, here abuts upon the coast. We see its dark forehead many hundred feet overhead, and the grassy platform beneath, now narrowed to a mere talus, sweeping upwards to its base from the shore,—steep, broken, lined thick with horizontal pathways, mottled over with ponderous masses of rock.

Among the blocks that load the beach, and render our onward progress difficult and laborious, we detect occasional fragments of an amygdaloidal basalt, charged with a white zeolite, consisting of crystals so extremely slender, that the balls, with their light fibrous contents, remind us of cotton apples divested of the seeds. There occur, though more rarely, masses of a hard white sandstone, abounding in vegetable impressions, which, from their sculptured markings, recall to memory the Sigilaria of the Coal Measures. Here and there, too, we find fragments of a calcareous stone, so largely charged with compressed shells, chiefly bivalves, that it may be regarded as a shell breccia.   There occur, besides, slabs of fibrous limestone, exactly resembling the limestone of the ichthyolite beds of the Lower Old Red ; and blocks of a hard gray stone, of silky lustre in the fresh fracture, thickly speckled with carbonaceous markings.   These frag-mentary masses,—all of them, at least, except the fibrous limestone, which occurs in mere plank-like bands,—represent distinct beds, of which this part of the island is composed, and which present their edges, like courses of ashlar in a build-ing, in the splendid section that stretches from the tall brow of the precipice to the beach ; though in the slopes of the talus, where the lower beds appear in but occasional protru-sions and landslips, we find some difficulty in tracing their order of succession.

Near the base of the slope, where the soil has been under-mined and the rock laid bare by the waves, there occur beds of a bituminous black shale,—resembling the dark shales so common in the Coal Measures,—that seem to be of fresh-water or estuary origin.   Their fossils, though numerous, are ill preserved ; but we detect in them scales and plates of fishes, at least two species of minute bivalves, one of which very much resembles a Cyclas ; and in some of the fragments, shells of Cypris lie embedded in considerable abundance.   After all that has been said and written by way of accounting for those alternations of lacustrine with marine remains which are of such frequent occurrence in the various formations, secondary and tertiary, from the Coal Measures downwards, it does seem strange enough that the estuary, or fresh-water lake, should so often in the old geologic periods have changed places with the sea.   It is comparatively easy to conceive that the inner Hebrides should have once existed as a broad ocean-sound, bounded on one or either side by Oolitic islands,

estuary origin: see Additional Note for p. 55

from which streams descended, sweeping with them, to the marine depths, productions, animal and vegetable, of the land. But it is less easy to conceive, that in that sound, the area covered by the ocean one year should have been covered by a fresh-water lake in perhaps the next, and then by the ocean again a few years after. And yet among the Oolitic deposits of the Hebrides evidence seems to exist that changes of this nature actually took place. I am not inclined to found much on the apparently fresh-water character of the bituminous shales of Eigg ;—the embedded fossils are all too obscure to be admitted in evidence : but there can exist no doubt, that fresh-water, or at least estuary formations, do occur among the marine Oolites of the Hebrides. Sir R. Murchison, one of the most cautious, as he is certainly one of the most distinguished, of living geologists, found in a northern district of Skye, in 1826, a deposit containing Cyclas, Paludina, Neritina,—all shells of unequivocally fresh-water origin,—which must have been formed, he concludes, in either a lake or estuary. What had been sea at one period had been estuary or lake at another. In every case, however, in which these intercalated deposits are restricted to single strata of no great thickness, it is perhaps safer to refer their formation to the agency of temporary land-floods, than to that of violent changes of level,—now elevating and now depressing the surface. There occur, for instance, among the marine Oolites of Brora, —the discovery of Mr Robertson of Inverugie,—two strata containing fresh-water fossils in abundance ; but the one stratum is little more than an inch in thickness,—the other little more than a foot ; and it seems considerably more probable, that such deposits should have owed their existence to extraordinary land-floods, like those which in 1829 devastated the province of Moray, and covered over whole miles of marine beach with the spoils of land and river, than that a sea-bottom should have been elevated, for their production, into a fresh-

---

Murchison: recorded in Murchison (1828); **Robertson**: Alexander Robertson F. G. S. (1816–1854) of Inverugie, Morayshire, an important geologist and collector (Andrews 1982) water lake, and then let down into a sea-bottom again. We find it recorded in the " Shepherd's Calendar," that after the thaw which followed the great snow-storm of 1794, there were found on a part of the sands of the Solway Frith known as the Beds of Esk, where the tide disgorges much of what is thrown into it by the rivers, " one thousand eight hundred and forty sheep, nine black cattle, three horses, two men, one woman, forty-five dogs, and one hundred and eighty hares, besides a number of meaner animals." A similar storm in an earlier time, with a soft sea-bottom prepared to receive and retain its spoils, would have formed a fresh-water stratum intercalated in a marine deposit.

Rounding the promontory, we lose sight of the Bay of Laig, and find the narrow front of the island that now presents itself exhibiting the appearance of a huge bastion. The green talus slopes upwards, as its basement, for full three hundred feet ; and a noble wall of perpendicular rock, that towers over and beyond for at least four hundred feet more, forms the rampart. Save towards the sea, the view is of but limited extent : we see it restricted, on the landward side, to the bold face of the bastion ; and in a narrow and broken dell that runs nearly parallel to the shore for a few hundred yards between the top of the talus and the base of the rampart,—a true covered way,—we see but the rampart alone. But the dizzy front of black basalt, dark as night, save where a broad belt of light-coloured sandstone traverses it in an angular direction, like a white sash thrown across a funeral robe,—the fantastic peaks and turrets in which the rock terminates atop, —the masses of broken ruins, roughened with moss and lichen, that have fallen from above, and lie scattered at its base,— the extreme loneliness of the place, for we have left behind us every trace of the human family,—and the expanse of solitary sea which it commands,—all conspire to render the scene a profoundly imposing one. It is one of those scenes

---

covered way: an earthen fortification of the time often had such a trench set into, or at the back of, the glacis (sloping outer rampart) surrounding it, providing cover from enemy fire. The path is indeed screened from the sea on one side, and overhung by the 'inner rampart' of Beinn Bhuidhe on the other side in which man feels that he is little, and that nature is great. There is no precipice in the island in which the puffin so delights to build as among the dark pinnacles overhead, or around which the silence is so frequently broken by the harsh scream of the eagle. The sun had got far adown the sky ere we had reached the covered way at the base of the rock. All lay dark below ; and the red light atop, half-absorbed by the dingy hues of the stone, shone with a gleam so faint and melancholy, that it served but to deepen the effect of the shadows.

The puffin, a comparatively rare bird in the inner Hebrides, builds, I was told, in great numbers in the continuous line of precipice which, after sweeping for a full mile round the Bay of Laig, forms the pinnacled rampart here, and then, turning another angle of the island, runs on parallel to the coast for about six miles more. In former times the puffin furnished the islanders, as in St Kilda, with a staple article of food, in those hungry months of summer in which the stores of the old crop had begun to fail, and the new crop had not yet ripened ; and the people of Eigg, taught by their necessities, were bold cragsmen. But men do not peril life and limb for the mere sake of a meal, save when they cannot help it ; and the introduction of the potatoe has done much to put out the practice of climbing for the bird, except among a few young lads, who find excitement enough in the work to pursue it for its own sake, as an amusement. I found among the islanders what was said to be a piece of the natural history of the puffin, sufficiently apocryphal to remind one of the famous passage in the history of the barnacle, which traced the lineage of the bird to one of the pedunculated cirripedes, and the lineage of the cirripede to a log of wood. The puffin feeds its young, say the islanders, on an oily scum of the sea, which renders it such an unwieldy mass of fat, that about the time when it should be beginning to fly, it becomes unable to

---

puffin: in its old sense of the bird now called the Manx Shearwater *Puffinus puffinus*, not in its modern sense of the colourfully beaked auk *Fratercula arctica*. Shearwaters were once eaten on Eigg (Dressler 1998) and still nest there; **pedunculated cirripedes**: goose barnacles, once thought to arise from floating logs on which they live, and (because of their feathery legs) to give rise to barnacle geese get out of its hole. The parent bird, not in the least puzzled, however, treats the case medicinally, and,—like mothers of another two-legged genus, who, when their daughters get over-stout, put them through a course of reducing acids to bring them down,—feeds it on sorrel-leaves for several days together, till, like a boxer under training, it gets thinned to the proper weight, and becomes able not only to get out of its cell, but also to employ its wings.

We pass through the hollow, and, reaching the farther edge of the bastion, towards the east, see a new range of prospect opening before us. There is first a long unbroken wall of precipice,—a continuation of the tall rampart overhead,—relieved along its irregular upper line by the blue sky. We mark the talus widening at its base, and expanding, as on the shores of the Bay of Laig, into an irregular grassy platform, that, sinking midway into a ditch-like hollow, rises again towards the sea, and presents to the waves a perpendicular precipice of red stone. The sinking sun shone brightly this evening; and the warm hues of the precipice, which bears the name of *Ru-Stoir*,—the Red Head,—strikingly contrasted with the pale and dark tints of the alternating basalts and sandstones in the taller cliff behind. The ditch-like hollow, which seems to indicate the line of a fault, cuts off this red headland from all the other rocks of the island, from which it appears to differ as considerably in texture as in hue. It consists mainly of thick beds of a pale red stone, which M'Culloch regarded as a trap, and which, intercalated with here and there a thin band of shale, and presenting not a few of the mineralogical appearances of what geologists of the school of the late Mr Cunningham term Primary Old Red Sandstone, in some cases has been laid down as a deposit of Old Red proper, abutting in the line of a fault on the neighbouring Oolites and basalts. In the geological map which I carried with me,—not one of high authority, however,—I

Ru-Stoir: see Additional Notes; **Mr Cunningham**: Robert James Hay Cunningham (1815-1842), who did field and survey work in different parts of Scotland (Waterston 1959; Livingstone 2003) – see Introduction for discussion of Miller's attitude to his work; **geological map**: see Additional Notes found it actually coloured as a patch of this ancient system. The Old Red Sandstone is largely developed in the neighbouring island of Rum, in the line of which the *Ru-Stoir* seems to have a more direct bearing than any of the other deposits of Eigg; and yet the conclusion regarding this red headland merely adds one proof more to the many furnished already, of the inadequacy of mineralogical testimony, when taken in evidence regarding the eras of the geologist. The hard red beds of *Ru-Stoir* belong, as I was fortunate enough this evening to ascertain, not to the ages of the Coccosteus and Pterichthys, but to the far later ages of the Plesiosaurus and the fossil crocodile. I found them associated with more reptilian remains, of a character more unequivocal, than have been yet exhibited by any other deposit in Scotland.

What first strikes the eye, in approaching the *Ru-Stoir* from the west, is the columnar character of the stone. The precipices rise immediately over the sea, in rude colonnades of from thirty to fifty feet in height ; single pillars, that have fallen from their places in the line, and exhibit a tenacity rare among the trap-rocks,—for they occur in unbroken lengths of from ten to twelve feet,—lie scattered below ; and in several places where the waves have joined issue with the precipices in the line on which the base of the columns rest, and swept away the supporting foundation, the colonnades open into roomy caverns, that resound to the dash of the sea. Wherever the spray lashes, the pale red hue of the stone prevails, and the angles of the polygonal shafts are rounded ; while higher up all is sharp-edged, and the unweathered surface is covered by a gray coat of lichens. The tenacity of the prostrate columns first drew my attention. The builder scant of materials would have experienced no difficulty in finding among them sufficient lintels for apertures from eight to twelve feet in width. I was next struck with the pecu-

---

inadequacy of mineralogical testimony: rocks of the same type or composition are not necessarily of the same age. In fact the red headland itself (but not the adjacent sedimentary rock, including the reptile bed) is actually a sill of volcanic rock of Tertiary age intruded into Jurassic – Miller's 'Oolitic' – sediments in such a way that it seems layered with them (Hudson and Allwright 2003) liar composition of the stone : it much rather resembles an altered sandstone, in at least the weathered specimens, than a trap, and yet there seemed nothing to indicate that it was an *Old Red* Sandstone.   Its columnar structure bore evidence to the action of great heat ; and its pale red colour was exactly that which the Oolitic sandstones of the island, with their slight ochreous tinge, would assume in a common fire.   And so I set myself to look for fossils.   In the columnar stone itself I expected none, as none occur in vast beds of the unaltered sandstones, out of some one of which I supposed it might possibly have been formed ; and none I found : but in a rolled block of altered shale of a much deeper red than the general mass, and much more resembling Old Red Sandstone, I succeeded in detecting several shells, identical with those of the deposit of blue clay described in a former chapter.   There occurred in it the small univalve resembling a Trochus, together with the oblong bivalve, somewhat like a Tellina ; and, spread thickly throughout the block, lay fragments of coprolitic matter, and the scales and teeth of fishes. Night was coming on, and the tide had risen on the beach ; but I hammered lustily, and laid open in the dark red shale a vertebral joint, a rib, and a parallelogramical fragment of solid bone, none of which could have belonged to any fish.   It was an interesting moment for the curtain to drop over the promontory of *Ru-Stoir :* I had thus already found in connection with it well nigh as many reptilian remains as had been found in all Scotland before,—for there could exist no doubt that the bones I laid open were such ; and still more interesting discoveries promised to await the coming morning and a less hasty survey.   We found a hospitable meal awaiting us at a picturesque old two-storey house, with, what is rare in the island, a clump of trees beside it, which rises on the northern angle of the Oolitic meniscus ; and after our day's hard work in the fresh sea-air, we did ample justice to the viands. Dark night had long set in ere we reached our vessel.

Next day was Saturday; and it behoved my friend the minister,—as scrupulously careful in his pulpit preparations for the islanders of Eigg as if his congregation were an Edinburgh one,—to remain on board, and study his discourse for the morrow. I found, however, no unmeet companion for my excursion in his trusty mate John Stewart. John had not very much English, and I had no Gaelic; but we contrived to understand one another wonderfully well; and ere evening I had taught him to be quite as expert in hunting dead crocodiles as myself. We reached the *Ru-Stoir*, and set hard to work with hammer and chisel. The fragments of red shale were strewed thickly along the shore for at least three quarters of a mile;—wherever the red columnar rock appeared, there lay the shale, in water-worn blocks, more or less indurated; but the beach was covered over with shingle and detached masses of rock, and we could nowhere find it *in situ*. A winter storm powerful enough to wash the beach bare might do much to assist the explorer. There is a piece of shore on the eastern coast of Scotland, on which for years together I used to pick up nodular masses of lime containing fish of the Old Red Sandstone; but nowhere in the neighbourhood could I find the ichthyolite bed in which they had originally formed. The storm of a single night swept the beach; and in the morning the ichthyolites lay revealed *in situ* under a stratum of shingle which I had a hundred times examined, but which, though scarce a foot in thickness, had concealed from me the ichthyolite bed for five twelvemonths together!

Wherever the altered shale of *Ru-Stoir* has been thrown high on the beach, and exposed to the influences of the weather, we find it fretted over with minute organisms, mostly the scales, plates, bones, and teeth of fishes. The organisms,

---

a piece of shore: location uncertain, but not Miller's well-known Cromarty site. Presumably one of the Black Isle or other Easter Ross fish sites as is frequently the case, seem indestructible, while the hard matrix in which they are embedded has weathered from around them. Some of the scales present the rhomboidal outline, and closely resemble those of the *Lepidotus Minor* of the Weald ; others approximate in shape to an isosceles triangle. The teeth are of various forms : some of them, evidently palatal, are mere blunted protuberances glittering with enamel,—some of them present the usual slim, thorn-like type common in the teeth of the existing fish of our coasts, —some again are squat and angular, and rest on rectilinear bases, prolonged considerably on each side of the body of the tooth, like the rim of a hat or the flat head of a scupper nail. Of the occipital plates, some present a smooth enamelled surface, while some are thickly tuberculated,—each tubercle bearing a minute depression in its apex, like a crater on the summit of a rounded hill. We find reptilian bones in abundance,—a thing new to Scotch geology,—and in a state of keeping peculiarly fine. They not a little puzzled John Stewart : he could not resist the evidence of his senses : they were bones, he said, real bones,—there could be no doubt of that : *there* were the joints of a back-bone, with the hole the brain-marrow had passed through ; and *there* were shank-bones and ribs, and fishes' teeth ; but how, he wondered, had they all got into the very heart of the hard red stones ? He had seen what was called wood, he said, dug out of the side of the Scuir, without being quite certain whether it was wood or no ; but there could be no uncertainty here. I laid open numerous vertebræ of various forms,—some with long spinous processes rising over the body or *centrum* of the bone,— which I found in every instance, unlike that of the Ichthyosaurus, only moderately concave on the articulating faces ; in others the spinous process seemed altogether wanting. Only two of the number bore any mark of the suture which unites, in most reptiles, the annular process to the centrum :

---

annular process: presumably the 'neural arch' over the spinal cord and forming the hole through which it passes in the others both centrum and process seemed anchylosed, as in quadrupeds, into one bone ; and there remained no scar to show that the suture had ever existed.   In some specimens the ribs seem to have been articulated to the sides of the centrum ; in others there is a transverse process, but no marks of articulation.   Some of the vertebræ are evidently dorsal, some cervical, one apparently caudal ; and almost all agree in showing in front two little eyelets, to which the great descending artery seems to have sent out blood-vessels in pairs. The more entire ribs I was lucky enough to disinter have, as in those of crocodileans, double heads ; and a part of a fibula, about four inches in length, seems also to belong to this ancient family.   A large proportion of the other bones are evidently Plesiosaurian.   I found the head of the flat humerus so characteristic of the extinct order to which the Plesiosaurus has been assigned, and two digital bones of the paddle, that, from their comparatively slender and slightly curved form, so unlike the digitals of its cogener the Ichthyosaurus, could have belonged evidently to no other reptile.   I observed, too, in the slightly-curved articulations of not a few of the vertebræ, the gentle convexity in the concave centre, which, if not peculiar to the Plesiosaurus, is at least held to distinguish it from most of its contemporaries.   Among the various nondescript organisms of the shale, I laid open a smooth angular bone, hollowed something like a grocer's scoop ; a three-pronged caltrop-looking bone, that seems to have formed part of a pelvic arch ; another angular bone, much massier than the first, regarding the probable position of which I could not form a conjecture, but which some of my geological friends deem cerebral ; an extremely dense bone, imperfect at each end, which presents the appearance of a cylinder slightly flattened ; and various curious fragments, which, with what our Scotch museums have not yet acquired,—entire reptilian fossils for the purposes of comparison,—might, I doubt not, be

---

dorsal, cervical, and caudal: referring here to body, neck and tail vertebrae respectively; in front two little eyelets: the two foramina or openings characteristic of the *bottom* side of each vertebra of a plesiosaur as it was oriented in the living animal; cerebral: head bone. Most of the bones mentioned here would have belonged to plesiosaurs easily assigned to their proper places. It was in vain that, leaving John to collect the scattered pieces of shale in which the bones occurred, I set myself again and again to discover the bed from which they had been detached. The tide had fallen; and a range of skerries lay temptingly off, scarce a hundred yards from the water's edge: the shale-beds might be among them, with Plesiosauri and crocodiles stretching entire; and fain would I have swam off to them, as I had done oftener than once elsewhere, with my hammer in my teeth, and with shirt and drawers in my hat; but a tall brown forest of kelp and tangle, in which even a seal might drown, rose thick and perilous round both shore and skerries; a slight swell was felting the long fronds together; and I deemed it better, on the whole, that the discoveries I had already made should be recorded, than that they should be lost to geology, mayhap for a whole age, in the attempt to extend them.

The water, beautifully transparent, permitted the eye to penetrate into its green depths for many fathoms around, though every object presented, through the agitated surface, an uncertain and fluctuating outline. I could see, however, the pink-coloured urchin warping himself up, by his many cables, along the steep rock-sides; the green crab stalking along the gravelly bottom; a scull of small rock-cod darting hither and thither among the tangle-roots; and a few large medusæ slowly flapping their continuous fins of gelatine in the opener spaces, a few inches under the surface. Many curious families had their representatives within the patch of sea which the eye commanded; but the strange creatures that had once inhabited it by thousands, and whose bones still lay sepulchred on its shores, had none. How strange, that the identical sea heaving around stack and skerry in this remote corner of the Hebrides should have once been thronged by reptile shapes more strange than poet ever imagined,—dragons, gorgons, and chimeras! Perhaps of all the extinct

age: century – despite Miller's survival, in fact, the deposit would not be seriously restudied until the 1960s (Hudson 2000, 2003); **cables:** *ie* the long tube feet of sea urchins reptiles, the Plesiosaurus was the most extraordinary.   An English geologist has described it, grotesquely enough, and yet most happily, as a snake *threaded* through a tortoise.   And here, on this very spot, must these monstrous dragons have disported and fed ; here must they have raised their little reptile heads and long swan-like necks over the surface, to watch an antagonist or select a victim ; here must they have warred and wedded, and pursued all the various instincts of their unknown natures.   A strange story, surely, considering it is a true one !   I may mention in the passing, that some of the fragments of the shale in which the remains are embedded have been baked by the intense heat into an exceedingly hard, dark-coloured stone, somewhat resembling basalt.   I must add further, that I by no means determine the rock with which we find it associated to be in reality an altered sandstone.   Such is the appearance which it presents where weathered ; but its general aspect is that of a porphyritic trap. Be it what it may, the fact is not at all affected, that the shores, wherever it occurs on this tract of insular coast, are strewed with reptilian remains of the Oolite.

The day passed pleasantly in the work of exploration and discovery ; the sun had already declined far in the west ; and, bearing with us our better fossils, we set out, on our return, by the opposite route to that along the Bay of Laig, which we had now thrice walked over.   The grassy talus so often mentioned continues to run on the eastern side of the island for about six miles, between the sea and the inaccessible rampart of precipice behind.   It varies in breadth from about two to four hundred yards ; the rampart rises over it from three to five hundred feet ; and a noble expanse of sea, closed in the distance by a still nobler curtain of blue hills, spreads away from its base : and it was along this grassy talus that our homeward road lay.   Let the Edinburgh reader imagine the fine walk under Salisbury Crags lengthened some twenty

---

English geologist: see Additional Notes; **baked**: the Reptile Bed's deep red colour in fact comes from the oxidation of the iron mineral siderite – but genuinely baked shale does occur on the beach here (J. D. Hudson, *pers. comm.* 2002); **walk**: at the foot of the rocky **Salisbury Crags**, part of the Arthur's Seat volcanic complex in Edinburgh

times,—the line of precipices above heightened some five or
six times,—the gravelly slope at the base not much increased
in altitude, but developed transversely into a green undulating belt of hilly pasture, with here and there a sunny slope
level enough for the plough, and here and there a rough wilderness of detached crags and broken banks ; let him further
imagine the sea sweeping around the base of this talus, with
the nearest opposite land—bold, bare, and undulating atop—
some six or eight miles distant; and he will have no very
inadequate idea of the peculiar and striking scenery through
which, this evening, our homeward route lay.   I have scarce
ever walked over a more solitary tract.   The sea shuts it in
on the one hand, and the rampart of rocks on the other ;
there occurs along its entire length no other human dwelling
than a lonely summer shieling ; for full one-half the way
we saw no trace of man ; and the wildness of the few cattle
which we occasionally startled in the hollows showed us that
man was no very frequent visitor among them.   About half
an hour before sunset we reached the midway shieling.

Rarely have I seen a more interesting spot, or one that,
from its utter loneliness, so impressed the imagination.   The
shieling, a rude low-roofed erection of turf and stone, with a
door in the centre some five feet in height or so, but with no
window, rose on the grassy slope immediately in front of the
vast continuous rampart.   A slim pillar of smoke ascends
from the roof, in the calm, faint and blue within the shadow
of the precipice, but it caught the sun-light in its ascent, and
blushed, ere it melted into the ether, a ruddy brown.   A
streamlet came pouring from above in a long white thread,
that maintained its continuity unbroken for at least two-
thirds of the way ; and then, untwisting into a shower of
detached drops, that pattered loud and vehemently in a rocky
recess, it again gathered itself up into a lively little stream,
and, sweeping past the shieling, expanded in front into a cir-

---

shieling: temporary summer habitation for transhumance (Scots) – see Introduction.
This shieling was at Rubha nan Tri Clach (Hudson 2000, 2003; Hudson and Allwright
2003)

cular pond, at which a few milch cows were leisurely slaking
their thirst. The whole grassy talus, with a strip, mayhap
a hundred yards wide, of deep green sea, lay within the shadow of the tall rampart ; but the red light fell, for many a
mile beyond, on the glassy surface ; and the distant Cuchullin Hills, so dark at other times, had all their prominent
slopes and jutting precipices tipped with bronze ; while here
and there a mist streak, converted into bright flame, stretched
along their peaks, or rested on their sides. Save the lonely
shieling, not a human dwelling was in sight. An island girl
of eighteen, more than merely good-looking, though much
embrowned by the sun, had come to the door to see who the
unwonted visitors might be, and recognised in John Stewart
an old acquaintance. John informed her in her own language that I was Mr Swanson's sworn friend, and not a *Moderate*, but one of their own people, and that I had fasted all
day, and had come for a drink of milk. The name of her
minister proved a strongly recommendatory one : I have not
yet seen the true Celtic interjection of welcome,—the kindly
" O o o,"—attempted on paper ; but I had a very agreeable
specimen of it on this occasion, *viva voce*. And as she set
herself to prepare for us a rich bowl of mingled milk and
cream, John and I entered the shieling. There was a turf
fire at the one end, at which there sat two little girls, engaged in keeping up the blaze under a large pot, but sadly
diverted from their work by our entrance ; while the other
end was occupied by a bed of dry straw, spread on the floor
from wall to wall, and fenced off at the foot by a line of
stones. The middle space was occupied by the utensils and
produce of the dairy,—flat wooden vessels of milk, a butter-
churn, and a tub half-filled with curd ; while a few cheeses,
soft from the press, lay on a shelf above. The little girls
were but occasional visitors, who had come, out of a juvenile
frolic, to pass the night in the place ; but I was informed by

---

Celtic ... welcome: 'O' is 'Alas' in Gaelic, so Miller was evidently mistaken! Probably
the girl was simply expressing wordless cries of surprise, hesitancy and shyness at the
unexpected visit of the great man

John that the shieling had two other inmates, young women, like the one so hospitably engaged in our behalf, who were out at the milking, and that they lived here all alone for several months every year, when the pasturage was at its best, employed in making butter and cheese for their master, worthy Mr M'Donald of Keill.   They must often feel lonely when night has closed darkly over mountain and sea, or in those dreary days of mist and rain so common in the Hebrides, when nought may be seen save the few shapeless crags that stud the nearer hillocks around them, and nought heard save the moaning of the wind in the precipices above, or the measured dash of the wave on the wild beach below.   And yet they would do ill to exchange their solitary life and rude shieling for the village dwellings and gregarious habits of the females who ply their rural labours in bands among the rich fields of the Lowlands, or for the unwholesome back-room and weary task-work of the city seamstress.   The sun-light was fading from the higher hill-tops of Skye and Glenelg, as we bade farewell to the lonely shieling and the hospitable island girl.

The evening deepened as we hurried southwards along the scarce visible pathway, or paused for a few seconds to examine some shattered block, bulky as a Highland cottage, that had fallen from the precipice above.   Now that the whole landscape lay equally in shadow, one of the more picturesque peculiarities of the continuous rampart came out more strongly as a feature of the scene than when a strip of shade rested along the face of the rock, imparting to it a retiring character, and all was sunshine beyond.   A thick bed of white sandstone, as continuous as the rampart itself, runs nearly horizontally about midway in the precipice for mile after mile, and, standing out in strong contrast with the dark-coloured trap above and below, reminds one of a belt of white hewn work in a basalt house-front, or rather——for there occurs above

Keill: Kildonnan Farm

a second continuous strip, of an olive hue, the colour assumed, on weathering, by a bed of amygdaloid—of a piece of dingy old-fashioned furniture, inlaid with one stringed belt of bleach'ed holly, and another of faded green-wood.   At some of the more accessible points I climbed to the line of white belting, and found it to consist of the same soft quartzy sandstone that in the Bay of Laig furnishes the musical sand.   Lower down there occur, alternating with the trap, beds of shale and of blue clay, but they are lost mostly in the talus.   Ill adapted to resist the frosts and rains of winter, their exposed edges have mouldered into a loose soil, now thickly covered over with herbage ; and, but for the circumstance that we occasionally find them laid bare by a water-course, we would scarce be aware of their existence at all.   The shale exhibits every-where, as on the opposite side of the *Ru-Stoir*, faint impres-sions of a minute shell resembling a Cyclas, and ill-preserved fragments of fish-scales.   The blue clay I found at one spot where the pathway had cut deep into the hill-side, richly charged with bivalves of the species I had seen so abundant in the resembling clay of the Bay of Laig ; but the closing twilight prevented me from ascertaining whether it also con-tained the characteristic univalves of the deposit, and whether its shells,—for they seem identical with those of the altered shales of the *Ru-Stoir*,—might not be associated, like these, with reptilian remains.   Night fell fast, and the streaks of mist that had mottled the hills at sunset began to spread gray over the heavens in a continuous curtain ; but there was light enough left to show me that the trap became more co-lumnar as we neared our journey's end.   One especial jutting in the rock presented in the gloom the appearance of an an-cient portico, with pediment and cornice, such as the travel-ler sees on the hill-sides of Petræa in front of some old tomb ; but it may possibly appear less architectural by day.   At length, passing from under the long line of rampart, just as the stars that had begun to twinkle over it were disappearing, one after one, in the thickening vapour, we reached the little bay of Kildonan, and found the boat waiting us on the beach.   My friend the minister, as I entered the cabin, gathered up his notes from the table, and gave orders for the tea-kettle ; and I spread out before him—a happy man—an array of fossils new to Scotch Geology.   No one not an enthusiastic geologist or a zealous Roman Catholic can really know how vast an amount of interest may attach to a few old bones.   Has the reader ever heard how fossil relics once saved the dwelling of a monk, in a time of great general calamity, when all his other relics proved of no avail whatever ?

Thomas Campbell, when asked for a toast in a society of authors, gave the memory of Napoleon Bonaparte ; significantly adding, " he once hung a bookseller."   On a nearly similar principle I would be disposed to propose among geologists a grateful bumper in honour of the revolutionary army that besieged Maestricht.   That city, some seventy-five or eighty years ago, had its zealous naturalist in the person of M. Hoffmann, a diligent excavator in the quarries of St Peter's mountain, long celebrated for its extraordinary fossils. Geology, as a science, had no existence at the time ; but Hoffmann was doing, in a quiet way, all he could to give it a beginning ;—he was transferring from the rock to his cabinet, shells, and corals, and crustacea, and the teeth and scales of fishes, with now and then the vertebræ, and now and then the limb-bone, of a reptile.   And as he honestly remunerated all the workmen he employed, and did no manner of harm to any one, no one heeded him.   On one eventful morning, however, his friends the quarriers laid bare a most extraordinary fossil,—the occipital plates of an enormous saurian, with jaws four and a half feet long, bristling over with teeth, like *chevaux de frise ;* and after Hoffmann, who got the block in which it lay embedded, cut out entire, and transferred to his

---

Campbell: see note for p. 10; **enormous saurian**: a classic specimen of *Mosasaurus*, a large carnivorous marine lizard house, had spent week after week in painfully relieving it from the mass, all Maestricht began to speak of it as something really wonderful. There is a cathedral on St Peter's mountain,—the mountain itself is church-land ; and the lazy canon, awakened by the general talk, laid claim to poor Hoffmann's wonderful fossil as *his* property. He was lord of the manor, he said, and the mountain and all that it contained belonged to him. Hoffmann defended his fossil as he best could in an expensive lawsuit ; but the judges found the law clean against him ; the huge reptile head was declared to be " treasure trove" escheat to the lord of the manor ; and Hoffmann, half broken-hearted, with but his labour and the lawyer's bills for his pains, saw it transferred by rude hands from its place in his museum, to the residence of the grasping churchman. The huge fossil head experienced the fate of Dr Chalmers' two hundred churches. Hoffmann was a philosopher, however, and he continued to observe and collect as before ; but he never found such another fossil ; and at length, in the midst of his ingenious labours, the vital energies failed within him, and he broke down and died. The useless canon lived on. The French Revolution broke out ; the republican army invested Maestricht ; the batteries were opened ; and shot and shell fell thick on the devoted city. But in one especial quarter there alighted neither shot nor shell. All was safe around the canon's house. Ordinary relics would have availed him nothing in the circumstances, —no, not "the three kings of Cologne," had he possessed the three kings entire, or the jaw-bones of the " eleven thousand virgins ;" but there was virtue in the jaw-bones of the Mosasaurus, and safety in their neighbourhood. The French *savans*, like all the other *savans* of Europe, had heard of Hoffmann's fossil, and the French artillery had been directed to play wide of the place where it lay. Maestricht surrendered ; the fossil was found secreted in a vault, and sent away

---

Dr Chalmers' two hundred churches: Chalmers and the Evangelicals had made great efforts to build more than two hundred churches, which had to be left at the Disruption – see Introduction; three kings ... eleven thousand virgins: Cologne Cathedral held the supposed relics of the Three Kings from the East who visited the infant Jesus, and in the same city St Ursula's Church claimed the remains of eleven thousand martyred virgins to the *Jardin des Plantes* at Paris, maugre the canon, to delight there the heart of Cuvier ; and the French, generously addressing themselves to the heirs of Hoffmann as its legitimate owners, made over to them a considerable sum of money as its price. They reversed the finding of the Maestricht judges ; and all save the monks of St Peter's have acquiesced in the justice of the decision.

Jardin des Plantes: literally the Paris botanic gardens, the precursor of, amongst other things, what is now the *Muséum national d'Histoire naturelle* where the *Mosasaurus* still rests; **Cuvier**: Georges Cuvier (1769-1832), the eminent palaeontologist and zoologist, and a key proponent of the interpretation of the fossil record as showing successive catastrophic mass extinctions (cf. p. 39)

CHAPTER VI.

I RECKON among my readers a class of non-geologists, who think my geological chapters would be less dull if I left out the geology; and another class of semi-geologists, who say there was decidedly too much geology in my last. With the present chapter, as there threatens. to be an utter lack of science in the earlier half of it, and very little, if any, in the latter half, I trust both classes may be in some degree satis-fied. It will bear reference to but the existing system of things,—assuredly not the last of the consecutive creations, —and to a species of animal that, save in the celebrated Guadaloupe specimens, has not yet been found locked up in stone. There have been much of violence and suffering in the old immature stages of being,—much, from the era of the Holoptychius, with its sharp murderous teeth and strong armour of bone, down to that of the cannibal Ichthyosaurus, that bears the broken remains of its own kind in its bowels, —much, again, from the times of the crocodile of the Oolite, down to the times of the fossil hyena and gigantic shark of the Tertiary. Nor, I fear, have matters greatly improved in that latest-born creation in the series, that recognises as its delegated lord the first tenant of earth accountable to his Maker. But there is a better and a last creation coming, in which man shall re-appear, not to oppress and devour his

---

creations: see Additional Note for p. 39; a species: humans; Guadaloupe specimens: see Additional Notes; first tenant accountable: humanity

fellow-men, and in which there shall be no such wrongs perpetrated as it is my present purpose to record,—" new heavens and a new earth, wherein dwelleth righteousness." Well
sung the Ayrshire ploughman, when musing on the great
truth that the present scene of being " is surely not the last,"
—a truth corroborated since his day by the analogies of a
new science,—

> " The poor, oppressed, honest man,
>   Had never sure been born,
> Had not there been some recompense
>   To comfort those that mourn."

It was Sabbath, but the morning rose like a hypochondriac
wrapped up in his night-clothes,—gray in fog, and sad with
rain.   The higher grounds of the island lay hid in clouds, far
below the level of the central hollow ; and our whole prospect from the deck was limited to the nearer slopes, dank,
brown, and uninhabited, and to the rough black crags that
frown like sentinels over the beach.   Now the rime thickened as the rain pattered more loudly on the deck ; and even
the nearer stacks and precipices showed as unsolid and spectral
in the cloud as moonlight shadows thrown on a ground of
vapour ; anon it cleared up for a few hundred yards, as the
shower lightened ; and then there came in view, partially at
least, two objects that spoke of man,—a deserted boat-harbour, formed of loosely piled stone, at the upper extremity of
a sandy bay ; and a roofless dwelling beside it, with two ruinous gables rising over the broken walls.   The entire scene
suggested the idea of a land with which man had done for
ever ;—the vapour-enveloped rocks,—the waste of ebb-un-
covered sand,—the deserted harbour,—the ruinous house,—
the melancholy rain-fretted tides eddying along the strip of
brown tangle in the foreground,—and, dim over all, the thick,
slant lines of the beating shower !—I know not that of themselves they would have furnished materials enough for a finish-

---

'new heavens …': after the Day of Judgement, after 'the earth … and the works that are
therein shall be burned up', Bible, 2 Peter 3:13; **Ayrshire ploughman**: Robert Burns;
'**The poor** …': from Burns' 'Man is made to mourn: a Dirge'

ed picture in the style of Hogarth's "End of all Things;" but right sure am I that in the hands of Bewick they would have been grouped into a tasteful and poetic vignette. We set out for church a little after eleven,—the minister encased in his ample-skirted storm-jacket of oiled canvass, and protected atop by a genuine *sou-wester*, of which the broad posterior rim sloped half a yard down his back ; and I closely wrapped up in my gray maud, which proved, however, a rather indifferent protection against the penetrating powers of a true Hebridean drizzle. The building in which the congregation meets is a low dingy cottage of turf and stone, situated nearly opposite to the manse windows. It had been built by my friend, previous to the Disruption, at his own expense, for a Gaelic school, and it now serves as a place of worship for the people.

We found the congregation already gathered, and that the very bad morning had failed to lessen their numbers. There were a few of the male parishioners keeping watch at the door, looking wistfully out through the fog and rain for their minister ; and at his approach nearly twenty more came issuing from the place,—like carder bees from their nest of dried grass and moss,—to gather round him, and shake him by the hand. The islanders of Eigg are an active, middle-sized race, with well-developed heads, acute intellects, and singularly warm feelings. And on this occasion at least there could be no possibility of mistake respecting the feelings with which they regarded their minister. Rarely have I seen human countenances so eloquently vocal with veneration and love. The gospel message, which my friend had been the first effectually to bring home to their hearts,—the palpable fact of his sacrifice for the sake of the high principles which he has taught,—his own kindly disposition,—the many services which he has rendered them, for not only has he been the minister, but also the sole medical man, of the Small Isles,

---

Hogarth's 'End of All Things': presumably the engraving by William Hogarth (1697-1764), 'Tail Piece – The end of everything ...', a scene of rack and ruin; **Bewick**: Thomas Bewick (1753-1828), the woodcut artist

and the benefit of his practice they have enjoyed, in every
instance, without fee or reward,—his new life of hardship
and danger, maintained for their sakes amid sinking health
and great privation,—their frequent fears for his safety when
stormy nights close over the sea,—and they have seen his
little vessel driven from her anchorage, just as the evening
has fallen,—all these are circumstances that have concurred
in giving him a strong hold on their affections.

The rude turf-building we found full from end to end, and
all a-steam with a particularly wet congregation, some of
whom, neither very robust nor young, had travelled in the
soaking drizzle from the farther extremities of the island.
And, judging from the serious attention with which they listened to the discourse, they must have deemed it full value
for all it cost them.   I have never yet seen a congregation
more deeply impressed, or that seemed to follow the preacher
more intelligently ; and I was quite sure, though ignorant of
the language in which my friend addressed them, that he
preached to them neither heresy nor nonsense.   There was
as little of the reverence of externals in the place as can well
be imagined : an uneven earthen floor,—turf-walls on every
side, and a turf-roof above,—two little windows of four panes
a-piece, adown which the rain-drops were coursing thick and
fast,—a pulpit grotesquely rude, that had never employed
the bred carpenter,—and a few ranges of seats of undressed
deal,—such were the mere materialisms of this lowly church
of the people ; and yet here, notwithstanding, was the living
soul of a Christian community,—understandings convinced
of the truth of the gospel, and hearts softened and impressed
by its power.

My friend, at the conclusion of his discourse, gave a brief
digest of its contents in English, for the benefit of his one
Saxon auditor ; and I found, as I had anticipated, that what
had so moved the simple islanders was just the old wondrous

Saxon: here, Scots Lowlander – Miller himself, of course

story, which, though repeated and re-repeated times beyond
number, from the days of the apostles till now, continues to
be as full of novelty and interest as ever,—" God so loved the
world, that he gave his only begotten Son, that whosoever be-
lieveth on Him should not perish, but have everlasting life."
The great truths which had affected many of these poor people to tears were exactly those which, during the last eighteen
hundred years, have been active in effecting so many moral
revolutions in the world, and which must ultimately triumph
over all error and all oppression.   On this occasion, as on
many others, I had to regret my want of Gaelic.   It was my
misfortune to miss being born to this ancient language, by
barely a mile of ferry.   I first saw the light on the southern
shore of the Frith of Cromarty, where the strait is narrowest,
among an old established Lowland community, marked by all
the characteristics, physical and mental, of the Lowlanders of
the southern districts ; whereas, had I been born on the northern shore, I would have been brought up among a Celtic
tribe, and Gaelic would have been my earliest language.   Thus
distinct was the line between the two races preserved, even
after the commencement of the present century.

In returning to the Betsey during the mid-day interval in
the service, we passed the ruinous two-gabled house beside
the boat-harbour.   During the incumbency of my friend's
predecessor it had been the public-house of the island, and
the parish minister was by far its best customer.   He was in
the practice of sitting in one of its dingy little rooms, day
after day, imbibing whisky and peat-reek ; and his favourite
boon companion on these occasions was a Roman Catholic
tenant who lived on the opposite side of the island, and who,
when drinking with the minister, used regularly to fasten his
horse beside the door, till at length all the parish came to
know that when the horse was standing outside the minister
was drinking within.   In course of time, through the natural

'God so loved …': Bible, John 3:16; **predecessor**: Rev. Maclean – see Introduction

gravitation operative in such cases, the poor incumbent became utterly scandalous, and was libelled for drunkenness before the General Assembly ; but as the island of Eigg lies
remote from observation, evidence was difficult to procure ;
and, had not the infatuated man got senselessly drunk one
evening, when in Edinburgh on his trial, and staggered, of
all places in the world, into the General Assembly, he would
probably have died minister of Eigg.   As the event happened, however, the testimony thus unwittingly furnished in the
face of the Court that tried him was deemed conclusive ;—
he was summarily deposed from his office, and my friend succeeded him.   Presbyterianism without the animating life is
a poor shrunken thing : it never lies in state when it is dead ;
for it has no body of fine forms, or trapping of imposing cere-
monies, to give it bulk or adornment : without the vitality
of evangelism it is nothing ; and in this low and abject state
my friend found the Presbyterianism of Eigg.   His predecessor had done it only mischief ; nor had it been by any
means vigorous before.   Rum is one of the four islands of the
parish ; and all my readers must be familiar with Dr Johnson's celebrated account of the conversion to Protestantism
of the people of Rum.   " The inhabitants," says the Doctor,
in his " Journey to the Western Islands," " are fifty-eight
families, who continued Papists for some time after the laird
became a Protestant.   Their adherence to their old religion
was strengthened by the countenance of the laird's sister, a
zealous Romanist ; till one Sunday, as they were going to
mass under the conduct of their patroness, Maclean met them
on the way, gave one of them a blow on the head with a yellow stick,—I suppose a cane, for which the Earse had no
name,—and drove them to the kirk, from which they have
never departed.   Since the use of this method of conversion,
the inhabitants of Eigg and Canna who continue Papists call
the Protestantism of Rum the religion of the yellow stick."

Dr Johnson's: Samuel Johnson (1709-1784), author and critic, undertook the tour
immortalised in Johnson (1775), and in his companion James Boswell's *Journal of a Tour
to the Hebrides*. The quote is from Johnson (1775, p.115). Perhaps to his surprise, he
found the Hebrideans congenial and hospitable, and his account was notably sympathetic
(Fenyő 2000)

Now, such was the kind of Protestantism that, since the days of Dr Johnson, had also been introduced, I know not by what means, into Eigg. It had lived on the best possible terms with the Popery of the island ; the parish minister had soaked day after day in the public-house with a Roman Catholic boon companion ; and when a Papist man married a Protestant woman, the woman, as a matter of course, became Papist also ; whereas when it was the man who was a Protestant, and the woman a Papist, the woman remained what she had been. Roman Catholicism was quite content with terms, actual though not implied, of a kind so decidedly advantageous ; and the Roman Catholics used good-humouredly to urge on their neighbours the Protestants, that, as it was palpable they had no religion of any kind, they had better surely come over to them, and have some. In short, all was harmony between the two Churches. My friend laboured hard, as a good and honest man ought, to impart to Protestantism in his parish the animating life of the Reformation ; and, through the blessing of God, after years of anxious toil, he at length fully succeeded.

I had got wet, and the day continued bad ; and so, instead of returning to the evening sermon, which began at six, I remained alone aboard of the vessel. The rain ceased in little more than an hour after, and in somewhat more than two hours I got up on deck to see whether the congregation was not dispersing, and if it was not yet time to hang on the kettle for our evening tea. The unexpected apparition of some one aboard the Free Church yacht startled two ragged boys who were manœuvring a little boat a stonecast away, under the rocky shores of *Eilean Chaisteil*, and who, on catching a glimpse of me, flung themselves below the thwarts for concealment. An oar dropped into the water ; there was a hasty arm and half a head thrust over the gunwale to secure it ; and then the urchin to whom they belonged again disappeared. Meanwhile the boat drifted slowly away : first one little head would appear for a moment over the gunwale, then another, as if reconnoitring the enemy ; but I still kept my place on deck ; and at length, tired out, the ragged little crew took to their oars, and rowed into a shallow bay at the lower extremity of the glebe, with a cottage, in size and appearance much resembling an ant-hill, peeping out at its inner extremity among some stunted bushes. I had marked the place before, and had been struck with the peculiarity of the choice that could have fixed on it as a site for a dwelling : it is at once the most inconvenient and picturesque on this side the island. A semicircular line of columnar precipices, that somewhat resembles an amphitheatre turned outside in,—for the columns that overlook the area are quite as lofty as those which should form the amphitheatre's outer wall,—sweeps round a little bay, flat and sandy at half-tide, but bordered higher up by a dingy, scarce passable beach of columnar fragments that have toppled from above. Between the beach and the line of columns there is a bosky talus, more thickly covered with brushwood than is at all common in the Hebrides, and scarce more passable than the rough beach at its feet. And at the bottom of this talus, with its one gable buried in the steep ascent,—for there is scarce a foot-breadth of platform between the slope and the beach,—and with the other gable projected to the tide-line on rugged columnar masses, stands the cottage. The story of the inmate,—the father of the two ragged boys,—is such a one as Crabbe would have delighted to tell, and as he could have told better than any one else.

He had been, after a sort, a freebooter in his time, but born an age or two rather late ; and the law had proved over strong for him. On at least one occasion, perhaps oftener,—for his adventures are not all known in Eigg,—he had been in prison for sheep-stealing. He had the dangerous art of subsisting without the ostensible means, and came to be feared and

---

Crabbe: George Crabbe (1754–1832) of Suffolk, author of gritty realist narrative poems about what life was really like for village folk. Miller might have had in mind the poem about an outcast, 'Peter Grimes', which forms part of *The Borough*

avoided by his neighbours as a man who lived on them without asking their leave.   With neither character nor a settled
way of living, his wits, I am afraid, must have been often
whetted by his necessities : he stole lest he should starve. For
some time he had resided in the adjacent island of Muck ;
but, proving a bad tenant, he had been ejected by the agent
of the landlord, I believe a very worthy man, who gave him
half a boll of meal to get quietly rid of him, and pulled down
his house, when he had left the island, to prevent his return.
Betaking himself, with his boys, to a boat, he set out in quest
of some new lodgment.   He made his first attempt or two
on the mainland, where he strove to drive a trade in begging,
but he was always recognised as the convicted sheep-stealer,
and driven back to the shore.   At length, after a miserable
term of wandering, he landed in the winter season on Eigg,
where he had a grown-up son a miller ; and, erecting a wretched shed with some spars and the old sail of a boat placed slantways against the side of a rock, he squatted on the beach, determined, whether he lived or died, to find a home on the
island.   The islanders were no strangers to the character of
the poor forlorn creature, and kept aloof from him,——none of
them, however, so much as his own son ; and, for a time, my
friend the minister, aware that he had been the pest of every
community among which he had lived, stood aloof from him
too, in the hope that at length, wearied out, he might seek
for himself a lodgment elsewhere.   There came on, however,
a dreary night of sleet and rain, accompanied by a fierce storm
from the sea ; and intelligence reached the manse late in the
evening, that the wretched sheep-stealer had been seized by
sudden illness, and was dying on the beach.   There could be
no room for further hesitation in this case ; and my friend
the minister gave instant orders that the poor creature should
be carried to the manse.   The party, however, which he had
sent to remove him found the task impracticable.   The night

was pitch dark ; and the road, dangerous with precipices, and blocked up with rough masses of rock and stone, they found wholly impassable with so helpless a burden.   And so, administering some cordials to the poor hapless wretch, they had to leave him in the midst of the storm, with the old wet sail flapping about his ears, and the half-frozen rain pouring in upon him in torrents.   He must have passed a miserable night, but it could not have been a whit more miserable than that passed by the minister in the manse.   As the wild blast howled around his comfortable dwelling, and shook the casements as if some hand outside were assaying to open them, or as the rain pattered sharp and thick on the panes, and the measured roar of the surf rose high over every other sound, he could think of only the wretched creature exposed to the fury of a tempest so terrible, as perchance wrestling in his death agony in the darkness beside the breaking wave, or as already stiffening on the shore.   He was early astir next morning, and almost the first person he met was the poor sheep-stealer, looking more like a ghost than a living man. The miserable creature had mustered strength enough to crawl up from the beach.   My friend has often met better men with less pleasure.   He found a shelter for the poor outcast ; he tended him, prescribed for him, and, on his recovery, gave him leave to build for himself the hovel at the foot of the crags.   The islanders were aware they had got but an indifferent neighbour through the transaction, though none of them, with the exception of the poor creature's son, saw what else their minister could have done in the circumstances.   But the miller could sustain no apology for the arrangement that had given him his vagabond father as a neighbour ; and oftener than once the site of the rising hovel became a scene of noisy contention between parent and son. Some of the islanders informed me that they had seen the son engaged in pulling down the stones of the walls as fast as the father raised them up ; and, save for the interference of the minister, the hut, notwithstanding the permission he gave, would scarce have been built.

On the morning of Monday we unloosed from our moorings, and set out with a light variable breeze for Isle Ornsay, in Skye, where the wife and family of Mr Swanson resided, and from which he had now been absent for a full month. The island diminished, and assumed its tint of diluting blue, that waxed paler and paler hour after hour, as we left it slowly behind us ; and the Scuir, projected boldly from its steep hill-top, resembled a sharp hatchet-edge presented to the sky. " Nowhere," said my friend, " did I so thoroughly realize the Disruption of last year as at this spot. I had just taken my last leave of the manse ; Mrs Swanson had staid a day behind me in charge of a few remaining pieces of furniture, and I was bearing some of the rest, and my little boy Bill, scarce five years of age at the time, in the yacht with me to Skye. The little fellow had not much liked to part from his mother, and the previous unsettling of all sorts of things in the manse had bred in him thoughts he had not quite words to express. The further change to the yacht, too, he had deemed far from an agreeable one. But he had borne up, by way of being very manly ; and he seemed rather amused that papa should now have to make his porridge for him, and to put him to bed, and that it was John Stewart, the sailor, who was to be the servant girl. The passage, however, was tedious and disagreeable ; the wind blew a-head, and heart and spirits failing poor Bill, and somewhat sea-sick to boot, he lay down on the floor, and cried bitterly to be taken home. ' Alas, my boy !' I said, ' you have no home now : your father is like the poor sheep-stealer whom you saw on the shore of Eigg. This view of matters proved in no way consolatory to poor Bill. He continued his sad wail, ' Home, home, home !' until at length he fairly sobbed himself asleep; and I never, on any other occasion, so felt the desolateness of my condition as when the cry of my boy,—' Home, home, home!'—was ringing in my ears."

We passed, on the one hand, Loch Nevis and Loch Hourn, two fine arms of the sea that run far into the mainland, and open up noble vistas among the mountains; and, on the other, the long undulating line of Sleat in Skye, with its inter-mingled patches of woodland and arable on the coast, and its mottled ranges of heath and rock above.   Towards evening we entered the harbour of Isle Ornsay, a quiet well-sheltered bay, with a rocky islet for a breakwater on the one side, and the rudiments of a Highland village, containing a few good houses, on the other.   Half a dozen small vessels were riding at anchor, curtained round, half-mast high, with herring-nets; and a fleet of herring-boats lay moored beside them a little nearer the shore.   There had been tolerable takes for a few nights in the neighbouring sea, but the fish had again disap-peared, and the fishermen, whose worn-out tackle gave such evidence of a long-continued run of ill luck, as I had learned to interpret on the east coast, looked gloomy and spiritless, and reported a deficient fishery.   I found Mrs Swanson and her family located in one of the two best houses in the vil-lage, with a neat enclosure in front, and a good kitchen-garden behind.   The following day I spent in exploring the rocks of the district,—a primary region with regard to or-ganic existence, "without *form* and void."   From Isle Orn-say to the Point of Sleat, a distance of thirteen miles, gneiss is the prevailing deposit; and in no place in the district are the strata more varied and interesting than in the neighbour-hood of Knockhouse, the residence of Mr Elder, which I found pleasingly situated at the bottom of a little open bay, skirted with picturesque knolls partially wooded, that present to the surf precipitous fronts of rock.   One insulated eminence, a gun-shot from the dwelling-house, that presents to the sea

---

primary region: see Additional Notes; 'without form and void': Bible, Genesis 1:1-2.
'In the beginning God created the heaven and the earth. And the earth was without form, and void; and darkness was upon the face of the deep'

two mural fronts of precipice, and sinks in steep grassy slopes
on two sides more, bears atop a fine old ruin.   There is a
blind-fronted massy keep, wrapped up in a mantle of ivy,
perched at the one end, where the precipice sinks steepest ;
while a more ruinous though much more modern pile of
building, perforated by a double row of windows, occupies
the rest of the area.   The square keep has lost its genealogy
in the mists of the past, but a vague tradition attributes its
erection to the Norwegians.   The more modern pile is said to
have been built about three centuries ago by a younger son
of M'Donald of the Isles ; but it is added that, owing to the
jealousy of his elder brother, he was not permitted to complete or inhabit it.   I find it characteristic of most Highland
traditions, that they contain speeches : they constitute true
oral specimens of that earliest and rudest style of historic
composition in which dialogue alternates with narrative.
" My wise brother is building a fine house," is the speech
preserved in this tradition as that of the elder son : " it is
rather a pity for himself that he should be building it on
another man's lands."   The remark was repeated to the
builder, says the story, and at once arrested the progress of
the work.   Mr Elder's boys showed me several minute pieces
of brass, somewhat resembling rust-eaten coin, that they had
dug out of the walls of the old keep ; but the pieces bore no
impress of the dye, and seemed mere fragments of metal
beaten thin by the hammer.

The gneiss at Knock is exceedingly various in its composition, and many of its strata the geologist would fail to recognise as gneiss at all.   We find along the precipices its two
unequivocal varieties, the schistose and the granitic, passing
not unfrequently, the former into a true mica schist, the latter into a pale feldspathose rock, thickly pervaded by needle-
like crystals of tremolite, that, from the style of the grouping, and the contrast existing between the dark green of the

---

dye: coiner's die

enclosed mineral, and the pale flesh-colour of the ground, frequently furnishes specimens of great beauty. In some pieces the tremolite assumes the common fan-like form; in some, the crystals, lying at nearly right angles with each other, present the appearance of ancient characters inlaid in the rock; in some they resemble the footprints of birds in a thin layer of snow; and in one curious specimen picked up by Mr Swanson, in which a dark linear strip is covered transversely by crystals that project thickly from both its sides, the appearance presented is that of a minute stigmaria of the Coal Measures, with the leaves, still bearing their original green colour, bristling thick around it. Mr Elder showed me, intercalated among the gneiss strata of a little ravine in the neighbourhood of Isle Ornsay, a thin band of a bluish-coloured indurated clay, scarcely distinguishable, in the hand specimen, from a weathered clay-stone, but unequivocally a stratum of the rock. I have found the same stone existing, in a decomposed state, as a very tenacious clay, among the gneiss strata of the hill of Cromarty; and oftener than once had I amused myself in fashioning it, with tolerable success, into such rude pieces of pottery as are sometimes found in old sepulchral tumuli. Such are a few of the rocks included in the general gneiss deposit of Sleat. If we are to hold, with one of the most distinguished of living geologists, that the stratified primary rocks are aqueous deposits altered by heat, to how various a chemistry must they not have been subjected in this district! In one stratum, so softened that all its particles were disengaged to enter into new combinations, and yet not so softened but that it still maintained its lines of division from the strata above and below, the green tremolite was shooting its crystals into the pale homogeneous mass; while in another stratum the quartz drew its atoms apart in masses that assumed one especial form, the feldspar drew its atoms apart into masses that assumed another and

---

Stigmaria ... leaves: Miller compared the mineral to one of the main roots of a coal forest 'tree', which he thought was a stem, with radiating rootlets – Miller's 'leaves'; aqueous deposits: rocks laid down under water, *eg* many sandstones; most distinguished: see Additional Notes

different form, and the glittering mica built up its multitudinous layers between.   Here the unctuous chlorite constructed its soft felt ; there the micaceous schist arranged
its undulating layers ; yonder the dull clay hardened amid
the intense heat, but, when all else was changing, retained
its structure unchanged.   Surely a curious chemistry, and
conducted on an enormous scale !

It had been an essential part of my plan to explore the
splendid section of the Lower Oolite furnished by the line of
sea-cliffs that, to the north of Portree, rise full seven hundred
feet over the beach ; and on the morning of Wednesday I
set out with this intention from Isle Ornsay, to join the mail
gig at Broadford, and pass on to Portree,—a journey of rather
more than thirty miles.   I soon passed over the gneiss, and
entered on a wide deposit, extending from side to side of the
island, of what is generally laid down in our geological maps
as Old Red Sandstone, but which, in most of its beds, quite
as much resembles a quartz rock, and which, unlike any Old
Red proper I have ever seen, passes, by insensible gradations,
into the gneiss.*   Wherever it has been laid bare in flat
tables among the heath, we find it bearing those mysterious
scratches on a polished surface which we so commonly find
associated on the main land with the boulder clay ; but here,
as in the Hebrides generally, the boulder clay is wanting.
To the tract of Red Sandstone there succeeds a tract of Lias,
which, also extending across the island, forms by far the most
largely-developed deposit of this formation in Scotland.   It
occupies a flat dingy valley, about six miles in length, and
that varies from two to four miles in breadth.   The dreary
interior is covered with mosses, and studded with inky pools,

---

* Professor Nicol of Aberdeen believes the Red Sandstones of the West
Highlands are of Devonian age, and the quartzite and limestone of Lower
Carboniferous.—*See Quarterly Journal of the Geological Society February*
1857.—W. S.

Nicol believes …: Now considered wrong. In fact this red sandstone, now termed the
Torridonian Sandstone, is of much older, Precambrian, age, while there are, in Skye alone,
tracts of Cambrian quartzite (metamorphosed sandstone) and limestone (also Cambrian
or possibly Ordovician) as well as Triassic sandstone and Jurassic limestone (Oldroyd
1996b)

in which the botanist finds a few rare plants, and which were dimpled, as I passed them this morning, with countless eddies, formed by myriads of small quick glancing trout, that seemed busily engaged in fly-catching.   The rock appears but rarely, —all is moss, marsh, and pool ; but in a few localities on the hill-sides, where some stream has cut into the slope, and disintegrated the softer shales, the shepherd finds shells of strange form strewed along the water-courses, or bleaching white among the heath.   The valley,—evidently a dangerous one to the night traveller, from its bogs and its tarns,—is said to be haunted by a spirit peculiar to itself,—a mischievous, eccentric, grotesque creature, not unworthy, from the monstrosity of its form, of being associated with the old monsters of the Lias.   Luidag—for so the goblin is called—has but one leg, terminating, like an ancient satyr's, in a cloven foot ; but it is furnished with two arms, bearing hard fists at the end of them, with which it has been known to strike the benighted traveller in the face, or to tumble him over into some dark pool.   The spectre may be seen at the close of evening hopping vigorously among the distant bogs, like a felt ball on its electric platform ; and when the mist lies thick in the hollows, an occasional glimpse may be caught of it even by day. But when I passed the way there was no fog : the light, though softened by a thin film of cloud, fell equally over the heath, revealing hill and hollow ; and I was unlucky enough not to see this goblin of the Liasic valley.

A deep indentation of the coast, which forms the bay of Broadford, corresponds with the hollow of the valley.   It is simply a portion of the valley itself occupied by the sea ; and we find the Lias, from its lower to its upper beds, exposed in unbroken series along the beach.   In the middle of the opening lies the green level island of Pabba, altogether composed of this formation, and which, differing, in consequence, both in outline and colour, from every neighbouring island and

---

electric platform: connected to a static electricity generator. The felt ball lying on it was charged up with the same charge, was repelled and jumped up in the air, falling back as the charge leaked, starting the cycle again hill, seems a little bit of flat fertile England, laid down, as if for contrast's sake, amid the wild rough Hebrides. Of Pabba and its wonders, however, more anon. I explored a considerable range of shore along the bay; but as I made it the subject of two after explorations ere I mastered its deposits, I shall defer my description till a subsequent chapter. It was late this evening ere the post-gig arrived from the south, and the night and several hours of the following morning were spent in travelling to Portree. I know not, however, that I could have seen some of the wildest and most desolate tracts in Skye to greater advantage. There was light enough to show the bold outlines of the hills,—lofty, abrupt, pyramidal, —just such hills, both in form and grouping, as a profile in black showed best; a low blue vapour slept in the calm over the marshes at their feet; the sea, smooth as glass, reflected the dusk twilight gleam in the north, revealing the narrow sounds and deep mountain-girdled lochs along which we passed; gray crags gleamed dimly on the sight; birch-feathered acclivities presented against sea and sky their rough bristly edges; all was vast, dreamy, obscure, like one of Martin's darker pictures: the land of the seer and the spectre could not have been better seen. Morning broke dim and gray, while we were yet several miles from Portree; and I reached the inn in time to see from my bed-room windows the first rays of the rising sun gleaming on the hill-tops.

Martin: John Martin (1789-1854), painter and engraver of dark tenebral mezzotints of Biblical, oriental and cosmical subjects such as the Flood and Belshazzar's Feast – and also several scenes of fighting Jurassic saurians

CHAPTER VII.

I BREAKFASTED in the travellers' room with three gentlemen from Edinburgh; and then, accompanied by a boy, whom I had engaged to carry my bag, set out to explore. The morning was ominously hot and breathless ; and while the sea lay moveless in the calm, as a floor of polished marble, mountain, and rock, and distant island, seemed tremulous all over, through a wavy medium of thick rising vapour. I judged from the first that my course of exploration for the day was destined to terminate abruptly ; and as my arrangements with Mr Swanson left me, for this part of the country, no second day to calculate upon, I hurried over deposits which in other circumstances I would have examined more carefully,——content with a glance. Accustomed in most instances to take long aims, as Cuddy Headrig did, when he steadied his musket on a rest behind the hedge, and sent his ball through Laird Oliphant's forehead, I had on this occasion to shoot flying ; and so, selecting a large object for a mark, that I might run the less risk of missing, I strove to acquaint myself rather with the general structure of the district than with the organisms of its various fossiliferous beds.

The long narrow island of Rasay lies parallel to the coast of Skye, like a vessel laid along a wharf, but drawn out from it, as if to suffer another vessel of the same size to take her

---

Cuddy Headrig: Headrigg is a ploughman turned insurgent in *Old Mortality*, Walter Scott's novel of the Covenanter uprising of 1679 around Clydesdale in the West of Scotland, and its defeat at Bothwell Bridge. After the downfall of the Stuarts in 1689, Headrigg returns with other exiles, and becomes involved in a skirmish with Olifant who has unjustly expropriated local lands during their absence

berth between ; and on the eastern shores of both Skye and
Rasay we find the same Oolitic deposits tilted up at nearly
the same angle.   The section presented on the eastern coast
of the one is nearly a duplicate of the section presented on
the eastern coast of the other.   During one of the severer
frosts of last winter I passed along a shallow pond, studded
along the sides with boulder stones.   It had been frozen over;
and then, from the evaporation so common in protracted
frosts, the water had shrunk, and the sheet of ice which had
sunk down over the central portion of the pond exhibited
what a geologist would term very considerable marks of dis-
turbance among the boulders at the edges.   Over one sharp-
backed boulder there lay a sheet tilted up like the lid of a
chest half-raised ; and over another boulder immediately behind it there lay another uptilted sheet, like the lid of a second
half-open chest ; and in both sheets, the edges, lying in nearly
parallel lines, presented a range of miniature cliffs to the
shore.   Now, in the two uptilted ice-sheets of this pond I
recognised a model of the fundamental Oolitic deposits Rasay
and Skye.   The mainland of Scotland had its representative
in the crisp snow-covered shore of the pond, with its belt of
faded sedges ; the place of Rasay was indicated by the inner,
that of Skye by the outer boulder ; while the ice-sheets, with
their shoreward-turned line of cliffs, represented the Oolitic
beds, that turn to the mainland their dizzy range of precipices,
varying from six to eight hundred feet in height, and then,
sloping outwards and downwards, disappear under mountain
wildernesses of overlying trap.   And it was along a portion
of the range of cliff that forms the outermost of the two uptilted lines, and which presents in this district of Skye a
frontage of nearly twenty continuous miles to the long Sound
of Rasay, that my to-day's course of exploration lay.   From
the top of the cliff the surface slopes downwards for about two
miles into the interior, like the half-raised chest-lid of my

illustration sloping towards the hinges, or the uptilted ice-table of the boulder sloping towards the centre of the pond; and the depression behind forms a flat moory valley, full fifteen miles in length, occupied by a chain of dark bogs and treeless lochans.   A long line of trap-hills rises over it, in one of which, considerably in advance of the others, I recognised the Storr of Skye, famous among lovers of the picturesque for its strange group of mingled pinnacles and towers; while directly crossing into the valley from the Sound, and then running southwards for about two miles along its bottom, is the noble sea-arm, Loch Portree, in which, as indicated by the name (the King's Port) a Scottish king of the olden time, in his voyage round his dominions, cast anchor.   The opening of the loch is singularly majestic;—the cliffs tower high on either side in graceful magnificence : but from the peculiar inward slope of the land, all within, as the loch reaches the line of the valley, becomes tame and low, and a black dreary moor stretches from the flat terminal basin into the interior.   The opening of Loch Portree is a palace gateway, erected in front of some homely suburb, that occupies the place which the palace itself should have occupied.

There was, however, no such mixture of the homely and the magnificent in the route I had selected to explore.   It lay under the escarpment of the cliff; and I purposed pursuing it from Portree to Holm, a distance of about six miles, and then returning by the flat interior valley.   On the one hand rose a sloping rampart, full seven hundred feet in height, striped longitudinally with alternating bands of white sandstone and dark shale, and capped atop by a continuous coping of trap, that lacked not massy tower, and overhanging turret, and projecting sentry-box ; while, on the other hand, spreading outwards in the calm from the line of dark trap-rocks below, like a mirror from its carved frame of black oak, lay the Sound of Rasay, with its noble background of island

and main rising bold on the east, and its long mountain vista
opening to the south.   The first fossiliferous deposit which
gave me occasion this morning to use my hammer occurs near
the opening of the loch, beside an old Celtic burying-ground,
in the form of a thick bed of hard sandstone, charged with
Belemnites,—a bed that must at one time have existed as a
widely-spread accumulation of sand,—the bottom, mayhap,
of some extensive bay of the Oolite, resembling the Loch Portree of the present day, in which eddy tides deposited the
sand swept along by the tidal currents of some neighbouring
sound, and which swarmed as thickly with Cephalopoda as
the loch swarmed this day with minute purple-tinged Medusæ. I found detached on the shore, immediately below this
bed, a piece of calcareous fissile sandstone, abounding in small
sulcated Terebratulæ, identical, apparently, with the Terebratula of a specimen in my collection from the inferior Oolite
of Yorkshire. A colony of this delicate Brachiopod must
have once lain moored near this spot, like a fleet of long-prow-
ed galleys at anchor, each one with its cable of many strands
extended earthwards from the single *dead-eye* in its umbone.
For a full mile after rounding the northern boundary of the
loch, we find the immense escarpment composed from top to
bottom exclusively of trap ; but then the Oolite again begins
to appear, and about two miles further on the section becomes truly magnificent,—one of the finest sections of this
formation exhibited anywhere in Britain, perhaps in the
world.   In a ravine furrowed in the face of the declivity by
the headlong descent of a small stream, we may trace all the
beds of the system in succession, from the Cornbrash, an upper deposit of the Lower Oolite, down to the Lias, the formation on which the Oolite rests. The only modifying circumstance to the geologist is, that though the sandstone beds
run continuously along the cliff for miles together, distinct as
the white bands in a piece of onyx, the intervening beds of

---

dead-eye in its umbone: perhaps a false back construction from 'umbones', plural of
'umbo'. The umbo or apex of the brachiopod shell commonly has a hole from which
emerges the pedicle or stalk fixing the animal to rocks. Nor is the metaphor particularly
apt – a dead-eye is a wooden block in a ship's rigging, used in various permutations to
fasten ropes to each other and adjust their respective lengths

shale are swarded over, save where we here and there see
them laid bare in some abrupter acclivity or deeper water-
course.   In the shale we find numerous minute Ammonites,
sorely weathered ; in the sandstone, Belemnites, some of them
of great size ; and dark carbonaceous markings, passing not
unfrequently into a glossy cubical coal.   At the foot of the
cliff I picked up an ammonite of considerable size and well-
marked character,—the *Ammonites Murchisonœ*, first discovered on this coast by Sir R. Murchison about fifteen years ago.
It measures, when full grown, from six to seven inches in
diameter : the inner whorls, which are broadly visible, are
ribbed; whereas the two, and sometimes the three outer ones,
are smooth,—a marked characteristic of the species.   My
specimen merely enabled me to examine the peculiarities of
the shell just a little more minutely than I could have done
in the pages of Sowerby ; for such was its state of decay, that
it fell to pieces in my hands.   I had now come full in view
of the rocky island of Holm, when the altered appearance of
the heavens led me to deliberate, just as I was warming in
the work of exploration, whether, after all, it might not be
well to scale the cliffs, and strike directly on the inn.   It
was nearly three o'clock ; the sky had been gradually darkening since noon, as if one thin covering of gauze after another had been drawn over it ; hill and island had first
dimmed and then disappeared in the landscape ; and now the
sun stood up right over the fast-contracting vista of the Sound,
round and lightless as the moon in a haze ; and the downward cataract-like streaming of the gray vapour on the horizon showed that there the rain had already broken, and was
descending in torrents.   We had been thirsty in the hot sun,
and had found the springs few and scanty ; but the boy now
assured me, in very broken English, that we were to get a
great deal more water than would be good for us, and that
it might be advisable to get out of its way.   And so, climb-

---

Ammonites murchisonae: actually discovered by Mrs Murchison (Sowerby and Sowerby
1812-1829, VI, pp. 95-96), as the gender of the specific name makes clear

ing to the top of the cliffs, along a water-course, we reached
the ridge, just as the fog came rolling downwards from the
peaked brow of the Storr into the flat moory valley, and the
melancholy lochans roughened and darkened in the rain. We
were both particularly wet ere we reached Portree.

In exploring our Scotch formations, I have had frequent
occasion, in Ross, Sutherland, Caithness, and now once more
in Skye, to pass over ground described by Sir R. Murchison ;
and in every instance have I found myself immensely his
debtor. His descriptions possess the merit of being true :
they are simple outlines often, that leave much to be filled
up by after discovery ; but, like those outlines of the skilful
geographer that fix the place of some island or strait, though
they may not entirely define it, they always indicate the exact
position in the scale of the formations to which they refer.
They leave a good deal to be done in the way of mapping out
the interior of a deposit, if I may so speak ; but they leave
nothing to be done in the way of ascertaining its place. The
work accomplished is *bona fide* work,—actual, solid, not to
be done over again,—work such as could be achieved in only
the school of Dr William Smith, the father of English Geology. I have found much to admire, too, in the sections of
Sir R. Murchison. His section of this part of the coast, for
example, strikes from the extreme northern part of Skye to
the island of Holm, thence to Scrapidale in Rasay, thence
along part of the coast of Scalpa, thence direct through the
middle of Pabba, and thence to the shore of the Bay of Laig.
The line thus taken includes, in regular sequence in the descending order, the whole Oolitic deposits of the Hebrides,
from the Cornbrash, with its overlying freshwater outliers of
mayhap the Weald, down to where the Lower Lias rests on
the primary red sandstones of Sleat. It would have cost
M'Culloch less exploration to have written a volume than it
must have cost Sir R. Murchison to draw this single line ;

William Smith: (1769-1839), the canal and mining engineer who demonstrated the
fundamental concept of using fossils to correlate rocks of the same age, and drew up a
geological map of England (Torrens 2003); **section … Laig**: a slip for Lucy – Miller
was evidently referring to Murchison's (1828, pl. 35) cross-section of the geology of Skye
which ends in 'Lucy Bay'

but the line once drawn, is work done to the hands of all after explorers.   I have followed repeatedly in the track of another geologist, of, however, a very different school, who explored, at a comparatively recent period, the deposits of not a few of our Scotch counties.   But his labours, in at least the fossiliferous formations, seem to have accomplished nothing for Geology,—I am afraid, even less than nothing.   So far as they had influence at all, it must have been to throw back the science.   A geologist who could have asserted only three years ago (" Geognostical Account of Banffshire," 1842), that the Old Red Sandstone of Scotland forms merely " a part of the great coal deposit," could have known marvellously little of the fossils of the one system, and nothing whatever of those of the other.   Had he examined ere he decided, instead of deciding without any intention of examining, he would have found that, while both systems abound in organic remains, they do not possess, in Scotland at least, a single species in common, and that even their types of being, viewed in the group, are essentially distinct.

The three Edinburgh gentlemen whom I had met at break-fast were still in the inn.   One of them I had seen before, as one of the guests at a Wesleyan soiree, though I saw he failed to remember that I had been there as a guest too.   The two other gentlemen were altogether strangers to me.   One of them,—a man on the right side of forty, and a superb spe-cimen of the powerful, six-feet-two-inch Norman Celt,—I set down as a scion of some old Highland family, who, as the broadsword had gone out, carried on the internal wars of the country with the formidable artillery of Statute and Decision. The other, a gentleman more advanced in life, I predicated to be a Highland proprietor, the uncle of the younger of the two,—a man whose name, as he had an air of business about him, occurred, in all probability, in the Almanac, in the list of Scotch advocates.   Both were of course high Tories,—I

another geologist … Banffshire: R. J. Hay Cunningham, in the *Transactions of the Highlands Agricultural Society of Scotland* (Waterston 1959) – he did not use fossils in correlating rocks, hence Miller's views. See Introduction and p. 73; **Wesleyan soiree:** Methodist meeting

was quite sure of that,—zealous in behalf of the Establishment, though previous to the Disruption they had not cared
for it a pin's point,—and prepared to justify the virtual sup-
pression of the toleration laws in the case of the Free Church.
I was thus decidedly guilty of what old Dr More calls a *pro-
sopolepsia*,—*i. e.* of the crime of judging men by their looks.
At dinner, however, we gradually ate ourselves into conversation : we differed, and disputed, and agreed, and then differed, disputed, and agreed again. I found first, that my
chance companions were really not very high Tories ; and
then, that they were not Tories at all ; and then, that the
younger of the two was very much a Whig, and the more advanced in life,—strange as the fact might seem,—very considerably a *Presbyterian* Whig ; and finally, that this latter
gentleman, whom I had set down as an intolerant Highland
proprietor, was a respected writer to the signet, a Free Church
elder in Edinburgh ; and that the other, his equally intolerant
nephew, was an Edinburgh advocate, of vigorous talent, much
an enemy of all oppression, and a brother contributor of my
own to one of the Quarterlies. Of all my surmisings regarding the stranger gentlemen, only two points held true,—they
were both gentlemen of the law, and both had Celtic blood
in their veins. The evening passed pleasantly ; and I can
now recommend from experience, to the hapless traveller who
gets thoroughly wet thirty miles from a change of dress, that
some of the best things he can resort to in the circumstances
are. a warm room, a warm glass, and agreeable companions.

On the morrow I behoved to return to Isle Ornsay, to set
out on the following day, with my friend the minister, for
Rum, where he purposed preaching on the Sabbath. To have
lost a day would have been to lose the opportunity of exploring the island, perhaps for ever ; and, to make all sure, I had
taken a seat in the mail gig, from the postman who drives
it, ere going to bed, on the morning of my arrival ; and now,

Dr More: Henry More (1614–1687), Cambridge academic and philosopher. Perhaps from
the *Spectator*, 8 June 1711; Quarterlies: heavyweight periodicals with reviews of new
books and essays on intellectual, social and political issues. Probably, here, the *North British
Review*, politically liberal and Christian but nonsectarian – its contributors included Free
Churchmen such as Miller (Houghton and Houghton 1966–1979; Shortland 1996d)

when it drove up, I went to take my place in it. The post-master of the village, a lean, hungry-looking man, interfered to prevent me. I had secured my seat, I said, two days previous. Ah, but I had not secured it from him. "I know nothing of you, I replied; but I secured it from one who deemed himself authorized to receive the fare; was he so? "Yes." "Could you have received it?" "No." "Show me a copy of your regulations." "I have no copy of regulations; but I have given the place in the gig to another." "Just so; and what say you, postman?" "That you took the place from me, and that *he* has no right to give a place to any one : I carry the Portree letters to him, but he has nothing to do with the passengers." A person present, the proprietor or stabler of the horse, I believe, also interfered on the same side; but what Carlyle terms the "gigmanity" of the postmaster was all at stake,—his whole influence in the mail-gig of Portree; and so he argued, and threatened withal, and, what was the more serious part of the business, the person he had given the seat to had taken possession of the gig; and so we had to compound the matter by carrying a passenger additional. The incident is scarce worth relating; but the postmaster was so vehement and terrible, so defiant of us all,—post, stabler, and simple passenger,—and so justly impressed with the importance of being postmaster of Portree, that, as I am in the way of describing rare specimens at any rate, I must refer to him among the rest, as if he had been one of the minor carnivoræ of a Skye deposit,—a cuttle-fish, that preyed on the weaker molluscs, or a hungry polypus, terrible among the animalculæ.

We drove heavily, and had to dismount and walk afoot over every steeper acclivity; but I carried my hammer, and only grieved that in some one or two localities the road should have been so level. I regretted it in especial on the southern and eastern side of Loch Sligachan, where I could see

---

Carlyle: Thomas Carlyle (1795–1881), philosopher and essayist; **gigmanity**: 'narrow middle-class philistinism' (*Chambers Dictionary*)

from my seat, as we drove past, the dark blue rocks in the
water-courses on each side the road, studded over with that
characteristic shell of the Lias, the *Gryphœa incurva*, and that
the dry-stone fences in the moor above exhibit fossils that
might figure in a museum.   But we rattled by.   At Broadford, twenty-five miles from Portree, and nine miles from
Isle Ornsay, I partook of a hospitable meal in the house of
an acquaintance ; and in little more than two hours after
was with my friend the minister at Isle Ornsay.   The night
wore pleasantly by.   Mrs Swanson, a niece of the late Dr
Smith of Campbelton, so well known for his Celtic researches
and his exquisite translations of ancient Celtic poetry, I found
deeply versed in the legendary lore of the Highlands.   The
minister showed me a fine specimen of Pterichthys which I
had disinterred for him, out of my first discovered fossiliferous deposit of the Old Red Sandstone, exactly thirteen years
before, and full seven years ere I had introduced the creature
to the notice of Agassiz.   And the minister's daughter, a
little chubby girl of three summers, taking part in the general entertainment, strove to make her Gaelic sound as like
English as she could, in my especial behalf.   I remembered,
as I listened to the unintelligible prattle of the little thing,
unprovided with a word of English, that just eighteen years
before, her father had had no Gaelic ; and wondered what
he would have thought, could he have been told, when he
first sat down to study it, the story of his island charge in
Eigg, and his Free Church yacht the Betsey.   Nineteen
years before, we had been engaged in beating over the Eathie
Lias together, collecting Belemnites, Ammonites, and fossil
wood, and striving in friendly emulation the one to surpass
the other in the variety and excellence of our specimens.
Our leisure hours were snatched, at the time, from college
studies by the one, from the mallet by the other : there were
few of them that we did not spend together, and that we

Smith: Rev. Dr John Smith (1747–1807), collaborator in translating the Bible into Gaelic;
my first … of the Old Red: the Cromarty beach site, made famous for its fossil fishes by
The Old Red Sandstone (Miller 1841, 1858, pp. 472–473); **Eathie Lias:** also made famous
by the same books. In fact an Upper Jurassic deposit

were not mutually the better for so spending.   I at least owe much to these hours,—among other things, views of theologic truth, that determined the side I have taken in our ecclesiastical controversy.   Our courses at an after period lay diverse ; the young minister had greatly more important business to pursue than any which the geologic field furnishes ; and so our amicable rivalry ceased early.   In the words in which an English poet addresses his brother,—the clergyman who sat for the picture in the " Deserted Village,"—my friend " entered on a sacred office, where the harvest is great and the labourers are few, and left to me a field in which the labourers are many, and the harvest scarce worth carrying away."

Next day at noon we weighed anchor, and stood out for Rum, a run of about twenty-five miles.   A kind friend had, we found, sent aboard in our behalf two pieces of rare antiquity,—rare anywhere, but especially rare in the lockers of the Betsey,—in the agreeable form of two bottles of semifossil Madeira,—Madeira that had actually existed in the grape exactly half a century before, at the time when Robespierre was startling Paris from its propriety, by mutilating at the neck the busts of other people, and multiplying casts and medals of his own ; and we found it, explored in moderation, no bad study for geologists, especially in coarse weather, when they had got wet and somewhat fatigued.   It was like Landlord Boniface's ale, mild as milk, had exchanged its distinctive flavour as Madeira for a better one, and filled the cabin with fragrance every time the cork was drawn. Old observant Homer must have smelt some such liquor somewhere, or he could never have described so well the still more ancient and venerable wine with which wily Ulysses beguiled one-eyed Polypheme :—

" Unmingled wine,
Mellifluous, undecaying, and divine,

'Deserted Village': poem by Oliver Goldsmith; **Landlord Boniface's ale**: possibly not a specific reference – Boniface was a generic name for innkeepers; '**Unmingled wine** …': Homer's *Odyssey*, translated by Alexander Pope, book 9, lines 238-245

Which now, some ages from his race concealed,
The hoary sire in gratitude revealed. * * *
Scarce twenty measures from the living stream
To cool one cup sufficed : the goblet crowned,
Breathed aromatic fragrances around."

Winds were light and variable.   As we reached the middle of the sound opposite Armadale, there fell a dead calm ; and the Betsey, more actively idle than the ship manned by the Ancient Mariner, dropped sternwards along the tide, to the dull music of the flapping sail.   The minister spent the day in the cabin, engaged with his discourse for the morrow ; and I, that he might suffer as little from interruption as possible, *mis*-spent it upon the deck.   I tried fishing with the yacht's set of lines, but there were no fish to bite,—got into the boat, but there were no neighbouring islands to visit,— and sent half a dozen pistol-bullets after a shoal of porpoises, which, coming from the Free Church yacht, must have astonished the fat sleek fellows pretty considerably, but did them, I am afraid, no serious damage.   As the evening began to close gloomy and gray, a tumbling swell came heaving in right ahead from the west ; and a bank of cloud, which had been gradually rising higher and darker over the horizon in the same direction, first changed its abrupt edge atop for a diffused and broken line, and then spread itself over the central heavens.   The calm was evidently not to be a calm long ; and the minister issued orders that the gaff-topsail should be taken down, and the storm-jib bent ; and that we should lower our topmast, and have all tight and ready for a smart gale a-head.   At half-past ten, however, the Betsey was still pitching to the swell, with not a breath of wind to act on the diminished canvass, and with but the solitary circumstance in her favour, that the tide ran no longer against her, as before.   The cabin was full of all manner of creakings ; the close lamp swung to and fro over the head of my friend ; and a refractory Concordance, after having twice travelled

---

lower our topmast: the topmast was a small mast which was used to extend the length of the main mast, and which could often be lowered in preparation for heavy weather, as here – there was no point in having it up if the gaff topsail had been taken down to reduce sail area. Putting up or **bending** the storm-jib in place of the normal jibsail would also reduce sail area – hence the **diminished canvass**; **Concordance**: index to the Bible from him along the entire length of the table, flung itself pettishly upon the floor. I got into my snug bed about eleven ; and at twelve, the minister, after poring sufficiently over his notes, and drawing the final score, turned into his. In a brief hour after, on came the gale, in a style worthy of its previous hours of preparation ; and my friend,—his Saturday's work in his ministerial capacity well over when he had completed his two discourses,—had to begin the Sabbath morning early as the morning itself began, by taking his stand at the helm, in his capacity of skipper of the Betsey. With the prospect of the services of the Sabbath before him, and after working all Saturday to boot, it was rather hard to set him down to a midnight spell at the helm, but, he could not be wanted at such a time, as we had no other such helmsman aboard. The gale, thickened with rain, came down, shrieking like a maniac, from off the peaked hills of Rum, striking away the tops of the long ridgy billows that had risen in the calm to indicate its approach, and then carrying them in sheets of spray aslant the furrowed surface, like snow-drift hurried across a frozen field. But the Betsey, with her storm-jib set, and her mainsail reefed to the cross, kept her weather bow bravely to the blast, and gained on it with every tack. She had been the pleasure yacht, in her day, of a man of fortune, who had used, in running south with her at times as far as Lisbon, to encounter, on not worse terms than the stateliest of her neighbours in the voyage, the swell of the Bay of Biscay ; and she still kept true to her old character, with but this drawback, that she had now got somewhat crazy in her fastenings, and made rather more water in a heavy sea than her one little pump could conveniently keep under. As the fitful gust struck her headlong, as if it had been some invisible missile hurled at us from off the hill-tops, she stooped her head lower and lower, like old stately Hardyknute under the blow of the "King of Norse," till at length the lee chain-

---

final score: last line; wanted: *ie* missing; tack: see Additional Notes; crazy: loose; Hardyknute … 'King of Norse': alluding to Lady Elizabeth Wardlaw's poem 'Hardyknute: a Scottish Fragment' in Thomas Percy's *Reliques of Ancient English Poetry* (1767); chain-plate: chain-plates are fastenings for the shrouds, rigging which provides lateral support for the mast. *Betsey* was heeling away from the wind, immersing her lee side

plate rustled sharp through the foam ; but, like a staunch
Free Churchwoman, the lowlier she bent, the more steadfastly
did she hold her head to the storm.   The strength of the opposition served but to speed her on all the more surely to the
desired haven.   At five o'clock in the morning we cast anchor in Loch Scresort,—the only harbour of Rum in which
a vessel can moor,—within two hundred yards of the shore,
having, with the exception of the minister, gained no loss in
the gale.   He, luckless man, had parted from his excellent
sou-wester ; a sudden gust had seized it by the flap, and hurried it away far to the lee.   He had yielded it to the winds,
as he had done the temporalities, but much more unwillingly, and less as a free agent.   Should any conscientious mariner pick up anywhere in the Atlantic a serviceable ochre-
coloured *sou-wester,* not at all the worse for the wear, I give
him to wit that he holds Free Church property, and that he
is heartily welcome to hold it, leaving it to himself to consider whether a benefaction to its full value, deducting salvage, is not owing, in honour, to the Sustentation Fund.

It was ten o'clock ere the more fatigued aboard could mus-
ter resolution enough to quit their beds a second time ; and
then it behoved the minister to prepare for his Sabbath labours ashore.   The gale still blew in fierce gusts from the
hills, and the rain pattered like small shot on the deck.   Loch
Scresort, by no means one of our finer island lochs, viewed
under any circumstances, looked particularly dismal this morning.   It forms the opening of a dreary moorland valley,
bounded on one of its sides, to the mouth of the loch, by a
homely ridge of Old Red Sandstone, and on the other by a
line of dark augitic hills, that attain, at the distance of about
a mile from the sea, an elevation of two thousand feet.   Along
the slopes of the sandstone ridge I could discern, through the
haze, numerous green patches, that had once supported a dense
population, long since " cleared off" to the backwoods of Ame-

---

staunch Free Churchwoman: no doubt worshipping out in the open – see Introduction;
Sustentation Fund: Free Church fund for cross-subsidizing poorer congregations, partly
through contributions from richer ones; **Old Red Sandstone**: not the Devonian stratum
of this age, in fact, but the much older Torridonian Sandstone of Precambrian age – see
Introduction

rica, but not one inhabited dwelling; while along a black moory acclivity under the hills on the other side I could see several groupes of turf cottages, with here and there a minute speck of raw-looking corn beside them, that, judging from its colour, seemed to have but a slight chance of ripening.   The hill-tops were lost in cloud and storm; and ever and anon as a heavier shower came sweeping down on the wind, the intervening hollows closed up their gloomy vistas, and all was fog and rhime to the water's edge.   Bad as the morning was, however, we could see the people wending their way, in threes and fours, through the dark moor, to the place of worship,—a black turf hovel, like the meeting-house in Eigg.   The appearance of the Betsey in the loch had been the gathering signal; and the Free Church islanders—three-fourths of the entire population—had all come out to meet their minister.

On going ashore, we found the place nearly filled.   My friend preached two long energetic discourses, and then returned to the yacht, a "worn and weary man."   The studies of the previous day, and the fatigues of the previous night, added to his pulpit duties, had so fairly prostrated his strength, that the sternest teetotaller in the kingdom would scarce have forbidden him a glass of our fifty-year-old Madeira.   But even the fifty-year-old Madeira proved no specific in the case.   He was suffering under excruciating headache, and had to stretch himself in his bed, with eyes shut but sleepless, waiting till the fit should pass,—every pulse that beat in his temples a throb of pain.

CHAPTER VIII.

THE geology of the island of Rum is simple, but curious.   Let
the reader take, if he can, from twelve to fifteen trap-hills,
varying from one thousand to two thousand three hundred
feet in height ; let him pack them closely and squarely together, like rum-bottles in a case-basket ; let him surround
them with a frame of Old Red Sandstone, measuring rather
more than seven miles on the side, in the way the basket surrounds the bottles ; then let him set them down in the sea a
dozen miles off the land,—and he shall have produced a second island of Rum, similar in structure to the existing one.
In the actual island, however, there is a defect in the inclosing basket of sandstone : the basket, complete on three of
its sides, wants the fourth ; and the side opposite to the gap
which the fourth should have occupied is thicker than the
two other sides put together.   Where I now write there is
an old dark-coloured picture on the wall before me.   I take
off one of the four bars of which the frame is composed,—
the end-bar,—and stick it on to the end-bar opposite, and then
the picture is fully framed on two of its sides, and doubly
framed on a third, but the fourth side lacks framing altogether.
And such is the geology of the island of Rum.   We find the
one loch of the island,—that in which the Betsey lies at anchor,—and the long withdrawing valley, of which the loch is

---

trap-hills: *ie* igneous rocks, not only basalt, as Miller made clear. They are now known
to be the varied rocks forming the exhumed and eroded roots of an ancient volcanic complex; **Old Red Sandstone**: again, in fact, the much older Torridonian Sandstone – see
Introduction

merely a prolongation, occurring in the double sandstone bar : it seems to mark—to return to my illustration—the line in which the superadded piece of frame has been stuck on to the frame proper.   The origin of the island is illustrated by its structure : it has left its story legibly written, and we have but to run our eye over the characters and read.   An extended sea-bottom, composed of Old Red Sandstone, already tilted up by previous convulsions, so that the strata presented their edges, tier beyond tier, like roofing slate laid aslant on a floor, became a centre of Plutonic activity.   The molten trap broke through at various times, and presenting various appearances, but in nearly the same centre ; here existing as an augitic rock, there as a syenite, yonder as a basalt or amygdaloid. At one place it uptilted the sandstone ; at another it over-flowed it : the dark central masses raised their heads above the surface, higher and higher with every earthquake throe from beneath ; till at length the gigantic Ben More attained to its present altitude of two thousand three hundred feet over the sea-level, and the sandstone, borne up from beneath like floating sea-wrack on the back of a porpoise, reached in long outside bands its elevation of from six to eight hundred.   And such is the piece of history, composed in silent but expressive language, and inscribed in the old geologic cha-racter, on the rocks of Rum.

The wind lowered and the rain ceased during the night, and the morning of Monday was clear, bracing, and breezy. The island of Rum is chiefly famous among mineralogists for its heliotropes or bloodstones ; and we proposed devoting the greater part of the day to an examination of the hill of Scuir More, in which they occur, and which lies on the opposite side of the island, about eight miles from the mooring ground of the Betsey.   Ere setting out, however, I found time enough, by rising some two or three hours before breakfast, to explore the Red Sandstones on the southern side of the loch.   They lie in this bar of the frame,—to return once more to my old illustration,—as if it had been cut out of a piece of cross-grained ·deal, in which the annular bands, instead of ranging lengthwise, ran diagonally from side to side ; stratum leans over stratum, dipping towards the west at an angle of about thirty degrees ; and as in a continuous line of more than seven miles there seem no breaks or repetitions in the strata, the thickness of the deposit must be enormous,—not less, I should suppose, than from six to eight thousand feet.   Like the Lower Old Red Sandstones of Cromarty and Moray, the red arenaceous strata occur in thick beds, separated from each other by bands of a grayish-coloured stratified clay, on the planes of which I could trace with great distinctness ripple markings ; but in vain did I explore their numerous folds for the plates, scales, and fucoid impressions which abound in the gray argillaceous beds of the shores of the Moray and Cromarty Friths.   It would, however, be rash to pronounce them non-fossiliferous, after the hasty search of a single morn-ing,—unpardonably so in one who had spent very many morn-ings in putting to the question the gray stratified beds of Ross and Cromarty, ere he succeeded in extorting from them the secret of their organic riches.

We set out about half-past ten for Scuir More, through the Red Sandstone valley in which Loch Scresort terminates, with one of Mr Swanson's people, a young active lad of twenty, for our guide.   In passing upwards for nearly a mile along the stream that falls into the upper part of the loch, and lays bare the strata, we saw no change in the character of the sand-stone.   Red arenaceous beds of great thickness alternate with grayish-coloured bands, composed of a ripple-marked micaceous slate and a stratified clay.   For a depth of full three thousand feet, and I know not how much more,—for I lacked time to trace it further,—the deposit presents no other variety : the thick red bed of at least a hundred yards succeeds the thin

---

ripple markings: *ie* the ripples left by water on the surface of the original sand gray band of from three to six feet, and is succeeded by a si-milar gray band in turn.   The ripple-marks I found as sharply relieved in some of the folds as if the wavy undulations to which they owed their origin had passed over them within the hour.   The comparatively small size of their alternating ridges and furrows give evidence that the waters beneath which they had formed had been of no very profound depth.   In the upper part of the valley, which is bare, trackless, and solitary, with a high monotonous sandstone ridge bounding it on the one side, and a line of gloomy trap-hills rising over it on the other, the edges of the strata, where they protrude through the mingled heath and moss, exhibit the mysterious scratchings and polishings now so generally connected with the glacial theory of Agassiz.   The scratchings run in nearly the line of the valley, which exhibits no trace of moraines ; and they seem to have been produced rather by the operation of those extensively developed causes, whatever their nature, that have at once left their mark on the sides and summits of some of our highest hills, and the rocks and boulders of some of our most extended plains, than by the agency of forces limited to the locality.   They testify, Agassiz would perhaps say, not regarding the existence of some local glacier that descended from the higher grounds into the valley, but respecting the existence of the great polar glacier.   I felt, however, in this bleak and solitary hollow, with the grooved and polished platforms at my feet, stretching away amid the heath, like flat tombstones in a graveyard, that I had arrived at one geologic inscription to which I still wanted the key. The vesicular structure of the traps on the one hand, identi-cal with that of so many of our modern lavas,—the ripple-markings of the arenaceous beds on the other, indistinguish-able from those of the sea-banks on our coasts,—the upturned strata and the overlying trap,—told all their several stories of fire, or wave, or terrible convulsion, and told them simply

---

scratchings: see Introduction; **moraines**: the lack of such moraines in the valley implies that it was formed by a much larger glacial icecap, not a mere local glacier and clearly ; but here was a story not clearly told. It summoned up doubtful, ever-shifting visions,—now of a vast ice continent, abutting on this far isle of the Hebrides from the Pole, and trampling heavily over it,—now of the wild rush of a turbid, mountain-high flood breaking in from the west, and hurling athwart the torn surface, rocks, and stones, and clay,—now of a dreary ocean rising high along the hills, and bearing onward with its winds and currents, huge icebergs, that now brushed the mountain-sides, and now grated along the bottom of the submerged valleys. The inscription on the polished surfaces, with its careless mixture of groove and scratch, is an inscription of very various readings.

We passed along a transverse hollow, and then began to ascend a hill-side, from the ridge of which the water sheds to the opposite shore of the island, and on which we catch our first glimpse of Scuir More, standing up over the sea, like a pyramid shorn of its top. A brown lizard, nearly five inches in length, startled by our approach, ran hurriedly across the path ; and our guide, possessed by the general Highland belief that the creature is poisonous, and injures cattle, struck at it with a switch, and cut it in two immediately behind the hinder legs. The upper half, containing all that anatomists regard as the vitals, heart, brain, and viscera, all the main nerves, and all the larger arteries, lay stunned by the blow, as if dead ; nor did it manifest any signs of vitality so long as we remained beside it ; whereas the lower half, as if the whole life of the animal had retired into *it*, continued dancing upon the moss for a full minute after, like a young eel scooped out of some stream, and thrown upon the bank ; and then lay wriggling and palpitating for about half a minute more. There are few things more inexplicable in the province of the naturalist than the phenomenon of what may be termed divided life,—vitality broken into two, and yet continuing to exist as vitality in both the dissevered

---

Scuir More: Sgorr Mhór, also known as Bloodstone Hill

pieces.   We see in the nobler animals mere glimpses of the phenomenon,—mere indications of it, doubtfully apparent for at most a few minutes.   The blood drawn from the human arm by the lancet continues to live in the cup until it has cooled and begun to coagulate ; and when head and body have parted company under the guillotine, both exhibit for a brief space such unequivocal signs of life, that the question arose in France during the horrors of the Revolution, whether there might not be some glimmering of consciousness attendant at the same time on the fearfully opening and shutting eyes and mouth of the one, and the beating heart and jerking neck of the other.   The lower we descend in the scale of being, the more striking the instances which we receive of this divisibility of the vital principle.   I have seen the two halves of the heart of a ray pulsating for a full quarter of an hour after they had been separated from the body and from each other.   The blood circulates in the hind leg of a frog for many minutes after the removal of the heart, which meanwhile keeps up an independent motion of its own.   Vitality can be so divided in the earthworm, that, as demonstrated by the experiments of Spalanzani, each of the severed parts carries life enough away to set it up as an independent animal ; while the polypus, a creature of still more imperfect organization, and with the vivacious principle more equally diffused over it, may be multiplied by its pieces nearly as readily as a gooseberry bush by its slips.   It was sufficiently curious, however, to see, in the case of this brown lizard, the least vital half of the creature so much more vivacious, apparently, than the half which contained the heart and brain.   It is not improbable, however, that the presence of these organs had only the effect of rendering the upper portion which contained them more capable of being thrown into a state of insensibility.   A blow dealt one of the vertebrata of the head at once renders it insensible.   It is after

scale of being: see Additional Note for p. 26; polypus: here, probably *Hydra*, a small freshwater relative of sea anemones this mode the fisherman kills the salmon captured in his wear, and a single blow, when well directed, is always sufficient ; but no single blow has the same effect on the earthworm ; and here it was vitality in the inferior portion of the reptile, —the earthworm portion of it, if I may so speak,—that refused to participate in the state of syncope into which the vitality of the superior portion had been thrown.   The nice and delicate vitality of the brain seems to impart to the whole system in connection with it an aptitude for dying suddenly, —a susceptibility of instant death, which would be wanting without it.   The heart of the rabbit continues to beat regularly long after the brain has been removed by careful excision, if respiration be artificially kept up ; but if, instead of amputating the head, the brain be crushed in its place by a sudden blow of a hammer, the heart ceases its motion at once. And such seemed to be the principle illustrated here.   But why the agonized dancing on the sward of the inferior part of the reptile ?—why its after painful writhing and wriggling ? The young eel scooped from the stream, whose motions it resembled, is impressed by terror, and can feel pain ; was *it* also impressed by terror, or susceptible of suffering ?   We see in the case of both exactly the same signs,—the dancing, the writhing, the wriggling ; but are we to interpret them after the same manner ?   In the small red-headed earthworm divided by Spalanzani, that in three months got upper extremities to its lower part, and lower extremities, in as many weeks, to its upper part, the dividing blow must have dealt duplicate feelings,—pain and terror to the portion below, and pain and terror to the portion above,—so far, at least, as a creature so low in the scale was susceptible of these feelings ; but are we to hold that the leaping, wriggling tail of the reptile possessed in any degree a similar susceptibility ?   *I* can propound the riddle, but who shall resolve it ?   It may be added, that this brown lizard was the only recent saurian I chanced to see in the Hebrides, and that, though large for its kind, its whole bulk did not nearly equal that of a single vertebral joint of the fossil saurians of Eigg.   The reptile, since his deposition from the first place in the scale of creation, has sunk sadly in those parts : the ex-monarch has become a low plebeian.

We came down upon the coast through a swampy valley, terminating in the interior in a frowning wall of basalt, and bounded on the south, where it opens to the sea, by the Scuir More.   The Scuir is a precipitous mountain, that rises from twelve to fifteen hundred feet direct over the beach.   M'Culloch describes it as inaccessible, and states that it is only among the debris at its base that its heliotropes can be procured ; but the distinguished mineralogist must have had considerably less skill in climbing rocks than in describing them, as, indeed, some of his descriptions, though generally very admirable, abundantly testify.   I am inclined to infer from his book, after having passed over much of the ground which he describes, that he must have been a man of the type so well hit off by Burns in his portrait of Captain Grose,—round, rosy, short-legged, quick of eye but slow of foot, quite as indifferent a climber as Bailie Nicol Jarvie, and disposed at times, like the elderly gentleman drawn by Crabbe, to prefer the view at the hill-foot to the prospect from its summit.   I found little difficulty in scaling the sides of Scuir More for a thousand feet upwards,—in one part by a route rarely attempted before,—and in ensconcing myself among the bloodstones.   They occur in the amygdaloidal trap of which the upper part of the hill is mainly composed, in great numbers, and occasionally in bulky masses ; but it is rare to find other than small specimens that would be recognised as of value by the lapidary.   The inclosing rock must have been as thickly vesicular in its original state as the scoria of a glass-house ; and all the vesicles, large and small, like the retorts and re-

---

ex-monarch: see Additional Notes; **Grose**: a 'fine, fat, fodgel [dumpy] wight,/O stature short but genius bright' in Burns' poem 'On the Late Captain Grose's Peregrinations thro' Scotland collecting the Antiquities of that Kingdom'; **Bailie Nicol Jarvie**: Glasgow bailie (burgh councillor and elected magistrate, Scots) in Scott's novel *Rob Roy*, an urbanite out of place in the Highlands; **glass-house**: *ie* glass-producing workshop, not horticultural

ceivers of a laboratory, have been vessels in which some curious chemical process has been carried on.   Many of them
we find filled with a white semi-translucent or opaque chalcedony ; many more with a pure green earth, which, where
exposed to the bleaching influences of the weather, exhibits
a fine verdigris hue, but which in the fresh fracture is generally of an olive green, or of a brownish or reddish colour.
I have never yet seen a rock in which this earth was so abundant as in the amygdaloid of Scuir More.   For yards together in some places we see it projecting from the surface in
round globules, that very much resemble green pease, and
that occur as thickly in the inclosing mass as pebbles in an
Old Red Sandstone conglomerate.   The heliotrope has formed
among it in centres, to which the chalcedony seems to have
been drawn, as if by molecular attraction.   We find a mass,
varying from the size of a walnut to that of a man's head, occupying some larger vesicle or crevice of the amygdaloid, and
all the smaller vesicles around it, for an inch or two, filled
with what we may venture to term satellite heliotropes, some
of them as minute as grains of wild mustard, and all of them
more or less earthy, generally in proportion to their distance
from the first formed heliotrope in the middle.   No one can
see them in their place in the rock, with the abundant green
earth all around, and the chalcedony, in its uncoloured state,
filling up so many of the larger cavities, without acquiescing
in the conclusion respecting the origin of the gem first suggested by Werner, and afterwards adopted and illustrated by
M'Culloch.   The heliotrope is merely a chalcedony, stained
in the forming with an infusion of green earth, as the coloured waters in the apothecary's window are stained by the
infusions, vegetable and mineral, from which they derive their
ornamental character.   The red mottlings which so heighten
the beauty of the stone occur in comparatively few of the
specimens of Scuir More.   They are minute jasperous forma-

---

green earth: probably mainly the green clay silicate mineral celadonite (of which this is
an old name), sometimes compact but sometimes powdery (Heddle 1901); **Werner**: see
Introduction

tions, independent of the inclosing mass ; and, from their resemblance to streaks and spots of blood, suggest the name by
which the heliotrope is popularly known.   I succeeded in
making up, among the crags, a set of specimens curiously illustrative of the origin of the gem.   One specimen consists of
white, uncoloured chalcedony ; a second, of a rich verdigris-
hued green earth ; a third, of chalcedony barely tinged with
green ; a fourth, of chalcedony tinged just a shade more deeply ; a fifth, tinged more deeply still ; a sixth, of a deep green
on one side, and scarce at all coloured on the other ; and a
seventh, dark and richly toned,—a true bloodstone,—thickly
streaked and mottled with red jasper.   In the chemical process that rendered the Scuir More a mountain of gems there
were two deteriorating circumstances, which operated to the
disadvantage of its larger heliotropes : the green earth, as if
insufficiently stirred in the mixing, has gathered, in many of
them, into minute soft globules, like air-bubbles in glass, that
render them valueless for the purposes of the lapidary, by filling them all over with little cavities ; and in not a few of the
others, an infiltration of lime, that refused to incorporate with
the chalcedonic mass, exists in thin glassy films and veins,
that, from their comparative softness, have a nearly similar
effect with the impalpable green earth in roughing the surface under the burnisher.

We find figured by M'Culloch, in his " Western Islands,"
the internal cavity of a pebble of Scuir More, which he picked up on the beach below, and which had been formed evidently within one of the larger vesicles of the amygdaloid.
He describes it as curiously illustrative of a various chemistry : the outer crust is composed of a pale-zoned agate, inclosing a cavity, from the upper side of which there depends a
group of chalcedonic stalactites, some of them, as in ancient
spar caves, reaching to the floor ; and bearing on its under
side a large crystal of carbonate of lime, that the longer sta-

---

spar caves: spar is an old word for transparent or translucent mineral, so a 'spar cave'
would be one encrusted with stalactites and stalagmites, and other calcareous deposits

lactites pass through.   In the vesicle in which this hollow
pebble was formed three consecutive processes must have
gone on.   First, a process of infiltration coated the interior
all around with layer after layer, now of one mineral substance, now of another, as a plasterer coats over the sides and
ceiling of a room with successive layers of lime, putty, and
stucco ; and had this process gone on, the whole cell would
have been filled with a pale-zoned agate.   But it ceased, and
a new process began.   A chalcedonic infiltration gradually
entered from above ; and, instead of coating over the walls,
roof, and floor, it hardened into a group of spear-like stalactites, that lengthened by slow degrees, till some of them had
traversed the entire cavity from top to bottom.   And then
this second process ceased like the first, and a third commenced.   An infiltration of lime took place ; and the minute
calcareous molecules, under the influence of the law of crys-
tallization, built themselves up on the floor into a large smooth-
sided rhomb, resembling a closed sarcophagus resting in the
middle of some Egyptian cemetery.   And then, the limestone
crystal completed, there ensued no after change.   As shown
by some other specimens, however, there was a yet farther
process : a pure quartzose deposition took place, that coated
not a few of the calcareous rhombs with sprigs of rock-crystal.   I found in the Scuir More several cellular agates in
which similar processes had gone on,—none of them quite so
fine, however, as the one figured by M'Culloch ; but there
seemed no lack of evidence regarding the strange and multifarious chemistry that had been carried on in the vesicular
cavities of this mountain, as in the retorts of some vast laboratory.   Here was a vesicle filled with green earth,—there
a vesicle filled with calcareous spar,—yonder a vesicle crust-
ed round on a thin chalcedonic shell with rock-crystal,—in
one cavity an agate had been elaborated, in another a heliotrope, in a third a milk-white chalcedony, in a fourth a jasper.

On what principle, and under what direction, have results so various taken place in vesicles of the same rock, that in many instances occur scarce half an inch apart ? Why, for instance, should that vesicle have elaborated only green earth, and the vesicle separated from it by a partition barely a line in thickness, have elaborated only chalcedony ? Why should this chamber contain only a quartzose compound of oxygen and silica, and that second chamber beside it contain only a calcareous compound of lime and carbonic acid ? What law directed infiltrations so diverse to seek out for themselves vesicles in such close neighbourhood, and to keep, in so many instances, each to its own vesicle ? I can but state the problem,—not solve it. The groupes of heliotropes clustered each around its bulky centrical mass seem to show that the principle of molecular attraction may be operative in very dense mediæ,—in a hard amygdaloidal trap even ; and it seems not improbable, that to this law, which draws atom to its kindred atom, as clansmen of old used to speed at the mustering signal to their gathering place, the various chemistry of the vesicles may owe its variety.

I shall attempt stating the chemical problem furnished by the vesicles here in a mechanical form. Let us suppose that every vesicle was a chamber furnished with a door, and that beside every door there watched, as in the draught doors of our coal-pits, some one to open and shut it, as circumstances might require. Let us suppose further, that for a certain time an infusion of green earth pervaded the surrounding mass, and percolated through it, and that every door was opened to receive a portion of the infusion. We find that no vesicle wants its coating of this earthy mineral. The coating received, however, one-half the doors shut, while the other half remained agap, and filled with green earth entirely. Next followed a series of alternate infusions of chalcedony, jasper, and quartz ; many doors opened and received some

---

draught doors: to ensure ventilation throughout a coal mine, some passages had to be blocked off with doors which were kept closed except when someone was actually passing through two or three coatings, that form around the vesicles skull-like shells of agate, and then shut ; a few remained open, and became as entirely occupied with agate as many of the previous ones had become filled with green earth.   Then an ample infusion of chalcedony pervaded the mass.   Numerous doors again opened ; some took in a portion of the chalcedony, and then shut ; some remained open, and became filled with it ; and many more that had been previously filled by the green earth opened their doors again, and the chalcedony pervading the green porous mass, converted it into heliotrope.   Then an infusion of lime took place.   Doors opened, many of which had been hitherto shut, save for a short time, when the green-earth infusion obtained, and became filled with lime ; other doors opened for a brief space, and received lime enough to form a few crystals.   Last of all, there was a pure quartzose infusion, and doors opened, some for a longer time, some for a shorter, just as on previous occasions.   Now, by mechanical means of this character,—by such an arrangement of successive infusions, and such a device of shutting and opening of doors,—the phenomena exhibited by the vesicles could be produced.   There is no difficulty in working the problem mechanically, if we be allowed to assume in our data successive infusions, well-fitted doors, and watchful door-keepers ; and if any one can work it chemically,—certainly without door-keepers, but with such doors and such infusions as he can show to have existed,—he shall have cleared up the mystery of the Scuir More.   I have given their various cargoes to all its many vesicles by mechanical means, at no expense of ingenuity whatever.   Are there any of my readers prepared to give it to them by means purely chemical ?

There is a solitary house in the opening of the valley, over which the Scuir More stands sentinel,—a house so solitary, that the entire breadth of the island intervenes between it and the nearest human dwelling.   It is inhabited by a shepherd

---

ingenuity: see Additional Notes

and his wife,—the sole representatives in the valley of a numerous population, long since expatriated to make way for a few flocks of sheep, but whose ranges of little fields may still be seen green amid the heath on both sides, for nearly a mile upwards from the opening.   After descending along the precipices of the Scuir, we struck across the valley, and, on scaling the opposite slope, sat down on the summit to rest us, about a hundred yards over the house of the shepherd.   He had seen us from below, when engaged among the bloodstones, and had seen, withal, that we were not coming his way ; and, " on hospitable thoughts intent," he climbed to where we sat, accompanied by his wife, she bearing a vast bowl of milk, and he a basket of bread and cheese.   And we found the refreshment most seasonable, after our long hours of toil, and with a rough journey still before us.   It is an excellent circumstance, that hospitality grows best where it is most needed.   In the thick of men it dwindles and disappears, like fruits in the thick of a wood ; but where man is planted sparsely, it blossoms and matures, like apples on a standard or espalier.   It flourishes where the inn and the lodging-house cannot exist, and dies out where they thrive and multiply.

We reached the cross valley in the interior of the island about half an hour before sunset.   The evening was clear, calm, golden-tinted ; even wild heaths and rude rocks had assumed a flush of transient beauty ; and the emerald-green patches on the hill-sides, barred by the plough lengthwise, diagonally, and transverse, had borrowed an aspect of soft and velvety richness, from the mellowed light and the broadening shadows.   All was solitary.   We could see among the deserted fields the grass-grown foundations of cottages razed to the ground ; but the valley, more desolate than that which we had left, had not even its single inhabited dwelling : it seemed as if man had done with it for ever.   The island, eighteen years before, had been divested of its inhabitants,

'on hospitable thoughts intent': Milton's 'Paradise Lost', book 5, line 449

amounting at the time to rather more than four hundred
souls, to make way for one sheep-farmer and eight thousand
sheep.　All the aborigines of Rum crossed the Atlantic ; and
at the close of 1828, the entire population consisted of but
the sheep-farmer, and a few shepherds, his servants : the
island of Rum reckoned up scarce a single family at this period for every five square miles of area which it contained.
But depopulation on so extreme a scale was found inconvenient ; the place had been rendered too thoroughly a desert
for the comfort of the occupant ; and on the occasion of a
clearing which took place shortly after in Skye, he accommodated some ten or twelve of the ejected families with sites
for cottages, and pasturage for a few cows, on the bit of morass beside Loch Scresort, on which I had seen their humble
dwellings.　But the whole of the once peopled interior remains a wilderness, without inhabitant,—all the more lonely
in its aspect from the circumstance that the solitary valleys,
with their plough-furrowed patches, and their ruined heaps
of stone, open upon shores every whit as solitary as themselves, and that the wide untrodden sea stretches drearily
around.　The armies of the insect world were sporting in the
light this evening by millions ; a brown stream that runs
through the valley yielded an incessant poppling sound, from
the myriads of fish that were ceaselessly leaping in the pools,
beguiled by the quick glancing wings of green and gold that
fluttered over them ; along a distant hill-side there ran what
seemed the ruins of a gray-stone fence, erected, says tradition,
in a remote age, to facilitate the hunting of the deer ; there
were fields on which the heath and moss of the surrounding
moorlands were fast encroaching, that had borne many a successive harvest ; and prostrate cottages, that had been the
scenes of christenings, and bridals, and blythe new-year's days;
—all seemed to bespeak the place a fitting habitation for man,
in which not only the necessaries, but also a few of the luxu-

ries of life, might be procured ; but in the entire prospect not
a man nor a man's dwelling could the eye command.   The
landscape was one without figures.   I do not much like extermination carried out so thoroughly and on system ;—it
seems bad policy ; and I have not succeeded in thinking any
the better of it though assured by the economists that there
are more than people enough in Scotland still.   There are, I
believe, more than enough in our workhouses,—more than
enough on our pauper-rolls,—more than enough huddled up,
disreputable, useless, and unhappy, in the miasmatic alleys
and typhoid courts of our large towns ; but I have yet to
learn how arguments for local depopulation are to be drawn
from facts such as these.   A brave and hardy people, favourably placed for the development of all that is excellent in
human nature, form the glory and strength of a country ;—
a people sunk into an abyss of degradation and misery, and
in which it is the whole tendency of external circumstances
to sink them yet deeper, constitute its weakness and its
shame ; and I cannot quite see on what principle the ominous increase which is taking place among us in the worse
class, is to form our solace or apology for the wholesale expatriation of the better.   It did not seem as if the depopulation of Rum had tended much to any one's advantage.   The
single sheep-farmer who had occupied the holdings of so many
had been unfortunate in his speculations, and had left the
island : the proprietor, his landlord, seemed to have been as
little fortunate as the tenant, for the island itself was in the
market ; and a report went current at the time that it was
on the eve of being purchased by some wealthy Englishman,
who purposed converting it into a deer-forest.   How strange
a cycle !   Uninhabited originally save by wild animals, it
became at an early period a home of men, who, as the gray
wall on the hill-side testified, derived, in part at least, their
sustenance from the chase.   They broke in from the waste

the furrowed patches on the slopes of the valleys,—they reared herds of cattle and flocks of sheep,—their number increased to nearly five hundred souls,—they enjoyed the average happiness of human creatures in the present imperfect state of being,—they contributed their portion of hardy and vigorous manhood to the armies of the country,—and a few of their more adventurous spirits, impatient of the narrow bounds which confined them, and a course of life little varied by incident, emigrated to America. Then came the change of system so general in the Highlands; and the island lost all its original inhabitants, on a wool and mutton speculation,—inhabitants, the descendants of men who had chased the deer on its hills five hundred years before, and who, though they recognised some wild island lord as their superior, and did him service, had regarded the place as indisputably their own. And now yet another change was on the eve of ensuing, and the island was to return to its original state, as a home of wild animals, where a few hunters from the mainland might enjoy the chase for a month or two every twelvemonth, but which could form no permanent place of human abode. Once more, a strange and surely most melancholy cycle!

There was light enough left, as we reached the upper part of Loch Scresort, to show us a shoal of small silver-coated trout, leaping by scores at the effluence of the little stream along which we had set out in the morning on our expedition. There was a net stretched across where the play was thickest; and we learned that the haul of the previous tide had amounted to several hundreds. On reaching the Betsey, we found a pail and basket laid against the companion-head, —the basket containing about two dozen small trout,—the minister's unsolicited teind of the morning draught; the pail filled with razor-fish of great size. The people of my friend are far from wealthy; there is scarce any circulating medium in Rum; and the cottars in Eigg contrive barely enough to

circulating medium: cash

earn at the harvest in the Lowlands, money sufficient to
clear with their landlord at rent-day.   Their contributions
for ecclesiastical purposes make no great figure, therefore, in
the lists of the Sustentation Fund.   But of what they have
they give willingly and in a kindly spirit ; and if baskets of
small trout, or pailfuls of spout-fish, went current in the Free
Church, there would, I am certain, be a per centage of both
the fish and the mollusc, derived from the Small Isles, in the
half-yearly sustentation dividends.   We found the supply of
both,—especially as provisions were beginning to run short
in the lockers of the Betsey,—quite deserving of our gratitude.   The razor-fish had been brought us by the worthy catechist of the island.   He had gone to the ebb in our special
behalf, and had spent a tide in laboriously filling the pail
with these "treasures hid in the sand;" thoroughly aware,
like the old exiled Puritan, who eked out his meals in a time
of scarcity with the oysters of New England, that even the
razor-fish, under this head, is included in the promises.   There
is a peculiarity in the razor-fish of Rum that I have not
marked in the razor-fish of our eastern coasts.   The gills of
the animal, instead of bearing the general colour of its other
parts, like those of the oyster, are of a deep green colour, resembling, when examined by the microscope, the fringe of a
green curtain.

We were told by John Stewart, that the expatriated inhabitants of Rum used to catch trout by a simple device of
ancient standing, which preceded the introduction of nets into
the island, and which, it is possible, may in other localities
have not only preceded the use of the net, but may have also
suggested it : it had at least the appearance of being a first
beginning of invention in this direction.   The islanders gathered large quantities of heath, and then tying it loosely into
bundles, and stripping it of its softer leafage, they laid the
bundles across the stream on a little mound held down by

'treasures hid in the sand': Bible, Deuteronomy 33:19, appropriate for these Disruption
times, as Miller's readers knew: 'They shall call the people unto the mountain; there they
shall offer sacrifices of righteousness: for they shall suck of the abundance of the seas, and
of treasures hid in the sand'; the old exiled Puritan: reference unknown, but evidently
to the Pilgrim Fathers in North America – Miller always sympathised with the Puritans

stones, with the tops of the heath turned upwards to the
current. The water rose against the mound for a foot or
eighteen inches, and then murmured over and through, occa-
sioning an expansion among the hard elastic sprays. Next a
party of the islanders came down the stream, beating the
banks and pools, and sending a still thickening shoal of trout
before them, that, on reaching the miniature dam formed by
the bundles, darted forward for shelter, as if to a hollow bank,
and stuck among the slim hard branches, as they would in
the meshes of a net. The stones were then hastily thrown
off,—the bundles pitched ashore,—the better fish, to the
amount not unfrequently of several scores, secured,—and the
young fry returned to the stream, to take care of themselves, and grow bigger. We fared richly this evening, after
our hard day's labour, on tea and trout ; and as the minister
had to attend a meeting of the Presbytery of Skye on the
following Wednesday, we sailed next morning for Glenelg,
whence he purposed taking the steamer for Portree. Winds
were light and baffling, and the currents, like capricious
friends, neutralized at one time the assistance which they
lent us at another. It was dark night ere we had passed
Isle Ornsay, and morning broke as we cast anchor in the
Bay of Glenelg. At ten o'clock the steamer heaved-to in
the bay to land a few passengers, and the minister went on
board, leaving me in charge of the Betsey, to follow him,
when the tide set in, through the Kyles of Skye.

CHAPTER IX.

No sailing vessel attempts threading the Kyles of Skye from the south in the face of an adverse tide. The currents of Kyle Rhea care little for the wind-filled sail, and battle at times, on scarce unequal terms, with the steam-propelled paddle. The Toward Castle this morning had such a struggle to force her way inwards as may be seen maintained at the door of some place of public meeting during the heat of some agitating controversy, when seat and passage within can hold no more, and a disappointed crowd press eagerly for admission from without. Viewed from the anchoring place at Glenelg, the opening of the Kyle presents the appearance of the bottom of a landlocked bay ;—the hills of Skye seem leaning against those of the mainland : and the tide-buffeted steamer looked this morning as if boring her way into the earth like a disinterred mole, only at a rate vastly slower. First, however, with a progress resembling that of the minute-hand of a clock, the bows disappeared amid the heath, then the midships, then the quarter-deck and stern, and then, last of all, the red tip of the sun-brightened union-jack that streamed gaudily behind. I had at least two hours before me ere the Betsey might attempt weighing anchor ; and, that they might leave some mark, I went and spent them ashore in the opening of Glenelg,—a gneiss district, nearly identical in structure with the district of Knock and Isle Ornsay. The upper part of the valley is bare and treeless, but not such its character where it opens to the sea ; the hills are richly wooded ; and cottages and corn-fields, with here and there a reach of the lively little river, peep out from among the trees. A group of tall roofless buildings, with a strong wall in front, form the central point in the landscape : these are the dismantled Berera Barracks, built, like the line of forts in .the great Caledonian Valley,—Fort George, Fort Augustus, and Fort William,—to overawe the Highlands at a time when the loyalty of the Highlander pointed to a king beyond the water ; but all use for them has long gone by, and they now lie in dreary ruin,—mere sheltering places for the toad and the bat. I found in a loose silt on the banks of the river, at some little distance below tide-mark, a bed of shells and coral, which might belong, I at first supposed, to some secondary formation, but which I ascertained, on examination, to be a mere recent deposit, not so old by many centuries as our last raised sea-beaches. There occurs in various localities on these western coasts, especially on the shores of the island of Pabba, a sprig coral, considerably larger in size than any I have elsewhere seen in Scotland ; and it was from its great abundance in this bed of silt that I was at first led to deem the deposit an ancient one.

We weighed anchor about noon, and entered the opening of Kyle Rhea. Vessel after vessel, to the number of eight or ten in all, had been arriving in the course of the morning, and dropping anchor, nearer the opening or farther away, each according to its sailing ability, to await the turn of the tide ; and we now found ourselves one of the components of a little fleet, with some five or six vessels sweeping up the Kyle before us, and some three or four driving on behind. Never, except perhaps in a Highland river big in flood, have I seen such a tide. It danced and wheeled, and came boil-

---

Berera: correctly Bernera; king beyond the water: one of the exiled Stuarts, *ie* James VII and II and his descendants; sprig coral: presumably what is in fact a calcareous alga, whose broken limy skeletons form 'maerl' beaches and sea-bed deposits ing in huge masses from the bottom; and now our bows heaved abruptly round in one direction, and now they jerked as suddenly round in another; and, though there blew a moderate breeze at the time, the helm failed to keep the sails steadily full.   But whether our sheets bellied out, or flapped right in the wind's eye, on we swept in the tideway, like a cork caught during a thunder shower in one of the rapids of the High Street.   At one point the Kyle is little more than a quarter of a mile in breadth; and here, in the powerful eddie which ran along the shore, we saw a group of small fishing-boats pursuing a shoal of sillocks in a style that blent all the liveliness of the chase with the specific interest of the angle.   The shoal, restless as the tides among which it disported, now rose in the boilings of one eddie, now beat the water into foam amid the stiller dimplings of another.   The boats hurried from spot to spot wherever the quick glittering scales appeared.   For a few seconds rods would be cast thick and fast, as if employed in beating the water, and captured fish glanced bright to the sun; and then the take would cease, and the play rise elsewhere, and oars would flash out amain, as the little fleet again dashed into the heart of the shoal. As the Kyle widened, the force of the current diminished, and sail and helm again became things of positive importance.   The wind blew a-head, steady though not strong; and the Betsey, with companions in the voyage against which to measure herself, began to show her paces.   First she passed one bulky vessel, then another: she lay closer to the wind than any of her fellows, glided more quickly through the water, turned in her stays like Lady Betty in a minuet; and, ere we had reached Kyle Akin, the fleet in the middle of which we had started were toiling far behind us, all save one vessel, a stately brig; and just as we were going to pass her too, she cast anchor, to await the change of the tide, which runs from the west during flood at Kyle Akin, as it runs from

---

sheets: nautical, the ropes controlling the trim of the sails. Miller apparently referred the term, wrongly, to the sails themselves; **High Street**: of Edinburgh; it slopes downwards; **turned in her stays like Lady Betty in a minuet**: see Additional Notes

the east through Kyle Rhea.   The wind had freshened ; and
as it was now within two hours of full sea, the force of the
current had somewhat abated ; and so we kept on our course,
tacking in scant room, however, and making but little way.
A few vessels attempted following us, but, after an inefficient
tack or two, they fell back on the anchoring ground, leaving
the Betsey to buffet the currents alone.   Tack followed tack
sharp and quick in the narrows, with an iron-bound coast on
either hand.   We had frequent and delicate turning : now
we lost fifty yards, now we gained a hundred.   John Stewart
held the helm ; and as none of us had ever sailed the way
before, I had the vessel's chart spread out on the companion-
head before me, and told him when to wear and when to
hold on his way,—at what places we might run up almost
to the rock edge, and at what places it was safest to give the
land a good offing.   Hurrah for the Free Church yacht
Betsey ! and hurrah once more !   We cleared the Kyle, leaving a whole fleet tide-bound behind us ; and, stretching out
at one long tack into the open sea, bore, at the next, right
into the bay at Broadford, where we cast anchor for the night,
within two hundred yards of the shore.   Provisions were
running short ; and so I had to make a late dinner this evening on some of the razor-fish of Rum, topped by a dish of tea.
But there is always rather more appetite than food in the
country ;—such, at least, is the common result under the
present mode of distribution : the hunger overlaps and out-
stretches the provision ; and there was comfort in the reflec-
tion, that with the razor-fish on which to fall back, it overlapped it but by a very little on this occasion in the cabin of
the Betsey.   The steam-boat passed southwards next morning, and I was joined by my friend the minister a little before breakfast.

   The day was miserably bad : the rain continued pattering
on the skylight, now lighter, now heavier, till within an hour

---

wear: to turn a sailing ship by moving her head first away from and then, if necessary,
back to the wind, with an intermediate position where the ship's stern is to the wind: the
opposite of 'tack' (see Additional Note for p. 141). But Miller probably meant 'tack',
which he used elsewhere in the passage. Wearing loses ground when one is seeking to sail
upwind

of sunset, when it ceased, and a light breeze began to unroll the thick fogs from off the landscape, volume after volume, like coverings from off a mummy,—leaving exposed in the valley of the Lias a brown and cheerless prospect of dark bogs and of debris-covered hills, streaked this evening with downward lines of foam.   The seaward view is more pleasing.   The deep russet of the interior we find bordered for miles along the edge of the bay with a many-shaded fringe of green ; and the smooth grassy island of Pabba lies in the midst, a polished gem, all the more advantageously displayed from the roughness of the surrounding setting.   We took boat, and explored the Lias in our immediate neighbourhood till dusk.   I had spent several hours among its deposits when on my way to Portree, and several hours more when on my journey across the country to the east coast ; but it may be well, for the sake of maintaining some continuity of description, to throw together my various observations on the formation, as if made at one time, and to connect them with my exploration of Pabba, which took place on the following morning.   The rocks of Pabba belong to the upper part of the Lias ; while the lower part may be found leaning to the south, towards the Red Sandstones of the Bay of Lucy. Taking what seems to be the natural order, I shall begin with the base of the formation first.

In the general indentation of the coast, in the opening of which the island of Pabba lies somewhat like a long green steam-boat at anchor, there is included a smaller indentation, known as the Bay or Cove of Lucy.   The central space in the cove is soft and gravelly ; but on both its sides it is flanked by low rocks, that stretch out into the sea in long rectilinear lines, like the foundations of dry-stone fences.   On the south side the rocks are red ; on the north they are of a bluish-gray colour ; their hues are as distinct as those of the coloured patches in a map ; and they represent geological periods that

---

Bay of Lucy: the inlet named on the Ordnance Survey map as Ob Lusa, 'Òb' being Gaelic for 'bay'. The cottage, or at least a cottage, is still there, as are the corals of the Lusa Coral Bed (Morton and Hudson 1995, J. D. Hudson, *pers. comm.* 2003)

lie widely apart. The red rocks we find laid down in most
of our maps as Old Red, though I am disposed to regard them
as of a much higher antiquity than even that ancient system ;
while the bluish-gray rocks are decidedly Liasic.* The cove
between represents a deep ditch-like hollow, which occurs in
Skye, both in the interior and on the sea-shore, in the line of
boundary betwixt the Red Sandstone and the Lias ; and it
"seems to have originated," says M'Culloch, "in the decomposition of the exposed parts of the formations at their junction." "Hence," he adds, "from the wearing of the materials at the surface, a cavity has been produced, which becoming subsequently filled with rubbish, and generally covered over with a vegetable soil of unusual depth, effectually
prevents a view of the contiguous parts." The first strata
exposed on the northern side are the oldest Liasic rocks anywhere seen in Scotland. They are composed chiefly of green-
ish-coloured fissile sandstones and calciferous grits, in which
we meet a few fossils, very imperfectly preserved. But the
organisms increase as we go on. We see in passing, near a
picturesque little cottage,—the only one on the shores of the
bay,—a crag of a singularly rough appearance, that projects
mole-like from the sward upon the beach, and then descending abruptly to the level of the other strata, runs out in a
long ragged line into the sea. The stratum, from two to three
feet in thickness, of which it is formed, seems wholly built up
of irregularly-formed rubbly concretions, just as some of the
garden-walls in the neighbourhood of Edinburgh are built of
the rough scoria of our glass-houses ; and we find, on examination, that every seeming concretion in the bed is a perfectly
formed coral of the genus Astrea. We have arrived at an
entire bed of corals, all of one species. Their surfaces, where-
ever they have been washed by the sea, are of great beauty :

* Sir R. Murchison considers these rocks Silurian. See "Quarterly
Journal" of the Geological Society, Anniversary Address.

---

red rocks ... bluish-gray ... Liasic: whatever Symonds meant in his ambiguous footnote, Miller was correct, these rocks being respectively the Torridonian Sandstone (much
older than the Old Red) and the Lias

nothing can be more irregular than the outline of each mass, and yet scarce anything more regular than the sculpturings on every part of it. We find them fretted over with polygons, like those of a honeycomb, only somewhat less mathematically exact, and the centre of every polygon contains its many-rayed star. It is difficult to distinguish between species in some of the divisions of corals : one Astrea, recent or extinct, is sometimes found so exceedingly like another of some very different formation or period, that the more modern might almost be deemed a lineal descendant of the more ancient species. With an eye to the fact, I brought with me some characteristic specimens of this Astrea* of the Lower Lias, which I have ranged side by side with the Astreæ of the Oolite I had found so abundant a twelvemonth before in the neighbourhood of Helmsdale. In some of the hand specimens, that present merely a piece of polygonal surface, bounded by fractured sides, the difference is not easily distinguishable : the polygonal depressions are generally smaller in the Oolitic species, and shallower in the Liasic one ; but not unfrequently these differences disappear, and it is only when compared in the entire unbroken coral that their specific peculiarities acquire the necessary prominence. The Oolitic Astrea is of much greater size than the Liasic one : it occurs not unfrequently in masses of from two to three feet in diameter ; and as its polygons are tubes that converge to the footstalk on which it originally formed, it presents in the average outline a fungous-like appearance ; whereas in the smaller Liasic coral, which rarely exceeds a foot in diameter, there is no such general convergency of the tubes ; and the form in one piece, save that there is a certain degree of flatness common to all, bears no resemblance to the form in another. Some of the recent Astreæ are of great beauty when inhabited by the living zoophites whose skeleton framework

* Probably one of the Isastrea of Edwards.

---

zoophites: *ie* zoophytes, here, the living individual coral animals each of which is equivalent to a tiny sea anemone

they compose.   Every polygonal star in the mass is the house
of a separate animal, that, when withdrawn into its cell, presents the appearance of a minute flower, somewhat like a
daisy stuck flat to the surface, and that, when stretched out,
resembles a small round tower, with a garland of leaves bound
round it atop for a cornice.   The *Astrea viridis*, a coral of
the tropics, presents on a ground of velvety brown myriads
of deep green florets, that ever and anon start up from the
level in their tower-like shape, contract and expand their petals, and then, shrinking back into their cells, straightway become florets again.   The Lower Lias presented in one of its
opening scenes, in this part of the world, appearances of similar beauty widely spread.   For miles together,—we know
not how many,—the bottom of a clear shallow sea was paved
with living Astreæ : every irregular rock-like coral formed a
separate colony of polypora, that, when in motion, presented
the appearance of continuous masses of many-coloured life,
and when at rest, the places they occupied were more thickly
studded with the living florets than the richest and most
flowery piece of pasture the reader ever saw, with its violets
or its daisies.   And mile beyond mile this scene of beauty
stretched on through the shallow depths of the Liasic sea.
The calcareous framework of most of the recent Astreæ are
white ; but in the species referred to,—the *Astrea viridis*,—
it is of a dark-brown colour.   It is not unworthy of remark,
in connection with these facts, that the Oolitic Astrea of
Helmsdale occurs as a white, or, when darkest, as a cream-
coloured petrifaction ; whereas the Liasic Astrea of Skye is
invariably of a deep earthy hue.   The one was probably a
white, the other a dingy-coloured coral.

    The Liasic bed of Astreæ existed long enough here to at-
tain a thickness of from two to three feet.   Mass rose over
mass,—the living upon the dead,—till at length, by a deposit
of mingled mud and sand,—the effect, mayhap, of some change

---

polypora: possibly error for polypifera, *ie* plural of polypifer of currents, induced we know not how,—the innumerable polypedes of the living surface were buried up and killed, and then, for many yards, layer after layer of a calciferous grit was piled over them.   The fossils of the grit are few and ill preserved ; but we occasionally find in it a coral similar to the Astrea of the bed below, and, a little higher up, in an impure limestone, specimens, in rather indifferent keeping, of a genus of polypifer which somewhat resembles the Turbinolia of the Mountain Limestone.   It presents in the cross section the same radiated structure as the *Turbinolia fungites*, and nearly the same furrowed appearance in the longitudinal one ; but, seen in the larger specimens, we find that it was a branched coral, with obtuse forky boughs, in each of which, it is probable, from their general structure, there lived a single polype.   It may have been the resemblance which these bear, when seen in detached branches, to the older Caryophyllia, taken in connection with the fact that the deposit in which they occur rests on the ancient Red Sandstone of the district, that led M'Culloch to question whether this fossiliferous formation had not nearly as clear a claim to be regarded as an analogue of the Carboniferous Limestone of England as of its Lias ; and hence he contented himself with terming it simply the Gryphite Limestone.   Sir R. Murchison, whose much more close and extensive acquaintance with fossils enabled him to assign to the deposit its true place, was struck, however, with the general resemblance of its polypifers to " those of the Madreporite Limestone of the Carboniferous series."   These polypifers occur in only the Lower Lias of Skye. *   I found no corals in its higher beds, though these are charged with other fossils, more characteristic of the formation, in vast abundance.   In not a few of the middle strata, composed of a mud-coloured fissile sandstone, the gryphites

* See a paper by the Rev. P. B. Brodie, on Lias Corals, " Edinburgh New Philosophic Journal," April 1857.

polypedes: perhaps an error for 'polypes', plural of 'polype', variant of 'polyp', or a misspelling of the plural of 'polypide', the polyp of a colonial animal

lie as thickly as currants in a Christmas cake ; and as they
weather white, while the stone in which they are embedded
retains its dingy hue, they somewhat remind one of the white-
lead tears of the undertaker mottling a hatchment of sable.
In a fragment of the dark sandstone, six inches by seven,
which I brought with me, I reckon no fewer than twenty-two
gryphites ; and it forms but an average specimen of the bed
from which I detached it.   By far the most abundant species
is that not inelegant shell so characteristic of the formation,
the *Gryphæa incurva*.   We find detached specimens scattered
over the beach by hundreds, mixed up with the remains of
recent shells, as if the *Gryphæa incurva* were a recent shell
too. They lie, bleached white by the weather, among the valves
of defunct oysters and dead buccinidæ ; and, from their resemblance to lamps cast in the classic model, remind one, in
the corners where they have accumulated most thickly, of the
old magician's stock in trade, who wiled away the lamp of
Aladdin from Aladdin's simple wife.   The *Gryphæa obliquita*
and *Gryphæa M'Cullochii* also occur among these middle strata
of the Lias, though much less frequently than the other.   We,
besides, found in them at least two species of Pecten, with two
species of Terebratula,—the one smooth, the other sulcated ;
a bivalve resembling a Donax ; another bivalve, evidently
a Gervillia, though apparently of a species not yet described ;
and the ill-preserved rings of large Ammonites, from ten
inches to a foot in diameter.   Towards the bottom of the
bay the fossils again become more rare, though they re-appear once more in considerable abundance as we pass along
its northern side ; but in order to acquaint ourselves with
the upper organisms of the formation, we have to take boat
and explore the northern shores of Pabba.   The Lias of Skye
has its three distinct groupes of fossils : its lower coraline
group, in which the Astrea described is most abundant ; its
middle group, in which the *Gryphæa incurva* occurs by mil-

---

white lead tears ... hatchment ... sable: the black-painted heraldic arms of a deceased
person, as used in a funeral, with conventional white lead paint tears – no doubt of the
same slightly curled teardrop shape as a *Gryphaea*

lions ; and its upper group, abounding in Ammonites, Nautili, Pinnæ, and Serpulæ.

Friday made amends for the rains and fogs of its disagreeable predecessor : the morning rose bright and beautiful, with
just wind enough to fill, and barely fill, the sail, hoisted high,
with miser economy, that not a breath might be lost ; and,
weighing anchor, and shaking out all our canvass, we bore
down on Pabba to explore.   This island, so soft in outline
and colour, is formidably fenced round by dangerous reefs ;
and, leaving the Betsey in charge of John Stewart and his
companion, to dodge on in the offing, I set out with the minister in our little boat, and landed on the north-eastern side of
the island, beside a trap-dyke that served us as a pier.   He
would be a happy geologist who, with a few thousands to
spare, could call Pabba his own.   It contains less than a
square mile of surface ; and a walk of little more than three
miles and a half along the line where the waves break at
high water brings the traveller back to his starting point ;
and yet, though thus limited in area, the petrifactions of its
shores might of themselves fill a museum.   They rise by
thousands and tens of thousands on the exposed planes of its
sea-washed strata, standing out in bold relief, like sculpturings on ancient tombstones, at once mummies and monuments,
—the dead, and the carved memorials of the dead.   Every
rock is a tablet of hieroglyphics, with an ascertained alphabet ; every rolled pebble a casket, with old pictorial records
locked up within.   Trap-dykes, beyond comparison finer than
those of the Water of Leith, which first suggested to Hutton
his theory, stand up like fences over the sedimentary strata,
or run out like moles far into the sea.   The entire island, too,
so green, rich, and level, is itself a specimen illustrative of
the effect of geologic formation on scenery.   We find its nearest neighbour,—the steep, brown, barren island of Longa,
which is composed of the ancient Red Sandstone of the dis-

Water of Leith ... Hutton: As a key part of his *Theory of the Earth*, James Hutton
realized during the eighteenth century that dykes were the remains of igneous rocks,
injected while molten into cracks in the surrounding rocks, then cooling and solidifying.
The dykes he observed included some in the valley of the Water of Leith, the river which
passes through Edinburgh (Hutton 1795, I, p. 153; McIntyre and McKirdy 2001)

trict,—differing as thoroughly from it in aspect as a bit of granite differs from a bit of clay-slate ; and the whole prospect around, save the green Liasic strip that lies along the bottom of the Bay of Broadford, exhibits, true to its various components, Plutonic or sedimentary, a character of picturesque roughness or bold sublimity. The only piece of smooth, level England, contained in the entire landscape, is the fossil-mottled island of Pabba. We were first struck, on landing this morning, by the great number of Pinnæ embedded in the strata,—shells varying from five to ten inches in length,— one species of the common flat type, exemplified in the existing *Pinna sulcata*, and another nearly quadrangular, in the cross section, like the *Pinna lanceolata* of the Scarborough limestone. The quadrangular species is more deeply crisped outside than the flat one. Both species bear the longitudinal groove in the centre, and, when broken across, are found to contain numerous smaller shells,—Terebratulæ of both the smooth and sulcated kinds, and a species of minute smooth Pecten resembling the *Pecten demissus*, but smaller. The Pinnæ, ere they became embedded in the original sea-bottom, long since hardened into rock around them, were, we find, dead shells, into which, as into the dead open shells of our existing beaches, smaller shells were washed by the waves. Our recent Pinnæ are all sedentary shells, some of them full two feet in length, fastened to their places on their deep-sea floors by flowing silky byssi,—cables of many strands,—of which beautiful pieces of dress, such as gloves and hose, have been manufactured. An old French naturalist, the Abbe Le Pluche, tells us that " the Pinna with its fleshy tongue" (foot), —a rude inefficient-looking implement for work so nice,— " spins such threads as are more valuable than silk itself, and with which the most beautiful stuffs that ever were seen have been made by the Sicilian weavers." Gloves made of the byssus of recent Pinnæ may be seen in the British Museum.

Abbe le Pluche: author of a popular eighteenth century illustrated book, *Spectacle de la Nature*, published in various English translations such as *Nature Display'd*; byssi: plural of byssus; here, the hardened threads that fasten certain bivalve shellfish to rocks

Associated with the numerous Pinnæ of Pabba, we found a delicately-formed Modiola, a small Ostrya, Plagiostoma, Terebratula, several species of Pectens, a triangular univalve resembling a Trochus, innumerable groupes of Serpulæ, and the star-like joints of Pentacrinites. The Gryphæ are also abundant, occurring in extensive beds ; and Belemnites of various species lie as thickly scattered over the rock as if they had been the spindles of a whole kingdom thrown aside in consequence of some such edict framed to put them down as that passed by the father of the Sleeping Beauty. We find, among the detached masses of the beach, specimens of Nautilus, which, though rarely perfect, are sufficiently so to show the peculiarities of the shell ; and numerous Ammonites project in relief from almost every weathered plane of the strata. These last shells, in the tract of shore which we examined, are chiefly of one species,—the *Ammonites spinatus*,—one of which, considerably broken, the reader may find figured in Sowerby's "Mineral Conchology," from a specimen brought from Pabba sixteen years ago by Sir R. Murchison. It is difficult to procure specimens tolerably complete. We find bits of outer rings existing as limestone, with every rib sharply preserved, but the rest of the fossil lost in the shale. I succeeded in finding but two specimens that show the inner whorls. They are thickly ribbed; and the chief peculiarity which they exhibit, not so directly indicated by Mr Sowerby's figure, is, that while the ribs of the outer whorl are broad and deep, as in the *Ammonites obtusus*, they suddenly change their character, and become numerous and narrow in the inner whorls, as in the *Ammonites communis*.

The tide began to flow, and we had to quit our explorations, and return to the Betsey. The little wind had become less, and all the canvass we could hang out enabled us to draw but a sluggish furrow. The stern of the Betsey " wrought no buttons" on this occasion ; but she had a good tide under

---

Pentacrinites ... joints: the stems of crinoids break up into little elements or 'joints' sometimes shaped like stars, as here; **'wrought no buttons'**: the allusion, if any, is unknown, and meaning uncertain – perhaps *Betsey* is sailing so slowly that she cannot even make a wake of the kind which is smooth and marked by button-like eddies

her keel ; and ere the dinner-hour we had passed through the
narrows of Kyle Akin.   The village of this name was designed by the late Lord M'Donald for a great sea-port town ;
but it refused to grow ; and it has since become a gentleman
in a small way, and does nothing.   It forms, however, a handsome group of houses, pleasantly situated on a flat green tongue
of land, on the Skye side, just within the opening of the Kyle ;
and there rises on an eminence beyond it a fine old tower,
rent open, as if by an earthquake, from top to bottom, which
forms one of the most picturesque objects I have almost ever
seen in a landscape.   There are bold hills all around, and
rocky islands, with the ceaseless rush of tides in front ; while
the cloven tower, rising high over the shore, is seen, in threading the Kyles, whether from the south or north, relieved dark
against the sky, as the central object in the vista.   We find
it thus described by the Messrs Anderson of Inverness, in
their excellent " Guide Book,"—by far the best companion
of the kind with which the traveller who sets himself to explore our Scottish Highlands can be provided.   " Close to the
village of Kyle Akin are the ruins of an old square keep,
called Castle Muel or Maoil, the walls of which are of a remarkable thickness.   It is said to have been built by the
daughter of a Norwegian king, married to a Mackinnon or
Macdonald, for the purpose of levying an impost on all vessels passing the Kyles, excepting, says the tradition, those of
her own country.   For the more certain exaction of this duty,
she is reported to have caused a strong chain to be stretched
across from shore to shore ; and the spot in the rocks to which
the terminal links were attached is still pointed out."   It was
high time for us to be home.   The dinner hour came ; but,
in meet illustration of the profound remark of Trotty-Veck,
not the dinner.   We had been in a cold Moderate district,
whence there came no half-dozens of eggs, or whole dozens
of trout, or pailfuls of razor-fish, and in which hard cabin-

---

Anderson: see Additional Note for p. 9; **Trotty-Veck**: Trotty Veck, the postman who
goes without his dinner in *The Chimes* of 1844, one of Charles Dickens's Christmas
Novels

biscuit cost us sixpence per pound.   And now our stores were exhausted, and we had to dine as we best could, on our last half-ounce of tea, sweetened by our last quarter of a pound of sugar.   I had marked, however, a dried thornback hanging among the rigging.   It had been there nearly three weeks before, when I came first aboard, and no one seemed to know for how many weeks previous; for, as it had come to be a sort of fixture in the vessel, it could be looked at without being seen.   But necessity sharpens the discerning faculty, and on this pressing occasion I was fortunate enough to see it. It was straightway taken down, skinned, roasted, and eaten; and, though rather rich in ammonia,—a substance better suited to form the food of the organisms that do not unite sensation to vitality, than organisms so high in the scale as the minister and his friend,—we came deliberately to the opinion, that, on the whole, we could scarce have dined so well on one of Major Bellenden's jack-boots,—" so thick in the soles," according to Jenny Dennison, "forby being tough in the upper leather."   The tide failed us opposite the opening of Loch Alsh; the wind, long dying, at length died out into a dead cälm; and we cast anchor in ten fathoms water, to wait the ebbing current that was to carry us through Kyle Rhea.

The ebb-tide set in about half an hour after sunset; and in weighing anchor to float down the Kyle,—for we still lacked wind to sail down it,—we brought up from below, on one of the anchor-flukes, an immense bunch of deep-sea tangle, with huge soft fronds and long slender stems, that had lain flat on the rocky bottom, and had here and there thrown out roots along its length of stalk, to attach itself to the rock, in the way the ivy attaches itself to the wall.   Among the intricacies of the true roots of the bunch, if one may speak of the true roots of an alga, I reckoned up from eighteen to twenty different forms of animal life,—Flustræ, Sertulariæ, Serpulæ, Anomiæ, Modiolæ, Astarte, Annelida, Crustacea,

thornback: ray, one of the fishmonger's 'skates'; **organisms that do not unite sensation to vitality**: plants; **Major Bellenden … Jenny Denison**: in Scott's novel *Old Mortality*, Jenny Dennison is a servant girl at Major Bellenden's sister's house of Tillietudlem, where they are besieged by insurgent Covenanters, food supplies run low, and the Major swears not to surrender till the garrison have eaten his old boots

and Radiata. Among the Crustaceans I found a female crab
of a reddish-brown colour, considerably smaller than the nail
of my small finger, but fully grown apparently, for the abdo-
minal flap was loaded with spawn ; and among the Echinoderms, a brownish-yellow sea-urchin about the size of a pistol-
bullet, furnished with comparatively large but thinly-set spines.
There is a dangerous rock in the Kyle Rhea, the Caileach stone,
on which the Commissioners for the Northern Lighthouses
have stuck a bit of board, about the size of a pot-lid, which,
as it is known to be there, and as no one ever sees it after
sunset, is really very effective, considering how little it must
have cost the country, in wrecking vessels.   I saw one of its
victims, the sloop of an honest Methodist, in whose bottom
the Caileach had knocked out a hole, repairing at Isle Ornsay ; and I was told, that if I wished to see more, I had only
just to wait a little.   The honest Methodist, after looking out
in vain for the bit of board, was just stepping into the shrouds,
to try whether he could not see the rock on which the bit of
board is placed, when all at once his vessel found out both
board and rock for herself.   *We* also had anxious looking out
this evening for the bit of board : one of us thought he saw
it right a-head ; and when some of the others were trying to
see it too, John Stewart succeeded in discovering it half a
pistol-shot astern.   The evening was one of the loveliest.   The
moon rose in cloudy majesty over the mountains of Glenelg,
brightening as it rose, till the boiling eddies around us curled
on the darker surface in pale circlets of light, and the shadow
of the Betsey lay as sharply defined on the brown patch of
calm to the larboard as if it were her portrait taken in black.
Immediately at the water-edge, under a tall dark hill, there
were two smouldering fires, that now shot up a sudden tongue
of bright flame, and now dimmed into blood-red specks, and
sent thick strongly-scented trails of smoke athwart the surface
of the Kyle.   We could hear, in the calm, voices from beside

---

Radiata: *eg* jellyfish, corals and sea anemones – here, probably just the last

them, apparently those of children ; and learned that they indicated the places of two kelp-furnaces,—things which have
now become comparatively rare along the coasts of the Hebrides. There was the low rush of tides all around, and the
distant voices from the shore, but no other sounds ; and, dim
in the moonshine, we could see behind us several spectral-look-
ing sails threading their silent way through the narrows, like
twilight ghosts traversing some haunted corridor.

It was late ere we reached the opening of Isle Ornsay ;
and as it was still a dead calm, we had to tug in the Betsey
to the anchoring ground with a pair of long sweeps. The
minister pointed to a low-lying rock on the left-hand side of
the opening,—a favourite haunt of the seal. "I took farewell
of the Betsey there last winter," he said. "The night had
worn late, and was pitch dark ; we could see before us scarce
the length of our bowsprit ; not a single light twinkled from
the shore ; and, in taking the bay, we ran bump on the skerry,
and stuck fast. The water came rushing in, and covered over
the cabin-floor. I had Mrs Swanson and my little daughter
aboard with me, with one of our servant-maids who had become attached to the family, and insisted on following us from
Eigg ; and, of course, our first care was to get them ashore.
We had to land them on the bare uninhabited island yonder,
and a dreary enough place it was at midnight, in winter, with
its rocks, bogs, and heath, and with a rude sea tumbling over
the skerries in front ; but it had at least the recommendation
of being safe, and the sky, though black and wild, was not
stormy. I had brought two lanthorns ashore : the servant
girl, with the child in her lap, sat beside one of them, in the
shelter of a rock ; while my wife, with the other, went walking up and down along a piece of level sward yonder, waving
the light, to attract notice from the opposite side of the bay.
But though it was seen from the windows of my own house
by an attached relative, it was deemed merely a singularly-

tug in the *Betsey* ... with ... long sweeps: *ie* row her in with long oars distinct apparition of Will o' the Wisp, and so brought us no assistance.   Meanwhile we had carried out a kedge astern of the Betsey, as the sea was flowing at the time, to keep her from beating in over the rocks ; and then, taking our few moveables ashore, we hung on till the tide rose, and, with our boat alongside ready for escape, succeeded in warping her into deep water, with the intention of letting her sink somewhere beyond the influence of the surf, which, without fail, would have broken her up on the skerry in a few hours, had we suffered her to remain there.   But though, when on the rock, the tide had risen as freely over the cabin sole inside as over the crags without, in the deep water the Betsey gave no sign of sinking.   I went down to the cabin ; the water was knee-high on the floor, dashing against bed and locker, but it rose no higher ;—the enormous leak had stopped, we knew not how ; and, setting ourselves to the pump, we had in an hour or two a clear ship.   The Betsey is clinker-built below.   The elastic oak planks had yielded inwards to the pressure of the rock, tearing out the fastenings, and admitted the tide at wide yawning seams ; but no sooner was the pressure removed, than out they sprung again into their places, like bows when the strings are slackened ; and when the carpenter came to overhaul, he found he had little else to do than to remove a split plank, and to supply a few dozens of drawn nails."

---

warping: nautical term, pulling on a hawser or cable attached to a fixed point, in this case a **kedge** anchor previously dropped some way astern of the yacht, to move the yacht towards the anchor

CHAPTER X.

THE anchoring ground at Isle Ornsay was crowded with coasting vessels and fishing boats; and when the Sabbath came round, no inconsiderable portion of my friend's congregation was composed of sailors and fishermen. His text was appropriate,—" He bringeth them into their desired haven;" and as his sea-craft and his theology were alike excellent, there were no incongruities in his allegory, and no defects in his mode of applying it, and the seamen were hugely delighted. John Stewart, though less a master of English than of many other things, told me he was able to follow the minister from beginning to end,—a thing he had never done before at an English preaching. The sea portion of the sermon, he said, was very plain : it was about the helm, and the sails, and the anchor, and the chart, and the pilot,—about rocks, winds, currents, and safe harbourage ; and by attending to this simpler part of it, he was led into the parts that were less simple, and so succeeded in comprehending the whole. I would fain see this unique discourse, preached by a sailor minister to a sailor congregation, preserved in some permanent form, with at least one other discourse,—of which I found trace in the island of Eigg, after the lapse of more than a twelvemonth,—that had been preached about the time of the Disruption, full in sight of the Scuir, with its impregnable hill-

He bringeth them: Bible, Psalms 107:30

fort, and in the immediate neighbourhood of the cave of Francis, with its heaps of dead men's bones.   One note stuck fast to the islanders.   In times of peril and alarm, said the minister, the ancient inhabitants of the island had two essentially different kinds of places in which they sought security ; they had the deep unwholesome cave, shut up from the light and the breath of heaven, and the tall rock summit, with its impregnable fort, on which the sun shone and the wind blew. Much hardship might no doubt be encountered on the one, when the sky was black with tempest, and rains beat or snows descended ; but it was found associated with no story of real loss or disaster,—it had kept safe all who had committed themselves to it ; whereas in the close atmosphere of the other there was warmth, and, after a sort, comfort ; and on one memorable day of trouble the islanders had deemed it the preferable sheltering place of the two.   And there survived mouldering skeletons, and a frightful tradition, to tell the history of their choice.   Places of refuge of these very opposite kinds, said the minister, continuing his allegory, are not peculiar to your island : never was there a day or a place of trial in which they did not advance their opposite claims : they are advancing them even now all over the world.   The one kind you find described by one great prophet as low-lying "refuges of lies," over which the desolating " scourge must pass," and which the destroying "waters must overflow ;" while the true character of the other may be learned from another great prophet, who was never weary of celebrating his "rock and his fortress."   " Wit succeeds more from being happily addressed," says Goldsmith, " than even from its native poignancy."   If my friend's allegory does not please quite as well in print and in English as it did when delivered *viva voce* in Gaelic, it should be remembered that it was addressed to an out-door congregation, whose minds were filled with the consequences of the Disruption,—that the bones of *Uamh Fraing*

---

refuges of lies ... waters must overflow: Bible, Isaiah 28:17-18, slightly misquoted; **rock and his fortress**: several possibilities exist in the Bible. Given the context of the Sgùrr Miller probably had in mind Psalm 18:2 which refers to a 'high tower', so **another great prophet** must be King David, who wrote the Psalms lay within a few hundred yards of them,—and that the Scuir, with the sun shining bright on its summit, rose tall in the back-ground, scarce a mile away.

On Monday I spent several hours in re-exploring the Lias of Lucy Bay and its neighbourhood, and then walked on to Kyle-Akin, where I parted from my friend Mr Swanson, and took boat for Loch Carron. The greater part of the following day was spent in crossing the country to the east coast in the mail-gig, through long dreary glens and a fierce storm of wind and rain. In the lower portion of the valley, occupied by the river Carron, I saw at least two fine groupes of moraines. One of these, about a mile and a half above the parish manse, marks the place where a glacier, that had once descended from a hollow amid the northern range of hills, had furrowed up the gravel and earth before it in long ridges, which we find running nearly parallel to the road ; the other group, which lies higher up the valley, and seems of considerably greater extent, indicates where one of those river-like glaciers that fill up long hollows, and impel their irresistible flood downwards, slow as the hour-hand of a time-piece, had terminated towards the sea. I could but glance at the appearances as the gig drove past, and point them out to a fellow passenger, the Establishment minister of * * *, remarking, at the same time, how much more dreary the prospect must have seemed than even it did to-day, though the fog was thick and the drizzle disagreeable, when the lateral hollows on each side were blocked up with ice, and overhanging glaciers, that ploughed the rock bare in their descent, glistened on the bleak hill-sides. I wore a gray maud over a coat of rough russet, with waistcoat and trowsers of plaid ; and the minister, who must have taken me, I suppose, for a southland shepherd looking out for a farm, gave me much information of a kind I might have found valuable had such been my condition and business, regarding the various dis-

maud ... russet ... plaid ... southland shepherd: see Introduction tricts through which we passed.   On one high-lying farm, the grass, he said, was short and thin, but sweet and wholesome, and the flocks throve steadily, and were never thinned by disease ; whereas on another farm that lay along the dank bottom of a valley, the herbage was rank and rich, and the sheep fed and got heavy, but braxy at the close of autumn fell upon them like a pestilence, and more than neutralized to the farmer every advantage of the superior fertility of the soil.   It was not uninteresting, even for one not a sheep-farmer, to learn that the life of the sheep is worth fewer years' purchase in one little track of country than in another adjacent one ; and that those differences in the salubrity of particular spots which obtain in other parts of the world with regard to our own species, and which make it death to linger on the luxuriant river-side, while on the arid plain or elevated hill-top there in health and safety, should exist in contiguous walks in the Highlands of Scotland in reference to some of the inferior animals.   The minister and I became wonderfully good friends for the time.   All the seats in the gig, both back and front, had been occupied ere he had taken his passage, and the postman had assigned him a miserable place on the narrow elevated platform in the middle, where he had to coil himself up like a hedgehog in its hole, sadly to the discomfort of limbs still stout and strong, but stiffened by the long service of full seventy years.   And, as in the case, made famous by Cowper, of the "softer sex" and the old-fashioned iron-cushioned arm-chairs, the old man had, as became his years, "'gan murmur."   I contrived, by sitting on the edge of the gig on the one side, and by getting the postman to take a similar seat on the other, to find room for him in front ; and there, feeling he had not to do with savages, he became kindly and conversible.   We beat together over a wide range of topics ;—the Scotch banks, and Sir Robert Peel's intentions regarding them,—the periodical press

---

fewer years' purchase: financial term, expressing value in terms of total likely yield – the sheep are worth less because they are more likely to die early and one will get fewer years' return; Cowper: from his poem 'The Task', book 1, 'I sing the Sofa', lines 70–71, 'The ladies first/'Gan murmur, as became the softer sex'; Scotch banks: see Additional Notes of Scotland,—the Edinburgh literati,—the Free Church even: he had been a consistent Moderate all his days, and disliked renegades, he said ; and I, of course, disliked renegades too. We both remembered that, though civilized nations give quarter to an enemy overpowered in open fight, they are still in the habit of shooting deserters.   In short, we agreed on a great many different matters ; and, by comparing notes, we made the best we could of a tedious journey and a very bad day. At the inn at Garve, a long stage from Dingwall, we alighted, and took the road together, to straighten our stiffened limbs, while the postman was engaged in changing horses.   The minister stopped short in the middle of a discussion.   We are not on equal terms, he said : you know who I am, and I don't know you : we did not start fair at the beginning, but let us start fair now.   Ah, we have agreed hitherto, I replied ; but I know not how we are to agree when you know who I am : are you sure you will not be frightened ?   Frightened !   said the minister sturdily ; no, by no man.   Then, I am the Editor of the *Witness*.   There was a momentary pause.   "Well," said the minister, "it's all the same : I'm glad we should have met.   Give me, man, a shake of your hand."   And so the conversation went on as before till we parted at Dingwall,—the Establishment clergyman wet to the skin, the Free Church editor in no better condition ; but both, mayhap, rather less out of conceit with the ride than if it had been ridden alone.

I had intended passing at least two days in the neighbourhood of Dingwall, where I proposed renewing an acquaintance, broken off for three-and-twenty years, with those bituminous shales of Strathpeffer in which the celebrated mineral waters of the valley take their rise,—the Old Red Conglomerate of Brahan, the vitrified fort of Knockferrel, the ancient tower of Fairburn, above all, the pleasure-grounds of Conon-side. I had spent the greater portion of my eighteenth and nineteenth years in this part of the country ; and I was curious

---

vitrified fort: see note for p. 363

to ascertain to what extent the man in middle life would verify the observations of the lad,—to recall early incidents, revisit remembered scenes, return on old feelings, and see who were dead and who alive among the casual acquaintances of nearly a quarter of a century ago.   The morning of Wednesday rose dark with fog and rain, but the wind had fallen ; and as I could not afford to miss seeing Conon-side, I sallied out under cover of an umbrella.   I crossed the bridge, and reached the pleasure-grounds of Conon-house.   The river was big in flood : it was exactly such a river Conon as I had lost sight of in the winter of 1821 ; and I had to give up all hope of wading into its fords, as I used to do early in the autumn of that year, and pick up the pearl muscles that lie so thickly among the stones at the bottom.   I saw, however, amid a thicket of bushes by the river-side, a heap of broken shells, where some herd-boy had been carrying on such a pearl fishery as I had sometimes used to carry on in my own behalf so long before ; and I felt it was just something to see it.   The flood eddied past, dark and heavy, sweeping over bulwark and bank.   The low-stemmed alders that rose on islet and mound seemed shorn of half their trunks in the tide ; here and there an elastic branch bent to the current, and rose and bent again ; and now a tuft of withered heath came floating down, and now a soiled wreath of foam.   How vividly the past rose up before me !—boyish day-dreams forgotten for twenty years,—the fossils of an early formation of mind, produced at a period when the atmosphere of feeling was warmer than now, and the immaturities of the mental kingdom grew rank and large, like the ancient Cryptogamiæ, and bore no specific resemblance to the productions of a present time.   I had passed in the neighbourhood the first season I anywhere spent among strangers, at an age when home is not a country, nor a province even, but simply a little spot of earth inhabited by friends and relatives ; and the rude verses,

---

muscles: mussels; **atmosphere**: see Additional Notes; **Cryptogamiae**: here, plants of the coal forests; **amidst strangers**: *ie* working away from home as an apprentice mason (Miller 1858) long forgotten, in which my joy had found vent when on the eve of returning to that home,—a home little more than twenty miles away,—came chiming as freshly into my memory as if scarce a month had passed since I had composed them beside the Conon.*

Three-and-twenty years form a large portion of the short life of man,—one-third, as nearly as can be expressed in unbroken numbers, of the entire term fixed by the psalmist, and full one-half, if we strike off the twilight periods of childhood and immature youth, and of senectitude weary of its toils. I found curious indications among the grounds of Conon-side, of the time that had elapsed since I had last seen them. There was a rectangular pond in a corner of a moor, near the public road, inhabited by about a dozen voracious, frog-eating pike, that I used frequently to visit. The water in the pond was exceedingly limpid; and I could watch from the banks every motion of the hungry, energetic inmates. And now I struck off from the river-side by a narrow tangled pathway, to visit it once more. I could have found out the place blindfold: there was a piece of flat brown heath that stretched round its edges, and a mossy slope that rose at its upper side, at the foot of which the taste of the proprietor had placed a rustic chair. The spot, though itself bare and moory, was nearly surrounded by wood, and looked like a clearing in an American forest. There were lines of graceful larches on two of its sides, and a grove of vigorous beeches that directly fronted the setting sun on a third; and I had often found it a place of delightful resort, in which to saunter alone in the calm summer evenings, after the work of the day was over. Such was the scene as it existed in my recollection. I came up to it this day through dripping trees, along a neglected pathway; and found, for the open space and the rectangular pond,

* The verses here referred to are introduced into " My Schools and Schoolmasters," chapter tenth.

---

term fixed by the psalmist: the Bible, Psalm 90:10, 'The days of our years are threescore years and ten' a gloomy patch of water in the middle of a tangled thicket, that rose some ten or twelve feet over my head.   What had been bare heath a quarter of a century before had become a thick wood ; and I remembered, that when I had been last there, the open space had just been planted with forest-trees, and that some of the taller plants rose half-way to my knee. Human lifetimes, as now measured, are not intended to witness both the seed-times and the harvests of forests,—both the planting of the sapling, and the felling of the huge tree into which it has grown ; and so the incident impressed me strongly.   It reminded me of the sage Shalum in Addison's antediluvian tale, who became wealthy by the sale of his great trees, two centuries after he had planted them.   I pursued my walk, to revisit another little patch of water which I had found so very entertaining a volume three-and-twenty years previous, that I could still recall many of its lessons ; but the hand of improvement had been busy among the fields of Conon-side ; and when I came up to the spot which it had occupied, I found but a piece of level arable land, bearing a rank swathe of grass and clover.*

Not a single individual did I find on the farm who had been there twenty years before.   I entered into conversation with one of the ploughmen, apparently a man of some intelligence ; but he had come to the place only a summer or two previous, and the names of most of his predecessors sounded unfamiliar in his ears : he knew scarce anything of the old laird or his times, and but little of the general history of the district.   The frequent change of servants incident to the large-farm system has done scarce less to wear out the oral antiquities of the country than has been done by its busy ploughs in obliterating antiquities of a more material cast. The mythologic legend and traditionary story have shared

* For a description of this pond see "My Schools and Schoolmasters," chapter tenth.

Shalum ... Addison: from the novel by Joseph Addison, *Shalum and Hilpa*, featuring very long-lived characters; **large-farm system**: as a result of Improvement – see Introduction; **oral antiquities**: *ie* spoken folklore and tradition

the same fate, through the influence of the one cause, which
has been experienced by the sepulchral tumulus and the ancient encampment under the operations of the other.   I saw
in the pillars and archways of the farm-steading some of the
hewn stones bearing my own mark,—an anchor, to which I
used to attach a certain symbolical meaning ; and I pointed
them out to the ploughman.   I had hewn these stones, I said,
in the days of the old laird, the grandfather of the present
proprietor.   The ploughman wondered how a man still in
middle life could have such a story to tell.   I must surely
have begun work early in the day, he remarked, which was
perhaps the best way for getting it soon over.   I remembered
having seen similar markings on the hewn-work of ancient
castles, and of indulging in, I daresay, idle enough speculations regarding what was doing at court and in the field, in
Scotland and elsewhere, when the old long-departed mechanics had been engaged in their work.   When this mark was
affixed, I have said, all Scotland was in mourning for the
disaster at Flodden, and the folk in the work-shed would have
been, mayhap, engaged in discussing the supposed treachery
of Home, and in arguing whether the hapless James had fallen
in battle, or gone on a pilgrimage to merit absolution for the
death of his father.   And when this other more modern mark
was affixed, the Gowrie conspiracy must have been the topic
of the day, and the mechanics were probably speculating,—
at worst not more doubtfully than the historians have done
after them,—on the guilt or innocence of the Ruthvens.   It
now rose curiously enough in memory, that I was employed
in fashioning one of the stones marked by the anchor,—a
corner stone in a gate-pillar,—when one of my brother-ap-
prentices entered the work-shed, laden with a bundle of newly-
sharpened irons from the smithy, and said he had just been
told by the smith that the great Napoleon Bonaparte was
dead.   I returned to the village of Conon Bridge, through

---

mark: mason's mark; **Flodden**: the English victory over James IV and the Scots in 1513;
Gowrie ... Ruthvens: in 1600 James VI was involved in a scuffle at Gowrie Castle as a
result, allegedly, of a conspiracy by the Master of Ruthven and his brother the Earl of
Gowrie who were, no doubt conveniently, killed in the fight

the woods of Conon House.   The day was still very bad : the
rain pattered thick on the leaves, and fell incessantly in large
drops on the pathways.   There is a solitary, picturesque burying-ground on a wooded hillock beside the river, with thick
dark woods all around it,—one of the two burying-grounds
of the parish of Urquhart,—which I would fain have visited,
but the swollen stream had risen high around, converting the
hillock into an island, and forbade access.   I had spent many
an hour among the tombs.   They are few and scattered, and
of the true antique cast,—roughened with death's heads, and
cross bones, and rudely sculptured armorial bearings ; and on
a broken wall, that marked where the ancient chapel once had
stood, there might be seen, in the year 1821, a small, badly
cut sun-dial, with its iron gnomon wasted to a saw-edged film,
that contained more oxide than metal.   The only fossils described in my present chapter are fossils of mind ; and the
reader will, I trust, bear with me should I produce one fossil
more of this somewhat equivocal class.   It has no merit to
recommend it,—it is simply an organism of an immature intellectual formation, in which, however, as in the Carboniferous period, there was provision made for the necessities of
an after time.*   If a young man born on the wrong side of
the Tweed for *speaking* English, is desirous to acquire the
ability of *writing* it, he should by all means begin by trying
to write it in verse.

I passed, on my return to Dingwall, through the village of
Conon Bridge ; and, remembering that one of the masons who
had hewn beside me in the work-shed so many years before
lived in the village at the time, I went direct to the house he
had inhabited, to see whether he might not be there still.   It

* These remarks refer to the poem " On Seeing a Sun-Dial in a Church-
Yard," which was introduced here when these chapters were first published
in the "Witness," but, having been afterwards inserted in the tenth chapter of " My Schools and Schoolmasters," is not here re-produced.

----

necessities of an after time: the coal, ironstone, limestone and fireclay laid down
during the Carboniferous that provided the critical resources for Britain and especially
Lowland Scotland in the Industrial Revolution (Torrens 2003); **Tweed**: river forming
part of the border between Scotland and England, and so by extension the whole border

was a low-roofed domicile beside the river, but in the days of
my old acquaintance it had presented an appearance of great
comfort and neatness ; and as there now hung an air of neglect about it, I inferred that it had found some other tenant.
I inquired, however, at the door, and was informed that Mr
* * * now lived higher up the street.   I would find him,
it was added, in the best house on the right-hand side,—the
house with a hewn front, and a shop in it.   He kept the shop,
and was the owner of the house, and had another house besides, and was one of the elders of the Free Church in Urquhart.   Such was the standing of my old acquaintance the
journeyman mason of twenty-three years ago.   He had been,
when I knew him, a steady, industrious, religious man,—
with but one exception the only contributor to missionary
and bible societies among a numerous party of workmen ;
and he was now occupying a respectable place in his village,
and was one of the voters of the county.   Let Chartism assert what it pleases on the one hand, and Toryism what it
may on the other, the property-qualification of the Reform
Bill is essentially a good one for such a country as Scotland.
In our cities it no doubt extends the political franchise to a
fluctuating class, ill-hafted in society, who possess it one year
and want it another ; but in our villages and smaller towns
it hits very nearly the right medium for forming a premium
on steady industry and character, and for securing that at
least the mass of those who possess it should be sober-minded
men, with a stake in the general welfare.   In running over
the histories of the various voters in one of our smaller towns,
I found that nearly one-half of the whole had, like my old
comrade at Conon Bridge, acquired for themselves, through
steady and industrious habits, the qualification from which
they derived their vote.   My companion failed to recognise
in the man turned of forty the smooth-cheeked stripling of
eighteen, with whom he had wrought so long before.   I soon

---

property qualification: the requirement to own or rent a certain minimum amount of
property to be entitled to have the **franchise** or vote in parliamentary elections; **one of
our smaller towns**: presumably Cromarty

succeeded, however, in making good my claim to his acquaintance. He had previously established the identity of the editor of his newspaper with his quondam fellow-workman, and a single link more was all the chain wanted. We talked over old matters for half an hour. His wife, a staid respectable matron, who, when I had been last in the district, was exactly such a person as her eldest daughter, showed me an Encyclopædia, with coloured prints, which she wished to send, if she knew but how, to the Free Church library. I walked with him through his garden, and saw trees loaded with yellow-cheeked pippins, where I had once seen only unproductive heath, that scantily covered a barren soil of ferruginous sand; and, unwillingly declining an invitation to wait tea,—for a previous engagement interfered,—I took leave of the family, and returned to Dingwall. The following morning was gloomy, and threatened rain; and, giving up my intention of exploring Strathpeffer, I took the morning coach for Invergordon, and then walked to Cromarty, where I arrived just in time for breakfast.

I marked from the top of the coach, about two miles to the north-east of Dingwall, beds of a deep gray sandstone, identical in colour and appearance with some of the gray sandstones of the Middle Old Red of Forfarshire, and learned that quarries had lately been opened in these beds near Montgerald. The Old Red Sandstone lies in immense development on the flanks of Ben-wevis; and it is just possible that the analogue of the gray flagstones of Forfar may be found among its upper beds. If so, the quarriers should be instructed to look hard for organic remains,—the broad-headed Cephalaspis, so characteristic of the formation, and the huge Crustacean, its contemporary, that disported in plates large as those of the steel mail of the later ages of chivalry. The geologists of Dingwall,—if Dingwall has yet got its geologists,—might do well to attempt determining the point. I

---

huge Crustacean: *Pterygotus* (q.v.); mail: in the sense of armour generally, including plate armour, not just the linked chains that comprise the usual meaning of 'mail' found the science much in advance in Cromarty, especially among the ladies,—its great patronizers and illustrators everywhere,—and, in not a few localities, extensive contributors to its hoards of fact. Just as I arrived, there was a pic-nic party of young people setting out for the Lias of Shandwick. They spent the day among its richly fossiliferous shales and limestones, and brought back with them in the evening Ammonites and Gryphites enough to store a museum. Cromarty had been visited during the summer by geologists speaking a foreign tongue, but thoroughly conversant with the occult yet common language of the rocks, and deeply interested in the stories which the rocks told. The vessels in which the Crown Prince of Denmark voyaged to the Faroe Isles had been for some time in the bay ; and the Danes, his companions, votaries of the stony science, zealously plied chisel and hammer among the Old Red Sandstones of the coast. A townsman informed me that he had seen a Danish Professor hammering like the tutelary Thor of his country among the nodules in which I had found the first Pterichthys and first Diplacanthus ever disinterred ; and that the Professor, ever and anon as he laid open a specimen, brought it to a huge smooth boulder, on which there lay a copy of the " Old Red Sandstone," to ascertain from the descriptions and prints its family and name. Shall I confess that the circumstance gratified me exceedingly ? There are many elements of discord among mankind in the present time, both at home and abroad,—so many, that I am afraid we need entertain no hope of seeing an end, in at least our day, to controversy and war. And we should be all the better pleased, therefore, to witness the increase of those links of union,—such as the harmonizing bonds of a scientific sympathy,—the tendency of which is to draw men together in a kindly spirit, and the formation of which involves no sacrifice of principle, moral or religious. I

Lias of Shandwick: actually various strata of the Middle and Upper Jurassic, 'Oolitic' in Miller's sense; occult: simply 'hidden except to those who know how to read it' – with none of today's magical connotations do not think that the foreigner, after geologizing in my company, would have had any very vehement desire, in the event of a war, to cut me down, or to knock me on the head. I am afraid this chapter would require a long apology, and for a long apology space is wanting. But there will be no egotism, and much geology, in my next.

CHAPTER XI.

I SPENT one long day in exploring the ichthyolite beds on both sides the Cromarty Frith, and another long day in re-newing my acquaintance with the Liasic deposit at Shand-wick.   In beating over the Lias, though I picked up a few good specimens, I acquired no new facts ; but in re-examin-ing the Old Red Sandstone and its organisms I was rather more successful.   I succeeded in eliciting some curious points not yet recorded, which, with the details of an interesting discovery made in the far north in this formation, I may be perhaps able to weave into a chapter somewhat more geo-logical than my last.

Some of the readers of my little work on the Old Red Sandstone will perhaps remember that I described the organ-isms of that ancient system as occurring in the neighbour-hood of Cromarty mainly on one platform, raised rather more than a hundred feet over the great Conglomerate ; and that on this platform, as if suddenly overtaken by some wide-spread catastrophe, the ichthyolites lie by thousands and tens of thousands, in every attitude of distortion and terror.   We see the spiked wings of the Pterichthys elevated to the full, as they had been erected in the fatal moment of anger and alarm, and the bodies of the Cheirolepis and Cheiracanthus bent head to tail, in the stiff posture into which they had

one platform ... catastrophe: see Additional Notes; spiked wings: the single pair of pectoral appendages in *Pterichthys* (now *Pterichthyodes*) and related forms, each encased in bone rather like a lobster's leg (Trewin 2003b)

curled when the last pang was over.   In various places in
the neighbourhood the ichthyolites are found *in situ* in their
coffin-like nodules, where it is impossible to trace the relation
of the beds in which they occur to the rocks above and below ; and I had suspected for years that in at least some of
the localities, they could not have belonged to the lower platform of death, but to some posterior catastrophe that had
strewed with carcases some upper platform.   I had thought
over the matter many a time and oft when I should have been
asleep,—for it is marvellous how questions of the kind grow
upon a man ; and now, selecting as a hopeful scene of inquiry
the splendid section under the Northern Sutor, I set myself
doggedly to determine whether the Old Red Sandstone in
this part of the country has not at least its two storeys of
organic remains, each of which had been equally a scene of
sudden mortality.   I was entirely successful.   The lower
ichthyolite bed occurs exactly one hundred and fourteen feet
over the great Conglomerate ; and three hundred and eighteen
feet higher up I found a second ichthyolite bed, as rich in
fossils as the first, with its thorny Acanthodians twisted half
round, as if still in the agony of dissolution, and its Pterichthyes still extending their spear-like arms in the attitude of
defence.   The discovery enabled me to assign to their true
places the various ichthyolite beds of the district.   Those in
the immediate neighbourhood of the town, and a bed which
abuts on the Lias at Eathie, belong to the upper platform ;
while those which appear in Eathie Burn, and along the
shores at Navity, belong to the lower.   The chief interest of
the discovery, however, arises from the light which it throws
on the condition of the ancient ocean of the Lower Old Red,
and on the extreme precariousness of the tenure on which
the existence of its numerous denizens was held.   In a section of little more than a hundred yards there occur at least
two platforms of violent death,—platforms inscribed with un-

Northern Sutor: one of the two Sutors, or headlands, making the entrance to the
Firth of Cromarty; **114 feet over the great Conglomerate**: *ie* within the geological
stratigraphical column, without allowing for tilting of the beds due to earth movement.
In principle and often in practice, beds at different 'heights' in the stratigraphical column
can be examined at the same topographical level today – *eg* as seashore exposures

equivocal evidence of two great catastrophes which over wide areas depopulated the seas.   In the Old Red Sandstone of Caithness there are many such platforms : storey rises over storey ; and the floor of each bears its closely-written record of disaster and sudden extinction.   Pompeii in this northern locality lies over Herculaneum, and Anglano over both.   We cease to wonder why the higher order of animals should not have been introduced into a scene of being that had so recently arisen out of chaos, and over which the reign of death so frequently returned.   In a somewhat different sense from that indicated by the poet of the " Seasons,"

" As yet the trembling *year* was unconfirmed,
    And *winter* oft at eve resumed the gale."

Lying detached in the stratified clay of the fish-beds, there occur in abundance single plates and scales of ichthyolites, which, as they can be removed entire, and viewed on both sides, illustrate points in the mechanism of the creatures to which they belonged that cannot be so clearly traced in the same remains when locked up in stone.   There is a vast deal of skilful carpentry exhibited—if carpentry I may term it—in the coverings of these ancient ichthyolites.   In the commoner fish of our existing seas the scales are so thin and flexible,— mere films of horn,—that there is no particularly nice fitting required in their arrangement.   The condition, too, through which portions of unprotected skin may be presented to the water, as over and between the rays of the fins, and on the snout and lips, obviates many a mechanical difficulty of the earlier period, when it was a condition, as the remains demonstrate, that no bit of naked skin should be exposed, and when the scales and plates were formed, not of thin horny films, but of solid pieces of bone.   Thin slates lie on the roof of a modern dwelling, without any nice fitting ;—they are scales of the modern construction : but it required much nice fitting to make thick flag-stones lie on the roof of an ancient

Pompeii ... Herculaneum: the Roman towns entombed when Vesuvius erupted in 79 CE; poet of the 'Seasons': James Thomson, 'Spring', lines 18-19 – in fact 'As yet the trembling year is unconfirm'd,/And Winter oft at eve resumes the breeze' cathedral ;—*they*, on the other hand, were scales of the ancient type.   Again, it requires no ingenuity whatever to suffer the hands and face to go naked,—and such is the condition of our existing fish, with their soft skinny snouts and membranous fins ; but to cover the hands with flexible steel gauntlets, and the face with such an iron mask as that worn by the mysterious prisoner of Louis XIV., would require a very large amount of ingenuity indeed ; and the ancient ichthyolites of the Old Red were all masked and gauntleted.   Now the detached plates and scales of the stratified clay exhibit not a few of the mechanical contrivances through which the bony coverings of these fish were made to unite—as in coats of old armour—great strength with great flexibility.   The scales of the Osteolepis and Diplopterus I found nicely bevelled atop and at one of the sides ; so that where they overlapped each other,—for at the joints not a needle-point could be insinuated, —the thickness of the two scales equalled but the thickness of one scale in the centre, and thus an equable covering was formed.   I brought with me some of these detached scales, and they now lie fitted together on the table before me, like pieces of complicated hewn work carefully arranged on the ground ere the workman transfers them to their place on the wall.   In the smaller-scaled fish, such as the Cheiracanthus and Cheirolepis, a different principle obtained.   The minute glittering rhombs of bone were set thick on the skin, like those small scales of metal sewed on leather that formed an inferior kind of armour still in use in eastern nations, and which was partially used in our own country just ere the buff coat altogether superseded the coat of mail.   I found a beautiful piece of jaw in the clay, with the enamelled tusks bristling on its brightly enamelled edge, like iron teeth in an iron rake.   Mr Parkinson expresses some wonder, in his work on fossils, that in a fine ichthyolite in the British Museum, not only the teeth should have been preserved, but also the lips ;

---

mysterious prisoner: no doubt the Man in the Iron Mask, imprisoned in France; **buff coat**: thick leather coat used as lightweight armour by seventeenth century soldiers such as Cromwell's Ironsides; **Parkinson ... work**: see Additional Notes

but we now know enough of the construction of the more
ancient fish, to cease wondering.   The lips were formed of
as solid bone as the teeth themselves, and had as fair a chance
of being preserved entire; just as the metallic rim of a toothed
wheel has as fair a chance of being preserved as the metallic
teeth that project from it.   I was interested in marking the
various modes of attachment to the body of the animal which
the detached scales exhibit.   The slater fastens on his slates
with nails driven into the wood : the tiler secures his tiles
by means of a raised bar on the under side of each, that locks
into a corresponding bar of deal in the framework of the
roof.   Now in some of the scales I found the art of the tiler
anticipated : there were bars raised on their inner sides, to
lay hold of the skin beneath ; while in others it was the
art of the slater that had been anticipated,—the scales had
been slates fastened down by long nails driven in slantwise,
which were, however, mere prolongations of the scale itself.
Great truths may be repeated until they become truisms, and
we fail to note what they in reality convey.   The great truth
that all knowledge dwelt without beginning in the adorable
Creator must, I am afraid, have been thus common-placed
in my mind; for at first it struck me as wonderful that the
humble arts of the tiler and slater should have existed in
perfection in the times of the Old Red Sandstone.

I had often remarked amid the fossiliferous limestones of
the Lower Old Red, minute specks and slender veins of a
glossy bituminous substance somewhat resembling jet, sufficiently hard to admit of a tolerable polish, and which emitted
in the fire a bright flame.   I had remarked, further, its apparent identity with a substance used by the ancient inhabitants of the northern part of the country in the manufacture
of their rude ornaments, as occasionally found in sepulchral
urns, such as beads of an elliptical form, and flat parallelograms, perforated edge-wise by some four or five holes a-piece ;

jet: Miller's hypothesis is yet to be tested, for the source of archaeological artifacts made
of true jet and similar materials such as cannel coal, shale and lignite, remains a significant
research problem today. But it is known that some Scottish artifacts were made of imported
jet from Whitby in Yorkshire, while a few of the others were made of cannel coal from
Inverbrora near Brora (Sheridan *et al.* 2002)

but I had failed hitherto in detecting in the stone, portions of sufficient bulk for the formation of either the beads or the parallelograms. On this visit to the ichthyolite beds, however, I picked up a nodule that inclosed a mass of the jet large enough to admit of being fashioned into trinkets of as great bulk as any of the ancient ones I have yet seen, and a portion of which I succeeded in actually forming into a parallelogram, that could not have been distinguished from those of our old sepulchral urns. It is interesting enough to think, that these fossiliferous beds, altogether unknown to the people of the country for many centuries, and which, when I first discovered them, some twelve or fourteen years ago, were equally unknown to geologists, should have been resorted to for this substance, perhaps thousands of years ago, by the savage aborigines of the district. But our antiquities of the remoter class furnish us with several such facts. It is comparatively of late years that we have become acquainted with the yellow chalk-flints of Banffshire and Aberdeen ; though before the introduction of iron into the country they seem to have been well known all over the north of Scotland. I have never yet seen a stone arrow-head found in any of the northern localities, that had not been fashioned out of this hard and splintery substance,—a sufficient proof that our ancestors, ere they had formed their first acquaintance with the metals, were intimately acquainted with at least the mechanical properties of the chalk-flint, and knew where in Scotland it was to be found. They were mineralogists enough, too, as their stone battle-axes testify, to know that the best toolmaking rock is the axe-stone of Werner ; and in some localities they must have brought their supply of this rather rare mineral from great distances. A history of those arts of savage life, as shown in the relics of our earlier antiquities, which the course of discovery served thoroughly to supplant, but which could not have been carried on without a knowledge of substances and qualities afterwards lost, until re-discovered by scientific curiosity, would form of itself an exceedingly curious chapter.   The art of the gun-flint maker (and it, too, promises soon to pass into extinction) is unquestionably a curious one, but not a whit more curious or more ingenious than the art possessed by the rude inhabitants of our country eighteen hundred years ago, of chipping arrow-heads with an astonishing degree of neatness out of the same stubborn material.   They found, however, that though flint made a serviceable arrow-head, it was by much too brittle for an adze or battle-axe ; and sought elsewhere than among the Banffshire gravels for the rock out of which these were to be wrought.   Where they found it in our northern provinces I have not yet ascertained.   It is but a short time since I came to know that they were before-hand with me in the discovery of the bituminous jet of the Lower Old Red Sandstone, and were excavators among its fossiliferous beds.   The vitrified forts of the north of Scotland give evidence of yet another of the obsolete arts.   Before the savage inhabitants of the country were ingenious enough to know the uses of mortar, or were furnished with tools sufficiently hard and solid to dress a bit of sandstone, they must have been acquainted with the *chemical* fact, that with the assistance of fluxes, a pile of stones could be fused into a solid wall, and with the *mineralogical* fact, that there are certain kinds of stones which yield much more readily to the heat than others. The art of making vitrified forts was the art of making ramparts of rock through a knowledge of the less obstinate earths and the more powerful fluxes.   I have been informed by Mr Patrick Duff of Elgin, that he found, in breaking open a vitrified fragment detached from an ancient hill-fort, distinct impressions of the serrated kelp-weed of our shores,—the identical flux which, in its character as the kelp of commerce, was so extensively used in our glass-houses only a few years ago.

---

vitrified forts: see note for p. 363; **Patrick Duff**: (1791–1861), Town Clerk of Elgin, important local geologist and fossil collector, and Secretary of the Elgin and Moray Scientific Association whose Museum features in *Cruise of the Betsey*; some of his collection is now in NMS (Andrews 1982; Willis 2002)

I was struck, during my explorations at this time, as I had been often before, by the style of grouping, if I may so speak, which obtains among the Lower Old Red fossils. In no deposit with which I am acquainted, however rich in remains, have all its ichthyolites been found lying together. The collector finds some one or two species very numerous ; some two or three considerably less so, but not unfrequent ; some one or two more, perhaps, exceedingly rare ; and a few, though abundant in other localities, that never occur at all. In the Cromarty beds, for instance, I never found a Holoptychius, and a Dipterus only once ; the Diplopterus is rare ; the Glyptolepis not common ; the Cheirolepis and Pterichthys more so, but not very abundant ; the Cheiracanthus and Diplicanthus, on the other hand, are numerous ; and the Osteolepis and Coccosteus more numerous still. But in other deposits of the same formation, though a similar style of grouping obtains, the proportions are reversed with regard to species and genera : the fish rare in one locality abound in another. In Banniskirk, for instance, the Dipterus is exceedingly common, while the Osteolepis and Coccosteus are rare, and the Cheiracanthus and Cheirolepis seem altogether awanting. Again, in the Morayshire deposits, the Glyptolepis is abundant, and noble specimens of the Lower Old Red Holoptychius—of which more anon—are to be found in the neighbourhood of Thurso, associated with remains of the Diplopterus, Coccosteus, Dipterus, and Osteolepis. The fact may be deemed of some little interest by the geologist, and may serve to inculcate caution, by showing that it is not always safe to determine regarding the place or age of subordinate formations from the per centage of certain fossils which they may be found to contain, or from the fact that they should want some certain organisms of the system to which they belong, and possess others. These differences may and do exist in contemporary deposits ; and I had a striking example, on

---

Banniskirk: in Caithness, just north of Achanarras; **per centage**: probably Charles Lyell's (1830-1833) then recent sub-division of the Tertiary into the Pliocene, Miocene, *etc*, on the basis of the percentage of their fossil molluscs still living today: he assumed that the lower the percentage, the older the stratum, because of the successive extinction of species this occasion, of their dependence on a simple law of instinct, which is as active in producing the same kind of phenomena now as it seems to have been in the earlier days of the Old Red Sandstone.   The Cromarty and Moray Friths, mottled with fishing boats (for the bustle of the herring fishers had just begun), stretched out before me.   A few hundred yards from the shore there was a yawl lying at anchor, with an old fisherman and a few boys angling from the stern for sillocks (the young of the coal-fish) and for small rock-cod.   A few miles higher up, where the Cromarty Frith expands into a wide land-locked basin, with shallow sandy shores, there was a second yawl engaged in fishing for flounders and small skate, —for such are the kinds of fish that frequent the flat shallows of the basin.   A turbot-net lay drying in the sun : it served to remind me that some six or eight miles away, in an opposite direction, there is a deep-sea bank, on which turbot, halibut, and large skate are found.   Numerous boats were stretching down the Moray Frith, bound for the banks of a more distant locality, frequented at this early stage of the herring fishing by shoals of herrings, with their attendant dog-fish and cod ; and I knew that in yet another deep-sea range there lie haddock and whiting banks.   Almost every variety of existing fish in the two friths has its own peculiar habitat ; and were they to be destroyed by some sudden catastrophe, and preserved by some geologic process, on the banks and shoals which they frequent, there would occur exactly the same phenomena of grouping in the fossiliferous contemporaneous deposits which they would thus constitute, as we find exhibited by the deposits of the Lower Old Red Sandstone.

The remains of Holoptychius occur, I have said, in the neighbourhood of Thurso.   I must now add, that very singular remains they are,—full of interest to the naturalist, and, in great part at least, new to Geology.   My readers, votaries of the stony science, must be acquainted with the masterly

paper of Mr Sedgwick and Sir R. Murchison "On the Old Red
Sandstone of Caithness and the North of Scotland generally,"
which forms part of the second volume (second series) of the
" Transactions of the Geological Society," and with the description which it furnishes, among many others, of the rocks
in the neighbourhood of Thurso.   Calcareo-bituminous flags,
grits, and shales, of which the paving flagstones of Caithness
may be regarded as the general type, occur on the shores, in
reefs, crags, and precipices ; here stretching along the coast
in the form of flat, uneven bulwarks ; there rising over it in
steep walls ; yonder leaning to the surf, stratum against stratum, like flights of stairs thrown down from their slant position to the level ; in some places severed by faults ; in others
cast about in every possible direction, as if broken and contorted by a thousand antagonist movements ; but in their
general bearing rising towards the east, until the whole cal·
careo-bituminous schists of which this important member of
the system is composed disappear under the red sandstones
of Dunnet Head.   Such, in effect, is the general description of
Mr Sedgwick and Sir R. Murchison, of the rocks in the neighbourhood of Thurso.   It indicates further, that in at least
three localities in the range there occur in the grits and shales,
scales and impressions of fish.   And such was the ascertained
geology of the deposit when taken up last year by an ingenious tradesman of Thurso, Mr Robert Dick, whose patient
explorations, concentrated mainly on the fossil remains of
this deposit, bid fair to add to our knowledge of the ich-
thyology of the Old Red Sandstone.   Let us accompany Mr
Dick in one of his exploratory rambles.   The various organisms which he disinterred I shall describe from specimens before me, which I owe to his kindness,—the localities in which
he found them, from a minute and interesting description, for
which I am indebted to his pen.

Leaving behind us the town at the bottom of its deep bay,

Mr Robert Dick: (1811–1866), baker of Thurso, geologist and botanist (Smiles 1878).
He fell on hard times and had to sell his fossil collection to John Miller (no relation), in
whose collection, now in NMS, Dick's specimens can no longer be distinguished (R. L.
Paton, *pers. comm.* 2000). However, Dick also gave material to Hugh Miller, some of which
can be identified in Miller's collection today from Miller's publications

we set out to explore a bluff-headed parallelogramical promontory, bounded by Thurso Bay on the one hand, and Murkle
Bay on the other, and which presents to the open sea, in the
space that stretches between, an undulating line of iron-bound
coast, exposed to the roll of the northern ocean. We pass two
stations in which the hard Caithness flagstones so well known
in commerce are jointed by saws wrought by machinery. As
is common in the Old Red Sandstone, in which scarce any
stratum solid enough to be of value to the workmen, whether
for building or paving, contains good specimens, we find but
little to detain us in the dark coherent beds from which the
flags are quarried. Here and there a few glittering scales
occur ; here and there a few coprolitic patches ; here and
there the faint impression of a fucoid ; but no organism sufficiently entire to be transferred to the bag. As we proceed
outwards, however, and the fitful breeze comes laden with the
keen freshness of the open sea, we find among the hard dark
strata in the immediate neighbourhood of Thurso Castle, a
paler-coloured bed of fine-grained semicalcareous stone, charged
with remains in a state of coherency and keeping better fitted to repay the labour of the specimen-collector. The inclosing matrix is comparatively soft : when employed in the
neighbouring fences as a building stone, we see it resolved by
the skyey influences into well-nigh its original mud ; whereas
the organisms which it contains are composed of a hard, scarce
destructible substance,—bone steeped in bitumen ; and the
enamel on their outer surfaces is still as glossy and bright as
the japan on a *papier-maché* tray fresh from the hands of the
workman. Their deep black, too, contrasts strongly with the
pale hue of the stone. They consist chiefly of scales, spines,
dermal plates, snouts, skull-caps, and vegetable impressions.
A little farther on, in a thick bed interposed between two
faults, the same kind of remains occur in the same abundance,
largely mingled with scales and teeth of Holoptychius, tuber-

---

fucoid: literally, a kind of seaweed. Miller appeared to use it as a generic term for certain
superficially seaweed-like fossil plants. As the Old Red Sandstone is in fact a freshwater
deposit, these still poorly understood plants are presumably a mixture of freshwater algae
with swamp and land plants; **resolved by the skyey influences**: broken up by wind, sun,
rain and frost; **tuberculated**: covered in small bumps or nodules

culated plates, and coprolitic blotches ; and further on still, in a rubbly flagstone, near where a little stream comes trotting merrily from the uplands to the sea, there occur skull-plates,—at least one of which has been disinterred entire,—large and massy as the helmets of ancient warriors. We have now reached the outer point of the promontory, where the seaward wave, as it comes rolling unbroken from the Pole, crosses, in nearing the shore, the eastward sweep of the great Gulf-stream, and then casts itself headlong on the rocks. The view has been extending with almost every step we have taken, and it has now expanded into a wide and noble prospect of ocean and bay, island and main, bold surf-skirted headlands, and green retiring hollows. Yonder, on the one hand, are the Orkneys, rising dim and blue over the foam-mottled currents of the Pentland Frith ; and yonder, on the other, the far-stretching promontory of Holborn Head, with the line of coast that sweeps along the opposite side of the bay ; here sinking in abrupt flagstone precipices direct into the tide ; there receding in grassy banks formed of a dark blue diluvium. The fields and dwellings of living men mingle in the landscape with old episcopal ruins and ancient burying-grounds ; and yonder, well-nigh in the opening of the Frith, gleams ruddy to the sun,—a true blood-coloured blush, when all around is azure or pale,—the tall Red Sandstone precipices of Dunnet Head. It has been suggested that the planet Mars may owe its red colour to the extensive development of some such formation as the Old Red Sandstone of our own planet : the existing formation in Mars may, at the present time, it is said, be a Red Sandstone formation. It seems much more probable, however, that the red flush which characterizes the whole of that planet,—its oceans as certainly as its continents,—should be rather owing to some widely-diffused peculiarity of the surrounding atmosphere, than to aught peculiar in the varied surface of land and water which that atmosphere surrounds; but certainly the extensive existence of such a red system might produce the effect. If the rocks and soils of Dunnet Head formed average specimens of those of our globe generally, we could look across the heavens at Mars with a disk vastly more rubicund and fiery than his own. The earth, as seen from the moon, would seem such a planet bathed in blood as the moon at its rising frequently appears from the earth.

We have rounded the promontory. The beds exposed along the coast to the lashings of the surf are of various texture and character,—here tough, bituminous, and dark; there of a pale hue, and so hard that they ring to the hammer like plates of cast iron; yonder soft, unctuous, and green,—a kind of chloritic sandstone. And these very various powers of resistance and degrees of hardness we find indicated by the rough irregularities of the surface. The softer parts retire in long trench-like hollows,—the harder stand out in sharp irregular ridges. Fossils abound : the bituminous beds glitter bright with glossy quadrangular scales, that look like sheets of black mica inclosed in granite. We find jaws, teeth, tubercled plates, skull-caps, spines, and fucoids,—"tombs among which to contemplate," says Mr Dick, "of which Hervey never dreamed." The condition of complete keeping in which we discover some of these remains, even when exposed to the incessant dash of the surf, seems truly wonderful. We see scales of Holoptychius standing up in bold relief from the hard cherty rock that has worn from around them, with all the tubercles and wavy ridges of their sculpture entire. This state of keeping seems to be wholly owing to the curious chemical change that has taken place in their substance. Ere the skeleton of the Bruce, disinterred entire after the lapse of five centuries, was re-committed to the tomb, there were such measures taken to secure its preservation, that, were it to be again disinterred even after as many centuries more had

chloritic: see note for pp. 101-102; Hervey: James Hervey (1714-1758), author of *Meditations among the Tombs*, a devotional work that dwelt upon death and mortality; the Bruce: King Robert I of Scotland passed, it might be found retaining unbroken its gigantic proportions. There was molten pitch poured over the bones in a state of sufficient fluidity to permeate all their pores, and fill up the central hollows, and which, soon hardening around them, formed a bituminous matrix, in which they may lie unchanged for more than a thousand years. Now, exactly such was the process of keeping to which nature resorted with these skeletons of the Old Red Sandstone. The animal matter with which they were charged has been converted into a hard black bitumen. Like the bones of the Bruce, they are bones steeped in pitch ; and so thoroughly is every pore and hollow still occupied, that, when cast into the fire, they flame like torches. In one of the beds at which we have now arrived Mr Dick found the occipital plates of a Holoptychius of gigantic proportions. The frontal plates measured full sixteen inches across, and from the nape of the neck to a little above the place of the eyes, full eighteen ; while a single plate belonging to the lower part of the head measures thirteen and a half inches by seven and a half. I have remarked, in my little work on the Old Red Sandstone,—founding on a large amount of negative evidence,—that a mediocrity of size and bulk seems to have obtained among the fish of the Lower Old Red, though, in at least the Upper formation, a considerable increase in both took place. A single piece of positive evidence, however, outweighs whole volumes of a merely negative kind. From the entire plate now in my possession, which is identical with one figured in Mr Noble of St Madoes' specimen, and from the huge fragments of the upper plates now before me, some of which are full five-eighth parts of an inch in thickness, I am prepared to demonstrate that this Holoptychius of the Lower Old Red must have been at least thrice the size of the *Holoptychius Nobilissimus* of Clashbennie.

Still we pass on, though with no little difficulty, over the

Mr Noble: Reverend James Noble (1800–1848), minister of St Madoes, had collected, from Clashbennie near by on the north bank of the Firth of Tay, not far from Perth, the first complete specimens of *Holoptychius nobilissimus* described by Louis Agassiz, who published the 'figure' to which Miller presumably referred (Andrews 1982) rough contorted crags, worn by the surf into deep ruts and uneven ridges, gnarled protuberances, and crater-like hollows. The fossiliferous beds are still very numerous, and largely charged with remains.   We see dermal bones, spines, scales, and jaws, projecting in high relief from the sea-worn surface of the ledges below, and from the weather-worn faces of the precipices above; for an uneven wall of crags, some thirty or forty feet high, now runs along the shore.   We have reached what seems a large mole, that, sloping downwards athwart the beach from the precipices, like a huge boat-pier, runs far into the surf.   We find it composed of a siliceous bed, so intensely compact and hard, that it has preserved its proportions entire, while every other rock has worn from around it.   For century after ce: torms of the fierce north-west sent their long ocean-nursed waves to dash against it in foam ; for century after century have the never-ceasing currents of the Pentland chafed against its steep sides, or eddied over its rough crest; and yet still does it remain unwasted and un-worn,—its abrupt wall retaining all its former steepness, and every angular jutting all the original sharpness of edge.   As we advance the scenery becomes wilder and more broken : here an irregular wall of rock projects from the crags towards the sea ; there a dock-like hollow, in which the water gleams green, intrudes from the sea upon the crags ; we pass a deep lime-encrusted cave, with which tradition associates some wild legends, and which, from the supposed resemblance of the hanging stalactites to the entrails of a large animal wounded in the chase, bears the name of Pudding-Gno; and then, turning an angle of the coast, we enter a solitary bay, that presents at its upper extremity a flat expanse of sand.   Our walk is still over sepulchres charged with the remains of the long-departed.   Scales of Holoptychius abound, scattered like coin over the surface of the ledges.   It would seem—to borrow from Mr Dick—as if some old lord of the treasury, who

---

Pudding-Gno: presumably a misreading or misspelling of what might be 'Pudding-Geo'. 'Geo' is the local term for the characteristic rectilinear inlets eroded along the faults and joints in the Old Red Sandstone cliffs

flourished in the days of the coal-money currency, had taken
a squandering fit at Sanday Bay, and tossed the dingy contents of his treasure-chest by shovelfuls upon the rocks. Mr
Dick found in this locality some of his finest specimens,
one of which—the inner side of the skull-cap of a Holoptychius, with every plate occupying its proper place, and the
large angular holes through which the eyes looked out still
entire—I trust to be able by and by to present to the public in a good engraving.   There occur jaws, plates, scales,
spines,—the remains of fucoids, too, of great size and in vast
abundance.   Mr Dick has disinterred from among the rocks
of Sanday Bay flattened carbonaceous stems four inches in
diameter.   We are still within an hour's walk of Thurso ;
but in that brief hour how many marvels have we witnessed !
—how vast an amount of the vital mechanisms of a perished
creation have we not passed over !   Our walk has been along
ranges of sepulchres, greatly more wonderful than those of
Thebes or Petræa, and mayhap a thousand times more ancient.
There is no lack of life along the shores of the solitary little
bay.   The shriek of the sparrow-hawk mingles from the cliffs
with the hoarse deep croak of the raven ; the cormorant on
some wave-encircled ledge hangs out his dark wing to the
breeze ; the spotted diver, plying his vocation on the shallows beyond, dives and then appears, and dives and appears
again, and we see the silver glitter of scales from his beak ;
and far away in the offing the sun-light falls on a scull of sea-
gulls, that flutter upwards, downwards, and athwart, now on
the sea, now in the air, thick as midges over some forest-brook
in an evening of midsummer.

But we again pass onwards, amid a wild ruinous scene of
abrupt faults, detached fragments of rock, and reversed strata :
again the ledges assume their ordinary position and aspect,
and we rise from lower to higher and still higher beds in the
formation,—for such, as I have already remarked, is the gene-

coal-money currency: the disc-like pieces of dark jetlike Jurassic shale found for
example near Dunrobin in Sutherland, and Kimmeridge in Dorset, England. They were
once thought to be prehistoric money, but are now considered wasters from lathe-turning,
for instance in the making of bangles

ral arrangement from west to east, along the northern coast of Caithness, of the Lower Old Red Sandstone. The great Conglomerate base of the formation we find largely developed at Port Skerry, just where the western boundary line of the county divides it from the county of Sutherland ; its thick upper coping of sandstone we see forming the tall cliffs of Dunnet Head; and the greater part of the space between, nearly twenty miles as the crow flies, is occupied chiefly by the shales, grits, and flagstones, which we have found charged so abundantly with the strangely-organised ichthyolites of the second stage of vertebrate existence. In the twenty intervening miles there are many breaks and faults, and so there may be, of course, recurrences of the same strata, and re-appearances of the same beds ; but, after making large allowance for partial foldings and repetitions, we must regard the development of this formation, with which the twenty miles are occupied, as truly enormous. And yet it is but one of three that occur in a single system. We reach the long flat bay of Dunnet, and cross its waste of sands. The incoherent coils of the sand-worm lie thick on the surface ; and here a swarm of buzzing flies, disturbed by the foot, rises in a cloud from some tuft of tangled sea-weed ; and here myriads of gray crustaceous sand-hoppers dart sidelong in the little pools, or vault from the drier ridges a few inches into the air. Were the trilobites of the Silurian system,—at one period, as their remains testify, more than equally abundant,—creatures of similar habits ? We have at length arrived at the tall sandstone precipices of Dunnet, with their broad decaying fronts of red and yellow ; but in vain may we ply hammer and chisel among them : not a scale, not a plate, not even the stain of an imperfect fucoid, appears. We have reached the upper boundary of the Lower Old Red formation, and find it bordered by a desert devoid of all trace of life. Some of the characteristic types of the formation re-appear in the upper deposits ; but though there is a reproduction of the original works in their more characteristic passages, if I may so speak, many of the readings are diverse, and the editions are all new.

It is one of the circumstances of peculiar interest with which Geology at its present stage is invested, that there is no man of energy and observation who may not rationally indulge in the hope of extending its limits by adding to its facts. Mr Dick, an intelligent tradesman of Thurso, agreeably occupies his hours of leisure, for a few months, in detaching from the rocks in his neighbourhood their organic remains ; and thus succeeds in adding to the existing knowledge of palæozoic life, by disinterring ichthyolites which even Agassiz himself would delight to figure and describe. Several of the specimens in my possession, which I owe to the kindness of Mr Dick, are so decidedly unique, that they would be regarded as strangers in the completest geological museums extant. It is a not uncurious fact, that when the Thurso tradesman was pursuing his labours of exploration among rocks beside the Pentland Frith, a man of similar character was pursuing exactly similar labours, with nearly similar results, among rocks of nearly the same era, that bound, on the coast of Cornwall, the British Channel. When the one was hammering in " Ready-money Cove," the other, at the opposite end of the island, was disturbing the echoes of " Pudding-Gno ;" and scales, plates, spines, and occipital fragments of palæozoic fishes rewarded the labours of both. In an article on the scientific meeting at York, which appeared in " Chambers' Journal" in the November of last year, the reading public were introduced to a singularly meritorious naturalist, Mr Charles Peach,* a private in the mounted guard (preventive

* Mr Peach has discovered fossils in the Durness limestone, which rests above the quartzite rock of the west of Scotland, that covers the Red Sandstone long believed to be OLD RED. The fossils are very obscure.— W. S. S.

scientific meeting at York: presumably the British Association for the Advancement of Science, September 1844, as reviewed by Chambers in *Chambers's Journal* for 23 November; **Charles Peach**: (1800–1886). He would later move to Caithness himself (Smiles 1878), and, still later, catalogue the Miller Collection in what is now NMS (Oldroyd 1996a; Taylor and Gostwick 2003) service), stationed on the southern coast of Cornwall, who has made several interesting discoveries on the outer confines of the animal kingdom, that have added considerably to the list of our British zoophites and echinodermata. The article, a finely-toned one, redolent of that pleasing sympathy which Mr Robert Chambers has ever evinced with struggling merit, referred chiefly to Mr Peach's labours as a naturalist; but he is also well known in the geological field.

Robert Chambers: (1802-1871), the editor, writer, and, with his brother William, publisher. *Chambers's Edinburgh Journal* published some of Miller's early work. Chambers was anonymous author of the pro–evolutionary *Vestiges* – see Introduction

CHAPTER XII.

MY term of furlough was fast drawing to a close. It was now Wednesday the 14th August, and on Monday the 19th it behoved me to be seated at my desk in Edinburgh. I took boat, and crossed the Moray Frith from Cromarty to Nairn, and then walked on, in a very hot sun, over Shakspeare's Moor to Boghole, with the intention of examining the ichthyolite beds of Clune and Lethenbarn, and afterwards striking across the country to Forres, through the forest of Darnaway, where the forest abuts on the Findhorn, at the picturesque village of Sluie. When I had last crossed the moor, exactly ten years before, it was in a tremendous storm of rain and wind ; and the dark platform of heath and bog, with its old ruinous castle standing sentry over it, seemed greatly more worthy of the genius of the dramatist, as cloud after cloud dashed over it, like ocean waves breaking on some low volcanic island, than it did on this clear, breathless afternoon, in the unclouded sunshine. But the sublimity of the moor on which Macbeth met the witches depends in no degree on that of the "heath near Forres," whether seen in foul weather or fair : its topography bears relation to but the mind of Shakspeare ; and neither tile-draining nor the plough will ever lessen an inch of its area.

The limestone quarry of Clune has been opened on the

----

tile-draining: 'improving' land by installing drains made of clay or 'tile' pipes, *etc* edge of an extensive moor, about three miles from the public road, where the province of Moray sweeps upwards from the broad fertile belt of corn-land that borders on the sea, to the brown and shaggy interior.   There is an old-fashioned bare-looking farm-house on the one side, surrounded by a few un-inclosed patches of corn ; and the moorland, here dark with heath, there gray with lichens, stretches away on the other. The quarry itself is merely a piece of moor that has been trenched to the depth of some five or six feet from the sur-face, and that presents, at the line where the broken ground leans against the ground still unbroken, a low uneven front-age, somewhat resembling that of a ruinous stone-fence.   It has been opened in the outcrop of an ichthyolite bed of the Lower Old Red Sandstone, on which in this locality the thin moory soil immediately rests, without the intervention of the common boulder clay of the country ; and the fish-envelop-ing nodules, which are composed in this bed of a rich lime-stone, have been burnt, for a considerable number of years, for the purposes of the agriculturist and builder.   There was a kiln smoking this evening beside the quarry ; and a few labourers were engaged with shovel and pickaxe in cutting into the stratified clay of the unbroken ground, and throw-ing up its spindle-shaped nodules on the bank, as materials for their next burning.   Antiquaries have often regretted that the sculptured marble of Greece and Egypt,—classic urns, to whose keeping the ashes of the dead had been con-signed, and antique sarcophagi, roughened with hieroglyphics, —should have been so often condemned to the lime-kiln by the illiterate Copt or tasteless Mohammedan ; and I could not help experiencing a somewhat similar feeling here.   The urns and sarcophagi, many times more ancient than those of Greece and Egypt, and that told still more wondrous stories, lay thickly ranged in this strange catacomb,—so thickly, that there were quite enough for the lime-kiln and the geologists

---

illiterate Copt or tasteless Mohammedan: meant literally rather than pejoratively: the first cannot read the hieroglyphic inscriptions, and the second cannot appreciate the artistic value of what to him are merely 'idols' too ; but I found the kiln got all, and this at a time when the collector finds scarce any fossils more difficult to procure than those of the Lower Old Red Sandstone.   I asked one of the labourers whether he did not preserve some of the better specimens, in the hope of finding an occasional purchaser.   Not now, he said : he used to preserve them in the days of Lady Cumming of Altyre ; but since her ladyship's death, no one in the neighbourhood seemed to care for them, and strangers rarely came the way.

The first nodule I laid open contained a tolerably well-preserved Cheiracanthus ; the second, an indifferent specimen of Glyptolepis ; and three others, in succession, remains of Coccesteus.   Almost every nodule of one especial layer near the top incloses its organism.   The colouring is frequently of great beauty.   In the Cromarty, as in the Caithness, Orkney, and Gamrie specimens, the animal matter with which the bones were originally charged has been converted into a dark glossy bitumen, and the plates and scales glitter from a ground of opaque gray, like pieces of japan-work suspended against a rough-cast wall.   But here, as in the other Morayshire deposits, the plates and scales exist in nearly their original condition, as bone that retains its white colour in the centre of the specimens, where its bulk is greatest, and is often beautifully tinged at its thinner edges by the iron with which the stone is impregnated.   It is not rare to find some of the better preserved fossils coloured in a style that reminds one of the more gaudy fishes of the tropics.   We see the body of the ichthyolite, with its finely arranged scales, of a pure snow-white.   Along the edges, where the original substance of the bone, combining with the oxide of the matrix, has formed a phosphate of iron, there runs a delicately shaded band of plum-blue ; while the outspread fins, charged still more largely with the oxide, are of a deep red.   The description of Mr Patrick Duff, in his "Geology of Moray," so re-

---

scarce any fossils more difficult to procure: surprising given the richness of these (actually Middle Old Red) deposits. Probably a reference to their then remoteness, the problems of travel in north Scotland and Orkney, and perhaps also a lack of commercial collectors; **Lady Cumming**: Lady Eliza Gordon Cumming (d. 1842), of Altyre House near Nairn. Her collection of local fossil fishes is now in NMS (Andrews 1982)

dolent of the quiet enthusiasm of the true fossil-hunter, especially applies to the ichthyolites of this quarry, and to those
of a neighbouring opening in the same bed,—the quarry of
Lethenbar. "The nodules," says Mr Duff, "which in their
external shape resemble the stones used in the game of curling, but are elliptical bodies instead of round, lie in the shale
on their flat sides, in a line with the dip. When taken out,
they remind one of water-worn pebbles, or rather boulders of
the shore. A smart blow on the edge splits them along on
the major axis, and exposes the interesting inclosure. The
practised geologist knows well the thrilling interest attending
the breaking up of the nodule : the uninitiated cannot sympathize with it. There is no time when a fossil looks so well
as when first exposed. There is a clammy moisture on the
surface of the scales or plates, which brings out the beautiful
colouring, and adds brilliancy to the enamel. Exposure to
the weather soon dims the lustre ; and even in a cabinet an
old specimen is easily known by its tarnished aspect."

I found at Clune no ichthyolite to which the geologists
have not been already introduced, or with which I had not
been acquainted previously in the Cromarty beds. The
Lower Old Red of Morayshire furnishes, however, at least
one genus not yet figured nor described, and of which, so far
as I am aware, only a single specimen has yet been found. It
seems to have been a small delicately-formed fish ; its head
covered with plates ; its body with round scales of a size intermediate between those of the Osteolepis and Cheiracanthus ;
its anterior dorsal fin placed, as in the Dipterus, Diplopterus,
and Glyptolepis, directly opposite to its ventral fins ; the enamelled surfaces of the minute scales were fretted with microscopic undulating ridges, that radiated from the centre to the
circumference; similar furrows traversed the occipital plates;
and the fins, unfurnished with spines, were formed, as in the
Dipterus and Diplopterus, of thick-set enamelled rays. The

Duff: (1842, p. 37); **one genus not yet figured or described**: indeed an unusual fish,
and not today recognizable – perhaps it did indeed go astray after Lady Eliza's death
(R. L. Paton, *pers. comm.* 2002)

posterior fins and tail of the creature were not preserved. I
may mention, for the satisfaction of the geologist, that I saw
this unique fossil in the possession of the late Lady Cumming
of Altyre, a few weeks previous to the lamented death of her
ladyship ; and that, on assuring her it was as new in relation
to the Cromarty and Caithness fish-beds as to those of Moray,
she intimated an intention of forthwith sending a drawing
of it to Agassiz ; but her untimely decease in all probability
interfered with the design, and I have not since heard of
this new genus of ichthyolite, or of her ladyship's interesting specimen, hitherto apparently its only representative and
memorial.   In the Morayshire, as in the Cromarty beds, the
limestone nodules take very generally the form of the fish
which they inclose : they are stone coffins, carefully moulded
to express the outline of the corpses within.   Is the fish entire ?—the nodule is of a spindle form, broader at the head
and narrower at the tail.   Is it slightly curved, in the attitude of violent death ?—the nodule has also its slight curve.
Is it bent round, so that the extremities of the creature meet ?
—the nodule, in conformity with the outline, is circular.   Is
it disjointed and broken ?—the nodule is correspondingly irregular.   In nine cases out of ten, the inclosing coffin, like
that of an old mummy, conforms to the outline of the organism which it incloses.   It is further worthy of remark, too,
that a large fish forms generally a large nodule, and a small
fish a small one.   Here, for instance, is a nodule fifteen inches
in length, here a nodule of only three inches, and here a nodule of intermediate size, that measures eight inches.   We
find that the large nodule contains a Cheirolepis thirteen
inches in length, the small one a Diplacanthus of but two and
a half inches in length, and the intermediate one a Cheiracanthus of seven inches.   The size of the fish evidently regu-
lated that of the nodule.   The coffin is generally as good a
fit in size as in form ; and the bulk of the nodule bears al-

most always a definite proportion to the amount of animal matter round which it had formed. I was a good deal struck, a few weeks ago, in glancing over a series of experiments conducted for a different purpose by a lady of singular ingenuity,—Mrs Marshall, the inventor and patentee of the beautiful marble-looking plaster, *Intonacco*,—to find what seemed a similar principle illustrated in the compositions of her various cements. These are all formed of a basis of lime, mixed in certain proportions with organic matter. The reader must be familiar with cements of this kind long known among the people, and much used in the repairing of broken pottery, such as a cement compounded of quicklime made of oyster-shells, mixed up with a glue made of skim-milk cheese, and another cement made also of quicklime mixed up with the whites of eggs. In Mrs Marshall's cements, the organic matter is variously compounded of both animal and vegetable substances, while the earth generally employed is sulphate of lime ; and the result is a close-grained marble-like composition, considerably harder than the sulphate in its original crystalline state. She had deposited, in one set of her experiments, the calcareous earth, mixed up with sand, clay, and other extraneous matters, on some of the commoner molluscs of our shores ; and universally found that the mass, incoherent everywhere else, had acquired solidity wherever it had been permeated by the animal matter of the molluscs. Each animal, in proportion to its size, is found to retain, as in the fossiliferous spindles of the Old Red Sandstone, its coherent nodule around it. One point in the natural phenomenon, however, still remains unillustrated by the experiments of Mrs Marshall. We see in them the animal matter giving solidity to the lime in immediate contact with it ; but we do not see it possessing any such affinity for it as to form, in an argillaceous compound, like that of the ichthyolite beds, a centre of attraction powerful enough to draw to-

earth: apparently in the old chemical sense of an inorganic compound as opposed to, for instance, a metal; **animal matter**: here, organic and nitrogenous compounds, such as those arising from the decay of the corpse gether the lime diffused throughout the mass.   It still remains for the geologic chemist to discover on what principle masses of animal matter should form the attracting nuclei of limestone nodules.

The declining sun warned me that I had lingered rather longer than was prudent among the ichthyolites of Clune ; and so, striking in an eastern direction across a flat moor, through which I found the schistose gneiss of the district protruding in masses resembling half-buried boulders, I entered the forest of Darnaway.   There was no path, and much underwood ; and I enjoyed the luxury of steering my course, out of sight of road and landmark, by the sun, and of being not sure at times whether I had skill enough to play the part of the bush-ranger under his guidance.   A sultry day had clarified and cooled down into a clear balmy evening ; the slant beam was falling red on a thousand tall trunks,—here gleaming along some bosky vista, to which the white silky woodmoths fluttering by scores, and the midge and the mosquito dancing by myriads, imparted a motty gold-dust atmosphere ; there penetrating in straggling rays far into some gloomy recess, and resting in patches of flame, amid the darkness, on gnarled stem, or moss-cushioned stump, or gray beard-like lichen.   I dislodged, in passing through the underwood, many a tiny tenant of the forest, that had a better right to harbour among its wild raspberries and junipers than I had to disturb them,—velvety night-moths, that had sat with folded wings under the leaves, awaiting the twilight, and that now took short blind flights of some two or three yards, to get out of my way,—and robust, well-conditioned spiders, whose elastic well-tightened lines snapped sharp before me as I pressed through, and then curled up on the scarce perceptible breeze, like broken strands of wool.   But every man, however Whiggish in his inclinations, entertains a secret respect for the powerful ; and though I passed within a few

---

it still remains: an important research area in palaeontology today is indeed how the chemistry of decay of a buried carcass can cause a nodule to form around it, sometimes so quickly as to preserve even the most delicate structures before they decay or are squashed under the weight of overlying sediment (*eg* Martill 1998); **Whiggish**: here, politically liberal feet of a large wasp's nest, suspended to a jutting bough of furze, the wasps I took especial care *not* to disturb.   I pressed on, first through a broad belt of the forest, occupied mainly by melancholy Scotch firs ; next through an opening, in which I found an American-looking village of mingled cottages, gardens, fields, and wood ; and then through another broad forest-belt, in which the ground is more varied with height and hollow than in the first, and in which I found only forest trees, mostly oaks and beeches.   I heard the roar of the Findhorn before me, and premised I was soon to reach the river ; but whether I should pursue it upwards or downwards, in order to find the ferry at Sluie, was more than I knew.   There lay in my track a beautiful hillock, that reclines on the one side to the setting sun, and sinks sheer on the other, in a mural sandstone precipice, into the Findhorn.   The trees open over it, giving full access to the free air and the sunshine ; and I found it as thickly studded over with berries as if it had been the special care of half a dozen gardeners. The red light fell yet redder on the thickly inlaid cranberries and stone-brambles of the slope, and here and there, though so late in the season, on a patch of wild strawberries ; while over all, dark, delicate blaeberries, with their flour-bedusted coats, were studded as profusely as if they had been peppered over it by a hailstone cloud.   I have seldom seen such a school-boy's paradise ; and I was just thinking what a rare discovery I would have deemed it had I made it thirty years sooner, when I heard a whooping in the wood, and four little girls, the eldest scarcely eleven, came bounding up to the hillock, their lips and fingers already dyed purple, and dropped themselves down among the berries with a shout.   They were sadly startled to find they had got a companion in so solitary a recess ; but I succeeded in convincing them that they were in no manner of danger from him ; and on asking whether there was any of them skilful enough to show me the way to Sluie, they told me they all lived there, and were on their way home from school, which they attended at the village in the forest. Hours had elapsed since the master had *let them go,* but in so fine an evening the berries would'nt, and so they were still in the wood. I accompanied them to Sluie, and was ferried over the river in a salmon coble. There is no point where the Findhorn, celebrated among our Scotch streams for the beauty of its scenery, is so generally interesting as in the neighbourhood of this village; forest and river, —each a paragon in its kind,—uniting for several miles together what is most choice and characteristic in the peculiar features of both. In no locality is the surface of the great forest of Darnaway more undulated, or its trees nobler; and nowhere does the river present a livelier succession of eddying pools and rippling shallows, or fret itself in sweeping on its zig-zag course, now to the one bank, now to the other, against a more picturesque and imposing series of cliffs. But to the geologist the locality possesses an interest peculiar to itself. The precipices on both sides are charged with fossils of the Upper Old Red Sandstone: they form part of a vast indurated grave-yard, excavated to the depth of an hundred feet by the ceaseless wear of the stream; and when the waters are low, the teeth-plates and scales of ichthyolites, all of them specifically different from those of Clune and Lethenbar, and most of them generically so, may be disinterred from the strata in handfuls. But the closing evening left me neither light nor time for the work of exploration. I heard the curfew in the woods from the yet distant town, and dark night had set in long ere I reached Forres. On the following morning I took a seat in one of the south coaches, and got on to Elgin an hour before noon.

Elgin, one of the finest of our northern towns, occupies the centre of a richly fossiliferous district, which wants only better sections to rank it among the most interesting in the

---

Sluie: Miller was apparently crossing the river a few kilometres south of Altyre House kingdom. An undulating platform of Old Red Sandstone, in which we see, largely developed in one locality, the lower formation of the Coccosteus, and in another, still more largely, the upper formation of the *Holoptychius Nobilissimus*, forms, if I may so speak, the foundation deposit of the district,— the true geologic plane of the country ; and, thickly scattered over this plane, we find numerous detached knolls and patches of the Weald and the Oolite, deposited like heaps of travelled soil, or of lime shot down by the agriculturist on the surface of a field. The Old Red platform is mottled by the outliers of a comparatively modern time : the sepulchral mounds of later races, that lived and died during the reptile age of the world, repose on the surface of an ancient burying-ground, charged with remains of the long anterior age of the fish ; and over all, as a general covering, rest the red boulder-clay and the vegetable mould. Mr Duff, in his valuable " Sketch of the Geology of Moray," enumerates five several localities in the neighbourhood of Elgin in which there occur outliers of the Weald ; though, of course, in a country so flat, and in which the diluvium lies deep, we cannot hold that all have been discovered. And though the outliers of the Oolite have not yet been ascertained to be equally numerous, they seem of greater extent ; the isolated masses detached from them by the denuding agencies lie thick over extensive areas ; and in working out the course of improvement which has already rendered Elginshire the garden of the north, the ditcher at one time touches on some bed of shale charged with the characteristic Ammonites and Belemnites of the system, and at another on some calcareous sandstone bed, abounding with its Pectens, its Plagiostoma, and its Pinnæ. Some of these outliers, whether Wealden or Oolitic, are externally of great beauty. They occur in the parish of Lhanbryde, about three miles to the east of Elgin, in the form of green pyramidal hillocks, mottled with trees, and at Linksfield, as a confluent

---

Weald ... Oolite ... outliers: see Additional Notes; **shot down:** dumped group of swelling grassy mounds. And from their insulated character, and the abundance of organisms which they inclose, they serve to remind one of those green pyramids of Central America in which the traveller finds deposited the skeleton remains of extinct races. It has been suggested by Mr Duff, in his "Sketch,"—a suggestion which the late Sutherland-shire discoveries of Mr Robertson of Inverugie have tended to confirm,—that the Oolite and Weald of Moray do not, in all probability, represent consecutive formations : they seem to bear the same sort of relation to each other as that mutually borne by the Mountain Limestone and the Coal Measures. The one, of lacustrine or of estuary origin, exhibits chiefly the productions of the land and its fresh waters ; the other, as decidedly of marine origin, is charged with the remains of animals whose proper home was the sea. But the productions, though dissimilar, were in all probability contemporary, just as the crabs and periwinkles of the Frith of Forth are contemporary with the frogs and lymnea of Flanders moss.

I had little time for exploration in the neighbourhood of Elgin ; but that little, through the kindness of my friend Mr Duff, I was enabled to economize. We first visited together the outlier of the Weald at Linksfield. It may be found rising in the landscape, a short mile below the town, in the form of a green undulating hillock, half cut through by a limestone quarry ; and the section thus furnished is of great beauty. The basis on which the hillock rests is formed of the well-marked calcareous band in the Upper Old Red, known as the Cornstone, which we find occurring here, as elsewhere, as a pale concretionary limestone of considerable richness, though in some patches largely mixed with a green argillaceous earth, and in others passing into a siliceous chert. Over the pale-coloured base, the section of the hillock is ribbed like an onyx : for about forty feet, bands of gray, green, and

Oolite and Weald: see Additional Note for p. 55; Flanders Moss: a large peat bog in the upper Forth valley in central Scotland; Coal Measures are not in fact contemporary with the Mountain Limestone of the Pennines, *etc* (at least as understood today). Certainly Miller (1891a, p. 71) did not regard these strata as being coeval in the Midland Valley blue clays alternate with bands of cream-coloured, light-green, and dark-blue limestones; and over all there rests a band of the red boulder-clay, capped by a thin layer of vegetable mould.   It is a curious circumstance, well fitted to impress on the geologist the necessity of cautious induction, that the boulder-clay not only *overlies*, but also *underlies*, this fresh-water deposit; a bed of unequivocally the same origin and character with that at the top lying intercalated, as if filling up two low flat vaults, between the upper surface of the Corn-stone and the lower band of the Weald.   It would, however, be as unsafe to infer that this intervening bed is older than the overlying ones, as to infer that the rubbish which choaks up the vaulted dungeon of an old castle is more ancient than the arch that stretches over it.   However introduced into the cavity which it occupies,—whether by land-springs or otherwise,—we find it containing fragments of the green and pale limestones that lie above, just as the rubbish of the castle dungeon might be found to contain fragments of the castle itself.   When the bed of red boulder-clay was inter-calated, the rocks of the overlying Wealden were exactly the same sort of indurated substances that they are now, and were yielding to the operations of some denuding agent. The alternating clays and limestones of this outlier, each of which must have been in turn an upper layer at the bottom of some lake or estuary, are abundantly fossiliferous.   In some the fresh-water character of the deposit is well marked : Cyprides are so exceedingly numerous in some of the bands, that they impart to the stone an Oolitic appearance; while others of a dark-coloured limestone we see strewed over, like the oozy bottom of a modern lake, with specimens of what seem Paludina, Cyclas, and Planorbus.   Some of the other shells are more equivocal : a Mytilus or Modiola, which abounds in some of the bands, may have been either a sea or a fresh-water shell; and a small oyster and Astarte seem de-

---

intercalated: see Additional Note for p. 199; **Oolitic**: here, in the primary sense of a granular rock texture, like that of fish roe cidedly marine. Remains of fish are very abundant,—scales, plates, teeth, ichthyodorulites, and in some instances entire ichthyolites. I saw, in the collection of Mr Duff, a small but very entire specimen of *Lepidotus minor*, with the fins spread out on the limestone, as in an anatomical preparation, and almost every plate and scale in its place. Some of his specimens of ichthyodorulites, too, are exceedingly beautiful, and of great size, resembling jaws thickly set with teeth, the apparent teeth being mere knobs ranged along the concave edge of the bone, the surface of which we see gracefully fluted and enamelled. What most struck me, however, in glancing over the drawers of Mr Duff, was the character of the Ganoid scales of this deposit. The Ganoid order in the days of the Weald was growing old ; and two new orders, —the Ctenoid and Cycloid,—were on the eve of taking its place in creation. Hitherto it had comprised at least two-thirds of all the fish that had existed ever since the period in which fish first began ; and almost every Ganoid fish had its own peculiar pattern of scale. But it would now seem as if well nigh all the simpler patterns were exhausted, and as if, in order to give the variety which nature loves, forms of the most eccentric types had to be resorted to. With scarce any exception save that furnished by the scales of the *Lepidotus minor*, which are plain lozenge-shaped plates, thickly japanned, the forms are strangely complex and irregular, easily expressible by the pencil, but beyond the reach of the pen. The remains of reptiles have been found occasionally, though rarely, in this outlier of the Weald,—the vertebra of a Plesiosaurus, the femur of some Chelonian reptile, and a large fluted tooth, supposed Saurian.

I would fain have visited some of the neighbouring outliers of the Oolite, but time did not permit. Mr Duff's collection, however, enabled me to form a tolerably adequate estimate of their organic contents. Viewed in the group, these

---

ichthyodorulites: fossil fin spines. Here, the cartilaginous bodies of sharks had rotted leaving only teeth and spines; order: relating to a classification of fishes by Louis Agassiz based on the structure of their scales, and used by Miller. Although soon superseded, it was an important early step in sorting out the diversity of fossil fishes (Oldroyd 1996a, Janvier 2003); reptiles: see Additional Note for p. 199

present nearly the same aspect as the organisms of the Upper Lias of Pabba.   There is in the same abundance large Pinnæ, and well-relieved Pectens, both ribbed and smooth ; the same abundance, too, of Belemnites and Ammonites of resembling type.   Both the Moray outliers and the Pabba deposit have their Terebratulæ, Gervilliæ, Plagiostoma, Cardiadæ, their bright Ganoid scales, and their imperfectly-preserved lignites. They belong apparently to nearly the same period, and must have been formed in nearly similar circumstances,—the one on the western, the other on the eastern coast of a country then covered by the vegetation of the Oolite, and now known, with reference to an antiquity of but yesterday, as the ancient kingdom of Scotland.   I saw among the Ammonites of these outliers at least one species, which, I believe, has not yet been found elsewhere, and which has been named, after Mr Robertson of Inverugie, the gentleman who first discovered it, *Ammonites Robertsoni*.   Like most of the genus to which it belongs, it is an exceedingly beautiful shell, with all its whorls free and gracefully ribbed, and bearing on its back, as its distinguishing specific peculiarity, a triple keel.   I spent the evening of this day in visiting, with Mr Duff, the Upper Old Red Sandstones of Scat-Craig.   In Elginshire, as in Fife and elsewhere, the Upper Old Red consists of three grand divisions,—a superior bed of pale yellow sandstone, which furnishes the finest building-stone anywhere found in the north of Scotland,—an intermediate calcareous bed, known technically as the Cornstone,—and an inferior bed of sandstone, chiefly, in this locality, of a grayish-red colour, and generally very incoherent in its structure.   The three beds, as shown by the fossil contents of the yellow sandstones above, and of the grayish-red sandstones below, are members of the same formation,—a formation which, in Scotland at least, does not possess an organism in common with the Middle Old Red formation, that of the Cephalaspis, as developed in Forfarshire, Stirling, and Ayr ; or the Lower Old Red formation, that of the Coccosteus, as developed in Caithness, Cromarty, Inverness, and Banff shires, and in so many different localities in Moray. The sandstones at Scat-Craig belong to the grayish-red base of the Upper Old Red formation. They lie about five miles south of Elgin, not far distant from where the palæozoic deposits of the coast-side lean against the great primary nucleus of the interior. We pass from the town, through deep rich fields, carefully cultivated and well inclosed : the country, as we advance on the moorlands, becomes more open ; the homely cottage takes the place of the neat villa ; the brown heath, of the grassy lea ; and unfenced patches of corn here and there alternate with plantings of dark sombre firs, in their mediocre youth. At length we near the southern boundary of the landscape,—an undulating moory ridge, partially planted ; and see where a deep gap in the outline opens a way to the upland districts of the province, a lively hill-stream descending towards the east through the bed which it has scooped out for itself in a soft red conglomerate. The section we have come to explore lies along its course : it has been the grand excavator in the densely occupied burial-ground over which it flows ; but its labours have produced but a shallow scratch after all,—a mere ditch, some ten or twelve feet deep, in a deposit the entire depth of which is supposed greatly to exceed a hundred fathoms. The shallow section, however, has been well wrought ; and its suit of fossils is one of the finest, both from the great specific variety which they exhibit, and their excellent state of keeping, that the Upper Old Red Sandstone has anywhere furnished.

So great is the incoherency of the matrix, that we can dig into it with our chisels, unassisted by the hammer. It reminds us of the loose gravelly soil of an ancient grave-yard, partially consolidated by a night's frost,—a resemblance still further borne out by the condition and appearance of its or-

ganic contents.   The numerous bones disseminated throughout the mass do not exist, as in so many of the Upper Old
Red Sandstone rocks, as mere films or impressions, but in their
original forms, retaining bulk as well as surface : they are
true grave-yard bones, which may be detached entire from the
inclosing mass, and of which, were we sufficiently well acquainted with the anatomy of the long-perished races to which
they belonged, entire skeletons might be reconstructed.   I
succeeded in disinterring, during my short stay, an occipital
plate of great beauty, fretted on its outer surface by numerous
tubercles, confluent on its anterior part, and surrounded on
its posterior portion, where they stand detached, by punctulated markings.   I found also a fine scale of *Holoptychius
Nobilissimus*, and a small tooth, bent somewhat like a nail
that had been drawn out of its place by two opposite wrenches,
and from the internal structure of which Professor Owen has
bestowed on the animal to which it belonged the generic name
Dendrodus.   I have ascertained, however, through the indispensable assistance of Mr George Sanderson, that the genus
Holoptychius of Agassiz, named from a peculiarity in the
sculpture of the scale, is the identical genus Dendrodus of
Professor Owen, named from a peculiarity in the structure
of the teeth.   Those teeth of the genus Holoptychius, whether
of the Lower or Upper Old Red, that belong to the second
or *reptile* row with which the creature's jaws were furnished,
present in the cross section the appearance of numerous
branches, like those of trees, radiating from a centre like
spokes from the nave of a wheel ; and their arborescent aspect suggested to the Professor the name Dendrodus.   It seems
truly wonderful, when one but considers it, to what minute
and obscure ramifications the variety of pattern, specific and
generic, which nature so loves to preserve, is found to descend.
We see great diversity of mode and style in the architecture
of a city built of brick ; but while the houses are different,

Professor Owen: see Additional Note for p. 127; Sanderson: Edinburgh lapidary (d.
1847) who pioneered thin-sectioning of geological material for microscopy; he processed
a number of fossils for Miller (Morrison-Low and Nuttall 2003)

the bricks are always the same. It is not so in nature. The bricks are as dissimilar as the houses. We find, for instance, those differences, specific and generic, that obtain among fishes, both recent and extinct, descending to even the microscopic structure of their teeth. There is more variety of pattern, —in most cases of very elegant pattern,—in the sliced fragments of the teeth of the ichthyolites of a single formation, than in the carved blocks of an extensive calico-print yard. Each species has its own distinct pattern, as if in all the individuals of which it consisted the same block had been employed to stamp it ; each genus has its own general *type* of pattern, as if the same inventive idea, variously altered and modified, had been wrought upon in all. In the genus Dendrodus, for instance, it is the generic type, that from a central nave there should radiate, spoke-like, a number of leafy branches ; but in the several species, the branches, if I may so express myself, belong to different shrubs, and present dissimilar outlines. There are no repetitions of earlier patterns to be found among the generically different ichthyolites of other formations. We see in the world of fashion old modes of ornament continually reviving : the range of invention seems limited ; and we find it revolving, in consequence, in an irregular, ever-returning cycle. But Infinite resource did not need to travel in a circle, and so we find no return or doublings in its course. It has appeared to me, that an argument against the transmutation of species, were any such needed, might be founded on those inherent peculiarities of structure that are ascertained thus to pervade the entire texture of the framework of animals. If we find one building differing from another merely in external form, we have no difficulty in conceiving how, by additions and alterations, they might be made to present a uniform appearance : transmutation, development, progression,—if one may use such terms,— seem possible in such circumstances. But if the buildings

---

carved blocks: *ie* woodcuts for fabric printing; **transmutation, development, progression**: often, as here, synonyms for what we today call biological evolution (Bowler 1989), although 'development' could also have its modern meaning of the 'ontogeny' or growth of the individual. Miller was wrong, in hindsight: all life on Earth shows the same 'brick and beam, bolt and nail' in its common biochemistry and genetics differ from each other, not only in external form, but also in every brick and beam, bolt and nail, no mere scheme of external alteration can induce a real resemblance. Every brick must be taken down, and every beam and bolt removed. The problem cannot be wrought by the remodelling of an old house : there is no other mode of solving it save by the erection of a new one.

Among the singularly interesting Old Red fossils of Mr Duff's collection I saw the impression of a large ichthyolite from the superior yellow sandstone of the Upper Old Red, which had been brought him by a country diker only a few days before. In breaking open a building stone, the diker had found the inside of it, he said, covered over with curiously carved flowers ; and, knowing that Mr Duff had a turn for curiosities, he had brought the flowers to him. The supposed flowers are the sculpturings on the scales of the ichthyolite ; and, true to the analogy of the diker, on at least a first glance, they may be held to resemble the rather equivocal florets of a cheap wall-paper, or of an ornamental tile. The specimen exhibits the impressions of four rows of oblong rectangular scales. One row contains seven of these, and another eight. Each scale averages about an inch and a quarter in length by about three quarters of an inch in breadth ; and the parallelogramical field which it presents is occupied by a curious piece of carving. By a sort of pictorial illusion, the device appears as if in motion : it would seem as if a sudden explosion had taken place in the middle of the field, and as if the numerous dislodged fragments, propelled all around by the central force, were hurrying to the sides. But these seeming fragments were not elevations in the original scale, but depressions. They almost seem as if they had been indented into it, in the way one sees the first heavy drops of a thunder shower indented into a platform of damp sea-sand ; and this last peculiarity of appearance seems to have suggested the

---

diker: builder of dykes, drystone field walls, in Scotland, not English ditcher; **Upper Old Red**: see Additional Notes

name which this sole representative of an extinct genus has
received during the course of the last few weeks from Agassiz. An Elgin gentleman forwarded to Neufchatel a singularly fine calotype of the fossil, taken by Mr Adamson of
Edinburgh, with a full-size drawing of a few of the scales ;
and from the calotype and the drawing the naturalist has decided that the genus is entirely new, and that henceforth it
shall bear the descriptive name of Stagonolepis, or drop-scale.
As I looked for the first time on this broken fragment of an
ichthyolite,—the sole representative and record of an entire
genus of creatures that had been once called into existence
to fulfil some wise purpose of the Creator long since accomplished,—I bethought me of Rogers' noble lines on the Torso,—

> " And dost thou still, thou mass of breathing stone,
> (Thy giant limbs to night and chaos hurled)
> Still sit as on the fragment of a world,
> Surviving all ?"

Here, however, was a still more wonderful Torso than that of
the dismembered Hercules, which so awakened the enthusiasm
of the poet. Strange peculiarities of being,—singular habits,
curious instincts, the history of a race from the period when
the all-producing Word had spoken the first individuals into
being, until, in circumstances unfitted for their longer existence, or in some great annihilating catastrophe, the last individuals perished,—were all associated with this piece of
sculptured stone ; but, like some ancient inscription of the
desert, written in an unknown character and dead tongue, its
dark meanings were fast locked up, and no inhabitant of earth
possessed the key.   Does that key anywhere exist, save in
the keeping of Him who knows all and produced all, and to
whom there is neither past nor future ?   Or is there a record
of creation kept by those higher intelligences,—the first-born
of spiritual natures,—whose existence stretches far into the
eternity that has gone by, and who possess, as their inheri-

Stagonolepis: see Additional Notes; **naturalist**: *ie* to J. L. R. Agassiz (1807-1873), then
the main authority on fossil fishes; **calotype** ... **Adamson**: see Additional Notes; **Rogers**
... **Torso**: the beginning of 'To the Fragment of a Statue of Hercules, Commonly called
the Torso' by Samuel Rogers (1806)

tance, the whole of the eternity to come ?   We may be at least assured, that nothing can be too low for angels to remember, that was not too low for God to create.

I took coach for Edinburgh on the following morning ; for with my visit to Scat-Craig terminated the explorations of my Summer Ramble.   During the summer of the present year I have found time to follow up some of the discoveries of the last.   In the course of a hasty visit to the island of Eigg, I succeeded in finding *in situ* reptile remains of the kind which I had found along the shores in the previous season, in detached water-rolled masses.   The deposit in which they occur lies deep in the Oolite.   In some parts of the island there rest over it alternations of beds of trap and sedimentary strata, to the height of more than a thousand feet ; but in the line of coast which intervenes between the farm-house of Keill and the picturesque shieling described in my fifth chapter, it has been laid bare by the sea immediately under the cliffs, and we may see it jutting out at a low angle from among the shingle and rolled stones of the beach for several hundred feet together, charged everywhere with the teeth, plates, and scales of Ganoid fishes, and, somewhat more sparingly, with the ribs, vertebræ, and digital bones of saurians.   But a full description of this interesting deposit, as its discovery belongs to the Summer Ramble of a year, the ramblings of which are not yet completed, must await some future time.

CHAPTER XIII.

SUPPLEMENTARY.

It is told of the "Spectator," on his own high authority, that having "read the controversies of some great men concerning the antiquities of Egypt, he made a voyage to Grand Cairo on purpose to take the measure of a pyramid, and that, so soon as he had set himself right in that particular, he returned to his native country with great satisfaction." My love of knowledge has not carried me altogether so far, chiefly, I daresay, because my voyaging opportunities have not been quite so great. Ever since my ramble of last year, however, I have felt, I am afraid, a not less interest in the geologic antiquities of Small Isles than that cherished by the "Spectator" with respect to the comparatively modern antiquities of Egypt; and as, in a late journey to these islands, the object of my visit involved but a single point, nearly as insulated as the dimensions of a pyramid, I think I cannot do better than shelter myself under the authority of the short-faced gentleman who wrote articles in the reign of Queen Anne. I had found in Eigg, in considerable abundance and fine keeping, reptile remains of the Oolite; but they had occurred in merely rolled masses, scattered along the beach. I had not discovered the bed in which they had been originally deposited, and could neither tell its place in the system, nor its relation to the other rocks of the island. The discovery was but a

'Spectator' … **Cairo**: a mock autobiographical article supposedly by the 'Spectator' himself, in fact Joseph Addison, in the first issue of the eponymous magazine in March 1711; **place in the system**: *ie* its source stratum and age half-discovery,—the half of a broken medal, with the date on the missing portion.   And so, immediately after the rising of the General Assembly in June last [1845], I set out to revisit Small Isles, accompanied by my friend Mr Swanson, with the determination of acquainting myself with the burial-place of the old Oolitic reptiles, if it lay anywhere open to the light.

We found the Betsey riding in the anchoring ground at Isle Ornsay, in her foul-weather dishabille, with her topmast struck and in the yard, and her cordage and sides exhibiting in their weathered aspect the influence of the bleaching rains and winds of the previous winter.   She was at once in an undress and getting old, and, as seen from the shore through rain and spray,—for the weather was coarse and boisterous, —she had apparently gained as little in her good looks from either circumstance as most other ladies do.   We lay storm-bound for three days at Isle Ornsay, watching from the window of Mr Swanson's dwelling the incessant showers sweeping down the loch.   On the morning of Saturday, the gale, though still blowing right ahead, had moderated ; the minister was anxious to visit this island charge, after his absence of several weeks from them at the Assembly ; and I, more than half afraid that my term of furlough might expire ere I had reached my proposed scene of exploration, was as anxious as he ; and so we both resolved, come what might, on doggedly beating our way adown the Sound of Sleat to Small Isles.   If the wind does not fail us, said my friend, we have little more than a day's work before us, and shall get into Eigg about midnight.   We had but one of our seamen aboard, for John Stewart was engaged with his potato crop at home ; but the minister was content, in the emergency, to rank his passenger as an able-bodied seaman ; and so, hoisting sail and anchor, we got under way, and, clearing the loch, struck out into the Sound.

---

topmast struck: taken down, for winter storage or heavy weather. Its removal and that of the associated rigging and sails would metaphorically leave the *Betsey* in **undress**; **in the yard**: meaning uncertain – possibly stored ashore, or (perhaps less probably) lashed to the yard or the adjacent mainmast (if the *Betsey* had a yard at all; a yard is a transverse spar carrying a single square sail)

We tacked in long reaches for several hours, now opening up in succession the deep withdrawing lochs of the mainland, now clearing promontory after promontory in the island district of Sleat. In a few hours we had left a bulky schooner, that had quitted Isle Ornsay at the same time, full five miles behind us ; but as the sun began to decline, the wind began to sink ; and about seven o'clock, when we were nearly abreast of the rocky point of Sleat, and about half-way advanced in our voyage, it had died into a calm ; and for full twenty hours thereafter there was no more sailing for the Betsey. We saw the sun set, and the clouds gather, and the pelting rain come down, and night fall, and morning break, and the noontide hour pass by, and still were we floating idly in the calm. I employed the few hours of the Saturday evening that intervened between the time of our arrest and nightfall, in fishing from our little boat for medusæ with a bucket. They had risen by myriads from the bottom as the wind fell, and were mottling the green depths of the water below and around far as the eye could reach. Among the commoner kinds,— the kind with the four purple rings on the area of its flat bell, which ever vibrates without sound, and the kind with the fringe of dingy brown, and the long stinging tails, of which I have sometimes borne from my swimming excursions the nettle-like smart for hours,—there were at least two species of more unusual occurrence, both of them very minute. The one, scarcely larger than a shilling, bore the common umbiliferous form, but had its area inscribed by a pretty orange-coloured wheel ; the other, still more minute, and which presented in the water the appearance of a small hazel-nut of a brownish-yellow hue, I was disposed to set down as a species of beroe. On getting one caught, however, and transferred to a bowl, I found that the brownish-coloured, melon-shaped mass, though ribbed like the beroe, did not represent the true outline of the animal : it formed merely the centre of a transparent gelatinous bell, which, though scarce visible in even the bowl, proved a most efficient instrument of motion.   Such were its contractile powers, that its sides nearly closed at every stroke, behind the opaque orbicular centre, like the legs of a vigorous swimmer ; and the animal, unlike its more bulky congeners,—that, despite of their slow but persevering flappings, seemed greatly at the mercy of the tide, and progressed all one way,—shot, as it willed, backwards, forwards, or athwart.   As the evening closed, and the depths beneath presented a dingier and yet dingier green, until at length all had become black, the distinctive colours of the acelpha,—the purple, the orange, and the brown,—faded and disappeared, and the creatures hung out, instead, their pale phosphoric lights, like the lanthorns of a fleet hoisted high to prevent collision in the darkness.   Now they gleamed dim and indistinct as they drifted undisturbed through the upper depths, and now they flamed out bright and green, like beaten torches, as the tide dashed them against the vessel's sides.   I bethought me of the gorgeous description of Coleridge, and felt all its beauty :—

> " They moved in tracks of shining white,
> And when they reared, the elfish light
>   Fell off in hoary flakes.
> Within the shadow of the ship
>   I watched their rich attire,—
> Blue, glassy green, and velvet black :
> They curled, and swam, and every track
>   Was a flash of golden fire."

A crew of three, when there are watches to set, divides wofully ill.   As there was, however, nothing to do in the calm, we decided that our first watch should consist of our single seaman, and the second of the minister and his friend. The clouds, which had been thickening for hours, now broke in torrents of rain, and old Alister got into his water-proof oil-skin and souwester, and we into our beds.   The seams of

---

acelpha: presumably misprint for acalephae, jellyfish; **Coleridge**: misquoting 'glassy' for 'glossy' from the version of 'Rime of the Ancient Mariner' in *Lyrical Ballads* by Wordsworth and his colleagues

the Betsey's deck had opened so sadly during the past winter, as to be no longer water-tight, and the little cabin re-
sounded drearily in the darkness, like some dropping cave, to
the ceaseless patter of the leakage.   We continued to sleep,
however, somewhat longer than we ought,—for Alister had
been unwilling to waken the minister ; but we at length got
up, and, relieving watch the first from the tedium of being
rained upon and doing nothing, watch the second was set to
do nothing and be rained upon in turn.   We had drifted
during the night-time on a kindly tide, considerably nearer
our island, which we could now see looming blue and indistinct through the haze some seven or eight miles away.   The
rain ceased a little before nine, and the clouds rose, revealing
the surrounding lands, island and main,—Rum, with its
abrupt mountain-peaks,—the dark Cuchullins of Skye,—and,
far to the south-east, where Inverness bounds on Argyllshire,
some of the tallest hills in Scotland,—among the rest, the
dimly-seen Ben-Nevis.   But long wreaths of pale gray cloud
lay lazily under their summits, like shrouds half drawn from
off the features of the dead, to be again spread over them,
and we concluded that the dry weather had not yet come.
A little before noon we were surrounded for miles by an immense but thinly-spread shoal of porpoises, passing in pairs
to the south, to prosecute, on their own behalf, the herring
fishing in Lochfine or the Gareloch ; and for a full hour the
whole sea, otherwise so silent, became vocal with long-breathed
blowings, as if all the steam-tenders of all the railways in
Britain were careering around us ; and we could see slender
jets of spray rising in the air on every side, and glossy black
backs and pointed fins, that looked as if they had been fashioned out of Kilkenny marble, wheeling heavily along the
surface.   The clouds again began to close as the shoal passed,
but we could now hear in the stillness the measured sound
of oars, drawn vigorously against the gunwale in the direc-

---

dropping cave: dripping cave – no doubt alluding to the occasion when Miller and
Swanson, as boys, were stranded overnight by the tide in such a cave near Cromarty
(Miller 1858, pp. 72-84); **Cuchillins**: Cuillin Hills; **Inverness**: *ie* Inverness-shire

tion of the island of Eigg, still about five miles distant, though the boat from which they rose had not yet come in sight. "Some of my poor people," said the minister, "coming to tug us ashore!" We were boarded in rather more than half an hour after,—for the sounds in the dead calm had preceded the boat by miles,—by four active young men, who seemed wonderfully glad to see their pastor; and then, amid the thickening showers, which had recommenced heavy as during the night, they set themselves to tow us unto the harbour. The poor fellows had a long and fatiguing pull, and were thoroughly drenched ere, about six o'clock in the evening, we had got up to our anchoring ground, and moored, as usual, in the open tide-way between *Eilan Chasteil* and the main island. There was still time enough for an evening discourse, and the minister, getting out of his damp clothes, went ashore and preached.

The evening of Sunday closed in fog and rain, and in fog and rain the morning of Monday arose. The ceaseless patter made dull music on deck and skylight above, and the slower drip, drip, through the leaky beams, drearily beat time within. The roof of my bed was luckily water-tight; and I could look out from my snuggery of blankets on the desolations of the leakage, like Bacon's philosopher surveying a tempest from the shore. But the minister was somewhat less fortunate, and had no little trouble in diverting an ill-conditioned drop that had made a dead set at his pillow. I was now a full week from Edinburgh, and had seen and done nothing; and, were another week to pass after the same manner,—as, for aught that appeared, might well happen,—I might just go home again, as I had come, with my labour for my pains. In the course of the afternoon, however, the weather unexpectedly cleared up, and we set out somewhat impatiently through the wet grass, to visit a cave a few hundred yards to the west of *Naomh Fraing,* in which it had been said the

---

Bacon's philosopher: 'It is a pleasure, to stand upon the shore, and to see ships tossed upon the sea', in 'Of truth', one of Francis Bacon's *Essays*; *Naomh Fraing*: another misspelling of *Uaimh Fhraing*, see note for p. 22

Protestants of the island might meet for the purposes of religious worship, were they to be ejected from the cottage
erected by Mr Swanson, in which they had worshipped hitherto.   We re-examined, in the passing, the pitch-stone dike
mentioned in a former chapter, and the charnel cave of Francis ; but I found nothing to add to my former descriptions,
and little to modify, save that perhaps the cave appeared
less dark, in at least the outer half of its area, than it had
seemed to me in the former year, when examined by torch-
light, and that the straggling twilight, as it fell on the ropy
sides, green with moss and mould, and on the damp bone-
strewn floor, overmantled with a still darker crust, like that
of a stagnant pool, seemed also to wear its tint of melancholy greenness, as if transmitted through a depth of sea-
water.   The cavern we had come to examine we found to be
a noble arched opening in a dingy-coloured precipice of augitic trap,—a cave roomy and lofty as the nave of a cathedral,
and ever resounding to the dash of the sea ; but though it
could have amply accommodated a congregation of at least five
hundred, we found the way far too long and difficult for at
least the weak and the elderly, and in some places inaccessible
at full flood ; and so we at once decided against the accommodation which it offered.   But its shelter will, I trust, scarce
be needed.

On our return to the Betsey, we passed through a straggling
group of cottages on the hill-side, one of which, the most dilapidated and smallest of the number, the minister entered,
to visit a poor old woman, who had been bed-ridden for ten
years.   Scarce ever before had I seen so miserable a hovel.
It was hardly larger than the cabin of the Betsey, and a thousand times less comfortable.   The walls and roof, formed of
damp grass-grown turf, with a few layers of unconnected stone
in the basement tiers, seemed to constitute one continuous
hillock, sloping upwards from foundation to ridge, like one of

---

the cavern we had come to examine: now named the Cathedral Cave; full flood; high
tide

the lesser moraines of Agassiz, save where the fabric here and there bellied outwards or inwards, in perilous dilapidation, that seemed but awaiting the first breeze. The low chinky door opened direct into the one wretched apartment of the hovel, which we found lighted chiefly by holes in the roof. The back of the sick woman's bed was so placed at the edge of the opening, that it had formed at one time a sort of partition to the portion of the apartment, some five or six feet square, which contained the fire-place ; but the boarding that had rendered it such had long since fallen away, and it now presented merely a naked rickety frame to the current of cold air from without. Within a foot of the bed-ridden woman's head there was a hole in the turf-wall, which was, we saw, usually stuffed with a bundle of rags, but which lay open as we entered, and which furnished a downward peep of sea and shore, and the rocky *Eilan Chasteil*, with the minister's yacht riding in the channel hard by. The little hole in the wall had formed the poor creature's only communication with the face of the external world for ten weary years. She lay under a dingy coverlet, which, whatever its original hue, had come to differ nothing in colour from the graveyard earth, which must so soon better supply its place. What perhaps first struck the eye was the strange flatness of the bed-clothes, considering that a human body lay below : there seemed scarce bulk enough under them for a human skeleton. The light of the opening fell on the corpse-like features of the woman, —sallow, sharp, bearing at once the stamp of disease and of famine ; and yet it was evident, notwithstanding, that they had once been agreeable,—not unlike those of her daughter, a good-looking girl of eighteen, who, when we entered, was sitting beside the fire. Neither mother nor daughter had any English ; but it was not difficult to determine, from the welcome with which the minister was greeted from the sick-bed, feeble as the tones were, that he was no unfrequent visitor.

---

sick woman's bed: a box bed, normal for privacy and warmth in single-roomed cottages. It was enclosed on three sides with wooden boarding and curtained in front. The boarding is partly missing on this particular bed

He prayed beside the poor creature, and, on coming away,
slipped something into her hand. I learned that not during
the ten years in which she had been bed-ridden had she received a single farthing from the proprietor, nor, indeed, had
any of the poor of the island, and that the parish had no session-funds. I saw her husband a few days after,—an old
worn-out man, with famine written legibly in his hollow cheek
and eye, and on the shrivelled frame, that seemed lost in his
tattered dress ; and he reiterated the same sad story. They
had no means of living, he said, save through the charity of
their poor neighbours, who had so little to spare ; for the
parish or the proprietor had never given them anything. He
had once, he added, two fine boys, both sailors, who had
helped them ; but the one had perished in a storm off the
Mull of Cantyre, and the other had died of fever when on a
West India voyage ; and though their poor girl was very duti-
ful, and staid in their crazy hut to take care of them in their
helpless old age, what other could she do in a place like Eigg
than just share with them their sufferings ? It has been recently decided by the British Parliament, that in cases of this
kind the starving poor shall not be permitted to enter the
law courts of the country, there to sue for a pittance to support life, until an intermediate newly-erected court, alien to
the Constitution, before which they must plead at their own
expense, shall have first given them permission to prosecute
their claims. And I doubt not that many of the English
gentlemen whose votes swelled the majority, and made it such,
are really humane men, friendly to an equal-handed justice,
and who hold it to be the peculiar glory of the Constitution,
as well shown by De Lolme, that it has not one statute-book
for the poor, and another for the rich, but the same law and
the same administration of law for all. They surely could
not have seen that the principle of their Poor Law Act for
Scotland sets the pauper beyond the pale of the Constitution

session-funds and Poor Law Act: see introduction; De Lolme: Jean-Louis De Lolme
(1741-1806), Swiss Calvinist Protestant lawyer, who published in 1768 *The Constitution of
England, or An Account of the English Government*, praising the British style of liberal
government through a balance of power, as the only one likely to guarantee true freedom

in the first instance, that he may be starved in the second. The suffering paupers of this miserable island cottage would have all their wants fully satisfied in the grave, long ere they could establish at their own expense, at Edinburgh, their claim to enter a court of law.   I know not a fitter case for the interposition of our lately formed "Scottish Association for the Protection of the Poor" than that of this miserable family; and it is but one of many which the island of Eigg will be found to furnish.

After a week's weary waiting, settled weather came at last; and the morning of Tuesday rose bright and fair.   My friend, whose absence at the General Assembly had accumulated a considerable amount of ministerial labour on his hands, had to employ the day professionally; and as John Stewart was still engaged with his potato crop, I was necessitated to sally out on my first geological excursion alone.   In passing vessel-wards, on the previous year, from the *Ru Stoir* to the farm-house of Keill, along the escarpment under the cliffs, I had examined the shores somewhat too cursorily during the one-half of my journey, and the closing evening had prevented me from exploring them during the other half at all; and I now set myself leisurely to retrace the way backwards from the farm-house to the *Stoir*.   I descended to the bottom of the cliffs, along the pathway which runs between Keill and the solitary midway shieling formerly described, and found that the basaltic columns over head, which had seemed so pictu-resque in the twilight, lost none of their beauty when viewed by day.   They occur in forms the most beautiful and fantastic; here grouped beside some blind opening in the precipice, like pillars cut round the opening of a tomb, on some rock-front in Petræa; there running in long colonnades, or rising into tall porticoes; yonder radiating in straight lines from some common centre, resembling huge pieces of fan-work, or bend-ing out in bold curves over some shaded chasm, like rows of

crooked oaks projecting from the steep sides of some dark ravine. The various beds of which the cliffs are composed, as
courses of ashlar compose a wall, are of very different degrees
of solidity : some are of hard porphyritic or basaltic trap ;
some of soft Oolitic sandstone or shale. Where the columns
rest on a soft stratum, their foundations have in many places
given way, and whole porticoes and colonnades hang perilously
forward in tottering ruin, separated from the living rock behind by deep chasms. I saw one of these chasms, some five
or six feet in width, and many yards in length, that descended
to a depth which the eye could not penetrate ; and another
partially filled up with earth and stones, through which, along
a dark opening not much larger than a chimney-vent, the
boys of the island find a long descending passage to the foot
of the precipice, and emerge into light on the edge of the
grassy talus half-way down the hill. It reminded me of the
tunnel in the rock through which Imlac opened up a way of
escape to Rasselas from the happy valley,—the "subterranean
passage," begun "where the summit hung over the middle
part," and that "issued out behind the prominence."

From the commencement of the range of cliffs, on half-way
to the shieling, I found the shore so thickly covered up by
masses of trap, the debris of the precipices above, that I could
scarce determine the nature of the bottom on which they rested. I now, however, reached a part of the beach where the
Oolitic beds are laid bare in thin party-coloured strata, and
at once found something to engage me. Organisms in vast
abundance, chiefly shells and fragmentary portions of fishes,
lie closely packed in their folds. One limestone bed, occurring
in a dark shale, seems almost entirely composed of a species
of small oyster ; and some two or three other thin beds, of
what appears to be either a species of small Mytilus or Avicula, mixed up with a few shells resembling large Paludina,
and a few more of the gaper family, so closely resembling ex-

---

Imlac: the wise philosopher and **Rasselas's** guide in Samuel Johnson's novel of 1759,
The History of Rasselas, Prince of Abissinia

isting species, that John Stewart and Alister at once chal-
lenged them as *smurslin*, the Hebridean name for a well-
known shell in these parts,—the *Mya truncata.* The remains
of fishes,—chiefly Ganoid scales and the teeth of Placoids,—
lie scattered among the shells in amazing abundance.   On
the surface of a single fragment, about nine inches by five,
which I detached from one of the beds, and which now lies
before me, I reckon no fewer than twenty-five teeth, and
twenty-two on the area of another.   They are of very various
forms,—some of them squat and round, like ill-formed small
shot,—others spiky and sharp, not unlike flooring nails,—some
straight as needles, some bent like the beak of a hawk,—
some, like the palatal teeth of the Acrodus of the Lias, resemble small leeches ; some, bearing a series of points ranged
on a common base, like masts on the hull of a vessel, the
tallest in the centre, belong to the genus Hybodus.   There
is a palpable approximation in the teeth of the leech-like form
to the teeth with the numerous points.   Some of the specimens show the same plicated structure common to both; and
on some of the leech backs, if I may so speak, there are
protuberant knobs, that indicate the places of the spiky points
on the hybodent teeth.   I have got three of each kind slit
up by Mr George Sanderson, and the internal structure appears to be the same.   A dense body of bone is traversed by
what seem innumerable roots, resembling those of woody
shrubs laid bare along the sides of some forest stream.   Each
internal opening sends off on every side its myriads of close-
laid filaments; and nowhere do they lie so thickly as in the line
of the enamel, forming, from the regularity with which they
are arranged, a sort of framing to the whole section.   It is
probable that the Hybodus,—a genus of shark which became
extinct some time about the beginning of the chalk,—united,
like the shark of Port Jackson, a crushing apparatus of palatal
teeth to its lines of cutting ones.   Among the other remains

---

Placoids: here, probably sharks and their kin; the shark of Port Jackson: a living
Australasian species, the Port Jackson Shark *Heterodontus portusjacksoni*

of these beds I found a dense fragment of bone, apparently reptilian, and a curious dermal plate punctulated with thick-set depressions, bounded on one side by a smooth band, and altogether closely resembling some saddler's thimble that had been cut open and straightened.

Following the beds downwards along the beach, I found that one of the lowest which the tide permitted me to examine,—a bed coloured with a tinge of red,—was formed of a denser limestone than any of the others, and composed chiefly of vast numbers of small univalves resembling Neritæ. It was in exactly such a rock I had found, in the previous year, the reptile remains; and I now set myself with no little eagerness to examine it. One of the first pieces I tore up contained a well-preserved Plesiosaurian vertebra; a second contained a vertebra and a rib; and, shortly after, I disinterred a large portion of a pelvis. I had at length found, beyond doubt, the reptile remains *in situ.* The bed in which they occur is laid bare here for several hundred feet along the beach, jutting out at a low angle among boulders and gravel, and the reptile remains we find embedded chiefly in its under side. It lies low in the Oolite. All the stratified rocks of the island, with the exception of a small Liasic patch, belong to the Lower Oolite, and the reptile-bed occurs deep in the base of the system,—low in its relation to the nether division, in which it is included. I found it nowhere rising to the level of high-water mark. It forms one of the foundation tiers of the island, which, as the latter rises over the sea in some places to the height of about fourteen hundred feet, its upper peaks and ridges must overlie the bones, making allowance for the dip, to the depth of at least sixteen hundred. Even at the close of the Oolitic period this sepulchral stratum must have been a profoundly ancient one. In working it out, I found two fine specimens of fish jaws, still retaining their ranges of teeth,—ichthyodorulites,—occipital plates of

---

curious dermal plate: almost certainly a crocodilian dermal scute (body armour plate)

various forms, either reptile or ichthyic,—Ganoid scales, of
nearly the same varieties of pattern as those in the Weald
of Morayshire,—and the vertebræ and ribs, with the digital,
pelvic, and limb-bones, of saurians.   It is not unworthy of
remark, that in none of the beds of this deposit did I find
any of the more characteristic shells of the system,—Ammonites, Belemnites, Gryphites, or Nautili.

I explored the shores of the island on to the *Ru Stoir*, and
thence to the Bay of Laig; but though I found detached
masses of the reptile bed occurring in abundance, indicating
that its place lay not far beyond the fall of ebb, in no other
locality save the one described did I find it laid bare.   I
spent some time beside the Bay of Laig in re-examining the
musical sand, in the hope of determining the peculiarities on
which its sonorous qualities depended.   But I examined and
cross-examined it in vain.   I merely succeeded in ascertaining, in addition to my previous observations, that the loudest
sounds are elicited by drawing the hand slowly through the
incoherent mass, in a segment of a circle, at the full stretch
of the arm, and that the vibrations which produce them communicate a peculiar titillating sensation to the hand or foot
by which they are elicited, extending in the foot to the knee,
and in the hand to the elbow.   When we pass the wet finger
along the edge of an ale-glass partially filled with water, we
see the vibrations thickly wrinkling the surface : the undulations which, communicated to the air, produce sound, render themselves, when communicated to the water, visible to
the eye ; and the titillating feeling seems but a modification
of the same phenomenon acting on the nerves and fluids of
the leg or arm.   It appears to be produced by the wrinklings
of the vibrations, if I may so speak, passing along sentient
channels.   The sounds will ultimately be found dependent, I
am of opinion, though I cannot yet explain the principle, on
the purely quartzose character of the sand, and the friction

---

musical sand: see Additional Note for p. 63

of the incoherent upper strata against under strata coherent and damp. I remained ten days in the island, and went over all my former ground, but succeeded in making no further discoveries.

On the morning of Wednesday, June 25th, we set sail for Isle Ornsay, with a smart breeze from the north-west. The lower and upper sky was tolerably clear, and the sun looked cheerily down on the deep blue of the sea ; but along the higher ridges of the land there lay long level strata of what the meteorologists distinguish as parasitic clouds. When every other patch of vapour in the landscape was in motion, scudding shorewards from the Atlantic before the still-increasing gale, there rested along both the Scuir of Eigg and the tall opposite ridge of the island, and along the steep peaks of Rum, clouds that seemed as if anchored, each on its own mountain-summit, and over which the gale failed to exert any propelling power. They were stationary in the middle of the rushing current, when all else was speeding before it. It has been shown that these parasitic clouds are mere local condensations of strata of damp air passing along the mountain-summits, and rendered visible but to the extent in which the summits affect the temperature. Instead of being stationary, they are ever-forming and ever-dissipating clouds,—clouds that form a few yards in advance of the condensing hill, and that dissipate a few yards after they have quitted it. I had nothing to do on deck, for we had been joined at Eigg by John Stewart ; and so, after watching the appearance of the stationary clouds for some little time, I went below, and, throwing myself into the minister's large chair, took up a book. The gale meanwhile freshened, and freshened yet more ; and the Betsey leaned over till her lee chain-plate lay along in the water. There was the usual combination of sounds beneath and around me,—the mixture of guggle, clunk, and splash,—of low, continuous rush, and bluff, loud blow,

which forms in such circumstances the voyager's concert.   I
soon became aware, however, of yet another species of sound,
which I did not like half so well,—a sound as of the washing
of a shallow current over a rough surface; and, on the minister coming below, I asked him, tolerably well prepared for
his answer, what it might mean.   "It means," he said, "that
we have sprung a leak, and a rather bad one; but we are
only some six or eight miles from the Point of Sleat, and
must soon catch the land."   He returned on deck, and I re-
sumed my book.   Presently, however, the rush became greatly
louder; some other weak patch in the Betsey's upper works
had given way, and anon the water came washing up from
the lee side along the edge of the cabin floor.   I got upon
deck to see how matters stood with us; and the minister,
easing off the vessel for a few points, gave instant orders to
shorten sail, in the hope of getting her upper works out of
the water, and then to unship the companion ladder, beneath
which a hatch communicated with the low strip of hold under
the cabin, and to bring aft the pails.   We lowered our fore-
sail; furled up the mainsail half-mast high; John Stewart
took his station at the pump; old Alister and I, furnished
with pails, took ours, the one at the foot, the other at the
head, of the companion, to hand up and throw over; a young
girl, a passenger from Eigg to the mainland, lent her assistance, and got wofully drenched in the work; while the minister, retaining his station at the helm, steered right on.   But
the gale had so increased, that, notwithstanding our diminished breadth of sail, the Betsey, straining hard in the rough
sea, still lay in to the gunwale; and the water, pouring in
through a hundred opening chinks in her upper works, rose,
despite of our exertions, high over plank, and beam, and cabin-
floor, and went dashing against beds and lockers.   She was
evidently filling, and bade fair to terminate all her voyagings
by a short trip to the bottom.   Old Alister, a seaman of

easing off the vessel for a few points: steering less close to the wind, a point of the
compass being 11.25 degrees or one thirty-second of the entire 360 degree circumference

thirty years' standing, whose station at the bottom of the cabin stairs enabled him to see how fast the water was gaining on the Betsey, but not how the Betsey was gaining on the land, was by no means the least anxious among us. Twenty years previous he had seen a vessel go down in exactly similar circumstances, and in nearly the same place ; and the reminiscence, in the circumstances, seemed rather an uncomfortable one.   It had been a bad evening, he said, and the vessel he sailed in, and a sloop, her companion, were pressing hard to gain the land.   The sloop had sprung a leak, and was straining, as if for life and death, under a press of canvass.   He saw her outsail the vessel to which he belonged, but, when a few bow-shots a-head, she gave a sudden lurch, and disappeared from the surface instantaneously, as a vanishing spectre, and neither sloop nor crew were ever more heard of.

There are, I am convinced, few deaths less painful than some of those untimely and violent ones at which we are most disposed to shudder.   We wrought so hard at pail and pump, —the occasion, too, was one of so much excitement, and tended so thoroughly to awaken our energies,—that I was conscious, during the whole time, of an exhilaration of spirits rather pleasurable than otherwise.   My fancy was active, and active, strange as the fact may seem, chiefly with ludicrous objects. Sailors tell regarding the flying Dutchman, that he was a hard-headed captain of Amsterdam, who, in a bad night and head wind, when all the other vessels of his fleet were falling back on the port they had recently quitted, obstinately swore that, rather than follow their example, he would keep beating about till the day of judgment.   And the Dutch captain, says the story, was just taken at his word, and is beating about still.   When matters were at the worst with us, we got under the lee of the point of Sleat.   The promontory interposed between us and the roll of the sea ; the wind gradually took off; and after having seen the water gaining fast and steadily on us for considerably more than an hour, we, in turn, began to gain on the water. It came ebbing out of drawers and beds, and sunk downwards along pannels and table-legs,—a second retiring deluge; and we entered Isle Ornsay with the cabin-floor all visible, and less than two feet water in the hold. On the following morning, taking leave of my friend the minister, I set off, on my return homewards, by the Skye steamer, and reached Edinburgh on the evening of Saturday.

END OF THE CRUISE OF THE BETSEY.

---

second retiring deluge: no doubt ironical – the first being Noah's Flood

RAMBLES OF A GEOLOGIST;

OR

TEN THOUSAND MILES OVER THE FOSSILIFEROUS DEPOSITS OF SCOTLAND.

RAMBLES OF A GEOLOGIST;

OR,

TEN THOUSAND MILES OVER THE FOSSILIFEROUS DEPOSITS OF SCOTLAND.*

CHAPTER I.

FROM circumstances that in no way call for explanation, my usual exploratory ramble was thrown this year (1847) from the middle of July into the middle of September; and I embarked at Granton for the north just as the night began to count hour against hour with the day. The weather was fine, and the voyage pleasant. I saw by the way, however, at least one melancholy memorial of a hurricane which had swept the eastern coasts of the island about a fortnight before, and filled the provincial newspapers with paragraphs of disaster. Nearly opposite where the Red Head lifts its mural front of Old Red Sandstone a hundred yards over the beach, the steamer passed a foundered vessel, lying about a mile and a half off the land, with but her topmast and the point of her peak over the surface. Her vane, still at the mast-head, was drooping in the

* This second title bears reference to the extent of the author's geologic excursions in Scotland during the nine years from 1840 to 1848 inclusive.

---

circumstances: probably illness in the Miller family (Hugh Miller, letter dated July 1847 to his mother Harriet, National Library of Scotland MS 7516 f.62). Perhaps also the death of Thomas Chalmers, the Evangelical leader, during the Free Church's General Assembly, and his burial on 4 June. Miller, being editor of the Free Church newspaper, would certainly have postponed his holiday till things were settled calm ; and its shadow, with that of the fresh-coloured *spar* to which it was attached, white atop and yellow beneath, formed a well-defined undulatory strip on the water, that seemed as if ever in the process of being rolled up, and yet still retained its length unshortened.   Every recession of the swell showed a patch of mainsail attached to the peak : the sail had been hoisted to its full stretch when the vessel went down.   And thus, though no one survived to tell the story of her disaster, enough remained to show that she had sprung a leak when straining in the gale, and that, when staggering under a press of canvass towards the still distant shore, where, by stranding her, the crew had hoped to save at least their lives, she had disappeared with a sudden lurch, and all aboard had perished.   I remembered having read, among other me-morabilia of the hurricane, without greatly thinking of the matter, that "a large sloop had foundered off the Red Head, —name unknown."   But the minute portion of the wreck which I saw rising over the surface, to certify, like some frail memorial in a churchyard, that the dead lay beneath, had an eloquence in it which the words wanted, and at once sent the imagination back to deal with the stern realities of the disas-ter, and the feelings abroad to expatiate over saddened hearths and melancholy homesteads, where for many a long day the hapless perished would be missed and mourned, but where the true story of their fate, though too surely guessed at, would never be known.

The harvest had been early ; and on to the village of Stone-haven, and a mile or two beyond, where the fossiliferous de-posits end and the primary begin, the country presented from the deck only a wide expanse of stubble.   Every farm-stead-ing we passed had its piled stack-yard ; and the fields were bare.   But the line of demarcation between the Old Red Sand-stone and the granitic districts formed also a separating line between an earlier and later harvest ; the fields of the less

---

melancholy homesteads: including, of course, Miller's own childhood home kindly subsoil derived from the primary rocks were, I could see, still speckled with sheaves ; and, where the land lay high, or the exposure was unfavourable, there were reapers at work. All along in the course of my journey northward from Aberdeen I continued to find the country covered with shocks, and labourers employed among them ; until, crossing the Spey I entered on the fossiliferous districts of Moray ; and then, as in the south, the champaign again showed a bare breadth of stubble, with here and there a ploughman engaged in turning it down. The traveller bids farewell at Stonehaven to not only the Old Red Sandstone and the early-harvest districts, but also to the rich wheat-lands of the country, and does not again fairly enter upon them until, after travelling nearly a hundred miles, he passes from Banffshire into the province of Moray. He leaves behind him at the same line the wheat-fields and the cottages built of red stone, to find only barley and oats, and here and there a plot of rye, associated with cottages of granite and gneiss, hyperstene and mica schist ; but on crossing the Spey, the red cottages re-appear, and fields of rich wheat-land spread out around them, as in the south. The circumstance is not unworthy the notice of the geologist. It is but a tedious process through which the minute lichen, settling on a surface of naked stone, forms in the course of ages a soil for plants of greater bulk and a higher order ; and had Scotland been left to the exclusive operation of this slow agent, it would be still a rocky desert, with perhaps here and there a strip of alluvial meadow by the side of a stream, and here and there an insulated patch of rich soil among the hollows of the crags. It might possess a few gardens for the spade, but no fields for the plough. We owe our arable land to that comparatively modern geologic agent, whatever its character, that crushed, as in a mill, the upper parts of the surface-rocks of the kingdom, and then overlaid them with their own debris and rubbish to the depth of from

shocks: of corn; comparatively modern geologic agent: now considered to be the glaciers and other erosive phenomena of the Ice Ages – see Introduction one to forty yards. This debris, existing in one locality as a boulder-clay more or less finely comminuted, in another as a grossly pounded gravel, forms, with few exceptions, that subsoil of the country on which the existing vegetation first found root; and, being composed mainly of the formations on which it more immediately rests, it partakes of their character,—bearing a comparatively lean and hungry aspect over the primary rocks, and a greatly more fertile one over those deposits in which the organic matters of earlier creations lie diffused. Saxon industry has done much for the primary districts of Aberdeen and Banff-shires, though it has failed to neutralize altogether the effects of causes which date as early as the times of the Old Red Sandstone; but in the Highlands, which belong almost exclusively to the non-fossiliferous formations, and which were, on at least the western coasts, but imperfectly subjected to that grinding process to which we owe our subsoils, the poor Celt has permitted the consequences of the original difference to exhibit themselves in full. If we except the islands of the Inner Hebrides, the famine of 1846 was restricted in Scotland to the primary districts.

I made it my first business, on landing in Aberdeen, to wait on my friend Mr Longmuir, that I might compare with him a few geological notes, and benefit by his knowledge of the surrounding country. I was, however, unlucky enough to find that he had gone, a few days before, on a journey, from which he had not yet returned; but, through the kindness of Mrs Longmuir, to whom I took the liberty of introducing myself, I was made free of his stone-room, and held half an hour's conversation with his Scotch fossils of the Chalk. These had been found, as the readers of the *Witness* must remember from his interesting paper on the subject, on the hill of Dudwick, in the neighbourhood of Ellon, and were chiefly impressions—some of them of singular distinctness and beauty—in yellow flint. I saw among them several speci-

---

Saxon: *ie* Lowlander; **Mr Longmuir**: Rev. John Longmuir (1803-1883), from 1840 minister of the *quoad sacra* Mariner's Chapel at Aberdeen, and from 1843 of the Mariner's Free Church; for some years lecturer in geology at King's College, Aberdeen (Scott 1915-1926, VI, pp. 12-13); **Chalk**: later eroded out and redeposited, as Miller explained (in Pliocene times, it is now considered: Merritt, Connell and Bridgland 2000) mens of the Inoceramus, a thin-shelled, ponderously-hinged conchifer, characteristic of the Cretaceous group, but which has no living representative ; with numerous flints, traversed by rough-edged, bifurcated hollows, in which branched sponges had once lain ; a well-preserved Pecten ; the impressions of spines of Echini of at least two distinct species ; and the nicely-marked impression of part of a Cidaris, with the balls on which the sockets of the club-like spines had been fitted existing in the print as spherical moulds, in which shot might be cast, and with the central ligamentary depression, which in the actual fossil exists but as a minute cavity, projecting into the centre of each hollow sphere, like the wooden fusee into the centre of a bomb-shell. This latter cast, fine and sharp as that of a medal taken in sulphur, seems sufficient of itself to establish two distinct points : in the first place, that the sili-ceous matter of which the flint is composed, though now so hard and rigid, must, in its original condition, have been as impressible as wax softened to receive the stamp of the seal; and, in the next, that though it was thus yielding in its cha-racter, it could not have greatly shrunk in the process of hard-ening. I looked with no little interest on these remains of a Scotch formation now so entirely broken up, that, like those ruined cities of the East which exist but as mere lines of wrought material barring the face of the desert, there has not " been left one stone of it upon another ;" but of which the fragments, though widely scattered, bear imprinted upon them, like the stamped bricks of Babylon, the story of its original condition, and a record of its *founders*. All Mr Longmuir's Cretaceous fossils from the hill of Dudwick are of flint,—a substance not easily ground down by the denud-ing agencies.

I found several other curious fossils in Mr Longmuir's col-lection. Greatly more interesting, however, than any of the specimens which it contains, is the general fact, that it should

---

fusee: fuze (military), here a conical plug of wood with a gunpowder-filled hole through its length, used to detonate (with a delay after ignition) a **bombshell**, a powder-filled hollow iron sphere then used as an explosive projectile in cannon and mortars; **sulphur**: when molten, sulphur was then used to take an impression of a medal, like modern plastic or rubber moulding materials

be the collection of a Free Church minister, sedulously attentive to the proper duties of his office, but who has yet
found time enough to render himself an accomplished geologist; and whose week-day lectures on the science attract
crowds, who receive from them, in many instances, their first
knowledge of the strange revolutions of which our globe has
been the subject, blent with the teachings of a wholesome
theology.   The present age, above all that has gone before,
is peculiarly the age of physical science; and of all the physical sciences, not excepting astronomy itself, geology, though
it be a fact worthy of notice, that not one of our truly accomplished geologists is an infidel, is the science of which
infidelity has most largely availed itself.   And as the theologian in a metaphysical age,—when scepticism, conforming to
the character of the time, disseminated its doctrines in the
form of nicely abstract speculations,—had, in order that the
enemy might be met in his own field, to become a skilful metaphysician, he must now, in like manner, address himself to
the tangibilities of natural history and geology, if he would
avoid the danger and disgrace of having his flank turned by
every sciolist in these walks whom he may chance to encounter.   It is those identical bastions and outworks that are *now*
attacked, which must be *now* defended; not those which were
attacked some eighty or a hundred years ago.   And as he
who succeeds in first mixing up fresh and curious truths, either
with the objections by which religion is assailed or the arguments by which it is defended, imparts to his cause all the
interest which naturally attaches to these truths, and leaves
to his opponent, who passes over them after him as at second
hand, a subject divested of the fire-edge of novelty, I can deem
Mr Longmuir well and not unprofessionally employed, in connecting with a sound creed the picturesque marvels of one of
the most popular of the sciences, and by this means introducing them to his people, linked, from the first, with right

associations. According to the old fiction, the look of the basilisk did not kill unless the creature saw before it was seen; —its mere *return* glance was harmless : and there is a class of thoroughly dangerous writers who in this respect resemble the basilisk. It is perilous to give them a first look of the public. They are formidable simply as the earliest popularizers of some interesting science, or the first promulgators of some class of curious little-known facts, with which they mix up their special contributions of error,—often the only portion of their writings that really belongs to themselves. Nor is it at all so easy to *counteract* as to *confute* them. A masterly confutation of the part of their works truly their own may, from its subject, be a very unreadable book : it can have but the insinuated poison to deal with, unmixed with the palatable pabulum in which the poison has been conveyed ; and mere treatises on poisons, whether moral or medical, are rarely works of a very delectable order. It seems to be on this principle that there exists no confutation of the " Constitution of Man" in which the ordinary reader finds amusement enough to carry him through ; whereas the work itself, full of curious miscellaneous information, is eminently readable; and that the "Vestiges of Creation,"—a treatise as entertaining as the "Arabian Nights,"—bids fair, not from the amount of error which it contains, but from the amount of fresh and interestingly-told truth with which the error is mingled, to live and do mischief when the various solidly-scientific replies which it has called forth are laid upon the shelf. Both the "Constitution" and the "Vestiges" had the advantage, so essential to the basilisk, of taking the first glance of the public on their respective subjects; whereas their confutators have been able to render them back but mere *return* glances. The only efficiently counteractive mode of looking down the danger, in cases of this kind, is the mode adopted by Mr Longmuir.

'**Constitution of Man**': see Additional Notes; '**Vestiges of Creation**': *ie Vestiges of the Natural History of Creation*, then anonymous – see Introduction

There was a smart frost next morning; and, for the first
few hours, my seat on the top of the Banff coach, by which
I travelled across the country to where the Gamrie and Banff
roads part company, was considerably more cool than agreeable. But the keen morning improved into a brilliant day,
with an atmosphere transparent as if there had been no atmosphere at all, through which the distant objects looked out
as sharp of outline, and in as well-defined light and shadow,
as if they had occupied the background, not of a Scotch, but
of an Italian landscape. A few speck-like sails, far away on
the intensely blue sea, which opened upon us in a stretch of
many leagues, as we surmounted the moory ridge over Macduff, gleamed to the sun with a radiance bright as that of
the sparks of a furnace blown to a white heat. The land,
uneven of surface, and open, and abutting in bold promontories on the frith, still bore the sunny hue of harvest, and
seemed as if stippled over with shocks from the ridgy hill
summits, to where ranges of giddy cliffs flung their shadows
across the beach. I struck off for Gamrie by a path that
runs eastward, nearly parallel to the shore,—which at one
or two points it overlooks from dark-coloured cliffs of grauwacke slate,—to the fishing village of Gardenstone. My
dress was the usual fatigue suit of russet, in which I find I
can work amid the soil of ravines and quarries with not only
the best effect, but with even the least possible sacrifice of
appearance : the shabbiest of all suits is a good suit spoiled.
My hammer-shaft projected from my pocket; a knapsack,
with a few changes of linen, slung suspended from my shoulders ; a strong cotton umbrella occupied my better hand ;
and a gray maud, buckled shepherd-fashion aslant the chest,
completed my equipment. There were few travellers on the
road, which forked off on the hill-side a short mile away, into
two branches, like a huge letter Y, leaving me uncertain
which branch to choose ; and I made up my mind to have

---

fatigue suit of russet, *etc*: see Introduction

the point settled by a woman of middle age, marked by a
hard, *manly* countenance, who was coming up towards me,
bound apparently for the Banff or Macduff market, and stooping under a load of dairy produce.   She too, apparently, had
her purpose to serve or point to settle; for as we met, she
was the first to stand; and, sharply scanning my appearance
and aspect at a glance, she abruptly addressed me.   " Honest
man," she said, " do you see yon house wi' the chimla ?'
" That house with the farm-steadings and stacks beside it ?'
I replied.   " Yes."   " Then I'd be obleeged if ye wald just
stap in as ye'r gaing east the gate, and tell *our* folk that the
stirk has gat fra her tether, an' 'ill brak on the wat clover.
Tell them to sen' for her *that* minute."   I undertook the
commission; and, passing the endangered stirk, that seemed
luxuriating, undisturbed by any presentiment of impending
peril, amid the rich swathe of a late clover crop, still damp
with the dews of the morning frost, I tapped at the door of
the farm-house, and delivered my message to a young good-
looking girl, in nearly the words of the woman :—" The gudewife bade me tell *them*," I said, " to send that instant for the
stirk, for she had gat fra her tether, and would brak on the
wat clover."   The girl blushed just a very little, and thanked
me; and then, after obliging me, in turn, by laying down
for me my proper route,—for I had left the question of the
forked road to be determined at the farm-house,—she set off
at high speed, to rescue the uuconscious stirk.   A walk of
rather less than two hours brought me abreast of the Bay of
Gamrie,—a picturesque indentation of the coast, in the formation of which the agency of the old denuding forces, ope-
rating on deposits of unequal solidity, may be distinctly traced.
The surrounding country is composed chiefly of Silurian
schists, in which there is deeply inlaid a detached strip of mouldering Old Red Sandstone, considerably more than twenty
miles in length, and that varies from two to three miles in

---

chimla: chimney; 'wald just ...': 'would just step in as you are going east along the road,
and tell our folk that the young cow has got [loose] from her tether, and will burst from
[eating] the wet clover' (Northeastern Scots)

breadth.   It seems to have been let down into the more
ancient formation,—like the keystone of a bridge into the
ringstones of the arch when the work is in the act of being
completed,—during some of those terrible convulsions which
cracked and rent the earth's crust, as if it had been an earthen
pipkin brought to a red heat and then plunged into cold
water.   Its consequent occurrence in a lower tier of the geological edifice than that to which it originally belonged has
saved it from the great denudation which has swept from the
surface of the surrounding country the tier composed of its
contemporary beds and strata, and laid bare the grauwacke
on which this upper tier rested.   But where it presents its
narrow end to the sea, as the older houses in our more ancient Scottish villages present their gables to the street, the
waves of the German Ocean, by incessantly charging against
it, propelled by the tempests of the stormy north, have hollowed it into the Bay of Gamrie, and left the more solid grauwacke standing out in bold promontories on either side, as
the headlands of Gamrie and Troup.

In passing downwards on the fishing village of Gardenstone, mainly in the hope of procuring a guide to the ichthyolite beds, I saw a labourer at work with a pick-axe, in a little
craggy ravine, about a hundred yards to the left of the path,
and two gentlemen standing beside him.   I paused for a
moment, to ascertain whether the latter were not brother-
workers in the geologic field.   "Hilloa!—here,"—shouted
out the stouter of the two gentlemen, as if, by some *clair-
voyant* faculty, he had dived into my secret thought; "come
here."   I went down into the ravine, and found the labourer
engaged in disinterring ichthyolitic nodules out of a bed of
gray stratified clay, identical in its composition with that of
the Cromarty fish-beds; and a heap of freshly-broken nodules,
speckled with the organic remains of the Lower Old Red
Sandstone,—chiefly occipital plates and scales,—lay beside

him.   "Know you aught of these ? said the stouter gentleman, pointing to the heap.   "A little," I replied ; "but
your specimens are none of the finest.   Here, however, is a
dorsal plate of Coccosteus ; and here a scattered group of
scales of Osteolepis ; and here the occipital plates of *Cheirolepis Cummingiæ ;* and here the spine of the anterior dorsal
of *Diplacanthus Striatus.*"   My reading of the fossils was at
once recognised, like the mystic sign of the freemason, as
establishing for me a place among the geologic brotherhood ;
and the stout gentleman producing a spirit-flask and a glass,
I pledged him and his companion in a bumper.   "Was I
not sure ?" he said, addressing his friend : "I knew by the
cut of his jib, notwithstanding his shepherd's plaid, that he
was a wanderer of the scientific cast."   We discussed the
peculiarities of the deposit, which, in its mineralogical character, and generically in that of its organic contents, resembles, I found, the fish-beds of Cromarty (though, curiously
enough, the intervening contemporary deposits of Moray and
the western parts of Banffshire differ widely, in at least their
chemistry, from both) ; and we were right good friends ere
we parted.   To men who travel for amusement, incident is
incident, however trivial in itself, and always worth something.   I showed the younger of the two geologists my mode
of breaking open an ichthyolitic nodule, so as to secure the
best possible section of the fish.   "Ah," he said, as he marked
a style of handling the hammer which, save for the fifteen
years' previous practice of the operative mason, would be
perhaps less complete,—"Ah, you must have broken open
a great many."   His own knowledge of the formation and
its ichthyolites had been chiefly derived, he added, from a certain little treatise on the "Old Red Sandstone," rather popular than scientific, which he named.   I of course claimed no
acquaintance with the work ; and the conversation went on.
    The ill luck of my new friends, who had been toiling among

the nodules for hours without finding an ichthyolite worth transferring to their bag, showed me that, without excavating more deeply than my time allowed, I had no chance of finding good specimens.   But, well content to have ascertained that the ichthyolite bed of Gamrie is identical in its composition, and, generically at least, in its organisms, with the beds with which I was best acquainted, I rose to come away.   The object which I next proposed to myself was, to determine whether, as at Eathie and Cromarty, the fossils here appear not only on the hill-side, but also crop out along the shore.   On taking leave, however, of the geologists, I was reminded by the younger of what I might have otherwise forgotten,—a raised beach in the immediate neighbourhood (first described by Mr Prestwich, in his paper on the Gamrie ichthyolites), which contains shells of the existing species at a higher level than elsewhere,—so far as is yet known,—on the east coast of Scotland.   And, kindly conducting me till he had brought me full within view of it, we parted.   The ichthyolites which I had just been laying open occur on the verge of that Strathbogie district in which the Church controversy raged so hot and high ; and by a common enough trick of the associative faculty, they now recalled to my mind a stanza which memory had somehow caught when the battle was at the fiercest.   It formed part of a satiric address, published in an Aberdeen newspaper, to the not very respectable non-intrusionists who had smoked tobacco and drank whisky in the parish church at Culsalmond, on the day of a certain forced settlement there, specially recorded by the clerks of the Justiciary Court.

> " Tobacco and whisky cost siller,
>   And meal is but scanty at hame ;
> But gang to the stane-mason M——r,
>   Wi' Old Red Sandstone fish he'll fill your wame."

Rather a dislocated line that last, I thought, and too much

Mr Prestwich … paper: Prestwich (1840), Andrews (1982, pp. 11, 57); **Strathbogie**: a district inland of Portsoy. The 'intrusion' of a minister at Marnoch in 1837, and the dispute's escalation, had played a major role in the run up to the Disruption. At Culsalmond in 1841, a patronage dispute led to the lock-out of the new minister. Miller ironically recalled allegations about the behaviour of some demonstrators in the style in which Zachary Boyd sings " Pharaoh and the Pascal." And as it is wrong to leave the beast of even an enemy in the ditch, however long its ears, I must just try and set it on its legs. Would it not run better thus?

> " Tobacco and whisky cost siller,
> An' meal is but scanty at hame ;
> But gang to the stane-mason M——r,"
> He'll pang wi' ichth'ólites your wame, —
> Wi' *fish !!* as Agassiz has ca'd 'em,
> In Greek, like themsel's, *hard* an' *odd,*
> That were baked in stane pies afore Adam
> Gaed names to the haddocks and cod.

Bad enough as rhyme, I suspect ; but conclusive as evidence to prove that the animal spirits, under the influence of the bracing walk, the fine day, and the agreeable rencounter at the fish-beds,—not forgetting the half-gill bumper,—had mounted very considerably above their ordinary level at the editorial desk.

The raised beach may be found on the slopes of a grass-covered eminence, once the site of an ancient hill-fort, and which still exhibits, along the rim-like edge of the flat area atop, scattered fragments of the vitrified walls. A general covering of turf restricted my examination of the shells to one point, where a landslip on a small scale had laid the deposit bare ; but I at least saw enough to convince me that the debris of the shell-fish used of old as food by the garrison had not been mistaken for the remains of a raised beach, —a mistake which in other localities has occurred, I have reason to believe, oftener than once. The shells, some of them exceedingly minute, and not of edible species, occur in layers in a siliceous stratified sand, overlaid by a bed of bluish-coloured silt. I picked out of the sand two entire specimens of a full-grown Fusus, little more than half an inch in length, —the *Fusus turricola ;* and the greater number of the fragments that lay bleaching at the foot of the broken slope, in

---

Zachary Boyd: (d. 1653), Presbyterian divine, writer, Rector of Glasgow University, and poet of notoriously erratic quality a state of chalky friability, seemed to be fragments of those smaller bivalves, belonging to the genera *Donax*, *Venus*, and *Mactra*, that are so common on flat sandy shores.   But when the sea washed over these shells, they could have been the denizens of at least no *flat* shore.   The descent on which they occur sinks downwards to the existing beach, over which it is elevated at this point two hundred and thirty feet, at an angle with the horizon of from thirty-five to forty degrees. Were the land to be now submerged to where they appear on the hill-side, the bay of Gamrie, as abrupt in its slopes as the upper part of Loch Lomond or the sides of Loch Ness, would possess a depth of forty fathoms water at little more than a hundred yards from the shore.   I may add, that I could trace at this height no marks of such a continuous ter-race around the sides of the bay as the waves would have infallibly excavated in the diluvium, had the sea stood at a level so high, or, according to the more prevalent view, had the land stood at a level so low, for any considerable time ; though the green banks which sweep around the upper part of the inflection, unscarred by the defacing plough, would scarce have failed to retain some mark of where the surges had broken, had the surges been long there.   Whatever may in this special case be the fact, however, I cannot doubt that in the comparatively modern period of the boulder clays, Scotland lay buried under water to a depth at least five times as great as the space between this ancient sea-beach and the existing tide-line.

Scotland lay buried under water: see Introduction

CHAPTER II.

I LINGERED on the hill-side considerably longer than I ought; and then, hurrying downwards to the beach, passed eastwards under a range of abrupt, mouldering precipices of red sandstone, to the village. From the lie of the strata, which, instead of inclining coastwise, dip towards the interior of the country, and present in the descent seawards the outcrop of lower and yet lower deposits of the formation, I found it would be in vain to look for the ichthyolite beds along the shore. They may possibly be found, however, though I lacked time to ascertain the fact, along the sides of a deep ravine, which occurs near an old ecclesiastical edifice of gray stone, perched, nest-like, half-way up the bank, on a green hummock that overlooks the sea. The rocks, laid bare by the tide, belong to the bed of coarse-grained red sandstone, varying from eighty to a hundred and fifty feet in thickness, which lies between the lower fish-bed and the great conglomerate, and which, in not a few of its strata, passes itself into a species of conglomerate, different only from that which it overlies, in being more finely comminuted. The continuity of this bed, like that of the deposit on which it rests, is very remarkable. I have found it occurring at many various points, over an area at least ten thousand square miles in extent, and bearing always the same well-marked character of a more thoroughly ground-down conglomerate than the great conglomerate on which it reposes. The underlying bed is composed of broken fragments of the rocks below, crushed, as if by some imperfect rudimentary process, like that which in a mill merely breaks the grain ; whereas, in the bed above, a portion of the previously-crushed materials seems to have been subjected to some further attritive process, like that through which, in the mill, the broken grain is ground down into meal or flour.

As I passed onwards, I saw, amid a heap of drift-weed stranded high on the beach by the previous tide, a defunct father-lasher, with the two defensive spines which project from its opercles stuck fast into little cubes of cork, that had floated its head above water, as the tyro-swimmer floats himself upon bladders ; and my previous acquaintance with the habits of a fishing village enabled me at once to determine why and how it had perished. Though almost never used as food on the eastern coast of Scotland, it had been inconsiderate enough to take the fisherman's bait, as if it had been worthy of being eaten ; and he had avenged himself for the trouble it had cost him, by mounting it on cork, and sending it off, to wander between wind and water, like the Flying Dutchman, until it died. Was there ever on earth a creature save man that could have played a fellow-mortal a trick at once so ingeniously and gratuitously cruel ? Or what would be the proper inference, were I to find one of the many-thorned ichthyolites of the Lower Old Red Sandstone with the spines of its pectorals similarly fixed on cubes of lignite ?—that there had existed in these early ages not merely *physical death*, but also *moral evil ;* and that the being who perpetrated the evil could not only inflict it simply for the sake of the pleasure he found in it, and without prospect of advantage to himself, but also by so adroitly reversing, fiend-like, the purposes of the benevolent Designer, that the

fishing-village: in this case, Cromarty

weapons given for the defence of a poor harmless creature should be converted into the instruments of its destruction. It was not without meaning that it was forbidden by the law of Moses to seethe a kid in its mother's milk.

A steep bulwark in front, against which the tide lashes twice every twenty-four hours,—an abrupt hill behind,—a few rows of squalid cottages built of red sandstone, much wasted by the keen sea-winds,—a wilderness of dunghills and ruinous pig-sties,—women seated at the doors, employed in baiting lines or mending nets,—groupes of men lounging lazily at some gable-end fronting the sea,—herds of ragged children playing in the lanes,—such are the components of the fishing village of Gardenstone. From the identity of name, I had associated the place with that Lord Gardenstone of the Court of Session who published, late in the last century, a volume of "Miscellanies in Prose and Verse," containing, among other clever things, a series of tart criticisms on English plays, transcribed, it was stated in the preface, from the margins and fly-leaves of the books of a "small library kept open by his Lordship" for the amusement of travellers at the inn of some village in his immediate neighbourhood ; and taking it for granted, somehow, that Gardenstone was the village, I was looking around me for the inn, in the hope that where his Lordship had opened a library I might find a dinner. But failing to discern it, I addressed myself on the subject to an elderly man in a pack-sheet apron, who stood all alone, looking out upon the sea, like Napoleon, in the print, from a projection of the bulwark. He turned round, and showed, by an unmistakeable expression of eye and feature, that he was what the servant girl in "Guy Mannering" characterizes as "very particularly drunk,"—not stupidly, but happily, funnily, conceitedly drunk, and full of all manner of high thoughts of himself. "It'll be an awfu' coorse nicht," he said, "fra the sea." "Very likely," I replied,

---

seethe …: Jewish dietary law, in Bible, Exodus 23:19 and 34:26 and Deuteronomy 14:21. It was ingratitude and perversion of God's gifts to use milk divinely intended for the young goat's sustenance to cook it; **Gardenstone**: Francis Garden (1721–1793), lawyer, judge, mineral collector and *bon viveur* (Livingstone 2003); **Court of Session**: Scots law, supreme civil court; **Guy Mannering**: novel by Scott; **coorse nicht**: coarse night (Scots) reiterating my query in a form that indicated some little confidence of receiving the needed information ; " I daresay you could point me out the public-house here ?"   " Aweel I wat, that I can ; but what's that ?' pointing to the straps of my knapsack ;—" are ye a sodger on the Queen's account, or ye'r ain ?'   " On my own, to be sure ; but have ye a public-house here ?'   " Ay, twa ; ye'll be a traveller ?'   " O yes, great traveller, and very hungry : have I passed the best public-house ?'   " Ay ; and ye'll hae come a gude stap the day ?" A woman came up, with spectacles on nose, and a piece of white seam-work in her hand ; and, cutting short the dialogue by addressing myself to her, she at once directed me to the public-house.   " Hoot, gudewife," I heard the man say, as I turned down the street, " we suld ha'e gotten mair oot o' him.   He's a great traveller yon, an' has a gude Scots tongue in his head."

Travellers, save when, during the herring season, an occasional fish-curer comes the way, rarely bait at the Gardenstone inn ; and in the little low-browed room, with its windows in the thatch, into which, as her best, the landlady ushered me, I certainly found nothing to identify the *locale* with that chosen by the literary lawyer for his open library. But, according to Ferguson, though " learning was scant, provision was good ;" and I dined sumptuously on an immense platter of fried flounders.   There was a little bit of cold pork added to the fare ; but, aware from previous experience of the pisciverous habits of the swine of a fishing village, I did what I knew the defunct pig must have very frequently done before me,—satisfied a keenly-whetted appetite on fish exclusively.   I need hardly remind the reader that Lord Gardenstone's inn was not that of Gardenstone, but that of Laurencekirk,—the thriving village which it was the special ambition of this law-lord of the last century to create ; and which, did it produce only its famed snuff-boxes, with the invisible hinges,

---

sodger: soldier; gude stap: Scots for 'good step', long way; Hoot: Scots exclamation expressing annoyance; Laurencekirk: in Kincardineshire, on the other side of Aberdeenshire from Gardenstown; snuff-boxes: Stiven (note, p. 286) started his artistic career decorating them (Andrews 1982, p. 70) would be rather a more valuable boon to the country than that secured to it by those law-lords of our own days, who at one fell blow disestablished the national religion of Scotland, and broke off the only handle by which their friends the politicians could hope to *manage* the country's old vigorous Presbyterianism. Meanwhile it was becoming apparent that the man with the apron had as shrewdly anticipated the character of the coming night as if he had been soberer. The sun, ere its setting, disappeared in a thick leaden haze, which enveloped the whole heavens; and twilight seemed posting on to night a full hour before its time. I settled a very moderate bill, and set off under the cliffs at a round pace, in the hope of scaling the hill, and gaining the high road atop which leads to Macduff, ere the darkness closed. I had, however, miscalculated my distance; I, besides, lost some little time in the opening of the deep ravine to which I have already referred as that in which possibly the fish-beds may be found cropping out; and I had got but a little beyond the gray ecclesiastical ruin, with its lonely burying-ground, when the tempest broke and the night fell.

One of the last objects which I saw, as I turned to take a farewell look of the bay of Gamrie, was the magnificent promontory of Troup Head, outlined in black on a ground of deep gray, with its two terminal stacks standing apart in the sea. And straightway, through one of those tricks of association so powerful in raising, as if from the dead, buried memories of things of which the mind has been oblivious for years, there started up in recollection the details of an ancient ghost-story, of which I had not thought before for perhaps a quarter of a century. It had been touched, I suppose, in its obscure, unnoted corner, as Ithuriel touched the toad, by the apparition of the insulated stacks of Troup, seen dimly in the thickening twilight over the solitary burying-ground. For it so chances that one of the main incidents of the story bears

---

manage: allusion to eighteenth century use of patronage (in both senses) by politicians such as Henry Dundas to 'manage' Scotland, in this case by using parish ministries as places for their clients and clients' clients; **Ithuriel … toad**: in Milton's 'Paradise Lost', IV, 798–812, the angel Ithuriel finds Satan hiding in Eden in the form of a toad, and touches him with his spear to restore him to his proper likeness: '… up he starts/Discovered and surprised …'

reference to an insulated sea-stack ; and it is connected altogether, though I cannot fix its special locality, with this part
of the coast.   The story had been long in my mother's family,
into which it had been originally brought by a great-grandfather of the writer, who quitted some of the seaport villages
of Banffshire for the northern side of the Moray Frith, about
the year 1718 ; and, when pushing on in the darkness, straining, as I best could, to maintain a sorely-tried umbrella
against the capricious struggles of the tempest, that now ta-
tooed furiously upon its back as if it were a kettle-drum, and
now got underneath its stout ribs, and threatened to send it
up aloft like a balloon, and anon twisted it from side to side,
and strove to turn it inside out like a Kilmarnock nightcap,
—I employed myself in arranging in my mind the details of
the narrative, as they had been communicated to me half an
age before by a female relative.

The opening of the story, though it existed long ere the
times of Sir Walter Scott or the Waverley novels, bears some
resemblance to the opening, in the " Monastery," of the story
of the White Lady of Avenel.   The wife of a Banffshire proprietor of the minor class had been about six months dead,
when one of her husband's ploughmen, returning on horseback from the smithy, in the twilight of an autumn evening,
was accosted, on the banks of a small stream, by a stranger
lady, tall and slim, and wholly attired in green, with her face
wrapped up in the hood of her mantle, who requested to be
taken up behind him on the horse, and carried across.   There
was something in the tones of her voice that seemed to thrill
through his very bones, and to insinuate itself, in the form
of a chill fluid, between his skull and the scalp.   The request,
too, appeared a strange one ; for the rivulet was small and
low, and could present no serious bar to the progress of the
most timid traveller.   But the man, unwilling ungallantly
to offend a lady, turned his horse to the bank, and she sprang

up lightly behind him. She was, however, a personage that could be better seen than felt : she came in contact with the ploughman's back, he said, as if she had been an ill-filled sack of wool ; and when, on reaching the opposite side of the streamlet, she leaped down as lightly as she had mounted, and he turned fearfully round to catch a second glimpse of her, it was in the conviction that she was a creature considerably less earthly in her texture than himself. She had opened, with two pale, thin arms, the enveloping hood, exhibiting a face equally pale and thin, which seemed marked, however, by the roguish, half-humorous expression of one who had just succeeded in playing off a good joke. " My dead mistress ! !" exclaimed the ploughman. " Yes, John, *your mistress*," replied the ghost. " But ride home, my bonny man, for it's growing late : you and I will be better acquainted ere long." John accordingly rode home, and told his story.

Next evening, about the same hour, as two of the laird's servant-maids were engaged in washing in an out-house, there came a slight tap to the door. " Come in," said one of the maids; and the lady entered, dressed, as on the previous night, in green. She swept past them to the inner part of the washing-room ; and, seating herself on a low bench, from which, ere her death, she used occasionally to superintend their employment, she began to question them, as if still in the body, about the progress of their work. The girls, however, were greatly too frightened to make any reply. She then visited an old woman who had nursed the laird, and to whom she used to show, ere her departure, greatly more kindness than her husband. And she now seemed as much interested in her welfare as ever. She inquired whether the laird was kind to her ; and, looking round her little smoky cottage, regretted she should be so indifferently lodged, and that her cupboard, which was rather of the emptiest at the time, should not be more amply furnished. For nearly a twelvemonth after,

scarce a day passed in which she was not seen by some of the
domestics; never, however, except on one occasion, after the
sun had risen, or before it had set.   The maids could see her
in the gray of the morning flitting like a shadow round their
beds, or peering in upon them at night through the dark win-
dow-panes, or at half-open doors.   In the evening she would
glide into the kitchen or some of the out-houses,—one of the
most familiar and least dignified of her class that ever held
intercourse with mankind,—and inquire of the girls how they
had been employed during the day; often, however, without
obtaining an answer, though from a cause different from that
which had at first tied their tongues.   For they had become
so regardless of her presence, viewing her simply as a trouble-
some mistress, who had no longer any claim to be heeded,
that when she entered, and they had dropped their conversation, under the impression that their visitor was a creature
of flesh and blood like themselves, they would again resume
it, remarking that the entrant was " only the green lady."
Though always cadaverously pale, and miserable looking, she
affected a joyous disposition, and was frequently heard to
laugh, even when invisible.   At one time, when provoked by
the studied silence of a servant girl, she flung a pillow at her
head, which the girl caught up and returned; at another, she
presented her first acquaintance, the ploughman, with what
seemed to be a handful of silver coin, which he transferred
to his pocket, but which, on hearing her laugh, he drew out,
and found to be merely a handful of slate shivers.   On yet
another occasion, the man, when passing on horseback through
a clump of wood, was repeatedly struck from behind the trees
by little pellets of turf; and, on riding into the thicket, he
found that his assailant was the green lady.   To her husband
she never appeared; but he frequently heard the tones of her
voice echoing from the lower apartments, and the faint peal
of her cold, unnatural laugh.

One day at noon, a year after her first appearance, the old nurse was surprised to see her enter the cottage ; as all her previous visits had been made early in the morning or late in the evening; whereas now,—though the day was dark and lowering, and a storm of wind and rain had just broken out, —still it *was* day. "Mammie," she said, "I cannot open the heart of the laird, and I have nothing of my own to give you ; but I think I can do something for you now. Go straight to the White House [that of a neighbouring proprietor], and tell the folk there to set out with all the speed of man and horse for the black rock in the sea, at the foot of the crags, or they'll rue it dearly to their dying day. Their bairns, foolish things, have gone out to the rock, and the tide has flowed round them ; and, if no help reach them soon, they'll be all scattered like sea-ware on the shore ere the fall of the sea. But if you go and tell your story at the White House, mammie, the bairns will be safe for an hour to come, and there will be something done by their mother to better you, for the news." The woman went, as directed, and told her story ; and the father of the children set out on horseback in hot haste for the rock,—a low, insulated skerry, which, lying on a solitary part of the beach, far below the line of flood, was shut out from the view of the inhabited country by a wall of precipices, and covered every tide by several feet of water. On reaching the edge of the cliffs, he saw the black rock, as the woman had described, surrounded by the sea, and the children clinging to its higher crags. But, though the waves were fast rising, his attempts to ride out through the surf to the poor little things were frustrated by their cries, which so frightened his horse as to render it unmanageable ; and so he had to gallop on to the nearest fishing village for a boat. So much time was unavoidably lost in consequence, that nearly the whole beach was covered by the sea, and the surf had begun to lash the feet of the pre-

---

sea-ware: seaweed on the beach (Scots)

cipices behind ; but until the boat arrived, not a single wave
dashed over the black rock ; though immediately after the
last of the children had been rescued, an immense wreath of
foam rose twice a man's height over its topmost pinnacle.

The old nurse, on her return to the cottage, found the
green lady sitting beside the fire. "Mammie," she said, "you
have made friends to yourself to-day, who will be kinder to
you than your foster-son. I must now leave you. My time
is out, and you'll be all left to yourselves ; but I'll have no
rest, mammie, for many a twelvemonth to come. Ten years
ago, a travelling pedlar broke into our garden in the fruit
season, and I sent out our old ploughman, who is now in Ireland, to drive him away. It was on a Sunday, and everybody else was in church. The men struggled and fought, and
the pedlar was killed. But though I at first thought of bringing the case before the laird, when I saw the dead man's pack,
with its silks and its velvets, and this unhappy piece of green
satin (shaking her dress), my foolish heart beguiled me, and
I bade the ploughman bury the pedlar's body under our ash
tree, in the corner of our garden, and we divided his goods
and money between us. You must bid the laird raise his
bones, and carry them to the churchyard ; and the gold, which
you will find in the little bowl under the tapestry in my room,
must be sent to a poor old widow, the pedlar's mother, who
lives on the shore of Leith. I must now away to Ireland to
the ploughman ; and I'll be e'en less welcome to him, mammie,
than at the laird's ; but the hungry blood cries loud against
us both,—him and me,—and we must suffer together. Take
care you look not after me till I have passed the knowe."
She glided away, as she spoke, in a gleam of light ; and when
the old woman had withdrawn her hand from her eyes, dazzled
by the sudden brightness, she saw only a large black gray-
hound crossing the moor. And the green lady was never
afterwards seen in Scotland. The little hoard of gold pieces,

however, stored in a concealed recess of her former apartment, and the mouldering remains of the pedlar under the ash tree, gave evidence to the truth of her narrative. The story was hardly wild enough for a night so drear and a road so lonely; its ghost-heroine was but a homely ghost-heroine, too little aware that the same familiarity which, according to the proverb, breeds contempt when exercised by the denizens of this world, produces similar effects when too much indulged in by the inhabitants of another. But the arrangement and restoration of the details of the tradition,—for they had been scattered in my mind like the fragments of a broken fossil,—furnished me with so much amusement, when struggling with the storm, as to shorten by at least one-half the seven miles which intervene between Gamrie and Macduff. Instead, however, of pressing on to Banff, as I had at first intended, I baited for the night at a snug little inn in the latter village, which I reached just wet enough to enjoy the luxury of a strong clear fire of Newcastle coal.

Mrs Longmuir had furnished me with a note of introduction to Dr Emslie of Banff, an intelligent geologist, familiar with the deposits of the district; and, walking on to his place of residence next morning, in a rain as heavy as that of the previous night, I made it my first business to wait on him, and deliver the note. Ere, however, crossing the Deveron, which flows between Banff and Macduff, I paused for a few minutes in the rain, to mark the peculiar appearance presented by the beach where the river disembogues into the frith. Occurring as a rectangular spit in the line of the shore, with the expanded stream widening into an estuary on its upper side, and the open sea on the lower, it marks the scene of an obstinate contest between antagonist forces,—the powerful sweep of the torrent, and the not less powerful waves of the stormy north-east; and exists, in consequence, as a long gravelly prism, which presents as steep an angle of descent to the waves on the one side as to the current on the other. It is a true river bar, beaten in from its proper place in the sea by the violence of the surf, and fairly stranded. Dr Emslie obligingly submitted to my inspection his set of Gamrie fossils, containing several good specimens of Pterichthys and Coccosteus, undistinguishable, like those I had seen on the previous day, in their state of keeping, and the character of the nodular matrices in which they lie, from my old acquaintance the Cephalaspians of Cromarty. The animal matter which the bony plates and scales originally contained has been converted, in both the Gamrie and Cromarty ichthyolites, into a jet-black bitumen ; and in both, the inclosing nodules consist of a smoke-coloured argillaceous limestone, which formed around the organisms in a bed of stratified clay, and at once exhibits, in consequence, the rectilinear lines of the stratification, mechanical in their origin, and the radiating ones of the sub-crystalline concretion, purely a trick of the chemistry of the deposit. ˙A Pterichthys in Dr Emslie's collection struck me as different in its proportions from any I had previously seen, though, from its state of rather imperfect preservation, I hesitated to pronounce absolutely upon the fact. I cannot now doubt, however, that it belonged to a species not figured nor described at the time ; but which, under the name *Pterichthys quadratus*, forms in part the subject of a still unpublished memoir, in which Sir Philip Egerton, our first British authority on fossil fish, has done me the honour to associate my humble name with his own ; and which will have the effect of reducing to the ranks of the Pterichthyan genus the supposed genera *Pamphractus* and *Homothorax*. A second set of fossils, which Dr Emslie had derived from his tile-works at Blackpots, proved, I found, identical with those of the Eathie Lias. As this Banffshire deposit had formed a subject of considerable discussion and difference among geologists, I was curious to examine it ; and the Doctor, though the day

---

memoir: Egerton (1848): *Pamphractus* and *Homothorax*: genera of fossil fishes which, Miller said, turn out to be the same as the previously described *Pterichthys* and so are subsumed within it. Now, however, considered to be synonyms of the similar genus *Bothriolepis* was still none of the best, kindly walked out with me, to bring under my notice appearances which, in the haste of a first examination, I might possibly overlook, and to show me yet another set of fossils which he kept at the works. He informed me, as we went, that the Grauwacke (Lower Silurian) deposits of the district, hitherto deemed so barren, had recently yielded their organisms in a slate quarry at Gamriehead ; and that they belong to that ancient family of the Pennatularia which, in this northern kingdom, seems to have taken precedence of all the others. Judging from what now appears, the Graptolite must be regarded as the first settler who squatted for a living in that deep-sea area of undefined boundary occupied at the present time by the bold wave-worn headlands and blue hills of Scotland ; and this new Banffshire locality not only greatly extends the range of the fossil in reference to the kingdom, but also establishes, in a general way, the fossiliferous identity of the Lower Silurian deposits to the north of the Grampians with that of Peebles-shire and Galloway in the south,—so far as I know, the only other two Scottish districts in which this organism has been found.

The argillaceous deposit of Blackpots occupies, in the form of a green swelling bank, a promontory rather soft than bold in its contour, that projects far into the sea, and forms, when tipped with its slim column of smoke from the tile-kiln, a pleasing feature in the landscape. I had set it down on the previous day, when it first caught my eye from the lofty cliffs of Gamrie-head, at the distance of some ten or twelve miles, as different in character from all the other features of the prospect. The country generally is moulded on a framework of primary rock, and presents headlands of hard, sharp outline, to the attrition of the waves ; whereas this single headland in the midst,—soft-lined, undulatory, and plump,—seems suited to remind one of Burns' young Kirk Alloway beauty disporting amid the thin old ladies that joined with her in

Lower Silurian: possibly an interpolation by Symonds; **Pennatularia ... graptolites**: see Additional Notes; **argillaceous deposit at Blackpots**: Pleistocene boulder clay including Jurassic material now considered to have been moved by glacial action from the Moray Firth floor – see Introduction; **Burns' young Kirk Alloway beauty**: see Additional Notes the dance. And it *is* a greatly younger beauty than the Cambrian and mica-schist protuberances that encroach on the sea on either side of it.   The sheds and kilns of a tile-work occupy the flat terminal point of the promontory; and as the clay is valuable, in this tile-draining age, for the facility with which it can be moulded into pipe-tiles (a purpose which the ordinary clays of the north of Scotland, composed chiefly of re-formations of the Old Red Sandstone, are what is technically termed too *short* to serve), it is gradually retreating inland before the persevering spade and mattock of the labourer.   The deposit has already been drawn out into many hundred miles of cylindrical pipes, and is destined to be drawn out into many thousands more,—such being one of the strange metamorphoses effected in the geologic formations, now that that curious animal the Bimana has come upon the stage; and at length it will have no existence in the country, save as an immense system of veins and arteries underlying the vegetable mould.   Will these veins and arteries, I marvel, form, in their turn, the *fossils* of another period, when a higher platform than that into which they have been laid will be occupied to the full by plants and animals specifically different from those of the present scene of things,—the existences of a happier and more finished creation?   My business to-day, however, was with the fossils which the deposit now contains, —not with those which it may ultimately form.

The Blackpots clay is of a dark-bluish or greenish-gray colour, and so adhesive, that I now felt, when walking among it, after the softening rains of the previous night and morning, as if I had got into a bed of bird-lime.   It is thinly charged with rolled pebbles, septaria, and pieces of a bituminous shale, containing broken Belemnites, and sorely-flattened Ammonites, that exist as thin films of a white chalky lime. The pebbles, like those of the boulder-clay of the northern side of the Moray Frith, are chiefly of the primary rocks and

a happier and more finished creation: heaven on earth, in the sense of Christian eschatology. The next and final 'creation' of life will be that which will take place after the Day of Judgement, which is itself to be the last of the 'catastrophes' of geological time – see Additional Note for p. 39

older sandstones, and were probably in the neighbourhood, in their present rolled form, long ere the re-formation of the inclosing mass ; while the shale and the septaria are, as shown by their fossils, decidedly Liasic. I detected among the conchifers a well-marked species of our northern Lias, figured by Sowerby from Eathie specimens,—the *Plagiostoma concentrica ;* and among the Cephalopoda, though considerably broken, the *Belemnite elongatus* and *Belemnite lanceolata,* with the *Ammonite Kœnigi (mutabilis),*—all Eathie shells. I, besides, found in the bank a piece of a peculiar-looking quartzose sandstone, traversed by hard jaspedeous veins of a brownish-gray colour, which I have never found, in Scotland at least, save associated with the Lias of our north-eastern coasts. Further, my attention was directed by Dr Emslie to a fine Lignite in his collection, which had once formed some eighteen inches or two feet of the trunk of a straight slender pine,—probably the *Pinites Eiggensis,*—in which, as in most woods of the Lias and Oolite, the annual rings are as strongly marked as in the existing firs or larches of our hill-sides.*

* Since the above was written, I have seen an interesting paper in "Hogg's Weekly Instructor," in which the Rev. Mr Longmuir of Aberdeen describes a visit to the Lias clay at Blackpots. Mr Longmuir seems to have given more time to his researches than I found it agreeable, in a very indifferent day, to devote to mine ; and his list of fossils is considerably longer. Their evidence, however, runs in exactly the same tract with that of the shorter list. He had been told at Banff that the clay contained "petrified tangles ;" and the first organisms shown him by the workmen, on his arrival at the deposit, were some of the "tangles" in question. "These," he goes on to say, "we found, as may have already been anticipated, to be pieces of Belemnites, well known on the other side of the Frith as 'thunderbolts,' and esteemed of sovereign efficacy in the cure of bewitched cattle." Though still wide of the mark, there is here an evident descent from the supernatural to the physical, from the superstitious to the true. "Satisfied that we had a mass of Lias clay before us, we set vigorously to work, in order either to find additional characteristic fossils, or obtain data on which to form a conjecture as to the history of this out-of-the-way deposit ; and our labour was not without its reward. We shall now present a brief account of the specimens we picked up. Observing a number of stones of different sizes, that had been thrown out, as they

paper: much of Longmuir (1848), reprinted more or less verbatim but erroneously punctuated so as to imply wrongly that Longmuir's 'Though still wide … to the true' is an interpolation of Miller's. The remainder of Longmuir's account described his impromptu geological lecture, laced with natural theology, to the workmen, who were said to have taken an intelligent interest

The Blackpots deposit is evidently a re-formation of a Liasic patch, identical, both in mineralogical character and in its organic remains, with the lower beds of the Eathie Lias ; while the fragments of shale which it contains belong chiefly

were struck, by the workman's shovel, we immediately commenced, and, like an inquisitor of old, knocked our victims on the head, that they might reveal their secrets ; or, like a Roman haruspex, examined their interior,— not, however, to obtain a knowledge of the future, but only to take a peep into the past. 1. Here, then, we take up, not a regular Lias lime nodule, but what appears to have formed part of one ; and the first blow has laid open part of a whorl of an Ammonite, which, when complete, must have measured three or four inches in diameter, and it is perfectly assimilated to the calcareous matrix. 2. Here is a mass of indurated clay ; and a gentle blow has exposed part of two Ammonites, smaller than the former, but their shells are white and powdery like chalk. 3. Another fragment is laid open ; and there, quite unmistakeably, lie the umbo and greater portion of the *Plagiostoma concentricum.* 4. Another fragment of a granular gritty structure presents a considerable portion of the interior of one of the shells of a Pecten, but whether the attached fragment is part of one of its ears, or of the other valve turned backward, is not so easily determined. 5. Here is a piece of Belemnite in limestone, and the fracture in the fossil presents the usual glistening planes of cleavage. 6. Next we take up a piece of distinctly laminated Lias, with Ammonites as thick as they can lie on the pages of this black book of natural history. 7. Once more we strike, and we have the cast and part of the shell of another bivalve ; but the valves have been jerked off each other, and have suffered a severe compound fracture ; nevertheless we can have little hesitation in pronouncing it a species of *unio.* 8. Here is another piece of limestone, with its small fragment of another shell, of very delicate texture, with finely marked traverse striæ. We are unwilling to decide on such slight evidence, but feel inclined to refer it to some species of Plagiostoma. 9. Here is a piece of pyrites, not quite so large as the fist, and so vegetable-like in its markings, that it might be mistaken for part of a branch of a tree. This is also characteristic of the Lias ; for when the shales are deeply impregnated with bitumen and pyrites, they undergo a slow combustion when heaped up with faggots and set on fire ; and in the cliffs of the Yorkshire coast, after rainy weather, they sometimes spontaneously ignite, and continue to burn for several months. 10. As we passed through the works, on our way to the clay, we observed a sort of reservoir, into which the clay, after being freed from its impurities, had been run in a liquid state ; the water had evaporated, and the drying clay had cracked in every direction. Here we find its counterpart in this large mass of stone ; only the clay here, mixed with a portion of lime, is petrified, and the fissures filled up with carbonate of lime ; thus forming the septaria, or cement-stone. We have dressed a specimen of it for our guide, who has a friend that will polish it, when the

---

pyrites: pyrite tends to oxidise to acidic iron sulphates in the presence of oxygen and water

to an upper Liasic bed. So rich is the dark-coloured tenacious argil of the Inferior Lias of Eathie, that the geologist
who walks over it when it is still moist with the receding
tide would do well to look to his footing ;—the mixture of
soap and grease spread by the ship-carpenter on his launch-
slips, to facilitate the progress of his vessel seawards, is not
more treacherous to the tread : while the Upper Liasic deposit which rests over it is composed of a dark slaty shale,

dark Lias will be strikingly contrasted with the white lime, and form
rather a pretty piece of natural mosaic. 11. Coming to a simple piece of
machinery for removing fragments of shale and stone from the clay, we
examined some of the bits so rejected, and found what we had no doubt
were fish-scales. 12. We have yet to notice certain long slender bodies,
outwardly brown, but inwardly nearly black, resembling whip-cord in
size. Are we to regard these as specimens of a fucus, perhaps the *filum*,
or allied to it, which is known in some places by the appropriate name of
sea-laces ? 13. Passing on to the office, we were shown a chop of wood that
had been found in the clay, and was destined for the Banff Museum. It is
about eighteen inches in length, and half as much in breadth ; and, although
evidently water-worn, yet we could count between twenty-five and thirty
concentric rings on one of its ends, which not only enabled us to form some
conjecture of its age previous to its overthrow, but also justified us in referring it to the coniferæ of the *vorwelt*, or ancient world."

Mr Longmuir makes the following shrewd remarks, in answering the
question, " Whether have we here a mass of Lias clay, as originally deposited, or has it resulted from the breaking up of Lias-shale ?" " The former alternative," says Mr Longmuir, " we have heard, has been maintained ; but we are inclined to adopt the latter, and that for the following
reasons :—1. This clay, judging from other localities, is not *in situ*, but has
every appearance of having been precipitated into a basin in the gneiss on
which it rests, having apparently under it, although it is impossible to say
to what extent, a bed of comminuted shells. 2. The fossils are all fragmentary and water-worn. This is especially the case with regard to the
Belemnites, the pieces averaging from one to two inches in length, no workman having ever found a complete specimen, such as occurs in the Lias-
shale at Cromarty, in which they may be found nine inches in length. 3.
But perhaps the most satisfactory proof, and one that in itself may be
deemed sufficient, is the frequent occurrence of pieces of Lias-shale, with
their embedded Ammonites; which clearly show that the Lias had been
broken up, tossed about in some violent agitation of the sea, and churned
into clay, just as some denudating process of a similar nature swept away
the chalk of Aberdeenshire, leaving on many of its hills and plains the
water-worn flints, with the characteristic fossils of the Cretaceous formation."

---

filum ... sea-laces: Sea Whip, the seaweed *Chorda filum* which has long, cylindrical
fronds like shoe-laces – but not, strictly, a realistic identification for these fossils, at least
in terms of the modern species

largely charged with bitumen.   And of a Liasic deposit of
this compound character, consisting in larger part of an inferior argillaceous bed, and in lesser part of a superior one of
dark shale, the tile-clay of Blackpots has been formed.

I had next to determine whether aught remained to indicate the period of its re-formation.   The tile-works at the
point of the promontory rest on a bed of shell-sand, composed
exclusively, like the sand so abundant on the western coast
of Scotland, of fragments of existing shells. These, however,
are so fresh and firm, that, though the stratum which they
form seems to underlie the clay at its edges, I cannot regard
them as older than the most modern of our ancient sea-mar-
gins.   They formed, in all probability, in the days of the old
coast line, a white shelly beach, under such a precipitous front
of the dark clay as argillaceous deposits almost always present to the undermining wear of the waves.   On the recession of the sea, however, to its present line, the abrupt, steep
front, loosened by the frosts and washed by the rains, would
of course gradually moulder down over them into a slope ;
and there would thus be communicated to the shelly stratum,
at least at its edges, an underlying character.   The true period of the re-formation of the deposit was, I can have no
doubt, that of the boulder-clay.   I observed that the septaria.
and larger masses of shale which the bed contains, bear, on
roughly-polished surfaces, in the line of their larger axes, the
mysterious groovings and scratchings of this period,—marks
which I have never yet known to fail in their chronological
evidence. It may be mentioned, too, simply as a fact, though
one of less value than the other, that the deposit occurs in
its larger development exactly where, in the average, the
boulder-clays also are most largely developed,—a little over
that line where the waves for so many ages charged against
the coast, ere the last upheaval of the land or the recession
of the sea sent them back to their present margin.   There
had probably existed to the west or north-west of the deposit,

perhaps in the middle of the open bay formed by the promontory on which it rests,—for the small proportion of other than Liasic materials which it contains serves to show that it could be derived from no great distance,—an outlier of the Lower Lias. The icebergs of the cold glacial period, propelled along the submerged land by some arctic current, or caught up by the gulf-stream, gradually grated it down, as a mason's labourer grates down the surface of the sandstone slab which he is engaged in polishing; and the comminuted debris, borne eastwards by the current, was cast down here. It has been stated that no Liasic remains have been found in the boulder-clays of Scotland. They are certainly rare in the boulder-clays of the northern shores of the Moray Frith; for there the nearest Lias, bearing in a western direction from the clay, is that of Applecross, on the other side of the island; and the materials of the boulder-deposits of the north have invariably been derived in the line, westerly in its general bearing, of the grooves and scratches of the iceberg era. But on the southern shore of the frith, where that westerly line passed athwart the Liasic beds of our eastern coast, organisms of the Lias are comparatively common in the boulder-clays; and here, at Blackpots, we find an extensive deposit of the same period formed of Liasic materials almost exclusively. Fragments of still more modern rocks occur in the boulder-clays of Caithness. My friend Mr Robert Dick of Thurso, to whose persevering labours and interesting discoveries in the Old Red Sandstone of his locality I have had frequent occasion to refer, has detected in a blue boulder-clay, scooped into precipitous banks by the river Thorsa, fragments both of chalk-flints and a characteristic conglomerate of the Oolite. He has, besides, found it mottled from top to bottom, a full hundred feet over the sea-level, and about two miles inland, with comminuted fragments of existing shells. But of this more anon.

river Thorsa: *ie* River Thurso, which passes through the town of the same name

CHAPTER III.

I PARTED from Dr Emslie, and walked on along the shore to Portsoy,—for three-fourths of the way over the prevailing grauwacke of the county, and for the remaining fourth over mica schist, primary limestone, hornblende slate, granitic and quartz veins, and the various other kindred rocks of a primary district. The day was still gloomy and gray, and ill suited to improve homely scenery ; nor is this portion of the Banff coast nearly so striking as that which I had travelled over the day before. It has, however, its spots of a redeeming character,—rocky recesses on the shore, half-beach, half-sward, rich in wild-flowers and shells,—where one could saunter in a calm sunny morning, with one's *bairns* about one, very delightfully ; and the interior is here and there agreeably undulated by diluvial hillocks, that, when the sun falls low in the evening, must chequer the landscape with many a pleasing alternation of light and shadow. The Burn of Boyne,—which separates, about two miles from Portsoy, a grauwacke from a mica-schist district,—with its bare, open valley, its steep limestone banks, and its gray, melancholy castle, long since roofless and windowless, and surrounded by a few stunted trees, bears a deserted and solitary shagginess about it, that struck me as wildly agreeable. It is such a valley as one might expect to meet a ghost in, in some still, dewy evening, as gloamin was darkening into uncertainty the outlines of the ancient ruin, and the newly-kindled stars looked down upon the stream.

It so happened, however, that my only story connected with either ruin or valley was as little a ghost story as might be. I remember that, when lying ill of fever on one occasion,—indisposed enough to see apparition after apparition flitting across the bed-curtains, like the figures of a magic lanthorn posting along the darkened wall, and yet self-possessed enough to know that they were but mere pictures in the eye, and to watch them as they rose,—I set myself to determine whether they were in any degree amenable to the will, or connected by the ordinary associative links of the metaphysician. Fixing my mind on a certain object, I strove to call it up in the character, not of an image of the conceptive faculty, but of a fever-vision on the retina. The image which I pictured to myself was that of a death's head, yellow and grim, and lighted up, as if from within, amid the darkness of a burial vault. But the death's head obstinately refused to rise. I had no control, I found, over the fever imagery. And the picture that rose instead, uncalled and unexpected, was that of a coal-fire burning brightly in a grate, with a huge tea-kettle steaming cheerily over it.

In traversing the bare height which, rising on the western side of the valley of the Boyne, owes its comparatively bold relief in the landscape to the firmness of the primary rock which composes it, I picked up a piece of graphic granite, bearing its inlaid characters of dark quartz on a ground of cream-coloured feldspar. This variety, however, though occasionally found in rolled boulders in the neighbourhood of Portsoy, is not the graphic granite for which the locality is famous, and which occurs in a vein in the mica schist of the eminence I was now traversing, about a mile to the east of the town. The prevailing ground of the granite of the vein is a flesh-coloured feldspar ; and the thickly-marked quartzose characters with which it is set, greatly smaller and paler than in the cream-coloured stone, bear less the antique Hebraic look, and would scarce deceive even the most credulous antiquary.   Antiquarians, however, *have* been sometimes deceived by weathered specimens of this graphic rock, in which the characters were of considerable size, and restricted to thin veins, covering the surface of a schistose groundwork.   Maupertuis, during his famous journey to Lapland, undertaken in 1737, to establish, from actual measurement, that the degrees of latitude are longer towards the pole than at the equator, and which demonstrated, of consequence, the true figure of the earth, travelled thirty leagues out of his way, through a wild country covered with snow, to examine an ancient monument, of which, he says, "the Fins and Laplanders frequently spoke, as containing in its inscription the knowledge of everything of which they were ignorant." He found it on the side of a mountain, buried in snow ; and ascertained, after kindling a great fire around it, in order to lay it bare, that it was a stone of irregular form, composed of various layers of unequal hardness, and that the characters, which were rather more than an inch in length, were written on "a layer of a species of flint," chiefly in two lines, with a few scattered signs beneath, while the rest of the mass was composed of a rock more soft and foliated.   Graphic granite, it may be mentioned, generally occurs, not in masses, but in veins and layers.   The inscription had been described in a previously published dissertation of immense erudition, as Runic ; but a Runic scholar of the party found he could make nothing of it.   The philosopher himself was struck by the frequent repetition of characters of nearly the same form on the stone ; but he was ingenious enough to get over the difficulty, by remembering that in our notation, after the Arabic manner, characters shaped exactly alike may be very

---

Maupertuis: Pierre de Maupertuis (1698-1757), natural philosopher, mathematician, and author of *The figure of the Earth* (1738). He was in Lapland to measure the distance which one degree of latitude subtended on the surface of the Earth, while another expedition made the same measurement in Peru. Comparison would show how far the Earth deviates from being a true sphere frequently repeated,—nay, as in some of the lines of the Lapland inscription, may succeed each other, as in the sums I. II. III. IIII. or X. XX. XXX.,—and yet very distinct and definite ideas attach to them all. Still, however, he could not, he says, venture on authoritatively deciding whether the inscription was a work of man or a sport of nature. He stood between his two conclusions, like our Edinburgh antiquarians between the two fossil Maries of Gueldres; and, richer in eloquence than most of the philosophers his contemporaries, was quite prepared, in his uncertainty, to give gilded mounting and a purple pall to both.

"Should it be no other than a sport of nature," he concludes, "the reputation which the stone bears in this country deserves that we should have given a description of it. If, on the other hand, what is on it be an inscription, though it certainly does not possess the beauty of the sculpture of Greece or Rome, it very possibly has the advantage of being the oldest in the universe. The country in which it is found is inhabited only by a race of men who live like beasts in the forests. We cannot imagine that they can have ever had any memorable event to transmit to posterity, nor, if ever they had had, that they could have invented the means. Nor can it be conceived that this country, with its present aspect, ever possessed more civilized inhabitants. The rigour of the climate and the barrenness of the land have destined it for the retreat of a few miserable wretches, who know no other. It seems, therefore, that the inscription must have been cut at a period when the country was situated in a different climate, and before some one of those great revolutions which, we cannot doubt, have taken place on our globe. The position that the earth's axis holds at present with respect to the ecliptic, occasions Lapland to receive the sun's rays very obliquely: it is therefore condemned to a long winter, adverse to man, as well as to all the productions of nature. No great move-

two fossil Maries of Gueldres: see Additional Notes; gilded mounting and a purple pall: a Roman Catholic style reliquary would only be given to relics accepted as authentic ment, possibly, in the heavens was necessary, however, to cause all its misfortunes. These regions may formerly have been those on which the sun shone most favourably; the polar circles may have been what now the tropics are, and the torrid zone have filled the place occupied by the temperate." Pretty well, Monsieur, for a philosopher! The various attempts made to unriddle the real history of graphic granite are, however, scarce less curious than the speculations connected with what may be termed its romance. It seems to be generally held, since the days of old Hutton, who, in his "Theory of the Earth," discussed the subject with his usual ingenuity, that the feldspathic basis of the stone first crystallized, leaving interstices between the crystals, partaking of a certain regularity of form,—a consequence of the regularity of the crystals themselves,—and of a certain irregularity from the eccentric dispositions which these manifest in their position and relations to each other; and that these interstices, being afterwards filled up with quartz, form the characters of the rock,—characters partaking enough of the first element of *regularity* to present their peculiar graphic appearance, and enough of the second element of *irregularity* to exhibit forms of an alphabet-like variety of outline. The chemist, however, in cross-questioning the explanation, has his puzzle to propound regarding it. Quartz, he says, being considerably less fusible than feldspar, would naturally consolidate first, and so would give form to the more fusible substance, instead of deriving form from it. On what principle, then, is it that, reversing its ordinary character, it should have been the last of the two substances to consolidate in the graphic granite?—a query to which there seems to be no direct reply, but which as little affects the fact that it *was* the substance which last consolidated, and which took form from the other, as the decision of the learned Strasburgers, which determined the impossibility of the long nose in Slaw-

---

learned Strasburgers ... Slawkenbergius's Tale: Chapter 4 in Laurence Sterne's novel, *The Life and Opinions of Tristram Shandy, Gent*

kenbergius's Tale, affected the actual existence of that remarkable feature. "It happens *to be*, notwithstanding your
objection," said the controversialists on the pro-nose side of
the question. "But it *ought not*," replied their opponents.

The rain again returned as I was engaged in examining
the graphic granite of the Portsoy vein ; the breeze from the
sea heightened into a gale, that soon fringed the coast with
a broad border of foam ; and I entered the town, which looked but indifferently well in its gray dishabille of haze and
spray, tolerably wet and worn, with but the prospect before
me of being weather-bound for the rest of the day. I found
an old-fashioned inn, kept by somewhat old-fashioned people,
who had lately come from the country to "open a public ;"
and ensconced myself by the fireside, in a huge many-win-
dowed room, that must have witnessed the county dinners of
at least a century ago. Soon wearying, however, of hearing
the rain beating mad-like ratans upon the panes, and availing myself of a comparatively "lucid interval," I sallied out,
wrapped up in my plaid, to examine the serpentine beds in
the neighbourhood, which produce what is so extensively
known as the Portsoy marble. The *beds* or *veins* of this substance,—for it is still a moot point whether they occur here
as mere insulated masses of contemporary origin with the
primary formations which surround them, or as Plutonic
dykes injected into fissures at a later period,—are of very
considerable extent, one of them measuring about twenty-five
yards across, and another considerably more than a quarter
of a mile ; and, had they but the solidity of the true marbles,
they would scarce fail to be regarded as valuable quarries of
a highly ornamental stone, admirably suited for the interior
decorations of the architect. But they are unluckily what
the quarrier would term rubbly,—traversed by an infinity of
cracks and fissures ; and it is rare indeed to find a continuous
mass out of which a chimney jamb or lintel could be fashion-

ed. The serpentine was wrought here considerably more than a century and a half ago, and exported to France, for the magnificent Palace of Versailles ; which, though regarded by the French nation, says Voltaire, as "a favourite without merit," Louis the Fourteenth persisted at the time in lavishly beautifying, and looked as far abroad as Portsoy for materials with which to adorn it. I have, however, seen it stated, that the greater part of a ship's cargo, brought afterwards to Paris on speculation, was suffered to lie unwrought for years in the stone-dealer's yard, and was ultimately disposed of as rubbish,—a consequence, probably, of its unfitness, from its shaky texture, for ornamental purposes on a large scale, though for ornaments of the smaller kind, such as boxes, vases, and plates, it has been pronounced unrivalled. " At Zöblitz, in Upper Saxony," says Professor Jamieson, " several hundred people are employed in quarrying, cutting, turning, and polishing the serpentine which occurs in that neighbourhood; and the various articles into which it is manufactured are carried all over Germany. The serpentine of Portsoy," he adds, "is, however, far superior to that of Zöblitz, in colour, hardness, and transparency, and, when cut, is very beautiful."

It is really a pretty stone ; and, bad as the evening was, it was by no means one of the worst of evenings for seeing it to advantage *in situ*, or among the rolled pebbles on the shore. The varnish-like gloss of the wet imparted to the undressed masses all the effect of polish, and brought out in their proper variegations of colour, every cloud, streak, and vein. Viewed in the mass, the general hue is green ; so much so, that an insulated stack, which stands abreast of one of the beds, a stone-cast in the sea, has greatly the appearance, at a little distance, of an immense mass of verdigris. But red, gray, and brown are also prevailing colours in the rock ; occasional veins and blotches of white give lightness to the darker portions ; and veins of hematitic and deep umbry tints, variety to the portions that are lighter. The greens vary from the palest olive to the deepest black-green of the mineralogist ; the reds and browns, from blood-red to dark chocolate, and from wood-brown to brownish-black ; and, thus various in shade, they occur in almost every possible variety of combination and form,—dotted, spotted, clouded, veined,—so that each separate pebble on the shore seems the representative of a rock different from the rocks represented by almost all the others. Though not much of a mineralogist, I could have spent considerably more time than the weather permitted me to employ this evening, in admiring the beauties of this beach of *marbles*, or rather,—as the real name, derived from those gorgeous, many-coloured cloudings that impart a terrible splendour to the skins of the snake and viper family, is not only the more correct, but also the more poetical of the two,—this beach of *serpentines*. I had, however, to compromise matters between the fierce wind and rain and the pretty rocks and pebbles, by adjourning to the workshop of the Portsoy lapidary, Mr Clark, and examining under cover his polished specimens, of which I purchased for a few shillings a characteristic and elegant little set. Portsoy is peculiarly rich in minerals ; and hence it reckons among its mechanics of the ordinary class, what perhaps no other village in Scotland of the same size and population possesses,— a skilful lapidary. Mr Clark's collection of the graphic granites, serpentines, and talcose and mica schists, of the district, with their associated minerals, such as schorl, talc, asbestos, amianthus, mountain cork, steatite, and schiller spar, will be found eminently worthy a visit by the passing traveller.

I made several inquiries in the village, though not, as it proved, in the right direction, regarding a poor old lady, several years dead, of whom I had known a very little considerably more than a quarter of a century before, and whose

---

steatite: perhaps talc or soapstone, not the same thing but both soft and greasy in texture grave I would have visited, bad as the night was, had I met any one who could have pointed it out to me. But ungrateful Portsoy seemed to have forgotten poor Miss Bond, who, in all her printed letters and little stories, so rarely forgot *it*. Have any of my readers ever seen the work (in two slim volumes), "Letters of a Village Governess," published in 1814 by Elizabeth Bond, and dedicated to Sir Walter Scott? If not, and should they chance to see, as I lately did, a copy on a stall (with uncut leaves, alas! and selling dog cheap), they might possibly do worse things than buy it.*

With better weather I could have spent a day or two very agreeably in Portsoy and its neighbourhood; but the rain dashed unceasingly, and made exploration under the cover of the umbrella somewhat resemble that of a sea-bottom under cover of the diving-bell. I could see but little at a time, and the little imperfectly. Miss Bond, in her "Letters," refers, in her light, pleasing style, to what in more favourable circumstances *might* be seen. "My troop of *light infantry*," she says, "keeps me so well employed here during the day, that the silence and repose of the evening is very delightful. In fine weather I walk by the sea-side, and scramble among the rugged rocks, many of which are inaccessible to human feet, forming a fine retreat for foxes. These animals often may be seen from the heights, sporting with their cubs in perfect safety. This day I went to see the works of an old *virtuoso*, who turns in marble, or rather granite [serpentine] all kinds of chimney-piece ornaments, rings, ear-rings, &c. Several specimens of his work, which must have cost him a vast deal of trouble, I thought very beautiful. It was in this neighbourhood that the celebrated Ferguson spent so much of his time. The globular stones on the gate of Durn are still to be seen, on which he mapped out the figuring of the

---

* A description of Miss Bond and of her "Letters," here referred to, is given in the fifth chapter of "My Schools and Schoolmasters."

---

diving-bell: a method of working underwater was to use a 'diving bell', an open-bottomed but otherwise mostly opaque chamber which trapped air in it – *ie* Miller is peering out of the bottom of the umbrella; **Miss Bond … *light infantry***: see Additional Notes; **Ferguson**: see Additional Notes terrestrial and celestial globes. I was told it was forbidden ground to approach the premises of Durn; but I could not resist the temptation of visiting the spot where the young philosopher had shown such early proofs of his genius; and I accordingly paid the forfeit of an *impertinent*, for the gentleman who resides there caught the prowler, and in genteel terms bade her go about her business, and never return. How ungracious! She was doing no harm."

The morning arose as gloomily as the evening had fallen; and I walked on in the rain to Cullen, fully disposed to sympathize by the way with the "hardy Byron,"—he of the "Narrative,"—who, from his ill-luck in weather, went among his sailors by the name of "Foul-weather Jack." In the sandy bay of Cullen, where the road, after inflecting inland for some five or six miles, comes again upon the sea, I found the surf charging home in long white lines six waves deep,—

> " Each stepping where his comrade stood,
> The instant that he fell."

The appearance was such as to impart no inadequate idea of the vast attritive power of ocean in wearing down the land. When pausing for a little abreast of the fishing village, partially sheltered by an old boat, to mark the fierce turmoil, it suddenly occurred to me,—as the tempest weltered around reef and skerry, and roared wildly, mile after mile, along the beach,—that the day and night were now just equal, and that it was the customary equinoctial storm that had broken out to accompany me on my journey. And so, calculating on a few days more of it, instead of waiting on in the hope of a fair afternoon to examine the outlier of Old Red which occurs in the neighbourhood of Cullen, I was content to see at a distance its mural-sided cliffs rising like broken walls through the flat sand; and, taking the road for Fochabers, with the intention of leaving exploration till fairer weather set in, I resolved on posting straight on, to join my relatives

---

forbidden: see also p. 458; **Byron**: the poet's grandfather, sailor and eventually Admiral, and author of *Narrative of the Honourable John Byron* describing his experiences when shipwrecked during Anson's circumnavigation of the globe; '**Each stepping …**': Walter Scott, 'Marmion: A Tale of Flodden Field', canto 6, verse 34 on the opposite side of the Frith. The deep-red colour of the boulder-clay, as exhibited by the wayside in the water-courses and the water,—for every runnel was tumbling down big and turbid with the rains,—intimated, when, after leaving Cullen some six or seven miles behind me, I passed from a bare moory region of quartz rock into a region of woods and fields, that I was again upon my ancient acquaintance, the Old Red Sandstone. And the section furnished by the Burn of Tynet showed me shortly after that the intimation was a correct one, and how generally it may be laid down as a rule, that at least the more impalpable portions of the boulder-clay are derived from the rocks on which it rests. The ichthyolite beds appear in the course of the burn. They have furnished several good specimens,—among the others, the specimen of Coccosteus figured by Mr Patrick Duff in his "Sketches of the Geology of Moray;" and they are, besides, curious, as being the first to exhibit to the traveller who explores from Gamrie westwards, that peculiar style of colouring which characterizes the Old Red ichthyolites of the shires of Moray and Nairn, and which differs so strikingly from the more sombre style exhibited by the other ichthyolites of Banffshire, with those of Cromarty, Ross, Caithness, and Orkney. Instead of bearing, like these, one uniform hue, as if deeply shaded with Indian ink, they are gorgeously attired, especially when newly laid open, in white, red, purple, and blue. The day, however, was ill suited for fishing Pterichthyes and Osteolepi out of the Tynet: the red water was roaring from bank to brae; here eddying along the half-submerged furze,—there tearing down the boulder-clays in raw, red land-slips; and so, casting but one eager glance at the bed where the fish lay, I travelled on, and entered the tall woods to the east of Fochabers. The rain ceased for a time; and I met in the woods an old pensioner, who had been evidently weather-bound in some public-house, and had now taken

---

pensioner: not in the modern sense, but, here, a pensioned-off former soldier (or, less probably, sailor) the opportunity of the fair interval to stagger to his dwelling. He was eminently, exuberantly happy,—there could not be two opinions on that head,—full of all manner of bright sunshiny thoughts and imaginations, rendered just a little tremulous and uncertain by the *summer-heat* exhalations of the imbibed moisture, like distant objects in a hot noonday landscape in July seen through volumes of rising vapour ; and a sheep's head and trotters, which he carried under his arm, was, I saw, to serve as a peace-offering to his wife at home. True, he had been taking a dram, but he was mindful of the family for all that. He confronted me with the air of an old acquaintance ; gave the military salute ; and then, laying hold of a corner of my plaid with his thumb and fore-finger,—"I know you," he said,—"I know *your kind* well ; ye're a Highland-Donald. Od, I've seen ye in the *thick o't.* Ye're *reugh* fellows when ye're bluid's up !" He had taken me for a grenadier of the 42d ; and I lacked the moral courage to undeceive him. I met nothing further on my way worthy of record, save and except a sheep's trotter, dropped by the old pensioner in one of his zig-zaggings to the extreme left ; but having no particular use for the trotter at the time and in the circumstances, I left it to benefit the next passer-by. I finished my journey of eighteen miles in capital style, and was within five minutes' walk of Fochabers when the horn of the mail-guard was sounding up the street. And, entering the village, I found the vehicle standing opposite the inn door, minus the horses.

The *insides* and *outsides* were sitting down to dinner together as I entered the inn ; and I felt, after my long walk, that it would be rather an agreeable matter to join with them. But in the hope of meeting my old friend Mr Joss, I requested to be shown, not into the passengers' room, but into that of the coachman and guard ; and with them I dined. It so chanced, however, that Mr Joss was not *out* that day ; and

---

reugh: rough (Scots); **grenadier**: man in the first or 'grenadier' company of an infantry battalion, usually selected from the taller and more intelligent men, which said something about Miller's appearance. During the eighteenth century they threw grenades in battle; **42d**: 42nd Regiment of Foot, better known as the Royal Highland Regiment (The Black Watch), in action in the Peninsular War, the Pyrenees crossing, and Waterloo the man in the red long coat was a stranger whom I had never seen before. I inquired of him regarding Mr Joss,— one of perhaps the most remarkable mail-guards in Europe. I have at least never heard of another who, like him, amuses his leisure on the coach-top with the " Principia" of Newton, and understands it. And the man, drawing his inference from the interest in Mr Joss which my queries evinced, asked me whether I myself was not a coach-guard. "No," I rather thoughtlessly replied, "I am not a coach-guard." Half a minute's consideration, however, led me to doubt whether I had given the right answer. "I am not sure," I said to myself, on second thoughts, "but the man has cut pretty fairly on the point ;—I daresay *I am* a sort of coach-guard. I have to mount my twice-a-week coach in all weathers, like any mail-guard among them all ; I have to start at the appointed hour, whether the vehicle be empty or full ; I have to keep a sharp eye on the opposition coaches ; I am responsible, like any other mail-guard, for all the parcels carried, however little I may have had to do with the making of them up ; I have always to keep my blunderbuss full charged to the muzzle, —not wishing harm to any one, but bound in duty to let drive at all and sundry who would make war upon the passengers, or attempt running the conveyance off the road ; and, finally, as my friend Mr Joss takes the " Principia" to *his* coach-top, I take pockets full of fossils to the top of mine, and amuse myself in fine days by working out, as I best can, the problems which they furnish. Yes, I rather think *I am* a coach-guard." And so, taking my seat beside my red-coated brother, who had guessed the true nature of my occupation so much more shrewdly than myself, I rode on to Elgin, where I passed the night.

It is difficult to arrange in the mind the geologic formations of Banffshire in their character as a series of deposits. The pages of the stony record which the county composes, like

---

'**Principia**': Sir Isaac Newton's classic work of mathematical physics those of an unskilfully-folded pamphlet, have been strangely mixed together, so that page last succeeds in some places to page first, and, of the intermediate pages, some appear at the beginning of the work, and some at the end. It is not until we reach the western confines of the county, some two or three miles short of the river Spey, its terminal boundary in this direction, that we find the beds comparatively little disturbed, and arranged chronologically in their original places. In the eastern and southern parts of the shire, rocks widely separated by the date of their formation have been set down side by side in patches, occasionally of but inconsiderable extent. Now the traveller passes over a district of grauwacke, now over a re-formation of the Lias; anon he finds himself on a primary limestone,—gneiss, syenite, clay-slate, or quartz-rock; and yet anon amid the fossils of some outlier of the Old Red. The geological map of the county is, like Joseph's coat, of many colours. I remember seeing, when a boy, more years ago than I am inclined to specify, some workmen engaged in pull-ing down what had been a house-painter's shop, a full cen-tury before. The painter had been in the somewhat slovenly habit of cleaning his brushes by rubbing them against a hard-cast wall, which was covered, in consequence, by a many-co-loured layer of paint, a full half-inch in thickness, and as hard as a stone. Taking a little bit home with me, I polished it by rubbing the upper surface smooth; and, lo! a geological map. The *strata* of variously hued pigment, spread originally over the uneven surface of the hard-cast wall, were cut open, by the *denudation* of the grindstone, into all manner of fan-tastic forms, and seemed thrown into all sorts of strange neigh-bourhoods. The *map* lacked merely the additional perplexity of a few bold *faults*, with here and there a decided *dike*, in order to render it on a small scale a sort of miniature tran-script of the geology of Banff; and I have very frequently found my thoughts reverting to it, in connection with deposits

of this broken character. On a rough *hard-cast* basis of granite I have laid down in imagination, as if by way of priming,
coat after coat of the primary rocks,—gneiss, and stratified
hornblend, and mica-schist, and quartz-rock, and clay-slate ;
and then, after breaking the coatings well up, and rubbing
them well down, and so spoiling and crumpling up the work
as to make their original order considerably a puzzle, I have
begun anew to paint over the rough surface with thick coatings of grauwacke and grauwacke-slate. When this part of
the operation was completed, I have again begun to break up
and grind down,—here letting a tract of grauwacke sink into
the broken primary,—there wearing it off the surface altogether,—yonder elevating the original granitic *hard-cast* till
it rose over all the coatings, Primary and Palæozoic. And
then I have begun to paint yet a third time with a thick Old
Red Sandstone pigment ; and yet again to break up and wear
down,—here to insert a tenon of the Old Red deep into a
mortise of the grauwacke, as at Gamrie,—there to dovetail it
into the clay-slate, as at Tomantoul,—yonder, after laying it
across the upturned quartz-rock, as at Cullen, to rub by much
the greater part of it away again, leaving but mere remainder-
patches and fragments, to mark where it had been. Lastly,
if I had none of the superior Palæozoic or Secondary formations to deal with, I have brushed over the whole, by way of
finish, with the variously-derived coatings of the superficial
deposits ; and thus, as I have said, I have often completed,
in idea, after the chance suggestion of the old painter's shop,
my portable models of the geology of disturbed districts like
the Banffshire one. The deposits of Moray are greatly less
broken. Denudation has partially worn them down ; but
they seem to have almost wholly escaped the previous crumpling process.

CHAPTER IV.

The prevailing yellow hue of the Elgin houses strikes the eye of the geologist who has travelled northwards from the Frith of Forth. He takes leave of a similar stone at Cupar-Fife,—a warmly-tinted yellow sandstone, peculiarly well suited for giving effect to architectural ornament; and after passing along the deep-red sandstone houses of the shires of Angus and Kincardine, and the gneiss, granite, hyperstene, and mica-schist houses of Aberdeen and Banff shires, he again finds houses of a deep red on crossing the Spey, and houses of a warm yellow tint on reaching Elgin,—geologically the Cupar-Fife of the north. And the story that the coloured buildings tell him is, that he has been passing, though by a somewhat circuitous route of a hundred and fifty miles, over an anticlinal geological section,—*down* in the scale till he reached Aberdeen and had gone a little beyond it, and then *up* again, until at Elgin he arrives at the same superior yellow bed of Old Red Sandstone which he had quitted at Cupar-Fife. Both beds contain the same organisms. The Holoptychius of Dura Den, near Cupar, must have sprung from the same original as the Holoptychius of the Hospital and Bishop-Mill quarries near Elgin; and it seems not improbable that the two beds, thus identical in their character and contents, may have existed, ere the upheaval of the Grampians broke their continuity, as an extended deposit, at the bottom of the same sea. But with this last and newest of the formations of the Old Red Sandstone the identity of the deposits to the south and north ceases. The strata which in the south overlie the yellow bed of the Holoptychius represent the Carboniferous period; the overlying strata in the north represent the Oolitic one. On the one side the miner sinks his shaft, and finds a true coal, composed of the Stigmaria, Calamites, Club-mosses, Ferns, and Araucarians of the Palæozoic era; he sinks his shaft on the other side, and finds but thin seams of an imperfect lignite, composed of the Cycadeæ, Pines, Sphenopteri, and Clathraria of the Secondary period. The flora which found its subsoil in the Old Red Sandstone north of the Grampians belonged to a scene of things so much more modern than the flora which found its subsoil in the Old Red Sandstone of the south, that all its productions were green and flourishing, waving beside lake, river, and sea, at a time when the productions of the other were locked up, as now, in sand and shale, lime and clay,—the dead mummies of ages long departed.

Another thoroughly wet morning! varied only from the morning of the preceding day by the absence of wind, and the greater weight of the persevering vertical rain, that leaped upwards in myriads of dancing little pyramids from the surface of every pool. I walked out under cover of my umbrella, to renew my acquaintance with the outlier of the Weald at Linksfield, and ascertain what sort of section it now presented under the quarrying operations of the lime-burners. There was, however, little to be seen; the bands of green and blue clays, alternating with strata of fossiliferous limestone, and layers of a gray shale thickly charged with minute shells of Cypris, were sadly blurred this morning by the trail of numerous slips from above, which had fallen during the rains, and softened into mud as they rushed down-

---

imperfect lignite: presumably the coal, of Jurassic age, then mined at Brora in Sutherland; Sphenopteri, more usually *Sphenopteris*, the foliage of a seed-fern, and Clathraria, an old term for a poorly preserved fossil plant, are Carboniferous forms, but Miller used these terms in the context of the 'Oolite' or Jurassic – perhaps a slip on his part

wards athwart the face of the quarry; and the arched band
of boulder-clay which so mysteriously underlies the deposit
was, save in a few parts, wholly covered up by the debris.
The occurrence of the clay here as an inferior bed, with but
the cornstone of the Old Red beneath, and all the beds of
the Weald resting over it, forms a riddle somewhat difficult
of solution; but it is palpably not reading it aright to regard
the deposit, with at least one geologist who has written on
the subject, as older than the rocks above. It is, on the contrary, as a vast amount of various and unequivocal evidence
demonstrates, incalculably more modern; nay, we find proof
of the fact here in that very bed which has been instanced
as rendering it doubtful: the clay of which the interpolation
is composed is found to contain fragments, not only of the
cornstone on which it rests, but also of the Wealden limestone and shales which it underlies. It forms the mere filling up of a flat-roofed cavern, or rather of two flat-roofed caverns,—for the limestone roof dipped in the centre to the
cornstone floor,—which, previous to the times of the boulder
clay, had lain open in what was then, as now, an old-world
deposit, charged with long extinct organisms, but which, during the iceberg period, was penetrated and occupied by the
clay, as run lime penetrates and occupies the interstices of a
dry-stone wall. It was no day for gathering fossils. I saw
a few ganoid scales, washed by the rain from the investing
rubbish, glittering on fragments of the limestone, with a few
of the characteristic shells of the deposit, chiefly Unionidæ;
but nothing worth bringing away. The adhesive clay of the
Weald, widely scattered by the workmen, and wrought into
mortar by the beating rains, made it a matter of some difficulty for the struggling foot to retain the shoe, and, sticking
to my soles by pounds at a time, rendered me obnoxious to
the old English nickname of "rough-footed Scot." And so,
after traversing the heaps, somewhat like a fly in treacle, I

---

mere filling up: see Additional Note for p. 199

had to yield to the rain above and the mud beneath, and to return to do in Elgin what cannot be done equally well in almost any other town of its size in Scotland,—pursue my geological inquiries under cover.

On this, as on other occcasions, I was struck by the complex and very various forms assumed by the ganoid scales of the Wealden. Throughout the Oolitic system generally, including the Lias, there obtains a singular complexity of type in these little glittering tiles of enamelled bone, which contrasts strongly with the greatly more simple style which obtained among the ganoids of the Palæozoic period. In many of these last, as in the Cœlacanth family, including the genera Holoptychius, Asterolepis, and Glyptolepis, in all their many species, with at least one genus of Dipterians, the genus Dipterus, the external outline and arrangement of scale was as simple as in any of the Cycloid family of the present time. Like slates on a roof, each single scale covered two, and was covered by two in turn ; and the only point of difference which existed in relation to the *laying down* of these massy *slates* of *bone*, and the laying down of the very thin ones of *horn* which cover fish such as the carp or salmon, was, that in the massier *slates*, the sides, or *cover*,—nicely bevelled, in order to preserve an equability of thickness throughout,—were so adjusted, that two scales at their edges, where they lay the one over the other, were not thicker than one scale at its centre. Even in the other ganoids, their contemporaries, such as the Osteolepis and Diplopterus, where the scales were ranged more in the tile fashion, side by side, there was, with much ingenious carpentry in the fitting, a general simplicity of form. It would almost appear, however, that ere the ganoid order reached the times of the Weald, the simple forms had been exhausted, and that nature, abhorring repetition, and ever stamping upon the scales some specific characteristic of the creature that bore them, was

---

Coelacanth family: a grouping of predatory bony fishes (today, however, with its meaning much more narrowly restricted to the true coelacanths); Asterolepis: see Additional Notes

obliged to have recourse to forms of a more complex and involved outline.   These latter-day scales send out nail-like
spikes laterally and atop, to lay hold of their neighbours, and
exhibit in their under sides grooves that accommodated the
nails sent out, in turn, by their neighbours, to lay hold upon
them.   Their forms, too, are indescribably various and fantastic.   It seems curious enough, that immediately after this
extremely *artificial* state of things, if I may so speak, the
two prevailing orders of the fish of the present day, the Cy-
cloids and Ctenoids, should have been ushered upon the scene,
and more than the original simplicity of scale restored.   There
took place a sudden re-action, from the fantastic and the complex to the simple and the plain.

It is further worthy of notice, that though many of the
ganoid scales of the Secondary systems, including those of
the Wealden, glitter as brightly in burnished enamel as the
more splendent scales of the Old Red Sandstone and Coal
Measures, there is a curious peculiarity exhibited in the structure of many of the older scales of the highly enamelled class,
which, so far as I have yet seen, does not extend beyond the
Palæozoic period.   The outer layer of the scale, which lies
over a middle layer of a cellular cancellated structure, and
corresponds, apparently, with that scarf-skin which in the human subject overlies the *rete mucosum,* is thickly set over
with microscopic pores, funnel-shaped in the transverse section, and which, examined by a good glass, in the horizontal
one resemble the puncturings of a sieve.   The Megalichthys
of the Coal Measures, with its various carboniferous congeners, with the genera Diplopterus, Dipterus, and Osteolepis
of the Old Red Sandstone,—all brilliantly enamelled fish,—
are thickly pore-covered.   But whatever purpose these pores
may have served, it seems in the Secondary period to have
been otherwise accomplished, if, indeed, it continued to exist.
It is a curious circumstance, that in no case do the pores seem

to pass *through* the scale.   Whatever their use, they existed merely as communications between the cells of the middle cancellated layer and the surface.   In a fish of the Chalk,— *Macropoma Mantelli,*—the exposed fields of the scales are covered over with apparently hollow, elongated cylinders, as the little tubes in a shower-bath cover their round field of tin, save that they lie in a greatly flatter angle than the tubes ; but I know not that, like the pores of the Dipterians and the Megalichthys, they communicated between the interior of the scale and its external surface.   Their structure is at any rate palpably different, and they bear no such resemblance to the pores of the human skin as that which the Palæozoic pores present.

The amount of design exhibited in the scales of some of the more ancient ganoids,—design obvious enough to be clearly read,—is very extraordinary.   A single scale of *Holoptychius Nobilissimus,*—fast locked up in its red sandstone rock, —laid by, as it were, for ever,—will be seen, if we but set ourselves to unravel its texture, to form such an instance of nice adaptation of means to an end as might of itself be sufficient to confound the atheist.   Let me attempt placing one of these scales before the reader, in its character as a flat counter of bone, of a nearly circular form, an inch and a half in diameter, and an eighth-part of an inch in thickness ; and then ask him to bethink himself of the various means by which he would impart to it the greatest possible degree of strength.   The human skull consists of two tables of solid bone, an inner and an outer, with a spongy cellular substance interposed between them, termed the *diploe ;* and such is the effect of this arrangement, that the blow which would fracture a continuous wall of bone has its force broken by the spongy intermediate layer, and merely injures the outer table, leaving not unfrequently the inner one, which more especially protects the brain, wholly unharmed.   Now, such also was the arrangement in the scale of the *Holoptychius Nobilissimus*. It consisted of its two well-marked tables of solid bone, corresponding in their dermal character, the outer to the cuticle, the inner to the true skin, and the intermediate cellular layer to the *rete mucosum;* but bearing an unmistakeable analogy also, as a mechanical contrivance, to the two plates and the *diploe* of the human skull. To the strengthening principle of the two tables, however, there were two other principles added. Cromwell, when commissioning for a new helmet, his old one being, as he expresses it, "ill set," ordered his friend to send him a "*fluted pot,*" *i. e.,* a helmet ridged and furrowed on the surface, and suited to break, by its protuberant lines, the force of a blow, so that the vibrations of the stroke would reach the body of the metal deadened and flat. Now, the outer table of the scale of the Holoptychius was a "fluted pot." The alternate ridges and furrows which ornamented its surface served a purpose exactly similar with that of the flutes and fillets of Cromwell's helmet. The inner table was strengthened on a different but not less effective principle. The human stomach consists of three coats ; and two of these, the outermost or peritoneal coat, and the middle or muscular coat, are so arranged, that the fibres of the one cross at nearly right angles those of the other. The violence which would tear the compact sides of this important organ along the fibres of the outer coat, would be checked by the transverse arrangement of the fibres of the middle coat, and *vice versa.* We find the cotton manufacturer weaving some of his stronger fabrics on a similar plan ;—they also are made to consist of two *coats ;* and what is technically termed the *tear* of the upper is so disposed that it lies at an angle of forty-five degrees with the *tear* of the coat which lies underneath. Now, the inner table of the scale of the Holoptychius was composed, on this principle, of various layers or coats, arranged the one over the other, so that the fibres of each lay at right angles with the fibres of the others in immediate contact with it. In the inner table of one scale I reckon nine of these alternating, variously-disposed layers ; so that any application of violence, which, in the language of the lath-splitter, would *run lengthwise along the grain* of four of them, would be checked by the *cross grain* in five. In other words, the line of the *tear* in five of the layers was ranged at right angles with the line of the *tear* in four. There were thus in a single scale, in order to secure the greatest possible amount of strength,—and who can say what other purposes may have been secured besides ?—three distinct principles embodied,—the principle of the two tables and *diploe* of the human skull,—the principle of the variously arranged coats of the human stomach,—and the principle of Oliver Crom- well's "fluted pot." There have been elaborate treatises written on those ornate flooring-tiles of the classical and mid- dle ages, that are occasionally dug up by the antiquary amid monastic ruins, or on the sites of old Roman stations. But did any of them ever tell a story half so instructive or so strange as that told by the incalculably more ancient ganoid *tiles* of the Palæozoic and Secondary periods ?

I called, on my way back from Linksfield, upon my old friend Mr Patrick Duff, and was introduced once more to his exquisite collection, with its unique ichthyolites of at least two genera of fishes of the Old Red,—the *Stagonolepis* and *Placothorax* of Agassiz,—which up to the present time are to be seen nowhere else ; and various other fine specimens of rare species, which, having sat for their portraits, have their forms preserved in the great work of the naturalist of Neufchatel. He showed me, with some triumph, one of his later acquisitions,—a fine specimen of Holoptychius from the upper yellow sandstone of Bishop-Mill, which exhibits the dorsal ridge covered with a line of large overlapping scales, not at all unlike those overlapping plates which cover the

portraits: paintings, for instance by Jonathan Stiven (c. 1799-1872), drawing master at Elgin Academy, which were used, eventually, as the masters for lithographic illustrations in the final publications – and see p. 208 for a mention of a photograph used in this way (Andrews 1982); the great work: Agassiz (1844-1845), *Poissons fossiles du Vieux Grès Rouge* ('Fossil fishes of the Old Red Sandstone') (Andrews 1982) tail of the lobster ; for which, by the way, they were mistaken by the workman who first laid the fossil open.   I examined, too, with some interest, fragments of a gigantic species of Pterichthys, belonging to an inferior division of the same Upper Old Red formation as the yellow stone, designated by Agassiz *Pterichthys major*, which must have attained to at least thrice the size, linearly, of even its bulkier congeners of the Lower formation of the Coccosteus.   After examining many a drawer, stored, from the deposits of the neighbourhood, with characteristic fossils of the Lias, the Weald, and the Oolite, and of the Upper and Lower Old Red, we set out together to expatiate amid the treasures of the Town Museum.

Among other recent additions to the Museum, there is an interesting set of the fishes of the Ganges, the donation of a gentleman long resident in India, to which Mr Duff called my attention, as illustrative, in some of the specimens, of the more characteristic ichthyolites of the Old Red Sandstone. One numerous family, the Pimelodi, abundantly represented in the Gangetic region, in not only the rivers, but also the ponds, tanks, and estuaries of the district, is certainly worthy the careful study of the geologist.   It approaches nearer, in some of its more strongly-marked genera, to the Coccosteus of the Lower Old Red, than any other tribe of existing fishes which I have yet seen.   The body of the Pimelodus, from the anterior dorsal downwards, is as naked as that of the eel ; whereas the head, and in several of the species the back, is armed with strong plates of naked bone, curiously fretted, as in many of the ichthyolites of the Lower, and more especially of the Upper Old Red Sandstone, into ridges of confluent tubercles, that radiate from the centre to the edges of the plates.   The dorsal plate, too, when detached, as in many of the species, from the plates of the head, bears upon its inner side a strong central ridge, that deepens as it descends, till it abruptly terminates a little short of the termination of the plate, exactly as in the dorsal plate of Coccosteus, which sunk its central ridge deep into the back of the animal. The point of resemblance to be mainly noticed, however, is the contrast furnished by the powerful armature of the head and back, with the unprotected nakedness of the posterior portions of the creature ;—a point specially noticeable in the Coccosteus, and apparent also, though in a lesser degree, in some of the other genera of the Old Red, such as the Pterichthyes and Asterolepides. From the snout of the Coccosteus down to the posterior termination of the dorsal plate, the creature was cased in strong armour, the plates of which remain as freshly preserved in the ancient rocks of the country as those of the Pimelodi of the Ganges on the shelves of the Elgin Museum ; but from the pointed termination of the plate immediately over the dorsal fin, to the tail, comprising more than one half the entire length of the animal, all seems to have been exposed, without the protection of even a scale, and there survives in the better specimens only the internal skeleton of the fish and the ray-bones of the fins. It was armed, like a French dragoon, with a strong helmet and a short cuirass ; and so we find its remains in the state in which those of some of the soldiers of Napoleon's old guard, that had been committed unstripped to the earth, may be dug up in the future on the fatal field of Borodino, or along the banks of the Dwina or the Wap. The cuirass lies still attached to the helmet, but we find only the naked skeleton attached to the cuirass. The Pterichthys to its strong helmet and cuirass added a posterior armature of comparatively feeble scales, as if, while its upper parts were shielded with plate armour, a lighter covering of ring or scale armour sufficed for the less vital parts beneath. In the Asterolepis the arrangement was somewhat similar, save that the plated cuirass was wanting : it was a strongly helmed warrior in slight scale armour ;

Asterolepides: *Asterolepis* and its relatives – but see note for p. 282; **dragoon**: see Additional Notes; **Borodino**: inconclusive battle of 1812 between Napoleon's *Grande Armée* and the Russian army under Kutuzov; **Dwina**: River Dvina, in what is now Belarus and Latvia; **Wap**: possible error for the nearby River Zap; **posterior armature**: *ie* scales covering the fish's rear body and tail for the disproportion between the strength of the plated head-piece and that of the scaly coat was still greater than in the Pterichthys. The occipital star-covered plates are, in some of the larger specimens, fully three-quarters of an inch in thickness, whereas the thickness of the delicately-fretted scales rarely exceeds a line.

Why this disproportion between the strength of the armature in different parts of the same fish should have obtained, as in Pterichthys and Asterolepis, or why, while one portion of the animal was strongly armed, another portion should have been left, as in Coccosteus, wholly exposed, cannot of course be determined by the mere geologist. His rocks present him with but the fact of the disproportion, without accounting for it. But the natural history of existing fish, in which, as in the Pimelodi, there may be detected a similar peculiarity of armature, may perhaps throw some light on the mystery. In Hamilton's "Fishes of the Ganges" I find but little reference made to the instincts and habits of the animals described : their deep-river haunts lie, in many cases, beyond the reach of observation ; and of the observations actually made, the descriptive naturalist, intent often on mere peculiarities of structure, is not unfrequently too careless. Hamilton describes the habitats of the various Indian species of Pimelodi, whether brackish estuaries, ponds, or rivers, but not their characteristic instincts. Of the Silurus, however, a genus of the same great family, I read elsewhere that some of the species, such as the *Silurus glanis*, being unwieldy in their motions, do not pursue their prey, which consists of small fishes, but lie concealed among the mud, and seize on the chance stragglers that come their way. And of the *Pimelodus gulio*, a little, strongly-helmed fish, with a naked body, I was informed by Mr Duff, on the authority of the gentleman who had presented the specimens to the Museum, that it burrowed in the holes of muddy banks, from which it shot out its armed head, and arrested, as they passed, the minute animals on which it preyed. The animal world is full of such compensatory defences : there is a half-suit of armour given to shield half the body, and a wise instinct to protect the rest. The *Pholas crispata* cannot shut its valves so as to protect its anterior parts, without raising them from off those parts which lie behind : like the Irishman in the haunted house, who attempted lengthening his blanket by cutting strips from the top and sewing them on to the bottom, it loses at the one end what it gains at the other ; but, hemmed round by the solid walls of the recess which it is its nature to hollow out for itself in shale or stone, the interior parts, though uncovered by the shell, are not exposed. By closing its valves anteriorly, it shuts the door of its little house, made, like that of the coney-folk of Scripture, in the rock ; and then, of the entire cell in which it dwells so secure, what is not shut door is impregnable wall. The remark of Paley, that the "human animal is the only one which is naked, and the only one which can clothe itself," is by no means quite correct. One half the hermit crab is as naked as the "human animal," and even less fitted for exposure ; for it consists of a thin-skinned, soft, unmuscular bag, filled with delicate viscera ; but not even the human animal is more skilful in clothing himself in the spoils of other animals than the hermit crab in wrapping up its naked bag in the strong shell of some dead fusus or buccinum, which it carries about with it in all its peregrinations, as at once clothes, armour, and house. Nature arms its front, and it is itself wise enough to arm its rear. Now, it seems not improbable that the half-armed Coccosteus, a heavy fish, indifferently furnished with fins, may have burrowed, like the recent *Silurus glanis* or *Pimelodus gulio*, in a thick mud,— of the existence of which in vast quantity, during the times of the Old Red Sandstone, the dark Caithness flagstones, the fetid breccia of Strathpeffer, and the gray stratified clays of

---

coney-folk of the Scripture: rock hyraxes rather than rabbits – 'which make their houses in the rocks' (Bible, Proverbs 30:24); **Paley**: William Paley (1743-1805), author of *Natural Theology*, the classic statement of the argument for divine creation from the design of living animals; 'human animal ...': Paley (1809, p. 213); **burrowed**: not current thinking today – but a serious hypothesis all the same

Cromarty, Moray, and Banff, unequivocally testify; and that it may have thus not only succeeded in capturing many of its light-winged contemporaries, which it would have vainly pursued in open sea, but may have been enabled also to present to its enemies, when assailed in turn, only its armed portions, and to protect its unarmed parts in its burrow. It is further worthy of notice, that many of the Pimelodi are furnished with spines, not, like those ichthyodorulites which occur so frequently in the older Secondary and Palæozoic divisions, unfinished in appearance at their lower extremity, as if, like the spines of the ancient Acanthodi, or those of the recent dog-fish *(Spinax acanthias)*, they had been simply embedded in the flesh, but bearing, like the wings of the Pterichthys, an articulated aspect. Those of the *Pimelodus rita* and *Pimelodus gagata* are of singular beauty; and when the creatures have no further use for them, and the mud of the Ganges has been consolidated into shale or baked into flagstone around them, they will make very exquisite fossils. A correct drawing of the plates and spines of some of the members of the Pime-lodi family, with a portion of the internal skeletons, arranged in their proper places, but divested of those more destructible parts to which they are attached, would serve admirably to show what strange forms fish not greatly removed from the ordinary type may assume in the fossil state, and might throw some light on the extraordinary appearance assumed, as ichthyolites, by the old family of the Cephalaspians.

The geological department of the Elgin Museum is not yet very complete. The private collections of the locality, by forestalling, greatly restrict the supply from the rich deposits in the neighbourhood, and have an unquestioned right to do so. The Museum contains, however, several interesting organisms. I saw, among the others, a specimen of Diplop-terus, that showed the form and position of the fins of this rather rare ichthyolite much better than any of the Moray-

---

articulated: *ie* properly jointed to the skeleton; **Cephalaspians**: *Cephalaspis* and related fishes, in the sense of Louis Agassiz who grouped the fish *Cephalaspis* (now *Zenaspis*) with *Coccosteus*, amongst other fishes, in the Cephalaspidae. Nowadays they are placed in completely different groups, *Zenaspis* being a jawless fish ('agnathan') and *Coccosteus* a jawed fish and a placoderm (Janvier 2003)

shire specimens portrayed by Agassiz in his great work; and
beside it, one of the two specimens of *Pterichthys oblongus*
which he figures, and on which he establishes the species. The
other individual,—a Cromarty specimen,—graces my little
collection.   The gloomy day passed pleasantly in decipher-
ing, with so accomplished a geologist as Mr Duff, these curious
hieroglyphics of the old world, that tell such wonderful stories,
and in comparing *viva voce*, as we were wont to do long years
before in lengthy epistles, our respective notions regarding
the true key for laying open their more occult meanings. And,
after sharing with him in his family dinner, I again took my
seat on the mail, as a chill, raw evening was falling, and rode
on, some six or eight and twenty miles, to Campbelton. The
rain pattered drearily through the night on my bed-room window ; and as frequent exposure to the wet had begun to tell
on a constitution not altogether so strong as it had once been,
I awakened oftener than was quite comfortable, to hear it.
The morning, however, was dry, though gray and sunless ;
and, taking an early breakfast at the inn, I traversed the flat
gravelly points of Ardersier and Fortrose, that, projecting
like moles far into the Frith, narrow the intervening ferry
to considerably less than one-third the width which it would
present were they away.   The origin of these long detrital
promontories, which form, when viewed from the heights on
either side, so peculiar a feature in the landscape, and which,
were they directly opposite, instead of being set down a mile
awry, would shut up the opening altogether, has not yet been
satisfactorily accounted for.   One special theory assigns their
formation to the agency of the descending tide, striking in
zig-gig style, in consequence of some peculiarity of the coast-
line or of the bottom, from side to side of the Frith, and de-
positing a long trail of sand and gravel, at nearly right angles
with the beach, first on the one shore and then on the other.
But why the tide, which runs in various zig-zag crossings in

the course of the Frith, should have the effect here, and nowhere else, of raising two vast mounds, each a full mile and
a quarter in length, with an average breadth of from two to
five furlongs, is by no means very apparent. Certainly the
present tides of the Frith could not have formed them, nor
could they have been elevated to their present average height
of ten or twelve feet over the flood-line in a sea standing at
the existing level. If they in reality originated in this cause,
it must have been ere the latter upheavals of the land or re-
cessions of the sea, when the great Caledonian Valley existed
as a narrow ocean sound, swept by powerful currents. Upon
another and entirely different hypothesis, these flat promontories have been regarded as the remains, levelled by the
waves, and gapped direct in the middle by the tide, of a vast
transverse morain of the great valley, belonging to the same
glacial age as the lateral morains some ten or fifteen miles
higher up, that extend from the immediate neighbourhood of
Inverness to the mansion-house of Dochfour. But this hypothesis, like the other, is not without its difficulties. Why, for
instance, should the promontories be a mile awry? There is,
however, yet another mode of accounting for their formation,
which I am not in the least disposed to criticise.

They were constructed, says tradition, through the agency
of the arch-wizard Michael Scott. Michael had called up the
hosts of Faery to erect the cathedral of Elgin and the cha-
nonry kirk of Fortrose, which they completed from foundation to ridge, each in a single night,—committing, in their
hurry, merely the slight mistake of locating the building intended for Elgin in Fortrose, and that intended for Fortrose
in Elgin ; but, their work over and done, and when the magician had no further use for them, they absolutely refused to
be *laid ;* and, like a *posse* of Irish labourers thrown out of
a job, came thronging round him, clamouring for more employment. Fearing lest he should be torn in pieces,—a ca-

---

great valley: Great Glen

tastrophe which has not unfrequently happened in such circumstances in the olden time, and of which those recent philan-
thropists who engage themselves in finding work for the unemployed may have perhaps entertained some little dread in
our own days,—he got rid of them for the time by setting
them off in a body to run a mound across the Moray Frith
from Fortrose to Ardersier.   Toiling hard in the evening of
a moonlight night, they had proceeded greatly more than two-
thirds towards the completion of the undertaking, when a
luckless Highlander passing by bade God-speed the work,
and, by thus breaking the charm, arrested at once and for
ever the construction of the mound, and saved the navigation of Inverness.

I stood for a few seconds at the Burn of Rosemarkie, un-
decided whether I should take the Scarfs-Craig road,—a break-
neck path which runs eastwards along the cliffs, and which,
though the rougher, is the more direct Cromarty line of the
two,—or the considerably better though longer line of the
White Bog, which strikes upwards along the burn in a westerly direction, and joins the Cromarty and Inverness highway
on the moor of the Maolbuie.   I had got into a part of the
country where every little locality, and every more striking
feature in the landscape, has its associated tradition; and the
pause of a few moments at the two roads recalled to my memory the details of a ghost-story, long regarded in the district in which it was best known as one of the most authentic of its class, but which seems by no means inexplicable on
natural principles.*

* The story here referred to is narrated in "Scenes and Legends of the
North of Scotland," chap. xxv.

CHAPTER V.

ROSEMARKIE, with its long narrow valley and its red abrupt *scaurs,** is chiefly interesting to the geologist for its vast beds of the boulder-clay. I am acquainted with no other locality in the kingdom where this deposit is hollowed into ravines so profound, or presents precipices so imposing and lofty. The clay lies thickly over most part of the Black Isle and the peninsula of Easter Ross,—both soft sandstone districts,—bearing everywhere an obvious relation, as a deposit, to both the form and the conditions of exposure of the existing land,— just as the accumulated snow of a long-lying snow-storm, exposed to the drifting wind, bears relation to the heights and hollows of the tracts which it covers. On the higher eminences the clay forms a comparatively thin stratum, and in not a few instances it has been wholly worn away ; while on the lower grounds, immediately over the old coast line, and in the sides of hollow valleys,—exactly such places as we might expect to see the snow occupying most deeply after a night of drift,—we find it accumulated in vast beds of from eighty to an hundred feet in thickness. One of these occurs in the opening of the narrow valley along which my course this morning lay, and is known far and wide,—for it forms a

---

* *Scaur*, Scotice, a precipice of clay. There is no single English word that conveys exactly the same idea.

marked feature in the landscape, and harbours in its recesses
a countless multitude of jackdaws,—as the "Kaes' Craig of
Rosemarkie." It presents the appearance of a hill that had
been cut sheer through the middle from top to base, and exhibits in its abrupt front a broad red perpendicular section of
at least a hundred feet in height, barred transversely by thin
layers of sand, and scored vertically by the slow action of the
rains.   Originally it must have stretched its vanished limb
across the opening, like some huge snow-wreath accumulated athwart a frozen rivulet ; but the incessant sweep of the
stream that runs through the valley has long since amputated
and carried it away ; and so only half the hill now remains.
The Keas' Craig resembles in form a lofty chalk cliff, square,
massy, abrupt, with no sloping fillet of vegetation bound
across its brow, but precipitous direct from the hill-top.   The
little ancient village of Rosemarkie stretches away from its
base on the opposite side of the stream ; and on its summit,
and along its sides, groupes of chattering jackdaws, each one
of them as reflective and philosophic as the individual immortalized by Cowper, look down high over the chimneys into
the streets.   The clay presents here, more than in almost any
other locality with which I am acquainted, the character of
a stratified deposit ; and the numerous bands of sand by which
the cliff is horizontally streaked from top to bottom we find
hollowed, as we approach, into a multitude of circular openings, like shot-holes in an old tower, which form breeding
places for the daw and the sand-martin.   The biped inhabitants of the cliff are greatly more numerous than the biped
inhabitants of the quiet little hamlet below ; and on Fortrose
fair-days, when, in virtue of an old feud, the Rosemarkie boys
were wont to engage in formidable bickers with the boys of
Cromarty, I remember, as one of the invading belligerents,
that, in bandying names with them in the fray, we delighted
to bestow upon them, as their hereditary sobriquet, given, of

---

individual immortalised by Cowper: in his poem 'The Jackdaw', in the collection
'Translations from Vincent Bourne'; Keas': not the New Zealand birds but an error for
Kaes', ie Jackdaws'

course, in allusion to their feathered neighbours, the designation of the "*Rosemarkie kaes.*" Cromarty, however, is two-thirds surrounded by the waters of a frith abounding in sea-fowl; and the little fellows of Rosemarkie, indignant at being classed with their *kaes*, used to designate us with hearty emphasis, in turn, as the "*Cromarty cooties,*" *i. e.* coots.

A little higher up the valley, on the western side, there occurs in the clay what may be termed a *group* of excavations, composing a piece of scenery ruinously broken and dreary, and that bears a specific character of its own which scarce any other deposit could have exhibited. The excavations are of considerable depth and extent,—hollows out of which the materials of pyramids might have been taken. The precipitous sides are fretted by jutting ridges and receding inflections, that present in abundance their diversified alternations of light and shadow. The steep descents form cycloid curves, that flatten at their bases, and over which the ferruginous stratum of mould atop projects like a cornice. Between neighbouring excavations there stand up dividing walls, tall and thin as those of our city buildings, and in some cases broken at their upper edges into rows of sharp pinnacles or inaccessible turf-coped turrets; while at the bottom of the hollows, washed by the runnels which, in the slow lapse of years, have been the architects of the whole, we find cairn-like accumulations of water-rolled stones,—the disengaged pebbles and boulders of the deposit. The boulders and pebbles project also from the steep sides, at all heights and of all sizes, like the primary masses inclosed in our ancient conglomerates, when exhibited in wave-worn precipices,—forcing upon the mind the conclusion that the boulder-clay is itself but an unconsolidated conglomerate of the later periods, which occupies nearly the same relative position to the existing vegetable mould, with all its recent productions, that the great conglomerate of the Old Red Sandstone occupies in relation

---

ferruginous substratum of mould: presumably Miller means the iron pan layer in the subsoil; vegetable mould: topsoil to the lower ichthyolite beds of that system, with their numerous extinct organisms.   But its buried stones are fretted with hieroglyphic inscriptions, in the form of strange scratchings and polishings, grooves, ridges, and furrows,—always associated with the boulder-clays,—which those of the more ancient conglomerates want, and which, though difficult to read, seem at length to be yielding up the story which they record.   Of this, however, more anon.   Viewed by moonlight, when the pale red of the clay where the beam falls direct is relieved by the intense shadows, these excavations of the valley of Rosemarkie form scenes of strange and ghostly wildness : the projecting, buttress-like angles,—the broken walls,—the curved inflections,—the pointed pinnacles,—the turrets, with their masses of projecting coping,—the utter lack of vegetation, save where the heath and the furze rustle far above,—all combine to form assemblages of dreary ruins, amid which, in the solitude of night, one almost expects to see spirits walk.   These excavations have been designated from time immemorial, by the neighbouring town's-people, as " the Danes ;" but whether the name be, as is most probable, merely a corruption of an appropriate enough Saxon word, " the dens," or derived, as a vague tradition is said to testify, from the ages of Danish invasion, it is not quite the part of the geologist to determine.   It may be worth mentioning, however, from its bearing on the point, that there are two excavations in the boulder-clay near Cromarty, one of which has been long known by the name of " the Morial's Den ;" while the other, greatly smaller in size, rejoices in the double diminutive of " the Little Dennie."   For an hour or so the Danes proved agreeable though somewhat silent companions; and then, climbing the opposite side of the valley, I gained the high road, and, walking on to Cromarty, found myself once more among " the old familiar faces."

In a few days the storm blew by ; and as the prolonged

---

dens: narrow valleys and ravines, often wooded (Scots, cognate with 'dean' or 'dene') – not animal lairs; 'the old familiar faces': the title of Charles Lamb's poem of bittersweet nostalgia, the point being that these remembered faces are no longer all there. Miller might indeed have felt that 'Ghost-like, I paced round the haunts of my childhood' rains had cleared out the deep ravines of the district, and given to the boulder-clay in which they are scooped a freshness in its section analogous to fresh fracture in rocks of harder consistency, I availed myself of the facilities afforded me in consequence, for exploring it once more. It has long constituted one of the hardest of the many riddles with which our Scottish deposits exercise the patience and ingenuity of the geologist. I remember a time when, after passing a day under its barren *scaurs*, or hid in its precipitous ravines, I used to feel in the evening as if I had been travelling under the cloud of night, and had seen nothing. It was a morose and taciturn companion, and had no speculation in it. I might stand in front of its curved precipices, red, yellow, or gray, according to the prevailing average colour of the rocks on which it rests, and mark their water-rolled boulders, of all qualities and sizes, sticking out in bold relief from the surface, like the rock-like protuberances that roughen the rustic basements of the architect, from the line of the wall; but I had no *open sesame* to form vistas through them into the recesses of the past. I saw merely the stiff pasty matrix of which they are composed, and the inclosed pebbles. But the boulder-clay has of late become more sociable; and, though with much hesitancy and irresolution, like old Mr Spectator on the first formal opening of his mouth,—a consequence, doubtless, in both cases of previous habits of silence long indulged,—it begins to tell its story. And a most curious story it is.

The morning was clear, but just a little chill; and a soft covering of snow, that had fallen during the storm on the flat summit of Benwevis, and showed its extreme tenuity by the paleness of its tint of watery blue, was still distinctly visible at the distance of full twenty miles. The sun, low in the sky,—for the hour was early,—cast its slant rays athwart the prospect, giving to each nearer bank and hillock,

---

rustic basements: eighteenth century buildings in the New Town of Edinburgh in particular often have a basement level below pavement level, with small sunken 'areas' or open basements in front. The street façade of the basement level is often done in masonry of a roughened 'rusticated' style, commonly with a globular texture akin to a sack of potatoes; old Mr Spectator: see note for p. 210

and to the more distant protuberances on the mountain-sides, those well-defined accompaniments of shadow that serve, by throwing the minor features of a landscape upon the eye in bold relief, to impart to it an air of higher finish and more careful filling up than it ever bears under a more vertical light. I took the road which, leading westward from the town towards Invergordon Ferry, skirts the Frith on the one hand, and runs immediately under the noble escarpment of green bank formed by the old coast line on the other. Fully two-thirds of the entire height of the rampart here, which rises in all about a hundred feet over the sea-level, is formed of the boulder-clay; and I am acquainted with no locality in which the deposit presents more strongly, for at least the first half mile, one of its marked scenic peculiarities. It is furrowed vertically on the slope, as if by enormous flutings in the more antique Doric style; and the ridges by which these are separated,—each from a hundred to a hundred and fifty feet in length, and from five-and-twenty to thirty feet in average height,—resemble those burial mounds with which the sexton frets the churchyard turf; with this difference, however, that they seem the burial mounds of giants, tall and bulky as those that of old warred against the gods. They are striking enough to' have caught the eye of the children of the place, and are known among them as the Giants' Graves. I could fain have taken their portrait in a calotype this morning, as they lay against the green bank,—their feet to the shore, and their heads on the top of the escarpment,—like patients on a reclining bed, and strongly marked, each by its broad bar of yellow light and of dark shadow, like the ebon and ivory buttresses of the poet. This little vignette, I would have said to the landscape-painter, represents the boulder-clay, after its precipitous banks—worn down, by the frosts and rains of centuries, into parallel runnels, that gradually widened into these hollow grooves—had sunk into the angle of inclination at which the disintegrating agents ceased to operate, and the green sward covered all up. You must be studying these peculiarities of aspect more than ever you studied them before. There is a time coming when the connoisseur will as rigidly demand the specific character of the various geologic rocks and deposits in your hills, *scaurs*, and precipices, as he now demands specific character in your shrubs and trees.

It is worthy the notice of the young geologist, who has just set himself to study the various effects produced on the surface of a country by the deposits which lie under it, that for about a quarter of a mile or so, the base of the escarpment here is bordered by a line of bogs, that bear in the driest weather their mantling of green. They are fed with a perennial supply of water, by a range of deep-seated springs, that come bursting out from under the boulder-clay; and one of their number, which bears, I know not why, the name of Samuel's Well, and yields its equable flow at an equable temperature, summer and winter, into a stone trough by the wayside, is not a little prized by the town's-people, and the seamen that cast anchor in the opposite roadstead, for the lightness and purity of its water. What is specially worthy of notice in the case is, the very definite beginning and ending of the chain of bogs. All is dry at the base of the escarpment, up to the point at which they commence; and then all is equally dry at the point at which they terminate. And of exactly the same extent,—beginning where the bogs begin, and ending where they end,—we may trace an ancient stratum of pure sand, of considerable thickness, intercalated between the base of the clay and the superior surface of the Old Red Sandstone. It is through this permeable sand that the profoundly seated springs find their way to the surface,— for the clay is impermeable; and where it comes in contact with the rock on either side of the arenaceous stratum, the

bogs cease. The chain of green bogs is a consequence of the
stratum of permeable sand. I have in vain sought this ancient layer of sand,—decidedly of the same era with the argillaceous bed which overlies it,—for aught organic. A single shell, so unequivocally of the period of the boulder-clay
as to occur at the base of the deposit, would be worth, I have
said, whole drawerfuls of fossils furnished by the better-known
deposits. But I have since seen in abundance shells of the
boulder-clay.

There is another scenic peculiarity of the clay, which the
neighbourhood of Cromarty finely illustrates, and of which
my walk this morning furnished numerous striking instances.
The Giants' Graves—to borrow from the children of the
place—occur on the steep slopes of the old coast line, or in
the sides of ravines, where the clay, as I have said, had once
presented a precipitous front, but had been gradually moulded,
under the attritive influences of the elements, into series of
alternating ridges and furrows, which, when they had flattened into the proper angle, the green sward covered up from
further waste. But the deep dells and narrow ravines in
which many ranges of these graves occur are themselves peculiarities of the deposit. Wherever the boulder-clay lies
thick and continuous, as in the parish of Cromarty, on a sloping table-land, every minute streamlet cuts its way to the
solid rock at the bottom, and runs through a deep dell, either
softened into beauty by the disintegrating process, or with all
its precipices standing up raw and abrupt over the stream.
Four of these ravines, known as the "Old Chapel Burn," the
"Ladies' Walk," the "Morial's Den," and the "Red Burn,"
each of them cutting the escarpment of the ancient coast line
from top to base, and winding far into the interior, occur in
little more than a mile's space ; and they lie still more thickly farther to the west. These dells of the boulder-clay, in
their lower windings,—for they become shallower and tamer

---

aught organic: *ie* Miller was looking for any fossils

as they ascend, till they terminate in the uplands in mere *drains*, such as a ditcher might excavate at the rate of a shilling or two per yard,—are eminently picturesque. On those gentler slopes where the vegetable mould has had time and space to accumulate, we find not a few of the finest and tallest trees of the district. There is a bosky luxuriance in their more sheltered hollows, well known to the schoolboy what time the fern begins to pale its fronds, for their store of hips, sloes, and brambles ; and red over the foliage we may see, ever and anon as we wend upwards, the abrupt frontage of some precipitous *scaur*, suited to remind the geologist, from its square form and flat breadth of surface, of the cliffs of the chalk. When viewed from the sea, at the distance of a few miles, these ravines seem to divide the sloping tracts in which they occur into large irregular fields, laid out considerably more in accordance with the principles of the landscape gardener than the stiffly squared rectilinear fields of the agriculturist. They are *ha-has* of Nature's digging ; and their bottom and sides in this part of the country we still find occupied in a few cases—though in many more they have been ravaged by the wasteful axe—by noble forest-*hedges*, tall enough to overtop, in at least their middle reaches, the tracts of table-land which they divide.

I passed, a little farther on, the quarry of Old Red Sandstone, with a huge bank of boulder-clay resting over it, in which I first experienced the evils of hard labour, and first set myself to lessen their weight by becoming an observer of geological phenomena. It had been deserted apparently for many years ; and the debris of the clay partially covered up, in a sloping talus, the frontage of rock beneath. Old Red Sandstone and boulder-clay, a broad bar of each !—such was the compound problem which the excavation propounded to me when I first plied the tool in it,—a problem equally dark at the time in both its parts. I have since got on a very

---

ha-has: sunken ditches, often with a wall or **hedge** concealed in them, used in eighteenth century park landscaping to control animals, for instance to keep them off the lawns of a great house, without blocking the view with walls or fences. This is an apt metaphor for how dens dissect the rising plateau hereabouts little way with the Old Red portion of the task; but alas for the boulder-clay portion of it! A bar of impenetrable shadow has rested long and obstinately over the newer deposit; and I scarce know whether the light which is at length beginning to play on its pebbly front be that of the sun or of a delusive meteor. But courage, patient hearts! the boulder-clay will one day yield up *its* secret too. Still further on by a few hundred yards, I could have again found use for the calotype, in transferring to paper the likeness of a protuberant picturesque cliff, which, like the Giants' Graves, could have belonged, of all our Scotch deposits, to only the boulder-clay. It stands out, on the steep acclivity of a furze-covered bank, abrupt as a precipice of solid rock, and yet seamed by the rain into numerous divergent channels, with pyramidal peaks between; and, combining the perpendicularity of a true cliff with the water-scooped furrows of a yielding clay, it presents a peculiarity of aspect which strikes, by its grotesqueness, eyes little accustomed to detect the picturesque in landscape. I remember standing to gaze upon it when a mere child; and the fisher children of the neighbouring town still tell that "*it has been prophesied*" it will one day fall, "and kill a man and a horse on the road below,"—a legend which shows it must have attracted *their* notice too.

I selected as the special scene of exploration this morning, a deep ravine of the boulder-clay, which had been recently deepened still more by the waters of a mill-pond, that had burst during a thunder-shower, and, after scooping out for themselves a bed in the clay some twelve or fifteen feet deep, where there had been formerly merely a shallow drain, had then tumbled into the ravine, and bared it to rock. The sandstones of the district, soft and not very durable, show the scratched and polished surfaces but indifferently well, and, when exposed to the weather, soon lose them; but in the bottom of the runnel by which the ravine is swept I

---

boulder-clay: from now on to p. 322, without warning, Miller made a long and complex digression on the boulder clay, ranging as far as Caithness before returning to the Bay of Cromarty found them exceedingly well marked,—the polish as decided as the soft red stone could receive, and the lines of scratching running in their general bearing due east and west, at nearly right angles with the course of the stream. Wherever the rock had been laid bare during the last few months, *there* were the markings; wherever it had been laid bare for a few twelvemonths, they were gone. I next marked a circumstance which has now for several years been attracting my attention, and which I have found an invariable characteristic of the true boulder-clay. Not only do the rocks on which the deposit rests bear the scratched and polished surfaces, but in every instance the fragments of stone which it incloses bear the scratchings also, if from their character capable of receiving and retaining such markings, and neither of too coarse a grain nor of too hard a quality. If of limestone, or of a coherent shale, or of a close, finely-grained sandstone, or of a yielding trap, they are scratched and polished,—invariably on one, most commonly on both their sides; and it is a noticeable circumstance, that the lines of the scratchings occur, in at least nine cases out of every ten, in the lines of their longer axes. When decidedly oblong or spindle-shaped, the scratchings run lengthwise, preserving in most cases, on the under and upper sides, when both surfaces are scratched, a parallelism singularly exact; whereas, when of a broader form, so that the length and breadth nearly approximate,— though the lines generally find out the longer axis, and run in that direction,—they are less exact in their parallelism, and are occasionally traversed by cross furrows. Of such certain occurrence is this longitudinal lining on the softer and finer-grained pebbles of the boulder-clay, that I have come to regard it as that special characteristic of the deposit on which I can most surely rely for purposes of identification. I am never quite certain of the boulder-clay when I do not detect it, nor doubtful of the true character of the deposit

when I do.   When examining, for instance, the accumulation of broken Liasic materials in the neighbourhood of Banff,
I made it my first care to ascertain whether the bank inclosed fragments of stone or shale bearing the longitudinal markings ; and felt satisfied, on finding that it did, that I had discovered the period of its re-formation.

CHAPTER VI.

FOR the greater part of a quarter of a century I had been finding organisms in abundance in the boulder-clay, but never anything organic that unequivocally belonged to its own period.   I had ascertained that it contains in Ross and Cromarty nodules of the Old Red Sandstone, which bear inside, like so many stone coffins, their well laid out skeletons of the dead; but then the markings on their surface told me that when the boulder-clay was in the course of deposition, they had been exactly the same kind of nodules that they are now. In Moray, it incloses, I had found, organisms of the Lias; but *they* also testify that they present an appearance in no degree more ancient at the present time than they did when first enveloped by the clay.   In East and West Lothian too, and in the neighbourhood of Edinburgh, I had detected in it occasional organisms of the Mountain Limestone and the Coal Measures; but these, not less surely than its Liasic fossils in Moray, and its Old Red ichthyolites in Cromarty and Ross, belonged to an incalculably more ancient state of things than itself; and—like those shrivelled manuscripts of Pompeii or Herculaneum, which, whatever else they may record, cannot be expected to tell aught of the catastrophe that buried them up—they throw no light whatever on the deposit in which they occur.   I at length came to regard the boulder-clay—

for it is difficult to keep the mind in a purely blank state on any subject on which one thinks a good deal—as representative of a chaotic period of death and darkness, introductory, mayhap, to the existing scene of things.

After, however, I had begun to mark the invariable connection of the clay, as a deposit, with the dressed surfaces on which it rests, and the longitudinal linings of the pebbles and boulders which it incloses, and to associate it, in consequence, with an ice-charged sea and the Great Gulf Stream, it seemed to me extremely difficult to assign a reason why it should be thus barren of remains. Sir Charles Lyell states, in his " Elements," that the " stranding of ice-islands in the bays of Iceland since 1835 has driven away the fish for several successive seasons, and thereby caused a famine among the inhabitants of the country ;" and he argues from the fact, " that a sea habitually infested with melting ice, which would chill and freshen the water, might render the same uninhabitable by marine mollusca." But then, on the other hand, it is equally a fact that half a million of seals have been killed in a single season on the meadow-ice a little to the north of Newfoundland, and that many millions of cod, besides other fish, are captured yearly on the shores of that island, though grooved and furrowed by ice-floes almost every spring. Of the seal family it is specially recorded by naturalists, that many of the species "are from choice inhabitants of the margins of the frozen seas towards both poles ; and, of course, in localities in which many such animals live, some must occasionally die." And though the grinding process would certainly have disjointed, and might probably have worn down and partially mutilated, the bones of the amphibious carnivora of the boulder period, it seems not in the least probable,' judging from the fragments of loose-grained sandstone and soft shale which it has spared, that it would have wholly destroyed them. So it happened, however, that from North Berwick

---

'Elements': Charles Lyell's *Elements of Geology* (1838 and later editions), a recasting of part of his *Principles*; 'stranding …': Lyell (1841, I, p. 243); **amphibious carnivora**: here, seals and walruses

to the Ord Hill of Caithness, I had never found in the boulder-clay the slightest trace of an organism that could be held
to belong to itself ; and as it seems natural to build on negative evidence, if very extensive, considerably more than mere
negative evidence, whatever the circumstances, will carry, I
became somewhat sceptical regarding the very existence of
boulder-fossils,—a scepticism which the worse than doubtful
character of several supposed discoveries in the deposit served
considerably to strengthen. The clay forms, when cut by a
water-course, or assailed on the coast by some unusually high
tide, a perpendicular precipice, which in the course of years
slopes into a talus ; and as it exhibits in most instances no
marks of stratification, the clay of the talus—a mere re-formation of fragments detached by the frosts and rains from
the exposed frontage—can rarely be distinguished from that
of the original deposit. Now, in these consolidated slopes it
is not unusual to find remains, animal and vegetable, of no
very remote antiquity. I have seen a human skull dug out of
the reclining base of a clay-bank once a precipice, fully six
feet from under the surface. It might have been deemed the
skull of some long-lived contemporary of Enoch,—one of the
accursed race, mayhap,

" Who sinned and died before the avenging flood."

But, alas ! the labourer dug a little farther, and struck his
pickaxe against an old rybat that lay deeper still. There
could be no mistaking the character of the champfered edge,
that still bore the marks of the tool, nor that of the square
perforation for the lock-bolt; and a rising theory, that would
have referred the boulder-clay to a period in which the polar
ice, set loose by the waters of the Noachian deluge, came
floating southwards over the foundered land, straightway
stumbled against it, and fell. Both rybat and skull had come
from an ancient burying-ground, that occupies a projecting
angle of the table-land above. I must now state, however,

Enoch: in the Bible, one of those living before the Flood, literally 'antediluvian', living to
an inordinate age, in his case 365 years (Genesis 4:17, 5:18-24); 'Who sinned ...': see
Additional Notes; Noachian deluge: the Biblical Flood – a joke on Miller's part, as in
reality he did not ascribe the boulder clay to it (Miller 1857, pp. 267-350); 'ancient
burying-ground': almost certainly of St Regulus's chapel at the east end of Cromarty

that my scepticism has thoroughly given way ; and that, slowly yielding to the force of positive evidence, I have become
as assured a believer in the *comminuted recent shells* of the
boulder-clay as in the belemnites of the Oolite and Lias, or
the ganoid ichthyolites of the Old Red Sandstone.

I had marked, when at Wick, on several occasions, a thick
boulder-clay deposit occupying the southern side of the harbour, and forming an elevated platform, on which the higher
parts of Pulteneytown are built ; but I had noted little else
regarding it than that it bears the average dark-gray colour
of the flagstones of the district, and that some of the granitic
boulders which protrude from its top and sides are of vast
size.   On my last visit, however, rather more than two years
ago, when sauntering along its base, after a very wet morning,
awaiting the Orkney steamer, I was surprised to find, where
a small slip had taken place during the rain, that it was mottled over with minute fragments of shells.   These I examined,
and found, so far as, in their extremely broken condition, I
dared determine the point, that they belonged in such large
proportion to one species,—the *Cyprina islandica* of Dr Fleming,—that I could detect among them only a single fragment of any other shell,—the pillar, apparently, of a large
specimen of *Purpura lapillus*.   Both shells belong to that
class of old existences,—long descended, without the pride
of ancient descent,—which link on the extinct to the recent
scenes of being.   *Cyprina islandica* and *Purpura lapillus*
not only exist as living molluscs in the British seas, but they
occur also as crag-shells, side by side with the dead races that
have no place in the present fauna.   At this time, however,
I could but think of them simply in their character as recent
molluscs ; and as it seemed quite startling enough to find them
in a deposit which I had once deemed representative of a
period of death, and still continued to regard as obstinately
unfossiliferous, I next set myself to determine whether it really

was the boulder-clay in which they occurred. Almost the first pebble which I disengaged from the mass, however, settled the point, by furnishing the evidence on which for several years past I have been accustomed to settle it;—it bore in the line of its longer axis, on a polished surface, the freshly-marked grooves and scratchings of the iceberg era. Still, however, I had my doubts, not regarding the deposit, but the shells. Might they not belong merely to the talus of this bank of boulder-clay ?—a re-formation, in all probability, not *more* ancient than the elevation of the most recent of the old coast lines,—perhaps greatly less so. Meeting with an intelligent citizen of Wick, Mr John Cleghorn, I requested him to keep a vigilant eye on the shells, and to ascertain for me, when opportunity offered, whether they occurred deep in the deposit, or were restricted to merely the base of its exposed front. On my return from Orkney, he kindly brought me a small collection of fragments, exclusively, so far as I could judge, of *Cyprina islandica,* picked up in fresh sections of the clay ; at the same time expressing his belief that they really belonged to the deposit as such, and were not accidental introductions into it from the adjacent shore. And at this point for nearly two years the matter rested, when my attention was again called to it by finding, in the publication of Mr Keith Johnston's admirable Geological Map of the British Islands, edited by Professor Edward Forbes, that other eyes than mine had detected shells in the boulder-clay of Caithness. "Cliffs of Pleistocene," says the Professor, in one of his notes attached to the map, "occur at Wick, containing boreal shells, especially *Astarte borealis.*"

I had seen the boulder-clay characteristically developed in the neighbourhood of Thurso ; but, during a rather hurried visit, had lacked time to examine it. The omission mattered the less, however, as my friend Mr Robert Dick is resident in the locality ; and there are few men who examine more

---

boreal: northern, here with connotations of Arctic forms which were evidence for the prevalence of cold climates when they were deposited; **Edward Forbes**: (1815–1854), important palaeontologist, geologist and marine biologist; *Cyprina islandica* (now *Arctica islandica*) and *Astarte borealis* are cold-water marine bivalves and fossils of them would be important evidence for cold climates during the Ice Ages

carefully or more perseveringly than he, or who can enjoy
with higher relish the sweets of scientific research.   I wrote
him regarding Professor Forbes's decision on the boulder-clay
of Wick and its shells ; urging him to ascertain whether the
boulder-clay of Thurso had not its shells also.   And almost
by return of post I received from him, in reply, a little packet·
of comminuted shells, dug out of a deposit of the boulder-
clay, laid open by the river Thorsa, a full mile from the sea,
and from eighty to a hundred feet over its level.   He had
detected minute fragments of shell in the clay about a twelvemonth before ; but a scepticism somewhat similar to my own,
added to the dread of being deceived by mere surface shells,
recently derived from the shore in the character of shell-sand,
or of the edible species carried inland for food, and then transferred from the ash-pit to the fields, had not only prevented
him from following up the discovery, but even from thinking
of it as such.   But he eagerly followed it up now, by visiting every bank of the boulder-clay in his locality within
twenty miles of Thurso, and found them all charged, from
top to bottom, with comminuted shells, however great their
distance from the sea, or their elevation over it.   The fragments lie thick along the course of the Thorsa, where the encroaching stream is scooping out the clay for the first time
since its deposition, and laying bare the scratched and furrowed pebbles.   They occur, too, in the depths of solitary
ravines far amid the moors, and underlie heath, and moss,
and vegetable mould, on the exposed hill-sides.   The farm-
house of Dalemore, twelve miles from Thurso as the crow
flies, and rather more than thirteen miles from Wick, occupies, as nearly as may be, the centre of the county ; and yet
there, as on the sea-shore, the boulder-clay is charged with
its fragments of marine shells.   Though so barren elsewhere
on the east coast of Scotland, the clay is everywhere in Caithness a shell-bearing deposit ; and no sooner had Mr Dick de-

termined the fact for himself, at the expense of many a fatiguing journey, and many an hour's hard digging, than he found that it had been ascertained long before, though, from the very inadequate style in which it had been recorded, science had in scarce any degree benefited by the discovery. In 1802 the late Sir John Sinclair, distinguished for his enlightened zeal in developing the agricultural resources of the country, and for originating its statistics, employed a mineralogical surveyor to explore the underground treasures of the district; and the surveyor's journal he had printed under the title of " Minutes and Observations drawn up in the course of a Mineralogical Survey of the County of Caithness, ann. 1802, by John Busby, Edinburgh." Now, in this journal there are frequent references made to the occurrence of marine shells in the blue clay. Mr Dick has copied for me the two following entries,—for the work itself I have never seen : —" 1802, Sept. 7th.—Surveyed down the river [Thorsa] to Geize ; found blue clay-marl, *intermixed with marine shells* in great abundance." " Sept. 12th.—Set off this morning for Dalemore. Bored for shell-marl in the ' grass-park ;' found it in one of the quagmires, but to no great extent. Bored for shell-marl in the ' house-park.' Surveyed by the side of the river, and found blue clay-marl in great plenty, *intermixed with marine shells, such as those found at Geize.* This place is supposed to be about twenty miles from the sea ; and is one instance, among many in Caithness, of *the ocean's covering the inland country at some former period of time.*"

The state of keeping in which the boulder-shells of Caithness occur is exactly what, on the iceberg theory, might be premised. The ponderous ice-rafts that went grating over the deep-sea bottom, grinding down its rocks into clay, and deeply furrowing its pebbles, must have borne heavily on its comparatively fragile shells. If rocks and pebbles did not escape, the shells must have fared but hardly. And very

---

the late Sir John Sinclair: of Ulbster (1754–1835), Caithness landowner, enthusiastic proponent of 'Improvement', first President of the Board of Agriculture, and editor of the first *Statistical Account of Scotland*

hardly they have fared : the rather unpleasant casualty of
being crushed to death must have been a greatly more common one in those days than in even the present age of railways and machinery.   The reader, by passing half a bushel
of the common shells of our shores through a barley-mill, as
a preliminary operation in the process, and by next subject-
ing the broken fragments thus obtained to the attritive influence of the waves on some storm-beaten beach for a twelvemonth or two, as a finishing operation, may produce, when he
pleases, exactly such a water-worn shelly debris as mottles
the blue boulder-clays of Caithness.   The proportion borne
by the fragments of one species of shell to that of all the
others is very extraordinary.   The *Cyprina islandica* is still
by no means a rare mollusc on our Scottish shores, and may,
on an exposed coast, after a storm, be picked up by dozens,
attached to the roots of the deep-sea tangle.   It is greatly
less abundant, however, than such shells as *Purpura lapillus,
Mytilus edule, Cardium edule, Littorina littorea,* and several
others ; whereas in the boulder-clay it is, in the proportion of
at least ten to one, more abundant than all the others put together.   The great strength of the shell, however, may have
in part led to this result ; as I find that its stronger and massier portions,—those of the umbo and hinge-joint,—are exceedingly numerous in proportion to its slimmer and weaker
fragments.   " The *Cyprina islandica,*" says Dr Fleming, in
his " British Animals," " is the largest British bivalve shell,
measuring sometimes thirteen inches in circumference, and,
exclusively of the animal, weighing upwards of nine ounces."
Now, in a collection of fragments of Cyprina sent me by Mr
Dick, disinterred from the boulder-clay in various localities
in the neighbourhood of Thurso, and weighing in all about
four ounces, I have detected the broken remains of no fewer
than *sixteen* hinge joints.   And on the same principle through
which the stronger fragments of Cyprina were preserved in so

Purpura lapillus, Mytilus edule, Cardium edule, Littorina littorea: all living forms
common on Scottish coasts today; **Dr Fleming**: John Fleming (1785-1857), from 1845
the Reverend Professor of Natural History at the Free Church College, Edinburgh
(previously Professor of Natural Philosophy at King's College, Aberdeen) (Andrews 1982).
The reference is to Fleming (1828, p. 444)

much larger proportion than the weaker ones, may Cyprina itself have been preserved in much larger proportion than its more fragile neighbours. Occasionally, however,—escaped, as if by accident,—characteristic fragments are found of shells by no means very strong,—such as *Mytilus, Tellina,* and *Astarte.* Among the univalves I can distinguish *Dentalium entale, Purpura lapillus, Turritella terebra,* and *Littorina littorea,* all existing shells, but all common also to at least the later deposits of the Crag. And among the bivalves Mr Dick enumerates,—besides the prevailing *Cyprina islandica,—Venus casina, Cardium edule, Cardium echinatum, Mytilus edule, Astarte danmoniensis (sulcata),* and *Astarte compressa,* with a *Mactra, Artemis,* and *Tellina.*[*] All the determined species here, with the exception of *Mytilus edule,* have, with many others, been found by the Rev. Mr Cumming in the boulder-clays of the Isle of Man ; and all of them are living shells at the present day on our Scottish coasts. It seems scarce possible to fix the age of a deposit so broken in its organisms, on the principle that would first seek to determine its per centage of extinct shells as the data on which to found. One has to search sedulously and long ere a fragment turns up sufficiently entire for the purpose of specific identification, even when it belongs to a well-known living shell ; and did the clay contain some six or eight per cent. of the extinct in a similarly broken condition (and there is no evidence that it contains a single per cent. of extinct shells), I know not how, in the circumstances, the fact could ever be determined. A lifetime might be devoted to the task of fixing their real proportion, and yet be devoted to it in vain. All that at present can be said is, that, judging from what appears, the boulder-clays of Caithness, and with them the boulder-clays of

[*] Mr Dick has since disinterred from out the boulder-clays of the Burn of Freswick, *Patella vulgata, Buccinum undatum, Fesus antiquus, Rostellaria, Pes pelicana,* a *Natica, Lutraria,* and *Balanus.*

Rostellaria, Pes pelicana: presumably an error for *Rostellaria pes-pelicani,* now *Aporrhais pespelicani,* the Common Pelican's Foot Shell, a sea snail or gastropod

Scotland generally, and of the Isle of Man,—for they are all palpably connected with the same iceberg phenomena, and occur along the same zone in reference to the sea-level,—were formed during the *existing* geological epoch.

These details may appear tediously minute ; but let the reader mark how very much they involve.   The occurrence of recent shells largely diffused throughout the boulder-clays of Caithness, at all heights and distances from the sea at which the clay itself occurs, and not only connected with the iceberg phenomena by the closest juxtaposition, but also testifying distinctly to its agency by the extremely comminuted state in which we find them, tell us, not only according to old John Busby, "that the ocean covered the inland country at some former period of time," but that it covered it to a great height at a time geologically recent, when our seas were inhabited by exactly the same mollusca as inhabit them now, and, so far as yet appears, by none others.   I have not yet detected the boulder-clay at more than from six to eight hundred feet over the level of the sea ; but the travelled boulders I have often found at more than a thousand feet over it ; and Dr John Fleming, the correctness of whose observations few men acquainted with the character of his researches or of his mind will be disposed to challenge, has informed me that he has detected the dressed and polished surfaces at least four hundred feet higher.   There occurs a greenstone boulder, of from twelve to fourteen tons weight, says Mr M'Laren, in his "Geology of Fife and the Lothians," on the south side of Black Hill (one of the Pentland range), at about fourteen hundred feet over the sea.   Now fourteen or fifteen hundred feet, taken as the extreme height of the dressings, though they are said to occur greatly higher, would serve to submerge in the iceberg ocean almost the whole agricultural region of Scotland.   The common hazel *(Corylus avellana)* ceases to grow in the latitude of the Grampians at from one thousand two hundred to one thousand five hundred feet over the sea-level; the common bracken *(Pteris aquilina)* at about the same height; and corn is never successfully culti- vated at a greater altitude. Where the hazel and bracken cease to grow, it is in vain to attempt growing corn.* In the period of the boulder-clay, then, when the existing shells of our coasts lived in those inland sounds and friths of the country that now exist as broad plains or fertile valleys, the sub-aerial superficies of Scotland was restricted to what are now its barren and mossy regions, and formed, instead of one con- tinuous land, merely three detached groupes of islands,—the small Cheviot and Hartfell group,—the greatly larger Gram- pian and Ben Nevis group,—and a group intermediate in size, extending from Mealfourvonny, on the northern shores of Loch Ness, to the Maiden Paps of Caithness.

The more ancient boulder-clays of Scotland seem to have been formed when the land was undergoing a slow process of subsidence, or, as I should perhaps rather say, when a very considerable area of the earth's surface, including the sea-bot- tom, as well as the eminences that rose over it, was the sub- ject of a gradual depression; for little or no alteration ap- pears to have taken place at the time in the *relative* levels of the higher and lower portions of the sinking area : the features of the land in the northern part of the kingdom, from the southern flanks of the Grampians to the Pentland Frith, seem to have been fixed in nearly the existing forms many ages before, at the close, apparently, of the Oolitic period, and at a still earlier age in the Lammermuir district, to the south. And so the sea around our shores must have deepened in the ratio in which the hills sank. The evidence of this process

* That similarity of condition in which the hazel and the harder cerealia thrive was noted by our north-country farmers of the old school, long ere it had been recorded by the botanist. Hence such remarks, familiarized into proverbs, as " A good *nut* year's a good *ait* year ;" or, " As the *nut* fills the *ait* fills."

slow process of subsidence: a problem minimised under the alternative glacial hypothesis – see Introduction of subsidence is of a character tolerably satisfactory. The dressed surfaces occur in Scotland, most certainly, as I have already stated on the authority of Dr Fleming, at the height of fourteen hundred feet over the present sea-level; it has been even said, at fully twice that height, on the lofty flanks of Schehallion,—a statement, however, which I have had hitherto no opportunity of verifying. They may be found, too, equally well marked, under the existing high-water line; and it is obviously impossible that the dressing process could have been going on at the higher and lower levels at the same time. When the icebergs were grating along the more elevated rocks, the low-lying ones must have been buried under from three to seven hundred fathoms of water,—a depth from three to seven times greater, be it remembered, than that at which the most ponderous iceberg could possibly have grounded, or have in any degree affected the bottom. The dressing process, then, must have been a bit-and-bit process, carried on during either a period of elevation, in which the rising land was subjected, zone after zone, to the sweep of the armed ice from its higher levels *downwards*, or during a period of subsidence, in which it was subjected to the ice, zone after zone, from its lower levels *upwards*. And that it was the lower, not the higher levels, that were first dressed, appears evident from the circumstance, that though on these lower levels we find the rocks covered up by continuous beds of the boulder-clay, varying generally from twenty to a hundred feet in thickness, they are, notwithstanding, as completely dressed under the clay as on the heights above. Had it been a rising land that was subjected to the attrition of the icebergs, the debris and dressings of the higher rocks would have protected the lower from the attrition; and so the thick accumulation of boulder-clay which overlies the old coast line, for instance, would have rested, not on dressed, but on undressed surfaces. The barer rocks of the lower levels might of course

---

dressed: *ie* in the stonemason's sense, worked, trimmed and smoothed off – a metaphor for the effects of what is now considered glacial abrasion exhibit their scratchings and polishings, like those of the higher; but wherever these scratchings and polishings occurred in the inferior zones, no thick protecting stratum of boulder-clay would be found overlying them; and, *vice versa*, wherever in these zones there occurred thick beds of boulder-clay, there would be detected on the rock beneath no scratchings and polishings. In order to *dress* the entire surface of a country from the sea-line and under it to the tops of its hills, and at the same time to cover up extensive portions of its low-lying rocks with vast deposits of clay, it seems a necessary condition of the process that it should be carried on piece-meal from the lower levels upwards,—not from the higher downwards.

It interested me much to find, that while from one set of appearances I had been inferring the gradual subsidence of the land during the period of the boulder-clay, the Rev. Mr Cumming of King William's College had arrived, from the consideration of quite a different class of phenomena, at a similar conclusion. "It appears to me highly probable," I find him remarking, in his lately published "Isle of Man," "that at the commencement of the boulder period there was a gradual sinking of this area [that of the island]. Successively, therefore, the points at different degrees of elevation were brought within the influence of the sea, and exposed to the rake of the tides, charged with masses of ice which had been floated off from the surrounding shores, and bearing on their under surfaces, mud, gravel, and fragments of hard rock." Mr Cumming goes on to describe, in his volume, some curious appearances, which seem to bear direct on this point, in connection with a boss of a peculiarly-compounded granite, which occurs in the southern part of the island, about seven hundred feet over the level of the sea. There rise on the western side of the boss two hills, one of which attains to the elevation of nearly seven hundred, and the other of nearly

eight hundred feet over it ; and yet both hills to their summits are mottled over with granite boulders, furnished by the
comparatively low-lying boss.   One of these travelled masses,
fully two tons in weight, lies not sixty feet from the summit
of the loftier hill, at an altitude of nearly fifteen hundred feet
over the sea.   Now, it seems extremely difficult to conceive
of any other agency than that of a rising sea or of a subsiding land, through which these masses could have been rolled
up the steep slopes of the hills.   Had the boulder period
been a period of elevation, or merely a stationary period, during which the land neither rose nor sank, the travelled boulders would not now be found resting at higher levels than
that of the parent rock whence they were derived.   We occasionally meet on our shores, after violent storms from the
sea, stones that have been rolled from their place at low ebb
to nearly the line of flood ; but we always find that it was
by the waves of the rising, not of the falling tide, that their
transport was effected.   For whatever removals of the kind
take place during an ebbing sea are invariably in an opposite
direction ;—they are removals, not from lower to higher
levels, but from higher to lower.

The upper subsoils of Scotland bear frequent mark of the
elevatory period which succeeded this period of depression.
The boulder-clay has its numerous intercalated arenaceous
and gravelly beds, which belong evidently to its own era ;
but the numerous surface-beds of stratified sand and gravel
by which in so many localities it is overlaid belong evidently to a later time.   When, after possibly a long protracted
period, the land again began to rise, or the sea to fall, the
superior portions of the boulder-clay must have been exposed
to the action of tides and waves ; and the same process of
separation of parts must have taken place on a large scale,
which one occasionally sees taking place in the present time
on a comparatively small one, in ravines of the same clay

swept by a streamlet. After every shower, the stream comes down red and turbid with the finer and more argillaceous portions of the deposit ; minute accumulations of sand are swept to the gorge of the ravine, or cast down in ripple-marked patches in its deeper pools; beds of pebbles and gravel are heaped up in every inflection of its banks ; and boulders are laid bare along its sides. Now, a separation, by a sort of washing process of an analogous character, must have taken place in the materials of the more exposed portions of the boulder-clay, during the gradual emergence of the land ; and hence, apparently, those extensive beds of sand and gravel which in so many parts of the kingdom exist, in relation to the clay, as a superior or upper subsoil ; hence, too, occasional beds of a purer clay than that beneath, divested of a considerable portion of its arenaceous components, and of almost all its pebbles and boulders. This *washed* clay,—a re-formation of the boulder deposit, cast down, mostly in insulated beds in quiet localities, where the absence of currents suffered the purer particles held in suspension by the water to settle,—forms, in Scotland at least, with, of course, the exception of the ancient fire-clays of the Coal Measures, the true brick and tile clays of the agriculturist and architect.

It is to these superior beds that all the recent shells yet found above the existing sea-level in Scotland, from the Dornoch Frith and beyond it, to beyond the Frith of Forth, seem to belong. Their period is much less remote than that of the shells of the boulder-clay, and they rarely occur in the same comminuted condition. They existed, it would appear, not during the chill twilight period, when the land was in a state of subsidence, but during the after period of cheerful dawn, when hill-top after hill-top was emerging from the deep, and the close of each passing century witnessed a broader area of dry land in what is now Scotland, than the close of the century which had gone before. Scandinavia is similarly

rising at the present day, and presents with every succeeding
age a more extended breadth of surface.   Many of the boulder-stones seem to have been cast down where they now lie,
during this latter time.   When they occur, as in many instances, high on bare hill-tops, from five to fifteen hundred
feet over the sea-level, with neither gravel nor boulder-clay
beside them, we of course cannot fix their period. They may
have been dropped by ice-floes or shore-ice, where we now
find them, at the commencement of the period of elevation,
after the clay had been formed ; or they may have been deposited by more ponderous icebergs during its formation, when
the land was yet sinking, though during the subsequent rise
the clay may have been washed from around them to lower
levels.   The boulders, however, which we find scattered over
the plains and less elevated hill-sides, with beds of the washed
gravel or sand interposed between them and the clay, must
have been cast down where they lie, during the elevatory ages.
For, had they been washed out of the clay, they would have
lain, not *over* the greatly lighter sands and gravels, but *under*
them.   Would that they could write their own histories!
The autobiography of a single boulder, with notes on the various floras which had sprung up around it, and the various
classes of birds, beasts, and insects by which it had been visited, would be worth nine-tenths of all the autobiographies
ever published, and a moiety of the remainder to boot.

A few hundred yards from the opening of this dell of the
boulder-clay, in which I have so long detained the reader,
there is a wooded inflection of the bank, formed by the old
coast line, in which there stood, about two centuries ago, a
meal-mill, with the cottage of the miller, and which was once
known as the scene of one of those supernaturalities that belong to the times of the witch and the fairy.   The upper
anchoring-place of the bay lies nearly opposite the inflection.
A shipmaster, who had moored his vessel in this part of the

---

this dell: Miller ended his long digression on the boulder clay and returned to where he
left off on p. 304, in the den to the west of Cromarty town; **bay**: Bay of Cromarty, west
of the town – part of the Cromarty Firth, on the opposite side of the Black Isle from
Rosemarkie and the Moray Firth

roadstead, some time in the latter days of the first Charles, was one fine evening sitting alone on deck, awaiting the return of his seamen, who had gone ashore, and amusing himself in watching the lights that twinkled from the scattered farm-houses, and in listening, in the extreme stillness of the calm, to the distant lowing of cattle, or the abrupt bark of the herdsman's dog. As the hour wore later, the sounds ceased, and the lights disappeared,—all but one solitary taper, that twinkled from the window of the miller's cottage. At length, however, it also disappeared, and all was dark around the shores of the bay, as a belt of black velvet. Suddenly a hissing noise was heard overhead ; the shipmaster looked up, and saw what seemed to be one of those meteors known as falling stars, slanting athwart the heavens in the direction of the cottage, and increasing in size and brilliancy as it neared the earth, until the wooded ridge and the shore could be seen as distinctly from the ship-deck as by day. A dog howled piteously from one of the outhouses,—an owl whooped from the wood. The meteor descended until it almost touched the roof, when a cock crew from within ; its progress seemed instantly arrested ; it stood still, rose about the height of a ship's mast, and then began again to descend. The cock crew a second time ; it rose as before ; and, after mounting considerably higher than at first, again sank in the line of the cottage, to be again arrested by the crowing of the cock. It mounted yet a third time, rising higher still ; and, in its last descent, had almost touched the roof, when the faint clap of wings was heard as if whispered over the water, followed by a still louder note of defiance from the cock. The meteor rose with a bound, and, continuing to ascend until it seemed lost among the stars, did not again appear. Next night, however, at the same hour, the same scene was repeated in all its circumstances : the meteor descended, the dog howled, the owl whooped, the cock crew. On the following morning the shipmaster visited the miller's, and, curious to ascertain how the cottage would fare when the cock was away, he purchased the bird ; and, sailing from the bay before nightfall, did not return until about a month after.

On his voyage inwards, he had no sooner doubled an intervening headland, than he stepped forward to the bows to take a peep at the cottage : it had vanished.   As he approached the anchoring ground, he could discern a heap of blackened stones occupying the place where it had stood ; and he was informed on going ashore, that it had been burnt to the ground, no one knew how, on the very night he had quitted the bay.   He had it re-built and furnished, says the story, deeming himself what one of the old schoolmen would perhaps term the *occasional* cause of the disaster.   He also returned the cock,—probably a not less important benefit,—and no after accident befel the cottage.   About fifteen years ago there was a human skeleton dug up near the scene of the tradition, with the skull, and the bones of the legs and feet, lying close together, as if the body had been huddled up twofold in a hole ; and this discovery led to that of the story, which, though at one time often repeated and extensively believed, had been suffered to sleep in the memories of a few elderly people for nearly sixty years.

schoolmen: mediaeval philosophers; occasional cause: event which determines the occasion, the time of action, of the effective cause (philosophy)

CHAPTER VII.

THE ravine excavated by the mill-dam showed me what I had never so well seen before,—the exact relation borne by the deep red stone of the Cromarty quarries to the ichthyolite beds of the system. It occupies the same place, and belongs to the same period, as those superior beds of the Lower Old Red Sandstone which are so largely developed in the cliffs of Dunnet Head in Caithness, and of Tarbet Ness in Ross-shire, and which were at one time regarded as forming, north of the Grampians, the analogue of the New Red Sandstone. I paced it across the strata this morning, in the line of the ravine, and found its thickness over the upper fish-beds, though I was far from reaching its superior layers, which are buried here in the sea, to be rather more than five hundred feet. The fossiliferous beds occur a few hundred yards below the dwelling-house of Rose Farm. They are not quite uncovered in the ravine; but we find their places indicated by heaps of gray argillaceous shale, mingled with their characteristic ichthyolitic nodules, in one of which I found a small specimen of Cheiracanthus. The projecting edge of some fossil-charged bed had been struck, mayhap, by an iceberg, and dashed into ruins, just as the subsiding land had brought the spot within reach of the attritive ice; and the broken heap thus detached had been shortly afterwards covered up, without mixture of any other deposit, by the red boulder-clay.   On the previous day I had detected the fish-beds in another new locality,— one of the ravines of the lawn of Cromarty House,—where the gray shale, concealed by a covering of soil and sward for centuries, had been laid bare during the storm by a swollen runnel, and a small nodule, inclosing a characteristic plate of Pterichthys, washed out.   And my next object in to-day's journey, after exploring this ravine of the boulder-clay, was to ascertain whether the beds did not also occur in a ravine of the parish of Avoch, some eight or nine miles away, which, when lying a-bed one night in Edinburgh, I remembered hav- ing crossed when a boy, at a point which lies considerably out of the ordinary route of the traveller.   I had remarked on this occasion, as the resuscitated recollection intimated, that the precipices of the Avoch ravine bore, at the unfrequented point, the peculiar aspect which I learned many years after to associate with the ichthyolitic member of the system ; and I was now quite as curious to test the truth of a sort of vig- nette landscape, transferred to the mind at an immature pe- riod of life, and preserved in it for full thirty years, as de- sirous to extend my knowledge of the fossiliferous beds of a system to the elucidation of which I had peculiarly devoted myself.

As the traveller reaches the flat moory uplands of the pa- rish, where the water stagnates amid heath and moss over a thin layer of peaty soil, he finds the underlying boulder-clay, as shown in the chance sections, spotted and streaked with patches of a grayish-white.   There is the same mixture of arenaceous and aluminous particles in the white as in the red portions of the mass ; for, as we see so frequently exemplified in the spots and streaks of the Red Sandstone formations, whether Old or New, the colouring matter has been discharged without any accompanying change of composition in the sub- stance which it pervaded ;—evidence enough that the red dye must be something distinct from the substance itself, just as the dye of a handkerchief is a thing distinct from the silk or cotton yarn of which the handkerchief has been woven. The stagnant water above, acidulated by its various vegetable solutions, seems to have been in some way connected with these appearances.   In every case in which a crack through the clay gives access to the oozing moisture, we see the sides bleached, for several feet downwards, to nearly the colour of pipe-clay ; we find the surface, too, when it has been divested of the vegetable soil, presenting for yards together the appearance of sheets of half-bleached linen : the red ground of the clay has been acted upon by the percolating fluid, as the red ground of a Bandona handkerchief is acted upon through the openings in the perforated lead, by the discharging chloride of lime.   The peculiar chemistry through which these changes are effected might be found, carefully studied, to throw much light on similar phenomena in the older formations.   There are quarries in the New Red Sandstone in which almost every mass of stone presents a different shade of colour from that of its neighbouring mass, and quarries in the Old Red the strata of which we find streaked and spotted like pieces of calico.   And their variegated aspect seems to have been communicated, in every instance, not during deposition, nor after they had been hardened into stone, but when, like the boulder-clay, they existed in an intermediate state.   Be it remarked, too, that the red clay here,— evidently derived from the abrasion of the red rocks beneath, —is in dye and composition almost identical with the substance on which, as an unconsolidated sandstone, the bleaching influences, whatever their character, had operated in the Palæozoic period, so many long ages befóre ;—it is a repetition of the ancient experiment in the Old Red, that we now see going on in the boulder-clay.   It is further worthy of notice, that the bleached lines of the clay exhibit, viewed hori-

---

perforated lead: *ie* a stencil made from sheet lead, for printing bandanna handkerchiefs

zontally, when the overlying vegetable mould has been removed, and the whitened surface in immediate contact with
it pared off, a polygonal arrangement, like that assumed by
the cracks in the bottom of clayey pools dried up in summer
by the heat of the sun.   Can these possibly indicate the
ancient rents and fissures of the boulder-clay, formed, immediately after the upheaval of the land, in the first process of
drying, and remaining afterwards open enough to receive what
the uncracked portions of the surface excluded,—the acidulated bleaching fluid ?

The kind of ferruginous pavement of the boulder-clay
known to the agriculturist as *pan*, which may be found extending in some cases its iron cover over whole districts,—
sealing them down to barrenness, as the iron and brass sealed
down the stump of Nebuchadnezzar's tree,—is, like the white
strips and blotches of the deposit, worthy the careful notice
of the geologist.   It serves to throw some light on the origin
of those continuous bands of clayey or arenaceous ironstone,
which in the older formations in which vegetable matter
abounds, whether Oolitic or Carboniferous, are of such common occurrence.   The *pan* is a stony stratum, scarcely less
indurated in some localities than sandstone of the average
hardness, that rests like a pavement on the surface of the
boulder-clay, and that generally bears atop a thin layer of
sterile soil, darkened by a russet covering of stunted heath.
The binding cement of the *pan* is, as I have said, ferruginous,
and seems to have been derived from the vegetable covering
above.   Of all plants, the heaths are found to contain most
iron.   Nor is it difficult to conceive how, in comparatively
flat tracts of heathy moor, where the surface-water sinks to
the stiff subsoil, and on which one generation of plants after
another has been growing and decaying for many centuries,
the minute metallic particles, disengaged in the process of decomposition, and carried down by the rains to the imperme-

---

Nebuchadnezzar's tree: Bible, Daniel 4. King Nebuchadnezzar dreamt of being told to
cut down a tree and 'leave the stump of his roots in the earth, even with a band of iron
and brass'

able clay, should, by accumulating there, bind the layer on
which they rest, as is the nature of ferruginous oxide, into a
continuous stony crust. Wherever this *pan* occurs, we find
the superincumbent soil doomed to barrenness,—arid and
sun-baked during the summer and autumn months, and, from
the same cause, overcharged with moisture in winter and
spring. My friend Mr Swanson, when schoolmaster of Nigg,
found a large garden attached to the school-house so invete-
rately sterile as to be scarce worth cultivation ; a thin stratum of mould rested on a hard impermeable pavement of *pan*,
through which not a single root could penetrate to the tenacious but not unkindly subsoil below. He set himself to
work in his leisure hours, and bit by bit laid bare and broke
up the pavement. The upper mould, long divorced from
the clay on which it had once rested, was again united to
it ; the piece of ground began gradually to alter its character
for the better ; and when I last passed the way, I found it,
though in a state of sad neglect, covered by a richer vegetation than it had ever borne under the more careful management of my friend. This ferruginous pavement of the boulder-clay may be deemed of interest to the geologist, as a curious instance of deposition in a dense medium, and as illustrative of the changes which may be effected on previously
existing strata, through the agency of an overlying vegetation.

I passed, on my way, through the ancient battle-field to
which I have incidentally referred in the story of the Miller
of Resolis.* Modern improvement has not yet marred it by
the plough ; and so it still bears on its brown surface many
a swelling tumulus and flat oblong mound, and—where the
high road of the district passes along its eastern edge—the
huge gray cairn, raised, says tradition, over the body of an

* For this story see " Scenes and Legends of the North of Scotland,"
chap. xxv.

ancient Pictish king. But the contest of which it was the scene belongs to a profoundly dark period, ere the gray dawn of Scottish history began. As shown by the remains of ancient art occasionally dug up on the moor, it was a conflict of the times of the stone battle-axe, the flint arrow-head, and the unglazed sepulchral urn, unindebted for aught of its symmetry to the turning-lathe,—times when there were heroes in abundance, but no scribes. And the cairn, about a hundred feet in length and breadth, by about twenty in height, with its long hoary hair of overgrown lichen waving in the breeze, and the trailing club-moss shooting upwards from its base along its sides, bears in its every lineament full mark of its great age. It is a mound striding across the stream of centuries, to connect the past with the present. And yet, after all, what a mere matter of yesterday its extreme antiquity is ! My explorations this morning bore reference to but the later eras of the geologist : the portion of the geologic volume which I was attempting to decipher and translate formed the few terminal paragraphs of its concluding chapter. And yet the *finis* had been added to them for thousands of years ere this latter antiquity began. The boulder-clay had been formed and deposited ; the land, in rising over the waves, had had many a huge pebble washed out of its last formed red stratum, or dropped upon it by ice-floes from above ; and these pebbles lay mottling the surface of this barren moor for mile after mile, bleaching pale to the rains and the sun, as the meagre and mossy soil received, in the lapse of centuries, its slow accessions of organic matter, and darkened around them. And then, for a few brief hours, the heath, no longer solitary, became a wild scene of savage warfare,—of waving arms and threatening faces,—and of human lives violently spilled, gushing forth in blood ; and, when all was over, the old weathered boulders were heaped up above the slain, and there began a new antiquity in re-

---

remains of ancient art: in the Victorian sense of 'art' as including technology or 'useful art'. What we should call artefacts lation to the pile in its gathered state, that bore reference to man's short lifetime, and to the recent introduction of the species. The child of a few summers speaks of the events of last year as long gone by ; while his father, advanced into middle life, regards them as still fresh and recent.

I reached the Burn of Killein,—the scene of my purposed explorations,—where it bisects the Inverness road ; and struck down the rocky ravine, in the line of the descending strata and the falling streamlet, towards the point at which I had crossed it so many years before. First I passed along a thick bed of yellow stone,—next over a bed of stratified clay. "The little boy," I said, "took correct note of what he saw, though without special aim at the time, and as much under the guidance of a mere observative instinct as Dame Quickly, when she took note of the sea-coal fire, the round table, the parcel-gilt goblet, and goodwife Keech's dish of prawns dressed in vinegar, as adjuncts of her interview with old Sir John when he promised to marry her. These are unequivocally the ichthyolitic beds, whether they contain ichthyolites or no." The first nodule I laid open presented inside merely a pale oblong patch in the centre, which I examined in vain with the lens, though convinced of its organic origin, for a single scale. Proceeding farther down the stream, I picked a nodule out of a second and lower bed, which contained more evidently its organism,—a finely-reticulated fragment, that at first sight reminded me of some delicate festinella of the Silurian system. It proved, however, to be part of the tail of a Cheiracanthus, exhibiting—what is rarely shown— the interior surfaces of those minute rectangular scales which in this genus lie over the caudal fin, ranged in right lines. A second nodule presented me with the spines of *Diplacanthus striatus ;* and still farther down the stream,—for the beds are numerous here, and occupy in vertical extent very considerable space in the system,—I detected a stratum of

---

Dame Quickly ... Sir John: Mistress Quickly and Falstaff in Shakespeare's play *The Merry Wives of Windsor*

bulky nodules charged with fragments of Coccosteus, belonging chiefly to two species,—*Coccosteus decipiens* and *Coccosteus cuspidatus*.   All the specimens bore conclusive evidence regarding the geologic place and character of the beds in which they occur ; and in one of the number, a specimen of *Coccosteus decipiens*, sufficiently fine to be transferred to my knapsack, and which now occupies its corner in my little collection, the head exhibits all its plates in their proper order, and the large dorsal plate, though dissociated from the nail-like attachment of the nape, presents its characteristic breadth entire.   It was the plates of this species, first found in the flagstones of Caithness, which were taken for those of a fresh-water tortoise ; and hence apparently its specific name, *decipiens ;*—it is the *deceiving* Coccosteus.   I disinterred, in the course of my explorations, as many nodules as lay within reach,—now and then longing for a pick-axe, and a companion robust and persevering enough to employ it with effect ; and after seeing all that was to be seen in the bed of the stream and the precipices, I retraced my steps up the dell to the highway.   And then, striking off across the moor to the north, —ascending in the system as I climbed the eminence, which forms here the central ridge of the old Maolbuie Common, —I spent some little time in a quarry of pale red sandstone, known, from the moory height on which it has been opened, as the quarry of the Maolbuie.   But here, as elsewhere, the folds of that upper division of the Lower Old Red in which it has been excavated contain nothing organic.   Why this should be so universally the case,—for in Caithness, Orkney, Cromarty, and Ross, wherever, in short, this member of the system is unequivocally developed, it is invariably barren of remains,—cannot, I suspect, be very satisfactorily explained. Fossils occur both over and under it, in rocks that seem as little favourable to their preservation ; but during that intervening period which its blank strata represent, at least the

---

organic: in the sense of an 'organism', *ie* a fossil

species of all the ichthyolites of the system seem to have changed, and, so far as is yet known, the *genus* Coccosteus died out entirely.

The Black Isle has been elaborately described in the last Statistical Account of the Parish of Avoch as comprising at least the analogues of three vast geologic systems. The Great Conglomerate, and the thick bed of coarse sandstone of corresponding character that lies over it, compose all which is not primary rock of that south-eastern ridge of the district which forms the shores of the Moray Frith ; and *they* are represented in the Account as Old Red Sandstone proper. Then, next in order,—forming the base of a parallel ridge,—come those sandstone and argillaceous bands to which the ichthyolite beds belong; and these, though at the time the work appeared their existence in the locality could be but guessed at, are described as representatives of the Coal Measures. Last of all there occur those superior sandstones of the Lower Old Red formation in which the quarry of the Maolbuie has been opened, and which are largely developed in the central or *back-bone* ridge of the district. "And these," says the writer, "we have little hesitation in assigning to the *New Red*, or variegated Sandstone formation." I remember that some thirteen years ago,—in part misled by authority, and in part really afraid to represent beds of such an enormous aggregate thickness as all belonging to one inconsiderable formation,—for such was the character of the Old Red Sandstone at the time,—I ventured, though hesitatingly, and with less of detail, on a somewhat similar statement regarding the sandstone deposits of the parish of Cromarty. But true it is, notwithstanding, that the stratified rocks of the Black Isle are composed generally, not of the analogues of three systems, but of merely a fractional portion of a single system,—a fact previously established in other parts of the district, and which my discovery of this day in the Burn of Killein served yet

last **Statistical Account**: the *New Statistical Account*, the second (1845) systematic survey of each parish in Scotland farther to confirm in relation to that middle portion of the tract in which the parish of Avoch is situated. The geologic records, unlike the Sybilline books, grow in volume and number as one pauses and hesitates over them ; demanding, however, with every addition to their bulk, a larger and yet larger sum of epochs and of ages.

The sun had got low in the western sky, and I had at least some eight or nine miles of rough road still before me ; but the day had been a happy and not unsuccessful one, and so its hard work had failed to fatigue. The shadows, however, were falling brown and deep on the bleak Maolbuie, as I passed, on my return, the solitary cairn ; and it was dark night long ere I reached Cromarty. Next morning I quitted the town for the upper reaches of the Frith, to examine yet further the superficial deposits and travelled boulders of the district.

I landed at Invergordon a little after noon, from the Leith steamer, that, on its way to the upper ports of the Moray and Dingwall Friths, stops at Cromarty for passengers every Wednesday ; and then passing direct through the village, I took the western road which winds along the shore towards Strathpeffer, skirting on the right the ancient province of the Munroes. The day was clear and genial ; and the wide-spreading woods of this part of the country, a little touched by their autumnal tints of brown and yellow, gave a warmth of hue to the landscape, which at an earlier season it wanted. A few slim streaks of semi-transparent mist, that barred the distant hill-peaks, and a few towering piles of intensely white cloud, that shot across the deep blue of the heavens, gave warning that the earlier part of the day was to be in all probability the better part of it, and that the harvest of observation which it was ultimately to yield might be found to depend on the prompt use made of the passing hour. What first attracts the attention of the geologist, in journeying west-

---

Sybilline [*recte* Sibylline] **books**: books of prophecy held by the Roman state. A prophetess, the Cumaean Sibyl, offered nine to King Tarquinius. She threw some on a fire each time he hesitated. Eventually he bought the remaining three for the price originally demanded for nine

wards, is the altered colour of the boulder-clay, as exhibited
in ditches by the way-side, or along the shore. It no longer
presents that characteristic red tint,—borrowed from the red
sandstone beneath,—so prevalent over the Black Isle, and in
Easter Ross generally ; but is of a cold leaden hue, not unlike
that which it wears above the Coal Measures of the south, or
over the flagstones of Caithness.   The altered colour here is
evidently a consequence of the large development, in Ferindonald and Strathpeffer, of the ichthyolitic members of the
Old Red, existing chiefly as fœtid bituminous breccias and
dark-coloured sandstones : the boulder-clay of the locality
forms the dressings, not of red, but of blackish-gray rocks ;
and, as almost everywhere else in Scotland, its trail lies to
the east of the strata, from which it was detached in the character of an impalpable mud by the age-protracted grindings
of the denuding agent.   It abounds in masses of bituminous
breccia, some of which, of great size, seem to have been drifted
direct from the valley of Strathpeffer, and are identical in
structure and composition with the rock in which the mineral
springs of the Strath have their rise, and to which they owe
their peculiar qualities.

    After walking on for about eight miles, through noble woods
and a lovely country, I struck from off the high road at the
pretty little village of Evanton, and pursued the course of the
river Auldgrande, first through intermingled fields and patches
of copsewood, and then through a thick fir wood, to where the
bed of the stream contracts from a boulder-strewed bottom
of ample breadth, to a gloomy fissure, so deep and dark, that
in many places the water cannot be seen, and so narrow, that
the trees which shoot out from the opposite sides interlace
their branches atop.   Large banks of the gray boulder-clay,
laid open by the river, and charged with fragments of dingy
sandstone and dark-coloured breccia, testify, along the lower
reaches of the stream, to the near neighbourhood of the ich-

Auldgrande: River Glass; **fissure:** the Black Rock Gorge (as it is now called) ends just
under 2 kilometres upstream from Evanton

thyolitic member of the Old Red ; but where the banks contract, we find only its lowest member, the Great Conglomerate.
This last is by far the most picturesque member of the system,—abrupt and bold of outline in its hills, and mural in
its precipices.   And nowhere does it exhibit a wilder or more
characteristic beauty than at the tall narrow portal of the
Auldgrande, where the river,—after wailing for miles in a pent-
up channel, narrow as one of the lanes of old Edinburgh, and
hemmed in by walls quite as perpendicular, and nearly twice
as lofty,—suddenly expands, first into a deep brown pool, and
then into a broad tumbling stream, that, as if permanently
affected in temper by the strict severity of the discipline to
which its early life had been subjected, frets and chafes in
all its after course, till it loses itself in the sea.   The banks,
ere we reach the opening of the chasm, have become steep,
and wild, and densely wooded ; and there stand out on either
hand, giant crags, that plant their iron feet in the stream ;
here girdled with belts of rank succulent shrubs, that love the
damp shade and the frequent drizzle of the spray ; and there
hollow and bare, with their round pebbles sticking out from
the partially decomposed surface, like the piled-up skulls in the
great underground cemetery of the Parisians.   Massy trees,
with their green fantastic roots rising high over the scanty
soil, and forming many a labyrinthine recess for the frog, the
toad, and the newt, stretch forth their gnarled arms athwart
the stream.   In front of the opening, with but a black deep
pool between, there lies a mid-way bank of huge stones.   Of
these, not a few of the more angular masses still bear, though
sorely worn by the torrent, the mark of the blasting iron, and
were evidently tumbled into the chasm from the fields above.
But in the chasm there was no rest for them, and so the arrowy
rush of the water in the confined channel swept them down,
till they dropped where they now lie, just where the widening bottom first served to dissipate the force of the current.

---

mark of the blasting iron: hole drilled by a 'jumper' for the insertion of black powder
charges when boulders were being broken up to clear the fields during 'Improvement' –
the sides of the holes would still be visible on the broken fragments

And over the sullen pool in front we may see the stern pillars of the portal rising from eighty to a hundred feet in height, and scarce twelve feet apart, like the massive obelisks of some Egyptian temple ; while, in gloomy vista within, projection starts out beyond projection, like column beyond column in some narrow avenue of approach to Luxor or Carnac. The precipices are green, with some moss or byssus, that, like the miner, chooses a subterranean habitat,—for here the rays of the sun never fall ; the dead mossy water beneath, from which the cliffs rise so abruptly, bears the hue of molten pitch ; the trees, fast anchored in the rock, shoot out their branches across the opening, to form a thick tangled roof, at the height of a hundred and fifty feet overhead ; while from the recesses within, where the eye fails to penetrate, there issues a combination of the strangest and wildest sounds ever yet produced by water : there is the deafening rush of the torrent, blent as if with the clang of hammers, the roar of vast bellows, and the confused gabble of a thousand voices. The sun, hastening to its setting, shone red, yet mellow, through the foliage of the wooded banks on the west, where, high above, they first curve from the sloping level of the fields, to bend over the stream ; or fell more direct on the jutting cliffs and bosky dingles opposite, burnishing them as if with gold and fire ; but all was coldly-hued at the bottom, where the torrent foamed gray and chill under the brown shadow of the banks ; and where the narrow portal opened an untrodden way into the mysterious recesses beyond, the shadow deepened almost into blackness. The scene lacked but a ghost to render it perfect. An apparition walking from within, like the genius in one of Goldsmith's essays, "along the surface of the water," would have completed it at once.

Laying hold of an overhanging branch, I warped myself upwards from the bed of the stream along the face of a precipice, and, reaching its sloping top, forced my way to the

---

byssus: *not* the holdfasts of molluscs, the sense used earlier, but an old genus of thread-like or filamentous plants living in damp and dark conditions, which became obsolete during the nineteenth century as botanists realised that it was an unworkable mixture of various plants. Given the reference on p. 397, Miller perhaps had some sort of moss in mind; **genius ... water**: see Additional Notes

wood above, over a steep bank covered with tangled underwood, and a slim succulent herbage, that sickened for want of
the sun.   The yellow light was streaming through many a
shaggy vista, as, threading my way along the narrow ravine
as near the steep edge as the brokenness of the ground permitted, I reached a huge mass of travelled rock, that had
been dropped in the old boulder period within a yard's length
of the brink.   It is composed of a characteristic granitic
gneiss of a pale flesh-colour, streaked with black, that, in the
hand-specimen, can scarce be distinguished from a true granite, but which, viewed in the mass, presents, in the arrangement of its intensely dark mica, evident marks of stratification, and which is remarkable, among other things, for furnishing almost all the very large boulders of this part of the
country.   Unlike many of the granitic gneisses, it is a fine
solid stone, and would cut well.   When I had last the pleasure of spending a few hours with the late Mr William Laidlaw, the trusted friend of Sir Walter Scott, he intimated to me
his intention,—pointing to a boulder of this species of gneiss,
—of having it cut into two oblong pedestals, with which he
purposed flanking the entrance to the mansion-house of the
chief of the Rosses,—the gentleman whose property he at
that time superintended.   It was, he said, both in appearance and history, the most remarkable stone on the lands of
Balnagown ; and so he was desirous that it should be exhibited at Balnagown Castle to the best advantage.   But as he
fell shortly after into infirm health, and resigned his situation,
I know not that he ever carried his purpose into effect.   The
boulder here, beside the chasm, measures about twelve feet
in length and breadth, by from five to six in height, and contains from eight to nine hundred cubic feet of stone.   On
its upper table-like surface I found a few patches of moss and
lichen, and a slim reddening tuft of the *Vaccinium myrtillus*,
still bearing, late as was the season, its half-dozen blaeberries.

---

the late Mr William Laidlaw: (1780–1845), friend, steward and amanuensis of
Walter Scott till the latter's bankruptcy, and then factor to Sir Charles Lockhart Ross of
Balnagown at the north end of the Firth of Cromarty

This pretty little plant occurs in great profusion along the steep edges of the Auldgrande, where its delicate bushes, springing up amid long heath and ling, and crimsoned by the autumnal tinge, gave a peculiar warmth and richness this evening to those bosky spots under the brown trees, or in immediate contact with the dark chasm on which the sunlight fell most strongly ; and on all the more perilous projections I found the dark berries still shrivelling on their stems. Thirty years earlier I would scarce have left them there; and the more perilous the crag on which they had grown, the more deliciously would they have eaten. But every period of life has its own playthings; and I was now chiefly engaged with the deep chasm and the huge boulder. Chasm and boulder had come to have greatly more of interest to me than the delicate berries, or than even that sovereign dispeller of ennui and low spirits, an adventurous scramble among the cliffs.

In what state did the chasm exist when the huge boulder, —detached, mayhap, at the close of a severe frost, from some island of the archipelago that is now the northern Highlands of Scotland,—was suffered to drop beside it, from some vast ice-floe drifting eastwards on the tide ? In all probability merely as a fault in the Conglomerate, similar to many of those faults which in the Coal Measures of the southern districts we find occupied by continuous dikes of trap. But in this northern region, where the trap-rocks are unknown, it must have been filled up with the boulder-clay, or with some still more ancient accumulation of debris. And when the land had risen, and the streams, swollen into rivers, flowed along the hollows which they now occupy, the loose rubbish would in the lapse of ages gradually wash downwards to the sea, as the stones thrown from the fields above were washed downwards in a later time; and thus the deep fissure would ultimately be cleared out. The boulder-stones lie thickly in this neighbourhood, and over the eastern half of Ross-shire,

and the Black Isle generally; though for the last century they
have been gradually disappearing from the more cultivated
tracts on which there were fences or farm-steadings to be built,
or where they obstructed the course of the plough. We find
them occurring in every conceivable situation,—high on hill-
sides, where the shepherd crouches beside them for shelter in
a shower,—deep in the open sea, where they entangle the nets
of the fisherman,—on inland moors, where in some remote
age they were painfully rolled together, to form the Druidical
circle or Picts'-house,—or on the margin of the coast, where
they had been piled over one another at a later time, as protecting bulwarks against the encroachments of the waves.
They lie strewed more sparingly over extended plains, or on
exposed heights, than in hollows sheltered from the west by
high land, where the current, when it dashed high on the
hill-sides, must have been diverted from its easterly course,
and revolved in whirling eddies.   On the top of the fine
bluff hill of Fyrish, which I so admired to-day, each time I
caught a glimpse of its purple front through the woods, and
which shows how noble a mountain the Old Red Sandstone
may produce, the boulders lie but sparsely.   I especially
marked, however, when last on its summit, a ponderous traveller of a vividly green hornblende, resting on a bed of pale-
yellow sandstone, fully a thousand feet over the present high-
water level.   But towards the east, in what a seaman would
term the *bight* of the hill, the boulders have accumulated in
vast numbers.   They lie so closely piled along the course of
the river Alness, about half a mile above the village, that it
is with difficulty the waters, when in flood, can force their
passage through.   For here, apparently, when the tide swept
high along the hill-side, many an ice-floe, detained in the shelter by the revolving eddy, dashed together in rude collision,
and shook their stony burdens to the bottom.   Immediately
to the east of the low promontory on which the town of Cro-

Picts' house: generic name (now obsolete) for the remains of prehistoric dwellings and
other structures, by no means all now considered to be Pictish

marty is built there is another extensive accumulation of boulders, some of them of great size. They occupy exactly the place to which I have oftener than once seen the drift-ice of the upper part of the Cromarty Frith, set loose by a thaw, and then carried seawards by the retreating tide, forced back by a violent storm from the east, and the fragments ground against each other into powder. And here, I doubt not, of old, when the sea stood greatly higher than now, and the ice-floes were immensely larger and more numerous than those formed, in the existing circumstances, in the upper shallows of the Frith, would the fierce north-east have charged home with similar effect, and the broken masses have divested themselves of their boulders.

The Highland chieftain of one of our old Gaelic traditions conversed with a boulder-stone, and told to it the story which he had sworn never to tell to man. I too, after a sort, have conversed with boulder-stones, not, however, to tell them any story of mine, but to urge them to tell theirs to me. But, lacking the fine ear of Hans Andersen, the Danish poet, who can hear flowers and butterflies talk, and understand the language of birds, I have as yet succeeded in extracting from them no such articulate reply

> " As Memnon's image, long renowned of old
> By fabling Nilus, to the quivering touch
> Of Titan's ray, with each repulsive string
> Consenting, sounded through the warbling air."

And yet who can doubt that, were they a little more communicative, their stories of movement in the past, with the additional circumstances connected with the places which they have occupied ever since they gave over travelling, would be exceedingly curious ones? Among the boulder group to the east of Cromarty, the most ponderous individual stands so exactly on the low-water line of our great Lammas tides, that, though its shoreward edge may be reached dry-shod from four

---

Memnon's image: Mark Akenside, *Pleasures of Imagination*, I, 109–112, somewhat misquoted: in fact, '... as old Memnon's image, long renowned/By fabling Nilus, to the quivering touch/Of Titan's ray, with each repulsive string/Consenting, sounded thro' the warbling air/Unbidden strains ...'

to six times every twelvemonth, no one has ever succeeded in walking dry-shod round it. I have seen a strong breeze from the west, prolonged for a few days, prevent its drying, when the Lammas stream was at its point of lowest ebb, by from a foot to eighteen inches,—an indication, apparently, that to that height the waters of the Atlantic may be heaped up against our shores by the impulsion of the wind. And the recurrence, during at least the last century, of certain ebbs each season, which, when no disturbing atmospheric phenomena interfere with their operation, are sure to lay it dry, demonstrate, that during that period no change, even the most minute, has taken place on our coasts, in the relative levels of sea and shore. The waves have considerably encroached, during even the last half-century, on the shores immediately opposite ; but it must have been, as the stone shows, simply by the attrition of the waves, and the consequent lowering of the beach,—not through any rise in the ocean, or any depression of the land. The huge boulder here has been known for ages as the *Clach Malloch*, or accursed stone, from the circumstance, says tradition, that a boat was once wrecked upon it during a storm, and the boatmen drowned. Though little more than seven feet in height, by about twelve in length, and some eight or nine in breadth, its situation on the extreme line of ebb imparts a peculiar character to the various productions, animal and vegetable, which we find adhering to it. They occur in zones, just as on lofty hills the botanist finds his agricultural, moorland, and alpine zones rising in succession as he ascends, the one over the other. At its base, where the tide rarely falls, we find two varieties of *Lobularia digitata*, dead-man's hand, the orange-coloured and the pale, with a species of sertularia ; and the characteristic vegetable is the rough-stemmed tangle, or cuvy. In the zone immediately above the lowest, these productions disappear : the characteristic animal, if animal it be, is a flat

---

Lammas stream: presumably the August low spring tide, Lammas being 1st August yellow sponge,—the *Halichondria papillaris*,—remarkable chiefly for its sharp siliceous spicula and its strong phosphoric smell; and the characteristic vegetable is the smooth-stemmed tangle, or queener. In yet another zone we find the common limpet and the vesicular kelp-weed; and the small gray balanus and serratèd kelp-weed form the productions of the top. We may see exactly the same zones occurring in broad belts along the shore,—each zone indicative of a certain overlying depth of water; but it seems curious enough to find them all existing in succession on one boulder. Of the boulder and its story, however, more in my next.

---

spicula: spicules, the little crystalline bodies shaped like needles or taking more complex forms, and which stiffen the bodies of many sponges

CHAPTER VIII.

THE natural, and, if I may so speak, topographical, history of the *Clach Malloch*,—including, of course, its zoology and botany, with notes of those atmospheric effects on the tides, and of that stability for ages of the existing sea-level, which it indicates,—would of itself form one very interesting chapter : its geological history would furnish another. It would probably tell, if it once fairly broke silence and became auto-biographical, first of a feverish dream of intense molten heat and overpowering pressure ; and then of a busy time, in which the free molecules, as at once the materials and the artizans of the mass, began to build, each according to its nature, under the superintendence of a curious chemistry,—here form-ing sheets of black mica, there rhombs of a dark-green horn-blende and a flesh-coloured feldspar, yonder amorphous masses of a translucent quartz. It would add further, that at length, when the slow process was over, and the entire space had been occupied to the full by plate, molecule, and crystal, the red fiery twilight of the dream deepened into more than mid-night gloom, and a chill unconscious night descended on the sleeper. The vast Palæozoic period passes by,—the scarce less protracted Secondary ages come to a close,—the Eocene, Miocene, Pliocene epochs are ushered in and terminate,—races begin and end,—families and orders are born and die ;

but the dead, or those whose deep slumber admits not of dreams, take no note of time; and so it would tell how its long night of unsummed centuries seemed, like the long night of the grave, compressed into a moment.

The marble silence is suddenly broken by the rush of an avalanche, that tears away the superincumbent masses, rolling them into the sea; and the ponderous block, laid open to the light, finds itself on the bleak shore of a desert island of the northern Scottish archipelago, with a wintry scene of snow-covered peaks behind, and an ice-mottled ocean before. The winter passes, the cold severe spring comes on, and day after day the field-ice goes floating by,—now gray in shadow, now bright in the sun. At length vegetation, long repressed, bursts forth, but in no profuse luxuriance. A few dwarf birches unfold their leaves amid the rocks; a few sub-arctic willows hang out their catkins beside the swampy runnels; the golden potentilla opens its bright flowers on slopes where the evergreen *Empetrum nigrum* slowly ripens its glossy crow-berries; and from where the sea-spray dashes at full tide along the beach, to where the snow gleams at midsummer on the mountain-summits, the thin short sward is dotted by the minute cruciform stars of the scurvy-grass, and the crimson blossoms of the sea-pink. Not a few of the plants of our existing sea-shores and of our loftier hill-tops are still identical in species; but wide zones of rich herbage, with many a fertile field and many a stately tree, intervene between the bare marine belts and the bleak insulated eminences; and thus the alpine, notwithstanding its identity with the littoral flora, has been long divorced from it; but in this early time the divorce had not yet taken place, nor for ages thereafter; and the same plants that sprang around the sea-margin rose also along the middle slopes to the mountain-summits. The landscape is treeless and bare, and a hoary lichen whitens the moors, and waves, as the years pass by, in pale tufts, from the disinterred stone, now covered with weather-stains, green and gray, and standing out in bold and yet bolder relief from the steep hill-side, as the pulverizing frosts and washing rains bear away the lesser masses from around it.　The sea is slowly rising, and the land, in proportion, narrowing its flatter margins, and yielding up its wider valleys to the tide ; the low green island of one century forms the half-tide skerry, darkened with algæ, of another, and in yet a third exists but as a deep-sea rock.　As its summit disappears, groupes of hills, detached from the land, become islands, skerries, deep-sea rocks, in turn.　At length the waves at full wash within a few yards of the granitic block. And now, yielding to the undermining influences, just as a blinding snow-shower is darkening the heavens, it comes thundering down the steep into the sea, where it lies immediately beneath the high-water line, surrounded by a wide float of pulverized ice, broken by the waves.　A keen frost sets in ; the half-fluid mass around is bound up for many acres into a solid raft, that clasps fast in its rigid embrace the rocky fragment ; a stream-tide, heightened by a strong gale from the west, rises high on the beach ; the consolidated ice-field moves, floats, is detached from the shore, creeps slowly outwards into the offing, bearing atop the boulder ; and, finally caught by the easterly current, it drifts away into the open ocean.　And then, far from its original bed in the rock, amid the jerkings of a cockling sea, the mass breaks through the supporting float, and settles far beneath, amid the green and silent twilight of the bottom, where its mosses and lichens yield their place to stony encrustations of deep purple, and to miniature thickets of arboraceous zoophites.

　　The many-coloured Acalephæ float by ; the many-armed Sepiadæ shoot over ; while shells that love the profounder depths,—the black Modiola and delicate Anomia,—anchor along the sides of the mass ; and where thickets of the deep-sea tangle spread out their long, streamer-like fronds to the tide, the strong Cyprina and many-ribbed Astarte shelter by scores amid the reticulations of the short woody stems and thick-set roots. A sudden darkness comes on, like that which fell upon Sinbad when the gigantic roc descended upon him ; the sea-surface is fully sixty fathoms over head ; but even at this great depth an enormous iceberg grates heavily against the bottom, crushing into fragments in its course, Cyprina, Modiola, Astarte, with many a hapless mollusc besides ; and furrows into deep grooves the very rocks on which they lie. It passes away ; and, after many an unsummed year has also passed, there comes another change. The period of depression and of the boulder-clay is over. The water has shallowed as the sea-line gradually sank, or the land was propelled upwards by some elevatory process from below ; and each time the tide falls, the huge boulder now raises over the waters its broad forehead, already hung round with flowing tresses of brown sea-weed, and looks at the adjacent coast. The country has strangely altered its features : it exists no longer as a broken archipelago, scantily covered by a semi-arctic vegetation, but as a continuous land, still whitened, where the great valleys open to the sea, by the pale gleam of local glaciers, and snow-streaked on its loftier hill-tops. But vast forests of dark pine sweep along its hill-sides or selvage its shores ; and the sheltered hollows are enlivened by the lighter green of the oak, the ash, and the elm. Human foot has not yet imprinted its sward ; but its brute inhabitants have become numerous. The cream-coloured coat of the wild bull,—a speck of white relieved against a ground of dingy green,—may be seen far amid the pines, and the long howl of the wolf heard from the nearer thickets. The gigantic elk raises himself from his lair, and tosses his ponderous horns at the sound ; while the beaver, in some sequestered dell traversed by a streamlet, plunges alarmed into his

---

gigantic elk: the so-called 'Irish Elk', actually Giant Deer, *Megaloceros giganteus*, now extinct

deep coffer-dam, and, rising through the submerged opening
of his cell, shelters safely within, beyond reach of pursuit.
The great transverse valleys of the country, from its eastern
to its western coasts, are still occupied by the sea,—they exist
as broad ocean-sounds ; and many of the detached hills rise
around its shores as islands.   The northern Sutor forms a
bluff high island, for the plains of Easter Ross are still submerged ; and the Black Isle is in reality what in later times
it is merely in name,—a sea-encircled district, holding a midway place between where the Sound of the great Caledonian
Valley and the Sounds of the Valleys of the Conan and Carron open into the German Ocean.   Though the climate has
greatly softened, it is still, as the local glaciers testify, ungenial and severe.   Winter protracts his stay through the later
months of spring ; and still, as of old, vast floats of ice, detached from the glaciers, or formed in the lakes and shallower
estuaries of the interior, come drifting down the Sounds every
season, and disappear in the open sea, or lie stranded along
the shores.

Ages have again passed : the huge boulder, from the further sinking of the waters, lies dry throughout the neaps, and
is covered only at the height of each stream-tide ; there is a
float of ice stranded on the beach, which consolidates around
it during the neap, and is floated off by the stream ; and the
boulder, borne in its midst, as of old, again sets out a voyaging.   It has reached the narrow opening of the Sutors, swept
downwards by the strong ebb current, when a violent storm
from the north-east sets in ; and, constrained by antagonist
forces,—the sweep of the tide on the one hand, and the roll
of the waves on the other,—the ice-raft deflects into the little
bay that lies to the east of the promontory now occupied by
the town of Cromarty.   And there it tosses, with a hundred
more jostling in rude collision ; and at length bursting apart,
the *Clach Malloch*, its journeyings for ever over, settles on its

Caledonian Valley: Great Glen

final resting-place. In a period long posterior it saw the ultimate elevation of the land. Who shall dare say how much more it witnessed, or decide that it did not form the centre of a rich forest vegetation, and that the ivy did not cling round it, and the wild rose shed its petals over it, when the Dingwall, Moray, and Dornoch Friths existed as sub-aerial valleys, traversed by streams that now enter the sea far apart, but then gathered themselves into one vast river, that, after it had received the tributary waters of the Shin and the Conon, the Ness and the Beauly, the Helmsdale, the Brora, the Findhorn, and the Spey, rolled on through the flat secondary formations of the outer Moray Frith,—Lias, and Oolite, and Greensand, and Chalk,—to fall into a gulf of the Northern Ocean which intervened between the coasts of Scotland and Norway, but closed nearly opposite the mouth of the Tyne, leaving a broad level plain to connect the coasts of England with those of the Continent! Be this as it may, the present sea-coast became at length the common boundary of land and sea. And the boulder continued to exist for centuries still later as a nameless stone, on which the tall gray heron rested moveless and ghost-like in the evenings, and the seal at mid-day basked lazily in the sun. And then there came on a night of fierce tempest, in which the agonizing cry of drowning men was heard along the shore. When the morning broke, there lay strewed around a few bloated corpses, and the fragments of a broken wreck; and amid wild execrations and loud sorrow the boulder received its name. Such is the probable history, briefly told, because touched at merely a few detached points, of the huge *Clach Malloch.* The incident of the second voyage here is of course altogether imaginary, in relation to at least this special boulder; but it is to second voyages only that all our positive evidence testifies in the history of its class. The boulders of the St Lawrence, so well described by Sir Charles Lyell, voyage by thousands every year ;* and there are few of my northern readers who have not heard of the short trip taken nearly half a century ago by the boulder of Petty Bay, in the neighbourhood of Culloden.

A Highland minister of the last century, in describing, for Sir John Sinclair's Statistical Account, a large sepulchral cairn in his parish, attributed its formation to an *earthquake !* Earthquakes, in these latter times, are introduced, like the heathen gods of old, to bring authors out of difficulties.   I do not think, however,—and I have the authority of the old critic for at least half the opinion,—that either gods or earthquakes should be resorted to by poets or geologists, without special occasion : they ought never to be called in except as a last resort, when there is no way of getting on without them.   And I am afraid there have been few more gratuitous invocations of the earthquake than on a certain occasion, some five years ago, when it was employed by the inmate of a north-country manse, at once to account for the removal of the boulder-stone of Petty Bay, and to annihilate at a blow the geology of the Free Church editor of the *Witness.*   I had briefly stated in one of my papers, in referring to this curious

---

* "In the river St Lawrence," says Sir Charles Lyell, "the loose ice accumulates on the shoals during the winter, at which season the water is low.   The separate fragments of ice are readily frozen together in a climate where the temperature is sometimes 30° below zero, and boulders become entangled with them ; so that in the spring, when the river rises on the melting of the snow, the rocks are floated off, frequently conveying away the boulders to great distances.   A single block of granite, fifteen feet long by ten feet both in width and height, and which could not contain less than fifteen hundred cubic feet of stone, was in this way moved down the river several hundred yards, during the late survey in 1837.   Heavy anchors of ships, lying on the shore, have in like manner been closed in and removed. In October 1836, wooden stakes were driven several feet into the ground, at one point on the banks of the St Lawrence, at high-water mark, and over them were piled many boulders as large as the united force of six men could roll.   The year after, all the boulders had disappeared, and others had arrived, and the stakes had been drawn out and carried away by the ice."—(" Elements," first edition, p. 138.)

---

boulder of Petty Bay: a boulder, up to 7 feet in diameter, which lay near a stream at around high tide level on the shore at Petty near Culloden and was a local landmark. One winter so much stream water froze over the boulder that the boulder gained partial flotation on an exceptionally high tide and was dragged 780 feet downshore by a violent blizzard (Miller 1859, pp. 69-70) incident, that the boulder of the bay had been "borne nearly three hundred yards outwards into the sea by an enclasping mass of ice, in the course of a single tide." "Not at all," said the northern clergyman; "the cause assigned is wholly insufficient to produce such an effect. All the ice ever formed in the bay would be insufficient to remove such a boulder a distance, not of three hundred, but even of *three* yards." The removal of the stone "*is referrible to an* EARTHQUAKE!" The country, it would seem, took a sudden lurch, and the stone tumbled off. It fell athwart the flat surface of the bay, as a soup tureen sometimes falls athwart the table of a storm-beset steamer, vastly to the discomfort of the passengers, and again caught the ground as the land righted. Ingenious, certainly! It does appear a little wonderful, however, that in a shock so tremendous nothing should have fallen off except the stone. In an earthquake on an equally great scale, in the present unsettled state of society, endowed clergymen would, I am afraid, be in some danger of falling out of their charges.

The boulder beside the Auldgrande has not only, like the *Clach Malloch*, a geologic history of its own, but, what some may deem of perhaps equal authority, a *mythologic* history also. The inaccessible chasm, impervious to the sun, and ever resounding the wild howl of the tortured water, was too remarkable an object to have escaped the notice of the old imaginative Celts; and they have married it, as was their wont, to a set of stories quite as wild as itself. And the boulder, occupying a nearly central position in its course, just where the dell is deepest, and narrowest, and blackest, and where the stream bellows far underground in its wildest combination of tones, marks out the spot where the more extraordinary incidents have happened, and the stranger sights have been seen. Immediately beside the stone there is what seems to be the beginning of a path leading down to the

water; but it stops abruptly at a tree,—the last in the descent,—and the green and dewy rock sinks beyond for more
than a hundred feet, perpendicular as a wall.   It was at the
abrupt termination of this path that a Highlander once saw a
beautiful child smiling and stretching out its little hand to
him, as it hung half in air by a slender twig.   But he well
knew that it was no child, but an evil spirit, and that if he
gave it the assistance which it seemed to crave, he would be
pulled headlong into the chasm, and never heard of more.
And the boulder still bears, it is said, on its side,—though I
failed this evening to detect the mark,—the stamp, strangely
impressed, of the household keys of Balconie.*

The sun had now got as low upon the hill, and the ravine
had grown as dark, as when, so long before, the Lady of Balconie took her last walk along the sides of the Auldgrande ;
and I struck up for the little alpine bridge of a few undressed
logs, which has been here thrown across the chasm, at the
height of a hundred and thirty feet over the water.   As I
pressed through the thick underwood, I startled a strange-
looking apparition in one of the open spaces beside the gulf,
where, as shown by the profusion of plants of *vaccinium*, the
blaeberries had greatly abounded in their season.   It was that
of an extremely old woman, cadaverously pale and miserable
looking, with dotage glistening in her inexpressive, rheum-
distilling eyes, and attired in a blue cloak, that had been
homely when at its best, and was now exceedingly tattered.
She had been poking with her crutch among the bushes, as
if looking for berries ; but my approach had alarmed her ;
and she stood muttering in Gaelic what seemed, from the
tones and the repetition, to be a few deprecatory sentences.
I addressed her in English, and inquired what could have
brought to a place so wild and lonely, one so feeble and help-

---

* The story of the Lady of Balconie and her keys is narrated in " Scenes
and Legends of the North of Scotland," chap. xi.

less. "Poor object!" she muttered in reply,—"poor object! —very hungry;" but her scanty English could carry her no further. I slipped into her hand a small piece of silver, for which she overwhelmed me with thanks and blessings; and, bringing her to one of the broader avenues, traversed by a road which leads out of the wood, I saw her fairly entered upon the path in the right direction, and then, retracing my steps, crossed the log-bridge. The old woman,—little, I should suppose from her appearance, under ninety,—was, I doubt not, one of our ill-provided Highland paupers, that starve under a law which, while it has dried up the genial streams of voluntary charity in the country, and presses hard upon the means of the humbler classes, alleviates little, if at all, the sufferings of the extreme poor. Amid present suffering and privation there had apparently mingled in her dotage some dream of early enjoyment,—a dream of the days when she had plucked berries, a little herd-girl, on the banks of the Auldgrande; and the vision seemed to have sent her out, far advanced in her second childhood, to poke among the bushes with her crutch.

My old friend the minister of Alness,—uninstalled at the time in his new dwelling,—was residing in a house scarce half a mile from the chasm, to which he had removed from the parish manse at the Disruption; and, availing myself of an invitation of long standing, I climbed the acclivity on which it stands, to pass the night with him. I found, however, that, with part of his family, he had gone to spend a few weeks beside the mineral springs of Strathpeffer, in the hope of recruiting a constitution greatly weakened by excessive labour, and that the entire household at home consisted of but two of the young ladies his daughters, and their ward the little Buchubai Hormazdji.

And who, asks the reader, is this Buchubai Hormazdji? A little Parsi girl, in her eighth year, the daughter of a Chris-

---

My old friend the minister of Alness: see Additional Notes

tian convert from the ancient faith of Zoroaster, who now
labours in the Free Church Mission at Bombay.   Buchubai,
his only child, was, on his conversion, forcibly taken from him
by his relatives, but restored again by a British court of law ;
and he had secured her safety by sending her to Europe, a
voyage of many thousand miles, with a lady, the wife of one
of our Indian missionaries, to whom she had become attached,
as her second but true mamma, and with whose sisters I now
found her.   The little girl, sadly in want of a companion this
evening, was content, for lack of a better, to accept of me as
a playfellow ; and she showed me all her rich eastern dresses,
and all her toys, and a very fine emerald, set in the oriental
fashion, which, when she was in full costume, sparkled from
her embroidered tiara.   I found her exceedingly like little
girls at home, save that she seemed more than ordinarily observant and intelligent,—a consequence, mayhap, of that early
development, physical and mental, which characterizes her
race.   She submitted to me, too, when I had got very much
into her confidence, a letter she had written to her papa from
Strathpeffer, which was to be sent him by the next Indian
mail.   And as it may serve to show that the style of little
girls whose fathers were fire-worshippers for three thousand
years and more differs in no perceptible quality from the
style of little girls whose fathers in considerably less than three
thousand were Pagans, Papists, and Protestants by turns, besides passing through the various intermediate forms of belief, I must, after pledging the reader to strict secrecy, submit it to his perusal :—

   " My dearest Papa,—I hope you are quite well.   I am
visiting mamma at present at Strathpeffer.   She is much
better now than when she was travelling.   Mamma's sisters
give their love to you, and mamma and Mr and Mrs F.
also.   They all ask you to pray for them, and they will pray
also.   There are a great many at water here for sick people

to drink out of. The smell of the water is not at all nice. I sometimes drink it. Give my dearest love to Narsion Skishadre, and tell her that I will write to her.—Dearest papa," &c.

It was a simple thought, which it required no reach of mind whatever to grasp,—and yet an hour spent with little Buchubai made it tell upon me more powerfully than ever before,—that there is in reality but one human nature on the face of the earth. Had I simply read of Buchubai Hormazdji corresponding with her father Hormazdji Pestonji, and sending her dear love to her old companion Narsion Skishadre, the names, so specifically different from those which we ourselves employ in designating our country folk, would probably have led me, through a false association, to regard the parties to which they attach as scarcely less specifically different from our country folk themselves. I suspect we are misled by associations of this kind when we descant on the peculiarities of race as interposing insurmountable barriers to the progress of improvement, physical or mental. We overlook, amid the diversities of form, colour, and language, the specific identity of the human family. The Celt, for instance, wants, it is said, those powers of sustained application which so remarkably distinguish the Saxon; and so we agree on the expediency of getting rid of our poor Highlanders by expatriation as soon as possible, and of converting their country into sheep-walks and hunting-parks. It would be surely well to have philosophy enough to remember what, simply through the exercise of a wise faith, the Christian missionary never forgets, that the peculiarities of race are not specific and ineradicable, but mere induced habits and idiosyncrasies engrafted on the stock of a common nature by accidents of circumstance or development; and that, as they have been wrought into the original tissue through the protracted operation of one set of causes, the operation of another and different set, wisely and perseve-

Hormazdji Pestonji: see Additional Notes; **development**: here used, apparently, in the modern sense of individual development and growth, not in the alternative sense of 'evolution'

ringly directed, could scarce fail to unravel and work them
out again. They form no part of the inherent design of man's
nature, but have merely stuck to it in its transmissive passage downwards, and require to be brushed off.   There was
a time, some four thousand years ago, when Celt and Saxon
were represented by but one man and his wife, with their
children and their children's wives ; and some sixteen or seven-
teen centuries earlier, all the varieties of the species,—Cau-
càsian and Negro, Mongolian and Malay,—lay close packed
up in the world's single family. In short, Buchubai's amusing prattle proved to me this evening no bad commentary on
St Paul's sublime enunciation to the Athenians, that God has
" made of one blood all nations of men to dwell on all the
face of the earth."   I was amused to find that the little girl,
who listened intently as I described to the young ladies all I
had seen and knew of the Auldgrande, had never before heard
of a ghost, and could form no conception of one now.   The
ladies explained, described, defined ; carefully guarding all
they said, however, by stern disclaimers against the ghost
theory altogether, but apparently to little purpose.   At length
Buchubai exclaimed, that she now knew what they meant,
and that she herself had seen a great many ghosts in India.
On explanation, however, her ghosts, though quite frightful
enough, turned out to be not at all spiritual : they were
things of common occurrence in the land she had come from,
—exposed bodies of the dead.

  Next morning—as the white clouds and thin mist-streaks
of the preceding day had fairly foretold—was close and wet ;
and the long trail of vapour which rises from the chasm of
the Auldgrande in such weather, and is known to the people
of the neighbourhood as the " smoke of the lady's baking,"
hung, snake-like, over the river. About two o'clock the rain
ceased, hesitatingly and doubtfully, however, as if it did not
quite know its own mind ; and there arose no breeze to shake

the dank grass, or to dissipate the thin mist-wreath that continued to float over the river under a sky of deep gray. But the ladies, with Buchubai, impatient to join their friends at Strathpeffer, determined on journeying notwithstanding; and, availing myself of their company and their vehicle, I travelled on with them to Dingwall, where we parted. I had purposed exploring the gray dingy sandstones and foetid breccias developed along the shores on the northern side of the bay, about two miles from the town, and on the sloping acclivities between the mansion-houses of Tulloch and Fowlis; but the day was still unfavourable, and the sections seemed untemptingly indifferent; besides, I could entertain no doubt that the dingy beds here are identical in place with those of Cadboll on the coast of Easter Ross, which they closely resemble, and which alternate with the lower ichthyolitic beds of the Old Red Sandstone; and so, for the present at least, I gave up my intention of exploring them.

In the evening, the sun, far gone down towards its place of setting, burst forth in great beauty; and, under the influence of a kindly breeze from the west, just strong enough to shake the wet leaves, the sky flung off its thick mantle of gray. I sauntered out along the high-road, in the direction of my old haunts at Cononside, with, however, no intention of walking so far. But the reaches of the river, a little in flood, shone temptingly through the dank foliage, and the cottages under the Conon woods glittered clear on their sweeping hill-side, "looking cheerily out" into the landscape; and so I wandered on and on, over the bridge, and along the river, and through the pleasure-grounds of Conon-house, till I found myself in the old solitary burying-ground beside the Conon, which, when last in this part of the country, I was prevented from visiting by the swollen waters. The rich yellow light streamed through the interstices of the tall hedge of forest-trees that encircles the eminence, once an island, and fell in fantastic

patches on the gray tomb-stones and the graves.   The ruinous
little chapel in the corner, whose walls a quarter of a century
before I had distinctly traced, had sunk into a green mound;
and there remained over the sward but the arch-stone of a
Gothic window, with a portion of the moulded transom attached, to indicate the character and style of the vanished
building.   The old dial-stone, with the wasted gnomon, has
also disappeared; and the few bright-coloured *throch-stanes,*
raw from the chisel, that had been added of late years to the
group of older standing, did not quite make up for what time
in the same period had withdrawn.   One of the newer inscriptions, however, recorded a curious fact.   When I had
resided in this part of the country so long before, there was
an aged couple in the neighbourhood, who had lived together,
it was said, as man and wife for more than sixty years; and
now, here was their tombstone and epitaph.   They had lived
on long after my departure; and when, as the seasons passed,
men and women whose births and baptisms had taken place
since their wedding-day were falling around them well stricken
in years, death seemed to have forgotten *them;* and when
he came at last, their united ages made up well nigh two
centuries.   The wife had seen her ninety-sixth and the husband his hundred and second birth-day.   It does not trans-
cend the skill of the actuary to say how many thousand
women must die under ninety-six for every one that reaches
it, and how many tens of thousands of men must die under
a hundred and two for every man who attains to an age so
extraordinary; but he would require to get beyond his tables
in order to reckon up the chances against the woman destined
to attain to ninety-six being courted and married in early life
by the man born to attain to a hundred and two.

  After enjoying a magnificent sunset on the banks of the
Conon, just where the scenery, exquisite throughout, is most
delightful, I returned through the woods, and spent half an

hour by the way in the cottage of a kindly-hearted woman, now considerably advanced in years, whom I had known, when she was in middle life, as the wife of one of the Conon-side hinds, and who not unfrequently, when I was toiling at the mallet in the burning sun, hot and thirsty, and rather loosely knit for my work, had brought me—all she had to offer at the time—a draught of fresh whey. At first she seemed to have wholly forgotten both her kindness and the object of it. She well remembered my master, and another Cromarty man who had been grievously injured, when undermining an old building, by the sudden fall of the erection; but she could bethink her of no third Cromarty man whatever. "Eh, sirs!" she at length exclaimed, "I daresay ye'll be just the sma' prentice laddie. Weel, what will young folk no come out o'? They were amaist a' stout big men at the wark except yoursel'; an' you're now stouter and bigger than maist o' them. Eh, sirs!—an' are ye still a mason?" "No; I have not wrought as a mason for the last fourteen years; but I have to work hard enough for all that." "Weel, weel, its our appointed lot; an' if we have but health an' strength, an' the wark to do, why should we repine?" Once fairly entered on our talk together, we gossipped on till the night fell, giving and receiving information regarding our old acquaintances of a quarter of a century before; of whom we found that no inconsiderable proportion had already sunk in the stream in which eventually we must all disappear. And then, taking leave of the kindly old woman, I walked on in the dark to Dingwall, where I spent the night. I could fain have called by the way on my old friend and brother-workman, Mr Urquhart,—of a very numerous party of mechanics employed at Conon-side in the year 1821 the only individual now resident in this part of the country; but the lateness of the hour forbade. Next morning I returned by the Conon road, as far as the noble bridge which strides across

---

for the last fourteen years: since around August 1833 – but he failed to count the last gravestone he ever carved, a headstone for his infant daughter Eliza who died in August 1839 and is buried in St Regulus's kirkyard, Cromarty (Bayne, 1871, II, p. 120)

the stream at the village, and which has done so much to
banish the water-wraith from the fords; and then striking
off to the right, I crossed, by a path comparatively little frequented, the insulated group of hills which separates the valley of the Conon from that of the Peffer.   The day was mild
and pleasant, and the atmosphere clear; but the higher hills
again exhibited their ominous belts of vapour, and there had
been a slight frost during the night,—at this autumnal season the almost certain precursor of rain.

---

water-wraith: in Highland folklore, the perils of fording fast-flowing Highland rivers,
of which the Conon was particularly dangerous, were 'personified ... by a frightful goblin,
that took a malignant delight in luring into its pools, or overpowering in its fords, the
benighted traveller' (Miller 1858, p. 202). But it became unemployed when proper bridges
were built

CHAPTER IX.

I WAS once more on the Great Conglomerate,—here, as elsewhere, a picturesque, boldly-featured deposit, traversed by
narrow mural-sided valleys, and tempested by bluff abrupt
eminences. Its hills are greatly less confluent than those of
most of the other sedimentary formations of Scotland ; and
their insulated summits, recommended by their steep sides
and limited areas to the old savage Vaubans of the Highlands, furnished, ere the historic eras began, sites for not a
few of the ancient hill-forts of the country. The vitrified
fort of Craig Phadrig, of the Ord Hill of Kessock, and of
Knock Farril,—two of the number, the first and last, being
the most celebrated erections of their kind in the north of
Scotland,—were all formed on hills of the Great Conglomerate. The Conglomerate exists here as a sort of miniature
Highlands, set down at the northern side of a large angular
bay of Palæozoic rock, which indents the *true* Highlands of
the country, and which exhibits in its central area a prolongation of the long moory ridge of the Black Isle, formed, as
I have already had occasion to remark, of an *upper* deposit
of the same lower division of the Old Red,—a deposit as
noticeable for affecting a confluent, rectilinear character in
its elevations, as the Conglomerate is remarkable for exhibiting a detached and undulatory one. Exactly the same

---

Vaubans: the seventeenth century Marquis de Vauban, Marshal of France, was one of
history's greatest military engineers

features are presented by the same deposits in the neighbourhood of Inverness; the *undulatory* Conglomerate composing, to the north and west of the town, the picturesque
wavy ridge comprising the twin-eminences of Munlochy Bay,
the Ord Hill of Kessock, Craig Phadrig, and the fir-covered
hill beyond in the line of the Great Valley; while on the
south and east, the *rectilinear* ichthyolitic member of the system, with the arenaceous beds that lie over it, form the continuous straight-lined ridge which runs on from beyond the
moor of the Leys to beyond the moor of Culloden.   There is
a pretty little loch in this dwarf Highlands of the Brahan
district, into which the old Celtic prophet Kenneth Ore, when,
like Prospero, he relinquished his art, buried " deep beyond
plummet sound" the magic stone in which he was wont to
see the distant and the future.   And with the loch it contains a narrow hermit-like dell, bearing but a single row of
fields, and these of small size, along its flat bottom, and whose
steep gray sides of rustic Conglomerate resemble Cyclopean
walls.   It, besides, includes among its hills the steep hill of
Knock Farril, which, rising bluff and bold immediately over
the southern slopes of Strathpeffer, adds so greatly to the
beauty of the valley, and bears atop perhaps the finest specimen of the vitrified fort in Scotland; and the bold frontage of cliff presented by the group to the west, over the pleasure grounds of Brahan, is, though on no very large scale,
one of the most characteristic of the Conglomerate formation
which can be seen anywhere.   It is formed of exactly such
cliffs as the landscape gardener would make if he could,—
cliffs with their rude prominent pebbles breaking the light
over every square foot of surface, and furnishing footing, by
their innumerable projections, to many a green tuft of moss,
and many a sweet little flower.   Some of the masses, too,
that have rolled down from the precipices among the Brahan
woods far below, and stand up, like the ruins of cottages,

Kenneth Ore: phonetic for Coinneach Odhar, the Brahan Seer. He had 'second sight',
the legendary ability of some Gaels to see beyond the normal limits of space and time;
'buried deep beyond plummet sound': Shakespeare's *The Tempest*, Act 5, Scene 1
– 'And deeper than did ever plummet sound/I'll drown my book …'

amid the trees, are of singular beauty,—worth all the imita-
tion-ruins ever erected, and obnoxious to none of the dispa-
raging associations which the mere show and make-believe of
the artificial are sure always to awaken.

Whatever exhibited an aspect in any degree extraordinary
was sure to attract the notice of the old Highlanders,—an
acutely observant race, however slightly developed their reflective powers ; and the great natural objects which excited
their attention we always find associated with some traditionary story.   It is said that in the Conglomerate cliffs above
Brahan, a retainer of the Mackenzie, one of the smiths of the
tribe, discovered a rich vein of silver, which he wrought by
stealth, until he had filled one of the apartments of his cottage with bars and ingots.   But the treasure, it is added, was
betrayed, by his own unfortunate vanity, to his chief, who
hanged him in order to serve himself his heir ; and no one
since his death has proved ingenious enough to convert the
rude rock into silver.   Years had, I found, wrought their
changes amid the miniature Highlands of the Conglomerate.
The sapplings of the straggling wood on the banks of Loch
Ousy,—the pleasant little lake, or lochan rather, of this upland region,—that I remembered having seen scarce taller
than myself, had shot into vigorous treehood; and the steep
slopes of Knock Farril, which I had left covered with their
dark screen of pine, were now thickly mottled over with half-
decayed stumps, and bore that peculiarly barren aspect which
tracts cleared of their wood so frequently assume in their transition state, when the plants that flourished in the shade have
died out in consequence of the exposure, and plants that love
the open air and the unbroken sunshine have not yet sprung
up in their place.   I found the southern acclivities of the
hill covered with scattered masses of vitrified stone, that had
fallen from the fortalice atop; and would recommend to the
collector in quest of a characteristic specimen, that instead of

vitrified: see Additional Notes

labouring, to the general detriment of the pile, in detaching one from the walls above, he should set himself to seek one here. The blocks, uninjured by the hammer, exhibit, in most cases, the angular character of the original fragments better than those forcibly detached from the mass, and preserve in fine keeping those hollower interstices which were but partially filled with the molten matter, and which, when shattered by a blow, break through and lose their character.

One may spend an hour very agreeably on the green summit of Knock Farril. And at almost all seasons of the year a green summit it is,—greener considerably than any other hill-top in this part of the country. The more succulent grasses spring up rich and strong within the walls, here and there roughened by tufts of nettles, tall and rank, and somewhat perilous of approach,—witnesses, say the botanists, that man had once a dwelling in the immediate neighbourhood. The green luxuriance which characterizes so many of the more ancient fortalices of Scotland seems satisfactorily accounted for by Dr Fleming, in his "Zoology of the Bass.' "The summits and sides of those hills which were occupied by our ancestors as *hill-forts*," says the naturalist, "usually exhibit a far richer herbage than corresponding heights in the neighbourhood with the mineral soil derived from the same source. It is to be kept in view, that these positions of strength were at the same time occupied as *hill-folds*, into which, during the threatened or actual invasion of the district by a hostile tribe, the cattle were driven, especially during the night, as to places of safety, and sent out to pasture in the neighbourhood during the day. And the droppings of these collected herds would, as takes place in analogous cases at present, speedily improve the soil to such an extent as to induce a permanent fertility." The further instance adduced by the Doctor, in showing through what protracted periods causes transitory in themselves may remain palpably influen-

---

Fleming ... 'Zoology of the Bass': Fleming's 'Zoology' was part of a set of articles comprising a volume on the Bass Rock, an island in the Firth of Forth off North Berwick, which was honoured as the place where Covenanters were imprisoned during the seventeenth century (M'Crie 1848, quote from pp. 407-408). Miller contributed the geological section tial in their effects, is curiously suggestive of the old meta-physical idea, that as every effect has its cause, "recurring from cause to cause up to the abyss of eternity, so every cause has also its effects, linked forward in succession to the end of time." On the bleak moor of Culloden the graves of the slain still exist as patches of green sward, surrounded by a brown groundwork of stunted heather. The animal matter, —once the nerves, muscles, and sinews of brave men,—which originated the change, must have been wholly dissipated ages ago. But the effect once produced has so decidedly main-tained itself, that it remains not less distinctly stamped upon the heath in the present day than it could have been in the middle of the last century, only a few years after the battle had been stricken.

The vitrification of the rampart which on every side in-closes the grassy area has been more variously, but less satis-factorily, accounted for than the green luxuriance within. It was held by Pennant to be an effect of volcanic fire, and that the walls of this and all our other vitrified strongholds are simply the crater-rims of extinct volcanoes,—a hypothesis wholly as untenable in reference to the hill-forts as to the lime-kilns of the country : the vitrified forts are as little vol-canic as the vitrified kilns. Williams, the author of the "Mineral Kingdom," and one of our earlier British geolo-gists, after deciding, on data which his peculiar pursuits en-abled him to collect and weigh, that they are *not* volcanic, broached the theory, still prevalent, as their name testifies, that they are artificial structures, in which vitrescency was designedly induced, in order to cement into solid masses accu-mulations of loose materials. Lord Woodhouselee advocated an opposite view. Resting on the fact that the vitrification is but of partial occurrence, he held that it had been pro-duced, not of design by the builders of the forts, but in the process of their demolition by a besieging enemy, who, find-

---

'recurring ...': possibly based on 'Concatenation of events' in Voltaire's *Philosophical Dictionary* (www.voltaire.ox.ac.uk); **Pennant**: Thomas Pennant (1726-1798), author of *A tour in Scotland 1769*; **Williams**: John Williams (1732-1795), 'mineral engineer' and mining consultant (Torrens 2002); **Lord Woodhouselee**: (1747-1813), historian, antiquarian, and Law Lord

ing, as he premised, a large portion of the ramparts composed
of wood, had succeeded in setting them on fire.   This hypothesis, however, seems quite as untenable as that of Pennant.
Fires not unfrequently occur in cities, among crowded groupes
of houses, where walls of stone are surrounded by a much
greater profusion of dry woodwork than could possibly have
entered into the composition of the ramparts of a hill-fort ;
but who ever saw, after a city-fire, masses of wall from eight
to ten feet in thickness fused throughout ?   The sandstone
columns of the aisles of the Old Greyfriars in Edinburgh,
surrounded by the woodwork of the galleries, the flooring,
the seating, and the roof, were wasted, during the fire which
destroyed the pile, into mere skeletons of their former selves;
but though originally not more than three feet in diameter,
they exhibited no marks of vitrescency.   And it does not seem
in the least probable that the stone-work of the Knock Farril rampart could, if surrounded by wood at all, have been
surrounded by an amount equally great, in proportion to its
mass, as that which enveloped the aisle-columns of the Old
Greyfriars.

The late Sir George Mackenzie of Coul adopted yet a fourth
view.   He held that the vitrification is simply an effect of
the ancient beacon-fires kindled to warn the country of an
invading enemy.   But how account, on this hypothesis, for
ramparts continuous, as in the case of Knock Farril, all round
the hill ?   A powerful fire long kept up might well fuse a
heap of loose stones into a solid mass ; the bonfire lighted on
the summit of Arthur Seat in 1842, to welcome the Queen
on her first visit to Scotland, particularly fused numerous detached fragments of basalt, and imparted, in some spots to
the depth of about half an inch, a vesicular structure to the
solid rock beneath.   But no fire, however powerful, could
have constructed a rampart running without break for several hundred feet round an insulated hill-top.   " To be satis-

---

Old Greyfriars: Miller witnessed this church's destruction by fire (Miller 1891b, pp.
191-205); the late Sir George Mackenzie of Coul: (1780-1848), pro–Clearance landlord, notable mineralogist, and friend of Robert Jameson (Livingstone 2003)

fied," said Sir George, " of the reason why the signal-fires
should be kindled on or beside a heap of stones, we have only
to imagine a gale of wind to have arisen when a fire was
kindled on the bare ground. The fuel would be blown about
and dispersed, to the great annoyance of those who attended.
The plan for obviating the inconvenience thus occasioned
which would occur most naturally and readily would be to
raise a heap of stones, on either side of which the fire might
be placed to windward ; and to account for the vitrification
appearing all round the area, it is only necessary to allow the
inhabitants of the country to have had a system of signals.
A fire at one end might denote something different from a
fire at the other, or in some intermediate part. On some
occasions two or more fires might be necessary, and sometimes
a fire along the whole line. It cannot be doubted," he adds,
" that the rampart was originally formed with as much regularity as the nature of the materials would allow, both in
order to render it more durable, and to make it serve the
purposes of defence." This, I am afraid, is still very unsa-
tisfactory. A fire lighted along the entire line of a wall inclosing nearly an acre of area could not be other than a very
attenuated, wire-drawn line of fire indeed, and could never
possess strength enough to melt the ponderous mass of rampart beneath, as if it had been formed of wax or resin. A
thousand loads of wood piled in a ring round the summit of
Knock Farril, and set at once into a blaze, would wholly fail
to affect the broad rampart below ; and long ere even a thousand, or half a thousand, loads could have been cut down, collected, and fired, an invading enemy would have found time
enough to moor his fleet and land his forces, and possess himself of the lower country. Again, the unbroken continuity
of the vitrified line militates against the signal-system theory.
Fire trod so closely upon the heels of fire, that the vitrescency
induced by the one fire impinged on and mingled with the

vitrescency induced by the others beside it. There is no other mode of accounting for the continuity of the fusion ; and how could definite meanings possibly be attached to the various parts of a line so minutely graduated, that the centre of the fire kindled on any one graduation could be scarce ten feet apart from the centre of the fire kindled on any of its two neighbouring graduations ? Even by day, the exact compartment which a fire occupied could not be distinguished, at the distance of half a mile, from its neighbouring compartments, and not at all by night, at any distance, from even the compartments farthest removed from it. Who, for instance, at the distance of a dozen miles or so, could tell whether the flame that shone out in the darkness, when all other objects around it were invisible, was kindled on the east or west end of an eminence little more than a hundred yards in length ? Nay, who could determine,—for such is the requirement of the hypothesis,—whether it rose from a compartment of the summit a hundred feet distant from its west or east end, or from a compartment merely ninety or a hundred and ten feet distant from it ? The supposed signal system, added to the mere beacon hypothesis, is palpably untenable.

The theory of Williams, however, which is, I am inclined to think, the true one in the main, seems capable of being considerably modified and improved by the hypothesis of Sir George. The hill-fort,—palpably the most primitive form of fortalice or stronghold originated in a mountainous country,—seems to constitute man's first essay towards neutralizing, by the art of fortification, the advantages of superior force on the side of an assailing enemy. It was found, on the discovery of New Zealand, that the savage inhabitants had already learned to erect exactly such hill-forts amid the fastnesses of that country as those which were erected two thousand years earlier by the Scottish aborigines amid the fastnesses of our own. Nothing seems more probable, therefore, than that the forts of eminences such as Craig Phadrig and Knock Farril, originally mere inclosures of loose, uncemented stones, may belong to a period not less ancient than that of the first barbarous wars of Scotland, when, though tribe battled with tribe in fierce warfare, like the red men of the West with their brethren ere the European had landed on their shores, navigation was yet in so immature a state in Northern Europe as to secure to them an exemption from foreign invasion. In an after age, however, when the roving Vikingr had become formidable, many of the eminences originally selected, from *their inaccessibility*, as sites for hillforts, would come to be chosen, from *their prominence in the landscape*, as stations for beacon-fires. And of course the previously erected ramparts, higher always than the inclosed areas, would furnish on such hills the conspicuous points from which the fires could be best seen. Let us suppose, then, that the rampart-crested eminence of Knock Farril, seen on every side for many miles, has become in the age of northern invasion one of the beacon-posts of the district, and that large fires, abundantly supplied with fuel by the woods of a forest-covered country, and blown at times into intense heat by the strong winds so frequent in that upper stratum of air into which the summit penetrates, have been kindled some six or eight times on some prominent point of the rampart, raised, mayhap, many centuries before. At first the heat has failed to tell on the stubborn quartz and feldspar which forms the preponderating material of the gneisses, granites, quartz rocks, and coarse conglomerate sandstones on which it has been brought to operate ; but each fire throws down into the interstices a considerable amount of the fixed salt of the wood, till at length the heap has become charged with a strong flux; and then one powerful fire more, fanned to a white heat by a keen, dry breeze, reduces the whole into a semi-fluid mass. The same effects have been produced on the materials of the

---

red men: Native Americans; **throws down ... fixed salt:** leaves wood ash, which contains potash, *etc*, a flux reducing the melting point of the stone – but see Ralston (1976) rampart by the beacon-fires and the alkali, that were produced, according to Pliny, by the fires and the soda of the Phœnician merchants storm-bound on the sands of the river Belus. But the state of civilization in Scotland at the time is not such as to permit of the discovery being followed up by similar results. The semi-savage guardians of the beacon wonder at the *accident*, as they well may ; but those happy accidents in which the higher order of discoveries originate occur in only the ages of cultivated minds ; and so they do not acquire from it the art of manufacturing glass. It could not fail being perceived, however, by intellects at all human, that the consolidation which the fires of one week, or month, or year, as the case happened, had effected on one portion of the wall, might be produced by the fires of another week, or month, or year, on another portion of it ; that, in short, a loose incoherent rampart, easy of demolition, might be converted, through the newly-discovered process, into a rampart as solid and indestructible as the rock on which it rested. And so, in course of time, simply by shifting the beacon-fires, and bringing them to bear in succession on every part of the wall, Knock Farril, with many a similar eminence in the country, comes to exhibit its completely vitrified fort where there had been but a loosely-piled hill-fort before. It in no degree militates against this compound theory,—borrowed in part from Williams and in part from Sir George,—that there are detached vitrified masses to be found on eminences evidently never occupied by hill-forts ; or that there are hill-forts on other eminences only partially fused, or hill-forts on many of the less commanding sites that bear about them no marks of fire at all. Nothing can be more probable than that in the first class of cases we have eminences that had been selected as beacon-stations, which had not previously been occupied by hill-forts ; and in the last, eminences that had been occupied by hill-forts which, from their want of

---

Pliny: in his *Natural History*, Pliny the Elder, the Roman historian and writer, told the story of the Phoenician merchants trading in soda who accidentally heated a mixture of soda and beach sand in their campfire, and thereby discovered how to make glass prominence in the general landscape, had not been selected as beacon-stations. And in the intermediate class of cases we have probably ramparts that were only partially vitrified, because some want of fuel in the neighbourhood had starved the customary fires, or because fires had to be less frequently kindled upon them than on the more important stations ; or, finally, because these hill-forts, from some disadvantage of situation, were no longer used as places of strength, and so the beacon-keepers had no motive to attempt consolidating them throughout by the piecemeal application of the vitrifying agent. But the old Highland mode of accounting for the present appearance of Knock Farril and its vitrified remains is perhaps, after all, quite as good in its way as any of the modes suggested by the philosophers.*

I spent some time, agreeably enough, beside the rude rampart of Knock Farril, in marking the various appearances exhibited by the fused and semi-fused materials of which it is composed,—the granites, gneisses, mica-schists, hornblendes, clay-slates, and red sandstones of the locality. One piece of rock, containing much lime, I found resolved into a yellow opaque substance, not unlike the coarse earthenware used in the making of ginger-beer bottles ; but though it had been so completely molten that it had dropped into a hollow beneath in long viscid trails, it did not contain a single air-vesicle ; while another specimen, apparently a piece of fused mica-schist, was so filled with air-cells, that the dividing partitions were scarcely the tenth of a line in thickness. I found bits of schistose gneiss resolved into a green glass ; the Old Red Sandstone basis of the Conglomerate, which forms the hill, into a semi-metallic scoria, like that of an iron-smelter's furnace ; mica into a gray waxy-looking stone, that

---

* This mode is described in a traditionary story regarding a gigantic tribe of *Fions*, narrated in " Scenes and Legends of the North of Scotland," chap. iv.

---

old Highland mode: allegedly Knockfarril was the stronghold of 'Fions', legendary giants. One day the men went out hunting, leaving the women and children at home. One of the less capable hunters came home early and was teased by the women, so he set fire to their house over their heads (Miller 1835, pp. 82-84) scratched glass ; and pure white quartz into porcellanic trails of white, that ran in one instance along the face of a darker-coloured rock below, like streaks of cream along the sides of a burnt china jug.   In one mass of pale large-grained granite I found that the feldspar, though it had acquired a vitreous gloss on the surface, still retained its peculiar rhomboidal cleavage ; while the less stubborn quartz around it had become scarce less vesicular and light than a piece of pumice. On some of the other masses there was impressed, as if by a seal, the stamp of pieces of charcoal ; and so sharply was the impression retained, that I could detect on the vitreous surface the mark of the yearly growths, and even of the medullary rays, of the wood.   In breaking open some of the others, I detected fragments of the charcoal itself, which, hermetically locked up in the rock, had retained all its original carbon.   These last reminded me of specimens not unfrequent among the trap-rocks of the Carboniferous and Oolitic systems.   From an intrusive overlying wacke in the neighbourhood of Linlithgow I have derived for my collection pieces of carbonized wood in so complete a state of keeping, that under the microscope they exhibit unbroken all the characteristic reticulations of the coniferæ of the Coal Measures.

I descended the hill, and, after joining my friends at Strath-peffer,—Buchubai Hormazdji among the rest,—visited the Spa, in the company of my old friend the minister of Alness. The thorough identity of the powerful effluvium that fills the pump-room with that of a muddy sea-bottom laid bare in warm weather by the tide, is to the dweller on the sea-coast very striking.   It *is* identity,—not mere resemblance.   In most cases the organic substances undergo great changes in the bowels of the earth.   The animal matter of the Caithness ichthyolites exists, for instance, as a hard, black, insoluble bitumen, which I have used oftener than once as sealing-wax : the vegetable mould of the Coal Measures has been converted

wacke: old geological rock name, which can mean a clayey or silty sandstone, or a decomposed basalt – the latter meaning being implied by Miller's 'intrusive'; Spa: Miller's son Hugh (1850–1896) would become a professional geologist with the Geological Survey, and would take part in a survey of the spa's geology (Robins and McMillan 1989) into a fire-clay, so altered in the organic pabulum, animal and vegetable, whence it derived its fertility, that, even when laid open for years to the meliorating effects of the weather and the visits of the winged seeds, it will not be found bearing a single spike or leaf of green. But here, in smell at least, that ancient mud, swum over by the Diplopterus and Diplacanthus, and in which the Coccosteus and Pterichthys burrowed, has undergone no change. The soft ooze has become solid rock, but its odoriferous qualities have remained uñaltered. I next visited an excavation a few hundred yards on the upper side of the pump-room, in which the gray fetid breccia of the Strath has been quarried for dyke-building, and examined the rock with some degree of care, without, however, detecting in it a single plate or scale. Lying over that Conglomerate member of the system which, rising high in the Knock Farril range, forms the southern boundary of the valley, it occupies the place of the lower ichthyolitic bed, so rich in organisms in various other parts of the country ; but here the bed, after it had been deposited in thin horizontal laminæ, and had hardened into stone, seems to have been broken up, by some violent movement, into minute sharp-edged fragments, that, without wear or attrition, were again consolidated into the breccia which it now forms. And its ichthyolites, if not previously absorbed, were probably destroyed in the convulsion. Detached scales and spines, however, if carefully sought for in the various openings of the valley, might still be found in the original laminæ of the fragments. They must have been amazingly abundant in it once ; for so largely saturated is the rock with the organic matter into which they have been resolved, that, when struck by the hammer, the impalpable dust set loose sensibly affects the organs of taste, and appeals very strongly to those of smell. It is through this saturated rock that the mineral springs take their course. Even the surface-waters of the valley, as they

largely saturated: much of the organic material is now considered to derive from blooms of freshwater algae in Lake Orcadie, the large freshwater lake in and around which the Old Red Sandstone of the Moray Firth region and the Orkneys was deposited in Devonian times

pass over it contract in a perceptible degree its peculiar taste
and odour.   With a little more time to spare, I would fain
have made this breccia of the Old Red the subject of a few
simple experiments.   I would have ground it into powder,
and tried upon it the effect both of cold and hot infusion.
Portions of the water are sometimes carried in casks and bottles, for the use of invalids, to a considerable distance ; but
it is quite possible that a little of the *rock*, to which the water
owes its qualities, might, when treated in this way, have all
the effects of a considerable quantity of the *spring*.   It might
be of some interest, too, to ascertain its qualities when crushed,
as a soil, or its effect on other soils ; whether, for instance,
like the old sterile soils of the Carboniferous period, it has
lost, through its rock-change, the fertilizing properties which
it once possessed ; or whether it still retains them, like some
of the coprolitic beds of the Oolite and Greensand, and might
not, in consequence, be employed as a manure.   A course of
such experiments could scarce fail to furnish with agreeable
occupation some of the numerous annual visitants of the Spa,
who have to linger long, with but little to engage them, waiting for what, if it once fairly leave a man, returns slowly,
when it returns at all.

In mentioning at the dinner-table of my friend my scheme
of infusing rock in order to produce Spa water, I referred to
the circumstance that the Belemnite of our Liasic deposits,
when ground into powder, imparts to boiling water a peculiar taste and smell, and that the infusion, taken in very small
quantities, sensibly affects both palate and stomach.   And I
suggested that Belemnite water, deemed sovereign of old, when
the Belemnite was regarded as a thunderbolt, in the cure of
bewitched cattle, might be in reality medicinal, and that the
ancient superstition might thus embody, as ancient superstitions not unfrequently do, a nucleus of fact.   The charm, I
said, might amount to no more than simply the administra-

Greensand: certain strata of Cretaceous age in England. In some places, particularly
near Cambridge, certain layers were mined for phosphatic nodules derived from faecal
remains – 'coprolites' – and other biological sources; **thunderbolt**: see Additional Notes

tion of a medicine to sick cattle, that did harm in no case, and good at times. The lively comment of one of the young ladies on the remark amused us all. If an infusion of stone had cured, in the last age, cattle that were bewitched, the Strathpeffer water, she argued, which was, it seems, but an infusion of stone, might cure cattle that were sick now; and so, though the biped patients of the Strath could scarce fail to decrease when they knew that its infused stone contained but the strainings of old mud and the juices of dead unsalted fish, it was gratifying to think that the poor Spa might still continue to retain its patients, though of a lower order. The pump-room would be converted into a rustic, straw-thatched shed, to which long trains of sick cattle, affected by weak nerves and dyspepsia, would come streaming along the roads every morning and evening, to drink and gather strength.

The following morning was wet and lowering, and a flat ceiling of gray cloud stretched across the valley, from the summit of the Knock Farril ridge of hills on the one side, to the lower flanks of Ben Wyvis on the other. I had purposed ascending this latter mountain,—the giant of the northeastern coast, and one of the loftiest of our second-class Scottish hills anywhere,—to ascertain the extreme upper line at which travelled boulders occur in this part of the country. But it was no morning for wading knee-deep through the trackless heather; and after waiting on, in the hope the weather might clear up, watching at a window the poorer invalids at the Spa, as they dragged themselves through the rain to the water, I lost patience, and sallied out, beplaided and umbrellaed, to see from the top of Knock Farril how the country looked in a fog. At first, however, I saw much fog, but little country; but as the day wore on, the flat mist-ceiling rose higher, till it rested on but the distant hills, and the more prominent features of the landscape began to stand out amid the general gray, like the stronger lines and masses in a half-finished drawing, boldly dashed off in the neutral tint of the artist. The portions of the prospect generically distinct are, notwithstanding its great extent aud variety, but few ; and the partial veil of haze, by glazing down its distracting multiplicity of minor points, served to bring them out all the more distinctly. There is, first, stretching far in a southern and eastern direction along the landscape, the rectilinear ridge of the Black Isle,—not quite the sort of line a painter would introduce into a composition, but true to geologic character. More in the foreground, in the same direction, there spreads a troubled cockling sea of the Great Conglomerate. Turning to the north and west, the deep valley of Strathpeffer, with its expanse of rich level fields, and in the midst its old baronial castle, surrounded by coeval trees of vast bulk, lies so immediately at the foot of the eminence, that I could hear in the calm the rush of the little stream, swollen to thrice its usual bulk by the rains of the night. Beyond rose the thick-set Ben Wyvis,—a true gneiss mountain, with breadth enough of shoulders, and amplitude enough of base, to serve a mountain thrice as tall, but which, like all its cogeners of this ancient formation, was arrested in its second stage of growth, so that many of the slimmer granitic and porphyritic hills of the country look down upon it, as Agamemnon, according to Homer, looked down upon Ulysses.

" Broad is his breast, his shoulders larger spread,
Though great Atrides overtops his head."

All around, as if toppling, wave-like, over the outer edges of the comparatively flat area of Palæozoic rock which composes the middle ground of the landscape, rose a multitude of primary hill-peaks, barely discernible in the haze ; while the long withdrawing Dingwall Frith, stretching on towards the open sea for full twenty miles, and flanked on either side by ridges of sandstone, but guarded at the opening by two squat granitic columns, completed the prospect, by adding to it its

---

second stage of growth: see Additional Notes; 'Broad is his breast ...': Homer's *Iliad*, in Alexander Pope's translation, book III; **Dingwall Frith**; *ie* Firth of Cromarty

last great feature. All was gloomy and chill; and as I turned me down the descent, the thick wetting drizzle again came
on; and the mist-wreaths, after creeping upwards along the
hill-side, began again to creep down. When I had first visited the valley, more than a quarter of a century before, it
was on a hot breathless day of early summer, in which, though
the trees in fresh leaf seemed drooping in the sunshine, and
the succulent luxuriance of the fields lay aslant, half-prostrated
by the fierce heat, the rich blue of Ben Wyvis, far above, was
thickly streaked with snow, on which it was luxury even to
look. It gave one iced fancies, wherewithal to slake, amid
the bright glow of summer, the thirst in the mind. The
recollection came strongly upon me, as the fog from the hill-
top closed dark behind, like that sung by the old blind Englishman, which

> " O'er the marish glides,
> And gathers ground fast at the lab'rer's heel,
> Homeward returning."

But the contrast had nothing sad in it; and it was pleasant
to feel that it had not. I had resigned many a baseless hope
and many an idle desire since I had spent a vacant day amid
the sunshine, now gazing on the broad placid features of the
snow-streaked mountain, and now sauntering under the tall
ancient woods, or along the heath-covered slopes of the valley; but in relation to never-tiring, inexhaustible nature, the
heart was no fresher at that time than it was now. I had
grown no older in my feelings or in my capacity of enjoyment; and what then was there to regret?

I rode down the Strath in the omnibus which plies between
the Spa and Dingwall, and then walked on to the village of
Evanton, which I reached about an hour after nightfall, some-
what in the circumstances of the " damp stranger," who gave
Beau Brummel the cold. There were, however, no Beau
Brummels in the quiet village inn in which I passed the night,

---

first visited: as a young mason (Miller 1858); **Englishman**: Milton using evening mist as
a simile for cherubim descending on Eden as Adam and Eve depart, 'Paradise Lost', book
XII, lines 630–632; 'damp stranger': Beau Brummell (1778–1840), Regency fop and wit,
explained a cold as 'the wretch of an innkeeper' putting him 'into the coffee-room with a
damp stranger'. Possibly from *Blackwood's Edinburgh Magazine* for June 1844

and so the effects of the damp were wholly confined to myself. I was soundly pummelled during the night by a frightful female, who first assumed the appearance of the miserable
pauper woman whom I had seen beside the Auldgrande, and
then became the Lady of Balconie ; and, though sufficiently
indignant, and much inclined to resist, I could stir neither
hand nor foot, but lay passively on my back, jambed fast beside the huge gneiss boulder and the edge of the gulf. And
yet, by a strange duality of perception, I was conscious all
the while that, having got wet on the previous day, I was
now suffering from an attack of nightmare ; and held that it
would be no very serious matter even should the lady tumble
me into the gulf, seeing that all would be well again when I
awoke in the morning. Dreams of this character, in which
consciousness bears reference at once to the fictitious events
of the vision and the real circumstances of the sleeper, must
occupy, I am inclined to think, very little time,—single moments, mayhap, poised midway between the sleeping and wak-
ing state. Next day (Sunday) I attended the Free Church
in the parish, where I found a numerous and attentive congregation,—descendants, in large part, of the old devout Munroes of Ferindonald,—and heard a good solid discourse. And
on the following morning I crossed the sea at what is known
as the Fowlis Ferry, to explore, on my homeward route, the
rocks laid bare along the shore in the upper reaches of the
Frith.

I found but little by the way : black patches of bitumen
in the sandstone of one of the beds, with a bed of stratified
clay, inclosing nodules, in which, however, I succeeded in detecting nothing organic; and a few fragments of clay-slate
locked up in the Red Sandstone, sharp and unworn at their
edges, as if derived from no great distance, though there be
now no clay-slate in the eastern half of Ross ; but though
the rocks here belong evidently to the ichthyolitic member of

the Old Red, not a single fish, not a "nibble" even, repaid the patient search of half a day.   I, however, passed some time agreeably enough among the ruins of Craighouse. When I had last seen, many years before, this old castle,* the upper storeys were accessible ; but they were now no longer so. Time, and the little herdboys who occasionally shelter in its vaults, had been busy in the interval ; and, by breaking off a few projecting corners by which the climber had held, and by effacing a few notches into which he had thrust his toe-points, they had rendered what had been merely difficult impracticable. I remarked that the huge kitchen chimney of the building, —a deep hollow recess, which stretches across the entire gable, and in which, it is said, two thrashers once plied the flail for a whole winter,—bore less of the stain of recent smoke than it used to exhibit twenty years before ; and inferred that there would be fewer wraith-lights seen from the castle at nights than in those days of *evil spirits* and illicit stills, when the cottars in the neighbourhood sent more smuggled whisky to market than any equal number of the inhabitants of almost any other district in the north.   It has been long alleged that there existed a close connection between the more ghostly spirits of the country and its distilled ones.   " How do you account," said a north country minister of the last age (the late Rev. Mr M'Bean of Alves) to a sagacious old elder of his Session, " for the almost total disappearance of the ghosts and fairies that used to be so common in your young days ?" "Tak my word for't, minister," replied the shrewd old man, " it's a' owing to the *tea ;* whan the *tea* cam in, the ghaists an' fairies gaed out. Weel do I mind whan at a' our neebourly meetings,—bridals, christenings, lyke-wakes, an' the like,— we entertained ane anither wi' rich nappy ale ; an' whan the verra dowiest o' us used to get warm i' the face, an' a little confused in the head, an' weel fit to see amaist onything whan

* See " My Schools and Schoolmasters," chap. xi.

on the muirs on our way hame.   But the tea has put out the nappy ; an' I have remarked, that by losing the nappy we lost baith ghaists an' fairies."

Quitting the ruin, I walked on along the shore, tracing the sandstone as I went, as it rises from lower to higher beds; and where it ceases to crop out at the surface, and gravel and the red boulder-clays take the place of rock, I struck up the hill, and, traversing the parishes of Resolis and Cromarty, got home early in the evening.   I had seen and done scarcely half what I had intended seeing or doing : alas, that in reference to every walk which I have yet attempted to tread, this special statement should be so invariably true to fact !—alas, that all my full purposes should be coupled with but half realizations! But I had at least the satisfaction, that though I had accomplished little, I had enjoyed much ; and it is something, though not all, nor nearly all, that, since time is passing, it should pass happily.   In my next chapter I shall enter on my tour to Orkney.   It dates one year earlier (1846) than the tour with which I have already occupied so many chapters ; but I have thus inverted the order of *time*, by placing it last, that I may be able so to preserve the order of *space* as to render the tract travelled over in my narrative continuous from Edinburgh to the northern extremity of Pomona.

Pomona: Mainland or Hrossey, the largest island in the Orkney archipelago

CHAPTER X.

A TWELVEMONTH had gone by since a lingering indisposition, which bore heavily on the springs of life, compelled me to postpone a long-projected journey to the Orkneys, and led me to visit, instead, rich level England, with its well-kept roads and smooth railways, along which the enfeebled invalid can travel far without fatigue. I had now got greatly stronger; and, if not quite up to my old thirty miles per day, nor altogether so bold a cragsman as I had been only a few years before, I was at least vigorous enough to enjoy a middling long walk, and to breast a tolerably steep hill. And so I resolved on at least glancing over, if not exploring, the fossiliferous deposits of the Orkneys, trusting that an eye somewhat practised in the formations mainly developed in these islands might enable me to make some amends for seeing comparatively little, by seeing well. I took coach at Invergordon for Wick early in the morning of Friday; and, after a weary ride, in a bleak gusty day, that sent the dust of the road whirling about the ears of the sorely-tossed "outsides," with whom I had taken my chance, I alighted in Wick, at the inn-door, a little after six o'clock in the evening. The following morning was wet and dreary ; and a tumbling sea, raised by the wind of the previous day and night, came rolling into the bay ; but the waves bore with them no steamer ; and when, some

England: recorded in *First impressions of England and its people* (Miller 1847)

five hours after the expected time, she also came rolling in, her darkened and weather-beaten sides and rigging gave evidence that her passage from the south had been no holiday trip. Impatient, however, of looking out upon the sea for hours, from under dripping eaves, and through the dimmed panes of streaming windows, I got aboard with about half-a-dozen other passengers; and while the Wick goods were in the course of being transferred to two large boats alongside, we lay tossing in the open bay. The work of raising box and package was superintended by a tall elderly gentleman from the shore, peculiarly Scotch in his appearance,—the steam company's agent for this part of the country.

"That," said an acquaintance, pointing to the agent, "is a very extraordinary man,—in his own special walk, one of the most original-minded, and at the same time most thoroughly practical, you perhaps ever saw. That is Mr Bremner of Wick, known now all over Britain for his success in raising foundered vessels, when every one else gives them up. In the lifting of vast weights, or the overcoming the *vis inertiæ* of the hugest bodies, nothing ever baffles Mr Bremner. But come, I must introduce you to him. He takes an interest in your peculiar science, and is familiar with your geological writings."

I was accordingly introduced to Mr Bremner, and passed in his company the half-hour which we spent in the bay, in a way that made me wish the time doubled. I had been struck by the peculiar style of masonry employed in the harbour of Wick, and by its rock-like strength. The gray ponderous stones of the flagstone series of which it is built, instead of being placed on their flatter beds, like common ashlar in a building, or horizontal strata in a quarry, are raised on end, like staves in a pail or barrel, so that at some little distance the work looks as if formed of upright piles or beams jambed fast together. I had learned that Mr Bremner had

---

Bremner: James Bremner (1784–1856), shipbuilder, civil engineer, and salvage engineer been the builder, and adverted to the peculiarity of his style of building. "You have given a vertical tilt to your strata," I said : "most men would have preferred the horizontal position. It used to be regarded as one of the standing rules of my old profession, that the 'broad bed of a stone' is the best, and should be always laid 'below.'" "A good rule for the land," replied Mr Bremner, "but no good rule for the sea. The greatest blunders are almost always perpetrated through the misapplication of good rules. On a coast like ours, where boulders of a ton weight are rolled about with every storm like pebbles, these stones, if placed on what a workman would term their best beds, would be scattered along the shore like sea-wrack, by the gales of a single winter. In setting aside the prejudice," continued Mr Bremner, "that what is indisputably the best bed for a stone on dry land is also the best bed in the water on an exposed coast, I reasoned thus :—The surf that dashes along the beach in times of tempest, and that forms the enemy with which I have to contend, is not simply water, with an onward impetus communicated to it by the wind and tide, and a re-active impetus in the opposite direction,—the effect of the backward rebound, and of its own weight, when raised by these propelling forces above its average level of surface. True, it is all this ; but it is also something more. As its white breadth of foam indicates, it is a subtile mixture of water and *air*, with a powerful *upward* action,—a consequence of the air struggling to effect its escape ; and this upward action must be taken into account in our calculations, as certainly as the other and more generally recognised actions. In striking against a piece of building, this subtile mixture dashes through the interstices into the interior of the masonry, and, filling up all its cavities, has, by its upward action, a tendency to *set the work afloat*. And the broader the beds of the stones, of course the more extensive are the surfaces which it has to act upon. One of

these flat flags, ten feet by four, and a foot in thickness, would
present to this upheaving force, if placed on end, a superficies
of but *four* square feet ; whereas, if placed on its broader
base, it would present to it a superficies of *forty* square feet.
Obviously, then, with regard to this aerial upheaving force,
that acts upon the masonry in a direction in which no precautions are usually adopted to bind it fast,—for the existence of the force itself is not taken into account,—the greater
bed of the stone must be just ten times over a worse bed
than its lesser one ; and on a tempestuous foam-encircled
coast such as ours, this aerial upheaving force is in reality,
though the builder may not know it, one of the most formidable forces with which he has to deal.   And so, on these
principles, I ventured to set my stones on end,—on what was
deemed their *worst*, not their *best* beds,—wedging them all
fast together, like staves in an anker ; and there, to the scan-
dal of all the old rules, are they fast wedged still, firm as
a rock."   It was no ordinary man that could have originated
such reasonings on such a subject, or that could have thrown
himself so boldly, and to such practical effect, on the conclusions to which they led.

Mr Bremner adverted, in the course of our conversation,
to a singular appearance among the rocks a little to the east
and south of the town of Wick, that had not, he said, attracted
the notice it deserved.   The solid rock had been fractured by
some tremendous blow, dealt to it externally at a considerable
height over the sea-level, and its detached masses scattered
about like the stones of an ill-built harbour broken up by a
storm.   The force, whatever its nature, had been enormously
great.   Blocks of some thirty or forty tons weight had been
torn from out the solid strata, and piled up in ruinous heaps,
as if the compact precipice had been a piece of loose brick-
work, or had been driven into each other, as if, instead of
being composed of perhaps the hardest and toughest sedi-

mentary rock in the country, they had been formed of sun-dried clay. " I brought," continued Mr Bremner, " one of your itinerant geological lecturers to the spot, to get his opinion ; but he could say nothing about the appearance : it was not in his books." " I suspect," I replied, " the phenomenon lies quite as much within your own province as within that of the geological lecturer. It is in all probability an illustration, on a large scale, of those floating forces with which you operate on your foundered vessels, joined to the forces, laterally exerted, by which you drag them towards the shore. When the sea stood higher, or the land lower, in the eras of the raised beaches, along what is now Caithness, the abrupt mural precipices by which your coast here is skirted must have secured a very considerable depth of water up to the very edge of the land ;—your coast-line must have resembled the side of a mole or wharf : and in that glacial period to which the thick deposit of boulder-clay immediately over your harbour yonder belongs, icebergs of very considerable size must not unfrequently have brushed the brows of your precipices. An iceberg from eighty to a hundred feet in thickness, and perhaps half a square mile in area, could not, in this old state of things, have come in contact with these cliffs without first catching the ground outside ; and such an iceberg, propelled by a fierce storm from the north-east, could not fail to lend the cliff with which it came in collision a tremendous blow. You will find that your shattered precipice marks, in all probability, the scene of a collision of this character : some hard-headed iceberg must have set itself to run down the land, and got wrecked upon it for its pains." My theory, though made somewhat in the dark,—for I had no opportunity of seeing the broken precipice until after my return from Orkney,—seemed to satisfy Mr Bremner ; nor, on a careful survey of the phenomenon, the solution of which it attempted, did I find occasion to modify or give it up.

With just knowledge enough of Mr Bremner's peculiar province to appreciate his views, I was much impressed by their broad and practical simplicity ; and bethought me, as we conversed, that the character of the thinking, which, according to Addison, forms the staple of all writings of genius, and which he defines as "simple but not obvious," is a character which equally applies to *all* good thinking, whatever its special department.   Power rarely resides in ingenious complexities : it seems to eschew in every walk the elaborately attenuated and razor-edged mode of thinking,—the thinking akin to that of the old metaphysical poets,—and to select the broad and massive style.   Hercules, in all the representations of him which I have yet seen, is the *broad* Hercules.   I was greatly struck by some of Mr Bremner's views on deep-sea founding.   He showed me how, by a series of simple, but certainly not obvious contrivances, which had a strong air of practicability about them, he could lay down his erection, course by course, in-shore, in a floating caisson of peculiar construction, beginning a little beyond the low-ebb line, and warping out his work piece-meal, as it sank, till it had reached its proper place, in, if necessary, from ten to twelve fathoms water, where, on a bottom previously prepared for it by the diving-bell, he had means to make it take the ground exactly at the required line.   The difficulty and vast expense of building altogether by the bell would be obviated, he said, by the contrivance, and a solidity given to the work otherwise impossible in the circumstances : the stones could be laid in his floating caisson with a care as deliberate as on the land.   Some of the anecdotes which he communicated to me on this occasion, connected with his numerous achievements in weighing up foundered vessels, or in floating off wrecked or stranded ones, were of singular interest ; and I regretted that they should not be recorded in an autobiographical memoir.   Not a few of them were humor-

'simple but not obvious': possibly derived from an article in *The Spectator*, 58, for 7 May 1711 ously told, and curiously illustrative of that general ignorance regarding the "strength of materials" in which the scientific world has been too strangely suffered to lie, in this the world's most mechanical age ; so that what ought to be questions of strict calculation are subjected to the guessings of a mere common sense, far from adequate, in many cases, to their proper resolution. "I once raised a vessel," said Mr Bremner,—"a large collier, choak-full of coal,—which an English projector had actually engaged to raise with huge bags of India rubber, inflated with air. But the bags, of course taxed far beyond their strength, collapsed or burst ; and so, when I succeeded in bringing the vessel up, through the employment of more adequate means, I got not only ship and cargo, but also a great deal of good India rubber to boot." Only a few months after I enjoyed the pleasure of this interview with the Brindley of Scotland, he was called south, to the achievement of his greatest feat in at least one special department,—a feat generally recognised and appreciated as the most herculean of its kind ever performed,—the raising and warping off of the Great Britain steamer from her perilous bed in the sand of an exposed bay on the coast of Ireland. I was conscious of a feeling of sadness as, in parting with Mr Bremner, I reflected, that a man so singularly gifted should have been suffered to reach a period of life very considerably advanced, in employments little suited to exert his extraordinary faculties, and which persons of the ordinary type could have performed as well. Napoleon,—himself possessed of great genius,—could have estimated more adequately than our British rulers the value of such a man. Had Mr Bremner been born a Frenchman, he would not now be the mere agent of a steam company, in a third-rate seaport town.

The rain had ceased, but the evening was gloomy and chill ; and the Orcades, which, on clearing the Caithness coast, came as fully in view as the haze permitted, were enveloped in

---

Brindley: James Brindley (1716–1772), leading civil engineer; **Great Britain**: Isambard Kingdom Brunel's screw steamship S. S. *Great Britain*, then an exceptionally large ship, and salvaged in the summer of 1847 by James Bremner and his son Alexander (Corlett 1975); **Orcades**: archaic name for the Orkneys an undress of cloud and spray, that showed off their flat low features to no advantage at all. The bold, picturesque Hebrides look well in any weather; but the level Orkney Islands, impressed everywhere, on at least their eastern coasts, by the comparatively tame character borne by the Old Red flagstones, when undisturbed by trap or the primary rocks, demand the full-dress auxiliaries of bright sun and clear sky, to render their charms patent. Then, however, in their sleek coats of emerald and purple, and surrounded by their blue sparkling sounds and seas, with here a long dark wall of rock, that casts its shadow over the breaking waves, and there a light fringe of sand and broken shells, they are, as I afterwards ascertained, not without their genuine beauties. But had they shared in the history of the neighbouring Shetland group, that, according to some of the older historians, were suffered to lie uninhabited for centuries after their first discovery, I would rather have been disposed to marvel this evening, not that they had been unappropriated so long, but that they had been appropriated at all. The late member for Orkney, not yet unseated by his Shetland opponent, was one of the passengers in the steamboat ; and, with an elderly man, an ambitious schoolmaster, strongly marked by the peculiarities of the genuine dominie, who had introduced himself to him as a brother voyager, he was pacing the quarter-deck, evidently doing his best to exert, under an unintermittent hot-water *douche* of queries, the patient courtesy of a Member of Parliament on a visit to his constituency. At length, however, the troubler quitted him, and took his stand immediately beside me ; and, too sanguinely concluding that I might take the same kind of liberty with the schoolmaster that the schoolmaster had taken with the Member, I addressed to him a simple query in turn. But I had mistaken my man : the schoolmaster permitted to unknown passengers in humble russet no such sort of familiarities as those permitted by the Member ; and so I met with a prompt rebuff, that at once set me down. I was evidently a big, forward lad, who had taken a liberty with the master. It is, I suspect, scarce possible for a man, unless naturally very superior, to live among boys for some twenty or thirty years, exerting over them all the while a despotic authority, without contracting those peculiarities of character which the master-spirits,—our Scotts, Lambs, and Goldsmiths,—have embalmed with such exquisite truth in our literature, and which have hitherto militated against the practical realization of those unexceptionable abstractions in behalf of the status and standing of the teacher of youth which have been originated by men less in the habit of looking about them than the poets. It is worth while remarking how invariably the strong common sense of the Scotch people has run every scheme under water that, confounding the character of the "village schoolmaster" with that of the "village clergyman," would demand from the schoolmaster the clergyman's work.

We crossed the opening of the Pentland Frith, with its white surges and dark boiling eddies, and saw its twin lighthouses rising tall and ghostly amid the fog on our lee. We then skirted the shores of South Ronaldshay, of Burra, of Copinshay, and of Deerness; and, after doubling Moul Head, and threading the sound which separates Shapinshay from the Mainland, we entered the Frith of Kirkwall, and caught, amid the uncertain light of the closing evening, our earliest glimpse of the ancient Cathedral of St Magnus. It seems at first sight as if standing solitary, a huge hermit-like erection, at the bottom of a low bay,—for its humbler companions do not make themselves visible until we have entered the harbour by a mile or two more, when we begin to find that it occupies, not an uninhabited tract of shore, but the middle of a gray straggling town, nearly a mile in length.

Lamb: Charles Lamb (1775-1834), essayist and humorist; **common sense**: see Additional Notes

We had just light enough to show us, on landing, that the
main thoroughfare of the place, very narrow and very crooked, had been laid out, ere the country beyond had got high-
ways, or the proprietors carts and carriages, with an exclusive eye to the necessities of the foot-passenger,—that many
of the older houses presented, as is common in our northern
towns, their gables to the street, and had narrow slips of
closes running down along their fronts,—and that as we
receded from the harbour, a goodly portion of their number
bore about them an air of respectability, long maintained, but
now apparently touched by decay.   I saw, in advance of one
of the buildings, several vigorous-looking planes, about forty
feet in height, which, fenced by tall houses in front and rear,
and flanked by the tortuosities of the street, had apparently
forgotten that they were in Orkney, and had grown quite as
well as the planes of public thoroughfares grow elsewhere.
After an abortive attempt or two made in other quarters, I
was successful in procuring lodgings for a few days in the
house of a respectable widow lady of the place, where I found
comfort and quiet on very moderate terms.   The cast of faded
gentility which attached to so many of the older houses of
Kirkwall,—remnants of a time when the wealthier Udallers
of the Orkneys used to repair to their capital at the close of
autumn, to while away in each other's society their dreary
winters,—reminded me of the poet Malcolm's "Sketch of
the Borough,"—a portrait for which Kirkwall is known to
have sat,—and of the great revolution effected in its evening
parties, when "tea and turn-out" yielded its place to "tea
and turn-in."   But the churchyard of the place, which I had
seen, as I passed along, glimmering with all its tombstones
in the uncertain light, was all that remained to represent
those "great men of the burgh," who, according to the poet,
used to "pop in on its card and dancing assemblies, about
the eleventh hour, resplendent in top-boots and scarlet vests,"

---

the poet Malcolm: Lt. John Malcolm (1792-1835), author of various works of poetry,
sketches and essays, see pp. 417-418; 'Sketch of the Borough', *etc*: various quotations
from 'The Borough' in *Poems, Tales and Sketches*; see Additional Notes

or of its "suppression-of-vice sisterhood of moral old maids," who kept all their neighbours right by the terror of their tongues. I was somewhat in a mood, after my chill and hungry voyage, to recall with a hankering of regret the vision of its departed suppers, so luxuriously described in the "Sketch,"—suppers at which "large rounds of boiled beef smothered in cabbage, smoked geese, mutton hams, roasts of pork, and dishes of dog-fish and of Welsh rabbits melted in their own fat, were diluted by copious draughts of strong home-brewed ale, and etherealized by gigantic bowls of rum punch." But the past, which is not ours, who, alas, can recall! And, after discussing a juicy steak and a modest cup of tea, I found I could regard with the indifferency of a philosopher, the perished suppers of Kirkwall.

I quitted my lodgings for church next morning about three quarters of an hour ere the service commenced ; and, finding the doors shut, sauntered up the hill that rises immediately over the town. The thick gloomy weather had passed with the night ; and a still, bright, clear-eyed Sabbath looked cheerily down on green isle and blue sea. I was quite unprepared by any previous description, for the imposing assemblage of ancient buildings which Kirkwall presents full in the foreground, when viewed from the road which ascends along this hilly slope to the uplands. So thickly are they massed together, that, seen from one special point of view, they seem a portion of some magnificent city in ruins,—some such city, though in a widely different style of architecture, as Palmyra or Baalbec. The Cathedral of St Magnus rises on the right, the castle-palace of Earl Patrick Stuart on the left, the bishop's palace in the space between ; and all three occupy sites so contiguous, that a distance of some two or three hundred yards abreast gives the proper angle for taking in the whole group at a glance. I know no such group elsewhere in Scotland. The church and palace of Linlith-

gow are in such close proximity, that, seen together, relieved
against the blue gleam of their lake, they form one magnificent pile ; but we have here a taller, and, notwithstanding
its Saxon plainness, a nobler church, than that of the southern burgh, and at least one palace more.   And the associations connected with the church, and at least one of the pa-
laces, ascend to a remoter and more picturesque antiquity.
The castle-palace of Earl Patrick dates from but the time of
James the Sixth ; but in the palace of the bishop, old grim
Haco died, after his defeat at Largs, "of grief," says Buchanan, "for the loss of his army, and of a valiant youth his
relation ;" and in the ancient Cathedral, his body, previous
to its removal to Norway, was interred for a winter.   The
church and palace belong to the obscure dawn of the national
history, and were Norwegian for centuries before they were
Scotch.

As I was coming down the hill at a snail's pace, I was
overtaken by a countryman on his way to church.   "Ye'll
hae come," he said, addressing me, "wi' the great man last
night ?'   "I came in the steamer," I replied, "with your
Member, Mr Dundas."   "O, aye," rejoined the man ; "but
I'm no sure he'll be our Member next time.   The Voluntaries yonder, ye see," jerking his head, as he spoke, in the direction of the United Secession chapel of the place, "are awfu'
strong, and unco radical ; an' the Free Kirk folk will soon
be as bad as them.   But I belong to the Establishment; and I
side wi' Dundas."   The aristocracy of Scotland committed,
I am afraid, a sad blunder when they attempted strengthening their influence as a class by seizing hold of the Church pa-
tronages.   They have fared somewhat like those sailors of
Ulysses who, in seeking to appropriate their master's wealth,
let out the winds upon themselves ; and there is now, in consequence, a perilous voyage and an uncertain landing before
them.   It was the patronate wedge that struck from off the

Haco ... Largs: the Scots defeated King Hakon of Norway in 1263, decisively halting
Scandinavian expansion and reinforcing Scots control of the Western Isles; Buchanan:
George Buchanan (1506-1582), Reformer, poet, dramatist, scholar, and author of *A history
of Scotland* – the quote is from Aikman (1827, I, p. 380); Member: of the Westminster
Parliament; Ulysses: see Additional Notes; wedge: *ie* patronage

Scottish Establishment at least nine-tenths of the Dissenters of the kingdom,—its Secession bodies, its Relief body, and, finally, its Free Church denomination,—comprising in their aggregate amount a great and influential majority of the Scotch people. Our older Dissenters,—a circumstance inevitable to their position as such,—have been thrown into the movement party : the Free Church, in her present transition state, sits loose to all the various political sections of the country; but her natural tendency is towards the movement party also; and already, in consequence, do our Scottish aristocracy possess greatly less political influence in the kingdom of which they owe almost all the soil, than that wielded by their brethren the Irish and English aristocracy in their respective divisions of the empire. Were the representation of England and Ireland as liberal as that of Scotland, and as little influenced by the aristocracy, Conservatism, on the passing of the Reform Bill, might have taken leave of office for evermore. And yet neither the English nor Irish are naturally so Conservative as the Scotch. The patronate wedge, like that appropriated by Achan, has been disastrous to the people, for it has lost to them the great benefits of a religious Establishment, and very great these are ; but it threatens, as in the case of the sons of Carmi of old, to work more serious evil to those by whom it was originally coveted,—"evil to themselves and all their house." As I approached the Free Church, a squat, sun-burned, carnal-minded "old wee wifie," who seemed passing towards the Secession place of worship, after looking wistfully at my gray maud, and concluding for certain that I could not be other than a Southland drover, came up to me, and asked, in a cautious whisper, "Will ye be wantin' a coo ?" I replied in the negative ; and the wee wifie, after casting a jealous glance at a group of gravefeatured Free Church folk in our immediate neighbourhood, who would scarce have tolerated Sabbath trading in a Sece-

---

Dissenters: the Secession and Relief churches, earlier secessions from the Establishment; Achan ... sons of Carmi: Bible, Joshua 7. When Jericho fell, its contents were cursed. Achan son of Carmi broke this prohibition by appropriating some of the spoil, bringing dire results to himself and his family; Southland drover: ie someone travelling to buy cattle to be herded to the Lowlands and England for fattening and sale; coo: cow (Scots) der, tucked up her little blue cloak over her head, and hied away to the chapel.

In the Free Church pulpit I recognised an old friend, to whom I introduced myself at the close of the service, and by whom I was introduced, in turn, to several intelligent members of his session, to whose kindness I owed, on the following day, introductions to some of the less accessible curiosities of the place. I rose betimes on the morning of Monday, that I might have leisure enough before me to see them all, and broke my first ground in Orkney as a geologist in a quarry a few hundred yards to the south and east of the town. It is strange enough how frequently the explorer in the Old Red finds himself restricted in a locality to well nigh a single organism,—an effect, probably, of some gregarious instinct in the ancient fishes of this formation, similar to that which characterizes so many of the fishes of the present time, or of some peculiarity in their constitution, which made each choose for itself a peculiar habitat. In this quarry, though abounding in broken remains, I found scarce a single fragment which did not belong to an exceedingly minute species of Coccosteus, of which my first specimen had been sent me a few years before by Mr Robert Dick, from the neighbourhood of Thurso, and which I at that time, judging from its general proportions, had set down as the young of the *Coccosteus cuspidatus.* Its apparent gregariousness, too, quite as marked at Thurso as in this quarry, had assisted, on the strength of an obvious enough analogy, in leading to the conclusion. There are several species of the existing fish, well known on our coasts, that, though solitary when fully grown, are gregarious when young. The coalfish, which as the sillock of a few inches in length congregates by thousands, but as the colum-saw of from two and a half to three feet is a solitary fish, forms a familiar instance; and I had inferred that the Coccosteus, found solitary, in

---

old friend: Rev. William Sinclair, born Edinburgh 1811; attended Edinburgh University, assistant at St Paul's, then, after the Disruption, 'laboured at Ellon' before being ordained at Grange in 1843, and was then translated to Kirkwall in 1845 where he died in 1874 (Ewing 1914, p. 317; Smith 1907, pp. 121-123) most instances, when at its full size, had, like the coal-fish, congregated in shoals when in a state of immaturity.   But a more careful examination of the specimens leads me to conclude that this minute gregarious Coccosteus, so abundant in this locality that its fragments thickly speckle the strata for hundreds of yards together—(in one instance I found the dorsal plates of four individuals crowded into a piece of flag barely six inches square)—was in reality a distinct species. Though not more than one-fourth the size, measured linearly, of the *Coccosteus decipiens*, its plates exhibit as many of those lines of increment which gave to the occipital buckler of the creature its tortoise-like appearance, and through which plates of the buckler species were at first mistaken for those of a Chelonian, as are exhibited by plates of the larger kinds, with an area ten times as great ; its tubercles, too, some of them of microscopic size, are as numerous ;—evidences, I think,— when we take into account that in the bulkier species the lines and tubercles increased in number with the growth of the plates, and that, once formed, they seem never to have been affected by the subsequent enlargement of the creature, —that this ichthyolite was not an *immature*, but really a *miniature* Coccosteus.   We may see on the plates of the full-grown Coccosteus, as on the shells of bivalves, such as *Cardium echinatum*, or on those of spiral univalves, such as *Buccinum undatum*, the diminutive markings which they bore when the creature was young ; and on the plates of this species we may detect a regular gradation of tubercles from the microscopic to the minute, as we may see on the plates of the larger kinds a regular gradation from the minute to the full-sized.   The average length of the dwarf Coccosteus of Thurso and Kirkwall, taken from the snout to the pointed termination of the dorsal plate, ranges from one and a-half to two inches ; its entire length from head to tail probably from three to four.   It was from one of Mr Dick's specimens

of this species that I first determined the true position of
the eyes of the Coccosteus,—a position which some of my
lately-found ichthyolites conclusively demonstrate, and which
Agassiz, in his restoration, deceived by ill-preserved specimens, has fixed at a point considerably more lateral and posterior, and where eyes would have been of greatly less use
to the animal.   About a field's breadth below this quarry of
the *Coccosteus minor*,—if I may take the liberty of extem-
porizing a name, until such time as some person better qualified furnishes the creature with a more characteristic one,
—there are the remains, consisting of fosse and rampart,
with a single cannon lying red and honeycombed amid the
ruins, of one of Cromwell's forts, built to protect the town
against the assaults of an enemy from the sea.   In the few
and stormy years during which this ablest of British gover-
nors ruled over Scotland, he seems to have exercised a singularly vigilant eye.   The claims on his protection of even
the remote Kirkwall did not escape him.

   The antiquities of the burgh next engaged me ; and, as
became its dignity and importance, I began with the Cathedral, a building imposing enough to rank among the most
impressive of its class anywhere, but whose peculiar *setting*
in this remote northern country, joined to the associations of
its early history with the Scandinavian Rollos, Sigurds, Einars,
and Hacos of our dingier chronicles, serve greatly to enhance
its interest.   It is a noble pile, built of a dark-tinted Old
Red Sandstone,—a stone which, though by much too sombre
for adequately developing the elegancies of the Grecian or
Roman architecture, to which a light delicate tone of colour
seems indispensable, harmonizes well with the massier and
less florid styles of the Gothic.   The round arch of that ancient Norman school which was at one time so generally recognised as Saxon, prevails in the edifice, and marks out its
older portions.   A few of the arches present on their ring-

Rollos ... chronicles: given names common in passages dealing with early mediaeval
Orkney in the old Icelandic sagas and chronicles, such as *Orkneyinga saga* ('History of
the Orkneymen') (Hewison 1998, Thomson 2001). The Earls of Orkney and their sons
included various Sigurds, Einars and Hakons. Rollo may refer to Hrolf or Rolf, first Duke
of Normandy. Miller used **dingier** in the old sense of darker or dimmer

stones those characteristic toothed and zig-zag ornaments that
are of not unfamiliar occurrence on the round squat door-
ways of the older parish churches of England ; but by much
the greater number exhibit merely a few rude mouldings,
that bend over ponderous columns and massive capitals, un-
fretted by the tool of the carver.   Though of colossal magnificence, the exterior of the edifice yields in effect, as in all
true Gothic buildings,—for the Gothic is greatest in what
the Grecian is least,—to the sombre sublimity of the interior.
The nave, flanked by the dim deep aisles, and by a double
row of smooth-stemmed gigantic columns, supporting each a
double tier of ponderous arches, and the transepts, with their
three tiers of small Norman windows, and their bold semicircular arcs, demurely gay with toothed or angular carvings,
that speak of the days of Rolf and Torfeinar, are singularly
fine,—far superior to aught else of the kind in Scotland;
and a happy accident has added greatly to their effect.   A
rare Byssus,—the *Byssus aeruginosa* of Linnæus,—the *Lepra-
sia aeruginosa* of modern botanists,—one of those gloomy ve·
getables of the damp cave and dark mine whose true habitat
is rather under than upon the earth, has crept over arch, and
column, and broad bare wall, and given to well nigh the entire interior of the building a close-fitted lining of dark velvety green, which, like the Attic rust of an ancient medal,
forms an appropriate covering to the sculpturings which it en-
wraps without concealing, and harmonizes with at once the
dim light and the antique architecture.   Where the sun
streamed upon it, high over head, through the narrow windows above, it reminded me of a pall of rich green velvet.
It seems subject, on some of the lower mouldings and damper
recesses, especially amid the tombs and in the aisles, to a decomposing mildew, which eats into it in fantastic map-like
lines of mingled black and gray, so resembling Runic fret-
work, that I had some difficulty in convincing myself that the

---

Torfeinar: Torf-Einar, a Norse Earl of Orkney; **Byssus**: see note for p. 337; **Attic**:
uncertain, possibly error for 'antic', an old variant spelling of 'antique'

tracery which it forms,—singularly appropriate to the architecture,—was not the effect of design.   The choir and chan-
cel of the edifice, which at the time of my visit were still employed as the parish church of Kirkwall, and had become a
" world too wide" for the shrunken congregation, are more
modern and ornate than the nave and transepts ; and the
round arch gives place, in at least their windows, to the pointed
one.   But the unique consistency of the pile is scarce at all
disturbed by this mixture of styles.   It is truly wonderful
how completely the forgotten architects of the darker ages
contrived to avoid those gross offences against good taste and
artistic feeling into which their successors of a greatly more
enlightened time are continually falling.   Instead of idly
courting ornament for its own sake, they must have had as
their proposed object the production of some definite effect,
or the development of some special sentiment.   It was perhaps well for them, too, that they were not so overladen as
our modern architects with the *learning* of their profession.
Extensive knowledge requires great judgment to guide it.   If
that high genius which can impart its own homogeneous character to very various materials be wanting, the more multifarious a man's ideas become, the more is he in danger of
straining after a heterogeneous patch-work excellence, which
is but excellence in its components, and deformity as a whole.
Every new vista opened up to him on what has been produced
in his art elsewhere presents to him merely a new avenue
of error.   His mind becomes a mere damaged kaleidoscope,
full of little broken pieces of the fair and the exquisite, but
devoid of that nicely reflective machinery which can alone
cast the fragments into shapes of a chaste and harmonious
beauty.
    Judging from the sculptures of St Magnus, the stone-cutter
seems to have had but an indifferent command of his trade
in Orkney, when there was a good deal known about it else-

---

world: an old man's leggings in Shakespeare's *As You Like It*, Act 2, Scene 7: 'His youthful hose, well saved, a world too wide for his shrunk shank …'

where. And yet the rudeness of his work here, much in keeping with the ponderous simplicity of the architecture, serves but to link on the pile to a more venerable antiquity, and speaks less of the inartificial than of the remote. I saw a grotesque hatchment high up among the arches, that, with the uncouth carvings below, served to throw some light on the introduction into ecclesiastical edifices of those ludicrous sculptures that seem so incongruously foreign to the proper use and character of such places. The painter had set himself, with, I doubt not, fair moral intent, to exhibit a skeleton wrapped up in a winding-sheet; but, like the unlucky artist immortalized by Gifford, who proposed painting a lion, but produced merely a dog, his skill had failed in seconding his intentions, and, instead of achieving a Death in a shroud, he had achieved but a monkey grinning in a towel. His contemporaries, however, unlike those of Gifford's artist, do not seem to have found out the mistake, and so the betowelled monkey has come to hold a conspicuous place among the solemnities of the Cathedral. It does not seem difficult to conceive how unintentional ludicrosities of this nature, introduced into ecclesiastical erections in ages too little critical to distinguish between what the workman had purposed doing and what he had done, might come to be regarded, in a less earnest but more knowing age, as precedents for the introduction of the intentionally comic and grotesque. Innocent accidental monkeys in towels may have thus served to usher into serious neighbourhoods monkeys in towels that were such with malice *prepense*.

I was shown an opening in the masonry, rather more than a man's height from the floor, that marked where a square narrow cell, formed in the thickness of the wall, had been laid open a few years before. And in the cell there was found depending from the middle of the roof a rusty iron chain, with a bit of barley-bread attached. What could the

---

Gifford: William Gifford (1756–1826), satirist and author of *Baviad* and *Maeviad* chain and bit of bread have meant? Had they dangled in the remote past over some northern Ugolino? or did they form in their dark narrow cell, without air-hole or outlet, merely some of the reserve terrors of the Cathedral, efficient in bending to the authority of the Church the rebellious monk or refractory nun? Ere quitting the building, I scaled the great tower,—considerably less tall, it is said, than its predecessor, which was destroyed by lightning about two hundred years ago, but quite tall enough to command an extensive, and, though bare, not unimpressive prospect. Two arms of the sea, that cut so deeply into the mainland on its opposite sides as to narrow it into a flat neck little more than a mile and a half in breadth, stretch away in long vista, the one to the south, and the other to the north; and so immediately is the Cathedral perched on the isthmus between, as to be nearly equally conspicuous from both. It forms in each, to the inward-bound vessel, the terminal object in the landscape. There was not much to admire in the town immediately beneath, with its roofs of gray slate,—almost the only parts of it visible from this point of view,—and its bare treeless suburbs; nor yet in the tract of mingled hill and moor on either hand, into which the island expands from the narrow neck, like the two ends of a sand-glass; but the long withdrawing ocean-avenues between, that seemed approaching from south and north to kiss the feet of the proud Cathedral,— avenues here and there enlivened on their ground of deep blue by a sail, and fringed on the lee—for the wind blew freshly in the clear sunshine—with their border of dazzling white, were objects worth while climbing the tower to see. Ere my descent, my guide hammered out of the tower-bells, on my special behalf, somewhat, I daresay, to the astonishment of the burghers below, a set of chimes handed down entire, in all the notes, from the times of the monks, from which also the four fine bells of the Cathedral have descended as an

---

Ugolino: from Dante's *Inferno*, canto 33. Imprisoned with his children, who died before him, he ate their corpses when maddened with hunger, and was therefore punished in hell heir-loom to the burgh. The chimes would have delighted the heart of old Lisle Bowles, the poet of

" Well-tun'd bell's enchanting harmony."

I could, however, have preferred listening to their music, though it seemed really very sweet, a few hundred yards further away; and the quiet clerical poet,—the restorer of the Sonnet in England,—would, I doubt not, have been of the same mind. The oft-recurring tones of those bells that ring throughout his verse, and to which Byron wickedly proposed adding a *cap*, form but an ingredient of the poetry in which he describes them; and they are represented always as distant tones, that, while they mingle with the softer harmonies of nature, never overpower them.

" How sweet the tuneful bells responsive peal !
* * * * * *
And, hark ! with lessening cadence now they fall,
And now, along the white and level tide,
They fling their melancholy music wide !
Bidding me many a tender thought recall
Of happy hours departed, and those years
When, from an antique tower, ere life's fair prime,
The mournful mazes of their mingling chime
First wak'd my wondering childhood into tears !"

From the Cathedral I passed to the mansion of old Earl Patrick,—a stately ruin, in the more ornate castellated style of the sixteenth century. It stands in the middle of a dense thicket of what are *trying* to be trees, and have so far succeeded, that they conceal, on one of the sides, the lower storey of the building, and rise over the *spring* of the large richly-decorated turrets. These last form so much nearer the base of the edifice than is common in our old castles, that they exhibit the appearance rather of hanging towers than of turrets,—of towers with their foundations cut away. The projecting windows, with their deep mouldings, square mullions, and cruciform shot-holes, are rich specimens of their peculiar style; and, with the double-windowed turrets with

---

Lisle Bowles: William Lisle Bowles (1762–1850), poet and antiquarian. The main quotation comprises most of his sonnet 'The Bells, Ostend'. During the 1810s he had been involved in a dispute with Byron the poet about what sort of poetry people should then be writing, so Byron's *cap* presumably referred to the jester's or fool's cap with bells which they range, they communicate a sort of *high-relief* effect to the entire erection, " the exterior proportions and ornaments of which," says Sir Walter Scott, in his Journal, " are very handsome."   Though a roofless and broken ruin, with the rank grass waving on its walls, it is still a piece of very solid masonry, and must have been rather stiff working as a quarry.   Some painstaking burgher had, I found, made a desperate attempt on one of the huge chimney lintels of the great hall of the erection,—an apartment which Sir Walter greatly admired, and in which he lays the scene in the " Pirate" between Cleveland and Jack Bunce ; but the lintel, a curious example of what, in the exercise of a little Irish liberty, is sometimes termed a *rectilinear arch*, defied his utmost efforts ; and, after half-picking out the keystone, he had to give it up in despair.   The bishop's palace, of which a handsome old tower still remains tolerably entire, also served for a quarry in its day ; and I was scarce sufficiently distressed to learn, that on almost the last occasion on which it had been wrought for this purpose, one of the two men engaged in the employment suffered a stone, which he had loosed out of the wall, to drop on the head of his companion, who stood watching for it below, and killed him on the spot.

the 'Pirate': Scott's novel set in Shetland and Orkney

CHAPTER XI.

THE "upper storey" of the bishop's palace, in which grim old Haco died,—thanks to the economic burghers who converted the stately ruin into a quarry,—has wholly disappeared. Though the death of this last of the Norwegian invaders does not date more than ten years previous to the birth of the Bruce, it seems to belong, notwithstanding, to a different and greatly more ancient period of Scottish history; as if it came under the influence of a sort of aerial perspective, similar to that which makes a neighbouring hill in a fog appear as remote as a distant mountain when the atmosphere is clearer. Our national wars with the English were rendered familiar to our country folk of the last age, and for centuries before, by the old Scotch "*Makkaris*," Barbour and Blind Harry, and in our own times by the glowing narratives of Sir Walter Scott,—magicians who, unlike those ancient sorcerers that used to darken the air with their incantations, possessed the rare power of dissipating the mists and vapours of the historic atmosphere, and rendering it transparent. But we had no such chroniclers of the time, though only half an age further removed into the past,

> " When Norse and Danish galleys plied
> Their oars within the Frith of Clyde,
> And floated Haco's banner trim
> Above Norweyan warriors grim,
> Savage of heart and large of limb."

'*Makkaris*': see p. 423; **Barbour**: John Barbour (c.1320-1395), author of 'The Brus', on Robert I the Bruce; **Blind Harry**: late fifteenth century author of 'The Wallace', on the Scottish patriot and national liberator; both poems were much read, often in prose versions, down to Miller's time and beyond. The young Miller read both (1858, pp. 40-41); '**When Norse …**': 'For Norse …' in original, Scott's 'Marmion', canto 3, verse 20, lines 5-9

And hence the thick haze in which it is enveloped. Curiously enough, however, this period, during which the wild Scot had to contend with the still wilder wanderers of Scandinavia in fierce combats that he was too little skilful to record, and which appears so obscure and remote to his descendants, presents a phase comparatively near, and an outline proportionally sharp and well-defined, to the intelligent peasantry of Iceland. *Their* Barbours and Blind Harries came a few ages sooner than ours, and the fog, in consequence, rose earlier; and so, while Scotch antiquaries of no mean standing can say almost nothing about the expedition or deathbed of Haco, even the humbler Icelanders, taught from their Sagas in the long winter nights, can tell how, harassed by anxiety and fatigue, the monarch sickened, and recovered, and sickened again; and how, dying in the bishop's palace, his body was interred for a winter in the Cathedral, and then borne in spring to the burying-place of his ancestors in Norway. The only clear vista on the death of Haco which now exists is that presented by an Icelandic chronicler; to which, as it seems so little known even in Orkney that the burying-place of the monarch is still occasionally sought for in the Cathedral, I must introduce the reader. I quote from an extract containing the account of Haco's expedition against Scotland, which was "translated from the original Icelandic by the Rev. James Johnstone, chaplain to his Britannic Majesty's Envoy Extraordinary at the court of Denmark," and appeared in the "Edinburgh Magazine" for 1787.

" King Haco," says the chronicler, " now in the seven and fortieth year of his reign, had spent the summer in watchfulness and anxiety. Being often called to deliberate with his captains, he had enjoyed little rest; and when he arrived at Kirkwall, he was confined to his bed by his disorder. Having lain for some nights, the illness abated, and he was on foot for three days. On the first day he walked about in his apart-

---

Icelandic chronicler: Sturla Þórðarson, the author of *Hákonar saga Hákonarsonar*. Johnstone's translation is in Goldsmid (1885, pp. 60–64) ments; on the second he attended at the bishop's chapel to hear mass; and on the third he went to Magnus Church, and walked round the shrine of St Magnus, Earl of Orkney. He then ordered a bath to be prepared, and got himself shaved. Some nights after, he relapsed, and took again to his bed. During his sickness he ordered the Bible and Latin authors to be read to him. But finding his spirits were too much fatigued by reflecting on what he had heard, he desired Norwegian books might be read to him night and day: first the lives of saints; and, when they were ended, he made his attendants read the Chronicles of our Kings, from Holden the Black, and so of all the Norwegian monarchs in succession, one after the other. The king still found his disorder increasing. He therefore took into consideration the pay to be given to his troops, and commanded that a merk of fine silver should be given to each courtier, and half a merk to each of the masters of the lights, chamberlain, and other attendants on his person. He ordered all the silver-plate belonging to his table to be weighed, and to be distributed if his standard silver fell short. * * * King Haco received extreme unction on the night before the festival of St Lucia. Thorgisl, Bishop of Stravanger, Gilbert, Bishop of Hamar, Henry, Bishop of Orkney, Albert Thorleif, and many other learned men, were present; and, before the unction, all present bade the king farewell with a kiss. * * * The festival of the Virgin St Lucia happened on a Thursday; and on the Saturday after, the king's disorder increased to such a degree, that he lost the use of his speech; and at midnight Almighty God called King Haco out of this mortal life. This was matter of great grief to all those who attended, and to most of those who heard of the event. The following barons were present at the death of the king:—Briniolf Johnson, Erling Alfson, John Drottning, Ronald Urka, and some domestics who had been near the king's person during his ill-

ness. Immediately on the decease of the king, bishops and
learned men were sent for to sing mass. * * * On Sunday the royal corpse was carried to the upper hall, and laid
on a bier.   The body was clothed in a rich garb, with a garland on its head, and dressed out as became a crowned monarch.   The masters of the lights stood with tapers in their
hands, and the whole hall was illuminated.   All the people
came to see the body, which appeared beautiful and animated;
and the king's countenance was as fair and ruddy as while he
was alive.   It was some alleviation of the deep sorrow of
the beholders to see the corpse of their departed sovereign
so decorated.   High mass was then sung for the deceased.
The nobility kept watch by the body during the night.   On
Monday the remains of King Haco were carried to St Magnus Church, where they lay in state that night.   On Tuesday the royal corpse was put in a coffin, and buried in the
choir of St Magnus Church, near the steps leading to the
shrine of St Magnus, Earl of Orkney.   The tomb was then
closed, and a canopy was spread over it.   It was also determined that watch should be kept over the king's grave all
winter.   At Christmas the bishop and Andrew Plytt furnished entertainments, as the king had directed; and good presents were given to all the soldiers.   King Haco had given
orders that his remains should be carried east to Norway, and
buried near his fathers and relatives.   Towards the end of
winter, therefore, that great vessel which he had in the west
was launched, and soon got ready.   On Ash Wednesday the
corpse of King Haco was taken out of the ground: this happened the third of the nones of March.   The courtiers followed the corpse to Skalpeid, where the ship lay, and which
was chiefly under the direction of the Bishop Thorgisl and
Andrew Plytt.   They put to sea on the first Saturday in Lent;
but, meeting with hard weather, they steered for Silavog.
From this place they wrote letters to Prince Magnus, ac-

quainting him with the news, and then sailed for Bergen.
They arrived at Laxavog before the festival of St Benedict.
On that day Prince Magnus rowed out to meet the corpse.
The ship was brought near to the king's palace, and the body
was carried up to a summer-house. Next morning the corpse
was removed to Christ's Church, and was attended by Prince
Magnus, the two queens, the courtiers, and the town's people.
The body was then interred in the choir of Christ's Church;
and Prince Magnus addressed a long and gracious speech to
those who attended the funeral procession. All the multitude present were much affected, and expressed great sorrow
of mind."

So far the Icelandic chronicle. Each age has as certainly
its own mode of telling its stories as of adjusting its dress or
setting its cap; and the mode of this northern historian is
somewhat prolix. I am not sure, however, whether I would
not prefer the simple minuteness with which he dwells on
every little circumstance, to that dissertative style of history
characteristic of a more reflective age, that for series of facts
substitutes bundles of theories. Cowper well describes the
historians of this latter school, and shows how, on selecting
some little-known personage of a remote time as their hero,

> " They disentangle from the puzzled skein
> In which obscurity has wrapped them up,
> The threads of politic and shrewd design
> That ran through all his purposes, and charge
> His mind with meanings that he never had,
> Or, having, kept concealed."

I have seen it elaborately argued by a writer of this class,
that those wasting incursions of the Northmen which must
have been such terrible plagues to the southern and western
countries of Europe, ceased in consequence of their conversion to Christianity; for that, under the humanizing influence of religion, they staid at home, and cultivated the arts
of peace. But the hypothesis is, I fear, not very tenable.

'They disentangle ...': from William Cowper's *The Task*, Book 3, 'The Garden', lines
145-150, coming just after his self-description as a wounded deer that has left the herd.
Not surprisingly, Miller omitted the continuation: '... Some drill and bore/The solid
earth, and from the strata there/Extract a register, by which we learn/That He who
made it, and reveal'd its date/To Moses, was mistaken in its age'

Christianity, in even a purer form than that in which it first found its way among the ancient Scandinavians, and when at least as generally recognised nationally as it ever was by the subjects of Haco, has failed to put down the trade of aggressive war. It did not prevent honest, obstinate George the Third from warring with the Americans or the French : it only led him to enjoin a day of thanksgiving when his troops had slaughtered a great many of the enemy, and to ordain a fast when the enemy had slaughtered, in turn, a great many of his troops. And Haco, who, though he preferred the lives of the saints, and even of his ancestors, who could not have been very great saints, to the Scriptures, seems, for a king, to have been a not undevout man in his way, and yet appears to have had as few compunctious visitings on the score of his Scottish war as George the Third on that of the French or the American one. Christianity, too, ere his invasion of Scotland, had been for a considerable time established in his dominions, and ought, were the theory a true one, to have operated sooner. The Cathedral of St Magnus, when he walked round the shrine of its patron saint, was at least a century old. The true secret of the cessation of Norwegian invasion seems to have been the consolidation, under vigorous princes, of the countries which had lain open to it,—a circumstance which, in all the later attempts of the invaders, led to results similar to those which broke the heart of tough old Haco in the bishop's palace at Kirkwall.

From the ruins I passed to the town, and spent a not uninstructive half-hour in sauntering along the streets in the quiet of the evening, acquainting myself with the general aspect of the people. I marked, as one of the peculiar features of the place, groupes of tidily-dressed young women, engaged at the close-heads with their straw plait,—the prevailing manufacture of the town,—and enjoying at the same time the fresh air and an easy chat. The special contribution made by the lassies of Orkney to the dress of their female neigh-bours all over the empire, has led to much tasteful dressing among themselves. Orkney, on its gala days, is a land of ladies. What seems to be the typical countenance of these islands ùnites an aquiline but not prominent nose to an oval face. In the ordinary Scotch and English countenance, when the nose is aquiline it is also prominent, and the face is thin and angular, as if the additional height of the central feature had been given it at the expense of the cheeks, and of lateral shavings from off the chin. The hard Duke-of-Wellington face is illustrative of this type. But in the aquiline type of Orkney the countenance is softer and fuller, and, in at least the female face, the general contour greatly more handsome. Dr Kombst, in his ethnographic map of Britain and Ireland, gives to the coast of Caithness and the Shetland Islands a purely Scandinavian people, but to the Orkneys a mixed race, which he designates the Scandinavian-Gaelic. I would be inclined, however,—preferring rather to found on those traits of person and character that are still patent, than on the un-authenticated statements of uncertain history,—to regard the people as essentially one from the northern extremity of Shetland to the Ord Hill of Caithness. Beyond the Ord Hill, and on to the northern shores of the Frith of Cromarty, we find, though unnoted on the map, a different race,—a race strongly marked by the Celtic lineaments, and speaking the Gaelic tongue. On the southern side of the Frith, and ex-tending on to the Bay of Munlochy, the purely Scandinavian race again occurs. The sailors of the Danish fleet which four years ago accompanied the Crown Prince in his expe-dition to the Faroe Islands were astonished when, on land-ing at Cromarty, they recognised in the people the familiar cast of countenance and feature that marked their country folk and relatives at home ; and found that they were simply Scandinavians like themselves, who, having forgotten their

---

Dr Kombst: a German ethnographer. This map was published in atlases in 1843 and 1848, and in later editions thereof (Withers 1984, pp. 90-92)

Danish, spoke Scotch instead. Rather more than a mile to the west of the fishing village of Avoch there commences a Celtic district, which stretches on from Munlochy to the river Nairne ; beyond which the Scandinavian and Teutonic-Scandinavian border that fringes the eastern coast of Scotland extends unbroken southwards through Moray, Banff, and Aberdeen, on to Forfar, Fife, the Lothians, and the Mearns. These two intercalated patches of Celtic people in the northern tract,—that extending from the Ord Hill to the Cromarty Frith, and that extending from the Bay of Munlochy to the Nairne,—still retaining, as they do, after the lapse of ages, a sharp distinctness of boundary in respect of language, character, and personal appearance, are surely great curiosities. The writer of these chapters was born on the extreme edge of one of these patches, scarce a mile distant from a Gaelic-speaking population ; and yet, though his humble ancestors were located on the spot for centuries, he can find trace among them of but one Celtic name ; and their language was exclusively the Lowland Scotch. For many ages the two races, like oil and water, refused to mix.

I spent the evening very agreeably with one of the Free Church elders of the place, Mr George Petrie, an accomplished antiquary ; and found that his love of the antique, joined to an official connection with the county, had cast into his keeping a number of curious old papers of the sixteenth, seventeenth, and eighteenth centuries,—not in the least connected, some of them, with the legal and civic records of the place, but which had somehow stuck around these, in their course of transmission from one age to another, as a float of brushwood in a river occasionally brings down along with it, entangled in its folds, uprooted plants and aquatic weeds, that would otherwise have disappeared in the cataracts and eddies of the upper reaches of the stream. Dead as they seemed, spotted with mildew, and fretted by the moth, I found them

---

George Petrie: the most important Orkney archaeologist of the nineteenth century, and (later) the first excavator of the Neolithic settlement of Skara Brae (Hewison 1998; Watters *et al.* 1996)

curiously charged with what had once been intellect and emo-
tion, hopes and fears, stern business and light amusement.
I saw, among the other manuscripts, a thin slip of a book,
filled with jottings, in the antique square-headed style of notation, of old Scotch tunes, apparently the work of some
musical county-clerk of Orkney in the seventeenth century;
but the paper, in a miserable state of decay, was blotted crimson and yellow with the rotting damps, and the ink so faded,
that the notation of scarce any single piece in the collection
seemed legible throughout. Less valuable and more modern,
though curious from their eccentricity, there lay, in company
with the music, several pieces of verse, addressed by some
Orcadian Claud Halcro of the last age, to some local patron,
in a vein of compliment rich and stiff as a piece of ancient
brocade. A peremptory letter, bearing the autograph signature of Mary Queen of Scots, to Torquil M'Leod of Dunve-
gan, who had been on the eve, it would seem, of marrying a
daughter of Donald of the Isles, gave the Skye chieftain "to
wit" that, as he was of the blood royal of Scotland, he could
form no matrimonial alliance without the royal permission,
—a permission which, in the case in point, was not to be
granted. It served to show that the woman who so ill liked
to be thwarted in her own amours could, in her character
as the Queen, deal despotically enough with the love affairs
of other people. Side by side with the letter of Mary there
were several not less peremptory documents of the times of
the Commonwealth, addressed to the Sheriff of Orkney and
Shetland, in the name of his Highness the Lord Protector,
and that bore the signature of George Monck. I found them
to consist chiefly of dunning letters,—such letters as those
duns write who have victorious armies at their back,—for
large sums of money, the assessments laid on the Orkneys by
Cromwell. Another series of letters, some ten or twelve
years later in their date, form portions of the history of a

Claud Halcro: a genial poetaster and enthusiast for the works of John Dryden, in Scott's
novel *The Pirate*

worthy covenanting minister, the Rev. Alexander Smith of Colvine, banished to North Ronaldshay from the extreme south of Scotland, for the offence of preaching the gospel, and holding meetings for social worship in his own house ; and, as if to demonstrate his incorrigibility, one of the series,—a letter under his own hand, addressed from his island prison to the Sheriff-Depute in Kirkwall,—showed him as determined and persevering in the offence as ever. It was written immediately after his arrival. "The poor inhabitants," says the writer, "so many as I have yet seen, have received me with much joy. *I intend, if the Lord will, to preach Christ to them next Lord's day*, wt.out the least mixture of anything that may smell of sedition or rebellion. If I be farther troubled for yt, I resolve to suffer with meekness and patience." The Galloway minister must have been an honest man. Deeming preaching his true vocation,—a vocation from the exercise of which he dared not cease, lest he should render himself obnoxious to the woe referred to by the apostle, —he yet could not steal a march on even the Sheriff, whose professional duty it was to prevent him from doing *his ;* and so he fairly warned him that he purposed breaking the law. The next set of papers in the collection dated after the Revolution, and were full charged with an enthusiastic Jacobitism, which seems to have been a prevalent sentiment in Orkney from the death of Queen Anne, until the disastrous defeat at Culloden quenched in blood the hopes of the party. There is a deep cave still shown on the shores of Westray, within sight of the forlorn Patmos of the poor Covenanter, in which, when the sun got on the Whig side of the hedge, twelve gentlemen, who had been engaged in the rebellion of 1745, concealed themselves for a whole winter. So perseveringly were they sought after, that during the whole time they dared not once light a fire, nor attempt fishing from the rocks to supply themselves with food ; and, though they escaped the

---

covenanting: see Introduction; **woe**: probably Bible, 1 Corinthians 9: 16, by the Apostle Paul, 'For though I preach the gospel, I have nothing to glory of: for necessity is laid upon me; yea, woe is unto me, if I preach not the gospel!'; **Patmos ... Whigs ... 1745**: see Additional Notes search, they never, it is said, completely recovered the horrors of their term of dreary seclusion, but bore about with them, in broken constitutions, the effects of the hardships to which they had been subjected. They must have had full time and opportunity, during that miserable winter, for testing the justice of the policy that had sent poor Smith into exile, from his snug southern parish in the Presbytery of Dumfries, to the remotest island of the Orkneys. The great lesson taught in Providence during the seventeenth and part of the eighteenth century to our Scottish countryfolk seems to have been the lesson of toleration ; and as they were slow, stubborn scholars, the lash was very frequently and very severely applied. One of the Jacobite papers of Mr Petrie's collection,—a triumphal poem on the victory of Gladsmuir, —which, if less poetical than the Ode of Hamilton of Bangour on the same subject, is in no degree less curious,—serves to throw very decided light on a passage in literary history which puzzled Dr Johnson, and which scarce any one would think of going to Orkney to settle.

Johnson states, in his Life of the poet Thomson, that the "first operation" of the act passed in 1739 "for licensing plays" was the "prohibition of 'Gustavus Vasa,' a tragedy of Mr Brook." "Why such a work should be obstructed," he adds, "it is hard to discover." We learn elsewhere,— from the compiler of the "Modern Universal History," if I remember aright,—that "so popular did the prohibitory order of the Lord Chamberlain render the play," that, "on its publication the same year, not less than a thousand pounds were the clear produce." It was not, however, until more than sixty years after, when both Johnson and Brook were in their graves, that it was deemed safe to license it for the stage. Now, the fact that a drama, in itself as little dangerous as "Cato" or "Douglas," should have been prohibited by the Government of the day, in the first instance, and should have

---

Battle of Gladsmuir: better known as Prestonpans, Charles Stuart's army's victory over the Government forces in 1745; **Johnson ... Thomson**: Samuel Johnson on James Thomson (1700-1748) in *Lives of the English Poets with prefaces, biographical and critical*, volume 48 (1779)

brought the author, on its publication, so large a sum in the second, can be accounted for only by a reference to the keen partizanship of the period, and the peculiar circumstances of parties. The Jacobites, taught by the rebellion of 1715 at once the value of the Highlands and the incompetency of the Chevalier St George as a leader, had begun to fix their hopes on the Chevalier's son, Charles Edward, at that time a young but promising lad; and, with the tragedy of Brook before them, neither they nor the English Government of the day could have failed to see the foreigner George the Second typified—unintentionally, surely, on the part of Brook, who was a "Prince of Wales" Whig—in the foreigner Christiern the Second, the Scotch Highlanders in the Mountaineers of Dalecarlia, and the young Prince in Gustavus. In the Jacobite manuscript of Mr Petrie's collection, the parallelism is broadly traced; nor is it in the least probable, as the poem is a piece of sad mediocrity throughout, that it is a parallelism which was originated by its writer. It must have been that of his party; and led, I doubt not, five years before, to the prohibition of Brook's tragedy, and to the singular success which attended its publication. The passage in the manuscript suggestive of this view takes the form of an address to the victorious prince, and runs as follows :—

> " Meanwhile, unguarded youth, thou stoodst alone ;
> The cruel Tyrant urged his Armie on ;
> But Truth and Goodness were the Best of Arms ;
> And, fearless Prince, Thou smil'd at Threatened harms.
> Thus, Glorious Vasa worked in Swedish mines,—
> Thus, Helpless, Saw his Enemy's Designs,—
> Till, roused, his Hardy Highlanders arose,
> And poured Destruction on their foreign foes."

I rose betimes next morning, and crossed the Peerie [little] Sea, a shallow prolongation of the Bay of Kirkwall, cut off from the main sea by an artificial mound, to the quarry of Pickoquoy, somewhat notable, only a few years ago, as the

---

Chevalier St George and Charles Edward: the Old and Young Pretenders, the latter better known as 'Bonnie Prince Charlie'. The Chevalier was the 'heir' of the exiled James VII and II sole locality in which shells had been detected in the Old Red Sandstone of Scotland. But these have since been found in the neighbourhood of Thurso, by Mr Robert Dick, associated with bones and plates of the Asterolepis, and by Mr William Watt on the opposite side of the Mainland of Orkney, at Marwick Head. So far as has yet been ascertained, they are all of one species, and more nearly resemble a small Cyclas than any other shell. They are, however, more deeply sulcated in concentric lines, drawn, as if by a pair of compasses, from the umbone, and somewhat resembling those of the genus Astarte, than any species of Cyclas with which I am acquainted. In all the specimens I have yet seen, it appears to be rather a thick dark epidermis that survives, than the shell which it covered ; nay, it seems not impossible that to its thick epidermis, originally an essentially different substance from that which composed the calcareous case, the shell may have owed its preservation as a fossil ; while other shells, its contemporaries, from the circumstance of their having been unfurnished with any such covering, may have failed to leave any trace of their existence behind them. It seems at least difficult to conceive of a sea inhabited by many genera of fishes, each divided into several species, and yet furnished with but one species of shell. I found the quarry of Pickoquoy,—a deep excavation only a few yards beyond the highwater mark, and some two or three yards under the highwater level,—deserted by the quarrymen, and filled to the brim by the overflowing of a small stream. I succeeded, however, in detecting its shells *in situ*. They seem restricted chiefly to a single stratum, scarcely half an inch in thickness, and lie, not thinly scattered over the platform which they occupy, but impinging on each other, like all the gregarious shells, in thickly-set groupes and clusters. There occur among them occasional scales of Dipteri ; and on some of the fragments of rock long exposed around the quarry-mouth to the weather

---

shells: almost certainly not bivalve molluscs, rare or unknown here in the Old Red Sandstone, but the very similar paired 'valves' of *Asmussia*, a conchostracan crustacean or 'clam-shrimp'

I found them assuming a pale nacreous gloss,—an effect, it is not improbable, of their still retaining, attached to the epidermis, a thin film of the original shell.   The world's history must be vastly more voluminous now, and greatly more varied in its contents, than when the stratum which they occupy formed the upper layer of a muddy sea-bottom, and they opened their valves by myriads, to prey on the organic atoms which formed their food, or shut them again, startled by the shadow of the Dipterus, as he descended from the upper depths of the water to prey upon them in turn.   The palate of this ancient ganoid is furnished with a curious dental apparatus, formed apparently, like that of the recent wolf-fish, for the purpose of crushing shells.

About mid-day I set out by the mail-gig for Stromness. For the first few miles the road winds through a bare, solitary valley, overlooked by ungainly heath-covered hills of no great altitude, though quite tall enough to prevent the traveller from seeing anything but themselves.   As he passes on, the valley opens in front on an arm of the sea, over which the range of hills on the right abruptly terminates, while that on the left deflects into a line nearly parallel to the shore, leaving a comparatively level strip of moory land, rather more than a mile in breadth, between the steeper acclivities and the beach.   A tall naked house rises between the road and the sea.   Two low islands immediately behind it, only a few acres in extent,—one of them bearing a small ruin on its apex,—give a little variety to the central point in the prospect which the naked house forms ; but the arm of the sea, bordered, at the time I passed, by a broad brown selvage of seaweed, is as tame and flat as a Dutch lake ; the background beyond, a long monotonous ridge, is bare and treeless ; and in front lies the brown moory plain, bordered by the dull line of hills, and darkened by scattered stacks of peat.   The scene is not at all such a one as a poet would, for its own sake, de-

---

arm of the sea: Bay of Firth

light to fancy; and yet, in the recollection of at least one very pleasing poet, its hills, and islands, and blue arm of the sea, its brown moory plain, and tall naked house rising in the midst, must have been surrounded by a sunlit atmosphere of love and desire, bright enough to impart to even its tamest features a glow of exquisiteness and beauty. Malcolm the poet was born, and spent his years of boyhood and early youth, in the tall naked house; and the surrounding landscape is that to which he refers in his "Tales of Flood and Field," as rising in imagination before him, bright in the red gleam of the setting sun, when, on the steep slopes of the Pyrenees, the "silent stars of night were twinkling high over his head," and the "tents of the soldiery glimmering pale through the gloom." The tall house is the manse of the parish of Frith and Stennis; and the poet was the son of the Rev. John Malcolm, its minister. Here, when yet a mere lad, dreaming, in the quiet obscurity of an Orkney parish, far removed from the seat of war and the literary circles, of poetic celebrity and military renown, he addressed a letter to the Duke of Kent, the father of our Sovereign Lady the reigning Monarch, expressing an ardent wish to obtain a commission in the army then engaged in the Peninsula. The letter was such as to excite the interest of his Royal Highness, who replied to it by return of post, requesting the writer to proceed forthwith to London; for which he immediately set out, and was received by the Duke with courtesy and kindness. He was instructed by him to take ship for Spain, in which he arrived as a volunteer; and, joining the army, engaged at the time in the siege of St Sebastian, under General Graham, he was promoted shortly after, through the influence of his generous patron, to a lieutenancy in the 42d Highlanders. He served in that distinguished regiment on to the closing campaign of the Pyrenees; but received at the battle of Toulouse a wound so severe as to render him ever after incapable of active bodily

Malcolm the poet: see note for p. 390

exertion ; and so he had to retire from the army on half-pay, and a pension honourably earned. The history of his career as a soldier he has told with singular interest, in one of the earlier volumes of " Constable's Miscellany ;" and his poems abound in snatches of description painfully true, drawn from his experience of the military life,—of scenes of stern misery and grim desolation, of injuries received, and of sufferings inflicted,—that must have contrasted sadly in his mind, in their character as gross realities, with the dreamy visions of conquest and glory in which he had indulged at an earlier time. The ruin of St Sebastian, complete enough, and attended with circumstances of the horrible extreme enough, to appal men long acquainted with the trade of war, must have powerfully impressed an imaginative susceptible lad, fresh from the domesticities of a rural manse, in whose quiet neighbourhood the voice of battle had not been heard for centuries, and surrounded by a simple people, remarkable for the respect which they bear to human life. In all probability, the power evinced in his description of the siege, and of the utter desolation in which it terminated, is in part owing to the fresh impressibility of his mind at the time. Such, at least, was my feeling regarding it, as I caught myself muttering some of its more graphic passages, and saw, from the degree of alarm evinced by the boy who drove the mail-gig, that the sounds were not quite lost in the rattle of that somewhat rickety vehicle, and that he had come to entertain serious doubts respecting the sanity of his passenger :—

" Sebastian, when I saw thee last,
    It was in Desolation's day,
  As through thy voiceless streets I passed,
    Thy piles in heaps of rubbish lay ;
  The roofless fragments of each wall
  Bore many a dent of shell and ball ;
  With blood were all thy gateways red,
  And thou,—a city of the dead !

With fire and sword thy walks were swept ;
Exploded mines thy streets had heaped
In hills of rubbish ; they had been
Traversed by gabion and fascine,
With cannon lowering in the rear
In dark array,—a deadly tier,—
Whose thunder-clouds, with fiery breath,
Sent far around their iron death.
The bursting shell, in fragments flung
Athwart the skies, at midnight sung,
Or, on its airy pathway sent,
Its meteors swept the firmament.
Thy castle, towering o'er the shore,
Reeled on its rock amidst the roar `
Of thousand thunders, for it stood
In circle of a fiery flood ;
And crumbling masses fiercely sent
From its high frowning battlement,
Smote by the shot and whistling shell,
With groan and crash in ruin fell.

Through desert streets the mourner passed,
Midst walls that spectral shadows cast,
Like some fair spirit wailing o'er
The faded scenes it loved of yore ;
No human voice was heard to bless
That place of waste and loneliness.

I saw at eve the night-bird fly,
And vulture dimly flitting by,
To revel o'er each morsel stolen
From the cold corse, all black and swoln,
That on the shattered ramparts lay,
Of him who perished yesterday,—
Of him whose pestilential steam
Rose reeking on the morning beam,—
Whose fearful fragments, nearly gone,
Were blackening from the bleaching bone.

The house-dog bounded o'er each scene
Where cisterns had so lately been :
Away in frantic haste he sprung,
And sought to cool his burning tongue.
He howled, and to his famished cry
The dreary echoes gave reply ;
And owlet's dirge, through shadows dim,
Rolled back in sad response to him."

The father was succeeded in his parish by the brother of Malcolm,—a gentleman to whom, during my stay in Orkney, I took the liberty of introducing myself in his snug little Free Church manse at the head of the bay, and in whose possession I found the only portrait of the poet which exists. It is that of a handsome and interesting-looking *young* man, though taken not many years before his death; for, like the greater number of his class, he did not live to be an old one, dying under forty.   His brother the clergyman kindly accompanied me to two quarries in the neighbourhood of his new domicile, which I found, like almost all the dry-stone fences of the district, speckled with scales, occipital plates, and gill-covers, of Osteolepides and Dipteri, but containing no entire ichthyolites.   He had taken his side in the Church controversy, he told me, firmly, but quietly; and when the Disruption came, and he found it necessary to quit the old manse, which had been a home to his family for well nigh two generations, and in which both he and his brother had been born, he scarce knew what his people were to do, nor in what proportion he was to have followers among them. Somewhat to his surprise, however, they came out with him almost to a man; so that his successor in the parish church had sometimes, he understood, to preach to congregations scarcely exceeding half a dozen.   I had learned elsewhere how thoroughly Mr Malcolm was loved and respected by his parishioners; and that unconsciousness on his own part of the strength of their affection and esteem, which his statement evinced, formed, I thought, a very pleasing trait, and one that harmonized well with the finely-toned unobtrusiveness and unconscious elegance which characterized the genius of his deceased brother.   A little beyond the Free Church manse the road ascends between stone walls, abounding in fragments of ichthyolites, weathered blue by exposure to the sun and wind; and the top of the eminence forms the water-

---

brother of Malcolm: Rev. William Malcolm (1784-1857) (Ewing 1914, p. 260; Smith 1907, p. 192)

shed in this part of the Mainland, and introduces the traveller to a scene entirely new. The prospect is of considerable
extent; and, what seems strange in Orkney, nowhere presents the traveller—though it contains its large inland lake
—with a glimpse of the sea.

CHAPTER XII.

THE Orkneys, like the mainland of Scotland, exhibit their higher hills and precipices on their western coasts : the Ward Hill of Hoy attains to an elevation of sixteen hundred feet ; and there are some of the precipices which skirt the island of which it forms so conspicuous a feature, that rise sheer over the breakers from eight hundred to a thousand. Un-_ like, however, the arrangement on the mainland, it is the newer rocks that attain to the higher elevations : the heights of Hoy are composed of that arenaceous upper member of the Lower Old Red Sandstone,—the last formed of the Palæozoic deposits of Orkney,—which overlies the ichthyolitic flagstones and shales of Caithness at Dunnet Head, and the ichthyolitic nodular beds of Inverness, Ross, and Cromarty, at Culloden, Tarbet Ness, within the Northern Sutor, and along the bleak ridge of the Maolbuie.   It is simply a tall upper storey of the formation, erected along the western line of coast in the Orkneys, which the eastern line wholly wants. Its screen of hills forms a noble background to the prospect which opens on the traveller as he ascends the eminence beyond the Free Church manse of Frith and Stennis.   A large lake, bare and treeless, like all the other lakes and lochs of Orkney, but picturesque of outline, and divided into an upper and lower sheet of water by two low, long promontories, that jut out from opposite sides, and so nearly meet as to be connected by a thread-like line of road, half-mound half-bridge, occupies the middle distance.   There are moory hills and a few rude cottages in front ; and on the promontories, conspicuous in the landscape, from the relief furnished by the blue ground of the surrounding waters, stand the tall stones of Stennis,—one group on the northern promontory, the other on the south.   A gray old-fashioned house, of no very imposing appearance, rises between the road and the lake.   It is the house of Stennis or Turmister, in which Scott places some of the concluding scenes of the " Pirate,'' and from which he makes Cleveland and his fantastic admirer Jack Bunce witness the final engagement, in the bay of Stromness, between the Halcyon sloop of war and the savage Goffe. Nor does it matter anything that neither sea nor vessels can be seen from the house of Turmister : the fact which would be so fatal to a dishonest historian tells with no effect against the honest "*maker*," responsible for but the management of his tale.

I got on to Stromness ; and finding, after making myself comfortable in my inn, that I had a fine bright evening still before me, longer by some three or four degrees of north latitude than the July evenings of Edinburgh, I set out, hammer in hand, to explore.   Stromness is a long, narrow, irregular strip of a town, fairly thrust by a steep hill into the sea, on which it encroaches in a broken line of wharf-like bulwarks, along which, at high water, vessels of a hundred tons burden float so immediately beside the houses, that their pennants on gala days wave over the chimney-tops.   The steep hill forms part of a granitic axis, about six miles in length by a mile in breadth, which forms the backbone of the district, and against which the Great Conglomerate and lower schists of the Old Red are upturned at a rather high angle. It is wrapped round in some places by a thin caul of the

---

'*maker*': 'maker' (or makar) is archaic Scots for 'poet'. 'Makaris' (p. 403) is the plural

stratified primary rocks. Immediately over the town, on the
brow of the eminence, where the granitic axis had been laid
bare in digging a foundation for the Free Church manse, I
saw numerous masses of schistose-gneiss, passing in some of
the beds into a coarse-grained mica-schist, and a lustrous
hornblendic slate, that had been quarried from over it, and
which may be still seen built up into the garden-wall of the
erection. I walked out towards the west, to examine the
junction of the granite and the Great Conglomerate, where
it is laid bare by the sea, little more than a quarter of a mile
outside the town. There was a horde of noisy urchins a
little beyond the inn, who, having seen me alight from the
mail-gig, had determined in their own minds that I was engaged in the political canvass going forward at the time, but
had not quite ascertained my side. They now divided into
two parties ; and when the one, as I passed, set up a "Hurra
for Dundas," the other met them from the opposite side of
the street, with a counter cry of "Anderson for ever." Immediately after clearing the houses, I was accosted by a man
from the country. " Ye'll be seeking beasts," he said :
" what price are cattle gi'en the noo ?' " Yes, seeking *beasts*,"
I replied, " but very old ones : I have come to hammer
your rocks for petrified fish." " I see, I see," said the man ;
" I took ye by ye'er gray plaid for a drover ; but I ken something about the stane fish too : there's lots o' them in the
quarries at Skaill."

I found the Great Conglomerate in immediate contact with
the granite, which is a ternary of the usual components, somewhat intermediate in colour between that of Peterhead and
Aberdeen, and which at this point bears none of the caul of
stratified primary rock by which it is overlaid on the brow
of the hill. When the Great Conglomerate, which is mainly
composed of it here, was in the act of forming, this granite
must have been one of the surface rocks of the locality, and

in no respect a different stone from what it is now. The widely-spread Conglomerate base of the Old Red Sandstone, which presents, over an area of so many thousand square miles, such an identity of character, that specimens taken from the neighbourhood of Lerwick, in Shetland, can scarce be distinguished from specimens detached from the hills which rise over the Great Caledonian Valley, contains in various places, as under the Northern Sutor, for instance, and along the shores of Navity, fragments of rock which have not been detected *in situ* in the districts in which they occur as agglomerated pebbles. In general, however, we find it composed of the debris of those very granites and gneisses which, as in the case of the granitic axis here, were forced through it, and through the overlying deposits, by deep-seated convulsions, long posterior in date to its formation. It appears to have been formed in a vast oceanic basin of primary rock,— a Palæozoic Hudson's or Baffin's Bay,—partially surrounded, mayhap, by bare primary continents, swept by numerous streams, rapid and headlong, and charged with the broken debris of the inhospitable regions which they drained. The graptolite-bearing grauwacke of Banffshire seems to have been the only fossiliferous rock that occurred throughout the entire extent of this ancient northern basin. The Conglomerate of Orkney, like that of Moray and Ross, varies from fifty to a hundred yards in thickness. It is not overlaid in this section by the thick bed of coarse-grained sandstone, so well-marked a member of the formation at Cromarty, Nigg, and Gamrie, and along the northern shores of the Beauly Frith; but at once passes into those gray bituminous flagstones so immensely developed in Caithness and the Orkneys. I traced the formation upwards this evening, walking along the edges of the upheaved strata, from where the Conglomerate leans against the granite, till where it merges into the gray flagstones, and then pursued these from older and lower to newer and higher layers, anxious to ascertain at what distance over the base the more ancient organisms of the system first appear, and what their character and kind. And little more than a hundred *yards* over the granite, and somewhat less than a hundred *feet* over the upper stratum of the Great Conglomerate, I found what I sought,—a well-marked bone, perhaps the oldest vertebrate remain yet discovered in Orkney, embedded in a light grayish-coloured layer of hard flag.

What, asks the reader, was the character of the ancient denizen of the Palæozoic basin of which it had formed a part? Was it a large or small fish, or of a high or low order? Not certainly of a low order, and by no means of a small size. The organism in the rock was a specimen of that curious nail-shaped bone of the Asterolepis which occurs as a central ridge in the single plate that occupies in this genus the wide curve of the under jaw ; and as it was fully five inches in length from head to point, the plate to which it belonged must have measured at least ten inches across, and the frontal occipital buckler with which it was associated, one foot two inches in length (not including the three accessory plates at the nape), by ten inches in breadth. And if built, as it probably was, in the same massy proportions as its brother Cœlacanths the Holoptychius or Glyptolepis, the individual to which the nail-shaped bone belonged must have been, judging from the size of the corresponding parts in these ichthyolites, at least twice as large an animal as the splendid Clashbennie Holoptychius of the Upper Old Red, now in the British Museum. The bulkiest ichthyolites yet found in any of the divisions of the Old Red system are of the genus Asterolepis ; and to this genus, and to evidently an individual of no inconsiderable size, this oldest of the organisms of Orkney belonged. I was so interested in the fact, that before ultimately leaving this part of the country I brought Dr Garson, Stromness, and Mr William Watt, jun., Skaill, both

---

Asterolepis: see Additional Note for p. 282, and Introduction; **buckler**: old word for shield, which Miller used to describe the larger bony plates of his fossil fishes; **Clashbennie Holoptychius**: see note for p. 184; **Dr Garson**: Dr George Garson of Stromness (Miller 1864, p. 6fn); **Mr William Watt jun.**: see Additional Notes very intelligent palæontologists, to mark the place and character of the fossil, that they might be able to point it out to geological visitors in the future, or, if they preferred removing it to their town Museum, to indicate to them the stratum in which it had lain. For the present I merely request the reader to mark, in the passing, that the most ancient organic remain yet found in the Old Red of this part of the country, nay, judging from its place, *one* of the most ancient yet found in Scotland,—so far as I know, absolutely the *most* ancient,—belonged to a ganoid as bulky as a large porpoise, and which, as shown by its teeth and jaws, possessed that peculiar organization which characterized the reptile fish of the Upper Devonian and Carboniferous periods. As there are, however, no calculations more doubtful or more to be suspected than those on which the size and bulk of the extinct animals are determined from some surviving fragment of their remains,—plate or bone,—I must attempt laying before the scientific reader at least a portion of the data on which I found.

This figure represents not inadequately one of the most characteristic plates of the Asterolepis. A very considerable fragment of what seems to be the same plate has been figured by Agassiz, from a cast of one of the huge specimens of Professor Asmus ("Old Red," Table 32, Fig. 13); but as no evidence regarding its true place had turned up at the time, it was supposed by the naturalist to form part of the opercular covering of the animal. It belonged, however, to a different portion of the head. In almost all the fish that appear at our tables the space which occurs within the arched sweep of the lower jaws is mainly occupied by a complicated osseous mechanism, known to anatomists as the hyoid bone

'Old Red': *ie* Agassiz's monograph, *Poissons fossiles du Vieux Grès Rouge* (1844-1845); hyoid: see note for p. 428

and branchiostegous rays ; and which serves both to support the branchial arches and the branchiostegous membrane. Now, in the fish of the Old Red Sandstone, if we except some of the Acanthodians, we find no trace of this piece of mechanism : the arched space is covered over with dermal plates of bone, as a window is filled up with panes. Three plates, resembling very considerably the three divisions of a pointed Gothic window, furnished with a single central mullion, divided atop into two branches, occupied the space in the genera Osteolepis and Diplopterus ; and two plates resembling the divisions of a pointed Gothic window, whose single central mullion does *not* branch atop, filled it up in the genera Holoptychius and Glyptolepis. In the genus Asterolepis this arch-shaped space was occupied, as I have said, by a single plate,—that represented in the wood-cut ; and the nail-shaped bone rose on its internal surface along the centre,— the nail-head resting immediately beneath the centre of the arch, and the nail-point bordering on the isthmus below, at which the two shoulder-bones terminated. Now, in all the specimens which I have yet examined, the form and proportions of this plate are such that it can be very nearly inscribed in a semicircle, of which the length of the nail forms the radius. A nail five inches in length must have belonged to a plate ten inches in its longer diameter. I have ascertained further, that this longer diameter was equal to the shorter diameter of the creature's frontal buckler, measured across about two-thirds of its entire length from the nape ; and that a transverse diameter of ten inches at this point was associated in the buckler with a longitudinal diameter of fourteen inches from the nape to the snout. Thus five inches along the nail represent fourteen inches along the occipital shield. The proportion, however, which the latter bore to the entire body in this genus has still to be determined. The corresponding frontal shield in the Coccosteus was equal

---

branchial arches: the bony arches supporting the gills; the **hyoid** (p. 427) and the **branchiostegous rays** and **membrane** are also parts of the head of bony fishes to about one-fifth the creature's entire length, and in the Osteolepis and Diplopterus, to nearly one-seventh its length ; while the length of the *Glyptolepis leptopterus*, a fish of the same family as the Asterolepis, was about five and a half times that of its occipital shield. If the Asterolepis was formed in the proportions of the Diplopterus, the ancient individual to which this nail-like bone belonged must have been about eight feet two inches in length ; but if moulded, as it more probably was, in the proportions of the Glyptolepis, only six feet five inches. All the Cœlacanths, however, were exceedingly massive in proportion to their length : they were fish built in the square, muscular, thick-set, Dirk-Hatterick and Balfour-of-Burley style ; and of the Russian specimens, some of the larger bones must have belonged to individuals of from twice to thrice the length of the Stromness one.

Passing upwards along the strata, step by step, as along a fallen stair, each stratum presenting a nearly perpendicular front, but losing, in the downward slant of the *tread*, as a carpenter would say, the height attained in the *rise*, I came, about a quarter of a mile farther to the west, and several hundred feet higher in the formation, upon a fissile dark-coloured bed, largely charged with ichthyolites. The fish I found ranged in three layers,—the lower layer consisting almost exclusively of Dipterians, chiefly Osteolepides ; the middle layer, of Acanthodians, of the genera Cheiracanthus and Diplacanthus ; and the upper layer, of Cephalaspides, mostly of one species, the *Coccosteus decipiens*. I found exactly the same arrangement in a bed considerably higher in the system, which occurs a full mile farther on,—the Dipterians at the bottom, the Acanthodians in the middle, and the Cephalaspides atop ; and was informed by Mr William Watt, a competent authority in the case, that the arrangement is comparatively a common one in the quarries of Ork-

---

Dirk-Hatterick: a dangerous smuggler in Walter Scott's novel *Guy Mannering*: Balfour-of-Burley style: Balfour of Burley was the Covenanter leader and assassin of Archbishop Sharp, portrayed in Scott's *Old Mortality* as austere and sinister in expression, and strong and muscular in body; Cephalaspides: see p. 291

ney.   How account for the phenomenon ?   How account for
the three storeys, and the apportionment of the floors, like
those of a great city, each to its own specific class of society ?
Why should the first floor be occupied by Osteolepides, the
second by Cheiracanthi and their cogeners, and the third by
Coccostei ?   Was the arrangement an effect of normal differences in the constitutions of the several families, operated
upon by some deleterious gas or mineral poison, which, though
it eventually destroyed the whole, did not so simultaneously,
but consecutively,—the families of weakest constitution first,
and the strongest last ?   Or were they exterminated by some
disease, that seized upon the families, not at once, but in
succession ?   Or did they visit the locality serially, as the
haddock now visits our coasts in spring, and the herring
towards the close of summer ; and were then killed off,
whether by poison or disease, as they came ?   These are
questions which may never be conclusively answered.   It is
well, however, to observe, as a curious geological fact, that
peculiar arrangement of the fossils by which they are suggested, and to record the various instances in which it occurs.   The minerals which I remarked among the schists
here as most abundant are a kind of black ironstone, exceedingly tough and hard, occurring in detached masses, and a
variety of bright pyrites disseminated among the darker flagstones, either as irregularly-formed, brassy-looking concretions
of small size, or spread out on their surfaces in thin leaf-like
films, that resemble, in some of the specimens, the icy foliage
with which a severe frost encrusts a window-pane.   Still
further on I came upon a vein of galena ; but a miner's excavation in the solid rock, a little above high-water mark,
quite as dark and nearly as narrow as a fox-earth, showed
me that it had been known long before, and, as the workings
seemed to have been deserted for ages, known to but little
purpose.   The crystals of ore, small and thinly scattered, are

embedded in a matrix of barytes, stromnite, and other kindred minerals, and the thickness of the entire vein is not very considerable. I have since learned, from the "Statistical Account of the Parish of Sandwick," that the workings of the mine penetrate into the rock for about a hundred yards, but that it has been long abandoned, "as a speculation which would not pay."

I observed scattered over the beach, in the neighbourhood of the lead mine, considerable quantities of the hard chalk of England; and, judging there could be no deposits of the hard chalk in this neighbourhood, I addressed myself, on my way back, to a kelp-burner engaged in wrapping up his fire for the night with a thick covering of weed, to ascertain how it had come there. "Ah, master," he replied, "that chalk is all that remains of a fine large English vessel, that was knocked to pieces here a few years ago. She was ballasted with the chalk; and as it is a light sort of stone, the surf has washed it ashore from that low reef in the middle of the tideway where she struck and broke up. Most of the sailors, poor fellows, lie in the old churchyard, beside the broken ruin yonder. It is a deadly shore this to seafaring-men." I had understood that the kelp-trade was wholly at an end in Orkney; and, remarking that the sea-weed which he employed was chiefly of one kind,—the long brown fronds of tang dried in the sun,—I inquired of him to what purpose the substance was now employed, seeing that barilla and the carbonate of soda had supplanted it in the manufacture of soap and glass, and why he was so particular in selecting his weed. "It's some valuable medicine," he said, "that's made of the kelp now: I forget its name; but it's used for bad sores and cancer; and we must be particular in our weed, for it's not every kind of weed that has the medicine in't. There's most of it, we're told, in the leaves of the tang." "Is the name of the drug," I asked, "iodine?" "Ay, that must

be just it," he replied,—"iodine ;" but it doesn't make such
a demand for the kelp as the glass and the soap."   I afterwards learned that the kelp-burner's character of this strip
of coast, as peculiarly fatal to the mariner, was borne out by
many a sad casualty, too largely charged with the wild and
the horrible to be lightly forgotten.   The respected Free
Church clergyman of Stromness, Mr Learmonth, informed
me that, ere the Disruption, while yet minister of the parish,
there were on one sad occasion eight dead bodies carried of
a Sabbath morning to his manse door.   Some of the incidents connected with these terrible shipwrecks, as related
with much graphic effect by a boatman who carried me across
the sound, on an exploratory ramble to the island of Hoy,
struck me as of a character considerably beyond the reach of
the mere dealer in fiction.   The master of one hapless vessel,
a young man, had brought his wife and only child with him
on the voyage destined to terminate so mournfully ; and when
the vessel first struck, he had rushed down to the cabin to
bring them both on deck, as their only chance of safety.   He
had, however, unthinkingly shut the cabin-door after him ;
a second tremendous blow, as not unfrequently happens in
such cases, so affected the framework of the sides and deck,
that the door was jambed fast in its frame.   And long ere
it could be cut open,—for no human hand could unfasten it,
—the vessel had filled to the beams, and neither the master
nor his wife and child were ever seen more.   In another
ship, wrecked within a cable-length of the beach, the mate,
a man of Herculean proportions, and a skilful swimmer,
stripped and leaped overboard, not doubting his ability to
reach the shore.   But he had failed to remark what in such
circumstances is too often forgotten, that the element on which
he flung himself, beaten into foam against the shallows, was,
according to Mr Bremner's shrewd definition, not water,
but a mixture of water and air, specifically lighter than the

---

Mr Learmonth: Rev. Peter Learmonth (1801–1858), minister until 1843 and then Free
Church minister, both of Stromness (Ewing 1914, p. 206; Smith 1907)

human body ; and so at the shore, though so close at hand, he never arrived, disappearing almost at the vessel's side. "The ground was rough," said my informant, "and the sea ran mountains high ; and I can scarce tell you how I shuddered on finding, long ere his corpse was thrown up, his two eyes detached from their sockets, staring from a wreath of sea-weed." There is in this last circumstance, horrible enough surely for the wildest German tale ever written, a unique singularity, which removes it beyond the reach of invention.

At my inn I found a pressing invitation awaiting me from the Free Church manse, which I was urged to make my home so long as I remained in that part of the country. A geologist, however, fairly possessed by the enthusiasm without which weak man can accomplish nothing,—whether he be a deer-stalker or a mammoth-fancier, or angle for live salmon or dead Pterichthyes,—has a trick of forgetting the right times of dining and taking tea, and of throwing the burden of his bodily requirements on early extempore breakfasts and late suppers ; and so, reporting myself a man of irregular habits and bad hours, whose movements could not in the least be depended upon, I had to decline the hospitality which would fain have adopted me as its guest, notwithstanding the badness of the character that, in common honesty, I had to certify as my own. Next morning I breakfasted at the manse, and was introduced by Mr Learmonth to two gentlemen of the place, who had been kindly invited to meet with me, and who, from their acquaintance with the geology of the district, enabled me to make the best use of my time, by cutting direct on those cliffs and quarries in the neighbourhood in which organic remains had been detected, instead of wearily re-discovering them for myself. There is a small but interesting museum in Stromness, rich in the fossils of the locality ; and I began the geologic business of the day by devoting an hour to the examination of its organ-

---

right times of dining: the formal meal of 'dinner' would have been at something like 4 or 5 pm, in the process of its decades-long shift from the middle of the day to the evening

isms, chiefly ichthyolites.   I saw among them several good
specimens of the genus Pterichthys, and of what is elsewhere
one of the rarer genera of the Dipterians,—the Diplopterus.
A well-marked individual of the latter genus had, I found,
been misnamed Dipterus by some geological visitor who had
recently come the way,—a mistake which, as in both ichthyolites the fins are similarly placed, occasionally occurs, but
which may be easily avoided, when the specimens are in a
tolerable state of preservation, by taking note of a few well-
marked characteristics by which the genera are distinguished.
In both Dipterus and Diplopterus the bright enamel of the
scales was thickly punctulated by microscopic points,—the
exterior terminations of funnel-shaped openings, that communicated between the surface and the cells of the middle
table of the scale ; but the form of the scales themselves was
different,—that of the Dipterus being nearly circular, and
that of the Diplopterus, save on the dorsal ridge, rhomboidal.
Again, the lateral line of the Diplopterus was a raised line,
running as a ridge along the scales ; whereas that of the Dipterus was a depressed one, existing as a furrow.   Their heads,
too, were covered by an entirely dissimilar arrangement of
plates.   The rounded snout-plate of the Diplopterus was suddenly contracted to nearly one-half its breadth by two semicircular inflections, which formed the orbits of the eyes ; full
in the centre, a little above these, a minute lozenge-shaped
plate seemed as if inlaid in the larger one, the analogue, apparently, of the anterior frontal; and over all there expanded
a broad plate, the superior frontal, half-divided vertically by
a line drawn downwards from the nape, which, however,
stopt short in the middle ; and fretted transversely by two
small but deeply-indented rectangular marks, which, crossing
from the central to two lateral plates, assumed the semblance
of connecting pins.   The snout of the Dipterus was less round ;
it bore no mark of the eye-orbits ; and the frontal buckler,

broader in proportion to its length than that of the Diplopterus, consisted of many more plates. I may here mention
that the frontal buckler of Diplopterus has not yet been
figured nor described; whereas that of Dipterus, though unknown as such, has been given to the world as the occipital covering of a supposed Cephalaspian,—the Polyphractus.
Polyphractus is, however, in reality a synonym for Dipterus,
—the one name being derived from a peculiarity of the animal's fins; the other, from the great number of its occipital
plates. There is no science founded on mere observation that
can be altogether free, in its earlier stages, from mistakes of
this character,—mistakes to which the palæontologist, however skilful, is peculiarly liable. The teeth of the two genera
were essentially different. Those of the Dipterus, exclusively
palatal, were blunt and squat, and ranged in two rectangular
patches;* while those of the Diplopterus bristled along its
jaws, and were slender and sharp. Their tails, too, though
both heterocercal, were diverse in their type. In each, an
angular strip of gradually-diminishing scales,—a prolongation
of the scaly coat which protected the body, and which covered here a prolongation of the vertebral column,—ran on to
the extreme termination of the upper lobe; but there was in
the Diplopterus a greatly larger development of fin on the
superior or dorsal side of the scaly strip than on that of the
Dipterus. If the caudal fin of the Osteolepis be divided longitudinally into six equal parts, it will be found that one of
these occurs on the upper side of the vertebral prolongation,
and five on the under; in the caudal fin of the Diplopterus

---

* I can entertain no doubt that the angular groupes of palatal teeth
figured by Agassiz and the Russian geologists as those of a supposed Placoid
termed the Ctenodus, are in reality groupes of the palatal teeth of Dipterus. In some of my specimens the frontal buckler of Polyphractus is
connected with the gill-covers and scales of Dipterus, and bears in its
palate what cannot be distinguished from the teeth of Ctenodus. The three
genera resolve themselves into one.

so divided, rather more than *two* parts will be found to occur
on the upper side, and rather less than four on the under;
while in the caudal fin of the Dipterus the development seems
to have been restricted to the under side exclusively; at
least, in none of the many individuals which I have examined
have I found any trace of caudal rays on the upper side. These
are minute and somewhat trivial particulars; but the geologist may find them of use; and the non-geologist may be disposed to extend to them some little degree of tolerance, when
he considers that they distinguished two largely-developed
genera of animals, to which the Author of all did not deem
it unworthy his wisdom to impart, in the act of creation, certain marked points of resemblance, and other certain points
of dissimilarity.

From the Museum, accompanied by one of the gentlemen
to whom Mr Learmonth had introduced me at breakfast, and
who obligingly undertook to act as my guide on the occasion,
I set out to visit a remarkable stack on the sea-coast, about
four miles north and west of Stromness. We scaled together
the steep granitic hill immediately over the town, and then
cut on the stack, straight as the bird flies, across a trackless
common, bare and stony, and miserably pared by the *flaughter*
spade. The landed proprietors in this part of the mainland
are very numerous, and their properties small; and there are
vast breadths of undivided common that encircle their little
estates, as the Atlantic encircles the Orkneys.   But the state
in which I found the unappropriated parts of the district had
in no degree the effect of making me an opponent of appro-
priation or the landholders.   Our country, had it been left
as a whole to all its people, as the Communist desiderates,
would ere now be of exceedingly little value to any portion
of them.   The soil of the Orkney commons has been so repeatedly pared off and carried away for fuel, that there are
now wide tracts on which there is no more soil to pare, and

which present, for the original covering of peaty mould, a continuous surface of pale boulder-clay, here and there mottled by detached tufts of scraggy heath, and here and there roughened by projections of the underlying rock. All is unredeemable barrenness. On the other hand, wherever a bit of private property appears, though in the immediate neighbourhood of these ruined wastes, the surface is swarded over, and the soil is the better, not the worse, for the services which it has rendered to man in the past. Whatever the Chartist and the Leveller may think of the matter, it is, I find, virtually on behalf of the many that the soil has been appropriated by the few. After passing from off the tract of moor which overlies the granitic axis of the district, to a tract equally moory which spreads over the gray flagstones, I marked, more especially in the hollows and ravines, where minute springs oose from the rock, vast quantities of bog-iron embedded in the soil, and presenting greatly the appearance of the scoria of a smith's forge. The apparent scoria here is simply a reproduction of the iron of the underlying flagstones, transferred, through the agency of water, to that stratum of vegetable mould and boulder-clay which represents the recent period.

I found the stack which I had been brought to see forming the picturesque centre of a bold tract of rock scenery. It stands out from the land as a tall insulated tower, about two hundred feet in height, sorely worn at its base by the breakers that ceaselessly fret against its sides, but considerably broader atop, where it bears a flat cover of sward on the same level with the tops of the precipices which in the lapse of ages have receded from around it. Like the sward-crested hummock left by a party of labourers, to mark the depth to which they have cut in removing a bank or digging a pond, it remains to indicate how the attrition of the surf has told upon the iron-bound coast; demonstrating that lines of precipices hard as iron, and of giddy elevation, are in full retreat before the

---

Leveller: the best known Levellers were a seventeenth century English egalitarian radical movement crushed by Cromwell in 1649, but there were other 'Levellers', for instance in southwestern Scotland in the eighteenth century, and Ireland dogged perseverance of an assailant that, though baffled in each single attack, ever returns to the charge, and gains by an aggregation of infinitesimals,—the result of the whole. From the edge of a steep promontory that commands an inflection of the coast, and of the wall of rock which sweeps round it, I watched for a few seconds the sea,—greatly heightened at the time by the setting in of the flood-tide,—as it broke, surge after surge, against the base of the tall dark precipices; and marked how it accomplished its work of disintegration. The flag-stone deposit here abounds in vertical cracks and flaws; and in the line of each of the many fissures which these form the waves have opened up a cave ; so that for hundreds of yards together the precipices seem as if founded on arch-divided piers, and remind one of those ancient prints or drawings of Old London Bridge in which a range of tall sombre buildings is represented as rising high over a line of arches ; or of rows of lofty houses in those cities of southern Europe in which the dwellings fronting the streets are perforated beneath by lines of squat piazzas, and present above a dingy and windowless breadth of wall. In course of time the piers attenuate and give way ; the undermined precipices topple down, parting from the solid mass behind in those vertical lines by which they are traversed at nearly right angles with their line of stratification; the perpendicular front which they had covered comes to be presented, in consequence, to the sea; its faults and cracks gradually widen into caves, as those of the fallen front had gradually widened at an earlier period; in the lapse of centuries, it too, resigning its place, topples over headlong, an undermined mass ; the surge dashes white and furious where the dense rock had rested before ; and thus, in its slow but irresistible march, the sea gains upon the land. In the peculiar disposition and character of the prevailing strata of Orkney, as certainly as in the power of the tides which sweep athwart its coasts, and the wide extent of sea which, stretching around it, gives the waves scope to gather bulk and momentum, may be found the secret of the extraordinary height to which the surf sometimes rises against its walls of rock. During the fiercer tempests, masses of foam shoot upwards against the precipices, like inverted cataracts, fully two hundred feet over the ordinary tide-level, and, washing away the looser soil from their summits, leaves in its place patches of slaty gravel, resembling that of a common sea-beach. Rocks less perpendicular, however great the violence of the wind and sea, would fail to project upwards bodies of surf to a height so extraordinary. But the low angle at which the strata lie, and the rectangularity maintained in relation to their line of bed by the fissures which traverse them, give to the Orkney precipices,—remarkable for their perpendicularity and their mural aspect,—exactly the angle against which the waves, as broken masses of foam, beat up to their greatest possible altitude. On a tract of iron-bound coast that skirts the entrance of the Cromarty Frith I have seen the surf rise, during violent gales from the north-west especially, against one rectangular rock, known as the White Rock, fully an hundred feet; while against scarcely any of the other precipices, more sloping, though equally exposed, did it rise more than half that height.

CHAPTER XIII.

WE returned to Stromness along the edge of the cliffs, gradually descending from higher to lower ranges of precipices,
and ever and anon detecting ichthyolite beds in the weathered
and partially decomposed strata.   As the rock moulders into
an incoherent clay, the fossils which it envelopes become not
unfrequently wholly detached from it, so that, on a smart
blow dealt by the hammer, they leap out entire, resembling,
from the degree of compression which they exhibit, those mi-
mic fishes carved out of plates of ivory or of mother-of-pearl,
which are used as counters in some of the games of China or
the East Indies.   The material of which they are composed,
a brittle jet, though better suited than the stone to resist the
disintegrating influences, is in most cases greatly too fragile
for preservation.   One may, however, acquire from the fragments a knowledge of certain minute points in the structure
of the ancient animals to which they belonged, respecting
which specimens of a more robust texture give no evidence.
The plates of Coccosteus sometimes spring out as unbroken
as when they covered the living animal, and, if the necessary
skill be not wanting, may be set up in their original order.
And I possess specimens of the head of Dipterus in which
the nearly circular gill-covers may be examined on both surfaces, interior and exterior, and in which the cranial portion

shows not only the enamelled plates of the frontal buckler, but also the strange mechanism of the palatal teeth, with the intervening cavities that had lodged both the brain and the occipital part of the spine. The fossils on the top of the cliffs here are chiefly Dipterians of the two closely allied genera, Diplopterus and Osteolepis.

A little farther on, I found, on a hill-side in which extensive slate-quarries had once been wrought, the remains of Pterichthys existing as mere patches, from which the colour had been discharged, but in which the almost human-like outline of both body and arms were still distinctly traceable; and farther on still, where the steep wall of cliffs sinks into a line of grassy banks, I saw in yet another quarry, ichthyolites of all the three great ganoid families so characteristic of the Old Red,—Cephalaspians, Dipterians, and Acanthodians, —ranged in the three-storied order to which I have already referred as so inexplicable. The specimens, however, though numerous, are not fine. They are resolved into a brittle bituminous coal, resembling hard pitch or black wax, which is always considerably less tenacious than the matrix in which they are inclosed; and so, when laid open by the hammer, they usually split through the middle of the plates and scales, instead of parting from the stone at their surfaces; and resemble, in consequence, those dark, shadow-like profiles taken in Indian ink by the limnèr, which exhibit a correct outline, but no details. We find, however, in some of the genera, portions of the animal preserved that are rarely seen in a state of keeping equally perfect in the ichthyolites of Cromarty, Moray, or Banff,—those terminal bones of the Coccosteus, for instance, that were prolonged beyond the plates by which the head and upper parts of the body were covered. Wherever the ichthyolites are inclosed in nodules, as in the more southerly counties over which the deposit extends, the nodule terminates, in almost every case, with the massier portions of the organism ; for the thinner parts, too inconsiderable to have served as attractive nuclei to the stony matter when the concretion was forming, were left outside its pale, and so have been lost; whereas, in the northern districts of the deposit, where the fossils, as in Caithness and Orkney, occur in flagstone, these slimmer parts, when the general state of keeping is tolerably good, lie spread out on the planes of the slabs, entire often in their minutest rays and articulations. The numerous Coccostei of this quarry exhibit, attached to their upper plates, their long vertebral columns, of many joints, that, depending from the broad dorsal shields of the ichthyolite, remind one of those skeleton fishes one sometimes sees on the shores of a fishing village, in which the bared backbone joints on, cord-like, to the broad plates of the skull. None of the other fishes of the Old Red Sandstone possessed an internal skeleton so decidedly osseous as that of the Coccosteus, and none of them presented externally so large an extent of naked skin,—provisions which probably went together. For about three-fifths of the entire length of the animal the surface was unprotected by dermal plates; and the muscles must have found the fulcrums on which they acted in the internal skeleton exclusively. And hence a necessity for greater strength in their interior framework than in that of fishes as strongly fenced round externally by scales or plates as the coleoptera by their elytrine, or the crustacea by their shells. Even in the Coccosteus, however, the ossification was by no means complete ; and the analogies of the skeleton seem to have allied it rather with the skeletons of the sturgeon family than with the skeletons of the sharks or rays. The processes of the vertebræ were greatly more solid in their substance than the vertebræ themselves,—a condition which in the sharks and rays is always reversed ; and they frequently survive, each with its little sprig of bone, formed like the letter Y, that attached

---

coleoptera by their elytrine [today usually 'elytra']: beetles by their characteristic hard wing covers; processes: here, the bony protrusions, or bones attached to, the vertebrae it to its centrum, projecting from it, in specimens from which the vertebral column itself has wholly disappeared. I found frequent traces, during my exploratory labours in Orkney, of the dorsal and ventral fins of this ichthyolite ; but no trace whatever of the pectorals or of the caudal fin. There seem to have been no pectorals ; and the tail, as I have already had occasion to remark, was apparently a mere point, unfurnished with rays.

In descending from the cliffs upon the quarries, my companion pointed to an angular notch in the rock-edge, apparently the upper termination of one of the numerous vertical cracks by which the precipices are traversed, and which in so many cases on the Orkney coast have been hollowed by the waves into long open coves or deep caverns. It was up there, he said, that about twelve years ago the sole survivor of a ship's crew contrived to scramble, four days after his vessel had been dashed to fragments against the rocks below, and when it was judged that all on board had perished. The vessel was wrecked on a Wednesday. She had been marked, when in the offing, standing for the bay of Stromness ; but the storm was violent, and the shore a lee one ; and as it was seen from the beach that she could scarce weather the headland yonder, a number of people gathered along the cliffs, furnished with ropes, to render to the crew whatever assistance might be possible in the circumstances. Human help, however, was to avail them nothing. Their vessel, a fine schooner, when within forty yards of the promontory, was seized broadside by an enormous wave, and dashed against the cliff, as one might dash a glass-phial against a stone-wall. One blow completed the work of destruction ; she went rolling in entire from keel to mast-head, and returned, on the recoil of the broken surge, a mass of shapeless fragments, that continued to dance idly amid the foam, or were scattered along the beach. But of the poor men, whom the spectators had seen but a few seconds before running wildly about the deck, there remained not a trace ; and the saddened spectators returned to their homes to say that all had perished. Four days after,—on the morning of the following Sabbath, —the sole survivor of the crew, saved, as if by miracle, climbed up the precipice, and presented himself to a group of astonished and terrified country people, who could scarce regard him as a creature of this world.   The fissure, which at the top of the cliff forms but a mere angular inflection, is hollowed below into a low-roofed cave of profound depth, into the farther extremity of which the tide hardly ever penetrates.   It is floored by a narrow strip of shingly beach ; and on this bit of beach, far within the cave, the sailor found himself, half a minute after the vessel had struck and gone to pieces, washed in, he knew not how.   Two pillows and a few dozen red herrings, which had been swept in along with him, served him for bed and board ; a tin cover enabled him to catch enough of the fresh-water droppings of the roof to quench his thirst ; several large fragments of wreck that had been jambed fast athwart the opening of the cave broke the violence of the wind and sea ; and in that doleful prison, day after day, he saw the tides sink and rise, and lay, when the surf rolled high at the fall of the tide, in utter darkness even at mid-day, as the waves outside rose to the roof, and inclosed him in a chamber as entirely cut off from the external atmosphere as that of a diving bell.   He was oppressed in the darkness, every time the waves came rolling in and compressed his modicum of air, by a sensation of extreme heat, —an effect of the condensation ; and then, in the interval of recession, and consequent expansion, by a sudden chill.   At low ebb he had to work hard in clearing away the accumulations of stone and gravel which had been rolled in by the previous tide, and threatened to bury him up altogether.   At length he succeeded, after many a fruitless attempt, in gaining an upper ledge that overhung his prison-mouth ; and, by a path on which a goat would scarce have found footing, he scrambled to the top. His name was Johnstone ; and the cave is still known as " Johnstone's Cave." Such was the narrative of my companion.

A little farther on, the undulating bank, into which the cliffs sink, projects into the sea as a flat green promontory, edged with hills of indurated sand, and topped by a picturesque ruin, that forms a pleasing object in the landscape. The ruin is that of a country residence of the bishops of Orkney during the disturbed and unhappy reign of Scotch Episcopacy, and bears on a flat tablet of weathered sandstone the initials of its founder, Bishop George Grahame, and the date of its erection, 1633. With a green cultivated oasis immediately around it, and a fine open sound, overlooked by the bold, picturesque cliffs of Hoy, in front, it must have been, for at least half the year, an agreeable, and, as its remains testify, a not uncomfortable habitation. But I greatly fear Scottish clergymen of the Establishment, whether Presbyterian or Episcopalian, when obnoxious, from their position or their tenets, to the great bulk of the Scottish people, have not been left, since at least the Reformation, to enjoy either quiet or happy lives, however extrinsically favourable the circumstances in which they may have been placed. Bishop Grahame, only five years after the date of the erection, was tried before the famous General Assembly of 1638 ; and, being convicted of having " all the ordinar faults of a bishop," he was deposed, and ordered within a limited time " to give tokens of repentance, under paine of excommunication." " He was a curler on the ice on the Sabbath day," says Baillie,— " a setter of tacks to his sones and grandsones, to the prejudice of the Church ; he oversaw adulterie ; slighted charming ; neglected preaching and doing of anie good ; and held portions of ministers' stipends for building his cathedral."

---

promontory: *ie* Breck Ness; the famous General Assembly of 1638 ... Baillie ... cathedral: see Additional Notes

The concluding portion of his life, after his deposition, was spent in obscurity ; nor did his successor in the bishoprick, subsequent to the re-establishment of Episcopacy at the Re-storation,—Bishop Honeyman,—close his days more happily. He was struck in the arm by the bullet which the zealot Mitchell had intended for Archbishop Sharp ; and the shat-tered bone never healed ; " for, though he lived some years after," says Burnet, " *they* were forced to lay open the wound every year, for an exfoliation ;" and his life was eventually shortened by his sufferings. All seemed comfortable enough, and quite quiet enough, in the bishop's country-house to-day. There were two cows quietly chewing the cud in what appa-rently had been the dignitary's sitting-room, and patiently awaiting the services of a young woman who was approaching at some little distance with a pail. A large gray cat, that had been sunning herself in a sheltered corner of the court-yard, started up at our approach, and disappeared through a slit hole. The sun, now gone far down the sky, shone brightly on shattered gable-tops, and roofless, rough-edged walls, re-vealing many a flaw and chasm in the yielding masonry ; and their shadows fell with picturesque effect on the loose litter, rude implements, and gapped dry-stone fence, of the neglected farm-yard which surrounds the building.

I have said that the flat promontory occupied by the ruin is edged by hills of indurated sand. Existing in some places as a continuous bed of a soft gritty sandstone, scooped wave-like a-top, and varying from five to eight feet in thickness, they form a curious example of a subaerial formation,—the sand of which they are composed having been all blown from the sea-beach, and consolidated by the action of moisture on a calcareous mixture of comminuted shells, which forms from twenty to twenty-five per cent. of their entire mass. I found that the sections of the bed laid open by the encroachments of the sea were scarce less regularly stratified than those of a

<hr>

Mitchell ... Sharp: Mitchell, an extremist Presbyterian or Covenanter, attempted to kill Archbishop James Sharp of St Andrews in 1668, in protest at the oppressive imposition of Episcopalianism and the persecution of the Covenanters (Sharp was eventually success-fully assassinated in 1679 by another Covenanter). Miller's source was *History of My Own Times* (1838, p. 187) by the ecclesiastic Gilbert **Burnet** (1643-1715) subaqueous deposit, and that it was hollowed, where most exposed to the weather, into a number of spherical cells, which gave to those parts of the surface where they lay thickest, somewhat the aspect of a rude Runic fret-work,—an appearance not uncommon in weathered sandstones. With more time to spare, I could fain have studied the deposit more carefully, in the hope of detecting a few peculiarities of structure sufficient to distinguish subaerially-formed from subaqueously-deposited beds of stone. Sandstones of subaerial formation are of no very unfrequent occurrence among the recent deposits. On the coast of Cornwall there are cliffs of considerable height, that extend for several miles, and have attained a degree of solidity sufficient to serve the commoner purposes of the architect, which at one time existed as accumulations of blown sand. " It is around the promontory of New Kaye," says Dr Paris, in an interesting memoir on the subject, " that the most extensive formation of sandstone takes place. Here it may be seen in different stages of induration, from a state in which it is too friable to be detached from the rock upon which it reposes, to a hardness so considerable, that it requires a violent blow from a sledge-hammer to break it. Buildings are here constructed of it ; the church of Cranstock is entirely built with it ; and it is also employed for various articles of domestic and agricultural uses. The geologist who has previously examined the celebrated specimen from Guadaloupe will be struck with the great analogy which it bears to this formation." Now, as vast tracts of the earth's surface,—in some parts of the world, as in Northern Africa, millions of square miles together,—are at present overlaid by accumulations of sand, which have this tendency to consolidate and become lasting subaerial formations, destined to occupy a place among the future strata of the globe, it seems impossible but that also in the old geologic periods there must have been, as now, sand-wastes and subaerial formations. And as the re-

---

subaerially: above water (literally, under air), for instance, blown sand dunes; **subaqueously**: under water, for instance, a sandbank deposited in a river; **New Kaye**: Newquay in Cornwall: **treatise**: Paris (1818, p. 6) presentatives of these may still exist in some of our sandstone quarries, it might be well to be possessed of a knowledge of the peculiarities by which they are to be distinguished from deposits of subaqueous origin.   In order that I might have an opportunity of studying these peculiarities where they are to be seen more extensively developed than elsewhere on the eastern coast of Scotland, I here formed the intention of spending a day, on my return south, among the sand-wastes of Moray,—a purpose which I afterwards carried into effect. But of that more anon.

On the following morning, availing myself of a kind invitation, through Dr Garson, from his brother, a Free Church minister resident in an inland district of the Mainland, in convenient neighbourhood with the northern coasts of the island, and with several quarries, I set out from Stromness, taking in my way the Loch and Standing Stones of Stennis, which I had previously seen from but my seat in the mail-gig as I passed.   Mr Learmonth, who had to visit some of his people in this direction, accompanied me for several miles along the shores of the loch, and lightened the journey by his interesting snatches of local history, suggested by the various objects that lay along our road,—buildings, tumuli, ancient battle-fields, and standing stones.   The loch itself, an expansive sheet of water fourteen miles in circumference, I contemplated with much interest, and longed for an opportunity of studying its natural history.   Two promontories,—those occupied by the Standing Stones,—shoot out from the opposite sides, and approach so near as to be connected by a rustic bridge.   They divide the loch into two nearly equal parts, the lower of which gives access to the sea, and is salt in its nether reaches and brackish in its upper ones, while the higher is merely brackish in its nether reaches, and fresh enough in its upper ones to be potable.   The shores of both were strewed, at the time I passed, by a line of wrack, consisting, for the first few miles,

---

Dr Garson's brother: John Garson (1813-1884) was assistant in the unified parishes of Birsay and Harray until the Disruption, when each became a separate Free Church parish, and Garson was ordained in Birsay (Ewing 1914, p. 165, *pace* Smith 1907, p, 175 who has a Mr Garson as Free Church minister of Birsay and Harray); **inland district**: *ie* Birsay; **Loch of Stennis**: two lochs, today the Loch of Stenness and the Loch of Harray from where the lower loch opens to the sea, of only marine plants, then of marine plants mixed with those of fresh-water growth, and then, in the upper sheet of water, of lacustrine plants exclusively. And the fauna of the loch, like its flora, is, I was led to understand, of the same mixed character; the marine and fresh-water animals having each their own reaches, with certain debateable tracts between, in which each expatiates with more or less freedom, according to its nature and constitution,—some of the sea-fishes advancing far on the fresh water, and others, among the proper denizens of the lake, encroaching far on the salt. The common fresh-water eel strikes out, I was told, farthest into the sea-water; in which, indeed, reversing the habits of the salmon, it is known in various places to deposit its spawn : it seeks, too, impatient of a low temperature, to escape from the cold of winter, by taking refuge in water brackish enough in a climate such as ours to resist the influence of frost. Of the marine fishes, on the other hand, I found that the flounder got greatly higher than any of the others, inhabiting reaches of the lake almost entirely fresh. A memoir on the Loch of Stennis and its productions, animal and vegetable, such as a Gilbert White of Selborne could produce, would be at once a very valuable and very curious document. By dividing it into reaches, in which the average saltness of the water was carefully ascertained, and its productions noted, with the various modifications which these underwent as they receded upwards or downwards from their proper habitat towards the line at which they could no longer exist, much information might be acquired, of a kind important to the naturalist, and not without its use to the geological student. I have had an opportunity elsewhere of observing a curious change which fresh-water induces on the flounder. In the brackish water of an estuary it becomes, without diminishing in general size, thicker and more fleshy than when in its legitimate habitat the sea; but the flesh

---

Gilbert White: (1720-1795), curate of Selborne in Hampshire, which he immortalised in loving detail in *The Natural History and Antiquities of Selborne* (1789)

loses in quality what it gains in quantity ;—it is flabby and insipid, and the margin-fin lacks always its delicious strip of transparent fat. I fain wish that some intelligent resident on the shores of Stennis would set himself carefully to examine its productions, and that then, after registering his observations for a few years, he would favour the world with its natural history.

The Standing Stones,—second in Britain, of their kind, to only those of Stonehenge,—occur in two groupes; the smaller group (composed, however, of the taller stones) on the southern promontory ; the larger on the northern one. Rude and shapeless, and bearing no other impress of the designing faculty than that they are stuck endwise in the earth, and form, as a whole, regular figures on the sward, there is yet a sublime solemnity about them, unsurpassed in effect by any ruin I have yet seen, however grand in its design or imposing in its proportions. Their very rudeness, associated with their ponderous bulk and weight, adds to their impressiveness. When there is art and taste enough in a country to hew an ornate column, no one marvels that there should be also mechanical skill enough in it to set it up on end ; but the men who tore from the quarry these vast slabs, some of them eighteen feet in height over the soil, and raised them where they now stand, must have been ignorant savages, unacquainted with machinery, and unfurnished, apparently, with a single tool. And what, when contemplating their handiwork, we have to subtract in idea from their minds, we add, by an involuntary process, to their bodies: we come to regard the feats which they have accomplished as performed by a power not mechanical, but gigantic. The consideration, too, that these remains,— eldest of the works of man in this country,—should have so long survived all definite tradition of the purposes which they were raised to serve, so that we now merely know regarding them that they were religious in their uses,—products of that

---

Standing Stones: the southern, smaller, group is now usually called the Stones of Stenness, and the northern, circular, group the Ring of Brogar ineradicable instinct of man's nature which leads him in so many various ways to attempt conciliating the Powers of another world,—serves greatly to heighten their effect. History at the time of their erection had no existence in these islands : the age, though it sought, through the medium of strange, unknown rites, to communicate with Heaven, was not knowing enough to communicate, through the medium of alphabet or symbol, with posterity. The appearance of the obelisks, too, harmonizes well with their great antiquity and the obscurity of their origin. For about a man's height from the ground they are covered thick by the shorter lichens,—chiefly the gray-stone parmelia,—here and there embroidered by golden-hued patches of the yellow parmelia of the wall ; but their heads and shoulders, raised beyond the reach alike of the herd-boy and of his herd, are covered by an extraordinary profusion of a flowing beard-like lichen of unusual length, —the lichen *calicarus* (or, according to modern botanists, *Ramalina scopulorum*), in which they look like an assemblage of ancient Druids, mysteriously stern and invincibly silent and shaggy as the bard of Gray, when

> " Loose his beard and hoary hair
> Streamed like a meteor on the troubled air."

The day was perhaps too sunny and clear for seeing the Standing Stones to the best possible advantage. They could not be better placed than on their flat promontories, surrounded by the broad plane of an extensive lake, in a waste, lonely, treeless country, that presents no bold competing features to divert attention from them as the great central objects of the landscape ; but the gray of the morning, or an atmosphere of fog and vapour, would have associated better with the misty obscurity of their history, their shaggy forms, and their livid tints, than the glare of a cloudless sun, that brought out in hard, clear relief their rude outlines, and gave to each its sharp dark patch of shadow. Gray-coloured objects, when

---

'Loose his beard ...': from Thomas Gray's 'The Bard'

tall and imposing, but of irregular form, are seen always to
most advantage in an uncertain light,—in fog or frost-rhime,
or under a scowling sky, or, as Parnell well expresses it,
"amid the livid gleams of night."   They appeal, if I may so
express myself, to the sentiment of the ghostly and the spectral, and demand at least a partial envelopment of the obscure.   Burns, with the true tact of the genuine poet, de-
velops the sentiment almost instinctively in an exquisite
stanza in one of his less-known songs, "The Posey,"—

> "The hawthorn I will pu', *wi' its locks o' siller gray,*
> Where, *like an aged man, it stands at break o' day.*"

Scott, too, in describing these very stones, chooses the early
morning as the time in which to exhibit them, when they
"stood in the gray light of the dawning, like the phantom
forms of antediluvian giants, who, shrouded in the habili-
ments of the dead, come to revisit, by the pale light, the earth
which they had plagued with their oppression, and polluted
by their sins, till they brought down upon it the vengeance
of long-suffering heaven."   On another occasion he introduces
them as "glimmering, a grayish white, in the rising sun, and
projecting far to the westward their long gigantic shadows."
And Malcolm, in the exercise of a similar faculty with that
of Burns aud of Scott, surrounds them, in his description,
with a somewhat similar atmosphere of partial dimness and
obscurity :—

> "The hoary rocks, of giant size,
> That o'er the land in circles rise,
> Of which tradition may not tell,
> Fit circles for the wizard's spell,
> Seen far *amidst the scowling storm,*
> Seem each a tall and phantom form,
> *As hurrying vapours o'er them flee,*
> Frowning in grim security,
> While, like a dread voice from the past,
> Around them moans the autumnal blast."

There exist curious analogies between the earlier stages of

Parnell 'amid the livid gleams of night': Thomas Parnell's (1679-1718) poem, 'A
night-piece on death', lines 18-19; Scott: from his novel *The Pirate*, in the final parting
scene between Cleveland, the eponymous pirate, and Minna Troil, the dark-haired sister
of the main heroine, who is in love with him – see p. 454; Malcolm: see note for p. 417;
'The hoary …': from 'Orkney', in *Poems, Tales and Sketches* (see p. 390)

society and the more immature periods of life,—between the savage and the child; and the huge circle of Stennis seems suggestive of one of these. It is considerably more than four hundred feet in diameter; and the stones which compose it, varying from three to fourteen feet in height, must have been originally from thirty-five to forty in number, though only sixteen now remain erect. A mound and fosse, still distinctly traceable, run round the whole; and there are several mysterious-looking tumuli outside, bulky enough to remind one of the lesser morains of the geologist. But the circle, notwithstanding its imposing magnitude, is but a huge child's house after all,—one of those circles of stones which children lay down on their village-green, and then, in the exercise of that imaginative faculty which distinguishes between the young of the human animal and those of every other creature, convert, by a sort of conventionalism, into a church or dwelling-house, within which they seat themselves, and enact their imitations of the employments of their seniors, whether domestic or ecclesiastical. The circle of Stennis was a circle, say the antiquaries, dedicated to the sun. The group of stones on the southern promontory of the lake formed but a half-circle, and it was a half-circle dedicated to the moon. To the circular sun the great rude children of an immature age of the world had laid down a circle of stones on the one promontory; to the moon, in her half-orbed state, they had laid down a half-circle on the other; and in propitiating these material deities, to whose standing in the old Scandinavian worship the names of our *Sun*day and *Mon*day still testify, they employed in their respective inclosures, in the exercise of a wild unregulated fancy, uncouth irrational rites, the extremeness of whose folly was in some measure concealed by the horrid exquisiteness of their cruelty. We are still in the nonage of the species, and see human society sowing its wild oats in a thousand various ways, very absurdly often, and often very wickedly ; but matters seem to have been greatly worse when, in an age still more immature, the grimly-bearded, six-feet children of Orkney were laying down their stone-circles on the green.   Sir Walter, in the parting scene between Cleveland and Mina Troil, which he describes as having taken place amid the lesser group of stones, refers to an immense slab " lying flat and prostrate in the middle of the others, supported by short pillars, of which some relics are still visible," and which is regarded as the sacrificial stone of the erection.   " It is a current belief," says Dr Hibbert, in an elaborate paper in the " Transactions of the Scottish Antiquaries," " that upon this stone a victim of royal birth was immolated.   Halfdan the Long-legged, the son of Harold the Fair-haired, in punishment for the aggressions of Orkney, had made an unexpected descent upon its coasts, and acquired possession of the Jarldom.   In the autumn succeeding, Halfdan was retorted upon, and, after an inglorious contest, betook himself to a place of concealment, from which he was the following morning unlodged, and instantly doomed to the Asæ. Einar, the Jarl of Orkney, with his sword carved the captive's back into the form of an eagle, the spine being longitudinally divided, and the ribs being separated by a transverse cut as far as the loins.   He then extracted the lungs, and dedicated them to Odin for a perpetuity of victory, singing a wild song, —' I am revenged for the slaughter of Rognvalld : this have the Nornæ decreed.   In my fiording the pillar of the people has fallen.   Build up the cairn, ye active youths, for victory is with us.   From the stones of the sea-shore will I pay the Long-legged a hard seat.' "   There is certainly no trace to be detected, in this dark story, of a golden age of the world : the golden age is, I would fain hope, an age yet to come. There at least exists no evidence that it is an age gone by. It will be the full-grown *manly* age of the world when the race, as such, shall have attained to their years of discretion.

Dr Hibbert: Samuel Hibbert (1782–1848), later Samuel Hibbert Ware, geologist and antiquarian (Andrews 1982). The quote is from Hibbert (1831, p. 117)

They are at present in their froward boyhood, playing at the mischievous games of war, and diplomacy, and stock-gambling, and site-refusing ; and it is not quite agreeable for quiet honest people to be living amongst them.   But there would be nothing gained by going back to that more infantine state of society in which the Jarl Einar carved into a red eagle the back of Halfdan the Long-legged.

---

site-refusing: refusing permission for the building of a Free Church – see Introduction

CHAPTER XIV.

WHILE yet lingering amid the Standing Stones, I was joined by Mr Garson, who had obligingly ridden a good many miles to meet me, and now insisted that I should mount and ride in turn, while he walked by my side, that I might be fresh, he said, for the exploratory ramble of the evening.   I could have ventured more readily on taking the command of a vessel than of a horse, and with fewer fears of mutiny; but mount I did; and the horse, a discreet animal, finding he was to have matters very much his own way, got upon honour with me, and exerted himself to such purpose, that we did not fall greatly more than a hundred yards behind Mr Garson.   We traversed in our journey a long dreary moor, so entirely ruined, like those which I had seen on the previous day, by belonging to everybody in general, as to be no longer of the slightest use to anybody in particular.   The soil seems to have been naturally poor; but it must have taken a good deal of spoiling to render it the sterile, verdureless waste it is now; for even where it had been poorest, I found that in the island-like appropriated patches by which it is studded, it at least bears, what it has long ceased to bear elsewhere, a continuous covering of green sward.   But if disposed to quarrel with the commons of Orkney, I found in close neighbourhood with them that with which I could have no quarrel,—

numerous small properties farmed by the proprietors, and forming, in most instances, farms by no means very large. There are parishes in this part of the mainland divided among from sixty to eighty landowners.

A nearly similar state of things seems to have obtained in Scotland about the beginning of the eighteenth century, and for the greater part of the previous one.   I am acquainted with old churchyards in the north of Scotland that contain the burying-grounds of from six to ten landed proprietors, whose lands are now merged into single properties. And, in reading the biographies of our old covenanting ministers, I have often remarked as curious, and as bearing in the same line, that no inconsiderable proportion of their number were able to retire, in times of persecution, to their own little estates.   It was during the disastrous wars of the French Revolution,—wars the effects of which Great Britain will, I fear, never fully recover,—that the smaller holdings were finally absorbed.   About twenty years ere the war began, the lands of England were parcelled out among no fewer than two hundred and fifty thousand families ; before the peace of 1815, they had fallen into the hands of thirty-two thousand.   In less than half a century, that base of actual proprietorship on which the landed interest of any country must ever find its surest standing, had contracted in England to less than one-seventh its former extent.   In Scotland the absorption of the great bulk of the lesser properties seems to have taken place somewhat earlier ; but in it also the revolutionary war appears to have given them the final blow ; and the more extensive proprietors of the kingdom are assuredly all the less secure in consequence of their extinction. They were the smaller stones in the wall, that gave firmness in the setting to the larger, and jambed them fast within those safe limits determined by the line and plummet, which it is ever perilous to overhang.   Very extensive territorial properties, wherever they exist, create almost necessarily—human nature being what it is—a species of despotism more oppressive than even that of great unrepresentative governments. It used to be remarked on the Continent, that there was always less liberty in petty principalities, where the eye of the ruler was ever on his subjects, than under the absolute monarchies.* And in a country such as ours, the accumulation of landed property in the hands of comparatively a few individuals has the effect often of bringing the territorial privileges of the great landowner into a state of antagonism with the civil and religious rights of the people, that cannot be other than perilous to the landowner himself. In a district divided, like Orkney, among many owners, a whole country-side could not be shut up against its people by some ungenerous or intolerant proprietor,—greatly at his own risk and to his own hurt,—as in the case of Glen Tilt or the Grampians; nor, when met for purposes of public worship,

* There is a very admirable remark to this effect in the "Travelling Memorandums" of the late Lord Gardenstone, which, as the work has been long out of print, and is now scarce, may be new to many of my readers :—" It is certain, and demonstrated by the experience of ages and nations," says his Lordship, in referring to the old principalities of France, "that the government of petty princes is less favourable to the security and interests of society than the government of monarchs, who possess great and extensive territories. The race of great monarchs cannot possibly preserve a safe and undisturbed state of government, without many delegations of power and office to men of approved abilities and practical knowledge, who are subject to complaint during their administration, and responsible when it is at an end; or yet without an established system of laws and regulations; so that no inconsiderable degree of security and liberty to the subject is almost inseparable from, and essential to, the subsistence and duration of a great monarchy. But it is easy for petty princes to practise an arbitrary and irregular exercise of power, by which their people are reduced to a condition of miserable slavery. Indeed, very few of them, in the course of ages, are capable of conceiving any other means of maintaining the ostentatious state, the luxurious and indolent pride, which they mistake for greatness. I heartily wish that this observation and censure may not, in some instances, be applicable to great landed proprietors in some parts of Britain."—"Travelling Memorandums," vol. i. p. 123. 1792.

Glen Tilt ... Grampians: see Additional Notes; Memorandums: *Travelling Memorandums made in a Tour upon the Continent of Europe in the year 1792* by Lord Gardenstone (see note for p. 247) could the population of a parish be chased from off its bare moors, at his instance, by the constable or the sheriff-officer, to worship God agreeably to their consciences amid the mire of a cross road, or on the bare sea-beach uncovered by the ebb of the tide. The smaller properties of the country, too, served admirably as stepping-stones, by which the proprietors or their children, when possessed of energy and intellect, could mount to a higher walk of society. Here beside me, for instance, was my friend Mr Garson, a useful and much-esteemed minister of religion in his native district; while his brother, a medical man of superior parts, was fast rising into extensive practice in the neighbouring town. They had been prepared for their respective professions by a classical education; and yet the stepping-stone to positions in society at once so important and so respectable was simply one of the smaller holdings of Orkney, derived to them as the descendants of one of the old Scandinavian Udallers, and which fell short, I was informed, of a hundred a-year.

Mr Garson's dwelling, to which I was welcomed with much hospitality by his mother and sisters, occupies the middle of an inclined hollow or basin, so entirely surrounded by low, moory hills, that at no point,—though the radius of the prospect averages from four to six miles,—does it command a view of the sea. I scarce expected being introduced in Orkney to a scene in which the traveller could so thoroughly forget that he was on an island. Of the parish of Harray, which borders on Mr Garson's property, no part touches the sea-coast; and the people of the parish are represented by their neighbours, who pride themselves upon their skill as sailors and boatmen, as a race of lubberly landsmen, unacquainted with nautical matters, and ignorant of the ocean and its productions. A Harray man is represented, in one of their stories, as entering into a compact of mutual forbearance with a lobster,—to him a monster of unknown

---

cross road … sea beach: the road, and, Miller implied, the beach would be Crown land, and therefore often the only land for miles not owned by the local landlord, and where the Free Church could meet without needing his permission. In fact, however, some Scottish foreshores are owned by private landowners powers and formidable proportions,—which he had at first attempted to capture, but which had shown fight, and had nearly captured him in turn. "Weel, weel, let a-be for let a-be," he is made to say ; "if thou doesna clutch me in thy grips, I'se no clutch thee in mine." It is to this primitive parish that David Vedder, the sailor-poet of Orkney, refers, in his "Orcadian Sketches," as "celebrated over the whole archipelago for the peculiarities of its inhabitants, their singular manners and habits, their uncouth appearance, and homely address. Being the most landward district in Pomona," he adds, "and consequently having little intercourse with strangers, it has become the stronghold of many ancient customs and superstitions, which modern innovation has pushed from off their pedestals in almost all the other parts of the island. The permanency of its population, too, is mightily in favour of ' old use and wont,' as it is almost entirely divided amongst a class of men yclept *pickie*, or petty lairds, each ploughing his own fields and reaping his own crops, much in the manner their great-great-grandfathers did in the days of Earl Patrick. And such is the respect which they entertain for their hereditary beliefs, that many of them are said still to cast a lingering look, not unmixed with reverence, on certain spots held sacred by their Scandinavian ancestors."

After an early dinner I set out for the barony of Birsay, in the northern extremity of the mainland, accompanied by Mr Garson, and passed for several miles over a somewhat dreary country, bare, sterile, and brown, studded by cold, broad, treeless lakes, and thinly mottled by groupes of gray, diminutive cottages, that do not look as if there was much of either plenty or comfort inside. But after surmounting the hills that form the northern side of the interior basin, I was sensible of a sudden improvement on the face of the country. Where the land slopes towards the sea, the shaggy heath

---

David Vedder: (1790-1854), Orcadian sailor, ship's captain and finally customs officer in several ports of the East Coast of Scotland. He published poetry, sketches, and other literary works gives place to a green luxuriant herbage ; and the frequent patches of corn seem to rejoice in a more genial soil. The lower slopes of Orkney are singularly rich in wild flowers,—richer by many degrees than the fat loamy meadows of England. They resemble gaudy pieces of carpeting, as abundant in petals as in leaves : their luxuriant blow of red and white, blue and yellow, seems as if competing, in the extent of surface which it occupies, with their general ground of green. I have remarked a somewhat similar luxuriance of wild flowers in the more sheltered hollows of the bleak north-western coasts of Scotland. There is little that is rare to be found among these last, save that a few Alpine plants may be here and there recognised as occurring at a lower level than elsewhere in Britain ; but the vast profusion of blossoms borne by species common to the greater part of the kingdom imparts to them an apparently novel character. We may detect, I am inclined to think, in this singular profusion, both in Orkney and the bleaker districts of the mainland of Scotland, the operation of a law not less influential in the animal than in the vegetable world, which, when hardship presses upon the life of the individual shrub or quadruped, so as to threaten its vitality, renders it fruitful in behalf of its species. I have seen the principle strikingly exemplified in the common tobacco plant, when reared in a northern county in the open air. Year after year it continued to degenerate, and to exhibit a smaller leaf and a shorter stem, until the successors of what in the first year of trial had been vigorous plants of from three to four feet in height, had in the sixth or eighth become mere weeds of scarce as many inches. But while the more flourishing, and as yet undegenerate plant, had merely borne a-top a few florets, which produced a small quantity of exceedingly minute seeds, the stunted weed, its descendant, was so thickly covered over in its season with its pale yellow bells, as to present the appearance of a nosegay ; and the seeds produced were not only bulkier in the mass, but also individually of much greater size. The tobacco had grown productive in proportion as it had degenerated and become poor. In the common scurvy grass, too, remarkable, with some other plants, as I have already had occasion to mention, for taking its place among both the productions of our Alpine heights and of our sea-shores, it will be found that in proportion as its habitat proves ungenial, and its stems and leaves become dwarfish and thin, its little white cruciform flowers increase, till, in localities where it barely exists, as if on the edge of extinction, we find the entire plant forming a dense bundle of seed-vessels, each charged to the full with seed. And in the gay meadows of Orkney, crowded with a vegetation that approaches its northern limit of production, we detect what seems to be the same principle, chronically operative ; and hence, it would seem, their extraordinary gaiety. Their richly-blossoming plants are the poor productive *Irish* of the vegetable world ;* for Doubleday seems to

---

* The exciting effects of a poor soil, or climate, or of severe usage, on the productive powers of various vegetable species, have been long and often remarked. Flavel describes, in one of his ingenious emblems, illustrative of the influence of affliction on the Christian, an orchard tree, which had been beaten with sticks and stones, till it presented a sorely stunted and mutilated appearance; but which, while the fairer and more vigorous trees around it were rich in only leaves, was laden with fruit,—a direct consequence, it is shown, of the hard treatment to which it had been subjected. I have heard it told in a northern village, as a curious anecdote, that a large pear tree, which, during a vigorous existence of nearly fifty years, had borne scarce a single pear, had, when in a state of decay, and for a few years previous to its death, borne immense crops of from two to three bolls each season. And the skilful gardener not unfrequently avails himself of the principle on which both phenomena seem to have occurred,—that exhibited in the beaten and that in the decaying tree,—in rendering his barren plants fruitful. He has recourse to it even when merely desirous of ascertaining the variety of pear or apple which some thriving sapling, slow in bearing, is yet to produce. Selecting some bough which may be conveniently lopped away without destroying the symmetry of the tree, he draws his knife across the bark, and inflicts on it a wound, from which, though death may not ensue for some two or three twelvemonths, it cannot ulti-

---

Doubleday: Thomas Doubleday (1790–1870), dramatist, radical politician, and author of *The true law of population shewn to be connected with the food of the people* (1842; outline of argument previously in *Blackwood's Edinburgh Magazine*). Darwin later used his arguments similarly in, *eg, Variation of Plants and Animals under Domestication*; **Flavel**: presumably John Flavel (d. 1691), Presbyterian divine and author of popular devotional essays be quite in the right in holding that the law extends to not only the inferior animals, but to our own species also. The lean, ill-fed sow and rabbit rear, it has been long known, a greatly more numerous progeny than the same animals when well cared for and fat ; and every horse and cattle breeder knows, that to over-feed his animals proves a sure mode of rendering them sterile. The sheep, if tolerably well pastured, brings forth only a single lamb at a birth ; but if half-starved and lean, the chances are that it may bring forth two or three. And so it is also with the greatly higher human race. Place them in circumstances of degradation and hardship so extreme as almost to threaten their existence as individuals, and they increase, as if in behalf of the species, with a rapidity without precedent in circumstances of greater comfort. The aristocratic families of a country are continually running out ; and it requires frequent creations to keep up the House of Lords ; while our poor people seem increasing in some districts in almost the mathematical ratio. The county of Sutherland is already more populous than it was previous to the great clearings. In Skye, though fully two-thirds of the population emigrated early in the latter half of the last century, a single generation had scarce passed ere the gap was completely filled ; and miserable Ireland, had the human family no other breeding-place or nursery,

---

mately recover. Next spring the wounded branch is found to bear its bunches of blossoms ; the blossoms set into fruit ; and while in the other portions of the plant all is vigorous and barren as before, the dying part of it, as if sobered by the near prospect of dissolution, is found fulfilling the proper end of its existence. Soil and climate, too, exert, it has been often remarked, a similar influence. In the united parishes of Kirkmichael and Culicuden, in the immediate neighbourhood of Cromarty, much of the soil is cold and poor, and the exposure ungenial ; and " in most parts, where hardwood has been planted," says the Rev. Mr Sage of Resolis, in his " Statistical Account," " it is stinted in its growth, and bark-bound. Comparatively young trees of ash," he shrewdly adds, " *are covered with seed,—an almost infallible sign that their natural growth is checked.* The leaves, too, fall off about the beginning of September."

would of itself be sufficient in a very few ages to people the world.

We returned, taking in our way the cliffs of Marwick Head, in which I detected a few scattered plates and scales, and which, like nine-tenths of the rocks of Orkney, belong to the great flagstone division of the formation. I found the dry-stone fences on Mr Garson's property still richer in detached fossil fragments than the cliffs ; but there are few erections in the island that do not inclose in their walls portions of the organic. We find ichthyolite remains in the flagstones laid bare along the wayside,—in every heap of road-metal,—in the bottom of every stream,—in almost every cottage and fence. Orkney is a land of defunct fishes, and contains in its rocky folds more individuals of the waning ganoid family than are now to be found in all the existing seas, lakes, and rivers of the world. I enjoyed in a snug upper room a delectable night's rest, after a day of prime exercise, prolonged till it just touched on toil, and again experienced, on looking out in the morning on the wide flat basin around, a feeling some-what akin to wonder, that Orkney should possess a scene at once so extensive and so exclusively inland.

Towards mid-day I walked on to the parish manse of Sand-wick, armed with a letter of introduction to its inmate, the Rev. Charles Clouston,—a gentleman whose descriptions of the Orkneys, in the very complete and tastefully written Guide-Book of the Messrs Anderson of Inverness, and of his own parish in the "Statistical Account of Scotland," had, both from the high literary ability and the amount of scientific ac-quirement which they exhibit, rendered me desirous to see. I was politely received, though my visit must have been, as I afterwards ascertained, at a rather inconvenient time. It was now late in the week, and the coming Sabbath was that of the communion in the parish ; but Mr Clouston obligingly devoted to me at least an hour, and I found it a very profit-

---

Clouston: see Additional Notes; communion: in Presbyterian practice this sacrament only took place at intervals of several months, and was therefore a major event for which the minister had to be well prepared

able one.   He showed me a collection of flags, with which
he intended constructing a grotto, and which contained numerous specimens of Coccosteus, that he had exposed to the
weather, to bring out the fine blue efflorescence,—a phosphate
of iron which forms on the surface of the plates.   They reminded me, from their peculiar style of colouring, and the
grotesqueness of their forms, of the blue figuring on pieces
of buff-coloured china, and seemed to be chiefly of one species, very abundant in Orkney, the *Coccosteus decipiens.*   We
next walked out to see a quarry in the neighbourhood of the
manse, remarkable for containing in immense abundance the
heads of Dipteri,—many of them in a good state of keeping,
with all the multitudinous plates to which they owe their
pseudo-name, Polyphractus, in their original places, and bearing unworn and untarnished their minute carvings and delicate enamel, but existing in every case as mere detached
heads.   I found three of them lying in one little slaty fragment of two and a half inches by four, which I brought along
with me.   Mr Clouston had never seen the curious arrangement of palatal plates and teeth which distinguishes the Dipterus ; and, drawing his attention to it in an ill-preserved
specimen which I found in the coping of his glebe-wall, I restored, in a rude pencil sketch, the two angular patches of
teeth that radiate from the elegant dart-head in the centre
of the palate, with the rhomboidal plate behind.   " We have
a fish, not uncommon on the rocky coasts of this part of the
country," he said,—" the Bergil or Striped Wrasse *(Labrus
Balanus),*—which bears exactly such patches of angular teeth
in its palate.   They adhere strongly together ; and, when
found in our old Pict's houses, which occasionally happens,
they have been regarded by some of our local antiquaries as
artificial,—an opinion which I have had to correct, though
it seems not improbable that, from their gem-like appearance,
they may have been used in a rude age as ornaments.   I

think I can show you one disinterred here some years ago." It interested me to find, from Mr Clouston's specimen, that the palatal grinders of this recent fish of Orkney very nearly resemble those of its *Dipterus* of the Old Red Sandstone. The group is of nearly the same size in the modern as in the ancient fish, and presents the same angular form; but the individual teeth are more strongly set in the Bergil than in the Dipterus, and radiate less regularly from the inner rectangular point of the angle to its base outside. I could fain have procured an Orkney Bergil, in order to determine the general pattern of its palatal dentition with what is very peculiar in the more ancient fish,—the form of the lower jaw; and to ascertain farther, from the contents of the stomach, the species of shell-fish or crustaceans on which it feeds; but, though by no means rare in Orkney, where it is occasionally used as food, I was unable, during my short stay, to possess myself of a specimen.

Mr Clouston had, I found, chiefly directed his palæontological inquiries on the vegetable remains of the flagstones, as the department of the science in which, in relation to Orkney, most remained to be done; and his collection of these is the most considerable in the number of its specimens that I have yet seen. It, however, serves but to show how very extreme is the poverty of the flora of the Lower Old Red Sandstone. The numerous fishes of the period seem to have inhabited a sea little more various in its vegetation than in its molluscs. Among the many specimens of Mr Clouston's collection I could detect but two species of plants,—an imperfectly preserved vegetable, more nearly resembling a club-moss than aught I have seen, and a smooth-stemmed fucoid, existing as a mere coaly film on the stone, and distinguished chiefly from the other by its sharp-edged, well-defined outline, and from the circumstance that its stems continue to retain the same diameter for a considerable distance, and this,

---

a sea little more varied in its vegetation: in fact, the Old Red Sandstone is now considered to have been a freshwater deposit, so that many of these still poorly known fossils are likely to be freshwater algae or land and swamp plants washed into fresh water too, after throwing off at acute angles numerous branches, nearly equal in bulk to the parent trunk.   In a specimen about two and a half feet in length, which I owe to the kindness of Mr Dick of Thurso, there are stems continuous throughout, that, though they ramify into from six to eight branches in that space, are quite as thick atop as at bottom. They are the remains, in all probability, of a long flexible fucoid, like those fucoids of the intertropical seas that, streaming slantwise in the tide, rise not unfrequently to the surface in fifteen and twenty fathoms water.   I saw among Mr Clouston's specimens no such lignite as the fragment of true coniferous wood which I had found at Cromarty a few years previous, and which, it would seem, is still unique among the fossils of the Old Red Sandstone.   In the chart of the Pacific attached to the better editions of " Cook's Voyages," there are several entries along the track of the great navigator that indicate where, in mid-ocean, trees, or fragments of trees, had been picked up.   The entries, however, are but few, though they belong to all the three voyages together : if I remember aright, there are only five entries in all,—two in the Northern and three in the Southern Pacific.   The floating tree, at a great distance from land, is of rare occurrence in even the present scene of things, though the breadth of land be great, and trees numerous ; and in the times of the Old Red Sandstone, when probably the breadth of land was *not* great, and trees *not* numerous, it seems to have been of rarer occurrence still.   But it is at least something to know that in this early age of the world trees there were.

I walked on to Stromness, and on the following morning, that of Saturday, took boat for Hoy,—skirting, on my passage out, the eastern and southern shores of the intervening island of Græmsay, and, on the passage back again, its western and northern shores.   The boatman, an intelligent man, —one of the teachers, as I afterwards ascertained, in the Free

Church Sabbath-school,—lightened the way by his narratives of storm and wreck, and not a few interesting snatches of natural history. There is no member of the commoner professions with whom I better like to meet than with a sensible fisherman, who makes a right use of his eyes. The history of fishes is still very much what the history of almost all animals was little more than half a century ago,—a matter of mere external description, heavy often and dry, and of classification founded exclusively on anatomical details. We have still a very great deal to learn regarding the character, habits, and instincts of these denizens of the deep,—much, in short, respecting that faculty which is in them through which their natures are harmonized to the inexorable laws, and they continue to live wisely and securely, in consequence, within their own element, when man, with all his reasoning ability, is playing strange vagaries in his ;—a species of knowledge this, by the way, which constitutes by far the most valuable part,—the *mental* department of natural history ; and the notes of the intelligent fisherman, gleaned from actual observation, have frequently enabled me to fill portions of the wide hiatus in the history of fishes which it ought of right to occupy. In passing, as we toiled along the Græmsay coast, the ruins of a solitary cottage, the boatman furnished us with a few details of the history and character of its last inmate, an Orkney fisherman, that would have furnished admirable materials for one of the darker sketches of Crabbe. He was, he said, a resolute, unsocial man, not devoid of a dash of reckless humour, and remarkable for an extraordinary degree of bodily strength, which he continued to retain unbroken to an age considerably advanced, and which, as he rarely admitted of a companion in his voyages, enabled him to work his little skiff alone, in weather when even better equipped vessels had enough ado to keep the sea. He had been married in early life to a religiously-disposed woman, a member of some dissenting body; but, living with him in the little island of Græmsay, separated by the sea from any place of worship, he rarely permitted her to see the inside of a church. At one time, on the occasion of a communion Sabbath in the neighbouring parish of Stromness, he seemed to yield to her entreaties, and got ready his yawl, apparently with the design of bringing her across the Sound to the town. They had, however, no sooner quitted the shore than he sailed off to a green little Ogygia of a holm in the neighbourhood, on which, reversing the old mythologic story of Calypso and Ulysses, he incarcerated the poor woman for the rest of the day till evening. I could see, from the broad grin with which the boatmen greeted this part of the recital, that there was, unluckily, almost fun enough in the trick to neutralize the sense of its barbarity. The unsocial fisherman lived on, dreaded and disliked, and yet, when his skiff was seen boldly keeping the sea in the face of a freshening gale, when every other was making for port, or stretching out from the land as some stormy evening was falling, not a little admired also. At length, on a night of fearful tempest, the skiff was marked approaching the coast, full on an iron-bound promontory, where there could be no safe landing. The helm, from the steadiness of her course, seemed fast lashed, and, dimly discernible in the uncertain light, the solitary boatman could be seen sitting erect at the bows, as if looking out for the shore. But as his little bark came shooting inwards on the long roll of a wave, it was found that there was no speculation in his stony glance : the misanthropic fisherman was a cold and rigid corpse. He had died at sea, as English juries emphatically express themselves in such cases, under "the visitation of God."

Ogygia: Calypso's island where she detained Odysseus (or Ulysses) in Homer's *Odyssey*

CHAPTER XV.

WE landed at Hoy, on a rocky stretch of shore, composed of the gray flagstones of the district. They spread out here in front of the tall hills composed of the overlying sandstone, in a green undulating platform, resembling a somewhat uneven esplanade spread out in front of a steep rampart. With the upper deposit a new style of scenery commences, unique in these islands : the hills, bold and abrupt, rise from fourteen to sixteen hundred feet over the sea-level ; and the valleys by which they are traversed,—no mere shallow inflections of the general surface, like most of the other valleys of Orkney,—are of profound depth, precipitous, imposing, and solitary. The sudden change from the soft, low, and comparatively tame, to the bold, stern, and high, serves admirably to show how much the character of a landscape may depend on the formation which composes it. A walk of somewhat less than two miles brought me into the depths of a brown, shaggy valley, so profoundly solitary, that it does not contain a single human habitation, nor, with one interesting exception, a single trace of the hand of man. As the traveller approaches by a path somewhat elevated, in order to avoid the peaty bogs of the bottom, along the slopes of the northern side of the dell, he sees, amid the heath below, what at first seems to be a rhomboidal piece of pavement of pale Old Red Sandstone, bearing atop a few stunted tufts of vegetation. There are no neighbouring objects of a known character by which to estimate its size; the precipitous hill-front behind is more than a thousand feet in height; the greatly taller Ward Hill of Hoy, which frowns over it on the opposite side, is at least five hundred feet higher; and, dwarfed by these giants, it seems a mere pavier's flag, mayhap some five or six feet square, by from eighteen inches to two feet in depth. It is only on approaching it within a few yards that we find it to be an enormous stone, nearly thirty feet in length by almost fifteen feet in breadth, and in some places, though it thins, wedge-like, towards one of the edges, more than six feet in thickness,—forming altogether such a mass as the quarrier would detach from the solid rock, to form the architrave of some vast gateway, or the pediment of some colossal statue. A cave-like excavation, nearly three feet square, and rather more than seven feet in depth, opens on its gray and lichened side. The excavation is widened within, along the opposite walls, into two uncomfortably short beds, very much resembling those of the cabin of a small coasting vessel. One of the two is furnished with a protecting ledge and a pillow of stone, hewn out of the solid mass; while the other, which is some five or six inches shorter than its neighbour, and presents altogether more the appearance of a place of penance than of repose, lacks both cushion and ledge. An aperture, which seems to have been originally of a circular form, and about two and a half feet in diameter, but which some unlucky herd-boy, apparently in the want of better employment, has considerably mutilated and widened, opens at the inner extremity of the excavation to the roof, as the hatch of a vessel opens from the hold to the deck; for it is by far too wide in proportion to the size of the apartment to be regarded as a chimney. A gray, rudely-hewn block of sandstone, which, though greatly too ponderous to be moved by any man of the ordinary strength, seems to have served the purpose of a door, lies prostrate beside the opening in front. And such is the famous Dwarfie Stone of Hoy,—as firmly fixed in our literature by the genius of Sir Walter Scott, as in this wild valley by its ponderous weight and breadth of base, and regarding which—for it shares in the general obscurity of the other ancient remains of Orkney—the antiquary can do little more than repeat, somewhat incredulously, what tradition tells him, viz., that it was the work, many ages ago, of an ugly, malignant goblin, half-earth half-air,—the Elfin Trolld,—a personage, it is said, that, even within the last century, used occasionally to be seen flitting about in its neighbourhood.

I was fortunate in a fine breezy day, clear and sunshiny, save where the shadows of a few dense piled-up clouds swept dark athwart the landscape. In the secluded recesses of the valley all was hot, heavy, and still ; though now and then a fitful snatch of a breeze, the mere fragment of some broken gust that seemed to have lost its way, tossed for a moment the white cannach of the bogs, or raised spirally into the air, for a few yards, the light beards of some seeding thistle, and straightway let them down again. Suddenly, however, about noon, a shower broke thick and heavy against the dark sides and gray scalp of the Ward Hill, and came sweeping down the valley. I did what Norna of the Fitful Head had, according to the novelist, done before me in similar circumstances,—crept for shelter into the larger bed of the cell, which, though rather scant, taken fairly lengthwise, for a man of five feet eleven, I found, by stretching myself diagonally from corner to corner, no very uncomfortable lounging-place in a thunder-shower. Some provident herd-boy had spread it over, apparently months before, with a littering of heath and fern, which now formed a dry, springy couch ; and as I lay wrapped up in my plaid, listening to the rain-drops as

---

Dwarfie Stone: in fact a tomb of the third millennium BCE; **Norna of the Fitful Head**: a self-styled spae-wife or witch, another character in Scott's *The Pirate*. Fitful Head itself is a promontory in Shetland they pattered thick and heavy a-top, or slanted through the broken hatchway to the vacant bed on the opposite side of the excavation, I called up the wild narrative of Norna, and felt all its poetry. The opening passage of the story is, however, not poetry, but good prose, in which the curious visitor might give expression to his own conjectures, if ingenious enough either to form or to express them so well. "With my eyes fixed on the smaller bed," the sorceress is made to say, "I wearied myself with conjectures regarding the origin and purpose of my singular place of refuge. Had it been really the work of that powerful Trolld to whom the poetry of the Scalds referred it? or was it the tomb of some Scandinavian chief, interred with his arms and his wealth, perhaps also with his immolated wife, that what he loved best in life might not in death be divided from him? or was it the abode of penance, chosen by some devoted anchorite of later days? or the idle work of some wandering mechanic, whom chance, and whim, and leisure, had thrust upon such an undertaking?" What follows this sober passage is the work of the poet. "Sleep," continues Norna, "had gradually crept upon me among my lucubrations, when I was startled from my slumbers by a second clap of thunder; and when I awoke, I saw through the dim light which the upper aperture admitted, the unshapely and indistinct form of Trolld the dwarf, seated opposite to me on the lesser couch, which his square and misshapen bulk seemed absolutely to fill up. I was startled, but not affrighted; for the blood of the ancient race of Lochlin was warm in my veins. He spoke, and his words were of Norse,—so old, that few save my father, or I myself, could have comprehended their import,—such language as was spoken in these islands ere Olave planted his cross on the ruins of heathenism. His meaning was dark also, and obscure, like that which the pagan priests were wont to deliver, in the name of their idols, to the tribes that as-

sembled at the *Helgafels.* * * * I answered him in nearly
the same strain ; for the spirit of the ancient Scalds of our
race was upon me ; and, far from fearing the phantom with
whom I sat cooped within so narrow a space, I felt the impulse of that high courage which thrust the ancient champions
and Druidesses upon contests with the invisible world, when
they thought that the earth no longer contained enemies
worthy to be subdued by them. * * * The Demon
scowled at me as if at once incensed and overawed ; and then,
coiling himself up in a thick and sulphurous vapour, he disappeared from his place.   I did not till that moment feel the
influence of fright, but then it seized me.   I rushed into the
open air, where the tempest had passed away, and all was
pure and serene."   Shall I dare confess, that I could fain
have passed some stormy night all alone in this solitary cell,
were it but to enjoy the luxury of listening, amid the darkness, to the dashing rain and the roar of the wind high among
the cliffs, or to detect the brushing sound of hasty footsteps
in the wild rustle of the heath, or the moan of unhappy spirits
in the low roar of the distant sea.   Or, mayhap,—again to borrow from the poet,—as midnight was passing into morning,

> " To ponder o'er some mystic lay,
> Till the wild tale had all its sway ;
> And in the bittern's distant shriek
> I heard unearthly voices speak,
> Or thought the wizard priest was come
> To claim again his ancient home !
> And bade my busy fancy range
> To frame him fitting shape and strange ;
> Till from the dream my brow I cleared,
> And smil'd to think that I had feared."

The Dwarfie Stone has been a good deal undervalued by
some writers, such as the historian of Orkney, Mr Barry ; and,
considered simply as a work of art or labour, it certainly does
not stand high.   When tracing, as I lay a-bed, the marks of
the tool, which, in the harder portions of the stone, are still

---

'To ponder …': Scott's *Marmion*, Introduction to canto II, lines 217-226 distinctly visible, I just thought how that, armed with pick and chisel, and working as I was once accustomed to work, I could complete such another excavation to order in some three weeks or a month. But then, I could not make my excavation a thousand years old, nor envelop its origin in the sun-gilt vapours of a poetic obscurity, nor connect it with the supernatural, through the influences of wild ancient traditions, nor yet encircle it with a classic halo, borrowed from the undying inventions of an exquisite literary genius. A half-worn pewter spoon, stamped on the back with the word *London*, which was found in a miserable hut on the banks of the Awatska by some British sailors, at once excited in their minds a thousand tender remembrances of their country. And it would, I suspect, be rather a poor criticism, and scarcely suited to grapple with the true phenomena of the case, that, wholly overlooking the magical influences of the associative faculty, would concentrate itself simply on either the workmanship or the materials of the spoon. Nor is the Dwarfie Stone to be correctly estimated, independently of the suggestive principle, on the rules of the mere quarrier who sells stones by the cubic foot, or of the mere contractor for hewn work who dresses them by the square one.

The pillow I found lettered over with the names of visitors; but the stone,—an exceedingly compact red sandstone, —had resisted the imperfect tools at the command of the traveller,—usually a nail or knife; and so there were but two of the names decipherable,—that of an " H. Ross, 1735," and that of a " P. Folster. 1830." The rain still pattered heavily overhead; and with my geological chisel and hammer I did, to beguile the time, what I very rarely do,—added my name to the others, in characters which, if both they and the Dwarfie Stone get but fair play, will be distinctly legible two centuries hence. In what state will the world then exist, or what sort of ideas will fill the head of the man who, when

the rock has well-nigh yielded up its charge, will decipher the
name for the last time, and inquire, mayhap, regarding the
individual whom it now designates, as I did this morning,
when I asked, "Who was this H. Ross, and who this P. Folster ?" I remember when it would have saddened me to think
that there would in all probability be as little response in the
one case as in the other ; but as men rise in years they become more indifferent than in early youth to "that life which
wits inherit after death," and are content to labour on and
be obscure.   They learn, too, if I may judge from experience,
to pursue science more exclusively for its own sake, with less,
mayhap, of enthusiasm to carry them on, but with what is at
least as strong to take its place as a moving force, that wind
and bottom of formed habit through which what were at
first acts of the will pass into easy half-instinctive prompt-
ings of the disposition.   In order to acquaint myself with the
fossiliferous deposits of Scotland, I have travelled, hammer
in hand, during the last nine years, over fully ten thousand
miles ; nor has the work been in the least one of dry labour,
—not more so than that of the angler, or grouse-shooter, or
deer-stalker : it has occupied the mere leisure intersstices of
a somewhat busy life, and has served to relieve its toils.   I
have succeeded, however, in accomplishing but little : besides,
what is discovery to-day will be but rudimentary fact to the
tyro-geologists of the future.   But if much has not been done,
I have at least the consolation of George Buchanan, when,
according to Melvill, "fand sitting in his chair, teiching his
young man that servit him in his chalmer to spell a, b, ab ;
e, b, eb.   'Better this,' quoth he, 'nor stelling sheipe.'"

The sun broke out in great beauty after the shower, glistening on a thousand minute runnels that came streaming down
the precipices, and revealing, through the thin vapoury haze,
the horizontal lines of strata that bar the hill-sides, like courses
of ashlar in a building.   I failed, however, to detect, amid

---

'That life ...': 'How vain that second life on others' breath/The estate which wits
inherit after death', nearly the end of Alexander Pope's 'Temple of Fame'; Melvill: see
Additional Notes

the general many-pointed glitter by which the blue gauze-like mist was bespangled, the light of the great carbuncle for which the Ward Hill has long been famous,—that wondrous gem, according to Sir Walter, "that, though it gleams ruddy as a furnace to them that view it from beneath, ever becomes invisible to him whose daring foot scales the precipices whence it darts its splendour." The Hill of Hoy is, however, not the only one in the kingdom that, according to tradition, bears a jewel in its forehead. The "great diamond" of the Northern Sutor was at one time scarce less famous than the carbuncle of the Ward Hill. I have been oftener than once interrogated on the western coast of Scotland regarding the "diamond rock of Cromarty;" and have been told by an old campaigner who fought under Abercrombie, that he has listened to the familiar story of its diamond amid the sand wastes of Egypt. But the diamond has long since disappeared; and we now see only the rock. Unlike the carbuncle of Hoy, it was never seen by day; though often, says the legend, the benighted boatman has gazed, from amid the darkness, as he came rowing along the shore, on its clear beacon-like flame, which, streaming from the precipice, threw a fiery strip across the water; and often have the mariners of other countries inquired whether the light which they saw so high among the cliffs, right over their mast, did not proceed from the shrine of some saint or the cell of some hermit. At length an ingenious ship-captain, determined on marking its place, brought with him from England a few balls of chalk, and took aim at it in the night-time with one of his great guns. Ere he had fired, however, it vanished, as if suddenly withdrawn by some guardian hand; and its place in the rock front has ever since remained as undistinguishable, whether by night or by day, as the scaurs and clefts around it. The marvels of the present time abide examination more patiently. It seems difficult enough to conceive, for instance, that the upper

---

old campaigner under Abercrombie: no doubt Miller's own Uncle Sandy who had served in the Royal Navy and was part of Sir Ralph Abercromby's amphibious force during the invasion of Egypt in 1801 (Miller 1858, pp. 37-38)

deposit of the Lower Old Red in this locality, out of which
the mountains of Hoy have been scooped, once overlaid the
flagstones of all Orkney, and stretched on and away to Dunnet Head, Tarbet Ness, and the Black Isle ; and yet such is
the story, variously authenticated, to which their nearly horizontal strata and their abrupt precipices lend their testimony.
In no case has this superior deposit of the formation of the
Coccosteus been known to furnish a single fossil ; nor did it
yield me on this occasion, among the Hills of Hoy, what it
had denied me everywhere else on every former one.   My
search, however, was by no means either very prolonged or
very careful.

I found I had still several hours of day-light before me ;
and these I spent, after my return on a rough tumbling sea
to Stromness, in a second survey of the coast, westwards from
the granitic axis of the island, to the bishop's palace, and the
ichthyolitic quarry beyond.   From this point of view the
high terminal Hill of Hoy, towards the west, presents what
is really a striking profile of Sir Walter Scott, sculptured in
the rock front by the storms of ages, on so immense a scale,
that the Colossus of Rhodes, Pharos and all, would scarce
have furnished materials enough to supply it with a nose.
There are such asperities in the outline as one might expect
in that of a rudely modelled bust, the work of a master, from
which, in his fiery haste, he had not detached the superfluous
clay ; but these interfere in no degree with the fidelity, I
had almost said spirit, of the likeness.   It seems well, as it
must have waited for thousands of years ere it became the
portrait it now is, that the human profile, which it preceded
so long, and without which it would have lacked the element
of individual truth, should have been that of Sir Walter.
Amid scenes so heightened in interest by his genius as those
of Orkney, he is entitled to a monument.   To the critical
student of the philosophy and history of poetic invention it

is not uninstructive to observe how completely the novelist
has appropriated and brought within the compass of one fiction, in defiance of all those lower probabilities which the
lawyer who pleaded before a jury court would be compelled
to respect, almost every interesting scene and object in both
the Shetland and Orkney islands. There was but little intercourse in those days between the two northern archipela-
gos. It is not yet thirty years since they communicated
with each other, chiefly through the port of Leith, where
their regular traders used to meet monthly ; but it was necessary, for the purposes of effect, that the dreary sublimities
of Shetland should be wrought up into the same piece of rich
tissue with the imposing antiquities of Orkney,—Sumburgh
Head and Roost with the ancient Cathedral of St Magnus
and the earl's palace, and Fitful Head and the sand-enveloped kirk of St Ringan with the Standing Stones of Stennis and the Dwarfie Stone of Hoy ; and so the little jury-
court probabilities have been sacrificed without scruple, and
that higher truth of character, and that exquisite portrait-
ure of external nature, which give such reality to fiction,
and make it sink into the mind more deeply than historic
fact, have been substituted instead. But such,—considerably
to the annoyance of the lesser critics,—has been ever the
practice of the greater poets. The lesser critics are all critics of the jury-court cast; while all the great masters of
fiction, with Shakspeare at their head, have been asserters of
that higher truth which is not letter, but spirit, and contemn-
ers of the mere judicial probabilities. And so they have
been continually fretting the little men with their extrava-
gances, and they ever will. What were said to be the ori-
ginals of two of Sir Walter's characters in the " Pirate" were
living in the neighbourhood of Stromness only a few years
ago. An old woman who resided immediately over the town,
in a little cottage, of which there now remains only the roof-

---

sand-enveloped kirk of St Ringan: St Ninian's Kirk in Shetland less walls, and of whom sailors, weather-bound in the port, used occasionally to purchase a wind, furnished him with the first conception of his Norna of the Fitful Head; and an eccentric shopkeeper of the place, who to his dying day used to designate the "Pirate," with much bitterness, as a "lying book," and its author as a "wicked lying man," is said to have suggested the character of Bryce Snailsfoot the pedlar. To the sorceress Sir Walter himself refers in one of his notes. "At the village of Stromness, on the Orkney main island, called Pomona, lived," he says, "in 1814 an aged dame called Bessie Millie, who helped out her subsistence by selling favourable winds to mariners. Her dwelling and appearance were not unbecoming her pretensions: her house, which was on the brow of the steep hill on which Stromness is founded, was only accessible by a series of dirty and precipitous lanes, and, for exposure, might have been the abode of Æolus himself, in whose commodities the inhabitant dealt. She herself was, as she told us, nearly one hundred years old, withered and dried up like a mummy. A clay-coloured kerchief, folded round her head, corresponded in colour to her corpse-like complexion. Two light-blue eyes that gleamed with a lustre like that of insanity, an utterance of astonishing rapidity, a nose and chin that almost met together, and a ghastly expression of cunning, gave her the effect of Hecate. She remembered Gow the pirate, who had been a native of these islands, in which he closed his career. Such was Bessie Millie, to whom the mariners paid a sort of tribute, with a feeling betwixt jest and earnest."

On the opposite side of Stromness, where the arm of the sea, which forms the harbour, is about a quarter of a mile in width, there is, immediately over the shore, a small square patch of ground, apparently a *planticruive*, or garden, surrounded by a tall dry-stone fence. It is all that survives —for the old dwelling-house to which it was attached was

---

Gow the pirate: John Gow, a Stromness mariner who turned pirate and returned to raid the Orkneys, but was caught and hanged in 1725, inspiring Scott's novel *The Pirate*; Aeolus: Greek god of the winds pulled down several years ago—of the patrimony of Gow the "Pirate;" and is not a little interesting, as having formed the central nucleus round which,—like those bits of thread or wire on which the richly saturated fluids of the chemist solidify and crystallize,—the entire fiction of the novelist aggregated and condensed under the influence of forces operative only in minds of genius. A white, tall, old-fashioned house, conspicuous on the hill-side, looks out across the bay towards the square inclosure, which it directly fronts. And it is surely a curious coincidence that, while in one of these two erections, only a few hundred yards apart, one of the heroes of Scott saw the light, the other should have proved the scene of the childhood of one of the heroes of Byron,

"Torquil, the nursling of the northern seas."

The reader will remember, that in Byron's poem of "The Island," one of the younger leaders of the mutineers is described as a native of these northern isles. He is drawn by the poet, amid the wild luxuriance of an island of the Pacific, as

"The blue-eyed northern child,
Of isles more known to man, but scarce less wild,—
The fair-haired offspring of the Orcades,
Where roars the Pentland with his whirling seas,—
Rocked in his cradle by the roaring wind,
The tempest-born in body and in mind,—
His young eyes, opening on the ocean foam,—
Had from that moment deemed the deep his home."

Judging from what I learned of his real history, which is well known in Stromness, I found reason to conclude that he had been a hapless young man, of a kindly, genial nature; and greatly "more sinned against than sinning," in the unfortunate affair of the mutiny with which his name is now associated, and for his presumed share in which, untried and unconvicted, he was cruelly left to perish in chains amid the horrors of a shipwreck. I had the honour of being introduced on the following day to his sister, a lady far advanced

---

Torquil ... Byron's poem: 'The Island', on the mutiny on H. M. S. *Bounty*, canto 4, line 113, and canto 2, lines 163–170. 'Torquil' was George Stewart (1726–1791), an officer on the *Bounty*, put ashore by the mutineers on Tahiti, arrested when he gave himself up to a Royal Navy ship, and drowned when it was wrecked (Wilson 1842, II, pp. 436–427); 'more sinned': Lear's speech in Shakespeare's *King Lear*, Act 3, Scene 2

in life, but over whose erect form and handsome features the
years seemed to have passed lightly, and whom I met at the
Free Church of Stromness, to which, at the Disruption, she
had followed her respected minister.   It seemed a fact as curiously compounded as some of those pictures of the last age
in which the thin unsubstantialities of allegory mingled with
the tangibilities of the real and the material, that the sister
of one of Byron's heroes should be an attached member of
the Free Church.

On my return to the inn, I found in the public room a
young German of some one or two and twenty, who, in making the tour of Scotland, had extended his journey into Orkney.   My specimens, which had begun to accumulate in the
room, on chimney-piece and window-sill, had attracted his
notice, and led us into conversation.   He spoke English well,
but not fluently,—in the style of one who had been more accustomed to read than to converse in it; and he seemed at
least as familiar with two of our great British authors,—
Shakspeare and Sir Walter Scott,—as most of the better-
informed British themselves.   It was chiefly the descriptions
of Sir Walter in the "Pirate" that had led him into Orkney.   He had already visited the Cathedral of St Magnus
and the Stones of Stennis; and on the morrow he intended
visiting the Dwarfie Stone; though I ventured to suggest
that, as a broad sound lay between Stromness and Hoy, and
as the morrow was the Sabbath, he might find some difficulty
in doing that.   His circle of acquirement was, I found, rather
literary than scientific.   It seemed, however, to be that of
a really accomplished young man, greatly better founded in
his scholarship than most of our young Scotchmen on quitting the national universities; and I felt, as we conversed together, chiefly on English literature and general politics, how
much poorer a figure I would have cut in his country than
he cut in mine.   I found, on coming down from my room

next morning to a rather late breakfast, that he had been out among the Stromness fishermen, and had returned somewhat chafed. Not a single boatman could he find in a populous seaport town that would undertake to carry him to the Dwarfie Stone on the Sabbath,—a fact, to their credit, which it is but simple justice to state. I saw him afterwards in the Free Church, listening attentively to a thoroughly earnest and excellent discourse, by the Disruption minister of the parish, Mr Learmonth; and in the course of the evening he dropped in for a short time to the Free Church Sabbath-school, where he took his seat beside one of the teachers, as if curious to ascertain more in detail the character of the instruction which had operated so influentially on the boatmen, and which he had seen telling from the pulpit with such evident effect. What would not his country now give,—*now*, while drifting loose from all its old moorings, full on the perils of a lee shore,—for the anchor of a faith equally steadfast! He was a Lutheran, he told me; but, as is too common in Germany, his actual beliefs appeared to be very considerably at variance with his hereditary creed. The creed was a tolerably sound one, but the living belief regarding it seemed to do little more than take cognizance of what he deemed the fact of its death.

I had carried with me a letter of introduction to Mr William Watt, to whom I have already had occasion to refer as an intelligent geologist; but the letter I had no opportunity of delivering. Mr Watt had learned, however, of my being in the neighbourhood, and kindly walked into Stromness, some six or eight miles, on the morning of Monday, to meet with me, bringing me a few of his rarer specimens. One of the number,—a minute ichthyolite, about three inches in length,—I was at first disposed to set down as new, but I have since come to regard it as simply an imperfectly-preserved specimen of a Cromarty and Morayshire species,—the

Mr William Watt: see p. 426

Glyptolepis microlepidotus; though its state of keeping is such as to render either conclusion an uncertainty. Another of the specimens was that of a fish, still comparatively rare, first figured in the first edition of my little volume on the " Old Red Sandstone," from the earliest found specimen, at a time while it was yet unfurnished with a name, but which has since had a place assigned to it in the genus Diplacanthus, as the species longispinus. The scales, when examined by the glass, remind one, from their pectinated character, of shells covering the walls of a grotto,—a peculiarity to which, when showing my specimen to Agassiz, while it had yet no duplicate, I directed his attention, and which led him to extemporize for it, on the spot, the generic name Ostralepis, or shell-scale. On studying it more leisurely, however, in the process of assigning to it a place in his great work, where the reader may now find it figured (Table XIV., fig. 8), the naturalist found reason to rank it among the Diplacanthi. Mr Watt's specimen exhibited the outline of the head more completely than mine ; but the Orkney ichthyolites rarely present the microscopic minutiæ ; and the shell-like aspect of the scales was shown in but one little patch, where they had left their impressions on the stone. His other specimens consisted of single plates of a variety of Coccosteus, undistinguishable in their form and proportions from those of the *Coccosteus decipiens,* but which exceeded by about one-third the average size of the corresponding parts in that species ; and of a rib-like bone, that belonged apparently to what few of the ichthyolites of the Lower Old Red seem to have possessed,—an osseous internal skeleton. This last organism was the only one I saw in Orkney with which I had not been previously acquainted, or which I could regard as new ; though possibly enough it may have formed part, not of an undiscovered genus, but of the known genus Asterolepis, of whose inner frame-work, judging from the Russian specimens

---

great work: see p. 286 and Andrews (1982)

at least, portions must have been bony.   After parting from
Mr Watt, I travelled on to Kirkwall, which, after a leisurely
journey, I reached late in the evening, and on the following
morning took the steamer for Wick.   I brought away with
me, if not many rare specimens or many new geological facts,
at least a few pleasing recollections of an interesting country
and a hospitable people.   In the previous chapter I indulged
in a brief quotation from Mr David Vedder, the sailor-poet
of Orkney; and I shall make no apology for availing myself, in the present, of the vigorous, well-turned stanzas in
which he portrays some of those peculiar features by which
the land of his nativity may be best recognised and most
characteristically remembered.

TO ORKNEY.

Land of the whirlpool,—torrent,—foam,
Where oceans meet in madd'ning shock;
The beetling cliff,—the shelving holm,—
    The dark insidious rock.
Land of the bleak,—the treeless moor,—
The sterile mountain, sered and riven,—
The shapeless cairn, the ruined tower,
    Scathed by the bolts of heaven,—
The yawning gulf,—the treacherous sand,—
I love thee still, MY NATIVE LAND.

Land of the dark,—the Runic rhyme,—
The mystic ring,—the cavern hoar,—
The Scandinavian seer, sublime
    In legendary lore.
Land of a thousand sea-kings' graves,—
Those tameless spirits of the past,
Fierce as their subject arctic waves,
    Or hyperborean blast,—
Though polar billows round thee foam,
I love thee!—thou wert once my home.

With glowing heart and island lyre,
Ah! would some native bard arise,
To sing, with all a poet's fire,
    Thy stern sublimities,—
The roaring flood,—the rushing stream,—
The promontory wild and bare,—

The pyramid, where sea-birds scream,
    Aloft in middle air,—
The Druid temple on the heath,
Old even beyond tradition's birth.

Though I have roamed through verdant glades,
In cloudless climes, 'neath azure skies,
Or pluck'd from beauteous orient meads,
    Flowers of celestial dies,—
Though I have laved in limpid streams,
That murmur over golden sands,
Or basked amid the fulgid beams
    That flame o'er fairer lands,
Or stretched me in the sparry grot,—
My country! THOU wert ne'er forgot.

END OF RAMBLES OF A GEOLOGIST.

GEOLOGY
THEN AND NOW

THE re-publication of *Cruise of the Betsey* should not be taken as an indication that all the science in it is necessarily considered valid today. Miller's catastrophism and antievolutionism, and views on the Ice Ages, have already been discussed in the Introduction. It would have been anachronistic to consider certain other issues when discussing Miller's work in the 1840s, and they are now briefly outlined, as they might otherwise confuse the reader who knows some geology. A few minor points are covered in the glossary and notes.

Plate tectonics is the key synthesis underlying the modern interpretation of Scottish geology. The pieces of crust now known as Scotland have moved around on the surface of the Earth, through different climatic zones, merging and splitting and merging again as time went on. As a twentieth century concept depending on evidence from worldwide geological surveys on land and under the seas, plate tectonics was unavailable to Miller finding fossils of subtropical animals in Hebridean rocks, or considering the importance of the Atlantic in forming the Old Red Sandstone conglomerate at Oban (p. 9). In fact, the Atlantic Ocean *postdates* the Old Red rocks, for it is a continuation and development of the continental rifting that separated Europe from North America in Mesozoic times. Around Scotland this created low-lying basins flooded by the 'Oolitic' seas and lagoons of brackish water with abundant snails and mussels, and in which plesiosaurs swam, as Miller so rightly perceived (p. 4). This later rifting was linked to the volcanic activity of Tertiary times which produced the layers of 'trap' lavas and intrusive 'sills' of Eigg, the fissures now filled with solidified basalt to form 'dykes', and the volcanoes of Rùm and the Cuillin of Skye (Miller's 'Cuchullin').

Stratigraphical table

The simplified table on page B3 is intended to clarify the relative age of the rock strata mentioned in *Cruise of the Betsey*. The equivalencies shown here are only very approximate: when Miller was writing, geologists were still developing their understanding of the sequence of strata, and the associated terminology (Secord 1986; Oldroyd 1990, 1996b). The table shows the terms which Miller uses, and their approximate modern equivalents.

The concept of 'Primary' rocks, formed during the original cooling of the Earth from a primeval molten mass, has no clear conceptual equivalent today (see

B1

Additional Note for p. 99); by Miller's time this was largely forgotten and in practice the term was applied to a mixture of igneous and metamorphic rocks often but by no means all of Precambrian age.

'Silurian' was originally a term for rocks older than the Old Red Sandstone but younger than the 'primary' rocks, thus roughly equivalent to the modern Cambrian, Ordovician and Silurian Periods. However, when Miller wrote, it was in process of being divided up into the modern Cambrian and a reduced Silurian, although the Ordovician had not then been established.

The Old Red Sandstone is of Devonian age. Miller's and his contemporaries' understanding of the relative positions of the various fish-bearing beds was in error by today's standards (Oldroyd 1996a). Partly because the Cromarty fish beds were close to the bottom of the Old Red Sandstone there, where it overlaps over the older rocks of the South Sutor, Miller accepted that they were Lower Old Red Sandstone. This was no doubt reinforced by his visit to Stromness recorded in *Cruise of the Betsey* where he found some of the same fishes, such as *Coccosteus*, in beds very close to the granite basement rocks. He regarded the *Cephalaspis* (now *Zenaspis*)-bearing beds of, for instance, the area around Forfar, as Middle Old Red Sandstone in age. Soon after his death, however, the Cromarty, Caithness and Stromness beds were reascribed to the Middle Old Red Sandstone, and the 'middle' beds to the Lower Old Red Sandstone.

Miller's 'Lias' roughly corresponds to our 'Lower Jurassic' and his 'Oolite' to our 'Middle and Upper Jurassic'. However, he misdates some outcrops, such as that at Eathie near Cromarty, as 'Lias', when they are in fact of Upper Jurassic age, which he would call 'Oolitic'.

Notes to the table opposite

* The Wealden rocks are a stratum found in England and laid down in freshwater or estuarine conditions. They are of Lower Cretaceous age. Miller, however, uses the term to denote a freshwater or estuarine variation of the much older mainly marine 'Oolite' rocks, *eg* on Eigg.
** In earlier usage 'Secondary' principally meant the sedimentary rocks derived from the 'Primary' rocks by erosion. Even in the 1830s it still included what is now termed the Devonian.

Modern terminology and dating		Terms or deposits Miller mentions (they do not form a continuous sequence)
ERA	**PERIOD**	
Quaternary	Holocene or Recent	peat
	Pleistocene 'Ice Ages'	eg boulder clay, erratic boulders
Ca. 1.6 million years before the present (BP)		Crag shells
Tertiary	Pliocene	Pliocene: Crag shells
	Miocene	Miocene
	Oligocene	
	Eocene	Eocene
	Palaeocene	
Ca. 65 million years BP		
Mesozoic	Cretaceous	Chalk Wealden*
= 'Secondary'** (now obsolete)	Jurassic	Oolite, including 'Wealden' sediments* and the coal of Brora (NB: geologists then ascribed the lavas of Eigg, *etc*, to this age, but they are now known to be Palaeocene)
		Lias
	Triassic	New Red Sandstone (part)
Ca. 245 million years BP		
Palaeozoic	Permian	New Red Sandstone (part)
	Carboniferous	Coal Measures, Mountain Limestone
	Devonian	Old Red Sandstone
	Silurian	Originally all 'Silurian' or 'Transition'. Includes the Grauwacke. In Miller's time increasingly being subdivided with the older beds termed 'Cambrian'
	Ordovician	
	Cambrian	
Ca. 570 million years BP		
Precambrian, including the gneiss of Skye and the Torridonian Sandstone of Skye, Rùm, *etc*		Miller misdates the 'Red Sandstone' of Skye and Rùm, ie what is now termed the Torridonian Sandstone, as Devonian Old Red Sandstone

GLOSSARY AND NOTES
TO *CRUISE OF THE BETSEY*

CRUISE OF THE BETSEY is replete with allusions to current events, biblical quotations, and writers, as well as now archaic expressions. Some have defied identification, but the most likely to be useful of those not already explained above are covered in the glossary and notes provided here.

Whether consciously or through errors of memory, Miller so often modified quotations, usually to meld better with his prose, that only significant errors are noted here, and it is often impossible to be sure which edition of a book he was using (the listing here of any one edition is simply for referencing, and should not be taken as a suggestion that Miller was using that particular variant). These notes also ignore the more obvious variations (often Scots) in spelling, and phonetic renderings of Gaelic language placenames. They omit formal references to standard sources of information such as the *Dictionary of National Biography* and similar works, Keay and Keay (2000), Sarjeant (1980-1996), and Cleevely (1983), and well-known publications such as poems and novels.

Miller naturally uses 1840s scientific terminology. Many of his terms are now obsolete and others have changed meaning, often in complex ways. For instance, his identification of igneous rocks such as greenstones and clinkstones (p. 9), and trachyte (p. 19) would be based on gross properties of colour, texture, and so on, that he could see and feel, whereas modern geologists use different classifications based partly on microscopic study (Oldroyd 1996a). I give broad equivalents for his scientific terms here, which will suffice for most readers. In particular, except for a few cases, mainly the Old Red Sandstone fishes, I do not modernize biological classification. Thus I do not try to explain in detail how, for instance, 'Pecten' as understood in the 1840s corresponds to the modern understanding of the mollusc genera now called *Pecten, Chlamys, Palliolum*, and so on, but simply translate it as 'scallop' – which may refer to anything from one particular scallop to all scallops. Moreover, to avoid introducing misleading specificity, I have not 'corrected' Miller's habit of using roman rather than italic script for genera, such as 'Pecten', almost as if they were vernacular names, when we would normally use *Pecten*. For comments on stratigraphy and geological ages, see the 'Geology then and now' section above.

Those wanting specific detail on geology and palaeontology as currently understood should consult the modern geological literature. To work out what Miller means in modern terms, the following may be helpful, as well as the various field guides, *etc*, recommended earlier. Oldroyd (1996a) is an excellent general appraisal of Miller's scientific work; see also Hudson (2000, 2003), and Hudson and Allwright (2003), particularly on Miller's fieldwork on Eigg; and Waterston (2002a, 2002b). For fossil fishes, Long (1995) is a good popular introduction, and Janvier (1996) a more technical one, while Andrews (1982), Janvier (2003), and Trewin (2003b) are particularly relevant to Miller.

Glossary of terms

A glossary of terms used in *Cruise of the Betsey* but not explained in the Introduction or Notes:

Acalephae: jellyfish
Acanthodians: a now extinct group of fossil fishes, characterised among other things by the structure of their fins, each fin (except the tail fin) comprising a spine supporting a web of skin like the sail of a yacht
Acrodus: fossil shark
advocate: lawyer who pleaded in the Scots courts
Aeolian harp: a stringed soundbox that resonates in air currents
ait: oat (Scots)
amianthus: asbestos
ammonites: extinct cephalopod molluscs with coiled shells similar to the modern Pearly Nautilus. Their shells are common fossils in many Mesozoic rocks
amygdaloidal: containing or relating to cavities, here especially in basalt lavas. The release of pressure on eruption of a lava flow allowed dissolved gases to come out of solution. These gases sometimes formed bubbles which remained when the lava cooled and solidified. These cavities might remain empty. However, mineral-rich 'hydrothermal' water, that had previously been heated by passage through hot rock, often percolated through the amygdaloidal basalt and deposited 'amygdaloidal' minerals such as zeolites and Rùm bloodstones in the cavities
anchylosed: fused, *ie* as two bones might be
animalculae: tiny animals, plankton, *etc*
Annelida: a group of worms, including ragworms and lugworms
Anomiae: oyster-like bivalves
anticlinal: adjective referring to an anticline, an upwards fold in rock layers
Araucarians: a group of coniferous trees including the modern monkey-puzzle pine
arenaceous: sandy
argil: clay
argillaceous: clay-rich
Artemis: bivalve
articulating faces: here, faces where two neighbouring bones such as vertebrae abut to form a flexible joint or 'articulation'

Astarte: a small clamlike bivalve; *Astarte compressa* and *Astarte danmonensis* (*sulcata*) [*recte damnoniensis*] are species of it

augitic: then, rich in the mineral augite, common in certain igneous rocks

Avicula: a bivalve

axe-stone of Werner: an old name for nephrite, an often dark green stone used, because of its homogeneity and toughness, for stone axes in prehistoric times

Balanus: acorn barnacle

barytes: the mineral barite, barium sulphate

Belemnites: extinct cephalopods related to the modern squid and externally similar to them, but having complex internal shells with airfilled buoyancy chambers. The belemnite shell had a dense, bullet-shaped ending or 'guard'. Belemnite guards were tough and resistant to destruction after death and are common fossils in many rocks of Mesozoic age

bent: when a sail is changed, the new sail is 'bent' or attached to the rigging

beroe: a sea-gooseberry or ctenophore, a translucent animal drifting in the sea much as jellyfish do but unrelated to them

bicker: porridge vessel made of wooden staves (Scots)

Bimana: old zoological term for humans 'with two hands' as opposed to the four-handed Quadrumana or apes and monkeys, and four-footed quadrupeds or remaining mammals

bivalve: a member of the Bivalvia, a major group of molluscs, with paired left and right shells or 'valves'; examples are clams, oysters, and mussels. Very common fossils

bloodstone: a siliceous mineral, green with red spots

brachiopods: marine shellfish superficially similar to bivalves but having top and bottom rather than left and right shells. Sometimes known as lamp-shells from their resemblance to an old clay oil lamp. Very common fossils, having been much more abundant and widely distributed than they are now

brae: steep side of a hill or valley (Scots)

brander: a wooden piled or latticed foundation for buildings on soft ground (Scots)

braxy: a sheep disease

breccia: coarse rock made up of angular stones (which can include shells or even bones), cemented together naturally

buccinidae: whelks

Buccinum: whelk; *Buccinum undatum* is the Common Whelk

bugle: glassy material as used for beads, *etc*

Cabul: Kabul, Afghanistan

Calamites: early 'horsetails' or sphenophytes

calcareo-argillaceous nodules: nodules of clayey limestone

cannach: cotton-grass

Cardiadae: cockles and related forms

Cardium echinatum: Rough Cockle

Cardium edule: Common Cockle

Caryophyllia: type of solitary coral

catechist: person, usually an elder (in the Presbyterian sense, see Introduction), who helps the minister by instructing and testing young people in Church doctrine, notably the *Shorter Catechism*

caudal fin: tail fin, as of fish

centrum: the main, roughly cylindrical, body of a vertebra

Cephalaspis: now *Zenaspis*. A type of fossil jawless fish, characteristic of (but not unique to) the Lower Old Red Sandstone (to Miller, the *Middle* Old Red Sandstone). It had a simple mouth and probably foraged for bits of food such as worms on the lake floor. It glided along using its muscular tail and front fins, and had an armoured head

Cephalopoda: the group of molluscs that includes octopuses, squids, belemnites and ammonites

Cestracion: a type of shark

chalcedony: a form, akin to agate, of the mineral silica

Chalk: the white limestone of Southern England and Yorkshire, now considered later Cretaceous in age

Chartism: a movement of the late 1830s and early 1840s, to extend political power to the working classes, notably by universal suffrage for all males

Cheiracanthus: Old Red Sandstone fish, an acanthodian (q.v.). It lacked teeth and swam with its mouth open, straining food particles with the gill rakers (bony rods supporting the gills)

Cheirolepis: Old Red Sandstone fish, an early bony fish and one of the first actinopterygian or ray–finned fishes. It was a fast–swimming hunter which could catch and eat fishes two-thirds its own size

Chelonian: member of the Chelonia, a group comprising the tortoises, terrapins and turtles

cherty: rich in silica, chert being a rock composed of this mineral (flint is a special variety of chert)

chlorite: now a group of greenish minerals, claylike and soft in texture

Cidaris: a kind of sea urchin with club–shaped spines

Cidarites: a kind of sea urchin with club–shaped spines

clinker-built: of wooden ships, the hull skinning made with planks which over-lap one another, in contrast to a smooth skin with the planks abutting one another edge on

clinkstone: old name for a variety of basalt, from its ringing like iron when hit with the hammer

Coccosteus minor: then a small species of *Coccosteus*. Now *Millerosteus minor*, placed in a different genus named in Miller's honour

Coccosteus: fossil fish of Old Red Sandstone age, found notably at Miller's classic Cromarty beach fossil site, described in his book *The Old Red Sandstone* (published 1841) – one species was named *Coccosteus milleri* in his honour (now *C. cuspidatus*). A placoderm (q.v.), *Coccosteus* was a streamlined predator with bony shearing jaws

columnar (of basalt, pitchstone, *etc*): lava flows sometimes crack on cooling and shrinking, to form more or less vertical columns. The Isle of Staffa and the Giant's Causeway on the Antrim coast are exceptionally dramatic examples of what is in fact a fairly common phenomenon

companion-head: the cover of the hatch down to the cabin (nautical)

conglomerate: sedimentary rock composed of rounded, waterworn pebbles and boulders, naturally cemented together

coprolitic matter: fossil faecal droppings

crag-shells: old name for fossil shells found in the Crag strata of, typically, East Anglia, now dated to the Pleistocene and Pliocene, *ie* roughly the Ice Ages and the period just before

Crustacea: lobsters, crabs, prawns, shrimps and relatives

Cryptogamiae: old grouping of 'lower' plants such as mosses, liverworts, and ferns which reproduce by spores rather than seeds

Ctenoid: relating to a classification of fishes by Louis Agassiz based on the structure of their scales, and used by Miller. This classification was soon superseded, but an important early step in sorting out the diversity of fossil fishes (Oldroyd 1996a; Janvier 2003). Ctenoid scales are thin, horny, and overlapping plates, one edge with a comblike fringe. Seen, for example, in modern perch

Culdee: a member of a Celtic Church monastic community

Cycadeae: cycads

Cyclas: *Cyrena*, a freshwater bivalve

Cycloid: relating to a classification of fishes by Louis Agassiz based on the structure of their scales, and used by Miller. This classification was soon superseded, but it was an important early step in sorting out the diversity of fossil fishes (Oldroyd 1996a; Janvier 2003). Cycloid scales are thin, horny and overlapping, and round in shape. Seen, for example, in modern herring and salmon

Cyprides: *ie Cypris* (q.v.) and related forms

Cyprina islandica: a clamlike bivalve, now *Arctica islandica*

Cypris: an ostracod, a tiny shelled water crustacean

Dentalium entale: now *D. entalis,* a scaphopod mollusc or tusk-shell

digital: relating to the finger or toe

diluvium: generic term for superficial deposits such as soil, boulder clay, *etc.* A hangover from the days when they were literally thought to be the sediment laid down by the 'Deluge' or Noah's Flood

Diplacanthus: a fossil fish of Middle Old Red Sandstone age, notably found at Miller's classic Cromarty beach fossil site, and described in his book *The Old Red Sandstone* (published 1841). *Diplacanthus* was an acanthodian (q.v.), probably grazing on algae or sieving small crustaceans from the water

Diplopterus: an Old Red Sandstone fish, a sarcopterygian (q.v.). *Diplopterus* is an old synonym for the fish now termed *Gyroptychius*, similar to *Osteolepis* (q.v.) but hunting in deeper water

Dipterus: an Old Red Sandstone fish. *Dipterus* was a lungfish, a particular type of sarcopterygian (q.v.), which breathed air at the surface when the water was stagnant. It had ridged toothplates to crush hard food like shellfish and soft food like worms

Donax: bivalve mollusc

donjon: castle

dowiest: saddest or dullest (Scots)

dykes: molten rock may sometimes pass upwards through more or less vertical fissures and congeal within them to form, usually, basalt rock. If they are exposed by erosion, the basalt is normally harder than the surrounding rock, and tends to be picked out as an upstanding wall-like feature, hence the name dyke (field wall, Scots)

Earse: Erse, *ie* Irish or, here, Scots Gaelic

echini: sea urchins

Echinoderms: a group including sea urchins, starfish, brittlestars and their relatives

Enaliosaurians: extinct marine reptiles, especially plesiosaurs and ichthyosaurs

exuviae: here, shells

factor: estate steward or manager (Scots)

father-lasher: an inshore fish often found in rockpools

feldspar: one of a group of crystalline minerals under this name, often a major component of igneous rocks such as granite (q.v.)

feldspathose rock: metamorphic rock rich in feldspar

festinella: a marine fossil comprising a bryozoan colony, polyps living in a skeleton rather resembling a piece of lace

Fesus antiquus: an evident misprint. True identity uncertain, but possibly what is now *Neptunea antiqua*, Red Whelk

fire-clay: seat earth, the clayey layer often underlying a coal seam, usually derived from the actual soil in which the plants forming the coal seam once grew

flaughter: spade for cutting turf

Flustrae: a group of bryozoans, including hornwrack. Bryozoans, known generally as sea-mats, are small colonial animals encrusting rocks or forming branching or, as in *Flustra*, leaflike growths

Fusus turricola: a species of gastropod

frith: now firth, wide inlet of the sea (Scots)

gaff topsail: a type of small sail above a mainsail

galena: mineral, lead sulphide

Ganoid: relating to a classification of fishes by Louis Agassiz based on the structure of their scales, and used by Miller. This classification was soon superseded, but it was an important early step in sorting out the diversity of fossil fishes (Oldroyd 1996a; Janvier 2003). Ganoid scales are large, bony, often enamelled and shiny, and often interlocking with each other, but not normally overlapping. Seen, for instance, in modern garpikes and sturgeons, and Old Red Sandstone fishes such as *Osteolepis*

gastropods: a group of molluscs including the snails and slugs, on land and in water

Gault: a stratum of the Cretaceous Period in England

Gervillia: bivalve mollusc

glebe: farmland allocated to the minister of a Church of Scotland parish

Glyptolepis: an Old Red Sandstone fish, a large predatory sarcopterygian (q.v.) with a body shape like a modern pike. Probably it had a similar lifestyle, lurking in ambush and rushing out with the acceleration conferred by its powerful body and tail to catch smaller fish with its large teeth and powerful jaws

gneiss: a type of metamorphic rock, formed by the alteration of older rocks by heat and pressure when buried deep in the earth, often similar to granite but with a more layered texture, and without the overtly platy, foliated texture of schist

granite: an igneous rock composed of visible crystals of quartz, feldspar and mica

graphic granite: granite with crystals arranged so regularly that the pattern resembles writing, especially when the rock is cut and polished

Grauwacke: also 'greywacke'. A lithological term for impure sandstone, but also often used to denote the sandstones and slates of a particular stratum, equivalent to the modern Lower Palaeozoic

Greenstone: old name for a variety of trap composed of the minerals hornblende and feldspar

Gryphaea incurva: an oyster

Gryphaea obliquata: an oyster

gryphites: fossil oysters such as *Gryphaea*, which is now popularly known as 'Devil's Toenails'

heliotrope: bloodstone (q.v.)

heterocercal: in tail fins, having a longer upper lobe than a lower one, as in sharks, but unlike many bony fish such as cod, which have equally sized upper and lower lobes symmetrical about the longitudinal axis of the body when seen from the side

Holoptychius: an Old Red Sandstone fish, a large predatory sarcopterygian (q.v.)

Homostius: an Old Red Sandstone fish. A large bottom-living placoderm (q.v.) fish, perhaps feeding on invertebrates. Much of the material which Miller ascribed to 'Asterolepis' is now referred to this genus

Homothorax: an Old Red Sandstone fish, now considered a synonym of the *Pterichthyodes*-like *Bothriolepis*

hornblende slate: slate with the mineral hornblende. Hornblende often occurs as coarse black crystals in igneous and metamorphic rock

Hybodus: fossil shark

hyperstene: rock rich in the hard dark mineral hypersthene

ichthyodorulite: fossil of a fish spine

ichthyolite: fossil fish

Ichthyosaurus: extinct marine reptile, like a dolphin in general appearance and habits

Inoceramus: bivalve like a large mussel, but unrelated to mussels

Isocardia: a bivalve mollusc

japan: enamel

jaspedeous: relating to jasper (q.v.)

jasper: a siliceous mineral, typically coloured red and yellow

kedge and halser: small anchor and cable ('hawser')

lacustrine: laid down in a lake environment

Lepidotus minor: now *Lepidotes*, a fossil bony fish of Mesozoic age, with thick enamelled scales

Lias (adjective **Liassic**): geological stratum, roughly equivalent to Lower Jurassic today

ligneous: woody

lignite: fossil wood, not completely carbonized to true coal

line: (dimensionally) an obsolete unit equal to one-twelfth of an inch, a little less than 2.2mm

Littorina littorea: Edible (or Common) Periwinkle

Lobularia digitata: now *Alcyonium digitatum*, a colonial soft coral commonly called 'Dead men's fingers'

London Clay: a geological stratum found in southern England, now considered Eocene (early Tertiary or Cenozoic) in age

Lutraria: a gaper or clamlike bivalve

lyke-wake: watch over the dead, often involving hospitality to mourners

lymnea: a freshwater snail

Macropoma: a coelacanth

Mactra: a clamlike bivalve

mactridae: a family (*ie* grouping in classification) of clamlike bivalves

maud: Lowland countryman's wrap – see Introduction

medusae: jellyfish

Megalichthys: an often very large predatory fish, a sarcopterygian (q.v.), of Carboniferous age

miasmatic: foul-smelling and badly ventilated, therefore disease-ridden according to the theories of the time

mica-schist: a metamorphic rock rich in the shining platy mineral mica, giving it a somewhat laminated texture

Modiola: a mussel

mole: masonry pier

moraines: mounds of rock, sand and clay debris left by glaciers in valleys and on plains, especially along their sides and at their ends where the ice has melted – rather like the mound left by a bulldozer

mountain cork: a descriptive term used for fibrous minerals when they occur in a matted, leathery form

Mountain Limestone: a geological stratum of Carboniferous age

muirs: moors (Scots)

Mya truncata: the Blunt Gaper, a clamlike mollusc

Mytilus edule: Common Mussel

nappy: frothy, strong, as of beer (Scots) – implying a special brewing as opposed to everyday household weak ale or small beer

Natica: a sea snail

Neritae: a group of gastropods

Neritina: a gastropod

New Red Sandstone: a rock of Permo-Triassic age in Britain

nondescript: in the old sense of not easily classified or identified; literally, new and undescribed, as by science

nummulites: the limy skeletons of certain large single-celled marine animals, often the size and shape of lentils or even small coins

obsidian: volcanic glass, usually black

occipital plates: bones of the head, *etc*, here of fish

Oiliva: presumably an error for *Oliva*, a gastropod

Oolite (adjective **Oolitic**): here, usually an expression of geological age, roughly equivalent, in modern chronology, to the Middle and Upper Jurassic

Osteolepis: an Old Red Sandstone fish, a sarcopterygian (q.v.). *Osteolepis* probably hunted smaller fish and crustaceans

Ostrea: oyster, such as *Ostrea acuminata*

Ostrya: *recte Ostrea*

Palaeozoic: Palaeozoic Era, now the Cambrian to Permian periods inclusive

Paludina: *Viviparus*, a freshwater snail

Pamphractus: an Old Red Sandstone fish, now considered a synonym of the *Pterichthyodes*-like *Bothriolepis*

Patella vulgata: Common Limpet

Pecten: scallop

pelvic arch: hip girdle (bones, anatomical)

Pentacrinites: a Jurassic genus of crinoid or sea lily, related to brittlestars and other echinoderms

Pholadomya aequalis: bivalve

Pholas crispata: now *Zirfaea crispata*, a piddock. Piddocks are bivalves which burrow in peat, clay, and soft rock

Pimelodus: a modern type of catfish

Pinnae: fanshells, a group of bivalve molluscs

pitchstone: volcanic rock that is somewhat glassy in texture, resembling solidified pitch, because of its rapid cooling, for instance when forced into cracks in pre-existing strata. It has a higher water content and is less translucent than obsidian (volcanic glass)

placoderms: an extinct group of fishes with armoured head and bodies, but unarmoured tails, and jaws sometimes armed with bony shearing plates rather than teeth proper

Placoids: relating to a classification of fishes by Louis Agassiz based on the structure of their scales, and used by Miller. This classification was soon super-seded, but it was an important early step in sorting out the diversity of fossil fishes (Oldroyd 1996a; Janvier 2003). Placoid scales were plate-like, irregularly arranged on the skin and detached from each other, and often bearing tubercles or rough points (Oldroyd 1996a). Seen, for instance, in sharks and their kin

Placothorax: a synonym for *Bothriolepis*, an Old Red Sandstone fish related to *Pterichthyodes*

Plagiostoma: another bivalve

Planorbis: freshwater snail

Planorbus: *ie Planorbis*

Plesiosaurus: a particular type of plesiosaur. Plesiosaurs comprised a group of extinct marine reptiles looking something like a sea lion but often, as with the Eigg animal, with an even longer neck

polyparious: of colonial polyps such as bryozoans

polypifer: whole colonial animal, a mass of individual polyps – often of coral

polypus: individual sessile tentacled animal such as a sea-anemone

porphyry: then, and today still informally, a term for an igneous rock containing distinct crystals scattered in a fine or glassy matrix

porringer: wooden bowl

processes: protrusions, especially on bones (anatomical)

Pterichthyodes: modern genus name for *Pterichthys* (q.v.)

Pterichthys: Old Red Sandstone fish (Janvier 2003; Trewin 2003b), found notably at Miller's classic Cromarty beach fossil site, described in his book *The Old Red Sandstone* (published 1841). A placoderm (q.v.), *Pterichthys* (now *Pterichthyodes*) had a flat belly and raised head and body armour, and eyes and nostrils on the top of its head. It probably lived on the lake floor. It may have eaten mud, digesting out any small particles of food. The Cromarty species was originally named *Pterichthys milleri* in honour of its discoverer Miller

Pterygotus: a large (up to 1-2m long) predatory aquatic arthropod found in the Old Red Sandstone. It was then considered to be a crustacean, but is now placed in the separate group of the superficially similar eurypterids or 'water scorpions'

Pullastra: possibly an error for *Venerupis pullastra*, now *V. senegalensis*, Pullet Carpet Shell, a clamlike bivalve

pumice: a light spongy lava, produced by the frothing of molten volcanic glass or obsidian

Purpura lapillus: now *Nucella lapillus*, Dog Whelk

pyrites: the mineral pyrite, iron sulphide

quadrupeds: mammals, more specifically the 'four-footed' ones, and therefore excluding primates (monkeys, apes, humans, *etc*)

Radiata: jellyfish, corals and sea anemones

raised beach: a former beach formed at a time of higher sea level relative to the land – a 'fossil beach' left high and dry, so to speak

ratans: rattans, continuous drumbeats

razor-fish: razorshells, *ie* molluscs not true fish

reefed: of a sail, reduced in area in preparation for heavy weather and high winds (nautical)

reefed to the cross: possibly a variant of 'close-reefed', reefed as far as possible

retainer: advocate's fee

rete mucosum: a layer in the skin

rough-stemmed tangle or cuvy: cuvie, *Laminaria hyperborea*, a large seaweed similar to oarweed proper

rybat:, dressed stone forming part of a window or doorway, *etc* (Scots)

salmon coble: salmon-fisher's boat

sarcopterygian: a member of the group of lobe-finned fishes recognisable by the fleshy base or 'lobe' of each paired fin. Sarcopterygians were common in Devonian times but are now extinct as fishes, except for the coelacanths. However, the amphibians, reptiles, birds and mammals are now considered to be descended from sarcopterygians

scalp of muscles: mussel-bed

scarf-skin: surface skin

schiller spar: bastite or lizardite, a serpentine mineral (see note for p. 269)

schorl: the mineral tourmaline

Secondary: what is now known as the Mesozoic Era, composing the Triassic, Jurassic and Cretaceous periods

Sepiadae: cuttlefish, *etc*

septaria: nodules of stone which have cracked through shrinkage at one stage and later had the cracks infilled by some other rock or mineral, giving a criss-cross pattern on the surface when cut (see p. 260 fn.)

serpentine: a magnesium-rich, hydrated, metamorphosed rock, typically fine-grained and variegated in colour like the skin of a 'serpent', and also known as soapstone

serpulae: wormtubes of limestone (secreted by the worms)

serrated kelp-weed: *Fucus serratus*, Serrated Wrack

Sertularia: a type of hydroid living in branching colonies – these hydroids are similar to and related to sea-anemones but much smaller

shrouds: the fixed or 'standing' rigging from the mast down to the ship's side, supporting the mast laterally

Sigilaria: *recte Sigillaria*, the fossil 'bark' or surface of the stem of certain coal forest 'trees'

sillock: young coalfish (Scots)

Silurus: a genus of catfish, often huge. Includes the Wels of the Danube

Slate: a metamorphic form of clay shale altered by heat and pressure deep down in the earth

spatangi: sea urchins, more specifically potato or heart urchins

spinous process: today, the 'neural spine' of the vertebra, projecting outwards and upwards (backwards in humans)

Squalidae: a family (*ie* grouping in classification) of sharks

storm-jib: a small jibsail (triangular sail between the main mast and the bow) used for heavy weather (nautical)

stromnite: a mixture of the minerals barite and strontianite, ores of the metals barium and strontium respectively

sulcated: deeply grooved or furrowed

syenite: a kind of granite

talcose: rich in the mineral talc

Tellina: a bivalve

Terebratula: a brachiopod or lamp-shell

Teredo navalis: shipworm, actually a wood-boring bivalve

ternary: mixture of three constituents, *eg* granite is a ternary of quartz, feldspar and mica

Tertiary: geological age, roughly equivalent to the modern Cenozoic without the most recent periods (Pleistocene and Holocene)

tesselated pavement: mosaic floor

throch-stanes: flat gravestones, perhaps lying on the ground but sometimes supported on four feet or low walls (Scots). When he was a mason Miller carved such gravestones, some of which can be seen at Cromarty, Rosemarkie and Nigg

toleration laws: guaranteeing religious freedom to Roman Catholics and Protestant Dissenters

trachyte: then a volcanic rock, rich in the mineral feldspar and recognised by its rough texture

transverse process: lateral process (anatomical)

trap: here, usually basalt, a dark, hard, finegrained rock, often, as here, cooled and solidified lava. Taken from the Swedish *trappa*, stair (also 'trap', Scots), via the characteristically staircase-like stepped terrain formed by such rocks (cf. p. 15), erosion having picked out the layers of successive lava flows. Such terrain is common on Eigg and in the Inner Hebrides generally

trap-dykes: dykes of basalt or 'trap' (q.v.)

trap-porphyry, a porphyry or type of fine-grained igneous rock with larger crystals of the mineral feldspar dispersed through it

tremolite: a needle-like mineral related to asbestos

trilobites: a group of marine animals, superficially like woodlice or slaters, but now extinct; important fossils in rocks of Cambrian to Permian age

Trochus: top shell, a type of gastropod

Turbinolia fungites: type of solitary coral

Turritella terebra: an auger shell, a gastropod with long tapering shell

Udaller: major landowner holding land as a freeman without feudal superior. Part of the 'allodial' tenurial system derived from the Norse period in the Northern Isles

umbo: the apex of each of the two shells or 'valves' of a bivalve mollusc

Unio: a freshwater mussel

univalve: mollusc with single shell, here a gastropod, though they also included
   tusk-shells
valve: one of the individual shells of a shelled animal such as a clam
Venus: a bivalve
Venus casina: a cockle-like bivalve
vertebral joint: a 'joint' in the sense of a single vertebra – rather than the
   articulation between two vertebrae
vesicular kelp-weed: *Fucus vesiculosus*, Bladder Wrack
Voluntaries: members of certain Presbyterian denominations which opposed
   State support for the Church of Scotland. The Free Church was not inher-
   ently Voluntarist in thinking, at least initially, for it considered itself the
   true Church, although temporarily divorced from its rightful relationship
   with the State
Wealden: see Additional Note for p. 55
Writer to the Signet: one of a group of solicitors who, in Scotland, had
   exclusive rights relating to writs in the supreme court of justice
yawl: here (p. 17), small boat, used as a ship to shore ferry in the manner of a
   modern yacht's dinghy
zeolite: a group of minerals typical of amygdaloids in lava, some being fibrous
   but others more solidly formed

Additional notes

page
9   Andersons: George and Peter Anderson, Inverness solicitors, amateur
     naturalists, and authors of *Guide to the Highlands and Islands of Scotland*
     (Anderson and Anderson 1863; the quote is from III, pp. 724–725). The
     original 1834 edition's section on geology was the first modern account of
     regional geology which the young Miller, isolated in Cromarty, encountered,
     and Miller's contact with George marked the beginning of his move into the
     wider geological community (Oldroyd 1996a; Collie 2003).

10   'tantly' and 'outrigger': nautical. *Betsey* was tauntly rigged, with a high
     mast and relatively large sail area for her size. 'Outrigger' in this context
     must mean a spar protruding from the stern, probably for the blocks and
     tackle controlling the mainsail, which again implies a sail area rather large for
     the hull (or, less probably, *Betsey* had two masts, in which case the outrigger
     would bear the mizzen sail's running rigging).

16   anchor ... stock: A traditional anchor lies with one of its flukes (the spade-
     like terminations) in the sea bed, and the other pointing upwards. A yacht
     anchored to a single anchor drifts downstream with the tide until the cable is
     taut. When the tide turns, the yacht drifts back till the cable is again taut in the

opposite direction. The cable then sometimes wraps itself around the upward fluke, and the now 'foul' anchor cannot keep a grip on the sea-bed; **stock**: the crossbar of a traditional anchor, set at right angles to the flukes. If it were downwards, the flukes would rest horizontally on the surface, without digging in as they should.

26   **'semi-reptile' and p. 125 'scale of being'**: Miller was referring to the similarities of the fishes *Holoptychius* and *Megalichthys* – for instance their crocodile-like teeth – to amphibians and reptiles in general ('reptiles' then tending to include amphibians as well). This was nothing to do with evolution, for Miller was an antievolutionist. Rather, Miller was implying that these groups lay close together within the Aristotelean Great Chain of Being (Henry 1996; Bowler 1989). The Chain was a fundamentally static concept, an antithesis of evolution. It attempted to represent the order and plenitude of divine Creation along a linear scale (later modified to incorporate branches, for instance) from the simplest to the most complex, with man close to the Creator at the apex. These fishes would therefore have been placed at the more 'advanced' end of the fishes, adjacent to the reptiles.

34   **trap**: that **along the base** is now considered a breccia of fragments of pitchstone in decomposed pitchstone, formed when the lava flowed over the valley floor. The bottom surface of the lava chilled and cracked in contact with the ground, and moisture in the earth flashed into steam, decomposing the adjacent pitchstone (J. D. Hudson, *pers. comm.* 2002).

37   **Lyells, Bucklands, Murchisons and Sedgwicks**: eminent British geologists who did much to develop the science. Charles Lyell (1797-1875) was author of the seminal *Principles of Geology* (1830-1833). William Buckland (1784-1856) was Professor of Geology at the University of Oxford, pioneering researcher of Pleistocene bone caves and much else, and author of *Geology and mineralogy considered with reference to natural theology* (1836), an important review aimed at the general public. Roderick Murchison (1792-1871), from Tarradale at the other end of the Black Isle from Cromarty, was author of *Siluria* and other works on the Palaeozoic rocks, and, from 1855, Director of the Geological Survey. Adam Sedgwick (1785-1873) was Professor of Geology at the University of Cambridge.

39   **three creations ago**: Miller was speaking of the successive geological deposits and their characteristic faunas. He, like many geologists then, thought of the history of life and the earth as periods interspersed with great catastrophes and mass extinctions, each of which was succeeded by a new divine creation of living things to fill the newly vacant world (though not all scientists agreed with the idea of serial divine creations). This succession of creations and mass extinctions, however they were replenished, was, at that time, the most

literal interpretation of the then very patchy fossil record. It has long been superseded by the acceptance of a continuous evolutionary descent from the first living things, if sometimes affected by occasional mass extinctions.

48   **Gouffing Jock**: an old Scottish Borders story reprised by James Hogg (1770–1835), variously Borders shepherd, farmer, novelist and poet, in one of his 'Shepherd's Calendar' articles originally published in *Blackwood's Edinburgh Magazine* and later reprinted on various occasions, the relevant article being 'Storms' in the issues for April and May 1819 (Hogg 1995, pp. 1-21, 257-259; Miller's paraphrase and quote correspond to p. 2). It is a tale, apparently of 1620 in the last lawless days of 'reiving' or armed robbery, about a farmer – rather than shepherd – John or Jock Scott, commonly called Gouffin' Jock (gouff, to talk foolishly, cackle [Scots]). Bowerhope Law is a hill next to St Mary's Loch in Selkirkshire.

55   **Weald**: normally a stratum of Lower Cretaceous age (named after the area in Southern England where it was first studied), and usually used as a chronological term. However, here and elsewhere Miller was effectively using the term 'Weald' in the sense of what would now be called a rock facies: in other words, an environmental variation denoting deposition in an 'estuarine' environment, as when he spoke (p. 200 and Miller 1859, pp. 124-127) of the Weald intercalating with the Oolite elsewhere in Scotland.

63   **how it should be at all sonorous**: a brave stab (also pp. 223-224) at explaining this intriguing phenomenon of 'musical' sand, now known to occur in many other places. How such sands 'sing' is still debated (Lindsay *et al.* 1976; Nori *et al.* 1997), but they typically comprise quartz grains of uniform size made slightly sticky by a surface water-silica layer, suggesting why they do not sing when grossly wet. Goldsack *et al.* (1997, p. 29) suggest that 'emission of a coherent wave sound pattern requires a minimal number of such particles to stick together, and such a loose cohesive mass of appropriately sized sand particles moving through the air, either tumbling down a dune or being shaken in a container, could act as a resonator'.

73   **'Ru Stoir' on Eigg**: MacCulloch (1819, III, p. 71) used 'Ru Stor', and Hay Cunningham (1839, p. 150) 'Ru Stoir Scalleadh'. 'Ru Stoir' is not on the modern Ordnance Survey map, nor is it, *pace* Miller, a credible phonetic rendition of the Gaelic for 'Red Head'. Possibly Miller confused *rubha*, 'headland', with *ruadh*, 'red' (as in 'Rob Roy'), in which the 'bh' and 'dh' are effectively silent. Then the name might be *Rubha Stòirr Sgàilleidh*, which might be translated as 'Headland of the Shadowed Cliff' (Hugh Cheape, *pers. comm.* 2003). This is an appropriate description, whether of the bluff face of the sill, or the dark north-facing cliff of Beinn Bhuidhe behind.

73   Miller's geological map 'not of high authority': Miller evidently used
      MacCulloch's book (1819). It contained the only detailed geological map of
      Eigg and Rùm till after Miller's visit, although MacCulloch's later free-
      standing *Map of the Geology of Scotland* of 1836, *etc*, also shows somewhat
      more detail on Eigg (Cumming 1981). However, neither can be the map
      Miller had on Eigg (pp. 73-74), as neither the 1819 map (NMS Library
      copies) nor the later map (BGS Library, Keyworth), shows any 'Old Red' on
      Eigg. Also, both NMS copies of the 1819 book show 'Ru Stor' coloured in as
      'trap', not sandstone, and, in the text, MacCulloch specifically denied that
      Eigg has any of the red sandstone found on Skye and Rùm. It is possible that
      Miller had a map afflicted with one of the colourist's errors which plagued
      MacCulloch (Cumming 1981). However, it seems more likely that Miller was
      carrying the 1842 map by William Rhind, which *does* show the northwestern
      part of Eigg as Old Red Sandstone (BGS Library, Keyworth). It was one of
      the few general maps of the region then published (Moir 1973-1983), and is
      a good candidate on the grounds of date, compactness, and, presumably,
      cheapness (given that at least some copies were published with a text on the
      'Geology of Scotland', and that these were often issued as part of an ordinary
      pocket atlas of Scotland, Lawson 1842). Miller's comment of 'no great
      authority' also seems consistent. William Rhind (1797-1874) trained as a
      doctor but made a living from popular science books. In geology he seems to
      be a minor figure with little original work to his name (Andrews 1982), and his
      map may well have been derivative rather than based on direct observation.

80   English geologist: Miller used a popular description for the long-necked
      plesiosaurs almost from the discovery of the first skeleton in the 1820s, still
      often used today – though now 'turtle' would be more appropriate than
      'tortoise'. The 'English geologist' is most probably Gideon Mantell (see p.
      52) whose version (Mantell 1844, II, p. 715) Miller might well have just read
      – but Mantell took it in turn from another writer whom he does not identify.

88   Guadaloupe specimens: found on the West Indian island of Guadeloupe,
      they appeared to be fossil human beings. In fact, however, the coral rock
      embedding the bones turned out to have been recently formed, and, in
      general, the then lack of any truly ancient fossil humans was consistent with
      the geologically very recent special divine creation of man and woman as
      told in Genesis (Lyell 1830-1833, II, p. 259; Torrens 1998). Unequivocal
      specimens of fossil humans were only found later in the nineteenth century.

99   primary region: in the old Wernerian theory, certain rocks were 'primary'
      in the sense of having been precipitated out from a hot, mineral-rich sea or
      primeval ocean in the early stages of the Earth's formation. By the time Miller
      wrote, 'primary' tended to mean the older rocks forming the deep bedrock,
      seemingly laid down before the appearance of living animals, or at least

fossilizable ones, hence '**primary ... with regard to organic existence**'. Miller appropriately quotes from Genesis 1, '**without form, and void**'.

101 most distinguished: Lyell (1830-1833, p. 374) defined the concept of 'metamorphic' rocks as 'stratified primary' deposits altered by heat, or, as we now put it, older sedimentary rocks altered by heat and pressure while buried deep within the Earth.

117 tack: Swanson and Miller wanted to sail into the wind to get to Rùm, but *Betsey*, like any sailing ship, could not sail directly into the wind. She could, however, sail obliquely to either side and partly upwind, so Swanson made progress in a series of 'tacks', the legs of a zig-zag course upwind, with the wind coming over her windward or **weather bow**.

127 ex-monarch: referring here to the plesiosaurs, *etc*, of Eigg – but very possibly a timely allusion to the naming of certain other giant fossil reptiles as 'dinosaurs' by the anatomist and zoologist Richard Owen (1804-1892) in 1842 (Torrens 1997). Much as Miller did with his 'Asterolepis' (see Introduction), Owen argued that the comparative degeneration of modern reptiles relative to dinosaurs was good evidence against the pre-Darwinian evolutionary concepts of the day, which suggested a simple progression from simple to complex animals. Owen later rose to become the first director of the British Museum (Natural History) in South Kensington, London, having masterminded its move from the British Museum in Bloomsbury.

127-132 heliotropes ... ingenuity: a careful, and valuable, field description of the main heliotrope, or bloodstone, occurrence on Rùm, before this was quarried out and covered over in later years (Harker 1908, p. 134), and a discussion on the formation of zonation within each bloodstone which appears to have been founded on that of MacCulloch (1819, I, pp. 497-506) but went well beyond it, especially Miller's apparently original attempt to devise a mechanism for the formation of adjacent but contrasting mineral assemblages (C. H. Emeleus, *pers. comm.* 2003). The problem of the formation of such minerals, especially agate, would continue to perplex mineralogists down to the present day (Heddle 1901; Macpherson 1989; Livingstone 2003).

141 turned in her stays like Lady Betty in a minuet: a multiple play on words. The dance 'Lady Betty Wood's Minuet' is in *Songs, Airs and Dances from the London Concert* of 1773, and one meaning of 'stays' is the metal or bone strips stiffening corsets, while a sailing ship such as *Betsey* (which is another diminutive for Elizabeth) can also be 'in stays'. When the ship is tacking, turning from one tack to another, it goes through the critical intermediate moment when it is head to wind and the sails provide no propulsion. The ship is then in stays, dependent on its momentum to maintain the turn.

The ability to pass rapidly through this critical stage is a valuable asset, because a sluggish ship risks 'missing stays', failing to complete the turn, and getting 'in irons', the bows pointing so close to the wind that the sails are unable to get any useful propulsion, the ship loses headway and starts to drift sternward.

160 **Scotch banks**: Peel, then Prime Minister, proposed to restrict the operations of Scottish banks on the English model. An ex-banker, Miller wrote critical articles, reprinted in 1844 as a pamphlet, *Words of warning to the people of Scotland, on Sir R. Peel's Scotch currency scheme* (Checkland 1975, p. 381).

162 **atmosphere**: alluding to the belief that the Earth had cooled down slowly over time, and that the life of any one period was adapted, by divine Providence, to the prevailing conditions – the coal forest plants, for instance, being suited to the hot and humid climate of that fairly early period.

171 **one platform**: Miller was saying that fossil fishes in the region of Cromarty are found at two main levels within the geological sequence – his 'platforms' do not exist as distinct features in the modern landscape. He was also suggesting that each level is the result of a single **catastrophe** in a sea. There has been no modern study specifically of the Cromarty sites, but as far as the Old Red Sandstone in the wider region is concerned, modern thinking (Trewin 1986; Trewin and Davidson 1999; Trewin and Hurst 1993; Trewin 2003b), is that these Old Red Sandstone beds were laid down in a large freshwater lake, of varying extent, covering much of what is now the Moray Firth, and Caithness, Orkney and Shetland. When the fish died, those corpses that sank to the deeper, anoxic part of the lake escaped scavenging and were buried in the sediment accumulating on the floor of the lake. In some areas the fish triggered the formation of nodules around them within the surrounding sediment, as at what is now Tynet Burn (which Miller visited on p. 274). Unlike Miller, we do not regard the postures of the corpses as indicating sudden death, but as artefacts of the ways in which the carcasses decay. However, current thinking on the abundant preservation of virtually complete fishes at certain levels – Miller's 'platforms' – is that each records a mass mortality in a specific area of the lake – local 'catastrophes', so to speak – caused by such things as blooms of toxic algae, or storms stirring up the deoxygenated water from the lake's depths. These produced many carcasses and also killed off the scavengers which would otherwise have destroyed them.

174 **Parkinson ... work**: James Parkinson (1755-1824), London surgeon, describer of the eponymous neurological disease, and fossil collector, wrote *Organic Remains of a Former World* (1804-1811), much used as a general work on fossils in the early nineteenth century. Miller referred to vol. III, p. 254.

199 Weald ... Oolite ... outliers: Miller accurately observed the Linksfield deposit (also pp. 280–281) and its paradox of older, Jurassic, strata overlying the relatively modern boulder clay. 'Outlier' is the geological term for an isolated exposure of a particular geological stratum surrounded on all sides by the underlying stratum and often forming higher ground, and Miller's use of the term implied that each outlier is formed *in situ*. However, Miller's interpretation of the boulder clay being washed into a cavity is now considered wrong, and his comparison to heaps of dumped soil was actually nearer the modern view. The Linksfield erratic is now interpreted as an enormous 'raft' picked up by a glacier from the floor of the Moray Firth, carried upwards and dumped over what is now dry land when the ice melted (Merritt, Connell, Hall and Peacock 2000), as are other similar 'outliers' in the area. In contrast, the Banffshire flints which Miller previously mentioned are thought to be a marine deposit formed when the sea was much higher – but laid down *before* the ice ages (Merritt, Connell and Bridgland 2000).

Miller's ascription of a 'Wealden' age was therefore ambiguous (p. 200 and Additional Note for p. 55), but in any case the Linksfield site and its fossils are now considered Rhaetian (latest Triassic) in age, and the 'femur of some Chelonian reptile', whatever it may be, is not now considered chelonian (Taylor and Cruickshank 1993; Storrs 1994).

207 Upper Old Red: the sandstones around Elgin were difficult to date. The lower ones were plainly Old Red Sandstone, of Devonian age, but the higher strata were suspected (correctly, we now consider) of being much later New Red Sandstone, of Permo-Triassic age, although they seemed to pass into the lower ones without the marked discontinuity which one would expect, corresponding to at least the entire Carboniferous period. This dating would become a crucially important issue in the 1850s when unequivocally reptilian fossils were discovered in the upper sandstones: if these really were Devonian, then they were anomalously early with major implications for the then understanding of the pattern of life, and its progress, if any, throughout geological time (Benton 1982, 1995b).

208 calotype ... Adamson: this photograph, using the calotype process, of *Stagonolepis* is the oldest known photograph of a fossil vertebrate, and one of the earliest of any fossil. It was used as the basis for drawing a lithograph in Agassiz's *Poissons fossiles du Vieux Grès Rouge* ('Fossil fishes of the Old Red Sandstone'). It was taken by the pioneering photographers Robert Adamson (1821-1848) and David Octavius Hill (note, p. 31), famous for their classic portraits of contemporaries such as Miller, and Duff himself with this very fossil (Andrews 1982; Stevenson 1981, 2002a, 2002b).

208 Stagonolepis: now known, from much more complete material, to be not a Devonian fish, but an armoured reptile distantly related to crocodiles, and of much later, Permo–Triassic, age (Benton 1995a, 1995b). Miller's comparison to a torso was closer than he knew, for the original specimen was part of the body armour of this reptile.

237 **'Constitution of Man'**: published 1828, a then notorious account of phrenology (of which 'reading the bumps' on heads was a debased version). In it George Combe (1788-1858) argued for a materialist view of human nature as being derived from the physical attributes of the brain. Its emphasis on natural law as a basis for moral law implied determinism and the denial of free will, and therefore fell foul of religious orthodoxy (Secord 2000).

257 **Pennatularia**: normally used to describe sea-pens. A sea-pen is a coral colony which lives not in a limy skeleton but the stem and branches of a horny skeleton shaped somewhat like a feather quill pen, with the 'nib' stuck in the sea floor mud. Miller was familiar with sea-pens netted by fishermen at Cromarty (Miller 1899b, pp. 307-308). But the fossils Miller was discussing are **graptolites**, now considered a completely different group of extinct marine colonial organisms. They are thought to have floated in the open ocean, living in branched horny skeletons which took various shapes, such as tuning-forks or fans. They are sometimes common in the rocks of Ordovician and Silurian age in the Southern Uplands of Scotland, laid down as fine mud on the deep ocean floor.

Dr Emslie's graptolites at Gamrie continue to puzzle geologists, partly because the single specimen of a graptolite labelled as being from Gamrie in the Miller Collection in NMS, and given to Miller by Emslie, in fact appears to be from Peeblesshire in the Borders (Trewin 1973). It is evident from the text of *Cruise of the Betsey* that Miller did not, at least on this occasion, visit the supposed locality at Gamrie-head. Possibly Miller had mislabelled a specimen given to him by Emslie, especially if it was some time before he could get home and do the necessary work.

257-258 **Burns' young Kirk Alloway beauty**: the 'winsome wench' in a 'cutty sark' or short chemise, one of the coven of witches dancing at Alloway Kirk, who chased the eponymous hero of Burns' poem 'Tam o' Shanter'.

267 **two fossil Maries of Gueldres**: topical reference to the mismanaged demolition in 1848, and (much later) rebuilding elsewhere, of Trinity College Church and Hospital just north of Edinburgh's Old Town, on which affair Miller commented at the time (Miller 1891c; Holmes 1988). The church's founder, Mary of Gueldres, consort of James II, was buried there, and her presumed remains were located and reburied at Holyrood Abbey before the church was demolished. However, the finding of a second high-status burial led to an extraordinary dispute between antiquaries over which burial was Mary, and in the end the second find was also reburied at Holyrood.

272 **Miss Bond ...** *light infantry*: Miss Bond was 'a kindly sort of person, fond
of children and mightily beloved by them in turn' who ran small boarding
schools in various locations, including Cromarty when Miller was a boy, but
died in poverty (Miller 1858, pp. 84–87). 'Light infantry' is a play on 'infant',
and perhaps also the old meaning of 'infantry' for children collectively, while
no doubt the children in question were indeed 'light'. But it is also a good
metaphor for children's habits, as light infantry such as riflemen deployed for
battle as dispersed skirmishers forward of the main body of infantry which
remained in tightly organized ranks.

272 **Ferguson**: the country farm-lad James Ferguson (1710–1776) who, through
his interest in mechanical contrivances and astronomy, rose to become an
astronomer, portrait painter, scientific lecturer, demonstrator and writer. The
globular stones were the stone spheres capping the gate pillars of the estate
of Durn.

282 **Asterolepis**: now known to be a mixture of fragmentary remains of different
large fishes. Miller's material of 'Asterolepis' was mostly the placoderm fish
Homostius with some pieces of the completely unrelated bony fish *Glyptolepis*
(Andrews 1982; R. L. Paton, *pers. comm.* 2002). Such errors were, and are, not
unusual in sorting out complex palaeontological problems on fragmentary
material.

288 **dragoon**: dragoons were originally raised as mounted infantry during the
seventeenth century. They were gradually converted to heavy cavalry during
the eighteenth century, each man partly armoured with a 'cuirass' or breast-
and back-plate, which was separate from the helmet, unlike placoderm fishes
such as *Pterichthyodes* which had a hinged connection between the head and
the thoracic armour, hence Miller's slightly confusing allusion. The cuirass
was obsolete in Britain by the end of the eighteenth century, although French
'cuirassiers' used it for longer.

309 **'Who sinned ...'**: misquotation from Scott, 'Vision of Don Roderick', verse
XIV, line 6, ' ... kings of giant race/That lived and sinn'd before the avenging
flood'. Antediluvian man was a theme treated by many poets between 1810
and 1850.

337 **genius ... water**: perhaps the Genius (*ie*, spirit of the place) in 'The History
of a Poet's Garden' (1773). It appears 'in a dark walk by which ran a prattling
brook' to Goldsmith contemplating the ruined gardens created by the poet
William Shenstone. This is indeed appropriate for Miller by the Auldgrande.
However, the quotation **'along the surface of the water'** does not match
Goldsmith's essay. Perhaps it is an error by Miller, or perhaps it is taken from
a completely different and so far untraced source.

353 My old friend the minister of Alness: the Flyters were also friends back to the previous generation on Miller's wife Lydia's side (Sutherland 2002). Rev. Alexander Flyter (1782-1866) was minister of Alness 1820-1843, and Alness Free Church 1843-1866. His wife Elizabeth was daughter of the Rev. Ronald Bayne of Kiltarlity, who was an important Evangelical and a family friend of Lydia's mother. Elizabeth's brother was the Rev. Charles Bayne of Fodderty, father of the journalist and writer Peter Bayne (1830-1890), who would later be Miller's official biographer (Bayne 1871; Scott 1915-1928, VI, p. 470, VII, p. 28; Sutherland 2002).

355 Hormazdji Pestonji: one of the first three Parsis of Bombay (now Mumbai) to be converted to Christianity by the work of Dr George Wilson and his colleagues (see p. 63; Smith 1879, pp. 133, 140). This caused much tension with the Parsi community, who reacted strongly by remarrying this convert's wife to another Parsi, and had to be compelled to give up his daughter by a case tried under the jurisdiction of the **British** law prevailing in Bombay. The **lady** caring for Buchubai must be Maria Mitchell, one of Alexander and Elizabeth Flyter's daughters (see Additional Note for p. 353), and married to the Rev. John Murray Mitchell, another missionary at Bombay. Moreover, George Wilson's first wife was Elizabeth Flyter's cousin Margaret Bayne. After Margaret's early death, her sisters Anna and Hay went out to Bombay to assist in the missionary work, and Hay married yet another Bombay missionary, the Rev. Robert Nesbit (Scott 1915-1928, II, p. 200, VII, pp. 703-704).

363 vitrified stone: many Scottish Iron Age forts, often on hilltops, were made of drystone walls with integral wooden reinforcement. 'Vitrified forts' are those fired so that the dry stones have, at least locally, partly melted into monolithic slaggy masses, as on Knockfarril. The original description of vitrified forts in the eighteenth century led to a controversy as to whether this was deliberate, to strengthen the walls, or the result of hostile action, for instance during an attack. Fieldwork and experiments with firing replica walls indicate that firing a fort wall damages rather than strengthens the wall, and that the wall as built does not contain enough wood to produce the degree of vitrification observed (Ralston 1986). Hence the current conclusion is that the forts were deliberately destroyed at leisure, with piles of firewood stacked around the walls: 'a premeditated act of intense symbolic power as the seats of a warrior aristocracy were permanently and spectacularly razed' (Armit 1997, p. 59). See also p. 177.

374 thunderbolt: this, following on from his earlier report (Miller 1841, p. 11), showed that 'thunderbolts' of folklore need not always be Mesolithic flint arrowheads (Taylor and Cheape 1999). Miller came across this tradition from a fellow workman in his first quarry near Eathie many years before, but perhaps because the tradition was already in disuse, he did not find out the original rationale. Presumably, if 'thunderbolts' or fairy arrows shot at cattle had caused their otherwise inexplicable illnesses, then they would act to cure them on the principle of sympathetic magic, the 'hair of the dog that bit you' (cf. Henderson and Cowan 2001, pp. 93-94).

376 **second stage of growth**: what Miller meant (as is clear from fuller discussion elsewhere, Miller 1899a, pp. 53-56) was that Ben Wyvis had completed only the first stage in the formation of many (but not all) mountains. These mountains were considered to have been heaved up by the injection of igneous rock beneath them to uplift wide domes of the country rock such as gneiss and mica-slate, like fluid-filled blisters as it were. If the process continued then 'the gneiss and mica-slate gave way a-top; and out of this lower dome there arose a higher dome of granite'. A further and final stage saw the development, in turn, of a 'third and last dome of porphyry'. Apparently he was following some variant of the theory of 'craters of elevation' by Christian Leopold von Buch (1744-1853) (Oldroyd 1996a, 1996b). Today, however, the formation of mountains is largely attributed to the crumpling of continental crust by the lateral movement of the plates of the earth's surface.

389 **common sense**: probably referring to a developing controversy within the Free Church over the running of schools. Miller supported nonsectarian but broadly Christian schools on a nationally organized and state-funded basis, open to any Presbyterian denomination (Roman Catholics would presumably operate their own schools). Others, including the faction ruling the Free Church, wanted Free Church schools open solely to Free Church members. This controversy was one of the issues over which Miller and *The Witness* drew away from the Church management, and it also led him to write the articles that became *My Schools and Schoolmasters* (Robb 1996).

390 **'Sketch of the Borough'**: in fact, 'The Borough' in *Poems, Tales and Sketches* (*eg*, Malcolm [1905], pp. 218-225). Miller's quotations are somewhat paraphrased and permuted, perhaps because he was working at home from notes, and away from a copy of Malcolm's book. By **'tea and turn-out'** Malcolm referred to an old social custom of providing tea but ejecting the guests late in the evening, hungry and supperless; he evidently preferred the newer custom of **'tea and turn-in'**, whereby the guests stayed to supper of the kind he so luxuriously described.

392 **sailors of Ulysses**: in Homer's *Odyssey*, Odysseus or Ulysses visits Aeolus, the King of the Winds, who gives him the winds safely contained in a leather bag. But when they are very nearly home, his sailors, thinking that it contains treasure, greedily open it and unleash the storms which blow them far away.

412 **Patmos**: the original Patmos was the Greek island to which St John the Divine was banished for preaching Christianity, and where he continued to preach, and wrote the Book of Revelation (Bible, Revelation 1:9). Miller's prose is perhaps rather confusing: his metaphorical 'Patmos' is North Ronaldsay to which, during the seventeenth century, Smith was exiled for his Covenanting activities. The twelve Jacobites, in complete contrast, were **engaged in the rebellion of 1745**. After the victory of the **Whigs**, which in this context means the anti-Jacobite, pro–Hanoverian faction, these Jacobites hid in the cave on Westray, which is a different island from North Ronaldsay.

426 **Mr William Watt jun.**: presumably William Graham Watt tertius (1776–1866), laird of Breckness and Skaill, and local historian and amateur archaeologist involved notably in the first excavation of the Neolithic village of Skara Brae near Skaill (Hewison 1998).

445 **General Assembly of 1638**: against Charles I's wishes, it abolished Episcopalianism and reasserted the primacy of Presbyterianism in Scotland, trying bishops for their offences; **curler on the ice**: playing the Scots game of curling, sliding stones on ice somewhat as bowls are used in lawn bowling – the problem was that Grahame did it on the Sabbath; **Baillie**: Robert Baillie of Jerviswood (c.1634-1684), linguist, scientist, mathematician and Covenanter, for which last he was executed in 1684. Miller quoted a section equivalent to Baillie (1841, I, p. 163); **setter of tacks to his sones and grandsones**: practising nepotism in letting Church property, presumably at deliberately low rentals; **oversaw adulterie; slighted charming**: ignored or failed to take action over adultery and witchcraft; **held portions of ministers' stipends for building his cathedral**: misused funds intended for ministers' salaries – either they went without or their parishioners made up the shortfalls. But Miller erroneously included the comment 'ordinar ['ordinary'] **faults of a bishop**', which applied to the Bishop of Moray.

458 **Glen Tilt ... Grampians**: Miller was always highly critical of lairds abusing their power, such as restricting access to land for selfish reasons, especially when this harmed public recreation and education – note his choice of quotation on p. 272. The Grampian Mountains in the central Highlands had recently been closed to the public by the Duke of Leeds, for the sake of game. Miller considered game a wasteful and frivolous use of land which also tended to criminalize country people. Glen Tilt was well known for its botany and the classic exposures of granitic veins which critically enabled the pioneering eighteenth century geologist James Hutton to demonstrate that granite is an igneous rock. The landowner, the Duke of Atholl, had just closed the glen, ignoring a long-standing right of way. When Professor Balfour of Edinburgh University (and, ironically, Hutton's closest living

relative) and his students sought to visit the glen on a botanical field trip, Atholl's employees barred the way. Atholl lost the ensuing court case brought by the Scottish Rights of Way Society (Miller 1862, pp. 112-121; Allen 2000).

464 **Clouston**: Rev. Charles Clouston (1800-1884), Establishment minister of Sandwick, amateur naturalist and meteorologist, and related by marriage to Rev. Learmonth of Stromness Free Church (Smith 1907; Hewison 1998). He was at one time President of Orkney Natural History Society which ran Stromness Museum. Miller mentions Clouston's finds elsewhere (Miller 1857, p. 432).

476 **Melvill**: the Reformer James Melvill or Melville (1556-1614). His brother was Andrew (1545-1622), theologian, fellow Reformer, and, alongside John Knox, one of the two founding fathers of Scottish Presbyterianism. The two brothers and their relatives had visited Buchanan in his **chalmer** (Scots, chamber). Buchanan actually completed his sentence '... nor stelling sheipe, or sitting ydle, quhilk is als ill' – Scots for '... than stealing sheep, or sitting idle, which is just as bad'. What Miller did not say, but many readers would know, was that Buchanan was on his deathbed, and the whole story is a testimony to Buchanan's Calvinist work ethic and unbending probity (Melville 1829, p. 86).

INDEX